TO VIRTUE

The Laws of interpersonal relationships — in business, home and society

RABBI AVROHOM EHRMAN

FIRST EDITION
First Impression … August 2002

Published and Distributed by
MESORAH PUBLICATIONS, LTD.
4401 Second Avenue / Brooklyn, N.Y 11232

Distributed in Europe by
LEHMANNS
Unit E, Viking Industrial Park
Rolling Mill Road
Jarow, Tyne & Wear, NE32 3DP
England

Distributed in Australia and New Zealand by
GOLDS WORLD OF JUDAICA
3-13 William Street
Balaclava, Melbourne 3183
Victoria, Australia

Distributed in Israel by
SIFRIATI / A. GITLER — BOOKS
6 Hayarkon Street
Bnei Brak 51127

Distributed in South Africa by
KOLLEL BOOKSHOP
Shop 8A Norwood Hypermarket
Norwood 2196, Johannesburg, South Africa

ARTSCROLL HALACHAH SERIES®
JOURNEY TO VIRTUE
© *Copyright 2002, by* MESORAH PUBLICATIONS
4401 Second Avenue / Brooklyn, N.Y. 11232 / (718) 921-9000 / www.artscroll.com

---

ISBN:
1-57819-759-7 (hard cover)
1-57819-760-0 (paperback)

Typography by CompuScribe at ArtScroll Studios, Ltd.

Printed in the United States of America by Noble Book Press Corp.
Bound by Sefercraft, Quality Bookbinders, Ltd., Brooklyn N.Y. 11232

לזכרון עולם בהיכל ה׳

לעילוי נשמת
אמי מורתי מרת חנה בת ר׳ ישראל ז״ל
Mrs. Hanni Ehrman ז״ל
נלב״ע ב׳ שבט תשנ״ב

ת.נ.צ.ב.ה.

לע״נ ר׳ שמואל פנחס ב״ר יעקב צבי עהרמאן ז״ל
מרת אסתר בת ר׳ שמואל ז״ל

ר׳ ישראל ב״ר מנשה שענקר ז״ל
מרת ריזל בת ר׳ אברהם ישראל ז״ל

לזכרון עולם בהיכל ה'

לעילוי נשמת

מורי חמי ר' שמואל בן הרב יצחק מרדכי גראס ז"ל

Mr. Sidney Gross ז"ל

נלב"ע ט"ו בשבט תשנ"ט

ת.נ.צ.ב.ה.

לע"נ הרב יצחק מרדכי בן הרב אברהם גראס ז"ל

מרת שרה בת ר' מאיר נתן ז"ל

ר' משה מרדכי בן ר' יהודה דוב סקס ז"ל

מרת יענטא דבורה בת ר' הירש וועלועל ז"ל

ת.נ.צ.ב.ה.

הסכמת הרב ש.י. נסים קרליץ שליט"א
ראש כולל חזון איש
רב אב"ד רמת אהרן

בס"ד עש"ק אחרי קדושים תשמ"ח

הנני בזה לחזק ולאמץ מעשה ידיו חכמה
ומלאכה של הרב המאה"ג י"א מרבים ר'
אברהם אהרמן שליט"א שחיבר חיבור רב
תועלת בעניינים שבין אדם לחבירו לברר
הלכותיהן ולעורר עליהם ויהי רצון שיתקבלו
הדברים לתועלת, ולימוד יביא לידי מעשה,
ויקוים בנו ורב שלום בניך.

ש.י. נסים קרליץ

[signature]

הוספת הגר"ש ואזנר שליט"א

ב"ה

הריני מצרף עצמי באהבה לדברים
האמורים למעלה בשבח המחברת לחיזוק
בדברים שבין אדם לחבירו, ויה"ר שהשי"ת
יהי' אתו בכל.

ע"ז באעה"ח
מצפה לרחמי ה'
שמואל הלוי ואזנר
רב אב"ד זכרון מאיר ב"ב

[signature]

All the approbations were given to the original Hebrew edition.
They appear here in the order in which they appear in that work.

בס״ד כ״ו׳ למב״י תשמ״ח

אל כבוד יקירנו הנכבד נאה מקיים ונאה
דורש הרה״ג מהר״א אהרמן שליט״א
אחדשה״ט וש״ת באהבה ויקר,

עברתי מעט בקונטרסיו על הלכות בין
אדם לחבירו התלוין בדיבור, הן בסור מרע והן
בעשה טוב, אשר אסף ולקט והוסיף נופך
משלו וערוך בטוטו״ד, והריני להחזיק
טיבותיה למר ולאמר לפעלו יישר כי הדברים
ראויין להוציאן לאור לזכות את הרבים אשר
לדאבוננו הכשלון רב בהם הן מפני שגגת
ידיעת חומר הדין והעון והן מפני אפיקורסיה
דדרא אשר הקהה הרגשי הקודש בזה, ובטוח
שמי שילמוד בספר זה יהי׳ לו לברכה ויתחזק
במילי שהן כבשונו של עולם, וכלל גדול
בתורה, והרבה מהצלחתו של אדם ברוחניות
וגשמיות תלויין בזה.

המכיר טובה ומוקירו דוש״ת

יהודא שפירא

הו"כ הרה"ג מוהר"א אהרמן שליט"א
אחד"ש כתרה"ט בהוקרה רבה!

מי אני כי אכתוב לו הערכה על חיבורו הנכבד, ואיך אתייצב
במקום הרבנים הגאונים שהסכימו עליו! רק זאת אוכל: לברך את
כת"ר שחפץ ה' בידו יצלח ויזכה שיתפשט ספרו ברבים להגדיל תורה
ולהאדיר ולהשיב רבים מעון, ויזכה כת"ר תמיד להיות ממזכי הרבים
ככוכבים לעולם ועד!

בכבוד רב כרום מעלת ערכו
ובברכת התורה

שלמה וולבה

ב"ה כ' תמוז תשמ"ח

כבוד ידידי הדגול ומאוד נעלה הרה"ג מוהר"ר אברהם עהרמן
שליט"א היושב באהלי תורה וי"ש בתוך ד' אמות של הלכה באתרא
קדישא בני ברק יצ"ו

פנה אלי לכתוב לו דברי הסכמה ועידוד על ספרו "קיצור דינים בין
אדם לחבירו" - ותמה אני איך אוכל ליתן הסכמה על קונטרס של
ההלכות החמורות הללו והלואי שאזכה להנצל בעצמי מלעבור בכל
יום ח"ו על העניינים הנשגבים ההם - והנה ההסכמות צריכות להנתן
ע"י גדולי התורה והיראה המושלמים על יצרם ויושבי על מדין, ולא
מנאי ומדכוותי - אולם במה שנוגע לברכה, אל נא תהי' ברכת הדיוט
כמוני קלה בעיניך, תלמידנו היקר מקדמת דנא, הנה ברך לקחתי וברך
ולא אשיבנה, ויה"ר שחפץ ה' בידך יצליח וספרך אשר כולו אומר כבוד
שמים ימצא חן בעיני אלקים ואדם שיהי' שם שמים מתאהב ומתקדש
ע"י לקרב לבבות איש אל אחיו, ולפרוש שלום ליוצא ולבא כדדרשו
רז"ל.

ממני הכותב בכל לב בידידות נאמנה
שמעון שוואב

בעזהי"ת

הרימותי ידי לעושה שמים וארץ שבעזהי"ת זכינו בזמנינו לחיבור רב
הכמות והאיכות בענינים שבין אדם לחבירו שחסרונו נרגש בכל פנה
וזוית. ומחברינו הרה"ג המופלא ומופלג בהפלגת חכמים ונבונים ירא
וחרד לדבר ה' לן באהלה של תורה בד' אמות של הלכה מו"ה אברהם
אהרמן שליט"א עשה נפלאות לאסוף בחיבור אחד כל הדברים
הנפזרים בספרים ספ"ק וטרח בעשר אצבעותיו לעשות דבר שלם וגם
להעלותם על מכבש הדפוס אשרי לו ואשרי חלקו מדזכה לנפשי' זכי
נמי לחברי' ואין ספק אצלי שבידו בכפו יבלענו כל רואותיו, כי כל בית
ובית בישראל הנאמן לה' ולתורתו ספר כזה הוא כמכה בפטיש
להשלימתו.

ובזה אצא בשים שלום טובה וברכה שיזכה עוד לעלות על במתי
ההצלחה ואושר האמיתי לשם ולתפארת ונזכה כולנו ביחד לקבל פני
משיח צדקנו בב"א.

ה' לפ' מטות מסעי שנת תשמ"ח לפ"ק

פה ברוקלין יצ"ו

משה שטרן

אב"ד דעברצין יצ"ו

הסכמת הרב יעקב פרלוב שליט"א
אדמו"ר מנאוואמינסק
ברוקלין נ.י.

בס"ד יום ה' ר"ח תמוז תשמ"ח

כבוד ידידי היקר והמופלא עולה ומתעלה בשבת תחכמוני בעיר התורה ב"ב שבאה"ק, הרה"ג מוהר"ר אברהם עהרמן שליט"א שפעת שלומים וישע רב.

אחדשה"ט בכל היקר,

קבלתי הגליונות מספרו הנכבד על הלכות שמירת הלשון ועוד הרבה מקצועות בענינים שבין אדם לחבירו, והנהו צרור של בשמים וסמא דחיי בהלכות קבועות וברורות הנוגעים למעשה על כל צעד ושעל, ויש בו זיכוי הרבים לאין ערוך בהדרכת המדות לפי משפטי ההלכה באופן מסודר ומועיל אשר אין ספק כי יביא תועלת וברכה לכל בית ישראל. ובאמת הרי מערכת"ה נמצא במחיצתם של גדולי הדור באה"ק ולא ידעתי מה ראה עוד לבקש דברי הסכמה ועידוד מיושבי חו"ל, אמנם רצונו של אדם זהו כבודו, וכבודו אני דורש זה הרבה שנים מזמן ששקד על דלתות התורה פה בנוא יארק, ועלץ לבי לראותו תמיד וכעת ביותר משתגשג לאילנא רברבא כיד השם הטובה עליו. ועל כן אמינא לידידי ולפעלו הטוב יישר, ויהא חילו לאורייתא להפיץ מעיינותיו חוצה בעולם התורה והחרדים אל דבר השם. והמקום יהא בעזרו שיתקבל חיבורו באלפי ישראל להרבות כבוד שמים ולהגדיל תורה ויאדיר.

כעתירת ידידו מוקירו ומכבדו הדוש"ת בלו"נ.

יעקב פרלוב

יעקב [חתימה]

Table of Contents

⤳ Abuse and Conflict — Chapters 6-9

⤳ Distancing From Falsehood — Chapters 10-14

✢ Purity of Soul — Chapters 15-19

❧ Conflicting Values — Chapters 20-29

⤜ Financial Damages and Obligations — Chapters 30-37

❧ Honest Commerce — Chapters 38-43

⇝ Respect and Honor — Chapters 44-47

⇝ Financial Kindness — Chapters 48-55

Introduction

The Torah is replete with mitzvos and morality lessons regarding interpersonal relationships (*mitzvos bein adam l'chaveiro*). The *chesed* of our patriarch Avraham is part of every Jewish child's basic education. To love one's fellow Jew as oneself is a mitzvah that, according to *Chazal*, is a basic lesson in understanding the Torah. The *Beis HaMikdash* was destroyed because of the sin of hatred. Keep far away from falsehood. These lessons directly affect our day-to-day lives.

The lessons are not, however, merely general; the Torah teaches us mitzvos of a *halachic* nature, and *halachah* is very precise. What exactly is the meaning of love, and conversely, hatred? When do I come before my fellow and when does he take precedence? Which acts are deemed revenge and which constitute bearing a grudge? What is the precise definition of *machlokes*? When must one tell the truth and when is one forbidden from doing so? These examples, many of which are intertwined, involve mitzvos *D'Oraisa* and *D'Rabbanan*, as well as *lifnim me'shuras hadin*. Furthermore, values may occasionally conflict: by helping Reuven, I may harm Shimon. In reality, all mitzvos *bein adam l'chaveiro* are one beautiful tapestry of *chesed* and *emes* — but doing them properly requires precise knowledge of their *halachic* parameters.

The Chofetz Chaim codified the laws of *lashon hara* and simultaneously discussed many other *halachos* as well. An excellent *sefer*, *Nesivos Chaim* by HaRav Moshe Kofman *shlita* of Bnei Brak, delves into the *sugyos* of the Chofetz Chaim and many parallel issues. However, there did not exist a comprehensive *sefer* to guide a person through all the *"bein adam l'chaveiro"* aspects of daily life.

Halichos Olam was published in 1988 in a humble attempt to codify all of these *halachos* in the fashion of a *Kitzur Shulchan Aruch*, with a much-improved edition appearing in 1995. These *halachos* were worked on — *k'darkah shel Torah* — from the *sugyos*. A footnote was appended to each *halachah* to note its source; some are longer to elucidate the *sugya*. In addition, the *sefer Kodesh Yisrael* was published alongside *Halichos Olam* in order to expound on certain *sugyos* at length.

This *sefer* as presented to the English-speaking audience is an even greater improved version of *Halichos Olam*, with a different order of presentation. The book is divided into sections reflecting different aspects of life, as listed in the table of contents. Many realistic examples were added to better illustrate the *halachos*.

The sources of the *halachos* as noted in the footnotes are classical: *Tanach, Shas, Poskim, Chofetz Chaim* and *Ahavas Chesed*. The *sefer Nesivos Chaim* by Rabbi Kofman is extensively cited, along with his commentaries, *Nesiv Chaim, Shevilei Chaim, Zera Chaim* and *Mei Menuchos* on *shidduchim*. The reader is sometimes referred to footnotes in *Halichos Olam*, and to the *sefer Kodesh Yisrael* when further elucidation of a *din* is necessary.

I was privileged for many years to learn in the Kollel Chazon Ish, a bastion of Torah in Bnei Brak. Among its many *talmidei chachamim* are some of today's giants of Torah, including HaGaon HaRav Moshe Deutsch *zt"l*, and *yblt"a* HaGaon HaRav Nissim Karelitz *shlita*, HaGaon HaRav Yehuda Shapira *shlita*, and HaGaon HaRav Chaim Kanievsky *shlita*. Some questions were posed to the *gedolei Torah* in the *kollel*; these are quoted as "heard from a *gadol*."

It is crucially important to note that the purpose of *kitzur halachos* (shortened codified *halachah*) is not to *pasken halachos*, but to make people aware of the basic principles involved. Real-life situations may differ from what is presented in a *sefer*, and we must therefore always consult our rabbanim. In addition, in order to properly understand *halachah*, one must delve and toil in a *sugya* and merit *siyata d'Shmaya*.

Many people are completely unaware of the existence of certain *halachos bein adam l'chaveiro*. Furthermore, many of these *halachos* are intimately connected to *middos*, which are exceedingly difficult to change. Thus, individuals who believed themselves to be keeping *halachah* correctly prior to reading this *sefer* may suddenly become aware that they have been repeatedly violating explicit *halachos*. This phenomenon is not meant, *chas v'shalom*, to break a person; indeed, this is the great challenge of life. The Vilna Gaon taught that a person is given life solely to work on his *middos*. Above all, this effort leads to the greatest virtue of all — humility.

On a personal note, I, too, share in this struggle. It is easier to learn the relevant *sugyos* and publish the *sefarim* than to actually live a full Torah life. With this book, I share this struggle with you. May *Hashem Yisbarach* grant us the fulfillment of our weekly *tefillah*, "Purify our hearts to worship You with truth."

Vihi Noam Hashem Elokeinu Aleinu

Acknowledgments

The Torah states (*Devarim* 8:10), *And you shall eat and be satiated and you shall bless Hashem for the good land that He has given you.* In a larger sense, this teaches us to constantly recognize Hashem's goodness and thank Him for it.

I cannot begin to thank the A-mighty for His constant benevolence to me and to my family.

My fate was pleasant and also my inheritance was beautiful to me (*Tehillim* 16:6, translation of Rav S.R. Hirsch). Hashem, in His infinite kindness, has given me the opportunity of "sitting in the House of Hashem," studying His Holy Torah. One of His great kindnesses is the publication of this *sefer*, which will *iy"h* give the English-speaking public the opportunity to learn the *halachos* of interpersonal relationships, a *klal gadol baTorah*, "great rule of Torah living."

This *sefer* has a long history, involving a few anecdotes as well. Early one summer morning in 1985 my then-7-year-old son asked me why I had walked four *amos* without *tzitzis*. Although I knew that this was a *hiddur* in the mitzvah of *tzitzis* based on a Gemara in *Shabbos* (119b), I wondered how he knew of this concept. When I became aware that it is mentioned in the beginning of *Kitzur Shulchan Aruch*, it occurred to me that it was important to have a *"Kitzur Shulchan Aruch"* for the interpersonal mitzvos, which are mostly *D'Oraisa*. Thus was conceived the idea of *Halichos Olam*.

After the first *sefer* appeared in 1988, a Jew in Yerushalayim by the name of Reb Pinchos Rohr suggested that it be translated into English, and over the next few years, he vigorously campaigned that it happen.

A major obstacle to the translation of the *sefer* was financial considerations. In the early 90's, a visitor to our home overheard me comment, "When Hashem sends the money, we will translate the *sefer*." To our surprise, an envelope arrived not long after containing a hefty check with which to begin the translation. To this person, who wishes to remain anonymous, belongs a tremendous part in the *zechus harabbim* of this *sefer*. May Hashem bless them and their family.

Halichos Olam was first reprinted in a revised improved edition in 1995. Reb Pinchos then got to work translating the *sefer* and contacted ArtScroll. This gave me the privilege of meeting the Mesorah/ArtScroll team: Rav Nosson Scherman, Reb Avrohom Biderman, Reb Shmuel Blitz etc. Under their tutelage, the *sefer* was reformatted and reedited to ensure that it would be clearly understood by the reader.

On the advice of Rav Joseph Elias *shlita*, examples were added, greatly enhancing the *sefer*. I am indebted to the many dedicated women from all walks of life who read and edited the book. Their pointed questions constantly created greater clarity in the book's presentation. These include Mrs. Tamar Pierce, Mrs. Estie Allina-Turnauer, Mrs. Sara Ackman and Mrs. Gail Gundle, and Mrs. Elana Felder for Mesorah/ArtScroll.

I would also like to thank the following members of the Mesorah/Artscroll staff: Mrs. Mindy Stern, who proofread the book and clarified many points; Reb Eli Kroen and Reb Hershy Feuerwerker, who designed the beautiful cover; and Mrs. Leah Weiner, Tzini Hanover and Menucha Mitnick, who typeset the book.

My deepest thanks to my *chavrusa* of many years in the Kollel Chazon Ish, Reb Simcha Horowitz *shlita*, who worked with me to clarify many of the *sugyos* in *Halichos Olam*. I would also like to thank HaRav HaGaon Yaakov Gutman *shlita* for much advice when *Halichos Olam* was first being written. The printing of the first edition was sponsored by my uncle and aunt, Fred and Suzan Ehrman, to whom I have a special *hakaras hatov*.

I would like to thank my dear parents for raising me to Torah: my mother, Mrs. Hanni Ehrman *o"h*, and *yblt"a* my father, Mr. Maurice Ehrman *shlita*, who from my youngest years taught me *Chumash* and Gemara and followed my Torah learning throughout the years. His worldview *hashkafos* played a major role in this *sefer*.

My late father-in-law, Mr. Sidney Gross *z"l*, lived the concepts of doing *chesed*, as is well-known in Pittsburgh. Together with *tblt"a* my mother-in-law, Mrs. Beverly Gross, they built a home of Torah and *chesed* which was a model for many to follow.

I want to thank and pay tribute to our wonderful children who have taught us about life — its struggles and victories, and how to face them with courage, patience, and above all, *tefillah*, *emunah* and *bitachon*. May *Hashem Yisbarach* bless each one of our children and grandchildren: Yitzchak and Chana and children, Moshe and Sara Fogel and children, Yissochor and Tziril, Shlomo, Raizel, Elchonon, Ruchama, Yeruchem, Devorah and Esther with *chaim aruchim* filled with *ahavas Torah* and *yiras Shamayim*.

And finally, my wife Joy, *tichyeh. Noda ba'she'arim baalah* — if her husband's *sefer* is known at the "gates" where *bnei Torah* meet, it is to her credit. Besides her tremendous dedication to Torah in general, she was particularly dedicated to this *sefer*, from the first day that the idea was conceived. In the words of Rabbi Akiva, "Mine and yours is hers."

May we merit to express our appreciation to the Creator for all His Goodness, and may He, *kivyachol*, have *nachas* from us.

Overview

The mitzvos of the Torah can be divided into two basic categories: *mitzvos bein adam laMakom* (between man and his Creator) and *mitzvos bein adam l'chaveiro* (between man and his fellow). It is commonly understood that the first involves the "deeds" or "ceremony" of religion, while the latter stresses the moral and ethical values of a human being. *Mitzvos bein adam laMakom* cement man's relationship to Hashem, e.g. Shabbos renews a Jew's covenant with Hashem, *tefillah* creates an I-Thou relationship between man and G-d, and by avoiding forbidden foods and relationships, a person keeps his body sanctified to his Creator. On the other hand, *mitzvos bein adam l'chaveiro* create an ethical and moral society; a person is obligated to help his fellow and is forbidden from harming him.

On the surface, it would seem that the latter form the foundation of becoming a "mentsch," while the former are the basis of being a "Yid." Indeed, most of the mitzvos that capture the flavor of Jewish life are *bein adam laMakom,* such as *tefillah, tefillin,* Shabbos, Yom Tov and *kashrus.* Furthermore, the most severe punishments for *aveiros* are for violations of such mitzvos, e.g. Shabbos violation and forbidden relationships. Torah study, the basis of Jewish life, is included in this category as well. Thus, a situation has evolved where the "spiritual" mitzvos are considered the barometer of a person's religiosity, whereas the *mitzvos bein adam l'chaveiro,* while important, are not deemed as basic to *Yiddishkeit* as the others.

However, even a superficial perusal of *Tanach* and the teachings of *Chazal* proves the fallacy of this attitude — the *Neviim,* for example, repeatedly stressed the importance of justice and kindness. In fact, a simple reading of *Tanach* leaves the impression that the two most important issues for a Jew are avoiding idolatry and the proper fulfillment of *mitzvos bein adam l'chaveiro.*

These two issues are actually closely related: *For in deceit* (between each other) *they have refused to know Me, says Hashem* (Yirmiyahu 9:5). *Champion the cause of the poor, that is good, for this is knowledge of Me, says Hashem* (ibid. 22:16). *These are the things that you shall do* (to bring about the redemption): *Speak truth each man to his fellow, and in your gates judge with truth, justice and peace. You shall not think in your heart about the evil of your fellow* (think about a person's positive, rather than negative, attributes) *and do not love false swearing, for all these things I hate, says Hashem* (Zechariah 8:16-17).

Yerushalayim was destroyed when there were no longer any honest people left (Shabbos 119b).

The second Beis HaMikdash was destroyed for causeless hatred (Yoma 9a).

(When quoting these *pesukim* and *Chazal,* one must simultaneously stress that the Holy Nation has always been exemplary in all the virtues of ethics and morality. No nation has ever come even close to *klal Yisrael* in creating a society of kindness, justice and peaceful living. However, the Divine Voice, expressed through the mouth of the *Navi* and the hearts of the *Chachamim,* demands perfection; thus we are given strong reprimands and a constant stress on improvement.)

These are but a few of the thousands of *pesukim* and *ma'amarei Chazal* stressing this theme. Moreover, from the start, we are taught that Avraham was chosen to be the father of the Holy Nation *because he will teach his children to follow the ways of Hashem to do tzedakah and mishpat* (kindness and justice) (Bereishis 18:10). Thus it seems that these virtues alone constitute the "way of Hashem."

Does this mean that kindness and justice alone are important? Are not Shabbos and *kashrus, tefillin* and *succah, berachos, tefillah* and *limud Torah* equally important? If so, why did Hashem not state that

Avraham was chosen to teach his children to follow the ways of Hashem including observing the laws of Shabbos and *kashrus* and delving into Torah study? In order to answer this question we must understand our purpose in life.

The Torah tells us that man was created in the "image of Hashem" with a "likeness to Hashem." Rashi explains that man was created like a coin in a mint. When the metal is poured, the mint and coin fit perfectly. Similarly, the human being is the perfect vessel in which the Divine Presence, *kivyachol*, can rest. The person is a *mikdash* (see *Shemos* 25:8) and just as a *mikdash* must be pure, so must a person endeavor to purify his heart and deeds to be worthy of the Divine Presence. These concepts are included in the very essence of the creation of the human being in the "image of Hashem" with a "likeness to Hashem." Thus, the foundation and purpose of human life is to live a Divine-like life.

Our *Chachamim* have taught us that while Hashem is infinite and beyond the scope of human understanding, He nevertheless reveals Himself to us through His deeds. By studying Hashem's ways we can learn about Him and in our own paltry human way attempt to imitate His ways. Thus, the Torah commands us, *You shall go in His ways* (*Devarim* 28:9): Just as Hashem is compassionate so shall you be compassionate. All the attributes of Hashem are taught to us in the Torah so that we should imitate them and practice them in our own lives (*Rambam, Hilchos Dei'os* 1:5-6). *Chazal* taught us (*Kiddushin* 40b) that Talmud (i.e. Torah study) brings to good deeds, meaning that by studying Hashem's ways — the essence of Torah study — we can learn to imitate them and practice them in our own lives. This alone is the purpose of mankind.

In order to be able to imitate the ways of Hashem we have to know their basic principles, as told to us by King David: *All the ways of Hashem are kindness and truth* (*Tehillim* 25:10). *Hashem loves tzedakah and mishpat, the kindness of Hashem fills the earth* (ibid. 33:5). Thus the revelation of Hashem is through kindness and *tzedakah*, truth and *mishpat*. It is therefore understood that Hashem expressed His love for Avraham Avinu because Avraham will teach his children the way of Hashem to do *mishpat* and *tzedakah, for those are the ways of Hashem.*

However, the question still remains: If our purpose in life is to act with *tzedakah* and *mishpat*, enabling us to be Divine-like, what is the importance of *mitzvos bein adam laMakom*? Why can't a person be a fine Torah Jew solely by believing in Hashem and treating everyone with kindness and truth? Why is a *mechallel Shabbos,* for example, ostracized from *klal Yisrael?*

The answer is that the purpose of life is not the act of *tzedakah* or *mishpat per se,* but rather becoming that Divine-like person who acts with *tzedakah* and *mishpat.* Divine-like means pure — pure *tzedakah* and pure *mishpat.* Among the attributes of Hashem are *kedushah* and *taharah* (sanctity and purity). While the human being has attributes of selfishness that express themselves negatively, Hashem's ways are pure: His kindness is pure kindness, His truth is pure truth.

Thus, when Hashem described His love for Avraham Avinu who will teach his children the ways of Hashem to do *mishpat* and *tzedakah,* it means that he will teach them a way of life that will enable them to achieve such nobility of soul, such purity and sanctity, that they will intrinsically be doing kindness and truth — pure *tzedakah* and pure *mishpat.* This concept requires further elucidation.

Every person is created with a "likeness to Hashem," and therefore, even a base person occasionally performs an act of *tzedakah* or *mishpat,* and certain noble individuals perform many such acts. Avraham Avinu, however, took upon himself a far greater mission; he undertook to teach his children a way of life of following Hashem, expressing constant thanks to Him, and aspiring to Him. This creates a personality of Divine-like purity and sanctity, which, in turn, aspires to do deeds of *tzedakah* and *mishpat.* This way of life encompasses the entire Torah, and therefore, the *mitzvos bein adam laMakom* are a constant renewal of a Jew's covenant with Hashem to be loyal to Him, to thank Him for all His bounty and to follow His ways. These mitzvos teach all virtues — humility and kindness, strength and compassion — sanctifying the physical and enriching the spiritual.

Above all, mitzvos teach submission to Hashem, reminding a person that he is merely a creature and that his Creator provides for all his needs and guides his life. As knowledge of the Creator is the basis of life, Hashem's mitzvos, first and foremost, raise a person from the crassness of living a life void of this acknowledgment. This concept is expressed in every *berachah* when performing a mitzvah: "He has sanctified us with His mitzvos." A mitzvah is a commandment and we do as we are commanded — this is the basis of submission to Hashem. Here enters the realm of *halachah* — to know exactly what is permitted and what is prohibited. This is the basis of Hashem's Kingdom, for we have a King and are His loyal subjects. Acceptance of the "yoke of the Kingdom of Heaven" is a prerequisite for admission to the school of Avraham Avinu. Only a person who is able to humbly submit himself to the truth of Hashem can learn to live a Divine-like life of pure *tzedakah* and pure *mishpat*. Only after a person can admit that he is created by Hashem can he begin to enter the world of Divine-like purity and goodness. All "natural" human virtues of love and compassion, justice and truth, become sublimely elevated and purified by the Torah and fear of Hashem.

Our *Chachamim* teach us that "good" and "evil" were originally two separate entities that became intertwined after Adam sinned in *Gan Eden*, thus activating both forces in the human being. Thus, a person can perform an act of kindness — but for selfish reasons. He can stand up for justice — yet can look away when his own interests are involved. He can simultaneously be kind and cruel, a mix of good and the evil. But the Torah of Hashem teaches purity, wherein the good is purified from the evil and the evil is destroyed. Here lies the crucial difference between the Jewish people and the nations of the world. Although the Jewish people, too, are tainted with this mix of good and evil, we *aspire* to purity. Whereas the nations of the world have no understanding of the world of purity, the Jew lives it, studies it, and prays for it, for therein is the source of his soul. Thus we pray every Shabbos and Yom Tov, "purify our hearts to worship You in truth." The gate to this world of sublime purity is *yiras Shamayim*, fear of Heaven, and thus Yisrael are *"dorshei yirah,"* they desire *yiras Shamayim* (see *Rashi, Sanhedrin* 76b, s.v. *rovo*). This is the great achievement of Avraham Avinu — to create a nation that aspires to live the ways of Hashem by forming a personality which intrinsically performs *tzedekah* and *mishpat*.

We can now begin to understand the great paradox. On the one hand, knowingly violating the Shabbos, or not accepting the yoke of the Kingdom of Heaven, is tantamount to denying Hashem and His Torah; such a person is ostracized from *klal Yisrael*, even if he performs many acts of *tzedakah* and *mishpat*. On the other hand, a miserly Jew who does not give *tzedakah*, although condemned as cruel and compared to an idol worshiper, is still considered part of the body of the Jewish nation. Similarly, an individual who lies and cheats causes the *Shechinah* to depart from *klal Yisrael*, but is still considered a part of that *klal*. Further, speaking *lashon hara* is compared to violating the three cardinal sins of idol worship, immorality and murder; yet while those sins are punishable with the death penalty, the *baal lashon hara* is not punished so. In short, violation of *tzedakah* and *mishpat* is a violation of the very purpose of the Jewish nation, yet *halachah* views the idol worshiper and Shabbos violator with far more gravity. Why?

The answer is that the idol worshiper and the Shabbos violator are denying Hashem, the Creator of the world and Source of all *tzedakah* and *mishpat*. Denial of Hashem is inherently the worst violation of *tzedakah* and *mishpat*, for how can a creature say to his Creator, "I deny You; You are not relevant to my life"? On the other hand, Shabbos observance is in essence an affirmation of the purpose of the Jewish nation — to live Divine-like lives, doing *tzedakah* and *mishpat*. Even if one's life is lacking in terms of practicing *tzedakah* and *mishpat*, he still affirms through his Shabbos observance that following Hashem's ways (by doing *tzedakah* and *mishpat*) is the true way of life, and *he* is the one who is amiss in his actions. Someone who poisons his Divine-like soul by defiling his body with immorality and forbidden foods may perform many acts of *tzedakah* and *mishpat*, but they arise from a tainted source, and are thus impure and will eventually die out. This can be compared to a tree that has not been properly watered and pruned; it may produce luscious fruit for a short time because of its former vigor, but the weakness of the tree will ultimately be seen in its poor produce. Conversely, those who faithfully observe Shabbos and study Torah but do not properly practice *tzedakah* and *mishpat* are living a life that contradicts the essence of religion.

This is portrayed by the Rambam in *Hilchos Yom Tov* (6:17-18): *A person is obligated on the Yamim Tovim to be happy and in good cheer, he and his family. And while a person eats and drinks, he is obligated to feed the convert, the orphan and the widow with all the other impoverished. But someone who locks the doors of his courtyard, eats and drinks with his family, but does not feed the impoverished, this is not the rejoicing of mitzvah but the rejoicing of his stomach.*

Let us imagine a religious Jew sitting with his family in his *succah* on Chol HaMoed in an atmosphere of true Torah rejoicing. They discuss Torah thoughts, and sing songs of joy and closeness to Hashem. Just then a *meshulach* from a particular yeshivah appears at the door for the umpteenth time. As the man of the house opens his wallet to give him a few dollars, the scowl on his face betrays his feelings of impatience at being "nudged" so often, especially during such a wonderful and Torah'dik Succos meal.

We may feel that although the person was amiss in his performance of the mitzvah of *tzedakah*, he is still fulfilling the mitzvah of *simchas Yom Tov* in a beautiful way. Yet the Rambam tells us that his *simchas Yom Tov* is lacking as well, for his *simchah* is a *simchah* of the stomach!

The reason is simple, yet penetrating. The essence of the mitzvah of rejoicing on Yom Tov is to come close to Hashem, who radiates love to all His creations, and especially to His beloved people. When coming close to Hashem, a person automatically feels that love, as someone approaching a fire feels its warmth. Closeness to Hashem without a simultaneous feeling of love for all one's fellow Jews is not a true closeness to Hashem, but to something else entirely. Were the man in the *succah* truly striving for closeness to Hashem, he would have felt a kinship and empathy with the *meshulach*, and shared the *simchas* Yom Tov with him (even if he could not afford to help him).

Tefillah is the experience of "standing before Hashem," and so, a person who has *davened* with true *kavannah* will feel distaste for all evil and desire only *tzedakah* and *mishpat*. At the end of *Shemoneh Esrei* we beseech Hashem to "guard my tongue from evil"; at that moment the person detests evil for that is the nature of the experience of "standing before Hashem." If a person is angry at a certain individual, and still feels the same measure of fury after *davening Shemoneh Esrei* as he did before, he can be quite certain that he did not truly experience "standing before Hashem."

Shabbos is described in *Navi* as the day when a person divests himself of his personal "interests," a day that teaches us idealism and selflessness. When Shabbos is over, a person should feel a bit more idealistic than at its start, and should be filled with a resolve to hold onto that idealism and spirituality the entire week. If he feels no such positive feelings and emotions, then he has "missed" Shabbos.

Rabbeinu Yonah teaches us that a person who does not constantly and actively seek peace between people is devoid of *yiras Shamayim*. Furthermore, a *yerei Shamayim* will not only refrain from speaking *lashon hara* but is *incapable* of destroying someone with his speech.

All these topics share one common theme. It is not enough for a person to know that Hashem runs the world. He must know about Hashem — who He is and what He wants from a person. He must know that Hashem reveals Himself through love, kindness and truth, through *tzedakah* and *mishpat*.

Let the wise man not esteem himself for his wisdom, let the mighty one not esteem himself for his strength nor the wealthy one for his wealth. Rather in this let a person esteem himself — ponder and know Me for I am Hashem who does tzedakah and mishpat, for this I choose, says Hashem (Yirmiyahu 9:22-23).

Anyone who performs tzedakah and mishpat is considered as if he has filled the world with kindness (Succah 49b).

Rabbi Shimon bar Yochai explains in the Holy Zohar that all Atzilus (Hashem's revelation of His attributes) is called love (Reishis Chochmah, Ahavah, Chapter 2, Paragraph 1).

The *mitzvos bein adam l'chaveiro* are mitzvos of the Torah, like all the mitzvos, and anyone who professes to be religious must be meticulous in their details. But they are much more — they serve as a barometer of a person's religiosity. Closeness to Hashem inherently means feeling love for both Hashem and His creatures, and developing a personality that loves *tzedakah* and *mishpat*. Above all, these mitzvos are the area where the human being reflects the Divine attributes by practicing them in his relationships with his fellow man. This is the great purpose of the holy nation — to immerse in the study of the ways of Hashem and apply them to life. This is why Hashem referred to Avraham Avinu as beloved, for he shall teach his children to follow the ways of Hashem to do *tzedakah* and *mishpat*. When we failed in our task we were sentenced to destruction and exile, and each small step in the right direction brings us one step closer to our ultimate redemption, as we were promised that in the end Hashem will redeem us and bring us back to Him. *Tziyon will be redeemed with mishpat and its returnees with tzedakah (Yeshayahu 1:27)* — *bimheirah b'yameinu, Amen.*

➹ Love and Hate

Chapters 1-5

1

Love and Kindness

1. It is a mitzvah for every Jew to love every fellow Jew as he loves himself, as the Torah states (*Vayikra* 19:18), *You shall love your fellow as yourself.*[1]

Rabbi Akiva taught that this is the principle upon which the mitzvos of the Torah are based. Ben Azzai elaborated, quoting the verse regarding the creation of man (*Bereishis* 1:27), *in the likeness of Hashem he was created.* Thus, when we view another person, we are viewing the likeness of the Creator. The Jewish people, who committed themselves to enter a permanent covenant with Hashem to follow His ways, are considered children of Hashem. This is how we must perceive every other Jew. Furthermore, since we all have one "Father," we are all "related," which breeds natural closeness and feelings of affinity.[2]

2. The underlying principle of this mitzvah can be stated as follows: Whatever you desire for yourself you should also wish for your brother in Torah and mitzvos.[3] The Torah does not expect us to actu-

---

1. *Rambam, Hilchos Dei'os* 6:3.

2. *Toras Kohanim, Parshas Kedoshim* 4:12; *Raavad, Rabbeinu Hillel* (cf. *Rashi, Shabbos* 31a, s.v. *de'aluch*). See also *Avos D'Rabbi Nosson* 16:5, *Devarim* 14:1.

3. *Ramban* on this mitzvah (*Vayikra* 19:18).

ally love other people in the same way we love ourselves; this is impossible since by nature each person loves himself more than he loves others. Rather, the Torah is telling us that just as it is natural for each person to love himself, to wish only good for himself, not to begrudge himself wealth, intelligence, friendship, etc. or resent himself for having them, so also should he love all other Jews so much that he wants them to have all that their hearts desire, and feels no twinge of resentment toward those who have more than he does. Some people are content for others to have wealth but not intelligence or vice versa, yet this mitzvah commands us to preclude that attitude and learn to genuinely want our fellow Jews to have limitless quantities of all the good things in the world.[4]

3. This mitzvah includes the expression of love and caring for one's fellow in practical ways. For example, we are commanded to:

❑ Speak only in a positive manner about others.
❑ Be as protective of their money and property as of our own.
❑ Show the same degree of concern for their honor as we do for our own.[5]
❑ Help those in need to the best of our abilities.
❑ Camouflage their deficiencies just as we would wish our own faults to be overlooked.
❑ Try to deflect and defuse a person's anger at another individual through any means available.[6]

All types of kindness (emotional support; physical and financial assistance, large or small;[7] and even a friendly smile[8]) are included in this mitzvah.[9]

4. Some people behave in the opposite fashion, taking pleasure in other people's distress, emphasizing their mistakes and failings, and doing their best to instigate disputes. Such individuals often pride themselves on their great cunning in causing trouble for

---

4. Thus this mitzvah commands us to eliminate, as far as possible, the trait of jealousy (*Ramban* ibid.).

5. *Rambam* ibid.

6. *Shemiras HaLashon, Shaar HaTevunah,* Ch. 17.

7. *Pe'ah* 1:1.

8. *Kesubos* 111b.

9. *Mesillas Yesharim,* Ch. 19.

people. However, the Torah teaches that genuine wisdom and strength lie in using the talents Hashem gave us to observe this mitzvah by supporting other people and helping them get along with each other.[10]

To Whom Does This Mitzvah Apply

5. The mitzvah of loving a fellow Jew applies to anyone included in the category of "your fellow," namely any upright Jew who believes in the Thirteen Principles of Faith and observes the fundamentals of Torah Law. Even if such a person occasionally commits transgressions because of his baser desires and inclinations, he is still considered a brother in Torah and mitzvos.[11] In the present era, we consider all Jews to be included in this mitzvah (as well as all other interpersonal mitzvos), even those who are not observant, since they have not yet been exposed to true Torah values.[12]

6. The special quality which makes the Jewish people deserving of our love, to the extent that it is even a mitzvah to love them, is that they serve Hashem.[13] Indeed, the mitzvah of loving Jews is directly subordinate to the mitzvah of loving Hashem, as the Torah writes, *You shall love your fellow as yourself, I am Hashem.* Anyone who loves the King will also love His children and servants simply because they are His children and servants, and the greater the service they perform for Him, the more worthy they are of our love. Torah scholars and others who stand out in their service of Hashem are worthy of special love. The greatest Sages were noted for the exceptional affection they had for all Torah scholars.[14]

---

10. *Shemiras HaLashon* ibid.

11. *Rambam, Commentary on Mishnah, Sanhedrin,* Ch. 10 (at the end of the Thirteen Articles of Faith).

12. *Chazon Ish, Yoreh Deah* 2:28. Also *Chazon Ish, Orach Chaim* 87:14. See *Rambam, Hilchos Mamrim* 3:3. For further discussion see Ch. 23 par. 25 and fn. 33.

13. *Avos D'Rabbi Nosson* 16:5; *Shemiras HaLashon, Shaar HaTevunah,* Ch. 6, fn.; see *Mesillas Yesharim,* Ch. 19.

Note: Unfortunately, sometimes the sacred mitzvah of *ahavas Yisrael* is used as a vehicle for promoting anti-Torah values such as racism or nationalism. The barometer of *ahavas Yisrael* is twofold: (a) It fosters the quality of love and kindness, and (b) it includes all Jews and especially those noted for their devotion to Hashem. Someone who preaches *ahavas Yisrael* toward all — including secular — Jews, but feels animosity to certain groups whose devotion to Hashem leads them to declare a different political stance than his own is not preaching *ahavas Yisrael* at all.

14. *Shabbos* 119a.

The Sages relate that whenever King Yehoshafat would see a Torah scholar, he would get up from his throne and embrace and kiss him and call to him, "My master, my master! My teacher, my teacher!"[15]

7. In addition to the general mitzvah, there is a special mitzvah to love converts, as the Torah says (*Devarim* 10:19): *You shall love the proselyte.* Just as we are commanded to love Hashem, as it says (ibid. 6:5), *You shall love Hashem, your G-d,* so are we commanded to love converts. In fact, the Torah writes specifically of Hashem's special love for converts (ibid. 10:18).[16]

Reishis Chochmah[17] counts ten verses in *Sefer Devarim* which command us to love Hashem. The tenth and final verse is *You shall love the proselyte,* because love of a proselyte has an innate connection to love of Hashem. This can be explained in the following way: The tenth verse expresses Hashem's sovereignty. The prophet describes the essence of Hashem's kingdom (*Zechariah* 14:9): *And Hashem will be King over all the earth; on that day Hashem will be One and His Name will be One.* A member of the nations of the earth who has entered a covenant to follow Hashem and His Torah, has, in effect, crowned Hashem upon himself. Thus his own "individual world" is a living testimony to Hashem's Kingship and Oneness (cf. *Rashi, Devarim* 8:4).

8. Although the mitzvah of love applies only to fellow Jews, the traits of love and kindness that are inherent in the mitzvah carry over to all human beings. The Rambam[18] writes, "Even toward idol worshipers the Sages commanded us to visit their sick and sustain their poor along with the Jewish poor, for these are the ways of peace." It is written (*Tehillim* 145:9), *Hashem is good to all, and His compassion is on all His creations;* we, too, are enjoined to follow His ways and act in a similar fashion. Furthermore, it says (*Mishlei* 3:17), *Its [the Torah's] ways are ways of pleasantness and all its pathways are peace.* Therefore, a Torah personality acts pleasantly and with a peaceful demeanor to everyone. (See Chapter 2, footnote 1.)

Rabban Yochanan ben Zakkai was always the first to greet another person. Never did anyone greet him first, Jew or gentile.[19]

---

15. *Makkos* 24a.

16. *Rambam, Hilchos Dei'os* 6:4.

17. *Shaar Ahavah,* Ch. 1.

18. *Hilchos Melachim* 10:12.

19. *Berachos* 17a.

The Positive and Negative Commandments

9. Just as there is a positive commandment to do good for others as we would want done for ourselves, so there is also a negative commandment not to do to others anything we would not want to have done to ourselves. Anyone who treats others as he would not want to be treated himself violates a commandment of the Torah.[20]

> *The Midcity, USA Jewish community numbered about 500 families. Traditionally, the Gold, Silver, and Scholar families were the leaders of the community. The Gold and Silver families were the wealthiest, and the Scholar family was the most learned. One day, David Scholar, who owned a medium sized mini-market, approached Chaim Gold with a request. The local supermarket chain was up for sale, and he wanted Chaim Gold to invest and help him acquire it. Chaim said he would think about it. However, Chaim Gold already felt secretly envious of David Scholar's Torah knowledge, which he had acquired through years of diligent study. The possibility that David would also vie with him for a position of wealth in the community was just too much to bear. He invented an excuse and politely explained that he was "unfortunately" unable to help. Chaim Gold has violated the commandment to "love one's fellow as oneself."*

10. The degree of good or bad in an action or statement is judged relative to the recipient or subject rather than to the doer or speaker.

Reuven is in *kollel* and devotes many hours each day to his Torah studies. His friend Shimon is a working man. If Reuven praises Shimon by saying that he spends three hours learning daily, Reuven is credited with the mitzvah of loving other Jews. Shimon's allotment of three hours is considered highly praiseworthy, since his time is constricted by the demands of his job and other obligations. On the other hand, for Shimon to say that Reuven learns six hours per day would be highly derogatory, since far more is expected of a *kollel* student. Shimon's statement transgresses the positive commandment to love fellow Jews, as well as the prohibitions against *lashon hara*. In any given situation, the standard is the effect of an action or statement on the person to whom it relates, regardless of how it would affect a different person.[21]

---

20. Cf. *Shabbos* 31a: "Whatever is hateful to you, do not do to others"; see *Avos D'Rabbi Nosson* 16:5; see also *Toras Kohanim* on *Vayikra* 19:18 with the commentary of the *Chofetz Chaim*.

21. *Chofetz Chaim, Hilchos Lashon Hara* 5:6.

11. The mitzvah of loving fellow Jews applies to children as well, since they are considered our "fellows" no less than adults. Anything one does to make them happy, given their age and level of development, is included in the mitzvah. Conversely, anything one does to cause them pain or unhappiness violates this mitzvah (except, of course, when necessary for their education and upbringing). Therefore, whenever one brings children happiness (including one's own children), one should have the fulfillment of this mitzvah in mind.

> One Yom Kippur night, R' Yisrael Salanter, the founder of the Mussar movement, delayed davening with a minyan in order to placate a crying child, thus fulfilling the commandment of loving fellow Jews. Ignoring the child would have constituted a violation of this mitzvah.

Other Practical Applications of the Mitzvah

12. All acts of kindness that one person does for another, such as shopping for a neighbor, offering someone a lift, or helping with homework, are included in the mitzvah to "love one's fellow."[22] There are a number of practical kindnesses that the Sages have categorized as independent mitzvos, such as hospitality, visiting the sick, comforting mourners and bringing joy to a bride and groom. Practical assistance such as healing the sick, lending money, and giving charity are also categorized as independent mitzvos. (These will be explained in later chapters.) However, they are all also included in this general mitzvah of kindness and love of one's fellow.[23]

13. Just as we can fulfill the mitzvah of loving fellow Jews with kind acts, so we can also fulfill it through kindness in speech, because any kindness we do for others is counted as a mitzvah.[24] If one sees a person who appears burdened with sadness or difficulty (e.g. illness, poverty, etc.) one should attempt to reassure him and relieve his anxiety. In our time, many people suffer from low self-esteem. Anything one does to help someone else live a happier and more satisfying life is included in the mitzvah of kindness.

22. *Rambam, Hilchos Aveil* 14:1.

23. *Mesillas Yesharim*, Ch. 19.

24. See *Ahavas Chesed* Part 3, Ch. 8 for a lengthy discussion.

The Sages said that anyone who gives a coin to a needy person receives six blessings, while someone who mollifies him receives eleven.[25]

Even greeting someone with a smile can cheer a person up and warm his heart. In fact, the Sages require us to greet every person with a pleasant countenance (*Avos* 1:15), which is also included in the mitzvah of kindness.

The Sages taught that showing someone the white of one's teeth (i.e. in a smile) is a greater mitzvah than giving him milk to drink.[26]

Greetings

14. When one meets someone with whom one is accustomed to exchange greetings, it is a mitzvah to greet him first, as the Psalmist says, *Seek peace and pursue it* (*Tehillim* 34:15).[27] The greatest Sages made a point of being the first to greet everyone they met, even non-Jews in the street.[28] There is, however, no requirement to greet someone of the opposite sex (for reasons of propriety).[29] Anyone who fails to return a greeting is considered a "thief."[30]

Community Responsibility

15. Each community should have trained and experienced workers available to resolve conflicts among people, especially between quarreling spouses. Those who do this work should be good natured and happy, rather than quick-tempered or perverse, and should be capable of placating people and creating a positive and cheerful atmosphere. For their efforts they are assured of a place in the World to Come.[31]

Other Forms of Kindness

16. Included in the mitzvah of kindness is arranging for someone to do a favor for another, giving people useful suggestions or advis-

25. *Bava Basra* 9b.

26. *Kesubos* 111b.

27. *Berachos* 6b.

28. Ibid. 17a.

29. *Rabbeinu Yonah* in *Sefer HaYirah*. (Note: The sanctity of Jewish *tzenius* proscribes unnecessary idle conversation between men and women [*Avos* 1:5]. Similarly, greetings between men and women are discouraged except where they are necessary and appropriate.)

30. *Berachos* 6b.

31. *Iggeres HaTeshuvah* by *Rabbeinu Yonah,* 14.

ing them how to avoid potential harm.[32] Also included in the mitzvah is giving directions to people in need of them. See Chapter 56 for further discussion of this mitzvah and its enormous reward.

Preventing Harm

17. Just as this mitzvah commands us to help our fellows in any way we can, so too does it forbid us to cause others any harm, whether physical (to their bodies or their property) or emotional (through any kind of anguish or discomfort). Thus if we see another Jew's property in danger of suffering damage, we are required to protect it, as the Torah says (*Devarim* 22:3), *You shall not look away* (when you can save someone else's property). All the more so, if we see anyone in danger of suffering physical or emotional harm, we are required to do everything in our power to protect him, as the Torah says (*Vayikra* 19:16), *You shall not stand aside while your fellow's blood is being shed.*[33]

18. It is highly desirable for each community to have an organization of trained volunteers, on constant alert, to undertake all types of rescue activities as required. Just as the Torah commands us to make efforts to protect the property of our fellows, all the more so are we required to see to the needs of their owners.[34]

Many communities have a Hatzalah organization that provides medical care to sick and injured people.

19. One should constantly look for ways to give others the merit of helping people, for the Sages said that causing others to do good is greater than doing good oneself:[35]
(a) Identify a needed action.
(b) Consider who would be appropriate to perform it.
(c) Suggest the mitzvah to that person.
(d) Assist him to overcome any obstacles that may arise.

Teaching Torah

20. Included in the mitzvah of kindness is teaching Torah, especially in places where there is no one else to do so. Those who exert

---

32. *Ahavas Chesed* Part 3, Ch. 8.

33. *Shaarei Teshuvah* 3:70.

34. Ibid. 3:71.

35. *Bava Basra* 9a.

themselves to teach Torah fulfill the commandments of learning Torah and performing kindness simultaneously.[36]

Major yeshivos have sponsored community *kollels* which have enabled many people to study Torah.

Praying for Others

21. Included in the mitzvah of doing kindness to others is praying for their well-being and feeling for their concerns as if they were one's own. The Sages said that anyone who is in a position to pray for someone in need of prayer, and does not do so, is considered a sinner. In particular, if the needy person is a Torah scholar one should go to great lengths when praying for him.[37]

King David said, *And when they were sick I donned sackcloth, I afflicted myself with fasting (Tehillim* 35:13).

The Extent of One's Obligation

22. Rabbeinu Yonah writes: "A person is obligated to exert himself to be beneficial to his people and to attempt with persevering toil to search for helpful solutions to the problems of his friends, whether rich or poor. This is one of the most serious and fundamental obligations demanded of each person."[38]

---

36. *Succah* 49b. See *Halichos Olam* 69:2,3 and fn. *beis.*
37. *Berachos* 12b.
38. *Shaarei Teshuvah* 3:13.

2

The Torah Personality[1]

Following the Ways of Hashem

1. We are commanded to follow Hashem's ways, as the Torah says,
    You shall go in His ways (*Devarim* 28:9). The Sages gave the fol-
    lowing explanation: Just as He is compassionate, you should also be
    compassionate; just as He performs kindness, so you should also
    perform kindness. In other words, we should strive to imbue our-
    selves with all those qualities which the Torah reveals Hashem as
    having.[2] The aim of this mitzvah is the ultimate goal of the Torah:
    to mold a personality that, although living in the midst of human
    beings, is endowed with Divine-like attributes. The practical
    aspects of this mitzvah are discussed in the following paragraphs,
    and in more detail in Chapter 16. Some of the more profound appli-
    cations of this mitzvah are discussed in the concluding chapter of
    this book.

---

1. The Talmud states (*Sotah* 14a) that the Torah commences with a Divine act of lovingkindness and concludes with a Divine act of lovingkindness. We can derive from this statement
that a person should, through Torah study, develop a personality that emulates Divine
ways. This is a "Torah personality."

2. *Rambam, Hilchos Dei'os* 1:6; *Chofetz Chaim*, Introduction, Positive Commandment 6.

Avraham Avinu served all his guests himself, even the lowest of people. He learned this from Hashem who brings rain and provides food for all His creatures (see Kiddushin 32b).

2. Whenever the prophets described Hashem's "character traits," such as slow to anger, abundant in kindness, righteous, truthful, straightforward, strong, etc., their intention was to teach us the qualities we should embody in our conduct in order to emulate Hashem, to the extent that our limited abilities allow.[3]

❏ If a person provides sustenance for someone, he should think, "I am emulating Hashem Who provides sustenance to all."

❏ If a person helps a groom and bride rejoice at their wedding, he should think, "I am emulating Hashem Who brought rejoicing to Adam and Chavah in *Gan Eden*."

❏ If a person visits or heals a sick person, he should think, "I am emulating Hashem Who heals the sick and visits them" (cf. *Bereishis* 18:1).

❏ If a person smiles at someone and raises their spirits, he should think, "I am emulating Hashem Who radiates His countenance at a human being and brings him inner joy and peace" (cf. *Bamidbar* 6:25-26; *Tehillim* 80:20; *Yalkut* ad loc.).

❏ If a person is tempted by evil, and he remains strong, he should think, "I am emulating Hashem Who is strong and overcomes all evil."

3. In practical terms, this mitzvah is not measured through accomplishment but rather by effort. A person cannot be expected to overcome negative character traits outright, but he is obligated to make a slow but sure effort toward the goal of character refinement. The effort is the essence of the mitzvah, and failing to make this effort constitutes a violation of the commandment to go in Hashem's ways.[4]

A daily regimen of *mussar* study is certainly an attempt to improve one's character traits. The *Mishnah Berurah* writes that *mussar* study has precedence over *Mishnayos* (Torah study).[5]

---

3. *Rambam* ibid.

4. *Sefer HaChinuch*, Mitzvah 611.

5. *Mishnah Berurah* 1:13 and *Shaar HaTziyun* 26.

4. Therefore, if someone does not make this effort and as a result falls prey to his negative character traits (e.g. anger, insensitivity), he actively violates this commandment, apart from any other prohibitions involved, since he is commanded to go in Hashem's ways and he chose to do the opposite.

Judging Others Favorably

5. The Torah commands us to give others the benefit of the doubt and to judge them favorably, as the Torah states: *With righteousness shall you judge your fellow* (*Vayikra* 19:15). We are commanded to view people as basically upright, honest and good-hearted. It is illogical that such a person would willfully do evil. Therefore, if we see a person do something that appears evil, we must search for the extenuating circumstance that mitigates the evil and does not present the perpetrator as being an "evil person." As we shall explain, this mitzvah applies in different ways depending on the circumstances.[6]

6. *An Upright Person.* If someone who is known to be very meticulous in his Torah observance is seen doing something which appears wrong, one is required to look for ways to excuse the suspicious action and to give it a favorable interpretation. (If one cannot think of any good interpretation, he should nonetheless tell himself that the subject must have had a good reason for acting as he did, even if it is difficult to imagine such a reason from one's present perspective.) It is forbidden to suspect the subject of wrongdoing.

> *When Chanah, the mother of the prophet Shmuel, was praying in an unusual manner, Eli the Kohen suspected her of drunkenness. He thus violated this prohibition.*

7. *An Ordinary Person.* If the subject is an ordinary person (someone who generally acts properly but does occasionally stray), and if favorable and unfavorable interpretations of his action seem equally likely, then one is required to give him the benefit of the doubt and to assume that the favorable interpretation is correct. Even if the unfavorable interpretation seems much more likely, it is still a mitzvah to judge the subject favorably, although it is not absolutely required. In any case, one should not firmly conclude

---

6. *Chofetz Chaim,* Introduction, Positive Commandment 3; *Chofetz Chaim, Hilchos Lashon Hara* 3:7, *Be'er Mayim Chaim* ad loc. See also *Zera Chaim; Kodesh Yisrael,* Ch. 23.

that the subject definitely acted improperly; rather, one should endeavor to at least remain in doubt about the matter.

> *When Miriam was late for her appointment with Dinah, Dinah presumed that an urgent matter had caused the tardiness, rather than assuming that Miriam acted with disregard toward other people.*

8. *A Habitual Wrongdoer.* If one knows that the subject habitually follows his base passions and in general makes no attempt to act properly, then one should assume that he acted improperly or had selfish motivations even if the facts of a particular incident suggest that he was in the right.[7]

> *Mr. A is known to be a money-hungry businessman. One day he returned some money to its rightful owner. Although one hopes that this is the first sign of teshuvah, one should nevertheless suspect that he had some ulterior motive of profit, legal or otherwise.*

9. In practice, each situation has to be evaluated individually.[8] Thus, if someone who is known to be an upright observer of the standard mitzvos is seen openly violating a well-known law of Shabbos, since in this area he is righteous, one is required to assume that he did so for a valid reason (e.g. in order to save a life). It is only permitted to believe that his intentions were bad if investigation shows that the action had no justification whatsoever and that his desecration of the Sabbath could only have been willful and deliberate. If, however, the same person is heard speaking what appears to be *lashon hara*, then unless he is known to be exceptionally careful in those *halachos*, he has the status of an ordinary person (as in paragraph 7 above). It is therefore permitted to suspect that he intended to speak *lashon hara*, although it is still a mitzvah to give him the benefit of the doubt and to presume that he had a valid reason for doing so.

10. Conversely, if someone is known to be extremely lax concerning the *halachos* regulating human interactions (e.g. he is known to be insensitive to people's feelings), and one hears that he has insulted someone, it is not required to give him the benefit of the doubt and assume that the account of the incident was distorted, since the report is consistent with his known behavior patterns. Nevertheless, it is still a mitzvah to look for mitigating circumstances, such as that his

---

7. *Chofetz Chaim* ibid., Positive Commandment 3.

8. *Kodesh Yisrael,* Ch. 23.

upbringing and experience in life have not taught him how wrong such behavior is. If, however, the same person is seen desecrating the Shabbos, because his status as an ordinary Jew has not changed, it is required to assume that he had a legitimate reason.

11. *Look for Excuses.* An important principle in these matters is that it is nearly always possible to find some way to excuse, or at least to mitigate the severity of, any action or bad quality one sees. Often, a person's first reaction to a questionable incident is totally negative, to the extent that one feels completely certain that there could not possibly be any excuse for what happened. In general, however, such reactions result from not thinking carefully about the circumstances surrounding the event. One can nearly always reason that the subject did not fully understand the seriousness of what he was doing, or that his training and experience in life have led him to believe that his action was actually good, or even required, or some other rationale for the failing in question.

> *Avraham was the ultimate "negative" in the yeshivah. He regularly taunted other boys, and had no interest in learning. His only real enjoyment was to make jokes at other people's expense. David regularly complained to his parents about Avraham. One day David's mother said to him, "It sounds like there was something missing in Avraham's background. Why don't we investigate his situation at home?" After a few days, it became clear that Avraham received very little love, recognition and emotional support from his family, and was acting up in yeshivah to get some much-needed attention. David felt sorry for Avraham and his feelings about him changed radically.*

12. One way to search for mitigating circumstances is to consider that had we seen this same action or bad quality in a close friend or relative (and all the more so in ourselves), we would most certainly find some way to excuse or overlook it. It is only because a stranger is involved that we condemn this action or failing. However, the Torah commands us, *You shall love your fellow as yourself* (*Vayikra* 19:18), in order to exhort us to go to the same lengths to excuse the actions of others as we would go to overlook our own failings. Seen in this way, it is easy to recognize that there are infinite excuses and justifications we can (and do) give for our own actions, and that by changing our perspective we can reverse our attitude toward another person from one extreme to the other.

Do you ever excuse yourself by saying: "That's the way I am! That's the way I was brought up! It's impossible for me to change! All right, so I'm not perfect. Other people aren't perfect in other ways!"?

Next time you jump to condemn someone, put yourself in their place and say: "That's the way he is! That's the way he was brought up! It's impossible for him to change! All right, so he's not perfect. Other people aren't perfect in other ways!"

Note: These excuses are not to be used as a reason to continue wrong behavior. Rather, this way of thinking is meant to help us view another person in a different light, to replace anger with sadness for someone who does not see that what he is doing is wrong, and to empathize with him, for we, too, rationalize when we do wrong.

13. Someone who fails to seek ways to excuse the actions of his fellow Jew and judges him unfavorably not only violates these two commandments — *With righteousness shall you judge your fellow* and *You shall love your fellow as yourself* — but also lays the groundwork for violating a host of commandments involving *lashon hara*, *rechilus*, and many of the other commandments governing interpersonal relationships.

14. *Put Yourself in Their Position.* If, in spite of one's best efforts, it is impossible to find an excuse for someone's action or bad quality, remember the Sages' advice, *Do not judge your fellow until you are in his place* (*Avos* 2:5). Thus, one should imagine himself in the exact position as the object of one's condemnation: in the same job or circumstance, equally poor or wealthy, formed by similar education and experiences, faced with identical pressures. Then, consider if it can honestly be said that under those circumstances, he, too, would not act in the same manner.[9]

---

9. At this point, it is worthwhile to discuss one situation in which people are quick to condemn others and gloat over their failings. Reports sometimes circulate alleging financial improprieties on the part of Torah institutions, and people who otherwise observe Torah and mitzvos are quick to believe such reports as entirely true [see Ch. 13 par. 33 for reliability (halachically and otherwise) of information conveyed through the news media] and to condemn the administrators of those institutions in their minds and to speak *lashon hara* about them. As we have said, however, even if the evidence is weighted heavily against them, the Torah requires us to judge them favorably and to assume that the reports are untrue. Even if they are true, we must presume that the people involved were led astray by unscrupulous elements and were not aware of what they were doing, or were otherwise acting in innocence. Even if there was impropriety involved, we are required to imagine how we would feel and behave if the heavy burden of covering the ongoing expenses of an institution rested on our shoulders, and if we ourselves were faced with

15. *Contorted Reasoning.* The *gaon* R' Chaim Ozer Grodzinsky was
    once asked,[10] if Hashem created everything in the world for a
    good purpose, what is the purpose of contorted reasoning (*a krumme
    kop*). He answered that its purpose is to help us judge others favor-
    ably, and he cited as proof a number of stories related by the Sages in
    Tractate *Shabbos* (127b).

> *Once, in the time of the Sages, a Jew left his family and hired himself
> out as a farm laborer to a landowner at the other end of the country.
> At the end of three years, right before Yom Tov, the worker, eager to see
> his family again, requested his wages. When he asked for money, the
> employer responded, "I have no money." When he asked for produce,
> the employer said, "I have no produce." When he asked for land, the
> employer said, "I have no land." When he asked for livestock, the
> employer said, "I have no livestock." When he asked for sheets and pil-
> lows, the employer said, "I have no sheets and pillows." Depressed, the
> worker returned to his family empty-handed.*
>
> *After Yom Tov the employer came to the worker's home with full
> financial compensation plus three donkeys laden with food, drink and
> choice delicacies. When they sat down to dine together, the employer
> asked the worker, "When I said I had no money, what did you think?"
> The worker answered, "I presumed that a large amount of cheap mer-
> chandise became available and you had invested all your money in it."*
>
> *"When I said I had no livestock, what did you think?"*
>
> *The worker answered, "I presumed that they were rented out to
> others at that time."*

---

the unrelenting task of persuading people to donate hard-earned resources to those committed to a life of Torah. Would we respond any better to this challenge? Let us especially remember that those administrators have made a conscious decision to accept these
burdens for the sake of promoting Torah, when they could easily abandon their responsibilities and pursue a less demanding and more lucrative career. Seen in this light, can we
really think that people's condemnations of such individuals, whatever wrongdoings
they may be guilty of, stem from anything other than petty vanity and derisiveness?
Rather, if one hears a report condemning the administration of a Torah institution, our
reaction should be sadness for the desecration of Hashem's Name and sorrow for the person involved that he allegedly stooped to such low behavior. Simultaneously, if possible,
one should show readiness to help that institution recover from its financial difficulties.
However, this is *in no way intended* to excuse any illicit behavior on anyone's part. There
is absolutely no excuse or justification for misdealings of any kind, however great the
pressures may be. Clearly the Torah, which is the source and foundation of all Truth, has
no desire for dishonest funding to survive and flourish. Rather, these words are intended
solely to discourage people from gloating over the failures of others.

10. Heard from my rebbi, HaRav Yerucham Gorelik.

"When I said I have no land, what did you think?"

The worker answered, "I presumed that it, too, was rented out."

"When I said I have no produce, what did you think?"

The worker answered, "I presumed it was not tithed yet."

"When I said I have no sheets and pillows, what did you think?"

The worker answered, "I presumed that you vowed to give all your possessions to the Sanctuary."

The employer then explained, "The truth is that I vowed to give away all my possessions to the Sanctuary because my son Hurkenos does not study Torah with diligence and is therefore unworthy of inheriting them. And when I approached the Sages in the south they released me from my vow. Therefore, I can now pay your wages!"

From this we see that we should apply all our reasoning abilities, even those that seem contorted, when it is necessary to invent excuses and justifications for other people's actions and to judge them favorably. If we are able to do so, we will fulfill Hashem's will that we seek out the good in others, and we can be assured that He, too, will seek out the good in us and judge our actions favorably.[11]

16. *Judging Groups.* Just as it is a mitzvah to judge individual Jews favorably, it is also a mitzvah to judge groups of Jews favorably. For this reason, when one observes other groups whose practices may seem strange and unexplainable from one's own perspective, one should be careful not to judge them unfavorably and certainly not to disparage these groups, since this would also be *lashon hara.*[12]

During our lengthy and difficult exile, Jews have been scattered to the four corners of the earth, where they have been exposed to alien influences and subjected to many trials. As a result, each grouping of Jews has developed its own strengths and weaknesses in response to the varied experiences undergone over the course of the centuries and millennia. It is human nature to overlook the failings of one's group (if one is aware of them at all) and to consider them normal and natural, yet at the same time to consider other groups' failings strange and undesirable. Thus, when one comes

---

11. *Shabbos* 127b.

12. Certainly if one considers a practice wrong or contrary to the Torah, he is entitled (and possibly required) to explain his objections to the practice and to advise those who respect his opinion not to follow it. Nonetheless, one should always give those who do follow such practices the benefit of the doubt and presume at least that they believe that a valid *halachic* opinion supports their position or some other justification of which one is unaware.

into contact with Jews from other cultures, one should remind himself that had he grown up among them he would undoubtedly have turned out the same. Furthermore, the fact that he is different and does not share their communal failings (or what seem like failings in his eyes) is not the result of any innate superiority on his part, but simply because Hashem saw fit to bring him into the world in a particular place, time and situation. Therefore he has no right to consider himself any better than them, but rather is required to accept and love them as equally beloved members of Hashem's people. Someone who fails to do so, and looks down on Jews from other groups — all the more so if he actively disparages them — violates these commandments (see paragraph 13 above) and is considered a *baal lashon hara* and *baal leitzanus*.

17. We must be far more careful not to look down on the Jewish people as a whole, nor to speak disparagingly of their failings and deficiencies. Instead, we should always strive to stress the strengths and accomplishments of Hashem's chosen and beloved people, both in our conversations with others as well as in our prayers.

Sefer Shemiras HaLashon (*Shaar HaTevunah*, Chapter 7) cites a moving prayer from *Tanna D'Vei Eliyahu*, which we present here in abridged form:

> *Master of the World, see our affliction and champion our cause, remember always the insults and injustice we suffer incessantly, how many of our people study Your Torah constantly in spite of the fact that they have no income. Think of all the youths who do not know their left hand from their right and study Torah constantly, of the elderly people who go to Your synagogues morning and night and eagerly await Your salvation with total faith in You. Remember Your covenant with Your faithful ones, our ancestors Avraham, Yitzchak and Yaakov; remember Your Torah which commands us to help and support the poor and afflicted, and please support us so that we never stumble and fall; remember the widows and orphans who uphold Your Torah and mitzvos every day. Remember that we are Your possessions.*

Concludes the Chofetz Chaim: "From this we can learn how each person can invoke Divine Mercy on the Jewish people, because even today, despite everything, there are many who study Torah, keep mitzvos, support Torah, and do manifold acts of kindness and charity."

Cleaving to Torah Scholars

18. The Torah commands us to cleave to Torah scholars, as the verse states, *To Him shall you cleave* (*Devarim* 10:20). Since it is impossible to cleave directly to Hashem, the Sages explained that we can fulfill this mitzvah by cleaving to those who devote themselves to studying and upholding His Torah.[13] By cleaving to them we will emulate their behavior.[14] The Sages urged us[15] to make our homes into meeting places for Torah scholars, to sit in the dust of their feet and to drink in their words thirstily, all in order to learn from their actions.

One cleaves to Torah scholars through any possible association such as:

❏ Marrying off his daughter to a Torah scholar.

❏ Marrying the daughter of a Torah scholar.

❏ Helping a Torah scholar with his financial affairs (e.g. investing for him).

19. If someone sees a group of people acting in a manner opposite to the Torah's teachings (e.g. speaking *lashon hara*, engaging in *machlokes*,[16] etc.) and deliberately joins in their conversation, he violates the mitzvah of fearing Hashem and cleaving to Him, even if the group includes individuals who study Torah.[17]

20. In matters of interpersonal relations, one should be careful not to learn from other people's incorrect behavior, even if they study Torah or are individuals of consequence.[18] Although we have to be careful to avoid learning from them, we are still required to give them the benefit of the doubt and assume that they are unaware of the severity of their actions and the prohibitions involved.[19] (Alternately, the onlooker may be mistaken in his assessment of the situation.)

Because our present exile is primarily a result of our failings in the realm of interpersonal mitzvos, it is quite possible that even someone who studies Torah does not appreciate the severity involved.

---

13. *Rambam, Hilchos Dei'os* 6:2; *Kesubos* 111b.

14. *Chofetz Chaim*, Introduction, Positive Commandment 6.

15. *Avos* 1:4.

16. See the beginning of Ch. 9 for a thorough and precise definition of the term *machlokes*.

17. *Chofetz Chaim* ibid.

18. *Chovas HaShemirah* (by the Chofetz Chaim), Ch. 10.

19. Ibid.

The 24,000 students of Rabbi Akiva died in a period of a few weeks because they did not show each other sufficient honor.

Qualities of a Torah Personality

21. The Torah commands us, *You shall do what is "straight" and "good" (yashar vetov) in Hashem's eyes (Devarim 6:8)*. The Ramban explains this mitzvah as follows: The Torah gives us many rules governing particular areas, such as *lashon hara* and *rechilus*, vengeance and grudge-bearing, rescuing others from harm, honoring elders, caring for the disadvantaged, and so on. However, it cannot discuss each and every way in which we interact with people and the myriad social, economic and political activities in which we engage in order to maintain our lives. Therefore, the Torah conveys a general principle to guide our behavior: that Hashem desires what is good, honest, and straight; and wants us to do more than that which strict justice requires; and wants us to accept compromises, even when we could insist on our rights.[20]

22. The Sages taught[21] that Jerusalem was destroyed because people insisted on their rights and did not compromise. Apparently, this is not merely an abrogation of a positive commandment but indicates a lack of something very basic to the Torah personality.

23. The Sages taught:[22] Three traits distinguish disciples of Avraham: (a) A good eye; i.e. one who is genuinely happy about the success of others. At the same time, he is content with what he has and does not desire the possessions of others. (b) A humble spirit, who is not boastful or arrogant about possessions and achievements. (c) A lowly soul ("soul" here is the life force that endlessly pursues material and physical pleasures); i.e. he limits the pursuit of pleasure and diversion.

24. The Sages taught:[23] *Be among the disciples of Aharon, loving and pursuing peace, loving people and bringing them closer to Torah.*

---

20. *Ramban* in *Chumash* on verse cited. Note: Although in general a person should compromise, nevertheless a person who is the subject of constant abusive behavior which is demeaning and destroys one's self-esteem, should insist on his rights. Compromise in such situations doesn't help either side, and is neither *tov* (good) nor *yashar* (straight).

21. *Bava Metzia* 30b.

22. *Avos* 5:23.

23. Ibid. 1:12.

Even if someone has undesirable qualities, and is difficult to love, we are nonetheless encouraged to love him in order to bring him closer to the Torah.

> There were ruffians who lived in the neighborhood of Rabbi Zeira. Rabbi Zeira befriended them in the hope that they would change their ways. The Sages were displeased, as his efforts seemed to yield no results, and it was unbefitting that a giant sage of the stature of Rabbi Zeira should have dealings with such people. When Rabbi Zeira passed on, those people said to themselves, "Until now Rabbi Zeira interceded in Heaven for us, who will do so now?" They changed their ways and repented.[24]

---

24. *Sanhedrin* 37a.

3

Constructive Criticism

Introductory Remarks

1. If a Jew is seen acting improperly or conducting his life in a way
    not sanctioned by the Torah, it is a mitzvah to convince him to
return to the correct path and to persuade him that he is harming himself with his actions. This mitzvah is derived from the verse, *You shall
reprove[1] your fellow* (*Vayikra* 19:17).[2]

2. It is important to emphasize from the outset that the mitzvah of
    giving reproof or criticism is intended purely for the benefit of the
recipient, by helping him to improve himself and to become a better
servant of Hashem. As will be explained below, if one's criticism
makes the recipient feel inferior or wicked, not only has one not fulfilled this mitzvah, but has instead transgressed the accompanying
injunction, *do not bear a sin because of him.*[3]

---

1. The Hebrew word for reproof, *tochachah*, is derived from a root which means "to prove"
or "to demonstrate."

2. *Rambam, Hilchos Dei'os* 6:7-8.

3. *Arachin* 16b.

3. By fulfilling the mitzvah of reproof, a Jew expresses love for his fellow Jew. The recipient of proper reproof has the opportunity to take the rebuke to heart, correct his faults and develop his Torah personality. This is the sole measure of a person's success in this world, which is determined only in terms of his spiritual growth. Therefore, helping someone by reproving him is a sign of *genuine concern and love* for that person. Furthermore, as Rabbeinu Yonah writes, a concern for the spiritual welfare of others is a sign of loyalty to Hashem:

> *Every creature is required to be a loyal agent and vigilant servant in all his work for his Master. If a worker is truly faithful, he will not only do his own work efficiently, but will also observe his fellows to ensure that they are performing their tasks diligently, and to advise them and caution them to work properly. He does this because his primary concern is that the Master's work be done faithfully, and therefore he gives his fellow workers whatever form of support they need (Shaarei Teshuvah 3:19).*

Note: Some people feel they are Hashem's policemen in this world. They are quick to point out the flaws of others, but are usually unaware of their own faults. Furthermore, they do not express their reproof gently, with sensitivity and discretion. (See paragraphs 6 and 7.) This is not at all the mitzvah of reproof. The Torah ideal of reproof is that the rebuker is humble, knows his own faults and constantly works on self-improvement, because he understands the immense value of this task. Furthermore, he is aware that every human being has a unique personality with its own strengths and weaknesses, and his primary motivation in reproof is to help others improve themselves.

4. Since our entire existence in this world is granted to us as an opportunity to strive continually to correct our flaws and thereby be better servants of Hashem,[4] it is certainly to our benefit that other people help us recognize our flaws so that we can correct them. Therefore, when others reprove us, rather than becoming angry, we should be grateful that they are helping us accomplish our mission in life.

5. Someone who is in a position to correct another person who has acted improperly, and fails to do so, shares the punishment of the

---

4. *Even Sheleimah* 1:2.

wrongdoer, and it is considered as if he himself has committed the same offense.[5] Situations where a person is not considered to be in "a position to correct" are discussed later in this chapter.

Sensitivity and Discretion

6. The mitzvah of giving criticism requires great sensitivity and discretion, and must therefore be performed in private, while speaking gently and with empathy. One must explain that he has only the person's well-being at heart and wants solely to help him change his ways and improve his standing both in this world and in the World to Come. In performing this mitzvah it is forbidden to speak harshly, as the above verse continues, *do not bear a sin because of him.*[6]

7. Speaking gently in such situations is not just sound advice, it is an absolute requirement of the mitzvah. Therefore, someone who cannot be sensitive to the subject's feelings is considered to be incapable of performing this mitzvah,[7] and should not offer any criticism. Instead, such a person is advised to develop the skill of approaching people with softness and sensitivity to enable him to perform this mitzvah.[8]

8. From the verse cited above, *do not bear a sin because of him*, the Sages[9] derived the *halachah* that it is forbidden, even in private, to criticize anyone in a way that causes him embarrassment, all the more so in the presence of others.[10] This is also the source of the general prohibition against embarrassing anyone, as discussed in Chapter 6.

9. Even the most sensitive person will encounter situations in which no matter how gently he approaches someone in need of correc-

---

5. *Rambam* ibid.

6. Ibid.

7. *Sefer Keser Rosh* by R' Chaim of Volozhin, 143.

8. It should be noted that in certain situations, and with certain people, an outwardly harsh tone may be the most effective way of accomplishing the desired purpose (see *Shabbos* 105b), and may thus be in the recipient's best interests. Nonetheless, great caution is required to ensure that one's actions are intended solely for the recipient's benefit and will actually help rather than harm him. If at all possible, someone in such a situation should seek the guidance of an experienced rav or counselor.

9. *Arachin* 16b; see *Rashi* ad loc. and see *Rambam, Hilchos Dei'os* 6:8.

10. Cf. *Avos* 3:15: *One who humiliates his fellow in public, though he may have Torah and good deeds, has no share in the World to Come.*

tion, the subject will still be highly offended and embarrassed. In such cases, one should not give criticism at all.[11]

When Hashem's Honor Is at Stake

10. It is required to criticize someone in private only if the wrong was done in private, but if it was done publicly, constituting a desecration of Hashem's Name, then one must immediately do whatever is required to prevent any further desecration.[12] However, the reprover is still obligated to speak as softly and gently as possible under the circumstances. It is forbidden to speak more harshly, or to cause the subject any more embarrassment, than is absolutely required to achieve the desired purpose.

> *The story is told that there was once a Purim shpiel in the Radin yeshivah in which lashon hara was said. Immediately, the Chofetz Chaim said in a soft tone, "Even on Purim lashon hara is prohibited."*

11. The mitzvah of judging others favorably and giving them the benefit of the doubt does not apply in situations where it is a mitzvah to give criticism. Therefore, if a person is seen doing something which appears wrong, even if it is possible to place a favorable interpretation on his act, one should still give the subject gentle criticism, as discussed in paragraphs 6-8 above.[13] However, if one is not engaged in giving criticism, the requirement to give the subject the benefit of the doubt and to interpret his actions in the most favorable way possible remains in force.[14]

> *Rabbi Gold, a rebbi at a local high school, noticed Yosi, a generally wayward student, at the counter of a treife store. He recounted to himself the halachah: On the one hand, I have to give him the benefit of the doubt that he was only buying a soda and had nowhere else to go. On the other hand, it may not be so simple, and I therefore must get to the bottom of this matter.*

---

11. Heard from a *gadol,* based on *Arachin* 16b, "If there is someone today who knows how to give *tochachah* …"

12. *Mishnah Berurah* 608:10.

13. Heard from a *gadol.*

14. If the subject is an exceptional Torah scholar who excels in piety in all mitzvos, there may not be any requirement of reproof; even if he sinned we can presume that he will shortly repent on his own (*Berachos* 19b). See *Chofetz Chaim, Hilchos Lashon Hara* 4, *Be'er Mayim Chaim* 18, and *Shevilei Chaim* ad loc. 20 quoting *Zeh HaShaar.* However, this rule is not all inclusive, and each case must be dealt with individually.

How Long to Continue Criticizing

12. If the subject spurns criticism, one must continue to give it until the subject either accepts it or reaches the point of forcefully rejecting it.[15]

> *If my friend verbally abuses others, I will constantly think of ways to help him recognize the evil that he perpetrates. I will not give up unless he responds to me with extreme rage or physical violence.*

If One Knows in Advance That Criticism Will Be Rejected

13. The requirement to give constructive criticism applies only if there is some possibility that the subject will accept the criticism. As long as that possibility exists, one must continue his attempts to reprove the subject. (See Chapter 11, paragraph 11 for a historical example portraying this concept.) However, if one is certain from the outset that a subject who is ignorant of the matter at hand will reject criticism, there is no requirement of reproof.

Sometimes, an entire group of people act in a certain manner because of a mistaken belief that this action is permitted or even encouraged. Individuals who belong to such a group are highly unlikely to accept criticism. They will reject any criticism as stemming from what they consider an excessively stringent attitude. If so, it is better to remain silent, and to allow the wrongdoers to remain ignorant of the serious nature of what they will only persist in doing anyway.[16]

14. In some cases, the wrongdoers constitute only a segment of the community, but there is a danger that others will be influenced by their example if left unchecked. Even if the wrongdoers will definitely not accept the criticism, one is still required to take the initiative and express reproof in order to prevent others from copying their mistakes.[17]

---

15. The Sages said (*Arachin* 16b) that one is required to continue his attempts to improve another Jew's conduct until the subject attacks the reprover and adamantly refuses to listen further. Thus the prophets were extolled for their willingness to even undergo beatings for the sake of elevating the spiritual status of the people. See *Hagahos Maimoniyos* on *Rambam, Hilchos Dei'os* 6:5.

16. *Orach Chaim* 608:2, *Beur Halachah*, s.v. *vedavka*.

17. *Orach Chaim* ibid., *Rema, Mishnah Berurah* 5, *Shaar HaTziyun* 5.

15. The rule stated above, of keeping quiet so that the wrongdoers will continue to act out of ignorance, applies only if they are genuinely ignorant. If, however, it is obvious that they do actually realize that their actions are wrong, then it is required to protest, even if they clearly will not be moved. If the wrongdoers form a substantial group it is sufficient to rebuke them only once. This will prevent them from subsequently claiming that this individual witnessed their action and gave their behavior silent assent. If only one person is involved, one is required to continue giving criticism until the subject becomes angry and says he will not accept the criticism (as explained in paragraph 12).[18]

> *Before the Pesach intercession, David, a fine yeshivah student, asked his Rosh Yeshivah, "Since most people in the shul in which my father davens talk about business in shul on Shabbos, am I required to reprove them?" (There are three prohibitions involved: (1) discussing business on Shabbos; (2) speaking during davening and Torah reading; and (3) talking about mundane matters in shul.)*
>
> *The Rosh Yeshivah replied: "If the people believe that what they are doing is permissible, and will reject any gentle reproof as being exceedingly stringent, then you are not required to speak. However, if you judge a person as sensitive to Torah, and believe that gentle, private reproof may have a positive effect on him, you must reprove him. On the other hand, if the people know their actions are forbidden and persist nevertheless, you must protest, assuming that you can find an opportunity to do so in a manner which will not cause them to respond with anger." (See paragraphs 15 and 17.)*

When to Stop Criticizing

16. Once there is no further obligation to offer criticism [either because there never was one (as in paragraph 13) or because one has already fulfilled it (as in paragraph 12)], it is forbidden to continue to do so. As King Shlomo says, *Do not rebuke a scoffer, lest he hate you* (*Mishlei* 9:8). In this vein the Sages have said, "Just as it is a mitzvah to say something which will be heard, so it is also a mitzvah not to say something which will not be heard."[19]

---

18. *Orach Chaim* ibid., *Rema, Mishnah Berurah* 5. See par. 17 below for an important qualification to this rule.

19. *Yevamos* 65b.

Whom Not to Criticize

17. The rule that one is required to continue giving criticism applies only when the subject is a family member or a close friend, i.e. when one can be certain that any resulting anger will not lead to hatred, vengeance and feuding. Concerning other people, however, if there is such a likelihood (i.e. he is not a righteous person who constantly seeks self-improvement), it is better to remain silent than to risk arousing pointless antagonism.[20] In such cases, we say that since the subject will reject the criticism forcefully from the outset, there is no requirement to offer it.

18. In all cases, if there is any possibility that offering criticism will put one in danger, then there is no requirement to criticize.[21]

Criticizing Those Who Do Not Accept the Torah

19. The mitzvah of giving constructive criticism applies only to those who are included in the category of "your fellow"[22] (a term generally used in the Torah to refer to those who share the yoke of Torah and mitzvos). In the present era, however, when many Jews are presumed to have the status of *tinokos she'nishbu* (Jews who have grown up under alien influences and are unaware of their obligation to uphold the Torah and its mitzvos), it would seem that each case has to be judged on an individual basis. Thus, if someone rejects the Torah in general, but seems open to criticism on a particular matter (offered in private and with sensitivity to the subject's feelings), the obligation to offer criticism remains in force; indeed, there is a mitzvah in doing so. If it is clear, however, that criticism will not be accepted, then one should keep quiet, as stated in the verse cited earlier, *Do not rebuke a scoffer, lest he hate you.*

Accepting Criticism

20. One of the forty-eight ways to acquire Torah is a love of criticism.[23] One should not respond to criticism with the attitude,

---

20. *Sefer Chassidim* 413, cited in *Orach Chaim* 608, *Magen Avraham* and *Beur Halachah*.

21. *Mishnah Berurah* ibid. 7.

22. *Beur Halachah* ibid., s.v. *aval*.

23. Cf. *Avos* 6:6; see also *Sefer Mitzvos Ketanos*, Mitzvah 9, who writes that involved here are both a mitzvah, *Remove the foolishness of your heart (Devarim* 10:16), i.e. to love the criticism

"Why should I listen to this person, when he himself is guilty of the same transgression?"[24] Instead, if his words are true, one should tell himself that whatever the speaker's intentions, it is to one's benefit to accept his criticism and incorporate it into one's personality. The ideal form of Torah criticism is for both the giver and the recipient to act out of love for Hashem, and therefore to respect and love each other for wanting to be better servants of Hashem.[25]

> Rabbi Yochanan ben Nuri stated: Heaven and Earth can testify that many times Akiva suffered through me, because anything he did wrong I brought to the attention of the Rabbi, and Akiva constantly showed me more loving gratitude because of it, as the verse states (Mishlei ibid.), Do not rebuke a scoffer, lest he hate you, but rebuke the wise man and he will love you (Arachin 16b). Such are the makings of great teachers like Rabbi Akiva.

21. When one does not accept justified criticism and continues to do wrong despite all warnings, his sin becomes amplified. However, should he accept it, the moment he decides to improve his ways a reward is decreed in Heaven for this resolution as if he had already changed his behavior.[26]

---

as well as the one who gives it; and also the accompanying negative commandment, *Do not be stubborn any further.*

24. See *Arachin* 16b.

25. This is implied in *Tanna D'Vei Eliyahu,* cited in *Beur Halachah,* and also in *Sefer Mitzvos Ketanos* ibid. In this vein see *Tiferes Yisrael (Boaz)* on *Avos* 4:1: *Who is wise? He who learns from every person.*

26. *Shaarei Teshuvah* 2:11.

4

Hatred: The Prohibition and the Mitzvah

1. Anyone who hates another Jew transgresses the negative commandment, *You shall not hate your brother in your heart* (*Vayikra* 19:17).[1] Although "hatred" is generally understood to mean extreme dislike, in the Torah any amount of dislike or disdain because of aversion is considered "hatred."[2]

2. There are two categories of forbidden hatred: (a) an inward feeling of repugnance toward the object of one's hatred, and (b) openly expressed hatred, including actions taken to harm or offend the person or failing to do favors for him because of this hatred.[3]

"I won't lend this to him because I don't like him."

---

1. *Rambam, Hilchos Dei'os* 6:5.

2. The Torah gives no limits to "hatred," which implies that any amount of dislike or animosity is prohibited. See *Raavad, Toras Kohanim* 4:10 (also quoted by *Chofetz Chaim* ad loc.) that if someone doesn't lend an object to another because of dislike he violates the prohibition not to hate. See also *Rabbeinu Yonah* in *Shaarei Teshuvah* 3:215 who discusses what the Gemara in *Pesachim* 113b calls "hate" as "distancing from his companionship."

3. The inward hatred is described in the verse as "hating in your heart." See *Raavad* quoted in fn. 2 that outward hatred is included. See *Kehillos Yaakov, Arachin,* Ch. 4 for discussion of disagreement in *Rishonim.* See *Kodesh Yisrael,* Ch. 25 that for all practical purposes this *din* is unanimous.

3. It is forbidden to allow feelings of hatred for another Jew to fester in one's heart. One is required to take action to uproot such feelings and expunge them from his inner makeup. Besides being a prohibition in itself, hatred leads to many other sins, including *lashon hara* and *rechilus*, as well as revenge and grudge-bearing. It also prevents the Jewish soul from fulfilling its purpose of serving Hashem, since all other thoughts and emotions come to be refracted through the prism of this hatred.[4]

The Sages say that the second *Beis HaMikdash* was destroyed by the hatred which existed within it, even though it was also filled with Torah and acts of kindness.[5]

Practical Application

4. In the course of interpersonal relationships it is quite natural for one person to feel dislike toward another. Such instinctive feelings are not included in the Torah prohibitions since they are involuntary.[6] However, the Torah does command: (a) not to act negatively to this person on the basis of these feelings, and (b) not to allow the feelings to fester.[7] Rather, one must remember that Hashem created and lovingly provides for every person. Every human being (including oneself) has positive and negative aspects, and our reaction to negative traits of others should be sorrow and a desire to help them overcome those traits. (See Chapter 2 — The Torah Personality.)

When you feel, say, or hear the following types of statements, you should immediately remind yourself about the prohibition against hate.

❑ *"I hate ..."*
❑ *"I can't stand ..."*
❑ *"He/she is such an obnoxious person!"*
❑ *" I won't talk to him."*
❑ *"Nobody likes him!"*

The Torah teaches[8] us that when we feel dislike for someone we should perform acts of kindness for him; in this way our feelings toward him will slowly change.

---

4. *Shaarei Teshuvah* 3:39. See also *Kodesh Yisrael,* Ch. 39.

5. *Yoma* 9.

6. This rule can be derived from the prohibition of grudge-bearing. See Ch. 7 pars. 1-3.

7. See *Shaarei Teshuvah* ibid.

8. *Bava Metzia* 32b.

If you see two people who need help, one a friend and the other someone you dislike, you must first help the one you dislike.

5. If someone has been wronged, and feels anger at the perpetrator, he should not bear anger and hatred in silence. Rather, he should approach the wrongdoer privately and rebuke him in a soft tone, asking why he acted that way.[9] This is part of the mitzvah of rebuke, which is discussed in Chapter 7, paragraphs 1-3. If he does not do so, and fosters hatred in his heart, he violates the prohibition against hating one's brother.

> **Chayah:** *Dinah was just mean to me.*
> **Mother:** *You must be feeling very angry.*
> **Mother (at some future point):** *You can't walk around hating Dinah. Let's think of some way for you to tell Dinah how hurt you are! I wonder what she will say.*

To Whom Does the Mitzvah Apply

6. The Sages taught[10] that one should not only like certain Jews (e.g. Torah scholars) while hating others (e.g. unlearned people), but also should like all upstanding Jews and hate heretics and those who incite Jews to leave the Torah. As the Psalmist says, *As for those who hate You, Hashem, I hate them, and I quarrel with those who rise up against You! With utmost hatred I hate them, I regard them as my own enemies (Tehillim* 139:21-22). The Torah commands us, *You shall love your fellow as yourself, I am Hashem (Vayikra* 19:18), to teach us that we are to love others because Hashem created them, and we are thus forbidden to hate anyone who is considered our "fellow," that is, who keeps Shabbos and believes in the fundamentals of Torah.[11] In Chapter 1, paragraph 5, it is noted that in the present era all Jews are included in this precept even if they do not yet keep the Torah.

Sinas Chinam — Pointless Hatred

7. The Torah only forbids "pointless" hatred, where the dislike arose because of an individual's personality or other qualities.[12] If, how-

---

9. *Rambam, Hilchos Dei'os* 6:6.

10. *Avos D'Rabbi Nosson* 16:5, quoted in *Kitzur Shulchan Aruch* 29:13.

11. See *Rambam, Mishnah Sanhedrin,* Ch. 10, at the end of the discussion of the Thirteen Articles of Faith. See also *Kodesh Yisrael,* Ch. 20.

12. *Shabbos* 32b, *Rashi,* s.v. *sinas chinam.*

ever, one knows that a person is actually "wicked" (because one has personally seen him deliberately transgress a well-known prohibition, such as adultery or eating *treife*),[13] then it is a mitzvah to distance oneself from him both emotionally and practically.[14] This is a very delicate issue because the injunction to love and not to hate one's fellow still applies.[15] Thus, the Torah wants us to distance ourselves from him because of his actions, but simultaneously to feel love for him because he is still a "fellow" Jew.

The Mitzvah to Hate

8. As described in paragraphs 6 and 7, there are times when it is a mitzvah to hate. One might ask, "How is this congruent with the Torah personality of love and kindness?"

Every human being is endowed with a Divine spark that inspires him to love kindness, truth and justice. At the same time, there is an inner drive pushing him to be selfish and to single-mindedly fulfill all his desires and goals with a total disregard both for other people and for these positive values of human interaction. Most people waver between these two drives, sometimes following one, sometimes the other, and usually applying a combination of both.

Simultaneously, every person has natural tendencies toward love and hatred — love for those people or ideas for which he has an affinity, and hatred as a reaction to his feelings of aversion for others.

The legacy of our forefather Avraham, and the prime teaching of the Torah, is that a person develop his Divine spark, which will lead him to follow the ways of kindness and justice.[16] He must also strive to overcome, as much as possible, the trait of selfishness, which leads to all the vices of the world. As a person develops this Divine spark within himself, he will feel an affinity to those qualities and an aversion to vice.[17]

The prime method of developing this Divine spark and an ultimate appreciation of Torah, kindness and justice is to recognize the manifold infinite kindnesses of Hashem. Every person must contemplate that his very creation was due to the sheer kindness of Hashem, Who

---

13. See Ch. 23 par. 24 and fn. 32 for detailed definition of "wicked."

14. *Pesachim* 113b.

15. *Tosafos* ad loc. See also *Rambam, Mishnah Sanhedrin* ibid.; *Kodesh Yisrael*, Ch. 20.

16. *Bereishis* 18:19.

17. *Shaarei Teshuvah* 3:190.

constantly showers him with life, sustenance and an infinite number of seemingly natural miracles. The enormity of the precise workings of the human organism, as well as animals, plants, etc., multiplied by billions, will overwhelm any thinking individual as to the majesty and kindness of the Creator.

After deep contemplation and awareness of the kindness of Hashem, Who cares for him at every stage of life, King David came to the conclusion in *Tehillim* 139: *How dear are your friends (the righteous) to me ... As for those who hate you, Hashem*, who stand for all the selfish vices of life ... *With utmost hatred I hate them* ... Any affinity for them and what they stand for is a rejection of my affinity for You and what You stand for, and, simultaneously, a rejection of my own purpose of existence. Thus, O *lovers of Hashem, hate evil* (*Tehillim* 97:10).

9. It cannot be overemphasized that the mitzvah is to hate "evil," not people. Even if someone is classified as "wicked" because he willfully transgressed a known mitzvah of the Torah, he still remains a "brother" for whom we are obligated to perform all the required acts of kindness. Furthermore, it is forbidden to allow our hatred to be tinged with any feelings of personal dislike or vindictiveness. Anyone who feels personal hatred for such an individual violates the serious prohibition against hating a fellow Jew (*Vayikra* 19:17).[18]

How to Differentiate

10. How may one determine whether his dislike is motivated by the legitimate mitzvah of distancing himself from evil or by vindictiveness? It has been suggested that the following question be asked: Does my love for Torah scholars and righteous people emanate purely from love of Hashem and His Torah? Even if they were to cause me to feel hurt, would I continue to love them because of their devotion to serving Hashem and their inherent goodness? If so, one can be reasonably sure that just as this love is not tinged by personal bias, so too his dislike for those whom he sees committing transgressions is motivated by the mitzvah described by King Shlomo (*Mishlei* 8:13), *The fear of Hashem is to hate evil*. If, however, he would feel rancor and spite if a Torah scholar seemed to have hurt his feelings, then it is likely that his feelings about those who sin also

---

18. *Tosafos, Pesachim* 113b.

involve personal motives. Far from being included in the mitzvah of hating wrongdoers, they fall into the category of prohibited hatred.[19]

People Who Reject Torah

11. The principle that the mitzvah to hate is limited to the actions of the sinner but not to the person himself applies only to Jews who are "wicked," yet still accept the basic tenets of Hashem's Torah. However, in the case of individuals who have become so banded to evil that they willfully reject the Torah, it is a mitzvah to hate them without restraint, as the Psalmist says (*Tehillim* 139:21), *As for those who hate You, Hashem, I hate them.*[20] Even then, the Torah wants us to see beyond their wickedness and await their return. *Therefore we await You, Hashem ... to turn to You all the wicked of the earth* (Daily Prayers).

In a place where idols were uprooted, one recites, "Blessed are You ... Who has uprooted idol worship from this place. Just as it has been uprooted here so may it be uprooted from all other places and return those who worship them to You" (*Berachos* 57b; *Rambam, Hilchos Berachos* 10:9).

For then I will cause the nations a turnabout so they will all call to the Name of Hashem and worship Him with unity (*Tzefaniah* 3:9).

12. In today's times, irreligious Jews are not considered to be "rejecting the Torah" or "wicked," but rather "misguided." Therefore, all the laws pertaining to interpersonal relationships with fellow Jews fully apply to them. However, while feeling and acting with affinity toward such an individual, a Torah Jew must simultaneously mentally and emotionally reject his non-Torah lifestyle.

---

19. Cf. *Mitzvos HaLevovos*, Introduction to Ch. 2.

20. *Chofetz Chaim, Hilchos Lashon Hara* 8:5.

5

Lashon Hara — Evil Speech

1. Any statement that belittles a fellow Jew, whether true or false, is called *lashon hara*, "evil speech." According to the Torah, these statements, and the qualities they represent, are evil because:[1] (a) they can cause the subject of the statement damage; (b) they can cause him embarrassment; (c) the speaker is condemning a fellow Jew; and (d) the speaker is gloating[2] over the faults of others. Note: Cases where one says derogatory information for beneficial purposes are discussed in Chapter 21.

2. In this context, "condemning" refers to relating in an unfavorable manner a fact that is not necessarily derogatory. It also covers cases where the subject's action was unquestionably wrong, but the speaker improperly judged him a bad person. Since any upright person can make an error in judgment or fail to realize the severity of vio-

---

1. *Shaarei Teshuvah* 3:216; *Chofetz Chaim, Hilchos Lashon Hara* 3:6, *Be'er Mayim Chaim* 7; see also *Kodesh Yisrael*, Chs. 3,4.

2. Translator's Note: We have used the word "gloat" for the Hebrew expression *same'ach le'eid*, as found in the verse, *One who gloats over another's misfortune will not be absolved* (*Mishlei* 17:5).

lating a certain prohibition, the Torah considers it *lashon hara* to label him "bad" simply because he has done wrong.

> *A woman was visiting her daughter's school and noticed one of the teachers berating a girl in front of the class. Although the mother knew nothing about the background of the incident and did not trouble to investigate it, she condemned the teacher in her mind for employing poor teaching techniques. Were she to relate her one-sided judgment to others, she is guilty of lashon hara for placing an unfavorable interpretation on an incident that did not necessarily reflect badly on the teacher. (See Chapters 21, 23, 24, and 25 for guidance as to the proper course of action in various circumstances.)*

> *A businessman, desperate because of plummeting sales and mounting debts, agreed to partake in a venture which promised large profits but involved illegal activities. Before long his associates were caught, and he himself was indicted for a number of serious crimes. Consequently, he was widely censured in his circles as a rasha (wicked person) who brought the Orthodox Jewish community disgrace and the Torah's ethical standards into public disrepute. However, those who judged him so harshly should have taken into account the fact that he had always been an honest and upright individual who erred only because of his desperate situation. It would have been more appropriate to refer to him sadly as a Jew who was ensnared by his yetzer hara to commit a terrible aveirah (sin). Although the Torah in no way condones such behavior, it is wrong nevertheless to condemn him as totally evil on the strength of this one uncharacteristic episode, however reprehensible it may have been.*

3. Even when the circumstances of a particular situation make it clear that the perpetrator is a bad person, any unnecessary criticism is considered "gloating," motivated by pleasure in denigrating others, and is prohibited.

Two people were observing that there are people who create an impression of being extremely pious and stringent in their religious observances, while at the same time engaging in highly dishonest business practices. In the course of their discussion they spoke disdainfully about a particular businessman who was well known for his dishonesty. Although their assessment of him was accurate and they were justified in denouncing his behavior, it was completely unnecessary to mention him at all. Therefore, their speech is considered "gloating" over the failings of a fellow Jew and is prohibited.

4. It is not only forbidden to speak unfavorably about others in this manner, but even to entertain such thoughts in one's mind, as the prophet says, *You shall not think in your heart about the evil of your fellow* (*Zechariah* 8:10). We are therefore required to train ourselves to think favorably of others. (See Chapter 19, paragraph 5 for a discussion of the *halachah* derived from this verse.)

5. The prohibition against *lashon hara* is not limited to disparaging others, but includes any statement about one or more people that, if passed from person to person, would cause the subject physical or financial damage or any other kind of distress or anxiety.[3] (Injurious *lashon hara* is discussed in more detail in Chapter 8.)

Relevant Commandments

6. In addition to the sin of speaking ill about others, the speaker also violates the prohibition against talebearing, as the Torah says, *You shall not be a gossip peddler among your people* (*Vayikra* 19:16), which forbids revealing insulting and injurious information.[4] Thus, anyone who reveals derogatory information violates two prohibitions: (a) By speaking in an "evil" manner he violates the prohibition against "evil" speech. (b) By revealing damaging information he violates the Torah prohibition against being a peddler of gossip.

If someone speaks ill of another person in a situation where he is not revealing information (i.e. the listener already knows the story), although he violates the prohibition against evil speech, he does not violate the prohibition against gossip peddling.

7. Even if the disparaging information is well known, it is still a violation of this prohibition to repeat it if one's intention is to inform those who were unaware of the situation or to add further details.[5]

> "You didn't hear about it yet? It was in the papers, so I can tell you."

---

3. *Rambam, Hilchos Dei'os* 7:5.

4. *Chofetz Chaim, Hilchos Lashon Hara* 1:1.

5. *Rambam* ibid.

8. It is also forbidden to accept (i.e. to listen to or believe) *lashon hara*, as the Torah says, *Do not accept a false report (Shemos* 23:1). This prohibition includes statements that cause *lashon hara* to be believed.[6]

> *Rumors have circulated in a school that a particular student cheated on an exam. If one student tells another that she actually caught the suspect in the act of cheating, thereby persuading her to believe the rumors, the speaker is guilty of causing the listener to believe lashon hara.*

9. In sum, relating previously unknown information violates the prohibition against talebearing. *Lashon hara* that renders information more believable violates the prohibition against causing *lashon hara* to be believed. Even if neither category applies, any "evil" speech, as defined in paragraph 1, is prohibited.[7]

10. Many people err in thinking that if the listener is already aware of an event, then there is no prohibition against discussing it. This is wrong for three reasons:

(a) If the speaker adds any uncomplimentary details of which the listener is unaware, he is guilty of talebearing.

> **Mr. A:** *He hit those children with a big stick!*
> **Mr. B:** *Oh, it was a big stick …*

(b) If the statement convinces the listener to believe the story, the speaker violates the prohibition against causing *lashon hara* to be believed.

> *"You heard that he was caught embezzling? Well, I was there and saw exactly what happened." The listener will believe the story now that he has heard an eyewitness account.*

(c) Even if both are equally acquainted with the facts (so that the prohibitions against talebearing and accepting false reports do not apply), the discussion is still *lashon hara* if it has no constructive purpose but only serves to condemn others and gloat over their disreputable activities (as discussed in paragraph 3). Apart from the "evil" aspect of the speech itself, such conversation clearly violates the mitzvah of loving fellow Jews.

---

6. *Pesachim* 118a; *Chofetz Chaim*, Negative Commandment 2.

7. See fn. 1.

Do not say: I know it, and he knows it, so we can say whatever we want!

Habitual Speakers of *Lashon Hara*

11. A person who is aware of the prohibitions yet habitually speaks *lashon hara* is known as a *baal lashon hara*. The Torah likens him to those who commit the three major sins: idolatry, forbidden relationships and murder. Unless such a person repents, he can lose his portion in the World to Come[8] and we are forbidden to associate with him.[9] Although these strictures apply only to those who habitually engage in *lashon hara*, speaking *lashon hara* is forbidden under any circumstances, even on an occasional basis.

12. On the positive side, for every moment one refrains from speaking forbidden speech in this world, he earns the privilege of basking in the special light Hashem reserves for the righteous in the World to Come. This is a reward unimaginable not only to any finite creature, but even to the angels in heaven.[10]

The Extent to Which One Must Go to Avoid *Lashon Hara*

13. Even if one is ordered to speak *lashon hara* by his father or rebbi, it is forbidden to obey.[11] This applies even to *avak lashon hara*.[12]

14. One is even required to give away all his money to avoid transgressing the prohibition against *lashon hara*, as is the case with all other prohibitions in the Torah. Clearly, then, it is also forbidden to speak *lashon hara* simply to avoid being insulted or branded a fool. In this connection the Sages have said that it is better to be thought of as a fool all one's life than to be wicked in Hashem's eyes for even one moment.[13]

---

8. *Chofetz Chaim, Hilchos Lashon Hara* 1:3,4.

9. *Rambam, Hilchos Dei'os* 7:6.

10. *Chofetz Chaim* ibid. 1:7.

11. Ibid 1:5.

12. "Secondary" *lashon hara* (literally: the "dust" of *lashon hara*; see Ch. 17 for a full treatment of this topic).

13. Ibid. 1:6,7.

After school the boys were making fun of the math teacher. Shimon refused to take part in this "rap" session and was branded "frumie," "tzaddik," etc. In reality, Shimon was following the halachah, and will receive an unimaginable reward.

15. Even if the speaker is merely joking and does not intend to disparage the subject, his words are forbidden as *lashon hara*.[14] In addition, if one's intention is merely to "make the truth known," not to denigrate the subject, his words are still forbidden as *lashon hara*.[15]

"He never lifts a finger to help anyone; I think you should know the truth."

Forms of *Lashon Hara*

16. All forms of *lashon hara* are equally forbidden, whether it is spoken outright, expressed in writing, or simply hinted at indirectly.[16] The same applies to *lashon hara* conveyed by facial expressions, body language, or any other means of insulting or belittling someone.[17]

Yaakov: *When Reuven comes, he will help you.*
Yitzchak: (with cynical smile): *Sure, Reuven …*

17. It is forbidden to belittle someone even if the subject's name is not revealed; as long as the listener can discern his identity (either at that time or at a later date), such speech is forbidden as *lashon hara*.[18]

Teacher: *Why did you speak lashon hara?*
Leah: *I didn't say anyone's name.*
Teacher: *Are you sure that they will never figure it out?*

18. Even when a statement contains no derogatory information, it is still prohibited as *lashon hara* if it will somehow cause harm or embarrassment to the subject or to anyone else.[19]

---

14. Ibid. 3:3.

15. Ibid. 5:1.

16. Ibid. 1:8.

17. When "saying" or "speaking" *lashon hara* is mentioned, it is to be understood that all other means of conveying *lashon hara* are included as well.

18. Ibid. 3:4.

19. Ibid.; see *Be'er Mayim Chaim* 3.

Reuven related the information that Shimon was contemplating opening a business. When Shimon found out, he was upset because he did not want the news known yet.

19. There are individuals who mistakenly believe that they can avoid the prohibition against *lashon hara* by speaking or writing in a measured and seemingly impartial tone, or disguising their intent with articulate words and sophisticated mannerisms. This is a grave error, for as long as one's intent is to cause others to lower their estimation of the subject, one has spoken *lashon hara*, however "intelligently" or subtly that effect was achieved. It is also forbidden to "innocently" repeat information one knows to be *lashon hara*, as if unaware that the statements are derogatory.[20]

> ***(Playing the innocent):***
> ❑ *"I didn't think there was anything wrong."*
> ❑ *"Oh! I didn't know that was lashon hara."*

20. Similarly, it is forbidden to speak *lashon hara* when including oneself along with others even if he is more critical of himself. Since he criticizes them as well, his statement is still considered *lashon hara*.[21]

> *"Reuven and I were both speeding on the highway but I was going faster."*

21. It is forbidden to relate that someone violated a prohibition, whether a Torah prohibition or a Rabbinical one. It is also forbidden to comment that someone has a particular bad trait, such as arrogance, frivolity, or a short temper, or even that he once displayed a bad trait.[22]

22. It is forbidden to say that someone lacks a particular good quality, e.g. to say that a student is not diligent or intelligent, because such comments cause the listener to think less of the subject.[23]

> *"Ari is a good boy, but he is not a masmid (diligent yeshivah student)."*

23. The exact same information may be considered favorable in connection with one person but negative regarding another, depend-

---

20. Ibid. 3:5.

21. Ibid. 1:9.

22. Ibid. 5:2.

23. Ibid. 5:3,4.

ing on the particulars of each situation, including the person involved, the time and the place. Therefore, it is important that all relevant factors be taken into account before speaking, and if the effect will in any way be insulting or belittling, then the statement is prohibited as *lashon hara*.[24]

> ❑ *Mr. Gold, the president of the Gold Insurance Company, spends three hours a day studying Torah (highly complimentary).*
>
> ❑ *Chaim Black, a yeshiva student, spends three hours a day studying Torah (highly derogatory).*

24. It is important to note that a particular piece of information may be *lashon hara* when related to one person but not when told to another. Many forms of behavior are accepted in certain segments of society, yet considered reprehensible in others. Thus, if the statement will reflect badly on the subject in the eyes of the listener, it is *lashon hara*, even if the person who performed the action and the person who relates it consider it acceptable.

> *Reuven, a smoker, relates to Shimon, who is vehemently opposed to smoking and holds it to be prohibited by the Torah, that Levi has just started smoking. Although both Reuven and Levi feel that Levi has done nothing wrong, Reuven's statement is lashon hara, because Shimon will now think less of Levi.*

Numbers Make No Difference

25. It makes no difference whether *lashon hara* is said by only one person or by a group;[25] whether the subject of the *lashon hara* is present or not;[26] or even if one is speaking directly to the subject and another person happens to overhear the conversation (in circumstances where the speaker should have taken care not to be overheard). In all these cases it is forbidden to speak *lashon hara*.[27]

> *The teacher spoke to Mrs. Black about her daughter's problems within earshot of Mrs. Smith.*

---

24. Ibid. 5:6.

25. Ibid. 5:8.

26. Ibid. 2:1.

27. *Nesivos Chaim, Nesiv Chaim* 3:4, from *Shemiras HaLashon* Part 2, *Parshas Korach.*

26. The prohibition against *lashon hara* applies regardless of the number of listeners; indeed, the larger the group, the greater is the speaker's transgression.[28]

Lashon Hara Spoken to Non-Jews

27. While it is prohibited to speak *lashon hara* to a Jew, it is an even more serious transgression to speak it to a non-Jew. If a Jew hears derogatory information about another Jew, he is required not to believe it, and to extend to the person spoken about the benefit of the doubt and investigate the matter. However, when a non-Jew hears similar information (e.g. that a Jew is a liar or dishonest), it may be assumed that he will immediately believe it and repeat it to others. Not only is the potential damage to the subject greatly increased, but the unfavorable report will also bring dishonor and disrespect to the Jewish people as a whole.[29]

28. Any individual who informs on a Jew or a group of Jews to people who do not abide by Torah law, and as a result Jewish life or property is placed in jeopardy, has committed one of the most serious sins (see Chapter 31, paragraph 10). It is therefore of the utmost importance not to speak ill of any Jew in a manner that could put one in the position of informant.[30]

> When Rabbi Shimon bar Yochai made the statement, "All that the Romans built was done for selfish purposes," a student of his carelessly repeated it. Eventually, the Romans heard of the incident and decreed the death penalty on Rabbi Shimon, who was forced to flee and go into hiding for many years.

All Jews Are Included

29. It is forbidden to speak *lashon hara* about any Jew, whether he is a Torah scholar or an ignorant person (but the more learned the subject, the greater the offense), an adult or a child, a relative or a nonrelative. It is particularly important to note that it is forbidden to speak *lashon hara* about one's spouse, family, or spouse's family. All the more so must we refrain from denigrating an entire group, such as

---

28. *Chofetz Chaim, Hilchos Lashon Hara* 2:1.

29. Ibid. 8:12.

30. Ibid.

the Jews of a particular city or country, the followers of a particular rabbi or rebbe, the members of a particular movement (Chassidim, *Misnagdim*, etc.) or an ethnic group (e.g. Ashkenazic or Sephardic Jews). Most serious of all is *lashon hara* spoken about the Jewish people as a whole.[31]

30. It is forbidden to speak *lashon hara* to any Jew, even to one's spouse or close friends.[32]

31. The laws of *lashon hara* as they pertain to children are discussed in Chapter 29.

Lashon Hara About the Departed

32. The Sages prohibited relating disparaging information about the deceased in the strongest possible terms and imposed a *cherem* (excommunication) on anyone found guilty of this offense. This applies even if the subject was an unlearned person, and all the more so if he was a Torah scholar. It is forbidden to insult the departed scholar as a person, and it is considered even worse to insult or disparage his Torah teachings.[33]

---

31. *Chovas HaShemirah*, Ch. 9.

32. *Chofetz Chaim, Hilchos Lashon Hara* 8:1-4.

33. Ibid. 8:9.

➤ Abuse and Conflict

Chapters 6-9

6

Verbal Abuse[1]

The Prohibition Against Causing Distress

1. Anyone who verbally causes another person pain or anguish violates the commandment, *A person shall not aggrieve his fellow* (*Vayikra* 25:17).[2] This offense (*ona'as devarim*) is a more serious offense than *ona'as mamon*,[3] since money taken wrongfully can be repaid, while pain cannot be undone once it is inflicted. In addition, verbally causing distress affects the victim directly rather than through his money or property. The Sages taught that any abused person who cries out to Hashem will be answered.[4] Concerning this commandment the Torah writes, *You shall fear Hashem,* to teach us that even though the offender may claim

---

1. Although the term "abuse" generally denotes inflicting strong and consistent pain, according to the Torah even causing slight pain through one's words on a single occasion is prohibited.

2. *Rambam, Hilchos Mechirah* 14:18; *Choshen Mishpat* 228:1 based on *Bava Metzia* 58b, 59a. See also *Sefer HaChinuch* 338 for definition of *ona'as devarim* and see *Halichos Olam,* Ch. 26 fn. *beis.*

3. A form of cheating by charging more than is proper. See Ch. 39.

4. For most sins Hashem will not punish immediately. However, when an abused person cries out to Hashem, the sin of the perpetrator comes before Hashem and he is liable to swift punishment (*Choshen Mishpat* 228:2).

that he intended no harm, Hashem knows a person's true intentions and judges him accordingly.[5]

Women and Children

2. A husband has to be particularly careful not to cause his wife any distress, since women are sensitive and easily moved to tears.[6] Hashem is particularly responsive to such emotions, as the Sages said, "The gates of tears are never closed."[7] Similarly, it is forbidden to upset children unnecessarily or for older children to hit or torment younger ones.

Asking the Price of an Item

3. A person should not inquire as to the cost of an item if he does not intend to buy it, unless he specifically informs the storeowner that he merely wishes to know the price but will not make a purchase.[8]

> *Miriam: Abba, I'm going window shopping with my friends.*
> *Father: Be careful! Don't ask how much things are without any intention to buy. Imagine how a salesperson feels waiting to make a sale. When the girls walk in, his hopes go up. Then they ask, "How much does this cost?" and his heart beats a little faster... maybe this will be a sale. If they just walk out, and they obviously had no intention to buy, he is upset and feels "taken for a ride." In Heaven this is called ona'as devarim, and it is recorded, "These girls tormented the salesperson!"*

Reminding Someone of His Past

4. One should not remind a *baal teshuvah* of his background (or anyone else who is likely to be embarrassed by his personal or family history) since this will cause him embarrassment and distress. It is also wrong to embarrass someone by asking him for an opinion about a matter of which he is sure to be ignorant. The underlying principle is to think carefully before speaking and avoid causing another person embarrassment or distress, remembering that Hashem knows our true intentions.[9]

---

5. Ibid.

6. Ibid.

7. *Bava Metzia* 58b. See also *Choshen Mishpat* 228, *Sma* 5; *Halichos Olam*, Ch. 26 fn. *dalet*.

8. *Bava Metzia* ibid. and *Choshen Mishpat* 228:4.

9. Ibid.

Social Insults

5. It is common for friends in social settings to insult or provoke one another and to take pleasure in the discomfort they cause. This is forbidden as *ona'as devarim* and often violates other prohibitions as well.[10] Such behavior is prohibited even on Purim.[11] Anyone who has taken part in such talk is required to apologize to the wronged party and ask for forgiveness.

> *"Boy, did we get him," implies that the prohibition of ona'as devarim has been violated.*

6. Insulting someone in a synagogue is likely to lead to quarreling and *machlokes*. Furthermore, it is offensive to the Divine Presence which rests there. If merely insulting someone in the presence of a Torah scholar is considered a mark of *apikorsus*,[12] how much more so in the Divine Presence – in a synagogue. Therefore, extreme caution is required to avoid such practices.[13]

Further Examples

7. It is obviously impossible to list every action which violates this mitzvah, so each person must be on constant alert in all his interactions with others. For example, it is forbidden to belittle a person's opinions or Torah thoughts, or even any question he poses.

> *"Only a fool would ask such a question!"*

Similarly, it is prohibited to remind someone of any misguided or foolish behavior in his past, since it might distress or embarrass him.

> *"I remember when you ..."*

Even a gesture or facial expression can cause pain and thereby violate this prohibition. The basic principle is that any word or deed that causes anyone any distress or anguish of any kind is forbidden as *ona'as devarim*.[14]

---

10. Rabbi Ephraim Bilitzer of Jerusalem has written a pamphlet giving commonly found examples of *ona'as devarim* and *geneivas da'as*.

11. See *Mishnah Berurah* 695:13,14 and *Halichos Olam*, Ch. 26 fn. *ches*.

12. *Sanhedrin* 99b.

13. Bilitzer, op. cit., quoting *Mishnah Berurah* 151:2.

14. *Sefer HaChinuch* 338; see also *The Power of Words* by Rabbi Zelig Pliskin for many specific examples of *ona'as devarim*.

Gloating Over People's Misfortunes

8. One should not tell someone who has suffered adversity that he is being punished for his sins.[15]

> *"It's all your fault because ..."*

A child who verbally abuses another who has hurt himself should be taught that it is *ona'as devarim* and wrong.

> *"I'm glad you fell! You deserved it!"*

Belittling Nicknames

9. It is *ona'as devarim* to call anyone by a belittling nickname with the intention of causing him discomfort, even if he is so used to the name that it no longer embarrasses him.

- ❏ *"Old Man"*
- ❏ *"Baby Face"*
- ❏ *"Crazy Head"*

The Sages said that anyone who does this regularly can lose his place in the World to Come.[16]

10. It is a Torah transgression to make insulting remarks.

- ❏ *"You idiot!"*
- ❏ *"You're crazy,"*
- ❏ *"What's wrong with you?"*

This is particularly common among children, and parents and other adults have a responsibility to correct them and to set a good example.[17]

Other Distasteful Activities

11. It is forbidden to cause people discomfort not only with words, but through any other kind of action as well.[18] One should be careful not to do anything which will cause even slight discomfort to someone else:[19]

---

15. *Choshen Mishpat* 228:4.

16. Ibid. 228:5; *Rambam, Hilchos Teshuvah* 3:24.

17. *Orach Chaim* 343.

18. *Shaarei Teshuvah* 3:24.

19. *Chagigah* 5a.

❑ *Jumping a line in a bank or post office.*
❑ *Smoking near someone who objects to cigarette smoke.*[20]

Awakening a Sleeping Person

12. It is forbidden to awaken a sleeping person without his permission (except to do a mitzvah) or to make noise which prevents someone from falling asleep.[21]

Who Is Covered by the Prohibition

13. Strictly speaking, the prohibition against *ona'as devarim* applies only to inflicting pain on Jews who observe Torah and mitzvos. As we have noted, however,[22] in these times almost all non-observant Jews who have not had meaningful instruction in Torah are considered to be unaware of the consequences of their actions; thus, all the *halachos* governing interpersonal relations, including *ona'as devarim*, *lashon hara*, etc., apply to them as well.

14. Although non-Jews are not included in the prohibition of *ona'as devarim*, it is wrong to verbally abuse any human being needlessly. This is included in the mitzvah of going in Hashem's ways (i.e. to follow His practices to the extent we are able; see Chapter 2), as the Psalmist says (*Tehillim* 145:9), *Hashem is good to all, and His compassion is on all His creations.* Similarly, *Its* [the Torah's] *ways are ways of pleasantness and all its pathways are peace*[23] (*Mishlei* 3:17). We find that the Torah Sages in all generations were agreeable and friendly to everyone they encountered.

Giving Advice

15. When a person is asked for advice, he is required to weigh all the relevant considerations and give the best possible advice, exactly as if his own interests were involved. However, if his own interests lead him to suggest anything less than the best possible

---

20. If done in a public place or in someone else's home this may be included in the prohibition against causing damage by creating smoke odors that are distasteful to other people (see Ch. 31). This is independent of the health problems of "secondhand smoke" (i.e. inhaling smoke from other people's cigarettes), given the evidence that it is nearly as unhealthy as actual smoking.

21. Bilitzer, op. cit.; see also *Kitzur Shulchan Aruch* 143:4.

22. See Ch. 1 par. 5.

23. See *Rambam, Hilchos Melachim* 10:17.

solution, even if that advice is essentially sound but not the best course of action, he violates the commandment not to place a stumbling block before a blind person, as well as the imprecation, *Accursed is one who causes a blind person to go astray on the road* (*Devarim* 27:18). The Torah makes a point of stating, *You shall fear your G-d*, to teach us that a person can claim that his intentions are good, but Hashem knows our true intentions and judges us accordingly.[24]

16. However, if his best advice would be harmful to himself, then he is permitted to say, "The best thing for you to do is ... but since this will harm my interests, I ask you not to do it." If he is uncomfortable with this response, he may refrain from giving any advice at all, but on no account should he give advice not in the best interests of the questioner.

> *Mr. A and Mr. B owned two competing stores. Mr. B decided to retire, and put his business up for sale. Mr. A was considering buying it and achieving a monopoly. One day, David Chen approaches Mr. A for his advice as to whether he should buy Mr. B's business. Mr. A may answer: "I can't advise you. Ask someone else." Or, "It's a great business, but I am considering the purchase myself. Please do not buy it."*
> *He may not answer: "It's not a good idea for you to buy it."*

17. If the questioner has dishonorable intentions, it is a mitzvah to deceive him and thwart his plans.[25]

The Prohibition Against Embarrassing

18. It is forbidden to embarrass any Jew, as the Torah says, *Do not bear a sin because of him* (*Vayikra* 19:17). In other words, even when engaging in the mitzvah of rebuke, which of necessity will inevitably hurt another person's feelings (e.g. through constructive criticism), it is still forbidden to embarrass him. How much more severe is it to cause embarrassment when there is no justification at all![26] One who shames a person in front of others to the point that the embarrassment is evident on his face, loses his portion in the World to Come. (According to some opinions,[27] only someone who does this regularly loses his portion in the World to Come, but to do so even once is still a very grave

---

24. *Toras Kohanim* on *Vayikra* 19:14; *Rambam, Hilchos Rotze'ach* 12:14; *Mesillas Yesharim*, Ch. 11.

25. *Mesillas Yesharim* ibid.

26. *Rambam, Hilchos Dei'os* 6:8; Introduction to *Chofetz Chaim*, Negative Commandment 14.

27. *Rambam, Hilchos Teshuvah* 3:14.

transgression. Some are even of the opinion[28] that this borders on murder; if so, one would be required to give up his life rather than transgress the prohibition to embarrass someone in public.)

Common Social Settings

19. Extreme caution is required not to cause embarrassment to anyone, adult or child.[29] For example:

❏ *In social settings, people sometimes call each other by embarrassing names or remind them of events in their past of which they are ashamed.*

❏ *People may react to foolish remarks made unthinkingly with ridicule or derisive looks, causing the speaker intense chagrin.[30]*

❏ *Some people embarrass children in the presence of their friends.*

Causing Distress to Disadvantaged Members of Society

20. Someone who causes a convert distress violates several additional prohibitions, making his transgression even more severe.[31] It is also a severe prohibition to cause distress to a widow, orphan, or any other disadvantaged or misfortunate person,[32] even through a slight gesture or facial expression[33] (the punishment for this is death at the hands of Heaven).

The extreme gravity of this prohibition is portrayed by the following story.

When the Romans led Rabban Shimon (the Nasi) and Rabbi Yishmael (the Kohen Gadol) to be martyred, Rabban Shimon was upset because he didn't know for what sin he was being martyred. Said Rabbi Yishmael, "Perhaps a disadvantaged person came to you for a judgment or to ask a question and you made him wait until you

---

28. See *Shaarei Teshuvah* 3:139-141.

29. *Rambam, Hilchos Dei'os* 6:8.

30. Bilitzer, op. cit.

31. *Rambam, Hilchos Mechirah* 14:15.

32. See *Rashi* on *Shemos* 22:21.

33. *Mechilta, Parshas Mishpatim* (180:22). See also *Maseches Semachos* 8 and *Nachalas Yaakov* at loc. cit. There are different versions of the story of Rabban Shimon which follows. Quoted is the version of *Mechilta* with the addition of *Ramban* quoted in *Nachalas Yaakov.*

finished your drink, or donned your tallis or finished your nap. Yet the Torah says (Shemos 22:22-23), 'If you shall oppress them [in any way, however slight] ... My wrath shall be kindled, and I shall kill you with the sword.'" Rabban Shimon replied, *"Rebbi, you have comforted me!"* (Mechilta, Parshas Mishpatim 180:22).

21. The Rambam[34] writes:

A person is required to treat widows and orphans with care because they are depressed and dispirited. Even wealthy widows and orphans or those of kings require special consideration, as the Torah says, "Every widow and orphan you shall not oppress" (Shemos 22:21). How should one behave toward them? One should speak to them gently, and treat them always with respect. One should not force them to do unpleasant work or speak to them harshly, and should show greater concern for their money and property than one does for his own. Anyone who annoys or angers them, or causes them pain, or wrongs them or causes them any loss, transgresses a negative commandment. This applies all the more so to striking or insulting them. Although no lashes are given for this offense, the Torah specifies its punishment in clear terms: "My wrath shall be kindled and I shall kill you with the sword" (ibid. v. 23). The One at Whose Word the world came into being has made a covenant with them that any time they cry out from injustice they will be answered, as the Torah says, "For if he shall cry to Me, I shall surely hear his cry" (ibid. v. 22).

The above applies only to tormenting such people solely for one's own benefit, but a teacher is allowed to strike a student in order to teach him Torah or a trade, or to guide him in the correct path. Even then, the teacher should not treat the orphan the same way he does his other students but rather gently, with great compassion and respect, as the verse says, "For Hashem will take up their cause" (Mishlei 22:23).

These principles apply no less to an orphan who has lost only a father or a mother, and they remain in effect until the orphan is no longer dependent upon others to care for and guide him, and is able to manage his life as an adult.

---

34. *Hilchos Dei'os* 6:10.

22. If a widow or orphan is causing someone damage (e.g. by performing work poorly and causing her employer a loss), a rav should be consulted.

23. Any disadvantaged person is included in this prohibition. Although a disadvantaged person may act in an abnormal way out of despair, we must still be extremely careful with our reaction.

> *Those who laugh at or treat with disdain the hapless people who wander the streets, however abnormal and even deranged they may sometimes seem to us, obviously have no idea of the gravity of the prohibitions they are violating.*

Cursing Others

24. Cursing someone with any of Hashem's Names, even in a language other than Hebrew, is a serious Torah offense. Sadly, many people use common coarse expressions without realizing the gravity of their offense. Any cursing of another person, even without using one of Hashem's Names, is also prohibited. This includes saying, "May So-and-so not be blessed to Hashem," or any similar expression of negative wishes.[35]

Translator's Note: In a situation where a person is required to assert his rights at someone else's expense, or to express antagonism for a legitimate purpose (even then, one must treat the other person with as much respect and sensitivity as possible), the custom of the righteous is to conclude one's words with a sincere blessing for the other person's good health and prosperity.

---

35. *Kitzur Shulchan Aruch* 6:3.

7

Interpersonal Wrongs — Reproof, Vengeance and Grudges

Reproof

1. The Torah states: *You shall not hate your brother in your heart; you shall reprove your fellow and do not bear a sin because of him* (*Vayikra* 19:17). The Torah recognizes that it is natural for someone who has been wronged to harbor a grudge or even hatred against the wrongdoer. The aggrieved party is commanded not to nurse such resentment in his heart but rather to approach the wrongdoer and express his feelings: "Why did you do that to me? I feel hurt!"[1]

> **David:** *I'm so angry at Shlomie ... he embarrassed me in front of the whole class. I wish I could beat him up ... insult him. He deserves it!*
>
> **Mother:** *You cannot embarrass him and you cannot beat him up, but you can and should go over to him privately and say, "Why did you embarrass me?! I feel very hurt ... I don't like to be embarrassed."*

---

1. *Rambam, Hilchos Dei'os* 6:6.

2. Someone who does not approach the wrongdoer, and instead nurses hatred in his heart, violates the Torah prohibitions against hatred and grudge-bearing.[2]

The Ramban illustrates this point with the following incident from *Tanach*. When Amnon violated Avshalom's sister, Avshalom did not express his anger to Amnon but instead refused to speak to him as a result of his hatred. These are the ways of the "wicked."[3] (Avshalom should have expressed his anger and hurt openly to Amnon.)

3. The commandment to approach the wrongdoer is included in the mitzvah of reproof, and all the relevant *halachos* of that mitzvah apply here as well. Thus, the reproof must be given privately and in a gentle tone which does not cause the recipient any unnecessary embarrassment.[4] (The reproof can and should reflect one's deep hurt or sadness but should not be presented in a vindictive manner.) In particular, it must be stressed that *under no circumstances* is it permitted to embarrass the wrongdoer in public, however strong or justified one's hurt or resentment may seem.[5]

4. If the wrongdoer apologizes and asks for forgiveness, it is a mitzvah to be kindhearted and forgive him graciously.[6] If, however, he refuses to admit that he has done anything wrong and rejects the criticism, one should seek out a wise person who is capable of influencing him to see the error of his ways and to restore peace.[7] However, if all such measures fail, it is still completely forbidden to embarrass him in public over the incident.[8]

5. If one genuinely feels no resentment over an incident (i.e. when it is clear that the alleged wrongdoer did not realize the implications of his action), this is considered a praiseworthy attitude and there is no requirement to reprove. The Torah's concern is only that one not harbor hidden grudges, but that is not the case here.[9]

---

2. Ibid.

3. Ibid.

4. Ibid. 6:8.

5. Ibid. Note: There are exceptional circumstances where others may publicize injustice in order to right a wrong. See Ch. 24 par. 4.

6. *Rambam* ibid. 6:6.

7. See Ch. 21 pars. 6-9.

8. *Rambam* ibid. 6:8.

9. Ibid. 6:9.

Vengeance and Grudges

6. Hate, vengeance and grudge-bearing are extremely difficult to avoid. Every person is very sensitive to insults and hurt and feels pain as a result; his only natural recourse is vengeance, which — in the words of the *Mesillas Yesharim* — is "sweeter than honey." Here a Jew is *required* by Torah law (*D'Oraisa*) to rise above his low earthly inclinations and emulate the angels.[10] In the remainder of the chapter we will discuss the relevant Torah laws as well as practical ideas of how to implement them.

7. A Jew who takes revenge against another Jew violates the positive commandment, *You shall not take revenge* (*Vayikra* 19:18). The Sages gave the following example of revenge: A asks to borrow B's shovel and B refuses to lend it. The next day B asks to borrow A's hammer and A says, "I won't lend it to you, just like you didn't lend me your shovel."[11]

    In general, revenge includes any situation in which one person refuses to do a favor for another or harms another because the other person once refused him some favor or caused him harm.

8. According to some opinions, it is forbidden to take revenge even if one has been insulted and humiliated.[12] However, according to many others, revenge is not prohibited if one is humiliated to the point of feeling hurt from the insult.[13] Even so, it is only permitted to take revenge according to the amount of "pain" suffered. If the avenger oversteps that boundary even slightly, he violates the prohibition of revenge.[14] Furthermore, some opinions permit only passive revenge (as explained in paragraph 11) but not active revenge.[15] Also, revenge is permitted only if the wrongdoer actively inflicted humiliation. If the only offense was "withholding," although the person was humiliated, or even if he actually suffered (e.g. food was withheld from a starving person), revenge is prohibited according to all opinions.[16]

---

10. *Mesillas Yesharim*, Ch. 11.

11. *Rambam, Hilchos Dei'os* 7:7.

12. According to *Rambam* ibid. and *Chinuch*.

13. *Rashi* and most other Rishonim, *Yoma* 23a.

14. See *Rashi* ibid.; *Halichos Olam*, Ch. 24 fn. *lamed; Kodesh Yisrael*, Ch. 18.

15. See *Shaarei Teshuvah* 3:38; *Kodesh Yisrael*, Ch. 18.

16. *Yoma* 23a (see *Love Your Neighbor* by Rabbi Zelig Pliskin, p. 248).

Mr. Diamond called Mr. Pearl an idiot in front of the whole shul. Mr. Pearl was very embarrassed and hurt, and asked the rav if there was any way he was permitted to take revenge. The rav answered that according to some opinions he could insult Mr. Diamond in return, but he must be absolutely sure that the amount of pain inflicted will not be any more than that which he suffered. He must take into account (a) the type of name to be used (idiot, stupid, etc.); (b) the social standing of the person giving the insult and the recipient (the pain of insults can be measured according to the status of those involved); (c) how this person generally reacts to insults. "I," the rav concluded, "do not know how to measure these factors. Even if you can do so, I would advise you to refrain from taking revenge."

9. However, if the hurt was from any form of withholding a favor, even a most basic one of decency, then any revenge is prohibited according to all opinions. Examples: (a) being denied a desperately needed loan; (b) not getting an *aliyah* in shul on a *yahrzeit*; (c) seeing someone intentionally driving by in a snowstorm without offering a lift.

10. In practice, one should not rely on the lenient opinions because: (a) Even they hold that it is meritorious to act according to the first opinion;[17] (b) if the revenge is in any way disproportionate to the harm suffered, one will have transgressed the prohibition against taking revenge; and (c) as a general rule, where a Torah prohibition is involved, the stringent view is followed.[18]

Passive Revenge

11. Revenge can sometimes be accomplished through inaction.[19]

Mr. Stern owned a food store in a financially depressed neighborhood. He refused to give any credit for fear that he would never get paid. The customers nurtured a great deal of resentment. One day, Mr. Stern got into trouble with the local authorities. No one from the neighborhood came to his aid, and in fact, there was a certain sense of satisfaction that he "got what he deserved." Since the customers did not help him because of vengeful feelings, they have violated the prohibition against taking revenge.

17. *Sefer Mitzvos Gedolos* on the mitzvah not to take revenge.

18. Introduction to *Chofetz Chaim*, Negative Commandment 9, and *Be'er Mayim Chaim.*

19. *Rashi, Yoma* 23a. See *Kodesh Yisrael*, Ch. 18.

The Prohibition Against Bearing Grudges

12. Any time one Jew bears a grudge against another, he violates a negative commandment, as the Torah says, *You shall not bear a grudge against the members of your people* (*Vayikra* 19:18).

The Sages gave an example of grudge-bearing: A asks to rent a house from B and B refuses. Some time later B asks to rent or borrow something from A, and A answers, "Yes, I'll lend it to you, since I'm not like you and won't treat you the way you treated me."

If A shows any trace of lingering resentment over B's earlier act in the way he performs this favor for B (or if his resentment emerges in any form in a later interaction with B), he has violated this commandment. This holds true even if one only fosters resentment without acting on it.[20] Instead, the Torah requires that he slowly eradicate all resentment from his heart.

The "How-to" of Not Bearing Grudges

13. It is a normal human reaction to resent anyone who causes one hardship, even if it merely resulted from a refusal to do a favor. The greater the insult or injury the greater the resentment. This is *not* prohibited, as the Torah never legislates on involuntary feelings. The entire Torah relates only to freewill involving a person's voluntary choices regarding his reactions. However, the Torah *does* legislate on a person's freewill. When a person feels resentment he has two choices: He can choose to foster the resentment or he can choose to work slowly to eradicate it. (See paragraphs 14-15 for practical ways of achieving this.) If he *chooses* to foster the resentment, even if it never emerges in any practical form, he violates the prohibition against bearing grudges. The Torah expects us to *recognize our resentment and to slowly work on eradicating it.*[21]

> *Yaakov walked into the Rosh Yeshivah's office, visibly upset. "Rebbi," Yaakov said, "Berel just embarrassed me in front of the whole beis midrash. He said that I ... I feel like killing him. I can never walk in there again!"*
>
> *The Rosh Yeshivah first gave him a great deal of empathy, until Yaakov slowly calmed down and returned to the beis midrash. A few hours later the Rosh Yeshivah called him back in. "Yaakov," he said,*

---

20. *Rambam, Hilchos Dei'os* 7:8; *Chofetz Chaim*, Introduction, Negative Commandments 8,9; *Be'er Mayim Chaim* ibid.

21. See *Rashi, Yoma* 23a, s.v. *aini*; see also *Rambam, Hilchos Dei'os* 7:8; *Kodesh Yisrael*, Ch. 18.

"The Torah now gives you two choices. One is a great mitzvah. The other is an issur D'Oraisa (Torah prohibition). You can choose to work on slowly eradicating your resentment against Berel. I'll give you some ideas about how to do so shortly. Or you can choose the 'natural' course of fostering your resentment. I wish you much success in making the right decision and accomplishing it successfully."

Practical Ideas on How to Avoid Fostering Resentment

14. The Torah teaches us[22] that if a person feels resentment toward another he should express his feelings to that person. He is not permitted to insult him, verbally abuse him, or speak against him publicly. Rather, he should privately say, for example, "I feel very hurt because you ..." The focus is on how "I" feel hurt rather than on how "you" are bad. This is the mitzvah of rebuke that was discussed at the beginning of the chapter.

15. In some cases, the rebuke is impractical or insufficient to alleviate the level of anger one feels. Then a person has to work on his own thought processes and feelings in order to slowly eradicate his resentment.

Some of these thoughts as taught by our Sages are:

(A) Is It Important?

Someone who probes deeply into material affairs understands that all in this world is passing, and in the long run of no value, and it is improper for a thinking person to make an issue about meaningless matters.[23]

Ari came home very upset after buying a suit when he realized that he had been "persuaded" to buy a more expensive one than he needed. He was angry and felt cheated.

After Ari calmed down, his father took him to the children's playroom, where his 3-year-old brother Yitzi was playing with his friend Shimi. Just then Shimi grabbed Yitzi's marbles. Yitzi was furious and picked up a broom to hit Shimi. Ari instinctively took away the broom and held Yitzi until he was calm. The wise father commented, "Your money is the same as these marbles. They are both passing phenomena, and it isn't fitting for a fine yeshivah bachur like you to become impassioned over such things."

---

22. *Rambam* ibid. 6:6-8.

23. Ibid. 7:7.

(B) Dealing With Pain[24]

If a person honestly reflects on his own life, he will come to the conclusion that he is not perfect. Furthermore, every pain that he suffers in life serves to refine and purify his personality. The Sages taught[25] that as long as a person lives in serenity none of his sins are atoned for. Through trials and tribulations a person merits rapprochement with his Creator, as the verse states (*Mishlei* 3:12), *For the one whom Hashem loves, He rebukes, and he finds favor as a son to a father.* This applies as well to the emotional pain caused by insults. Even though the person who gave the insult is guilty of causing pain, the recipient should nevertheless consider this pain as Divinely ordained, as Hashem utilizes all sorts of wickedness as tools for refining the righteous. The Chofetz Chaim elaborates on this theme with the following allegory:

If a person slips and falls, thereby breaking his arm, the arm is not angry at the leg for being a careless fool. After all, the arm and the leg are all part of the same person. In the same way, the Sages taught that all the souls of the Jewish people are in reality different aspects of one unit. Although in the physical world each one has a separate existence, they are all connected in their spiritual source. Therefore, just as the arm doesn't blame the leg, it is improper for one Jew to blame another for his misfortune. Instead, he must realize that all misfortune is part of the Divine plan to refine His people, and make them worthy of the ultimate eternal pleasure of basking in His Presence.

A person should reflect to himself, "The perpetrator was just a tool in Hashem's hands for the purpose of refining me. Why should I be angry with him? If anything, I should thank him for helping me to achieve an immense reward" (see next paragraph).

(C) The Immense Reward of Overlooking Harm Inflicted by Others

(i) The Sages taught that whoever lives his life in a way that is not exacting and, in general, overlooks the harm that others do to him, will merit that in Heaven they will not be exacting with him and will overlook his faults and wrongdoings.[26]

> *Rav Huna became very ill. His friend Rav Pappa came to visit, and he told the family that all is lost, and they might as well prepare for Rav Huna's funeral. A few days later Rav Pappa saw Rav*

---

24. Paragraphs B and C are based on *Shemiras HaLashon, Shaar HaTevunah,* Chs. 6,8.
25. *Sifri,* mentioned in *Shaarei Teshuvah* 2:4.
26. *Rosh Hashanah* 17a. See fn. 30 for an important reservation.

*Huna in the beis midrash. Rav Huna said, "Don't feel bad,
because your prediction was true and I was destined to die. But
they decreed in Heaven that since I am not exacting with others,
they will not be exact with my faults, and I was granted new life."*

(ii) The Sages taught about those who receive insults and do not return
them, who hear themselves disgraced and do not reply, who act out of
love and rejoice in their afflictions, that of them Scripture says, *Those who
love Him will be like the powerfully rising sun (Shoftim 5:31).*[27] Analyzing the
Sages' statement closely, we see that it describes three distinct categories:[28]
(a) those who are insulted but do not give insults in return,[29] responding
instead with calm assertiveness;[30] (b) those who do not respond to insults
in any way; and (c) the very pious and righteous, who actually rejoice in
insults, because they recognize that these are the best afflictions since they
atone for their sins without causing any physical harm.

*The Sages taught that the Divine Throne has four "legs." Three are
held by the patriarchs Avraham, Yitzchak, and Yaakov. The fourth was
coveted by David, but he did not merit it, despite his lofty spiritual status and his composing of Tehillim. Toward the end of David's life, his
son Avshalom rebelled against him, as part of the Divine retribution for
the sin David had committed. Broken in spirit, he had to flee from
Jerusalem, accompanied by some of his faithful servants. Just then a
great scholar, Shimi ben Geira from the tribe of Benjamin, appeared,
throwing rocks and hurling epithets at him. "Run, run, wicked man of
blood, this is the retribution for usurping the kingdom of Shaul." King
David's faithful servant begged him for permission to kill Shimi. (The
halachah is that insulting a king incurs the death penalty.) King David
refused, saying: Shimi's words must be from a Divine source, and I
willingly accept this Divine retribution, for perhaps then I will merit*

---

27. *Yoma* 23a. See also Ra*mbam, Hilchos Dei'os* 2:3.

28. *Shemiras HaLashon, Shaar HaTevunah,* Ch. 8.

29. This is not a stringency but a requirement; it is forbidden to insult when one is insulted
(unless there is absolutely no other way to stop the perpetrator from further insults).
However, since this *halachah* is difficult to follow, the Sages taught that its reward is
immense (see *Kodesh Yisrael,* Ch. 19).

30. This is the lowest of the three categories, yet in many instances it is the preferred
method. The silence of someone with low self-esteem merely reinforces that trait ("See, I
am bad!"). Similarly, people in an abusive situation are not being righteous by being vic-
timized; they should learn how to be assertive without being insulting (which, incidental-
ly, is a great kindness to the abuser). However, if a person happens to be insulted, it is fitting to attempt to scale the heights of angelic behavior to reach category b or even c.

returning to Jerusalem. At that moment, it was decreed that David merited the fourth "leg" of the Divine Throne. Accepting this insult, which came at the lowest point in his life, gained him a stature that an entire lifetime of greatness and the merit of composing Tehillim had not.

Public Insults to Torah Scholars

16. The situations discussed until this point apply only to insults directed at ordinary people. However, if a Torah scholar is publicly insulted, it is an affront to the Torah itself. It is therefore not permitted to remain silent,[31] as silence implies that the Torah is an unimportant passing phenomenon. It is incumbent upon each person to uphold the honor of the Torah because that constitutes the honor of Hashem. Lack of honor for Hashem and His Torah implies their lack of importance, which is a contradiction to the entire purpose of Creation. Therefore, according to some opinions, the prohibition against revenge and grudge-bearing does not apply here at all.[32] However, according to the opinions cited in paragraph 8, which allow some degree of revenge for insults, no greater degree of revenge is permitted for the Torah scholar than for any other person. Nevertheless, others are required to defend his honor.[33] On a practical level, if a Torah scholar is insulted in public, his best course of action is to remain silent and allow others to act on his behalf; in this way all the relevant opinions are satisfied.

17. On the other hand, if a Torah scholar is insulted in private, it is praiseworthy for him to forgive the wrongdoer completely, even though he deserves to be ostracized from the community for his offense. This has always been the practice of the great scholars of Israel.[34] If one merely refuses to do a favor for a Torah scholar but does not insult him, even in public, any form of revenge or grudge-bearing is forbidden, despite the detestable nature of such behavior.[35]

---

31. *Yoma* 23a, cf. *Bamidbar* 31:2,3. Note: In the example of the previous paragraph, King David, too, was obligated take revenge because of his royal status, as a king is forbidden to abrogate his own honor. Nevertheless, David, in his fugitive status, decided not to act on momentary anger, but instead displayed angel-like humility. On his deathbed, when most people are filled with feelings of remorse and forgiveness, David instructed his son Shlomo to use his wisdom to fulfill the Divine duty of upholding the honor of the Monarchy of Israel by having Shimi killed. (See B*ehold a People by* Rabbi Avigdor Miller, p. 276.)

32. *Rambam, Hilchos Talmud Torah* 7:13.

33. *Yoma* 23a according to Ra*shi. See Kodesh Yisrael,* Ch. 18.

34. *Rambam* ibid. 7:13

35. According to *Rashi* and most opinions this is a Torah prohibition. See *Kodesh Yisrael,* Ch. 18.

8

Causing Animosity and Anguish: Rechilus and Lashon Hara

1. The Torah states, *You shall not be a rachil among your people* (*Vayikra* 19:16). A *rachil* is a professional peddler who goes from place to place. As the peddler wanders he sees and hears news that, if repeated, can cause animosity or distress. Speech that causes animosity is called *rechilus,* and speech that causes distress (physical, financial, mental or emotional) is a form of *lashon hara.* Thus, revealing statements such as "So-and-so said this about you" are prohibited even if true, because they cause anguish and resentment.[1]

> *A classic example of rechilus is when Doeg, the leading Torah scholar in King Shaul's court, reported to the king that Achimelech the Kohen gave David, a fugitive from the king, food and a weapon. The result was the murder of the entire population of Nov, the city of Kohanim. Doeg eventually lost his entire prestige as a Torah scholar, died young, and lost his portion in the World to Come.*

Note: Cases where derogatory information is said for beneficial purposes are discussed in Chapter 21.

---

1. *Chofetz Chaim, Hilchos Rechilus* 1:1; *Chofetz Chaim, Hilchos Lashon Hara* 5:2. See also *Ramban* on *Chumash* for explanation of *"rachil." Rechilus* is also considered *lashon hara.* The "evil" of *rechilus* is that it causes animosity among people with all the negative results of antagonism.

Rechilus — Causing Resentment and Conflict

2. Any statement which causes any kind of dislike or resentment among people is considered *rechilus*, even if there is nothing intrinsically derogatory in the action or fact related. There are even situations where the subject of the *rechilus* would not deny the facts if he were asked, either because he acted entirely properly or because his intent was completely different from that which was attributed to him. Nevertheless, the statement is prohibited as *rechilus* because it produces resentment.[2]

▸ Example 1: *Rechilus* — even if nothing is wrong with the action reported

Mr. A owned the local supermarket in town. Mr. B, after consulting a rav expert in monetary laws, is considering opening a competing store in the vicinity. If someone were to relate this information to Mr. A, he would be guilty of rechilus. Even though the story he is relating is not negative in and of itself, it is prohibited because in practice it causes resentment.

▸ Example 2: *Rechilus* — where the subject was in the right

Debby was twice caught cheating on school tests. The principal called in her teacher to discuss whether to take serious punitive action, or to simply reprimand her. They decided to postpone the decision for a day or two. In the meantime, the teacher called Debby in and related to her, without the principal's knowledge, that the latter was considering serious punitive action. The teacher is guilty of rechilus. Obviously, the principal is in the "right" and Debby in the "wrong," and the principal would readily verify the teacher's story. Should punitive action be taken, Debby will then be informed. In the meantime, the statement is prohibited as rechilus, since it has no beneficial purpose and only produces useless resentment on the part of Debby toward the principal.

▸ Example 3: *Rechilus* — where the subject had a different intent

Mr. Stone and Mr. Diamond each owned a large diamond-cutting factory — the two largest operations in the area. They were in fierce competition and zealously guarded their expert workers. One day, Chaim, a top worker for Mr. Stone, walked over to Mr. Diamond's factory dur-

---

2. *Chofetz Chaim, Hilchos Rechilus* 1:2.

ing his lunch hour to wish a friend mazel tov on his new baby. Chaim's fellow worker Yanki casually mentioned to Mr. Stone that Chaim had visited the other factory. Mr. Stone's immediate suspicion is that Mr. Diamond is trying to woo Chaim away. If Chaim were questioned, he would readily admit to the visit due to the innocent circumstances. However, Mr. Stone's suspicions may be aroused, producing animosity toward Chaim and fueling his antagonism toward Mr. Diamond. Yanki's statement was prohibited, and he is guilty of rechilus.

3. A statement can be prohibited as *rechilus* even if the speaker has no intention of causing the listener to dislike the subject, and even feels that the subject's action or statement is entirely justified.[3]

> **Reuven to Shimon:** *Why did you say that I am not successful in my work?*
> **Shimon:** *Because it is true. Even Levi agrees with me!*
> *Shimon is guilty of rechilus, even though he obviously agrees with Levi and did not specifically intend to cause antagonism between Reuven and Levi.*

4. All of the above rules apply even if the statement involved is entirely true, with no element of falsehood.[4] The worst form of *rechilus*, which is particularly abhorrent in Hashem's eyes, makes enemies out of friends who always treated each other with respect until now. However, even if the parties involved already bear intense hatred for each other, any statement that could further fuel their dispute is considered *rechilus*.[5] In practical terms, if two people are openly hostile to each other, any mention of the actions of one party toward the other is likely to stir up additional antagonism, and is therefore forbidden as *rechilus*.[6]

5. *Rechilus* is forbidden whether one speaks directly about the subject himself or simply mentions or alludes to his family, property, or anything else connected with the subject, in a way which might cause the listener to resent the subject or which might reawaken a prior resentment. Similarly, it is forbidden to relate any information about an organization or institution which might cause the listener to feel resentment about its membership or leaders.

---

3. Ibid. 1:3.

4. Ibid. 1:4.

5. Ibid.

6. Ibid. 4:2, and *Be'er Mayim Chaim* 3. See *Halichos Olam*, Ch. 7 fn. *ches.*

Do not say: *The National Organization of X decided to choose someone else as their guest of honor.*

The general rule is that any statement which can be expected to create antagonism or bad feelings of any kind among people is forbidden as *rechilus.*[7]

6. Given that any statement which can provoke conflicts is forbidden as *rechilus*, it follows that it makes no difference whether the statement is made to the subject himself or to his relatives, friends, students or followers; any affront to the subject's honor is likely to provoke resentment in any of these people and lead to antagonism.

> *Rivki told Sarah that she heard that Reb David made negative comments about Sarah's uncle. Sarah felt the pain of someone belittling her uncle, and felt resentment towards Reb David. Rivki has violated the prohibition against rechilus.*

Furthermore, relaying any provocative information to someone likely to repeat it is *rechilus*, since the report may eventually reach the wrong ears and cause disputes.[8]

Lashon Hara — Causing Anguish

7. Any statement that, if made public, would cause any Jew to suffer either physical harm, property damage, or any distress or anxiety, is considered *lashon hara.*[9]

8. Revealing any information in a manner that if it came to be known might adversely affect someone's interests or well-being is considered *lashon hara.*[10]

> ❏ ***Speaker:*** *Mr. Green is not well off.*
> ***Listener (to himself):*** *Important information if someone is looking for a business partner.*
> ❏ ***Speaker:*** *David has a weak constitution.*
> ***Listener (to himself):*** *Store that away for when he is looking for a shidduch.*

---

7. *Chofetz Chaim, Hilchos Rechilus* 4:11.

8. Ibid. 3:3.

9. *Rambam, Hilchos Dei'os* 7:5.

10. *Chofetz Chaim, Hilchos Lashon Hara* 5:5.

Note: There are times when it is beneficial to reveal information, as discussed in Chapter 21.

9. Talking about other people's possessions can be *lashon hara*, if doing so could damage a person financially, cause him anguish, or lower the listener's esteem for the person in any way.[11]

❑ *"That store always has second-rate merchandise."*

❑ *"He may be well-to-do, but his furniture is old and worn and his clothes look like shmattes."*

If Reuven receives a gift from Shimon, it is forbidden for Levi to deprecate the gift to Reuven since doing so will lower Reuven's esteem for Shimon.[12]

> **Reuven:** *Look at the expensive watch Shimon gave me for my bar mitzvah. (Intent: Shimon went out of his way to give me something special.)*
> **Levi:** *Ah! He got it on sale for $50. (Intent: He didn't do anything special for you; he just tried to make it "look good.")*

10. It is forbidden to reveal another person's secrets. For example, if one knows that someone plans to open a business he may not tell others if the subject does not yet want his plans known. However, if a particular piece of information is not at all derogatory or inflammatory, and the person involved has himself related it in the presence of at least three people without giving any indication that he objects to its becoming known, then there is considered to be adequate evidence that he does not mind if the information is publicized.[13]

> *A statement made in front of three people:*
> ❑ *"I am planning to leave in a month."*
>   *Permitted to reveal.*
> ❑ *"I am planning to leave in a month. Please keep this quiet."*
>   *Forbidden to reveal.*
> ❑ *"I am planning to leave in a month."*
>   *If you know someone will be upset at him for leaving, do not reveal.*

---

11. Ibid. 5:7.

12. See *Nesivos Chaim* ad loc.

13. *Rashi, Arachin* 16a; see also *Chofetz Chaim, Hilchos Lashon Hara* 5:2, *Be'er Mayim Chaim* 1; *Kodesh Yisrael*, Ch. 6.

The Prohibition Against Spreading *Rechilus*

11. The prohibitions against *rechilus* and causing anguish have all the parameters of the prohibition against *lashon hara*; they apply equally whether one speaks on one's own initiative or under pressure, even from one's parent or rebbi. It is forbidden even if refusing to do so will result in loss of money or even of one's source of livelihood.[14] Furthermore, *rechilus* and causing distress are forbidden whether the information is conveyed orally or in writing, through direct statements or through hints, allusions, gestures, facial expressions, etc. Even if a particular person knows all the facts of a situation and lacks only the identity of one of those involved, it is forbidden to divulge this information to him in any way.[15]

12. As with *lashon hara*, *rechilus* and causing distress are forbidden whether directed to only one individual or to a group of people and whether said in the subject's presence or not.[16] Also, the rules of *rechilus* and causing distress apply to everyone, including men and women, close friends, relatives, and even parents and spouses.[17]

Note: See Chapter 29 for a discussion of the related *halachos* of young children speaking to parents about their experiences.

13. The prohibitions against *lashon hara* and *rechilus* apply whether the listener is a Jew or a non-Jew; when *lashon hara* or *rechilus* is spoken to non-Jews it is an even greater transgression,[18] as they are more likely to react with vengeance.

> *When Yehudah ben Geirim heard R' Shimon bar Yochai make negative statements about the Romans, he casually repeated them. Eventually, when the Romans heard, they decreed the death penalty, forcing R' Shimon bar Yochai to flee for his life.*

Sadly, it occurs not infrequently that one Jew tries to belittle the merchandise or services of another, even to non-Jews. This is unquestionably prohibited, since it causes the subject both pain and monetary loss, at times even to the point of threatening his livelihood.[19]

---

14. *Chafetz Chaim, Hilchos Lashon Hara* 4:5-7.

15. Ibid. 4:9.

16. Ibid. 2:1, 3:1.

17. Ibid 7:1.

18. Ibid. 7:4, *Gittin* 56a.

19. Ibid.

14. Although *rechilus* about any Jew is forbidden, whether an adult or a child, a scholar or an unlearned person, it is an even more serious offense to speak *rechilus* about a Torah scholar, for three reasons: (a) There is more likely to be falsehood in *rechilus* about a Torah scholar than about an ordinary person. The nature of Torah study imbues in its students a love of truth and an innate desire to do what is right. Therefore, it is likely that the actions of the Torah scholar are justified or at least well-intentioned. (b) Just as it is a mitzvah to associate with Torah scholars, conversely it is forbidden to instigate bad feelings toward them. (c) People are likely to be more resentful of an injury done to them by a Torah scholar than by an ordinary person (since higher standards of behavior are expected of him). The intensity of disputes caused by this form of *rechilus* is therefore liable to be that much greater.[20]

> *Mr. Green overheard Rabbi Abrams, the rabbi of the West End Synagogue, make negative comments about Mr. Gold, the synagogue's president. If Mr. Green relates the comments so that Mr. Gold hears about them, a major feud could erupt. Although Mr. Gold generally has a good sense of humor, he would be upset to hear that these statements came from the rabbi. Mr. Green should consider that perhaps Rabbi Abrams was justified in his statements, in the circumstances in which they were related. However, even if the remarks were not warranted it would be a grievous violation of rechilus to repeat them.*

Note: One should not relay *rechilus* presuming that the recipient will take the comments in good humor; one never knows what feelings lie deep in a person's heart.

Applications of *Rechilus*

15. If a fact or story allows for several interpretations, one of which would fall into the category of *rechilus*, then it is forbidden to relate it to someone who is likely to place the unfavorable interpretation on it, or to someone who bears any kind of grudge against the subject which is likely to be reawakened by the present situation.[21]

> *David, the esteemed son-in-law of King Shaul and the savior of Israel, fled for his life when his father-in-law secretly turned against*

---

20. Ibid. 7:2.

21. Ibid. 2:2.

him. When he came to Nov, the city of the Kohanim, Achimelech the Kohen, unaware of the palace intrigue, innocently gave him food and a sword. Upon hearing that Achimelech had provided these items, King Shaul, whose mind was turned against David, could only conclude that Achimelech was in league with David against himself (I Shmuel, Ch. 22).

16. If one member of a partnership was considering leaving the business but then decided not to do so, it is forbidden to inform the other partners that the subject ever had such intentions. Similarly, if one side wanted to withdraw from a *shidduch*, or a teacher was seeking a new position, the information must be kept confidential. Even if the matter has become public knowledge, revealing it to the wrong people will certainly cause the subject distress and is forbidden as *rechilus*.[22]

> *Reb Moshe was a top rebbi in the local cheder of City A. City B's cheder offered him a substantial increase in salary to come teach for them. However, there were many practical details involved so Reb Moshe secretly made a trip to City B to discuss the offer and all its ramifications. Mr. Gold, a businessman from City A, happened to be visiting City B and noticed Reb Moshe at the cheder. Since Mr. Gold is now aware of the situation he may discuss it privately with Reb Moshe. However, if he mentions it to anyone else in City A, or even alludes to it, he is guilty of rechilus, because if Reb Moshe decides not to relocate, there will still be resentment that he considered leaving their cheder. Should Reb Moshe choose to consider the offer, he will then inform the appropriate parties.*

> *Esther is engaged to Yanki. However, she is having second thoughts about going through with the marriage. She calls two friends to discuss it with them. They are absolutely prohibited from even hinting a word about Esther's thoughts to anyone, because if word gets back to Yanki or his family there will obviously be resentment. However, if they are not sure what to advise their friend they may discuss it privately with a rav or another wise person who can be trusted to be discreet.*

---

22. Ibid. 2:4.

17. In some cases, one *rechilus* leads to another.[23]

> **Reuven to Shimon:** *Levi is a fool. (lashon hara)*
> **Shimon to Levi:** *Reuven said you are a fool. (rechilus)*
> *If Levi subsequently asks Reuven, "Why did you say that I am a fool?" Reuven will surmise that Shimon revealed his words to Levi and Levi will have violated the prohibition against rechilus.*

18. It is best not to relate potentially inflammatory information to anyone, even if one cautions the listener not to repeat it, and even if one knows him to be a person of discretion who can be counted on to respect such a request (a rare enough quality in itself). Furthermore, it is nearly impossible to relate such information without allowing derogatory elements to creep in, in which case one has violated the prohibition against *lashon hara.*[24]

> *"You know Rivki really doesn't like Leah. I can tell you because I know Leah will never find out!" (Will Leah never find out? Isn't the statement in itself disparaging, making it lashon hara?)*

"What Did He Say About Me?"

19. A asks B, "What did C say about me?" If telling the truth will cause resentment, B should resort to lying rather than speaking *rechilus.* B is first required to try other strategies in order to avoid lying, including diverting A's attention to some other matter, giving an ambiguous answer which is likely to be interpreted in a more favorable way, or telling A only part of what C said, leaving out the derogatory aspects of C's statement.[25] (See example after paragraph 21.)

20. One person should not ask another, "What did A say about me?" because such a question is an inducement to *rechilus* (e.g. "He said you're a nice person but ..."). Furthermore, as stated in Chapter 14, there is a prohibition against listening to and believing *rechilus.* Asking the question, "What did A say about me?" is an obvious prelude to believing the answer, even if it involves *rechilus.* Since a natural curiosity exists to ask this type of question, a person should be doubly on guard to avoid that particular form of inducement to *rechilus.*[26]

---

23. Ibid. 3:2.
24. Ibid. 3:3.
25. Ibid. 1:8.
26. Ibid. 5:5.

21. Conversely, if a person is asked, "What did A say about me?" he could mention the positive things that A has said. Alternately, he might answer that such questions are out of place and should not be answered (see example).

Analyzing a Problem

Esti, Sarah and Rivki were all good friends, until cliques started to develop in their class. One day Esti noticed Rivki whispering to Sarah. Esti suspected that they were talking about her, so she went to Sarah and asked, "What did she say about me?"

If Rivki did indeed say something negative, Sarah should not repeat it. She could (a) mention something positive that was said, or (b) claim the conversation was not about Esti, or (c) reply that she doesn't answer such questions because they induce rechilus.

Presuming that (b) is a lie, and (a) at least a partial lie, (c) would be the best alternative. However, if Sarah is not known to be consistent (i.e. she will repeat positive statements, but when negative speech is involved, she claims not to answer such questions), then her statement is obviously a thin cover-up of negative conversation. Therefore, (c) is forbidden, as it is at least avak rechilus, and possibly actual rechilus (see Chapter 17), making (a) or (b) the preferable response. If (a) is partially true it is preferred. However, if it will sound like a cover-up and is likely not to be believed, then Sarah must resort to (b). It is quite obvious that Esti should have never asked the question!

Note: Esti could be assertive and confront Rivki, saying, "Please do not talk about me."

9

The Prohibition of Machlokes and the Mitzvah to Seek Peace

1. If two or more people find themselves involved in a disagreement, the Torah strongly urges them to make whatever compromises and concessions are necessary to restore peace.[1] This is a mitzvah, as derived from the verse, *Seek peace and pursue it* (*Tehillim* 34:15). If they are unable to reach a compromise through their own efforts they should go to a *beis din* or select arbitrators. While the Sages condemned conflict and noted that peace does not come from dispute (even if each side is convinced that their approach will bring peace), it is not, strictly speaking, forbidden.[2]

---

1. These compromises are only in the realm of that which belongs to a person. He may compromise his rights, etc. but a person cannot compromise the Torah. HaRav Shimon Schwab once commented on the verse in *Mishlei* 23:24, *Acquire truth and do not sell it,* that the ideal of Torah is for truth and peace to exist simultaneously. However there are times when a person is in the unfortunate position of having to choose between truth and peace. In such a situation, King Shlomo teaches "Acquire truth" — even if you have to pay the expensive price of peace, and "do not sell it" — even if you could then acquire that precious commodity of peace. The *halachos* of *machlokes* for the sake of Heaven are discussed in paragraphs 14-21.

2. Cf. *Devarim* 25:1: *If there is a dispute between people, they shall approach the court, and they will judge them.* See *Rashi* ad loc.

2. Sadly, disputes sometimes degenerate to the point where the parties are divided into two camps, with the adherents of each side united not only by their mutual loyalty but also by antagonism toward their opponents. When a dispute stops being concerned solely with a particular issue (money, honor, policy, etc.) and enters the stage where either side relates to the conflict as a personal — "us" vs. "them" — situation, then it has become a *machlokes* (literally: division).[3]

> *Mr. Gold and Mr. Silver own two competing stores. Their competition is ruthless, with each claiming that the other engages in unfair business tactics. As long as their disagreements related to the issues and were not personal in nature, they were involved in a "dispute." However, when they stopped talking to each other and a feud developed between the Gold and Silver families, their dispute has degenerated into a "machlokes" and is strictly forbidden.*

3. The classic example of a *machlokes* is that of Korach and his followers,[4] who, as *Rashi* says, "took himself on one side to be divided from amongst the congregation." Otherwise stated, a situation was created in which "Korach's people" were estranged from "Moshe's people." Such a situation involving *machlokes* is forbidden by the Torah.

4. Anyone who creates a *machlokes* (i.e. turning a conflict over issues of substance, however justified, into a situation of antagonism between individuals or groups) transgresses a Torah prohibition, as derived from the verse, *Do not be like Korach and his assembly* (*Bamidbar* 17:5). Similarly, anyone who is in a position to settle a *machlokes* and fails to do so also violates this commandment. Apart from the basic prohibition, which is extremely grave in itself, *machlokes* leads people to commit a number of other very serious transgressions and renders them "wicked" in Hashem's eyes.[5]

5. Even if one side is absolutely right and the other absolutely wrong, *both* sides are obligated to make every effort to seek peace. Even if those in the wrong willfully continue to antagonize the others, the side in the right is still obligated to maintain efforts to make peace. Failing to do so violates the prohibition against upholding *machlokes*.[6]

---

3. *Kodesh Yisrael*, Ch. 25.

4. Cf. *Avos* 5:20: *What sort of machlokes was not for the sake of Heaven? That of Korach and his entire assembly.*

5. *Sanhedrin* 110a; *Shemiras HaLashon, Shaar HaZechirah*, Ch. 15.

6. *Shemiras HaLashon* ibid., see example.

Korach, Dasan and Aviram organized a mutiny against Moshe Rabbeinu. There was no question that Moshe Rabbeinu was right and the others wrong, yet he spared no effort to pacify them and restore peace. The Torah describes how Moshe sent messengers to Dasan and Aviram to speak to them, and the Sages comment that had Moshe not done so, he would have been guilty of upholding *machlokes*.

Machlokes Directed at a Torah Scholar

6. It is prohibited to create a *machlokes* even with someone of equal stature and wisdom, but it is a much graver offense if the *machlokes* is directed against a Torah scholar, whether or not he is one's personal rebbi. Creating a dispute with one's rebbi, however, is a far more serious offense.[7]

7. It is common for the parties in a *machlokes* to insult members of the other faction. This is forbidden as *lashon hara*. Insulting a Torah scholar is a far more serious offense; of such a person the Torah says (*Bamidbar* 15:31), *He has scorned the word of Hashem and broken His commandments; that person shall surely be cut off* (*kareis*).

8. A Torah scholar is defined according to each particular generation.

In our times, anyone who has spent many years laboring in Torah, and is an accomplished scholar, has the status of a Torah scholar.[8] The Sages stated most emphatically that insulting a Torah scholar is equivalent to insulting the word of Hashem and that one can lose his portion in the World to Come for this offense alone.[9] Although some opinions hold that this punishment applies only to those who regularly engage in such insults, all agree that even one transgression is considered most serious.[10] There are individuals who will instigate a feud with the rav or Torah scholars of their city when they feel their personal honor is at stake. This is tantamount to starting a feud with the Creator.

> *The atmosphere at the Green's Shabbos table was very agitated. Rabbi Black had publicly denounced the local modern day school and strongly urged his congregants to enroll their children in the more traditional school. Mrs. Green took it as a personal attack on her hus-*

---

7. *Sanhedrin* ibid.; *Shemiras HaLashon* ibid., Ch. 16.

8. *Shemiras HaLashon* ibid. See also Ch. 45 here, "Honor and Reverence of Torah Scholars."

9. *Shaarei Teshuvah* 3:147.

10. *Rambam, Hilchos Teshuvah* 3:14.

band, a prominent member of the shul and president of the modern school, where his children were students. The girls were especially upset because the rabbi had denounced the lack of a dress code in their school. "I'll dress how I want. No one is going to tell me what to do!" they exclaimed. Mr. Green waited for the family to calm down a bit, and then raised his hand for silence. He wanted to say something very important. "I realize that everyone feels very strongly about this," he started slowly, "but we have to remember that our rabbi is a Torah scholar. His honor is kavod Shamayim (honor of Hashem). I can't say that I am not hurt, and I certainly intend to speak to him privately in a respectful manner to ask for clarification and guidance. However, disrespectful talk and feuding are not permitted, and no matter how I feel I will not start a feud with a rav."

Disengaging From *Machlokes*

9. If a person finds himself so entangled in a *machlokes* that it will be difficult to extract himself, he must still make every possible effort to shun his companions and certainly not to listen to any of their *lashon hara*, for there is no other way to spare himself from sharing their punishment. Even though his standing in the circle may suffer, he should remember that it is better to endure embarrassment in this world than to be shamed for all eternity in the World to Come. The Sages have said of such a situation that it is better to be called a fool all one's life than to be wicked in Hashem's eyes for even one instant.[11]

10. Just as it is forbidden to take part in a *machlokes*, it is also forbidden to give aid to one side of a *machlokes*, even if one's father or another relative is involved. If a father orders his son to assist him in a *machlokes*, it is forbidden to comply, since the mitzvah of honoring parents does not apply when a parent orders a child to violate the Torah.[12]

The Mitzvah to Seek Peace

11. Anyone involved in any dispute (and certainly a *machlokes*) is required to do his utmost to restore peace. This includes compro-

---

11. *Shemiras HaLashon* ibid.

12. Ibid. Ch. 17. Even if the father seems to be in the right the child may not abet his *machlokes*. He should also suspect that perhaps the father is not actually in the right, because just as a person has a bias toward his own opinion, so is he naturally inclined to take his parents' side. When a person is biased, he does not think clearly and what may seem very clear to him may not be objectively clear at all.

mises on his honor, finances, etc. Similarly, any outsider who is in a position to calm and reconcile the parties is required to do so to the extent of his abilities, as we learn from the verse, *Seek peace and pursue it* (*Tehillim* 34:15).[13]

12. The obligation to pursue peace applies whether the parties involved are one's friends or enemies, and whether the dispute or *machlokes* is in the city where one lives or elsewhere. If one can settle a *machlokes* by traveling to another city he must do so. One is required not only to exert himself physically but also to spend his own money for this purpose.

> *Reuven and Shimon are feuding with one another in Eretz Yisrael. Levi, who lives in the United States, is a person whom they both respect and who has the capacity to restore peace. Levi must fly to Eretz Yisrael to restore peace. If there are no other funds available, he must spend his own money to procure a ticket (as with other mitzvos such as lulav, tefillin, etc. where a person is required to spend his own funds to perform the mitzvah; see Orach Chaim 656; Mishnah Berurah 8).*

13. Even if there is no immediate prospect of peace, one is still required to make every possible effort in the hope that he will eventually succeed. Furthermore, even if the disputants are incensed to the point of being incapable of listening to reason, he must still try to influence other parties who remain neutral not to get involved with either side. The Sages derived these principles from the verse cited above, *Seek peace and pursue it.*[14]

Failing to seek peace in any conflict is tantamount to spurning the yoke of Heaven; such a person is considered wicked.[15]

Machlokes for the Sake of Heaven

14. The principles discussed so far in this chapter apply to disputes involving personal honor, money, property, etc. However, when community leaders and other respected individuals stray from the path of righteousness and influence people to sin, then one is *required* to make a *machlokes* with them for the sake of Heaven.[16]

---

13. Ibid.
14. Ibid.
15. *Shaarei Teshuvah* 3:12.
16. Ibid. 3:59.

When Moshe Rabbeinu descended from Mount Sinai he found that some Jews had engaged in the sin of the Golden Calf, creating a looseness and laxness in the people as a whole. Therefore, Moshe initiated a conflict with his battle cry, "Who is for Hashem — come to me!"

When segments of the Jewish people adopted the habits of the Greeks, they uprooted the service in the *Beis HaMikdash*, and with the aid of their Syrian-Greek friends engaged in a campaign to destroy the relationship of the Jewish people with their Creator. Mattisyahu the Kohen and his sons took up the same battle cry, "Who is for Hashem — come to me!" and single-handedly started a war which eventually uprooted those elements from Eretz Yisrael and merited the miracle of Chanukah.

15. In such a situation, however, one must first make every effort to avoid the need for *machlokes,* and even after the start of a *machlokes* must continue to seek peace wherever possible, in the hope that the situation will change. Even though one's intention is for the sake of Heaven, he still violates the commandment not to persist in *machlokes* if he does not seek out opportunities to make peace.[17] (See example in paragraph 5.)

16. If despite continued efforts the wrongdoers continue in their ways, then one is required to vehemently oppose them. If one fails to do so, he violates the commandment, *Do not bear a sin because of [your fellow]* (*Vayikra* 19:17), and will be punished with them.[18]

Halachos of Machlokes for the Sake of Heaven

17. How can we know if a *machlokes* is genuinely for the sake of Heaven? The most reliable test is to examine how the parties to the dispute relate to each other in matters unrelated to their disagreement. If in all other areas they treat each other with sincere love and respect (as Jews are required to relate in all circumstances), we may conclude that their motives in disagreeing are genuinely for the sake of Heaven. If, however, they treat each other with hatred in other areas as well, as would true enemies, this is a clear

---

17. See *Sanhedrin* 110a.

18. *Shaarei Teshuvah* ibid.

sign that the *machlokes* is not for the sake of Heaven, and that the *Satan* is at work.[19]

18. Even though one is obligated to stand up in defense of the Torah, as described above, the utmost care must be taken to ensure that his actions are solely to *defend* the Torah. It is forbidden, however, to *persecute* opponents. Even if it is a righteous person who persecutes a wicked person, Hashem takes the side of the persecuted.[20]

19. In the course of a *machlokes,* any statement made which is not absolutely required, especially an attack against the other side, is a violation of the severe prohibition against *machlokes* and usually of other prohibitions as well (e.g. *lashon hara, ona'as devarim* and others). Anyone involved in a *machlokes* must constantly make fine distinctions between actions and statements that are necessary and those that are not essential. Furthermore, there must be constant definition of what constitutes an action in defense of the Torah and what is a persecution of the other side. Unfortunately, those involved are often so swayed by their emotions that it is impossible for them to assess situations and events rationally. Therefore, exceptional caution is required. A wise person who is involved in a *machlokes* for the sake of Heaven will consult a great Torah sage regarding any detail of his statements and actions.

20. However, if despite all these precautions a person finds himself required to engage in a *machlokes* for the sake of Heaven, he is not allowed to shirk his duty[21] with the excuse that the matter is too diffi-

---

19. *Sefer Yaaros Devash* by R' Yonasan Eibeshutz, cited in *Guard Your Tongue* by Rabbi Zelig Pliskin (*Hilchos Lashon Hara* 9:10). I have also seen written in the name of a *gadol* that R' Yonasan Eibeshutz appeared in a dream many years after his death and revealed that he and his well-known antagonist, R' Yaakov Emden, were dwelling together in *Gan Eden,* while all the others involved in their *machlokes* were in Gehinnom. Translator's note: There is a *mashal* of two world-class doctors with a common grandson who became seriously ill. They studied his case and came to opposite conclusions, with one declaring an operation vital and the other saying it would be fatal. One day their students heard them arguing, "You're going to kill the boy!" "No, YOU'RE going to kill him!" etc. They concluded that each one considered the other to be a murderer. But the students missed the point: Neither doubted the degree of the other's love for the boy, and no one had a better appreciation of the other's greatness and thought process. So it is in a *machlokes* between *gedolim;* the more they care about the Torah and *klal Yisrael* the greater the intensity of their argument. (I heard this *mashal* used to illustrate a *machlokes* between *gedolim.*)

20. *Shemiras HaLashon* ibid.

21. See par. 16.

cult to carry out properly. Rather, he must oppose the wrongdoers in a Torah manner to the best of his ability.

Torah Sages have time and again been involved in vehement opposition to anti-Torah elements, fearlessly saying what had to be said, while carefully avoiding unnecessary statements.

21. Anyone who is involved in a *machlokes* should bear in mind the story of Yerovam, king of Israel, and Aviyah, king of Judea.

The wicked Yerovam caused the entire Kingdom of Israel to sin with the Golden Calves, a sin which eventually led to the exile of the Ten Tribes, and, according to the Sages, caused Yerovam to lose his place in the World to Come. Aviyah, king of Judea, mobilized 400,000 men for a decisive battle with Yerovam (who still outnumbered him with a force of 800,000). Before the battle Aviyah implored the Ten Tribes in a public speech to forsake Yerovam and return to him. *"Hashem, G-d of Israel, gave kingship over Israel to David eternally ... But Yerovam son of Nevat, a servant of Shlomo ... rebelled against his master. Empty wicked people gathered around him ... And now you intend to stand defiantly before the kingdom of Hashem, which He has given to David's descendants. You have great numbers and with you are the Golden Calves that Yerovam made into gods ... But we have Hashem with us and we have not left Him ... For we observe the charge of Hashem, our G-d, and you have forsaken Him ... Children of Israel, do not wage war against Hashem ... for you will not succeed"* (II Divrei HaYamim 13:4-12).

Although Yerovam was winning at the start of the battle, Judea cried to Hashem and He gave them a decisive victory, slaying 500,000 from the Ten Tribes ... *And Aviyah pursued Yerovam ... And Hashem smote him and he died* (ibid. vs. 19-20).

The Sages note that chronologically, Aviyah died before Yerovam. Therefore, "Hashem smote him and he died" refers to Aviyah. They explain that one of the reasons for this punishment was because he was guilty of embarrassing Yerovam and his people publicly! (Apparently, he could have altered his speech so as not to include all of Yerovam's abominations.)[22]

If Aviyah was punished despite Yerovam's great wickedness, how much more so must we be careful to avoid embarrassing any Jew, even when the Torah requires us to engage in *machlokes*.

---

22. *II Divrei HaYamim* 13:4-20 (see *Rashi* and *Radak*); *Bereishis Rabbah* 65:20; *Vayikra Rabbah* 33:5.

➤ Distancing From Falsehood

Chapters 10-14

10

Truth and Falsehood

The Mitzvah to "Distance"

1. The Torah commands us to distance ourselves from falsehood (*Shemos* 23:7). (Our Sages' specific definition of falsehood will be explained in this chapter.) The commandment to "distance" ourselves obligates us to pay attention to our everyday speech so that we should not come to speak falsehood.[1] We must be especially careful not to speak any falsehood that might damage or deceive others.[2]

2. It is noteworthy that the Torah specifically commands us to "distance" ourselves from falsehood. There are two reasons for this: First, falsehood is abominable to Hashem, as King Shlomo wrote, *Lips of falsehood are an abomination to Hashem* (*Mishlei* 12:22).

Since it is so abominable, the Torah commands us to be "distant" from it, i.e. to avoid any breath of falsehood.

> *Misleading people is, in a sense, more serious than theft, because false speech is a serious sin; and we are obligated to stay within the parameters of truth, for truth is one of the foundations of the soul (Shaarei Teshuvah 3:184).*[3]

---

1. *Sefer Yere'im* section 235.

2. Ibid. See *Halichos Olam,* Ch. 29 fn. *beis.*

3. The human being consists of an inner life-force called the "soul" which gives life to the body. The Torah teaches us which actions are good and which are evil. Simultaneously, the Torah teaches us how to purify our inner life-force so that it should be worthy of being in

Second, a person's natural tendency is to say whatever is most to his advantage, whether or not it is true.[4] Therefore, the Torah warns us to be extra careful in our speech to distance ourselves from falsehood, i.e. never to come even close to speaking it.

When Falsehood Is Prohibited

3. Falsehood that results in any form of deception or damage to others is prohibited. However, in certain situations, where there is a legitimate purpose in speaking falsehood and where no one's interests are adversely affected, the Sages permitted it, subject to the conditions and restrictions detailed below.

4. Like *lashon hara*, falsehood is prohibited whether spoken out loud or conveyed through facial expressions, gestures, body language, etc.

The Nine Categories

5. Nine categories of forbidden falsehood are presented in this chapter, starting with the most severe:[5]

6. The *first* and most serious category encompasses any falsehood that causes injustice or loss to another person, such as disclaiming a debt of money or property, including wages owed to a worker. This violates the prohibition: *Do not deny falsely* (*Vayikra* 19:11). Similarly, cheating in business, which violates the commandment not to aggrieve others (ibid. 25:14) — by means of any deception, unfair pricing, or other form of dishonesty in business activity, including relations with partners and other associates — is prohibited by the Torah. It is also forbidden to use inaccurate weights and measures, or even to merely have them in one's possession (see Chapter 38).

7. The *second* category encompasses falsehood that does not in itself cause direct harm or loss, but is intended to lead to it. For exam-

---

the presence of its Creator. Both are crucial to the success of a human being in this world. However, not all "good" or "evil" are equal. Some are manifested mainly in the physical world of action; others are manifested more in the impurity of the soul. Rabbeinu Yonah teaches us that the "evil" of theft manifests itself mainly in the physical world of action; by robbing someone of his possessions, the thief has perpetrated an injustice. The evil that is manifested in the physical world by false speech is generally less than that manifested by the thief. However, the stain caused by false speech on the purity of the soul is greater because "truth" is a crucial component of the purity of the soul.

4. Cf. *Shaarei Teshuvah* 3:179, 184; *Yalkut Tehillim* 85 (834); also *Alei Shur* II, p. 524.

5. The source of these nine categories is *Shaarei Teshuvah* 3:178-186.

ple, when a swindler befriends his intended victim so that he will relax his guard, enabling the swindler to harm him later, the behavior falls into this category of falsehood. In these first two categories, the transgressor is guilty of both the falsehood, actual or implied, as well as causing any ensuing damage.

> *A and B are executives in a large corporation; A is B's boss. B, coveting A's job, makes a point of treating A with a great show of respect and loyalty. A decides to entrust B with more responsibility and puts him in charge of several important accounts. B then uses his position to cause several deals to fall through in a way that reflects badly on A, but leaves B looking blameless. As a result, A is fired and B is given his job. Even though B's earlier subservient behavior toward A did not harm A directly, his behavior was prohibited under this category of falsehood.*

8. The *third* category encompasses situations in which one person deceitfully prevents another from realizing a certain profit or advantage and diverts it to himself, or deceives someone into giving him a present. This may not cause any actual loss, but it still deprives someone from the expected benefit or profit, and he is therefore punished for his falsehood or deceit. The Sages said[6] that anyone who equivocates in his speech is like an idolater; just as an idolater employs the falsehood of idolatry to make his prayers succeed, so does a liar use falsehood to achieve success in his affairs.

> *Two students are tied for the highest honor at their upcoming high school graduation. One student (A) sends a friend to the principal to say that since the rival (B) is so humble and unassuming, she (B) would certainly prefer that the friend (A) be given the top honor. This is strictly prohibited falsehood.*

9. The *fourth* category encompasses deliberately misstating what one has heard, even though no advantage is derived from doing so. In a way, this is less serious than the previous cases, since no one suffers any harm or loss. On the other hand, the punishment is more severe; since the speaker gains nothing from his falsehood, the only explanation for it is that truth has no intrinsic value to him and is equal to falsehood in his eyes.

> *Yaakov and Chezkie were telling their friends about a camp outing. Yaakov told a story about a midnight intruder to their campfire.*

---

6. *Sanhedrin* 92a.

Chezkie interrupted him and said, "Stop making up stories. There was no midnight intruder." Yaakov answered, "Leave me alone! What difference does it make?"

10. The *fifth* category encompasses offering to do a favor or give a gift without intending to do so. This is duplicity, and the Torah speaks of a person who does such a thing as deceitful, as the Psalmist said, *Guard your tongue from evil and your lips from speaking deceit* (*Tehillim* 34:14). The Sages taught[7] that the term *hin tzedek*, "honest measure," (*Vayikra* 19:36) teaches us that our "yes" (Hebrew: *hin*) and our "no" should both be honest. In other words, just as we are commanded to use only honest weights and measures, so also are we commanded to speak only an honest "yes" and "no" and not to speak with hypocrisy.[8]

❏ *Child to parent: I will do my homework right after I finish playing.* (*To himself: I have no real intention of doing it then. At least I will put it off.*)

❏ *Wife to husband: Please clean up this room while I go to the PTA meeting.*
Husband: *All right.*
(*He has no intention of doing so, but it is more convenient not to make an issue of it.*)

11. The *sixth* category encompasses promising to do something with the intention of keeping one's word, and then deciding afterwards to renege on the promise. This is called a breach of trust and is forbidden, since those involved trusted that the promise would be kept.

There are three ways in which one's word can be considered a "promise":

(a) If the word "promise" is used.

(b) If the word given is for so small a favor that the recipient has no reason to doubt that it will be kept.

(c) If one gives his word in a public setting, since people naturally assume that such a commitment will be honored.

The common factor in these three cases is that the recipient has a specific reason to expect that the word will be kept. In contrast, if

---

7. *Bava Metzia* 49a.

8. If one genuinely intends to fulfill an offer at the time he makes it and only later changes his mind, it is not considered falsehood unless he gives the offer the force of a promise, as discussed in the following paragraph. See also Ch. 40.

none of these factors apply (i.e. he does not use the word "promise," the favor is not a small one, and he does not state it in public), he is permitted not to keep his word should a difficulty arise. If it is not very difficult, one should go *lifnim me'shuras hadin* (beyond the letter of the law) to keep his word.[9]

> *Word must be kept:*
> ❏ *"I promise to take you to see …"*
> ❏ *"I will take you home." (A five-minute drive.)*
> ❏ *At a public meeting: "I will work on setting up a committee." However:*
> ❏ *"I will take you to the airport" (a two-hour drive).*
> *The speaker may back down from his word. However, if the passenger says, for example, "I'm relying on you," and the speaker responds, "Yes, you can rely on me," that is considered a promise, because the passenger expects the speaker to keep his word.*

12. Someone who pledges to donate money to *tzedakah* (charity) and does not keep his word commits the sin of falsehood and he also violates the prohibition of profaning one's vow (*Bamidbar* 30:3), since a pledge to give *tzedakah* has the force of a vow. Even if one merely postpones fulfilling such a promise, he violates the commandment not to delay paying that which one has vowed to give (*Devarim* 23:22). In Chapter 55 the laws of vows and pledges to *tzedakah* are discussed.

13. The *seventh* category encompasses indicating that one has done someone a favor or spoken well of him, when one has not actually done so. This type of misleading, called *geneivas da'as* (literally: theft of mind), is discussed in Chapter 12.

14. The *eighth* category consists of praising oneself for good deeds or qualities one does not possess. Also, if honor is extended to one individual because of qualities that he is falsely presumed to have, he may not accept the honor.

> ❏ *"I donated $50,000 toward the construction of that building." (He actually donated only $40,000.)*
> ❏ *"Stand up for Reb David. He has completed Shas." (If he has learned only 70 percent of Shas he is required to say, "I have not yet learned all of Shas.")*

---

9. *Yerushalmi, Sheviis* 10; see Ch. 40.

❑ *"He deserves to be honored because he is a talmid chacham (Torah scholar)." (If he is not, he is required to say so.)*

15. The *ninth* category covers the kinds of falsehood that people say for their own pleasure or convenience. Such falsehood does not cause any loss to anyone, and it does not indicate a total lack of sensitivity to the value of truth (as in the fourth category), but is still forbidden, since one does derive some benefit from the falsehood. The prophet says, *They have accustomed their tongue to words of falsehood* (*Yirmiyahu* 9:4), to warn us to avoid even these kinds of falsehood.

> *Mother: What time did you go to sleep last night?*
> *Child: Uh, 9:30. (He really went to sleep at 11:00.)*

16. One should not offer a child something and then not give it.

Even if no "promise" was made, as described in paragraph 10, it is still forbidden to accustom a child to falsehood in any form, as in the prophet's warning cited in the previous paragraph.[10] Since a child, by nature, is constantly learning from everything he sees, we have to be especially careful to avoid any action from which he might learn to be insensitive to falsehood.

> *Mother: I will take you to the zoo. (She must take the child.)*
> *She may say: If we can, maybe we will go to the zoo. (She did not commit herself.)*

When It Is Permitted to Alter the Truth

17. In certain situations the Sages allowed an altering of the truth, subject to the provisions of paragraphs 21-23 below. For example, it is permitted, and indeed a mitzvah, to alter the truth to bring peace between two parties in a dispute, or between quarreling spouses. We find that even Hashem altered the truth in order to bring peace into a marriage.[11] The Sages also encourage us to follow the example of Aharon.

---

10. Similarly, the *halachah* is that when one is trying to persuade someone to do a mitzvah in which he is obligated but which he adamantly refuses to do (e.g. *chalitzah* or saving someone's life), it is permitted to offer him excess money for doing the mitzvah even though one does not intend to make good on the offer (*Choshen Mishpat* 264:7). With children, however, one should not do such a thing (e.g. "If you *daven*, I will give you a prize," and then not to do so because he had to *daven* anyway).

11. See *Rashi, Bereishis* 18:13, and *Yevamos* 65b.

> *When Aharon the Kohen would see that two people were fighting he would go to one, sit with him, and say, "Your friend feels so bad, he is so embarrassed because he feels he is at fault ...," and would stay with him until his feelings of animosity would completely dissipate. Then Aharon would go to the antagonist and sit with him and say, "Your friend feels so bad, he is so embarrassed because he feels he is at fault ...," and would stay with him until his animosity would completely dissipate. Then the two would meet on the street and they would embrace.*[12]

18. It is also permitted and even considered a mitzvah to praise a purchase, or to praise a bride to her groom, even if one has to thereby embellish the truth.[13]

> *How does one dance before the bride? (What does one say?)*
>
> *Beis Hillel says, "The bride is naah vachasuda" (an expression indicating beauty permeated with Divine love and grace).*
>
> *If an individual has made a purchase, a person should comment, "It's nice," or "You did well," even if he overpaid, or the object is not appropriate.*
>
> *In both cases the praise may not be true, but our purpose is to bring happiness to others.*

19. The Talmud lists[14] three specific situations in which the Sages would habitually alter the truth:

(a) If one is asked if he knows a particular tractate well, he is allowed to say "no" out of humility, even though he does actually know it.

(b) If one is asked if he slept on a particular bed, he is allowed to answer "no" out of discretion, so as to avoid discussing his private affairs.

(c) If one is asked by unscrupulous people whether he was properly received in a particular home, he is not allowed to speak excessively favorably about his reception so as not to encourage them to take unfair advantage of the host's hospitality.

20. It is permitted to alter the truth in order to protect money or property from theft or extortion.[15]

---

12. *Pirkei Avos* 1:12; *Avos D'Rabbi Nosson* 12:3.

13. *Kesubos* 17a. See also Ch. 26.

14. *Bava Metzia* 23b.

15. *Bava Kamma* 114a.

Mr. Gold owns two businesses: an insurance business and a real estate business. One of his largest insurance customers is the Smith Company. One day Mr. Smith saw a million-dollar mansion offered for sale by the Gold real estate company. As he is a good customer of Mr. Gold, he figured he could bargain him down considerably. After much negotiating Mr. Gold agreed to reduce the price by only 10 percent. Finally, Mr. Smith pulled out his ace card: Give me that mansion for $650,000 or I will take my business elsewhere. Since Mr. Smith was using extortion to force Mr. Gold to sell at a loss, Mr. Gold was permitted to alter the truth. "I'm sorry," he answered, "we are just an agent for a private anonymous seller who is demanding a minimum of $900,000 for the mansion."

Conditions for Permitted Falsehood

21. Altering the truth for any of the above purposes is permitted only if there is no other way to achieve the desired result (such as protecting property or instilling peace). If another way exists, however, such as diverting attention to a different topic, or making ambiguous statements, then it is forbidden to alter the truth.

22. If forced to alter the truth, one should still try to minimize the falsehood to the greatest possible extent.[16] When falsehood is prohibited, it is prohibited in any form, great or small, even by creating a false impression through partial truths. Even when it is permitted to alter the truth, we are still required to alter as little as possible (with saying half-truths, ambiguous statements, diversionary tactics, etc).[17] If, however, one judges that these strategies will only arouse the other party's suspicions and make matters worse, then to say an outright falsehood is permitted at the outset.[18]

> *When Yaakov Avinu came to his father impersonating Esav, as he was commanded to do, he avoided outright lying by saying, "I am ... Esav your eldest," leaving room for the ambiguous explanation, "I am who I am, Esav is your eldest" (Bereishis 27:19; see Rashi).*

---

16. *Chofetz Chaim, Hilchos Rechilus* 1:8.
17. Ibid.
18. *Niv Sefasaim*, Ch. 2 par. 12.

Dov is a competent but not diligent student. When he got engaged, the Rosh Yeshivah said to the father of the bride, "Dov is a good person and he knows how to learn." However, if the Rosh Yeshivah had said only, "He is a good person: he is kind, has derech eretz, etc.," the father would have wondered why he didn't mention his learning, and would have inferred something negative. So the Rosh Yeshivah added, "He knows how to learn." This expression usually implies a bright, diligent student, so in that sense, the Rosh Yeshivah's statement is not true. Since the Rosh Yeshivah was permitted to alter the truth, he did it in a way that the actual words were technically true, so as to minimize falsehood. Dov does know how to understand a Gemara and even "talk in learning." The father may possibly make an inference that Dov is an outstanding yeshivah student, which will help build a relationship with his new family. The Rosh Yeshivah has accomplished this without technically saying anything false.

23. Furthermore, falsehood is permitted only if it does not adversely affect anyone's interests. However, if it causes any type of harm as described above (e.g. loss of expected gain or *geneivas da'as*), whether to Jews or non-Jews, it is prohibited. Even fulfilling a mitzvah does not justify such falsehood.[19] This does not apply to protecting property from a thief or extortionist, because one does not have to suffer a loss so that another may gain.[20] Even in such a case, however, a person should try to minimize the falsehood as much as possible.

Exaggeration

24. The prohibitions against falsehood do not apply to blatant exaggerations that are obvious to the listener.[21]

❏ *"He is as tall as a skyscraper."*
❏ *"The entire city came to the wedding."*

---

19. *Shaarei Teshuvah* 3:181.

20. One is not permitted to protect one's own property at the expense of the property of others (see *Choshen Mishpat* 388, *Sma* 10). However, one is not required to suffer a loss in order for another person to realize a gain.

21. Heard from a *gadol*. See *Devarim* 9:1, and also *Chullin* 90b.

11
Flattery

The Prohibition Against Flattery

1. Flattery is prohibited as a form of falsehood. The nine categories of flattery are presented below, starting with the most serious.[1]

2. The *first* and most serious category is having definite knowledge that a person has acted in a way prohibited by the Torah (i.e. speaking *lashon hara* or *ona'as devarim*, wasting time allotted for Torah learning, cheating in business), and telling the wrongdoer, "You did nothing wrong." This is the most severe form of flattery, and specifically violates the following transgressions:

    (a) The positive commandment to rebuke wrongdoers. If the flatterer merely says nothing to the wrongdoer, he has violated this commandment. However, if he actually tells the person that he has done no wrong, he has not only failed to stand up for the truth, but has actively aided and abetted falsehood by portraying bad as good. This significantly increases the severity of his transgression.

---

1. The source of these nine categories is *Shaarei Teshuvah* 3:187-199.

Note: Even in those instances that a person is free of the obligation to rebuke (see Chapter 3), he is still prohibited from actively violating the mitzvah by encouraging evil.

(b) The commandment not to place a stumbling block before the blind (*Vayikra* 19:14). This forbids any action that encourages or enables a person to do a wrong he would not have otherwise committed. Here, the flatterer's action not only makes it more difficult for the wrongdoer to recognize his failings, but it also discourages him from doing the required *teshuvah*.

(c) If the wrongdoer has caused damage to another party through his actions, flattery not only discourages him from making the required restitution, it also encourages him to continue the behavior both toward this victim and others.

(d) The transgression against falsehood is particularly severe in this case, as the verse says, *One who justifies the wicked or inculpates the righteous, both of these are abominations to Hashem* (*Mishlei* 17:15).

(e) If the wrongdoer sinned in public and one then flatters him in the presence of others, the flattery constitutes a desecration of Hashem's Name.

3. This type of flattery is considered so serious a sin that one is required to place himself into moderate danger rather than transgress it.

> In the last decades before the destruction of the second Beis HaMikdash, the Romans ruled in the land of Israel, plundering and persecuting the people. At one point, Agrippas of the wicked House of Herod, who was close to the Roman emperor, became king. Upon ascending the throne he repented and piously ruled the land in a righteous manner consistent with Torah values.
>
> Once every seven years on the festival of Succos, the king reads the Book of Devarim in front of the entire nation. When Agrippas came to the passage, "You shall not permit someone who is not your 'brother' to rule," his eyes filled with tears because he was of Edomite lineage. (Yochanan Hurkenos conquered the Edomites, and forcibly converted them to be slaves, against the advice of the Sages. From this nation came Herod and his descendants who tyrannized the people and played a major role in bringing about the Destruction.)
>
> The people were in a quandary before their pious king who was crying because his kingdom was a violation of the Torah. Aside from their love and reverence for him, they knew that it would be danger-

ous to depose him because the Romans would punish them severely. They cried out, "You are our brother," thereby flattering him by falsifying the Torah. The Sages taught that when they did so, they were liable for the punishment of destruction. Eventually enemies poisoned the pious Agrippas. His wicked son, Agrippas II, played a major role in bringing on the invasion of the Romans who destroyed the Beis HaMikdash.[2]

4. The *second* category of flattery is extending honor to wicked people. Although the Torah considers this a grievous sin, most people do not appreciate its serious nature, which can be explained as follows:

> *A person with a healthy sense of justice who sees one person abusing another will instinctively place himself on the side of the victim against the abuser. Should he see someone else encourage the abuser and mock the victim, he will naturally react with fury and abhorrence.*
>
> *Likewise, a person who has elevated himself above worldly emotions sees with clarity the goodness of the Creator Who gives life and sustenance to all creatures and provides for all their needs. He will instinctively be infuriated by wicked people who constantly receive life and sustenance from the Creator and yet ignore and even mock His presence and goodness. Most people, however, are not on so elevated a level and therefore do not naturally feel this anger and disdain. Nevertheless, they should, at a minimum, refrain from honoring such wicked behavior.*

5. It is forbidden to praise a wicked person, whether or not he is present. Not only may one not praise the bad behavior of such an individual, but even any good, since if people were to only hear of his good actions, but not the bad, they may conclude that he is actually righteous and deserving of honor; and honor for the wicked destroys the world. Therefore, if one is in a situation where it is necessary to praise the good actions of wicked people, he should also mention their wickedness, as it says, *May the name of the wicked rot* (*Mishlei* 10:7).

Note: A "wicked" person is defined as a notoriously wicked individual who flaunts basic Torah values.

---

2. *Sotah* 41b. Note: The Sages taught that one who flatters will eventually fall either by the hand of the person he flattered, his son or his grandson. See *Torah Nation* by Rabbi Avigdor Miller regarding the major role Agrippas II played in bringing about the destruction of the *Beis HaMikdash*.

Mr. A abused his wife and children regularly until they left him. He adamantly refused to give his wife a get (divorce), making her an agunah, unable to remarry. At the same time, Mr. A was a wealthy man and heavy supporter of charitable institutions.

One day the Board of Directors of the Free Loan Society, which gave interest-free loans to impoverished people, called a meeting to devise new ways of soliciting funds. The rav of the city attended the meeting, as he was very involved in the society's activities.

Mr. Schwartz, the president of the society, opened the meeting by praising the founders and supporters of the society, most of whom were present. When he mentioned Mr. A, the rav slowly rose and declared in a soft voice, "While we lavishly praise Mr. A for his dedication to this mitzvah, we must also remember that he abused his family and refuses his wife a get, an abomination which cannot be overlooked."

The audience was shocked that the rav, who was extremely meticulous in the laws of lashon hara and all other interpersonal mitzvos, would publicly make such a statement. Someone called out, "What about the mitzvah of judging favorably? Don't the Sages say, 'Do not judge someone until you have been in his place'? Perhaps something in his background mitigates his guilt somewhat. Mr. A has been a generous and helpful supporter of the society's activities. Why can't we concentrate on his positive aspects?"

"Rabbi," another member added, "didn't you teach us that we learn from the verse, 'Hashem does not look for the evil in Yaakov,' that we, too, should overlook the evil in others?" The rav calmly responded, "All those lessons are very appropriate in other situations. But," he continued, raising his voice slightly, "if we give honor, or publicly mention the good deeds of a person who blatantly violates the Torah and every form of human decency in his personal life, then we are, in effect, guilty of giving a stamp of approval to his abusive behavior. We thereby deny the entire purpose of creation, namely that a human being develop Divine-like attributes; and I, for one, do not want to be a party to this. If we really want to help Mr. A achieve true honor," he continued, "we must pray that he mend his ways, and do everything in our power to help him reach this goal. When he gives his wife a get and begs forgiveness from his family, I will be the first one to stand and praise him for achieving the heights of teshuvah (repentance)."

6. The *third* category of flattery is to praise a wicked person in private.
In general, people are quick to believe praise and to then conclude that they are righteous.[3] Praising a wicked person even in private, which does not in any way elevate his public standing, nevertheless allows him to form a false impression of himself and makes it more difficult for him to change his ways. In particular, the Sages have said that anyone who flatters powerful people in order to gain honor will not escape disgrace.

> *Mr. G, a powerful member of the local federation, made a long and bitter speech at a council meeting against support of institutions of higher Torah study. Mr. A knew that Mr. G's position was all wrong, but being in need of Mr. G's favor, remained silent. Moreover, the next time he visited Mr. G he praised him as one of the greatest people in town. Mr. G immediately concluded that his opinions were acceptable even in Torah circles since Mr. A continued to adulate him. Mr. A has violated the third category of flattery.*

7. The *fourth* category is to ally oneself with wicked people, even for the purpose of doing mitzvos, because such a partnership is a form of honoring them. Even righteous individuals who form an alliance with the wicked will share their punishment.

> *Yehoshafat was one of the great pious kings of Judah. In his time the king of the Ten Tribes of Israel was the wicked Achav. After decades of animosity and war between Judah and the Ten Tribes, King Yehoshafat made the daring move of joining the two dynasties by taking Achav's daughter Atalia as a wife for his son Yehoram. Although his motives were for the sake of peace, it was wrong to ally with the wicked Achav, and the punishment of total destruction eventually befell not only Achav's dynasty, but Yehoshafat's as well. Atalia, who was wicked like her father, introduced idol worship in Judah, and poisoned the entire dynasty of King David — her own family. Only Divine intervention saved the dynasty when one baby was hidden in the attic of the Beis HaMikdash where he was raised to become king, and Atalia was put to death.[4]*

---

3. The only exceptions are those few who have achieved genuine humility. In this context, the Sages taught (*Avos D'Rabbi Nosson* 29) that if a person has friends, some of whom praise him and some who rebuke him, "love the rebukers and distance yourself from the praisers." The rebukers bring a person Eternal Life, while the praisers merely give him fleeting pleasure.

4. See *II Melachim* 11:1; *II Divrei HaYamim* 22:10, *Rashi*.

8. The *fifth* category is to claim that an individual is trustworthy when he is not. One should not declare a person trustworthy unless one personally knows him to be entirely reliable, since others who trust you may rely on his opinion or entrust him with their valuables and be subsequently deceived.

9. Included in this category is claiming that a person is learned and can be relied upon for *halachic* rulings when this is not the case.

If an unworthy individual is appointed rav or *dayan* because of political or financial considerations, it is considered tantamount to erecting an idol. The Sages said of such a person, *Woe to those who say to wood, "Arise," and to a silent stone, "Wake up." Will he teach? He is bound by gold and silver, there is no spirit within him (Chabakkuk 2:19).*[5]

10. The *sixth* category is to fail to reprove a person whom one has seen doing wrong, in a situation where there is reason to believe he would be moved by the reproof.

11. The *seventh* category is to fail to reprove a wrongdoer even if there is no reason to believe that he will be moved by the rebuke (as long as it is not clear that he will reject the rebuke).

> *At the time of the destruction of the first Beis HaMikdash there was a debate in the Heavenly Court about the fate of the righteous people of Jerusalem.*[6] *At first Hashem in His mercy decreed that they be saved. However, Justice argued that they were guilty for not rebuking the wicked. Hashem answered, "It is clear to Me that even if they had rebuked them they would not have succeeded, for the wicked would not repent." Justice retorted, "Even though it is clear to You, to them it is not clear." Hashem accepted the arguments of Justice and the righteous, too, suffered along with their wicked brothers.*[7]

However, if it is clear that they will reject the rebuke, one should remain silent. The Sages said of such a case that just as there is a mitzvah to tell people that which they will listen to, so also there is a mitzvah not to tell them what they will not listen to.[8]

---

5. *Sanhedrin* 7b.

6. When the Sages want to teach us the different aspects of Divine Wisdom and Justice, they employ the euphemism of "debate" so that we better understand the various concepts.

7. *Shabbos* 55a.

8. *Yevamos* 65b.

12. The *eighth* category is to remain silent when a group of people are mocking others or speaking *lashon hara*. In this case it is forbidden to remain silent, even if it is clear that they will not accept rebuke, for this silence is interpreted as acquiescence. Thus, if one is in the company of those speaking *lashon hara*, or disparaging a Torah scholar, or transgressing any other mitzvos of the Torah, he must either speak out, in order to honor the Torah and not let it be assumed that he shares their views, or immediately remove himself from their presence.

13. It was previously explained that the second category of flattery includes extending honor to wicked people. We must now differentiate between two kinds of honor: first, genuine praise given to those respected for their character and accomplishments, and second, the feigned honor shown to the wealthy or powerful, i.e. standing in their presence as if in fear. This second type of honor is not interpreted as genuine, but obviously arises from an ulterior motive such as monetary gain.

The *ninth* category precludes flattering a wicked person even with the latter type of honor. It is permitted, however, to show such "honor" to wealthy and powerful individuals who are not wicked.

> *Feigned honor may be displayed to an employer, unless he is an evil person.*

14. If a reasonable fear exists that a wicked person who cannot be deterred will actually cause harm if not treated properly, then it is permitted to extend the second kind of honor, i.e. standing in his presence and acting with feigned trepidation. However, treating such an individual with genuine respect, such as by speaking favorably of him out of his presence, is forbidden under any circumstances.

> *A rabid anti-Semite has become very powerful. The Jewish community may attempt to temper his hatred by means of gifts, etc. (see Bereishis 32:14-21).*

15. Even an upright person should not be praised for qualities he does not possess; this is considered flattery unless a worthy purpose will be achieved.

> *It is permitted for a person to praise a spouse for the sake of maintaining peace in the family, a rebbi in order to better learn Torah, or a student so that he will excel.*[9]

---

9. *Sefer Chovas HaShemirah*, Ch. 14.

12

Geneivas Da'as

Deception in Sales and Gifts

1. It is forbidden[1] to mislead a buyer, Jew or non-Jew, even if there is no monetary loss involved, including misrepresentation of an item that does not affect its value in any way.[2]

   Non-kosher meat may not be sold to a non-Jew as kosher, even though the kashrus of meat is of no significance to him.

2. However, one is not required to inform the recipient of a gift of a lack of value or quality that he assumed it to have, since the recipient has no reason to expect a gift to be perfect or superior. However, it is forbidden to claim or lead the recipient to believe that a gift is of superior value when it is not.[3]

---

1. The prohibition against *geneivas da'as* (literally: theft of knowledge, or misleading people) stems from the requirement to act in accordance with the truth and to distance ourselves from falsehood. In addition, it has many similar features to *ona'as devarim*. The two *halachos* are discussed together in *Choshen Mishpat* (228); *Sforno* (*Parshas Behar*) writes that *geneivas da'as* is included in the prohibition against *ona'as devarim*.

2. *Choshen Mishpat* 228:6.

3. *Tosafos* on *Chullin* 94b, also *Rosh* and *Rashba*; see also *Kodesh Yisrael*, Ch. 26.

If Reuven gives a tie to Shimon, who assumes it is silk, Reuven does not have to correct his false impression. However Reuven may not claim that it is silk, nor may he present it in a wrapping labeled "silk tie" because he is then deceiving Shimon.

3. It is particularly important not to give children a gift different in any way from their expectations, since they are incapable of grasping subtle distinctions and they will feel that the giver of the gift lied to them.[4]

Pretending to Be Doing a Favor

4. It is forbidden for a person to act as if he is doing a favor on another's behalf when he is not. Thus, one may not incessantly press someone to be his guest knowing that he will not consent, nor to persistently offer someone a gift that he knows will not be accepted.[5]

5. In general, the Torah requires us to be honest and straightforward in all our dealings and to avoid misrepresenting our true motives. If a statement misleads people by creating a false impression, it is forbidden as *geneivas da'as*, even if it is, strictly speaking, true.[6]

A Person Misleading Himself

6. Although it is forbidden to create a false impression of acting for the benefit of another person, if he reaches that conclusion completely on his own, one is not required to correct it.

Reuven meets Shimon on the road and thinks that Shimon came out especially to greet him. Shimon is not required to tell Reuven that the meeting was coincidental.[7]

7. Similarly, if an act was intended to honor another person, but an additional reason exists as well, one is not required to inform the other person of the other reason.

Ulla visited Rav Yehudah, who, delighted to see the beloved sage, opened a large barrel of wine in his honor. In reality, Rav Yehudah had originally planned to open the barrel in order to sell some of

---

4. See *Succah* 44b; *Kodesh Yisrael* ibid.

5. *Choshen Mishpat* 228:6, see *Sma* 6.

6. *Rambam, Hilchos Dei'os* 2:6.

7. *Choshen Mishpat* ibid.

its contents. He may say that he is opening the barrel in Ulla's honor, and is not required to inform him of the original reason.[8] *If, however, Rav Yehudah happened to be opening the wine barrel just as Ulla unexpectedly walked in, so that he really had only one motivation for doing so, he would be required to tell Ulla the true reason for his action. This is so despite the fact that had he known Ulla was coming, Rav Yehudah would have opened the barrel in his honor.*[9]

Common Forms of *Geneivas Da'as*

8. Certain forms of *geneivas da'as* are very common in today's world.[10]

(a) It is *geneivas da'as* for a storekeeper to give all his customers a reduction from the listed price, yet tell an acquaintance that he is giving him the lower price "because you are my good friend." Anything one says or does to make a person feel unjustifiably indebted to him is *geneivas da'as*.[11]

> **Wrong:** *You're my good friend; I am going to give you a special price. (The item is on sale.)*
> **Right:** *You're my good friend; I'm happy you came when the item is on sale.*

(b) Many of the claims made in the worlds of advertising, politics and public relations fall into the category of *geneivas da'as*, and also violate the prohibitions against falsehood and making promises one does not intend to keep.

(c) If someone claims that he has recommended a friend for some purpose when he did not in fact do so, he is guilty of *geneivas da'as*.

(d) It is forbidden for those who collect for charities to say that they are collecting for one cause when they are really collecting for another, or to claim that they are collecting for an institution or other charity when they really intend to keep most of the money for themselves.

---

8. *Chullin* 94a with *Tosafos* 94b, s.v. *veha*.

9. *Tosafos* ibid.

10. Rabbi Ephraim Bilitzer of Jerusalem has written a pamphlet listing commonly found examples of *ona'as devarim* and *geneivas da'as*.

11. *Rashi* on *Chullin* 94a.

Note: Many institutions rely on fundraisers, who are legitimately entitled to a fair commission. However, most of the money collected must go to the institution.

Cheating on Tests

9. It is *geneivas da'as* to copy answers from another student's test or homework, whether the teacher is a Jew or a non-Jew. Any money or benefit one receives through deceit is considered stolen.

> *A graduate whose academic degree is attained as a result of cheating or any other dishonest conduct is guilty of geneivas da'as, and any ensuing benefit (raises, promotions, etc.) are considered stolen.*[12]

---

12. *Igros Moshe, Choshen Mishpat* II:30

13

Accepting Lashon Hara

1. The verse, *Do not accept a false report (Shemos* 23:1*)*, prohibits believing *lashon hara*.[1] The Torah calls *lashon hara* a "false report" even though the facts may be true because *lashon hara*, by its very nature, is prone to be false. The Torah forbids us to believe words spoken in the manner that false reports are conveyed,[2] such as behind the person's back.

2. The definition of believing *lashon hara* is to accept as true any statement which causes the listener to lower his opinion of the subject.[3] Very often there is room to doubt that the facts of *lashon hara* are true, and even if they are true it is usually reasonable to suspect that additional information exists that would exonerate the subject. Therefore, the Torah forbids concluding that any unfavorable impression created by *lashon hara* is accurate.[4] Instead, we are required to suspect either that critical facts in a report are false, or that the report omits key information

---

1. *Pesachim* 118a.
2. See *Rashi, Sanhedrin* 7b, s.v. *shamoa; Rashi, Shevuos* 31a, s.v. *shaima shav; Kodesh Yisrael,* Ch. 11; see also par. 7.
3. *Shaarei Teshuvah* 3:213.
4. Ibid. 3:211.

(e.g. that if the subject actually committed the alleged act, he did not realize it was forbidden, or he did not do it with evil intentions, etc.).[5]

3. Since the Torah commands that we remain in doubt as to whether the subject did in fact act wrongly, the rule of *chazakah*[6] requires us to presume that he did no wrong at all in spite of this doubt. We must continue to treat him in practice as an upright person, as if the unfavorable report were never heard.[7] Thus, it is even forbidden to think any less of the subject as a result of the report, or all the more so to suspect that he has actually done any wrong. (Even though the possibility exists that the subject did indeed commit the alleged wrong, we must continue to consider him innocent, since it is *forbidden* to suspect an upright person of wrongdoing.[8] This is not intended to preclude being wary of people on a practical level, and taking measures to protect ourselves.[9])

> *Reuven and Shimon are two outstanding students in Yeshivas Eitz Chaim. While Reuven sets aside time for daily study of the laws of lashon hara, he has not yet been able to persuade Shimon to do so. One day a rumor spread in town that Mr. Gold, a prominent businessman who davens in the yeshivah every morning, had been caught engaging in illicit business deals. The next morning, Reuven greeted Mr. Gold with a cheerful "good morning" as usual, while all the other students ignored him. When Shimon questioned Reuven about his behavior, he answered, "None of the reports concerning Mr. Gold have been confirmed, and they therefore fall into the category of lashon hara which it is forbidden to accept. Under the rule of chazakah, we are required to treat Mr. Gold exactly the same as before, and we are not even allowed to suspect him of wrongdoing, much less to treat him coldly." As a result of this experience, Shimon also began to study the laws of lashon hara on a regular basis.*

4. The prohibition against believing *lashon hara* applies even in a situation where it is permitted to relate derogatory information. If the speaker is a righteous individual who is meticulous in the laws of

---

5. *Chofetz Chaim, Hilchos Lashon Hara* 6:1, and *Be'er Mayim Chaim* 1.

6. Literally: presumption, a general *halachic* principle which provides that a state which is known to have existed until now is presumed to remain in existence until proven otherwise, even if a doubt arises as to whether that state has changed.

7. Ibid. 6:10 and *Be'er Mayim Chaim* 25.

8. *Rambam, Hilchos Teshuvah* 4:4.

9. *Derech Eretz Rabbah* 5. See also Ch. 16 par. 24.

lashon hara, and he relates the information for a beneficial purpose, the listener is still forbidden to accept the negative impression of the subject as definitely true. Rather, he must remain in doubt and continue to consider the subject an upstanding person. Furthermore, if there is reason to believe that the information is false (e.g. if the speaker is known to exaggerate or to dislike the subject), then we are *required* to reject the derogatory information entirely and not even to entertain any doubts about the subject's character (see also paragraph 37).[10]

How to Avoid Believing *Lashon Hara*

5. Having stated these *halachos,* it must be stated that the natural inclination of most people is just the opposite. They will immediately believe any negative information they hear, especially if they are close to the source or consider him reliable, and are quick to judge people unfavorably on the basis of any disparaging report heard. The following paragraphs contain several insights to assist us in obeying the Torah and incorporating the proper thought patterns to overcome these instincts and avoid violating clearly stated *halachos.* The Torah prescribes two attitudes which, if internalized, will deter us from accepting *lashon hara.*[11]

6. The first is an ingrained love for our fellow human beings, just as Hashem loves all His creatures. When someone feels for others, he wants them to enjoy honor and respect and suffers when they are embarrassed or disgraced. If he hears bad about a person he loves, his first reaction is to push it from his mind and to search for any pretext to find it untrue. Since he does not want to believe any negative information, he will avoid doing so unless and until he is absolutely forced to.

> *If a parent is told that his son has committed a terrible crime, he will refuse to believe what he has heard, and will seek any possible means to reject it as false or at least exaggerated. However bad his son's previous behavior, he will still refuse to believe the worst of him until there is no longer any room for doubt. This is how the Torah wants us to react when we hear a negative report about any Jew.*[12]

---

10. *Chofetz Chaim, Hilchos Lashon Hara* 7:3. See also *Kodesh Yisrael,* Ch. 12.

11. See *Shaarei Teshuvah* 3:211.

12. Cf. *Nesiv Chaim* 6:1.

7. The second attitude expected of us is a deep-rooted love of truth, and conversely, an abhorrence of falsehood, as we are commanded, *Distance yourself from a false word* (Shemos 23:7). By its very nature *lashon hara* is prone to falsehood, since the speaker has the ear of the audience while the subject cannot defend himself. In order to protect oneself from hearing falsehood, one must avoid listening to a speaker who subtly interjects lies and embellishments without his audience realizing what they are hearing. Furthermore, *lashon hara* is especially prone to falsehood because the speaker is unlikely to have taken the trouble to verify the information.

8. Unfortunately, however, we live in exile and are constantly exposed to social influences diametrically opposed to those encouraged by the Torah, influences which make us more inclined to accept *lashon hara*. One such destructive quality is a desire to notice and discuss people's faults and a willingness to believe any negative report we hear about others. Another commonly found quality is insensitivity to falsehood. Sadly, purity of the soul is of little value in contemporary society; thus, a person who is indifferent to the entry of falsehood into his mind has no incentive to reject glib *lashon hara*.

9. Therefore, every individual living in today's world is required to attempt, to the best of his ability, to uproot these pervasive influences from his personality in order to adhere to the commandments of the Torah.[13]

On a practical level we should:

(a) Become accustomed to rejecting any negative thoughts which we have about others and any derogatory information we hear about them, unless a legitimate need exists, such as protecting ourselves or others from harm.

(b) Make a positive effort to recognize the good in others and to keep their positive qualities foremost in our minds at all times.

(c) Develop a personal and natural love of truth and dislike of falsehood.

These efforts will enable us to build and strengthen a personal foundation on which to observe the Torah in a natural way, and which, in particular, will protect us from violating the serious prohibitions against accepting *lashon hara*.

---

13. See *Shaarei Teshuvah* 3:211, 184; see also *Kodesh Yisrael*, Ch. 11.

Action on the Basis of *Lashon Hara* Is Forbidden

10. As merely believing *lashon hara* is forbidden, all the more so is it forbidden to take any harmful action on the strength of derogatory information one has heard. Even if the information comes from a trustworthy individual who is respected in the community, it may not be used to detract in any way from the subject's upstanding status.[14]

> *If a particular businessman is said to have engaged in dishonest business practices, it is forbidden to call him a thief, or even to treat him coldly and harbor an internal dislike for him.*

> *If a report circulates that an individual who is considered needy has deliberately created a false impression of poverty in order to elicit donations, it is forbidden to cease giving him charity until the rumor can be confirmed (as discussed in paragraph 32).15*

11. Although the Torah forbids accepting unsubstantiated rumors as truth, one may use them as the basis to conduct an investigation if there is a legitimate need to do so. When a community needs accurate information, the proper method is to appoint two people to investigate the matter and report their findings to a *beis din*. Once the testimony of two witnesses is accepted by a *beis din*, the Torah considers their report to be completely reliable, making it permissible to take action on its strength (see paragraph 32).

> *For years Berel has been collecting tzedakah in all the shuls in town where everyone considers him a worthy recipient and donates generously. One day a rumor spread that Berel actually had a large bank account in another city. The town's rav announced that since the rumors were unconfirmed, everyone was obligated to continue giving their customary tzedakah, although he would attempt to ascertain whether or not the claim was true. The rav appointed two reliable people to investigate, and they were able to establish through their contacts that Berel did indeed have a substantial bank account as rumored. Upon determining that Berel's confirmed assets were enough to disqualify him from receiving tzedakah, the rav convened a*

---

14. *Chofetz Chaim, Hilchos Lashon Hara* 6:11.

15. Ibid. in fn.

beis din. Berel was summoned and allowed to hear the testimony of the witnesses and was then given an opportunity to present his side of the story. Since Berel did not claim any extenuating circumstances as justification, the beis din ruled that he was no longer permitted to solicit tzedakah in town, and circulated an announcement to that effect.

What Is Included in the Prohibition

12. Just as the prohibition against speaking *lashon hara* applies to all categories of derogatory statements, so are all such statements included in the prohibition against accepting *lashon hara*. Thus, it is forbidden to believe a statement implying that someone is of bad character, or lacks intelligence, or that he acted improperly in his earlier years,[16] or any of the other matters discussed in Chapters 5 and 8. Furthermore, if a person accepts the unfavorable interpretation of a report which he knows to be true but which may be interpreted either favorably or unfavorably, he transgresses not only the commandment to judge others favorably,[17] but also the commandment not to accept *lashon hara*. This applies to *lashon hara* spoken about an ordinary Jew, and all the more so to *lashon hara* regarding a Torah scholar.[18]

13. Just as it is forbidden to speak *lashon hara* in front of several individuals, a group of people, or even in the presence of the subject, it is also forbidden to accept *lashon hara* spoken in these circumstances. And just as it is forbidden for several people to speak *lashon hara* together, it is also forbidden to accept *lashon hara* heard from more than one person.[19]

If the Subject Admits to the Report

14. If *lashon hara* is spoken in the presence of the subject who admits that the information is true, or apologizes for his action in a manner indicating an admission of guilt, then it is permitted to believe the report.[20] However, if the subject remains silent, it is forbidden to

---

16. Ibid. 6:9.

17. See above, Ch. 2.

18. *Chofetz Chaim, Hilchos Lashon Hara* 6:7-8.

19. Ibid. 7:1-3.

20. Translator's note: Even in this situation, however, one should be careful, since the subject may be deliberately accepting blame for something he did not do in order to placate his accuser or otherwise restore peace. In some cases it can be a mitzvah to do so, and even to say falsehood for this purpose, as discussed in Ch. 10 par. 17.

believe the *lashon hara*, for his silence does not necessarily constitute an acknowledgment of guilt. Even if his nature is to loudly protest anything not to his liking, it must be assumed that in this case he has overcome his nature or that he has kept quiet for another reason. Perhaps he judges that those present will think the worst of him no matter what he says; unfortunately many people are all too willing to believe any accusation they hear, even if the accused attempts to prove his innocence in a hundred different ways. The rule for *lashon hara* is that silence is not considered acquiescence.[21]

> **Teacher (in front of class):** *It is obvious that Yaakov cheated on this test.*
> **Yaakov:** *(silence)*
> *The class is not permitted to conclude that Yaakov cheated on the test.*

Listening to *Lashon Hara*

15. Just as it is forbidden to believe *lashon hara*, it is also forbidden to merely pay attention to it, even if the listener resolves not to believe any derogatory information he hears.[22] There are two reasons for this: For one thing, listening attentively is itself a form of acceptance because it shows that the listener attaches enough importance to the words to want to hear them. Furthermore, simply listening to *lashon hara* implies acceptance, reinforcing the speaker's resolve to continue as well as strengthening the likelihood that any additional listeners will believe his words, since they see others listening without protest. The listener thus becomes an accessory to evil gossip, and any connection with such gossip is considered evil by association. In addition, one also violates the prohibitions against placing a stumbling block before the blind by aiding and abetting those who violate the commandments.[23]

16. The following excerpt from the ethical will of the sage Rabbi Eliezer HaGadol clearly conveys the seriousness which the Sages attached to all participants in any conversation involving *lashon hara*.[24]

> *My son, do not sit in a group with those who speak ill of their fellows, for when their words ascend to Heaven they are recorded in a*

---

21. Ibid. 7:2 and *Be'er Mayim Chaim* 3.

22. *Shaarei Teshuvah* 3:212; see also a lengthy discussion in *Kodesh Yisrael*, Ch. 10.

23. *Shaarei Teshuvah* ibid.

24. Cited in *Chofetz Chaim, Hilchos Lashon Hara* 6:6.

ledger, and anyone present at the time is inscribed as having been part of their wicked group and having habituated in lashon hara.

Joining a Group Where *Lashon Hara* Is Spoken

17. It is common for people to converse in groups where, unfortunately, they speak *lashon hara* and other forms of forbidden speech. It is forbidden to join such a group; one who does so violates the commandment to cling to Hashem[25] which we can fulfill by associating with Torah scholars. Conversely, anyone who attaches himself to a group whose behavior is the exact opposite of that which is expected of Torah scholars violates this commandment. Furthermore, by merely joining a group already engaged in speaking *lashon hara*, one violates the prohibition against listening to *lashon hara*.[26]

> *At a Kiddush following davening one Shabbos morning, Chaim notices several groups of people in conversation. One group, including the rav, is discussing the weekly parshah while a second group is discussing educational methods in public schools. A third group is loudly discussing the selection of a new principal at the local day school and seems to be on the verge of disparaging one of the candidates. Further inspection finds a fourth group engaged in outright lashon hara about a prominent member of another shul. Chaim immediately realizes that he should join the first group, but he takes the opportunity to assess the situation according to his study of Sefer Chofetz Chaim, Chapter Six, as follows: To join the last group would be a clear violation of the prohibition against listening to lashon hara, while joining the third group (which was not yet speaking lashon hara) violates the commandment to cling to Hashem. On the other hand, by joining the rav's group, he will be fulfilling the commandment to cling to Hashem.*

If One Finds Himself in the Presence of People Speaking *Lashon Hara*

18. If one does find himself in the company of a group of people speaking *lashon hara*, no matter how he came to join them, he must now extricate himself from their midst. If that is not possible, he must

---

25. *Rambam, Hilchos Dei'os* 6:2.

26. *Chofetz Chaim, Hilchos Lashon Hara* 6:6 and *Be'er Mayim Chaim* 18.

at least take great care not to violate the Torah's prohibition against accepting *lashon hara*. To do so he must take the following three steps:[27]

(a) He should make a firm decision not to believe any *lashon hara* he hears.

(b) He should resolve that he does not wish to listen to any *lashon hara* that is being spoken.

(c) He should make every effort to remain totally impassive and to avoid any expression indicating his agreement. It is even better if he can adopt an expression of censure.

19. The Sages have taught that Hashem gave us "pointed" fingers so that we can put them in our ears to block out forbidden speech if there is no other way to avoid hearing it.[28]

The Requirement to Rebuke Speakers of *Lashon Hara*

20. If one finds himself in the company of people speaking *lashon hara*, he is required to rebuke them, as the Torah says, *You shall reprove your fellow* (*Vayikra* 19:17). Even if in his judgment his reproof will not deter them, as long as it will do no harm (as discussed below) he may not remain silent, allowing them to think that he condones their speech. Furthermore, he is also required to defend the honor of the subject of their attacks, who retains his presumption as being an upstanding person despite their *lashon hara*. Indeed, one of the primary reasons he is required to leave is to avoid being tempted or intimidated into remaining silent and thereby sharing in their punishment. If he cannot find an effective way of rebuking them into silence, he should employ any possible tactic (such as diverting the conversation to another topic) to prevent them from transgressing the Torah's prohibitions.[29]

> *The eighth-grade boys were pretty upset with their teacher. As they were walking home from school, the conversation turned to lashon hara about him. Chaim, who was well-versed in the laws of lashon hara, wanted to stop them, but he knew that it was out of the ques-*

---

27. Ibid.

28. Ibid.; *Kesubos* 5b. Translator's Note: Similarly, one can hum to oneself or utilize any other method of making surrounding conversations unintelligible. In this situation one should also remember the Sages' injunction that it is better to be thought of as a fool all one's life in this world than to be wicked in Hashem's eyes for even one moment.

29. *Chofetz Chaim, Hilchos Lashon Hara* 9:4.

tion to try to defend the teacher. Instead, he tried a different tactic: "Did you hear about last night's basketball game ... ?"

21. As stated above, the requirement to reprove those who are speakers of *lashon hara* applies only when such attempts will not lead to further harm. If, in one's judgment, any intervention will only make matters worse and cause even more *lashon hara* about the subject ("How could you defend him, don't you realize that he ...?") then it is best to remain silent and leave as soon as possible.[30]

When It Is Permitted to Suspect

22. Although it is forbidden to accept or believe *lashon hara,* a person is permitted to accept a report to the extent needed to forestall potential damage and should take the necessary measures to protect himself and others from harm.[31]

> *Reuven is told that Shimon is a thief. Reuven is forbidden to accept this as definitely true and cause Shimon damage or embarrassment as a result (since he must continue to view Shimon as an upright person until he sees conclusive proof to the contrary). Nevertheless, Reuven should suspect that some truth may be contained in the report so that practical steps may be taken to prevent damage. Therefore, if he was considering hiring Shimon he should refrain from doing so. Similarly, if Reuven knows that Levi may hire Shimon, he should warn him, "I have heard that Shimon is a thief, and while I do not know this to be true and we must continue treating him as an upright person, we should also consider the possibility that it is accurate and take steps to protect ourselves from harm."*

23. If one is approached by an individual who informs him that he wishes to speak *lashon hara* for the listener's own benefit (or the subject's, or any other party's), it is permitted to listen to what he has to say. It is also permitted to listen to forbidden *lashon hara* for the purpose of proving to the speaker that he is mistaken in his assessment of the situation, or to assuage his anger and restore peace.[32]

> *Mr. Brown was sitting with Mr. Gold in the Gold's living room, furiously describing all the terrible qualities of Mr. Silver and Mr.*

---

30. Ibid.

31. Ibid. 6:10.

32. Ibid. 6:4.

Diamond. Mr. Gold listened quietly. After Mr. Brown left, the Gold children asked their father, "How could you listen to all that lashon hara?" "I know him well," the father answered. "He feels much better now and won't go speaking about them to anyone else."

Note: Mr. Gold should have taken steps to prevent his children from listening to the lashon hara. Since they did hear it, he should attempt to persuade them not to accept the lashon hara. He could begin by saying, "That is how Mr. Brown sees the situation, but there is probably another side to the story."

As a general rule, it is permitted to listen to *lashon hara* if the intention is to bring about a beneficial result. Nevertheless, even when it is permitted to listen to *lashon hara*, it is still forbidden to accept it as definitely being true.[33]

Seeking Information About Others

24. A person is only permitted to listen to negative information as needed to conduct his affairs if the listener informs the speaker of the legitimate purpose in doing so. If this is not made clear, the speaker will still be speaking *lashon hara*, even though it is acceptable to relate the negative information. Since the speaker does not realize that the listener's purpose is beneficial, and his intention is simply to disparage the subject, the listener has, in effect, caused the speaker to speak *lashon hara*.[34]

> **Mrs. A:** *Oh, my son was just telling me about his friend, Yaakov C.*
>
> *[Mrs. B has been seeking information about Yaakov C, whom she is considering as a potential match for her daughter. She sees this as a perfect opportunity to get an honest opinion without engaging in lashon hara, since any negative information will be for a beneficial purpose. However, Mrs. B realizes that if Mrs. A isn't informed of her true motive in listening to the report, it will still be lashon hara, and decides to tell her, knowing that she won't lose out when keeping Hashem's mitzvos.]*
>
> **Mrs. B:** *Wonderful, I need information about Yaakov for a shidduch (she is not necessarily obligated to say for whom; see Chapter 27, paragraph 3).*

---

33. Ibid. 6:10.
34. Ibid. 6:2-4.

25. It is all the more forbidden to request information about a person without making it clear that the question has a beneficial purpose. Only when this purpose is clear to both the speaker and the listener does the conversation become permitted rather than a means of disparaging the subject. If one simply asks about another person without making it clear that he has a legitimate purpose in doing so, he causes the speaker to speak *lashon hara*.[35]

> *Right:*
> **Mr. A:** *I need information about Yitzie G; he applied for a job in my company.*
> **Mr. B:** *Well, I think …*
> *Wrong:*
> **Mr. A:** *Hi, what's doing? Hey, do you know Yitzie G from your shul? What is he like? Does he …?*

When Accepting *Lashon Hara* Is Permitted

26. In some situations it is permitted both to accept *lashon hara* and to believe it. This holds true if one is relying not just on the report itself (which, as explained in paragraph 7, is liable to be false) but also on information corroborated independently, as explained in the following paragraphs.

27. It is permitted to accept *lashon hara* about someone who is well-known for the flagrant transgression of universally known Torah prohibitions (e.g. Shabbos violations, adultery, or eating forbidden foods). Even if an individual is known to have rejected only one commandment, it is permitted to believe reports that he has also violated others. Since we have independent knowledge that this person rejects specific commandments, he is presumed likely to violate others as well. When someone speaks *lashon hara* about him the rule of *chazakah* does not apply, and we are not required to presume that he is innocent of what the report alleges.[36] Although few people today, if any, have the status of "wicked" (since Jews who do not adhere to the Torah in general are considered "captive infants who were raised by gentiles" — see Chapter 1, paragraph 5), we are nevertheless permitted to believe *lashon hara* about them. Although they are not consid-

---

35. Ibid. Causing someone to sin is included in the prohibition against placing a stumbling block before a blind person.

36. Ibid. 7:5 and *Be'er Mayim Chaim*.

ered "wicked," the fact remains that they do not act in conformity with the Torah and there is no reason to presume that a negative report is untrue. (However, this does not allow speaking or listening to *lashon hara* about them in the first place — see paragraph 31.)

28. Sometimes, a generally Torah-observant Jew is lax in the observance of certain well-known prohibitions (i.e. he has not rejected them but rather is lax for the sake of convenience). If one later hears that this person has left a Torah way of life completely, the Chofetz Chaim is uncertain whether the prohibition against accepting *lashon hara* applies, even though strong grounds existed previously to suspect that he might eventually abandon Torah and mitzvos. Therefore, it is best to be stringent and not believe the report until corroborating evidence is available, and treat him as before in the interim.[37]

> *A teenager has left the yeshivah and spends most of his time "on the street." He is known to willfully violate several prohibitions when he is with his friends. After a time, it is said that he has left Torah and mitzvos completely. One should not accept the information as true without corroborating evidence.*

29. If one is aware that a certain individual is weak in his observance of a particular area of the Torah (for example, he regularly engages in deceitful business practices), and that he does not seem to regard such practices as forbidden, often because "everybody does it," then it is permitted to believe reports that he is continuing this forbidden behavior, since he has already lost his presumption of righteousness in that area.

> **Mr. A:** *We contracted Mr. B to add a porch to our house. He said it wouldn't cost a penny over $15,000, but now he wants $25,000.*
>
> *Since the listener is aware that Mr. B habitually conducts his business in this manner, he may believe the story.*

30. Similarly, if one is aware that an individual belongs to a group that is known to be lax with certain *halachos*, and one knows that this person follows the practice of the group in one area, then it is permitted to believe reports that he is not careful in the practices of the group in other matters as well. This person cannot be

---

37. *Chofetz Chaim, Hilchos Lashon Hara,* Ch. 6, *Be'er Mayim Chaim* 28.

considered "wicked" since we can judge him favorably by saying that he is merely following the group's misguided notion that their practices are acceptable. However, we may still believe the reports due to the independent corroboration of his known affiliation with the group and his acceptance of some of its practices, and we need not rely exclusively on the report itself. Indeed, we would have been justified in suspecting that he accepted other leniences of his group even without hearing the report.

> The members of the ABC synagogue are known for behaving with a habitual lack of respect, arriving late, leaving early and holding lengthy conversations during davening. Reuven, Shimon and Levi share an apartment in the vicinity of the synagogue. Shimon and Levi attend another minyan where there is decorum during davening, while Reuven is a member of the ABC synagogue. Shimon and Levi notice that Reuven usually is late to leave for shul. One Shabbos, Shimon was invited to a bar mitzvah in the ABC synagogue, where he saw Reuven engaging in an ongoing conversation during davening. Shimon is not permitted to relate this incident to Levi (see paragraph 31), but if he does, Levi is permitted to believe it.

31. The fact that it is permitted to believe *lashon hara* when corroborating evidence exists, as explained above, applies only after the fact, i.e. when one has already heard the *lashon hara*. However, it is not in any way meant to permit speaking or listening to *lashon hara*, which is otherwise prohibited, even with corroborating evidence. One is only permitted to speak or to listen to *lashon hara* if there is a genuinely beneficial purpose to be accomplished, as discussed in Chapter 21. When there is corroborating evidence, however, it is permitted to believe the *lashon hara* regardless of whether it was originally heard in a permitted or prohibited fashion.[38]

What Constitutes Confirmation

32. As stated in paragraphs 10-11, rumors may not be believed unless they are confirmed. Confirmation takes place when there exist (a) a number of reports from (b) multiple sources (c) who are impartial. A number of reports is defined as the subject having been seen engaging in a consistent pattern of behavior over a period of

---

38. Ibid. 7:12; see also *Halichos Olam*, Ch. 6 fn. *pei.*

time; one episode does not prove negative character. Reports which originate from only one person are not considered reliable proof. Moreover, if the sources dislike the subject, the reports are never considered reliable. Very often, negative information is widely circulated and accepted, but upon investigation, it is revealed that all the reports originated from a single source or from individuals who dislike the subject and are therefore not reliable, or that only one incident is under discussion.[39]

> *Caution is advised when hearing: "Everyone knows it's true — it's the talk of the town!"*
>
> *(How does "everyone" know? From how many sources does the information originate, and are they impartial? How many separate events are they discussing?)*

Reports Based on the News Media

33. Special care is required to ascertain that the reports originate from honest and trustworthy sources. A great deal of our information originates in newspapers and other media where, unfortunately, the bottom line is usually holding the reader's attention (often by appealing to the baser aspects of human nature) rather than reporting events and quotes accurately and fairly. Even those who do wish to report the news accurately can themselves lack the complete information about events or their circumstances necessary to convey them properly. Furthermore, public figures may distort the truth or even fabricate outright falsehoods to serve their personal or political interests. As a result, many stories with, at best, the weakest connection to the truth receive general acceptance. Needless to say, the fact that such stories are widely circulated does not constitute halachically acceptable confirmation, as described above. While it is permitted to suspect that a story might be true in order to protect oneself from damage, it is forbidden to accept it as absolute truth or to take action that will harm anyone else on its strength.

> *Be alert to comments such as:*
> ❏ *"Of course it's true; there was a whole write-up about it in the paper."*
> ❏ *"It must be true; I heard it on the news."*

---

39. *Chofetz Chaim, Hilchos Lashon Hara, Ch. 7, Be'er Mayim Chaim 8.*

When Substantiating Evidence Is Not Sufficient

34. As stated above, while it is forbidden to accept *lashon hara* when relying exclusively on the forbidden statement, it may be believed if it is substantiated by independent evidence. However, this independent evidence must actually support the essence of the story, rather than its peripheral aspects (see examples below). Furthermore, if one does not have direct knowledge of the corroborating evidence but has only heard it from others or through media sources, then the evidence itself is no better than *lashon hara*. It is therefore forbidden to believe it, and all the more so, to believe any further *lashon hara* on its strength.[40]

35. Moreover, although an incriminating story may be true, the negative conclusion to be drawn about the subject may still be invalid. Even within the confines of a story, room always remains to judge the subject favorably (i.e. to ascribe a permissible motive to his actions, or to attribute them to ignorance of the *halachah*). If one hears a story which allows a favorable interpretation, he is required to give the subject the benefit of the doubt; if he instead judges the subject unfavorably, he violates the prohibition against accepting *lashon hara*.[41] If, however, the independent evidence supports the unfavorable conclusions, then it is permitted to accept the unfavorable conclusions as true.[42]

▶ *Example 1: Direct Evidence*

> *During the revolt of Avshalom, King David was told that Mephiboshes had hopes of regaining the throne of his grandfather King Shaul. After quelling the rebellion, David saw Mephiboshes dressed in mourning and heard him make statements indicating his disappointment in the outcome. Since King David himself saw the clothing of Mephiboshes and heard his words, he felt justified in believing the reports because he had direct evidence. (This example continues after paragraph 37.)*

▶ *Example 2: Direct Evidence*

> *A storekeeper heard reports that a neighborhood boy was expelled from yeshivah and had been idle at home for a few weeks. Upon hearing this, the storekeeper realized that he had frequently*

---

40. Ibid. 7:10-11.

41. See also Ch. 2 concerning violating the mitzvah to judge others favorably.

42. *Chofetz Chaim, Hilchos Lashon Hara* 7:10-11. See also Ch. 2.

noticed the boy in his store at different times of day, strongly suggesting that the boy was not regularly attending yeshivah. Since the boy did not seem ill (and his family is believed to be in good health), the storekeeper may rely on this direct evidence and believe the reports. (This example continues after paragraph 37.)

▸ *Example 3: Peripheral Evidence*

Rumors have spread that a local businessman is enmeshed in a court case because of unethical business dealings. One day a neighbor notices the subject's car parked downtown near the courthouse. Since this evidence is at best peripheral — the businessman may be visiting any of hundreds of offices in the area — it does not provide any basis whatsoever to believe the rumors.

▸ *Example 4: Direct but Unconvincing Evidence*

Reuven observes someone placing an order at the counter of a non-kosher restaurant. Since the man may just as well have been ordering a soft drink, we are required to give him the benefit of the doubt (as we are with all Torah-observant Jews; see Chapter 2), and to assume that he was not violating any prohibitions. Even if Reuven is later told that this man eats treife, he may not believe the report on the basis of what he witnessed. If, however, Reuven had seen the man sit down at a table with treife food, even without actually seeing him eat, and subsequently hears that this person eats treife, Reuven can believe the report based on his observations.

▸ *Example 5: Direct but Unreliable Evidence*

One day, a rumor spreads in shul that a prominent member had declared bankruptcy and left the country with $20 million, leaving his partners, investors, and creditors with serious losses. The next day a local newspaper carries a report loaded with many details. If anyone in shul had personally witnessed the details as reported in the paper he would have been permitted to use the information as a basis for believing the rumors. However, because the source is at best questionable (since newspaper articles are not halachically valid sources; see paragraph 33), the rumors remain unconfirmed.

36. Great caution must be exercised before concluding that any independent evidence actually supports a story or the negative inferences drawn from it, for the *yetzer hara* has enormous power to

cloud people's judgment in such matters.[43] Great shrewdness and perception are often required to get to the bottom of a story, and unless one is entirely certain that he has a clear understanding of the situation, it is better to give the benefit of the doubt and to assume that the negative reports are false or at least distorted. This is the way of those who genuinely wish to serve Hashem and to go in His ways; happy is their lot in this world and the next.[44]

If the Speaker Dislikes the Subject

37. We have learned that *lashon hara* supported by independent direct evidence may be believed. In other words, while the words have made some impression, we are not permitted to believe the story until independent direct evidence corroborates it. It would seem, however, that if one knows that the speaker dislikes the subject and wishes to malign him, then the story should be discounted as entirely false and should not even be allowed to make an impression. Thus, in order to believe any compelling evidence that comes to light, it must be so strong as to prove the truth of the statements entirely independently of the *lashon hara*.[45]

> In Example 1 (see paragraph 35), the source of King David's information was Tziva, the servant of Mephiboshes, who disliked his master and whom David knew to be a liar. Therefore, David should not have given the report any credence whatsoever. Had David merely found Mephiboshes dressed in mourning, he may have sought an explanation, but without hearing the report, he would not have concluded that Mephiboshes coveted the throne. Insofar as David believed Tziva's report on the basis of the corroborating evidence, he was guilty of accepting lashon hara.[46]
>
> In Example 2 if the storekeeper had not heard the report, he might have wondered why the boy was not in school but would not have concluded that he had been expelled from yeshivah. If the report originated with another boy who was known to despise the subject, the storekeeper is required to completely discount the information.

---

43. Ibid. in note.

44. See *Chofetz Chaim, Hilchos Lashon Hara* 7:7; *Nesiv Chaim* 15.

45. See *Kodesh Yisrael,* Ch. 12.

46. See the opinion of Rav (*Shabbos* 56a); also *Kodesh Yisrael* ibid.

When It Is Permitted to Believe *Lashon Hara* — and When to Act

38. Even in a situation where *lashon hara* supported by external evidence may be believed, it is still forbidden to repeat what one has heard; after all, even if one had personally witnessed the incriminating event it would be forbidden to relate it to others. However, when a legitimate need exists to relate what one has seen, such as for the other party's protection, then it is also permitted to repeat what one has heard. Nonetheless, one should caution the listener that the information is based on hearsay and circumstantial evidence, and that he does not have direct personal knowledge of the matter.[47]

39. Furthermore, even when it is permitted to believe the *lashon hara*, it is still forbidden to take physical action against the subject or to cause him monetary or property loss on the strength of hearing a report. Having personal knowledge of the corroborating evidence is not sufficient to allow one to take any punitive action against the subject. Had one personally witnessed the events, he would have been permitted to take action, but in this case, he does *not* have actual knowledge of the event.[48]

> *Reuven has had an item stolen from him and tells his friends that he has seen evidence suggesting that Shimon is the thief. It is forbidden for them to believe Reuven's claim, and it is all the more so forbidden for them to pressure Shimon to make him confess. Even if Reuven actually shows them circumstantial evidence that points to Shimon as the thief, they are still forbidden to take any action. They should certainly investigate the matter in order to help Reuven recover the stolen item, but if they punish Shimon in any way, they have violated the relevant prohibitions. This applies as well to anyone in a position of authority, such as an employer who takes action against one employee on the basis of the statement of another.[49]*

---

47. *Chofetz Chaim, Hilchos Lashon Hara* 7:12.

48. Ibid. 7:12, and in *Be'er Mayim Chaim* 28-30.

49. Ibid. 7:14.

14

Listening to and Accepting Rechilus

1. Just as accepting *lashon hara* is prohibited, so too is accepting *rechilus*, which is also included in the category of *lashon hara*. Thus, one is forbidden to accept as true a report that another person has acted or spoken against him since antagonism and resentment could result. Even if there is reason to believe that the facts of a report are true, it is forbidden to accept any negative implications of those facts and to allow oneself feelings of resentment as a result. Rather, one must always suspect that the subject acted as he did out of innocent motives and therefore the report does not provide justification for instigating a conflict.[1]

> *Mr. A: How can you speak favorably of him after what he said about you?*
>
> *Mr. B: He was probably given misinformation about me, because if he knew me, he wouldn't have said what he did. Also, different people view the same situation in different ways, so from his vantage point, he may feel that I acted wrongly. That doesn't mean that I was wrong, only that*

---

1. *Chofetz Chaim, Hilchos Rechilus* 5:1,6. See Ch. 13 for in-depth analysis of the prohibition to accept *lashon hara*. Many principles of this chapter are explained and analyzed in Ch. 13.

he perceived it that way. I certainly don't want to make an enemy of a person with a different point of view than mine, chas v'shalom.

2. We have learned that if one hears a report whose facts can be established as true but which can be interpreted in a way that is favorable to the subject, there is a mitzvah to give him the benefit of the doubt and judge him favorably.[2] In addition, if one judges him unfavorably, not only has he failed to observe the mitzvah of judging people favorably, but he has also violated the prohibition against accepting *rechilus*.[3]

3. An individual who does accept and believe *rechilus* violates the commandment not to accept a false report (*Shemos* 23:1). The Sages taught that *lashon hara* and *rechilus* kill three people: the one who speaks it, the one who hears it, and the one of whom it is spoken. This means that these forms of forbidden speech have the power to arouse intense hatred and resentment, which in some cases can lead to actual murder (see Chapter 8, paragraph 1).[4] On the other hand, the reward for not accepting *rechilus* is immense.

> *King Yerovam II was informed that the prophet Amos was speaking of his downfall.*
>
> *"Chas v'shalom," the king responded, "he wouldn't say that, and if he did, it comes from Hashem."*
>
> *Because King Yerovam II refused to be incited to condemn and punish Amos, he was granted the merit to expand the boundaries of Eretz Yisrael even further than Yehoshua bin Nun. This was despite the fact that Yerovam II, like the other kings of the Ten Tribes, followed the rites of the Golden Calves of Yerovam I. Before him, in the time of his grandfather Yehoachaz, the Ten Tribes were downtrodden by their enemies, but Hashem helped him lead his people to great success.*

Listening to *Rechilus*

4. Just as merely listening to *lashon hara* is forbidden, so too is it forbidden to listen to *rechilus*.[5] However, if the *rechilus* contains infor-

---

2. As discussed in Ch. 2, it is a mitzvah to judge an ordinary person favorably as long as the favorable interpretation is equally likely; but if the subject is a Torah scholar, then it is a mitzvah to give him the benefit of the doubt even if the unfavorable interpretation is much more likely than the favorable one.

3. *Chofetz Chaim, Hilchos Rechilus* 5:6.

4. Ibid. 5:1.

5. Ibid. 5:2.

mation necessary to protect oneself, it is permitted to listen.[6] Thus, if a person is told that someone intends to injure him (or anyone else) or to take some other action against his (or someone else's) interests, he is allowed to listen to the report and to suspect that it contains some truth in order to take steps to protect himself (and/or any other threatened parties). Even in this case, however, it is forbidden to accept the report as absolutely true. While taking protective measures based on the possibility that the report is true, one must at the same time continue to view its subject as an upright person, and to assume that the information is false or at least distorted. It is possible that the subject was acting with good intentions rather than out of a desire to do harm.

5. If it is forbidden to believe that such a report is true — even while taking steps to protect oneself — it follows that it is all the more forbidden to cause the subject any harm, loss, or even discomfort on the basis of the report. The Torah prohibits even nurturing a dislike of the person as a result. It is also forbidden to use this report as an excuse not to pay any debts or obligations owed to the subject, or to abstain from giving him *tzedakah*, loans, or any other personal assistance, as the Torah obligates us to extend to needy people.

> *Mr. Jacob purchased Mr. Silver's secondhand car for $7,500, and agreed to make three payments of $2,500. The car seemed to be in good shape and Mr. Jacob was satisfied with the deal. One evening, Mr. Black visited Mr. Jacob and remarked that he believed that Mr. Silver had put about 100,000 miles on the car and subsequently tampered with the odometer so that it showed only 35,000 miles. Mr. Jacob was furious and stopped payment on the next check. Mr. Jacob is guilty of accepting rechilus from Mr. Black. Mr. Jacob should have quietly discussed the matter with Mr. Silver; if Mr. Silver denies the charge and Mr. Jacob has no proof, he must presume that the story is false and continue making the payments as agreed. Mr. Jacob has the option of taking Mr. Silver to a din Torah if he remains suspicious that the story is true. In any event, stopping payments on the basis of Mr. Black's rechilus is prohibited. Furthermore, if Mr. Silver later requests a favor of Mr. Jacob, such as a ride to shul, it is prohibited for Mr. Jacob to refuse because of the ill feeling created by Mr. Black. (See also Chapter 7.)*

6. Ibid. 5:2. One should state that he is listening for a permitted purpose.

6. In short, we are not allowed to lower our estimation of the subject in any way as a result of the report. The fact that we are allowed to suspect that there might be some truth to the matter applies only to the extent of taking steps to protect against potential harm. However, in all other respects we are required to consider the report to be false.[7]

Taking the Initiative to Find Information

7. In order to take steps to protect one's interests (or those of others), it is not only permitted to listen to reports of threatening activities, but even to take the initiative to make relevant inquiries. Thus, if one sees someone acting in a manner which arouses suspicion that he intends to cause harm or damage, it is permitted to make inquiries as to the person's intentions in order to take necessary precautions. One need not remain silent out of fear that his questions might cause others to speak *lashon hara*.[8] Nevertheless, the inquirer is required to state explicitly that he is asking for a permitted objective. It is forbidden to pose the questions innocently, leading people to think that he wants to hear idle gossip, for in that case he would still be guilty of causing others to speak *lashon hara* or *rechilus*.[9]

> For years, Simon's Judaica has been providing religious articles to the Midcity, U.S.A. Jewish community. One year Mr. Simon realizes that sales are considerably down, and also notices that fewer people than usual had purchased lulavim from him. He begins to suspect that the people in town may be doubting his reliability, and asks his friend Mr. Levi to investigate the matter. When Mr. Levi does so, he may say, "I'm trying to find out why people aren't buying from Mr. Simon. I'd like to clear things up and help him." He may not say, "What's new in town? Looks like people don't buy from Mr. Simon anymore. Don't they trust him?"
>
> If Mr. Simon himself is inquiring he may ask, "Why don't people buy from me anymore?" making it clear that he is asking for his own benefit and not to elicit gossip.

---

7. Ibid.

8. Ibid. 5:3.

9. Ibid. *Hilchos Lashon Hara* 6:3.

Scope of the Prohibition

8. As with *lashon hara*, the prohibition against accepting *rechilus* applies whether the *rechilus* is spoken in private or in public,[10] whether or not it is spoken in the subject's presence,[11] whether it is said by only one person or by a number of people,[12] and whether it is said deliberately or unintentionally.[13] Even if one considers the source of the *rechilus* completely reliable because he is a close friend or relative or a person known to be of great integrity, it is nevertheless forbidden to accept his words as definitely true.[14]

> *Unfortunately, some people are careful not to accept lashon hara and rechilus in general, but relax their standards and believe everything they hear from family members and close friends.*

9. It is forbidden to accept *rechilus* as true whether the speaker is speaking for a legitimate purpose (such as warning of possible danger or damage) or merely to repeat gossip. However, in both cases one should take any necessary steps to prevent potential harm.[15]

Corroborating Evidence

10. Just as in a case of *lashon hara* where direct corroborating evidence proves that the story is true, and the *lashon hara* can be believed, this rule applies in *rechilus* as well. The evidence must address the main issues of the story rather than peripheral points. In addition, it is necessary to have direct knowledge of the supporting evidence, i.e. having seen it oneself rather than simply hearing about it from others.[16]

11. Furthermore, the evidence must directly implicate the subject as guilty. However, it is forbidden to reach a negative conclusion if the evidence merely indicates that a statement was made or an action taken, yet leaves room to judge the subject favorably (i.e. he didn't have a negative intention).[17] Once these conditions are met, and it is

---

10. Ibid. *Hilchos Rechilus* 6:1.

11. Ibid. 6:2. Even if the subject is silent, that is not proof of the truth of the matter. See Ch. 13 par. 14.

12. Ibid. 6:4.

13. Ibid. 6:8.

14. Ibid. 6:7. See Ch. 13.

15. See Ch. 13 par. 31.

16. Ibid. 6:7.

17. Ibid. 6:9.

permitted to believe the *rechilus*, it is still forbidden to relate this knowledge to others, including one's wife and family, except for a legitimate purpose such as to warn them against probable danger. It is certainly forbidden to take any action against the subject of the report or to cause him injury or even embarrassment.[18]

12. If someone is aware that a certain individual bears him enmity and has caused him considerable damage in the past, and is told that this enemy has once again taken harmful action of a sort no worse than the previous incident, it would seem that it is permitted to believe this report. The individual in question has already proven capable of causing harm at that level.[19]

13. In general, "supporting" evidence is never sufficient to hurt anyone or to cause monetary or property loss. Unfortunately, many people are misinformed in this matter and commit serious transgressions as a consequence.[20]

> *Reb David, a fundraiser for a yeshivah in Eretz Yisrael, was invited to stay in the Levi home. Mr. Levi was not only a baal tzedakah himself, but collected from many friends for various causes. Planning an upcoming trip to Eretz Yisrael, he asked friends for tzedakah money to distribute there. He accumulated over $5,000 in cash which he locked in the personal safe in his house, the keys to which were well hidden.*
>
> *The day before his trip he discovered the safe open and the money gone. He searched for his key and found that missing as well. Apparently this was an "inside job," with all evidence pointing to Reb David. Who else was in the house and could have known about the money? Furthermore, he must have felt that since he was collecting for a worthy cause in Eretz Yisrael, he was entitled to the additional funds destined to be distributed there.*
>
> *However, Mr. Levi has no direct proof that Reb David was the thief, and even supporting evidence is insufficient. Therefore, he cannot devise a plan to "recover" the money, nor may he call the authorities.*
>
> *Instead, Mr. Levi may: (a) Approach Reb David directly. If Reb David denies the charge, Mr. Levi may opt to (b) take Reb David to a din Torah. (See Choshen Mishpat 75:17, Beis Yosef and Rema.)*

---

18. Ibid.
19. Ibid. *Hilchos Lashon Hara* 7:5; see also above, Ch. 13 pars. 27-30.
20. Ibid. *Hilchos Rechilus* 6:9 and *Be'er Mayim Chaim* 20.

❊ Purity of Soul

Chapters 15-19

15

Leitzanus — Mockery and Cynicism

1. The term *leitzanus* refers to ridicule and cynicism directed toward a person or against any concept of positive value. The Torah considers it one of the most destructive character traits in existence, since the mockery of a cynic destroys the very fabric of man's fear of Heaven.[1]

> The "leitzanim" said that Yitzchak was conceived from Avimelech and not Avraham (Bereishis 25:19, Rashi). The implications of their cynicism involve the disintegration of the entire legacy of Avraham Avinu.

Aside from the prohibition of the *leitzanus* itself, it leads to many other sins. The trait of *leitzanus* brings on Divine retribution even in this world and ultimately results in the destruction of the cynic.[2]

---

1. Aside from the devastating nature of *leitzanus*, there is a Torah prohibition against it derived from the verse (*Devarim* 6:7), *You shall speak of them* [words of Torah] and not other things (*Yoma* 19b, *Chavas HaShemirah*, Ch. 9). This teaches us that our basic agenda is to lead a Torah life (all our activities — physical, financial, recreational — are to be in conformance with Torah, and we are to dedicate ourselves to Torah study and practice as much as possible given the constrictions of daily life). Words of no positive value and destructive to ourselves and our endeavor to follow Hashem are to be excluded from our speech.

2. *Avodah Zarah* 18b; *Mesillas Yesharim*, Ch. 5.

The cynic enjoys his mockery; he cannot accept any reproof (which he will merely mock as well). Therefore, the only hope for him is Divine retribution, for that he will be unable to mock. (See Mesillas Yesharim, Chapter 5.)

The Sages taught that someone who engages in *leitzanus* falls into Gehinnom.[3] Furthermore, the *leitz* is one of four categories of people who will not merit to bask in the Divine Presence.[4] (Nevertheless, an individual who is already enmeshed in this quality need not despair; see the last paragraph of this chapter for advice on how to break free of it.)

2. The prohibition against *leitzanus* includes reading heretical writings as well as any books and periodicals containing *leitzanus*, obscenity, profanity, etc., since they all debase and demoralize the Divine soul.[5]

Television and radio programs can easily fall into this category.

Leitzanus Directed Against Idolaters

3. Every form of *leitzanus* is forbidden except that directed against idolatry[6] or against those who scorn the Torah and its mitzvos.[7]

The prophet Yeshayahu mocked the idols of Babylonia in the following way. "Bel[8] kneeled and Nevo[8] bent over... they couldn't restrain themselves from holding back their 'load'" (a euphemism for bodily needs) (Yeshayahu 46:1,2).

If somone is known to be involved in immoral acts one can call him "gimmel" "shin": "gaifa" (adulterer) and "shoteh" (fool) (Megillah 25b).

However, one's intention when employing *leitzanus* even in a permitted situation must be to disprove and discredit the wrong beliefs

---

3. *Avodah Zarah* ibid.

4. *Sotah* 42a. The other three are people who regularly engage in *lashon hara* (see Ch. 5), flattery (see Ch. 11), and falsehood (see Ch. 10).

5. *Chovas HaShemirah* ibid.

6. *Megillah* 25b.

7. *Chovas HaShemirah*, Ch. 12.

8. Names of Babylonian idols. Note: Babylonia was the greatest world power and its idols constituted the sum total of culture and national purpose in life.

and actions of his target, and not simply for the pleasure of making fun of others.[9] He should also take great care that the listeners understand that his purpose is the noble one of discrediting evil and not the base one of humiliating people.[10]

> *The purpose of this mockery is to completely discredit false beliefs, ideas and ways of life in the eyes of every person, so that even in his weaker moments he will stay far away from them. (See Ohr Yechezkel, "Emunah," pp. 164-165.)*

4. The most serious *leitzanus* is mockery or cynicism directed against Hashem, His Torah and mitzvos; this is tantamount to heresy.[11] People who are committed to lives of Torah and mitzvos generally do not engage in such mockery. However, we do see less extreme forms of *leitzanus* which although not as well known are considered very severe. Rabbeinu Yonah presents five categories of this *leitzanus* in decreasing order of severity. All are forbidden and continuous involvement in them constitutes *leitzanus* as described in paragraph 1.[12]

Categories of *Leitzanus*

5. The *first* and most serious category is *leitzanus* intended to make people look bad in the eyes of others. This behavior is also prohibited as *lashon hara*.

> *"He is a stupid idiot."*

6. The *second* category involves deriding people not because one takes pleasure in their failings or wishes them ill, but simply because one looks down on their poverty, inferior status or any other lack of success.

> *Sadly, many people gloat over those less fortunate, as if poverty were a great disgrace, thinking that if only the poor person would work as hard as they do, he too could be prosperous and respectable.*

---

9. Translator's Note: In this context it is worthwhile to relate the well-known observation that there are two kinds of zealots, corresponding to a housewife and her pet cat. Although both of them want the cat to kill mice, the housewife's goal is the noble one of ridding the house of harmful pests while the cat's entire interest is its base enjoyment in catching and eating mice.

10. Cf. *Chofetz Chaim, Hilchos Lashon Hara* 9:3, *Be'er Mayim Chaim* 9.

11. *Sanhedrin* 99b.

12. The following section is based on *Shaarei Teshuvah* 3:174-7.

This attitude generally stems either from arrogance or from a feeling of complacency with the blessings of Hashem. It shows that one attributes his own success to personal strength and skill, as the Torah describes: *My strength and the might of my hand created for me all this wealth* (*Devarim* 8:14). Of such a person King Shlomo says, *One who makes fun of a poor person insults his Maker* (*Mishlei* 17:5), because he thinks that the poor person himself is responsible for his predicament instead of realizing that wealth and poverty are products of Hashem's decrees.[13]

❏ *"He is just a schnorrer."*
❏ *"That store is not for our 'class'; it's for poor people."*
❏ *"He never made it in life."*

7. Subconscious feelings of scorn for "have-nots" may bring a person to look down on Torah scholars who endure difficult conditions in order to dedicate themselves to a life of Torah. This is a particularly serious form of *leitzanus*, for it involves mockery of Torah and its scholars.

> **Father:** *What are your plans once you're married?*
> **Yaakov:** *I'd like to learn in kollel for a few years.*
> **Father:** *Oh! You want to be one of "them"?*

8. The *third* category of *leitzanus* includes the belittling of activities and events as foolish and useless without directly attacking the people involved, and even at times expressing respect for them.

> *A convention designed to strengthen Torah observance was described in the following way: "There are a lot of good people in that group but they waste their time with a lot of useless talk."*

This form of *leitzanus* can lead to statements tantamount to heresy (of which the people are often unaware), such as making fun of mitzvos.

> *"He's a nice fellow, but all he does is learn, learn, learn and live like a parasite off the generosity of others."*

This trait usually stems from a feeling of superiority over the one whose actions they wish to deride. Such individuals generally find it difficult or impossible to accept constructive criticism, which places

---

13. Cf. *Metzudas David.*

them in a spiritual quagmire. People caught in such a quagmire should learn how to slowly change their ways.

9. One common manifestation of this category of *leitzanus* is unfortunately so widespread and deeply entrenched as to require special attention. It has become routine for members of one group to make fun of or belittle the practices and customs of other groups, e.g. Chassidim and *Misnagdim;* Ashkenazim and Sephardim; Jews who originate from different countries or regions; and followers of various rebbes, *tzaddikim,* and *gedolim.* This practice is strictly forbidden. The customs of these groups were generally instituted by great *tzaddikim* for profound reasons far beyond the understanding of those who deride them.

❏ *"Those Chassidim spend all their time ..."*
❏ *"He is a litvishe bachur so he doesn't ..."*
❏ *"Sephardim ..."*

10. There are times when a parent or rebbi must tell a child or student that the actions of another person or group are improper. This should be accomplished without *leitzanus.*

> *"This is their way of avodas Hashem (serving Hashem) which they think is permissible. However, as we understand the Torah, this practice is incorrect and distances them from Torah. We respect them for doing as their rebbes taught, for which they probably will be rewarded. But we were taught differently."*

> *"In reality it is prohibited and shows terrible middos. Although they are mistaken in their actions, we still must respect them for the positive things they accomplish and realize that <u>they</u> perceive their bad behavior as good. Hashem judges each individual according to his ability to understand the Torah. It is not our business to judge others, for that is beyond human capacity (cf. Pesachim 54b; Rambam, Hilchos Teshuvah 3:1; Rabbeinu Yonah 2:19). While we will avoid their incorrect actions, we will respect the people for the good they do, and try to concentrate only on the merits of all Jews."*

11. The *fourth* category covers those who regularly spend time in fruitless activities and pointless talk, such as prohibited discussion of political affairs and developments.

"We spent two hours discussing all the details of the latest government scandal."

Two destructive consequences arise from such activity: The first is the proliferation of pointless talk, as the Sages said, *One who talks excessively brings on sin (Avos* 1:17); and the second is the waste of time that could be spent in Torah-related activity. The Torah says of a person who has an opportunity to engage in Torah and does not do so, *He has scorned the word of Hashem (Bamidbar* 15:31). In particular, someone who deliberately goes to a place where people gather for idle talk and activities violates the Psalmist's warning (*Tehillim* 1:1) not to sit in a "session of scorners."[14]

12. The *fifth* category involves making fun of people or their behavior simply for the sake of amusement, even if it is clear from the jokes that the speaker actually respects both the people involved and their conduct.

> *"Look at how Chaim Yankel davens, he's such a tzaddik!"*
> *(The speaker respects Chaim Yankel, as well as his efforts in tefillah, but he was just seeking amusement at his expense.)*

Note: Rabbeinu Yonah points out that this type of *leitzanus* is occasionally found in many people, including otherwise upright Jews. Therefore, it is important to make a great effort to work on eliminating any belittlement of others from one's speech.

Legitimate Humor

13. Although *leitzanus* is strictly forbidden, legitimate humor can be of great value, such as that which creates a cheerful and enthusiastic frame of mind desirable for Torah study and other worthwhile activities. The type of humor which cheers and encourages others is included in the mitzvah of doing acts of *chesed* (kindness).[15] However, jokes that only serve to belittle or are excessively light-headed[16] are included in the prohibition against *leitzanus*.[17] In

---

14. Cf. also *Avodah Zarah* 18b.

15. *Taanis* 22a.

16. In Hebrew *kalus rosh;* this refers to the giddiness which comes from excessive levity and laughter to the point that one loses control of himself like a drunk person. Cf. *Avos* 3:13 and *Tiferes Yisrael.*

17. Heard from a *gadol* that *se'chok* and *kalus rosh* are included in *leitzanus* (cf. *Avos* ibid.)

summary, jokes are an excellent tool to help pass through life's travail, provided they are neither at another's expense, nor at the expense of one's own soul.

> *Rav Beroka was in the marketplace talking with Eliyahu HaNavi, who pointed out two men as having a place in the World to Come. Rav Beroka engaged them in conversation to find out what great merit had made them so worthy. "We are jolly people," they said, "and when we see people who are depressed we speak to them and cheer them up. Furthermore, if we see two individuals engaged in conflict, we try to restore peace through good cheer."*[18]

Ingrained *Leitzanus*

14. A person who is aware that *leitzanus* has become ingrained in his character need not despair, even if his efforts to rid himself of this trait have not brought immediate results. The key to success in this area is steady and diligent work, and eventually Hashem will help set him free completely. At first, the greatest attention should be paid to avoiding the worst forms of *leitzanus*, followed by progressive work on the less serious degrees. It is especially helpful to set aside regular times to study relevant works of *mussar*. He should never give up even if relapses occur, but should regather his forces and continue these efforts, as King Shlomo said, *A tzaddik falls down seven times, and keeps rising* (*Mishlei* 24:16). If possible, one should seek the advice of Torah sages for encouragment to persevere. Furthermore, we may presume that from the moment a person *begins* to make efforts to free himself of this trait, he has removed himself from the category of habitual speakers of *leitzanus*. Even though his efforts have not yet yielded success, he will at least not be subject to the punishments described in paragraph 1, and should be aware that Hashem greatly cherishes his efforts at self-improvement.

> *The Vilna Gaon writes,*[19] *"Our greatest task in life and reason for existence is to improve our character."*

---

18. *Taanis* 22a.

19. *Even Sheleimah* 1:2; see also *Rambam, Hilchos Dei'os* 1:5-6 for a discussion of the mitzvah of following Hashem's ways.

16

Personal Behavior

1. The Torah's commandment, *You shall go in His ways* (*Devarim* 28:9), requires us to emulate Hashem's ways by working on improving our character traits, acquiring good qualities and correcting those that are poor.[1] A person is not "bad" for having negative traits; it is natural to be conceited[2] or to become angry when provoked. There are individuals whose nature is to be selfish or unkind and it is a mitzvah for such a person to improve himself by working on his character traits.

2. The mitzvah is fulfilled by *making efforts* to improve one's character traits.[3] A person must realize, however, that despite his best efforts he will often not succeed in acquiring and expressing sterling qualities. He should not be discouraged, but should "forgive" himself[4] and continue with his efforts. *The mitzvah is achieved by steady effort, not steady success.*

---

1. *Rambam, Hilchos Dei'os* 1:5,6.

2. *Mesillas Yesharim*, Ch. 23.

3. See *Sefer HaChinuch*, Mitzvah 611.

4. When a person does something wrong he is held accountable. Nevertheless, character traits and environmentally learned behaviors certainly play a factor in mitigating but not

Every single person has a unique combination of inborn character traits and environmentally learned behavior. The mitzvah is to strive to improve, employing these unique capabilities. Each small effort at improvement is a fulfillment of this positive commandment and is highly cherished in Heaven.[5]

While this is a general commandment covering all aspects of our behavior, the Torah specifically warns us to expend special effort to avoid certain exceptionally poor qualities.

Conceit

3. The Torah teaches us to avoid conceit and pride. Even a king is not allowed to become overly wealthy or to take an excess of wives so that he does not become haughty over his brethren (*Devarim* 17:20). If a king who must exercise firm control over his people is expected to remain humble and lowly in spirit, all the more so are ordinary people required to conduct themselves in such a manner.[6]

4. Although a person must cultivate a healthy self-image[7] and fully recognize his talents and achievements, he must not develop feelings of superiority as a result. Each individual is born into a unique

---

necessarily absolving his guilt. There are categories in *halachah* of intentional (*meizid*), unintentional (*shogeg*), and involuntary (*oness*). Many sub-categories exist within these categories. When a person knows what the proper behavior should be, but loses himself to his emotions and reacts wrongly, he usually regrets his actions immediately. This, in itself, is the beginning of *teshuvah* (repentance), and categorizing his behavior as intentional or unintentional is irrelevant. In any event, wrong behavior requires *teshuvah* and by his regret and continued efforts he has already started on the path to *teshuvah*. Rabbeinu Yonah teaches us (1:16) that for every degree of *teshuvah* there is corresponding forgiveness, i.e. the deeper the *teshuvah* penetrates the heart, the deeper is the corresponding forgiveness. However, even a shallow *teshuvah* evokes some level of forgiveness. It is crucial to integrate this principle into our personality — Hashem loves us and eagerly awaits every effort toward *teshuvah*. Therefore, when a person does not succeed, he should never give up or become discouraged, because his continued efforts are cherished in Heaven. As a parent lovingly perseveres and helps a child grow, how infinitely more so does Hashem stay with us every minute of our lives, constantly helping us and encouraging us to grow (see *Yeshayahu* 48:17; *Tehillim* 103:13-14). He is aware of our weaknesses, and forgives us at a level corresponding to our efforts at *teshuvah*. We, too, must have *emunah* (faith) in Hashem, and believe that He forgives us, and therefore, we, too, can forgive ourselves and not be pulled down by past failures. However, if a person refuses to make an effort to improve himself, and wishes to remain within the confines of improper behavior, then his wrong remains unmitigated and he should not forgive himself, for in Heaven, too, his wrong is not forgiven.

5. See *Sefer HaTanya* at length regarding *beinoni*.

6. *Shaarei Teshuvah* 3:34.

7. *Rabbeinu Yonah, Shaarei Avodah* (beginning).

environment with certain capabilities, and is measured solely according to his own accomplishments relative to those abilities. No human being can ever accurately judge another person and determine whether he is righteous or wicked.[8] Furthermore, even if one person truly is more righteous than another, he should remind himself that all human greatness is paltry compared to the infinite majesty of the Creator.[9] How can a person utilize the talents given to him by his Creator, and, standing before Him, attribute those talents to himself?

> *It is written in the Torah that Moshe Rabbeinu believed with perfect faith that he alone was the greatest prophet of Israel, while believing with the same perfect faith that he was the humblest of all men. (Both of these are written in the Torah, and Moshe, along with every Jew, was compelled to accept the veracity of every word in the Torah.) How could a truly humble person be aware of his own unique greatness both in the trait of humility and the area of prophecy? Moshe possessed an unparalled awareness of Hashem's presence and knew that compared to Him all human greatness is nothing. (Heard from HaRav Shimon Schwab.)*

> *King David was chastised by his wife Michal, daughter of King Shaul — after publicly "lowering" himself with song and dance in front of the Aron HaKodesh — for not maintaining proper dignity in public, even if only before the women. "Those women," David retorted, "are mothers in Israel. I should wish to reach their greatness in the World to Come" (Midrash Rabbah, Bamidbar 4:20). David well knew that he alone was the great king of Israel from whose seed will come the Mashiach, Hashem's instrument for the Final Redemption. He recognized as well that he was the greatest Torah scholar of his time. Yet, when he measured his accomplishments against his G-d-given capabilities, comparing himself to the self-sacrificing mothers of Israel, he perceived that they were greater than he. This is the meaning of "I will be humble in my eyes" (II Shmuel 6:22).*
>
> *In contrast, Bilam the wicked retorted to Hashem, "I may not be important to You, but to the kings of the world I am important" (Bamidbar 22:10, Rashi).*

---

8. *Rambam, Hilchos Teshuvah* 3:2; *Shaarei Teshuvah* 2:19; cf. *Pesachim* 54b.

9. Morning prayer: *Le'olam yehei adam* …; also, Yom Kippur *Ne'ilah* prayer.

None of us, however great his talents or achievements, is allowed to think of himself as better than the next person, however lowly that person may appear to be.

5. Conceit is a forbidden trait even if only in our thoughts, and all the more so in our actions. Anyone who considers himself superior to others is required to purge his mind of this belief,[10] and if he fails to do so and willingly allows such thoughts to persist, he violates the Torah's commandment, *that his heart does not become haughty over his brothers* (*Devarim* 17:20). Should his arrogance express itself through action, the violation is that much greater.

> *Conceit is one of the most severe sins, with the greatest destructive effects on the soul, as King Shlomo says, "All who are haughty of heart are abominable to Hashem" (Mishlei 16:5). Of what benefit are all the possessions and accomplishments in the world if one is acting in a way that is abominable in the eyes of Hashem? Furthermore, this quality causes people to commit many other transgressions by increasing the yetzer hara's power and distancing us from Hashem.*[11]

6. The Torah Sages offered advice as to how to achieve the desired degree of humility: treat each and every person as if he were better than you. If he is a greater Torah scholar, you are certainly required to respect him. Likewise, if an individual is wealthier than you, perhaps Hashem granted him his riches because he was worthy. There may be a Divine plan that he do mitzvos with his wealth, for which he must be respected. Conversely, if his wealth is inferior to yours, he bears less responsibility to maintain Torah institutions and support the poor and therefore carries less guilt over their plight. If he is inferior to you in wisdom, assume that he is more righteous than you, since his sins are considered relatively unintentional, while you are held more responsible for your sins *because* of your superior wisdom. It is possible to avoid any trace of conceit by

---

10. *Chovas HaShemirah*, Ch. 14. It should be noted that although the Torah sometimes does legislate thoughts (e.g. thoughts of forbidden relationships, conceit, idol worship), a person cannot control which thoughts come to him and therefore, his responsibility for these thoughts does not start at the moment they enter his mind. Rather, as soon as one becomes aware that a thought is forbidden, he is required to attempt to purge it from his mind by diverting his attention to other subjects (preferably Torah). Only if he fails to do so, and willingly allows the thought to linger in his mind for his enjoyment, is he considered to have violated the relevant prohibition (heard from a *gadol*).

11. *Shaarei Teshuvah* 3:34.

keeping such thoughts constantly in mind, thereby reaping great rewards both in this world and the next.[12]

Anger

7. Anger is another highly destructive quality that we are strongly cautioned to avoid. The Sages said that when a person is angry, it is as if he is worshiping idols, and all forms of Gehinnom have power over him.[13] People who are habitually angry tend to lead miserable lives.[14]

8. A person who is provoked will naturally feel anger, and sometimes this overwhelming feeling will be acted upon (through hostility, insults, physical abuse, breaking objects, etc.). In order to control anger one has to clearly distinguish between (a) feeling angry and (b) acting angrily. An individual who controls his anger during an argument is held in the highest esteem by our Sages.

> *The world continues to exist in the merit of someone who closes his mouth during an argument.*[15]

A person may feel very angry, but has learned to express his anger in ways that are not harmful. There is the even higher angelic level of the saintly Hillel who never even "felt" anger because his heart was so filled with love of Hashem and all His creations.[16] These are the goals toward which we are commanded to direct our efforts. However, a person should learn to know himself, and when he is angry he should not deny his feelings. He should admit to himself, "Yes, I am angry. Unfortunately, I am far from the level of Hillel," and search for ways to diminish his anger without harming others. This is the gateway to success; denying anger, however, is a recipe for failure.

9. Parents or teachers who must act angrily for the benefit of a child or student should train themselves to show anger outwardly, but to remain inwardly calm.[17] In general, punishment is most effective as an educational tool when the parent/teacher feels and acts calmly as it is meted out.

---

12. *Iggeres HaRamban.*
13. *Nedarim* 22a; *Shabbos* 105b.
14. *Pesachim* 113b.
15. *Chullin* 89a.
16. *Shabbos* 31a; *Mesillas Yesharim*, Ch. 11. This analysis of anger was explained to me by a Torah scholar.
17. *Rambam, Hilchos Dei'os* 2:3.

10. The Sages extolled the virtues of those who "climb the ladder" of self-training in interpersonal relationships.

> *Those who accept insults without insulting in return, hear themselves humiliated without replying, act out of love for Hashem and rejoice in such "afflictions," of them Scripture says, "Those who love Him will be like the powerfully rising sun" (Shoftim 5:31).*[18]

Conceit vs. Humility and Anger vs. Patience in Our Times

11. In contemporary times it is very difficult to achieve the virtues of humility, patience and tolerance. This requires an explanation.

In the present era, we are surrounded by many other cultures and are constantly bombarded in nearly every aspect of our lives with influences and stimuli alien to Torah values. Contemporary lifestyles make it especially difficult to even recognize the value of the Torah attributes of humility and patience (the opposite of conceit and anger), much less to attain them. Declining faith in Hashem makes it harder than ever to recognize that the satisfaction of personal desires is not the ultimate purpose of existence, but that there exists a Creator Who brought us into being and sustains us every moment of our lives, and to Whom we owe everything.

The thrust of modern technology is to constantly devise personal comforts with ever-improving ways to avoid pain and effort. This has become the *raison d'être* of the society in which we live. It is therefore hard to accept the notion that we do not have an inalienable right to always have our way, making our frustration level extremely low. Thus, an understanding of the Torah's eternal truth as to the virtues of humility, patience and selflessness is difficult to acquire, and it is an even greater difficulty to live accordingly.

12. However, it is precisely because awareness of the purity of the soul, and humility and patience are so difficult to acquire, that the reward for our efforts toward inward perfection is so immense. This quest to perfect our character traits is the form of service most valued by Hashem, certainly in our generation, and is indeed the purpose for which He created us[19] and continues to grant us life and

---

18. *Yoma* 23a. See Ch. 7 par. 15(Cii) for further analysis of these qualities.

19. *Even Sheleimah* 2:1.

freewill. Furthermore, as a person concentrates his attention toward achieving these goals, he will find inner peace and joy in life.

13. A person can often get discouraged because he feels that these efforts meet with failure after failure. However, one must always remember that it is the continual *effort* that counts and he should never despair or relax his endeavors. Even if years of effort appear to have brought no progress whatsoever in reaching a particular goal — such as controlling anger or verbal abuse — the very recognition that the goal is worthy of effort is in itself immeasurably important in Hashem's eyes. In addition, a person is usually blind to his own success, thinking himself a miserable failure, when in fact he has made enormous progress in correcting certain of his deficiencies.

Crude Speech

14. The Sages have said[20] that when a person speaks crudely, even a decree issued for seventy years of happiness will be reversed. They also stated that crude speech is liable to evoke serious punishment, as the prophet said, *"Therefore G-d will not rejoice over His youths, and He will not have compassion on His orphans and His widows, for it is all flattery and wickedness, and every mouth speaks foulness; and even so His wrath has not abated and His hand is still extended (to punish)"* (*Yeshayahu* 9:16). Three reasons are given for the severity of this offense:

(a) The Jewish soul is by nature modest and pure, and crude speech reflects corruption.

(b) The Torah calls Israel a *wise and discerning people* (*Devarim* 4:6). Anyone who speaks like those foolish and uninhibited individuals who reject the Torah, desecrates the sanctity of Israel and demonstrates that he is not among the wise who disdain such speech.

(c) Crude speech befouls the human mind, which is our most precious possession.

Listening to Crude Speech

15. Anyone who listens to crude speech, and does not close his ears or try to escape the company of those who speak it, is subject to

---

20. *Shabbos* 33a. Note: Rabbeinu Yonah lists six categories of *lashon hara*, i.e. speech that is "evil." These are: (a) untrue *lashon hara*; (b) true *lashon hara*; (c) *rechilus*; (d) *avak lashon hara* and *rechilus*; (e) crude speech; and (f) captiousness. In the following paragraphs we will discuss the *halachos* of the final two – crude speech and captiousness [faultfinding] (*Shaarei Teshuvah* 3:229-31 is the source of these paragraphs).

serious punishment, as King Shlomo says, *For the mouth of the estranged is a deep pit, those who anger Hashem will fall there* (*Mishlei* 22:14). If it is impossible to avoid listening (e.g. one who works in an office where others speak in a foul manner and is unable to find another job), one should at least recognize that such speech is poison to the soul and take constant steps to "detoxify" himself.[21]

Unseemly Speech

16. Certain modes of speech, while not exactly crude, are nonetheless unseemly. The Sages taught us never to allow even this form of speech to emerge from our mouths. It is better to utilize lengthy circumlocutions or strained euphemisms, than to speak in such an unseemly manner.[22] Furthermore, it is a mitzvah to choose words that are as refined as possible.[23]

> **Do not say:** *This stinks.*
> **Instead, say:** *There is a highly unpleasant odor.*
>
> **Do not say:** *This is as filthy as a pigsty.*
> **Instead, say:** *This place needs a <u>major</u> cleaning.*
>
> *In situations where one must convey negative information:*[24]
> **Do not say:** *He is a lazy good-for-nothing.*
> **Instead, say:** *He really has no interest in achieving any potential in life.*
>
> **Do not say:** *He is a big slob.*
> **Instead, say:** *He is not a neat person.*
>
> **Do not say:** *He is a stupid idiot.*
> **Instead, say:** *He is not very smart. (When it is necessary to emphasize the point one may add: That is an understatement.)*

17. There are two reasons to avoid unseemly speech: (a) to make sure that we never come even close to speaking crudely; (b) when we

---

21. See *Halichos Olam*, Ch. 21 fn. *hei*.

22. *Pesachim* 3a.

23. See *Rashi* on *Pesachim* 3a, s.v. *vetivchar*.

24. If these statements were said for no reason they are *lashon hara*. However, if there is a beneficial purpose (e.g. to convince someone not to enter an unsuitable *shidduch*; see Chs. 27-28), one should make sure to use the finer method of speech. Furthermore, since the implications of the more unseemly speech are stronger than those of the more refined speech, usage of the former is considered *lashon hara*.

are careful not to belittle anyone or anything, even inanimate objects, we are less likely to ever deprecate a human being; we are thus protected from speaking *lashon hara*.

> *A sage was once walking with his students when they passed the carcass of a dog. When some of the students commented on the unpleasant odor emanating from the carcass, the sage pointed out how beautifully white its teeth were. Thus, he trained his students to naturally comment on the good of their environment.*[25]

18. The Sages pointed out that in several places the Torah speaks in a long-winded fashion in order to teach us to use refined speech. In telling the story of the flood, the Torah speaks of certain animals as being "not clean" rather than *tamei*[26] to teach us never to unnecessarily speak in a slighting manner — even of an unclean animal.

The Affliction of a Negative Personality

19. A captious person[27] is one who habitually complains about other people's talk or behavior. Even when people act entirely properly and have no intention to offend, the captious person looks for reasons to take offense and to interpret innocent actions as deliberate affronts. Captious people have a "chip on their shoulder"; they constantly claim that they are being ill-treated when the truth is exactly the opposite — their relentless complaining afflicts everyone around them.

> ❑ *"Why is everyone out to get me?"*
> ❑ *"Why isn't breakfast ever ready on time?"*
> ❑ *"You just hate me."*

20. The Sages advised us to prevent captiousness by complaining as little as possible (even when there are valid grounds to do so) and avoid the sin of inadvertently injuring the feelings of others with unjustified complaints.[28]

Lack of Appreciation

21. Captious people are prone to be unappreciative of the favors people do for them; indeed, they often interpret favors as

---

25. *Chovos HaLevavos, Shaar HaKeniah*, Ch. 6.
26. Cf. *Bereishis 7:8*.
27. Captiousness is also a form of *lashon hara*. See fn. 20.
28. Cf. *Derech Eretz Zuta*, Chs. 1 and 9.

affronts and respond negatively, at times with vituperation, to any attempt to help them. Of such character traits King Shlomo said, *One who responds to good with evil, evil will not leave his house* (*Mishlei* 17:13).

> *After Reuven does Shimon a favor, Shimon, if he is captious, may respond, "Why does he bother me?" or, "What is his ulterior motive?"*

22. Sometimes this attitude leads those afflicted with it to think of the kindnesses Hashem does for them as forms of His vengeance and punishment and causes them to complain bitterly about matters that are, in reality, to their benefit.

> *This was the principal sin of the people in the incident of the spies, as the Torah says: You slandered in your tents and said, "Because of Hashem's hatred for us did He take us out of the land of Egypt" (Devarim 1:28). As Rashi explains, their slander, i.e. their lashon hara, was rooted in the distorted belief that Hashem hated them when in fact He loved them and it was they who unjustly felt hatred toward Him in return.*

Self-aggrandizement at the Expense of Others

23. It is forbidden to compare one's attributes, such as knowledge, good deeds, or wealth, with those of another individual in order to make oneself appear superior and the other person inferior. This applies not only to verbal statements but to gestures and facial expressions as well. Thus, one must take great care not to even hint about one's own advantages relative to others, even if the intention is merely to make oneself look good, not to make anyone else look bad.

> ❏ *I got a higher grade than he did.*
> ❏ *I know 400 Mishnayos and he knows only 300.*
> ❏ *I could have done a better job than he did.*

It is forbidden to do so even if there is no *lashon hara* involved.

> *"He is a nice fellow, but he doesn't have anything near what I have." (A lack of wealth is not a disgrace and the statement is not lashon hara unless it is harmful in context.)*

The Sages say that it is exceptionally difficult to repent for honoring oneself by degrading others, since one generally does not even recognize having done anything wrong. This is especially true if the object of his scorn was not present and was unaware of what was said. If one commits this sin on a regular basis he forfeits his place in the World to Come. Although according to some opinions this applies only when done regularly in the presence of the subject, it is still a grave sin to do so even once, even if the subject is not present.[29]

Suspecting Upright People

24. It is forbidden to suspect upright people of having committed transgressions, unless one has certain knowledge of their wrong-doing.[30] The word "suspect" has two applications; the first category is permitted and even encouraged, and the second is prohibited: (a) If a person wants to protect himself or others from harm, he will be careful to detect if someone is acting in a suspicious manner. Thus, the suspicion is used as a practical tool to protect from harm and is permitted. (b) If a person entertains suspicions about someone who thereby loses his upright status in the person's eyes, this type of suspicion is prohibited.

> **Son:** *Daddy, I think Reuven is the thief.*
> **Father:** *You don't know, you think. You are not permitted to perceive of him as a thief, call him a thief, or speak about him as if he were a thief. However, you can investigate the matter so that if he did steal, he can return the stolen goods. But remember, until you have concrete information, you must look at him as completely innocent.*

Note: If wrongdoing occurred in the home or classroom, the parent/teacher may follow up on suspicions for the purposes of education and chastisement. However, until the facts are clear they should not make any assumptions about who is guilty. In addition, the other children should be taught to avoid casting aspersions.

A suspicion for a constructive purpose is not only permitted but sometimes advisable.[31]

> *A man once came to Rabbi Yehoshua, who honored him with food and drink and gave him sleeping quarters on the roof. Rabbi Yeshoshua, suspecting that the man may be a thief, removed the ladder to the roof. In the middle of the night, the man awoke, gathered any utensils he*

---

29. *Rambam, Hilchos Teshuvah* 4:4 and 3:14. Introduction to *Chofetz Chaim, Be'er Mayim Chaim* par. 5.

30. *Yoma* 19b; *Rambam, Hilchos Teshuvah* 4:4.

31. *Derech Eretz Rabbah*, Ch. 5.

could find and wrapped them in his tallis. He then tried to escape with his stolen merchandise, but, unable to see in the dark that Rabbi Yehoshua had removed the ladder, fell and broke his neck. In the morning Rabbi Yehoshua found him. From here the Sages concluded, "One should honor everyone like Rabban Gamliel (the Nasi and one of the great Sages of his time) and simultaneously suspect them of being robbers."[32]

25. Harboring suspicions for no purpose is also a very difficult sin for which to repent, since it is easy to rationalize one's action by saying that one has committed no wrong and has, after all, only entertained the thought in his mind. The fact is, however, that such a mindset is in itself prohibited, since it is forbidden to conceive of an upright person as a sinner.[33] If the subject learns that one has held him under suspicion, one is required to ask him for forgiveness and to bless him.[34]

When Chanah came to Shiloh to pray for a child, Eli the Kohen presumed from her manner of prayer that she was drunk and he chastised her. In fact, Eli was guilty of suspecting an upright person. When he learned of his mistake, he appeased her and blessed her that Hashem should heed her request. Shortly thereafter she bore her first son, Shmuel (I Shmuel 1:1).

Compelling Others

26. It is forbidden for one person to compel others to serve him. Thus, if a person knows that other people are intimidated by him or are embarrassed to refuse him, he is not permitted to ask them to do anything, whether big or small, on his behalf unless they are willing to do so and it is to their benefit as well. This applies even to simple actions such as boiling water or going to the store for a small purchase. According to some opinions, this violates the commandment, *You shall not subjugate your brethren, the Children of Israel, through hard labor (Vayikra 25:46).*[35] One is permitted, however, to order one's children or Torah students to do such errands for him, since it is to their benefit because of the mitzvah to honor and serve one's parent or rebbi.[36]

---

32. Ibid.
33. *Rambam* ibid. See fn. 6 concerning the parameters of forbidden thoughts.
34. *Berachos* 31b.
35. *Shaarei Teshuvah* 3:60.
36. Ibid. See commentary of HaGaon Rav Chaim Kanievsky on *Maseches Avadim* par. 45 for a discussion of the opinions in *Rishonim*. See also *Halichos Olam*, Ch. 32 fns. *tes* and *yud*.

If you are an employer, principal, or important government official, be careful not to demand favors. However, if you are a parent or rebbi, do not hesitate to expect your children/students to do things for you; it is for their own good.

Stinginess

27. It is forbidden to be stingy or miserly. The Torah commands us to be generous and unselfish, as it says, *You shall surely give him, and let your heart not feel bad when you give him* (*Devarim* 15:10). It is not sufficient merely to give, however generously; we are obligated to make the quality of generosity a fundamental component of our personality.[37]

Note: This does not mean that a person should give away all his possessions. Rather, the Torah wants a person to integrate the quality of generosity into his personality while managing his affairs with prudence, being as generous as is financially possible and feasible.

> *A poor person once approached a famous Torah scholar who was entrusted with distributing funds to the poor. The scholar gave a certain sum to the poor person. When the recipient responded that he needed much more as this amount did not nearly meet his needs, the scholar responded with tears in his eyes, "I wish I could give you more."*

Compassion and Cruelty

28. It is forbidden to be cruel, and indeed, we are required to make compassion an integral part of ourselves, as the Torah says, *You shall not harden your heart or close your hand* (*Devarim* 15:7). Thus, although we may give generously to the poor, we are required to do so with kindness and compassion, rather than coldly or cruelly. The punishment for such cruelty is severe and bitter.[38]

29. Hashem has compassion for all, as the Psalmist says (*Tehillim* 145:9), *His compassion is on all His creations.*[39] We, too, are obligated to follow His ways. The Sages taught that when someone has compassion for others, Hashem has compassion for him.[40]

---

37. *Shaarei Teshuvah* 3:35.

38. Ibid. 3:36.

39. *Bava Metzia* 85a. Reb Chaim Vital in *Shaarei Kedushah,* Part 1 section 5, includes a listing of good qualities: to love all Hashem's creations, even gentiles.

40. *Shaarei Teshuvah* ibid., drawn from *Shabbos* 151b.

The Sages have said that Jews are distinguished by three traits: compassion, modesty, and kindness.[41]

30. Nonetheless, when one sees a wicked person leading innocent Jews astray and causing them to sin, it is forbidden to have compassion on him. One is required to do whatever possible to prevail over him and protect innocent Jews from sin, as the Torah says, *You shall not be compassionate nor cover up for him* (*Devarim* 13:9).[42] If, however, the wicked are in a position of power, one should not insult them or quarrel with them since it is unlikely to lead to positive results.[43]

31. It is forbidden to cause distress to any living creature.[44]

Unfortunately, some children make a game of tormenting animals and insects; they must be taught that this behavior is wrong and that they should be compassionate.

Envy

32. Envy is a destructive quality which can cause a person endless anguish in this world, and can eventually remove him from the World to Come.[45] Most people are afflicted with this malady to some extent. There are those who cannot enjoy their own blessings because they are envious of the success of others. Others are inwardly envious although they mouth happiness at the success of a peer.[46] The only cure for this malady is to realize that every blessing and success in the world comes from Hashem, and no one gains or loses because of someone else's success. When a person can integrate this truth into his personality — that neither his gain nor loss is dependent on another's success or failure — only then can he be cured of the malady of envy.[47]

33. It is forbidden to do anything to arouse the envy of others, and one should therefore take care not to show off his possessions or success. It is particularly forbidden (and unwise as well) to provoke the envy of other nations against Israel.[48]

---

41. *Yevamos* 79a.

42. *Shaarei Teshuvah* 3:37.

43. See *Halichos Olam*, Ch. 32 fn. *pei*.

44. *Bava Metzia* 32b.

45. *Pirkei Avos* 4:21; see *Tos. R' Akiva Eiger* ad loc.

46. *Mesillas Yesharim*, Ch. 11 from *Mishlei* 14:30.

47. *Mesillas Yesharim* ibid.

48. *Orach Meisharim*, Ch. 21 from *Taanis* 10b and *Megillah* 7a (*Bereishis* 42:1, *Rashi*).

When there was a famine in the land of Israel, our Patriarch Yaakov told his sons that although they have food, they must act as if they do not in order not to stir up the envy of their gentile neighbors.

It is wrong for even a wealthy person to have extravagant housing, jewelry or clothing or to make lavish celebrations in a manner that stirs up the envy of others, Jew or gentile. Such behavior, besides being against the Torah, has caused much suffering for the Jewish people throughout history.

Clear of Suspicion

34. It is forbidden to do anything that might cause people to suspect one of wrongdoing, even if the actions involved are entirely proper in themselves. This applies both to financial matters and all other Torah commandments (including Rabbinical decrees), as the Torah says, *You shall be vindicated from Hashem and from Israel* (*Bamidbar* 32:22). Also, King Shlomo says, *He shall find favor and good understanding in the eyes of God and man* (*Mishlei* 3:4).[49] In this vein, the Sages caution us to avoid not only that which is actually disreputable but also anything resembling it.[50]

Bold but Not Impudent

35. The Sages taught:[51] *Be bold as a leopard, light as an eagle, swift as a deer and strong as a lion to carry out the will of your Father in Heaven.*

This boldness is meant to encourage us not to feel fear or shame in the face of those who mock us for serving Hashem and doing His will. At the same time, one should never speak impudently, even to those who scoff at the service of Hashem, so as not to become accustomed to such behavior in situations where Hashem's honor is not involved.[52] Similarly, one should never get into fights over the performance of mitzvos (e.g. saying *Kaddish* or leading the services). Thus we find that even though it was a mitzvah to eat the *lechem hapanim* (the bread that was on the Table in the *Beis HaMikdash*),

---

49. *Shekalim* 3:2; see also *Orach Meisharim* 14:5 for a discussion with proofs.

50. *Chullin* 44b; see also *Orach Meisharim* ibid.

51. *Avos* 5:24.

52. *Mishnah Berurah* 1:5.

wise Kohanim would withdraw from participating in this mitzvah when their misguided fellows would fight to eat as much as possible.[53]

Ways of the Pious

36. The Sages taught:[54] Someone who loves his wife as himself, honors her more than he honors himself, guides his sons and daughters in a straight path, and marries them off at a young age, about him the verse says *(Iyov 5:24): And you will know that there is peace in your dwelling.*

Someone who loves his neighbors and makes an effort to be close to his relatives, who marries his sister's daughter,[55] and who lends money to an impoverished person at a critical moment, of him the verse says *(Yeshayahu 58:9): Then you shall call and Hashem will answer, cry out and He will say I am here.*

Human Dignity

37. One should always have great respect for the personal dignity of other people.[56]

The *Rambam*[57] cautions a judge who must administer justice: "All his actions should be performed purely for Heaven's sake, and let not human dignity be light in his eyes ... and certainly the dignity of the children of Avraham, Yitzchak, and Yaakov, who uphold Torah truths, that he should be wary not to slight their honor unless the honor of Hashem requires it."

---

53. *Kitzur Shulchan Aruch* 29:9, based on *Yoma* 39a.

54. *Yevamos* 62b.

55. In ancient times this was not an uncommon practice. The purpose was (see *Rashi* ad loc.) to ensure harmony and love between the spouses because a person is usually endeared to his relative. In modern terms this can be interpreted as suggesting that a man should look foremost for a spouse who will be dear and cherished by him as a person, and not for other advantages, so that there will be harmony in the home.

56. *Berachos* 19b.

57. *Hilchos Sanhedrin* 24:10.

17

Avak Lashon Hara

1. *Lashon hara* (evil talk) not only causes damage but is inherently evil.

Since Hashem is *tov* (good), all *ra* (evil) is anathema by definition and causes a person to be distanced from His Presence.[1] Therefore, even coming close to "evil" is prohibited. It is for this reason that the Torah prohibits statements that either resemble or lead to *lashon hara;* they are called *avak lashon hara*[2] (literally: the "dust" of *lashon hara*).[3] The prohibition against *avak lashon hara* is divided into four categories:[4]

(a) Statements that, while not directly insulting or belittling, imply the existence of negative information about the subject. (According to some opinions, this constitutes actual *lashon hara* and not merely *avak lashon hara*.)

(b) Statements that are liable to cause or result in *lashon hara*.

(c) Statements that would generally be permissible except in a situation where the listener will suspect the speaker of saying *lashon hara*.

---

1. *Sotah* 42a.

2. Generally *"avak"* is considered a Rabbinical prohibition; however, there are aspects of *avak lashon hara* that are Biblical (D'*Oraisa*).

3. Figuratively, as a person trails another person he will "pick up" the dust of his track; so too *avak lashon hara* "picks up" the dust of *lashon hara*; it trails it and resembles it.

4. See *Rambam, Hilchos Dei'os* 7:4; *Shaarei Teshuvah* 3:226; *Kodesh Yisrael,* Ch. 5.

(d) Associating with habitual speakers of *lashon hara*.

Now we shall consider each category in detail.

The First Category

2. Under the first category, any statement suggesting the existence of derogatory information about a person or group is prohibited.

❏ *"Who would have thought that he would turn out like that?"*

❏ *"Don't ask me about them! I don't want to tell you what happened."*

❏ *If someone needs food, one should not say, "Try in that house; they're always cooking there." The tone insinuates that the residents of the house are inveterate gluttons.*

According to some opinions, these statements are not merely *avak lashon hara* but *lashon hara* itself. However, all agree that such statements are forbidden.[5]

The Second Category

3. The second prohibited category includes any statement that might lead someone to speak *lashon hara*. Thus, one should not speak highly of someone in the presence of people who dislike him or do not get along with him. This also applies to people who simply do not properly appreciate the subject or who are likely to respond to favorable comments by pointing out his failings. Words of praise spoken in the presence of such people are forbidden as *avak lashon hara*.[6]

> *"David learns very well. He is an exceptional talmid chacham."*
>
> *"Yes, he learns well, but he doesn't earn a living."*
>
> *As the listener does not appreciate the greatness of Torah study, this praise should not have been told to him.*

> *Mr. C is trying to change Mr. A's negative opinion of Mr. B.*
>
> *Mr. C: Well, I know Mr. B personally. He is a really nice fellow, who means well.*
>
> *Mr. A: But I can't stand the way he …*

---

5. *Chofetz Chaim, Hilchos Lashon Hara* 9:1, and also 9:3 in the comment. See also *Halichos Olam*, Ch. 20 fn. *gimmel*.

6. *Chofetz Chaim* ibid. 9:1, 9:3, fn.

Note: It is a mitzvah to bring people to conciliation, but wisdom is needed to do so without causing greater conflict and additional lashon hara. If a question arises, consult an experienced person, but in general, it is better to desist than to risk causing additional conflict.

4. For this reason, if one knows that someone is not on good terms with the rabbi of a community, it is forbidden to inquire about his interactions with the rabbi, since he is liable to respond with a negative comment. Similarly, if two people are known not to be on good terms, it is *avak lashon hara* to say or do anything to remind either party of their discord and provoke an unfavorable reaction.[7]

> ❑ *Do not ask the shul president, "How was your meeting with the rabbi yesterday?" if they do not get along.*
> ❑ *If Mrs. A and Mrs. B dislike each others' children, do not ask Mrs. A, "Oh, and how are the B children?"*

5. *Sefer Chassidim*[8] writes that one should never praise one wealthy person to another, or a member of a profession or craft to an individual in the same field.

> *Do not say to shoemaker A, "You know, shoemaker B produces very fine shoes."*

One may, however, praise one pious individual to another, since the existence of others as pious as himself or even more so is a source of joy to such a person. Rather than feeling resentment, he will want to learn from their ways, as Moshe Rabbeinu says, *Would that the entire people of Hashem be prophets* (*Bamidbar* 11:29). However, it is best to determine if the listener will be glad or resentful to hear of another person's greater piety before speaking.

Be Careful With Praise

6. It is forbidden to speak about a person with excessive praise, since it is a common practice to include mention of a negative quality in order to temper the praise.[9]

---

7. Ibid.

8. Paragraph 64. *Sefer Chassidim* by Rabbi Yehudah HaChassid, one of the *Baalei Tosafos*, is a classical work quoted often by the *Poskim*.

9. *Chofetz Chaim, Hilchos Lashon Hara* 9:1, see also *Be'er Mayim Chaim* 5.

> *"Reuven is a wonderful person. He sets aside regular hours for Torah study, is kind, charitable, and well-liked ... except for the few times he lost his temper."*

Similarly, it is forbidden to offer praise tempered by the implication that the subject lacks another quality normally found in a person of such high caliber.

> *"What do you think of Rabbi Plony?"*
> *"In terms of his learning, he is a big talmid chacham"* (implying that a lack exists in some other aspect of his life).

7. It is also forbidden to praise someone before a large gathering, since there may be a listener present who enjoys disparaging anyone he hears being praised, and your words are liable to provoke *lashon hara* on his part. Such praise is permitted, however, if the subject is a well-known *tzaddik* (e.g. Rav Moshe Feinstein), since everyone knows that any negative statement about him is unfounded. One may also praise someone unknown to the audience, if the speaker judges that no one is likely to insult him. Even so, care must be taken not to praise the subject excessively.[10]

8. It is best to refrain from discussing the ways one has benefited from another person's kindness, since unscrupulous people may attempt to use the information to exploit the benefactor's generosity.[11]

> *Reb Reuven returned from a business trip and told all his friends that Reb Shimon provides his guests with full board for as long a stay as is needed, and caters to their every whim, just like in a hotel!*

Avak Rechilus

9. Just as there is a prohibition of *avak lashon hara* so too is there a prohibition of *avak rechilus*. Therefore if someone wants to praise one person to another he should take care that his praise not cause animosity between them.[12]

> *Reuven has extended Levi an interest-free loan. One day Levi met Shimon, Reuven's business partner.*

---

10. Ibid. 9:2.

11. Ibid. 9:3.

12. *Chofetz Chaim, Hilchos Rechilus* 8:2.

Levi: Oh, you are Reuven's partner; he did me a great kindness when he extended me a loan.
Beware: Shimon may be thinking: I thought we were short on cash. Why is he lending money?

School director to Mrs. Plony: Your husband really helped our school with that $5,000 donation yesterday.
Beware: She may be thinking: He did? Then he will tell me that we can't afford a vacation!

Fundraiser to Mr. Plony: Your wife volunteered to make one hundred fundraising calls next week.
Beware: He may be thinking: Why did she agree to do that … as it is we have almost no time together. Couldn't they find someone else?

10. One should not discuss a favor that was done for oneself with other people.[13]

> *Reuven:* Shimon, could you please drive me to the airport Sunday afternoon?
> *Shimon:* I'm sorry, but Sunday afternoons I'm usually busy.
> *Reuven:* But you took Levi last Sunday afternoon.
> *(Shimon thinks: Why does Levi have to tell people what I do for him!? He just gets me into trouble!)*

11. One should not repeat what one person said about another if he spoke in even slightly insulting terms.[14]

> *In Parshas Vayeira Sarah said: "How can I have children and my husband is an old man?" Hashem repeated her words to Avraham in the following way: Sarah said, "How can I have children and I am old?" Hashem changed her version because a husband could be sensitive to being referred to as an old man, even though only slight feelings of hurt are involved (Bereishis 18:12-13).*

---

13. Ibid 8:3.
14. Ibid 8:4.

Joining Discussions

12. One should not participate in a group that perpetually discusses other people, even if they are being praised, since it is nearly unavoidable that *lashon hara* will be spoken. Even if the subjects are great Torah Sages, a negative comment is inevitable as the discussion continues and comparisons are made.[15] As we have discussed,[16] the more learned and righteous the individual is, the more serious is the offense of speaking *lashon hara* about him.

13. From this we see the serious danger courted by those who congregate to discuss "Jewish politics" (including the worlds of Chassidim and yeshivos), since such conversations rarely fail to include *lashon hara* and *rechilus* about any given faction whose members are upstanding Jews. Even if no *lashon hara* is being spoken at the time one joins the discussion, it is *avak lashon hara* to merely participate because of the likelihood that *lashon hara* will ensue.

❑ *"The Chassidim are all ..." (Is this statement permitted? Is it even true?)*

❑ *"The people in that neighborhood are ..." (Is this statement permitted? Are "all" the people there ...? If you lived there, or grew up there, would you be any different?)*

Newspapers

14. Newspapers, as part of the media, are a form of communication. Were the writer/reporter speaking to us, we could listen attentively to some statements, while rejecting others as indecent and prohibited. So too, when these words are in print, we must be careful to read only selected articles and not others.[17]

---

15. *Chofetz Chaim, Hilchos Lashon Hara* 9, *Be'er Mayim Chaim* 7.

16. See Ch. 5 par. 29.

17. Reading newspapers is a classic example of a modern-day *halachic* question. As newspapers are full of immorality, crime and *lashon hara*, it can well be argued that they should be avoided completely. The Torah guideline for such questions is *Devarim* (17:10), *You shall do as they teach you*, meaning that we must follow the Sages of our times. In general, the Torah Sages in Eretz Yisrael have prohibited reading secular newspapers and have instead established religious dailies that do not report on news that is unfit to print. The Torah Sages in the U.S.A. have generally not prohibited reading the papers; however, as Rav Schwab said, a person must be very careful about what he reads. Obviously, this applies only to respectable papers, and does not include other mediums such as television that have been prohibited by our Torah Sages, because the likelihood of immorality and

HaRav Shimon Schwab compared reading a newspaper to shopping in a supermarket. An observant Jew will buy fruit, but avoid the treife products. Similarly, one may read newsworthy items but must avoid "treife" articles.

Not only are indecent articles considered *treife*, but articles containing *lashon hara* are prohibited as well, both to read and believe. The laws for reading and accepting written *lashon hara* fall into the same parameters as listening to and believing spoken *lashon hara*.

15. A "yellow journalism" newspaper, even if it is under Jewish ownership, exists solely to "scoop" headlines and insinuate negativity about various personalities and conflicts, and is considered the same as a *"baal lashon hara."* A person should completely avoid such newspapers and not peruse them even to check the weather. It goes without saying that any negativity implied therein should be disdained and must not be believed.

16. The communication media not only serves as a bearer of news, but also creates an environment which influences all who are exposed to it. Even "innocent" children's programs are usually full of poor character traits:

❏ *"He hit me, I'll beat him up."*
❏ *"You idiot!"*
❏ *"I'll tell everyone what you did."*

These programs have exactly the opposite effect of a Torah education. Unfortunately, children already receive a heavy dose of negative character traits from society. Allowing an even greater dosage through the media (TV, videos, radios, books) while simultaneously providing a Torah education is being self-contradictory. Furthermore, adults, too, are constantly influenced by society. Therefore, it is of the utmost importance to create an environment for oneself which encourages Torah values. It is a positive commandment in the Torah to cling to the company of those whose lives are dedicated to Torah study and its values.[18] Conversely, creating a negative environment

---

destructive effect is that much greater. While many people are careful to avoid immorality in the newspapers, there is not as great an awareness of the necessity to avoid *lashon hara* in these publications.

18. *Rambam, Hilchos Dei'os* 6:12.

(e.g. by pointless reading about violent crimes) violates this commandment and is self-destructive.

The Third Category

17. Under the third category of *avak lashon hara*, we are forbidden to make a statement that others might suspect of being *lashon hara*, even though it is entirely permissible. Therefore, in a situation where it is necessary to say something which might be interpreted as *lashon hara*, one must take care to explain to the listeners why his words are permitted.

> *"David, you cannot go to Chaim's house nor can he come here. He has poor character traits and I want you to stay away from him. This is not lashon hara because I am telling you for an important reason — so that you should have only very fine friends."*

If the explanation is inadequate and the listeners suspect him of speaking *lashon hara*, his statements are *avak lashon hara*.[19]

> *Mr. Silver considers Mr. Gold a fine person. Reb Yosef, who knows that Mr. Gold enjoys mocking people, tells Mr. Silver, "Stay away from Mr. Gold, he is a leitz" (a person who mocks people or mitzvos; see Chapter 15).*
>
> *Mr. Silver responds, "Don't tell me lashon hara about Mr. Gold." Reb Yosef had positive intentions, but since he misjudged the situation, and Mr. Silver now views him as a person who speaks lashon hara, Reb Yosef is guilty of violating "avak lashon hara."*

Lashon Hara With the Subject's Permission

18. If a person gives someone permission to speak *lashon hara* about him, the listener is allowed to repeat it.[20] However, he must state explicitly that he was given permission, since the listeners might otherwise suspect that he is speaking *lashon hara*, and his statements would then be forbidden as *avak lashon hara*.[21]

> ❏ *"Reuven told me that I could say that he thinks he acted like a fool."*
> ❏ *"She is upset at you. She said that I could tell you."*

---

19. *Chofetz Chaim, Hilchos Lashon Hara* 9:3; see *Guard Your Tongue* by Rabbi Zelig Pliskin, 9:9.

20. See *Chofetz Chaim* ibid. 1:9.

21. See *Halichos Olam*, Ch. 20 fn. *samech*.

The Fourth Category

19. Under the fourth category of *avak lashon hara* we are forbidden to associate with habitual speakers of *lashon hara*. This includes establishing a regular seat in a synagogue or *beis midrash*[22] in their vicinity, and all the more so joining their conversations.[23]

> *Malki and Rivki were assigned to be partners on a school trip, both on the bus and throughout the day. Malki complained to the teacher that she does not want to spend the time with Rivki because she constantly speaks lashon hara. Malki acted correctly and should be assigned another partner. (Perhaps Rivki can be taught to change her speaking habits or, if necessary, not have a partner.)*

Relating Confidential Information

20. Any conversation related in private may not be repeated, even if the information does not seem to reflect badly on any party. Nevertheless, if any reason exists to suspect that the speaker would prefer that the matter be kept in confidence, it should not be repeated without permission from the original source.[24]

> **Reuven:** *Come here, I want to tell you something.*
> **Shimon (to himself):** *"Come here" implies that Reuven wants to maintain privacy and does not wish to publicize this matter. Unless I get explicit permission from Reuven, I should not repeat the conversation.*

---

22. Apart from the prohibition of *avak lashon hara*, this is likely to lead to distraction during *tefillos* and failure to answer to *Kaddish, Kedushah,* etc.

23. *Chofetz Chaim* ibid. 9:4.

24. Ibid. 9:6; *Be'er Mayim Chaim* 27.

18

Teshuvah — Repentance

1. A person who commits a wrong action has an obligation to do
   teshuvah. (*Teshuvah* literally means "return." When a person does
   wrong he distances himself from the Source Who created him; thus
   he has a mitzvah to "return.") This is one of the positive commandments of the Torah.[1]

2. There are three basic conditions necessary to fulfill this mitzvah:
   The offender must:
   (a) regret his wrong;
   (b) resolve that he will no longer engage in such behavior;
   (c) confess his wrongdoing before Hashem.[2]
   Every *teshuvah* brings with it some degree of forgiveness; the deeper the *teshuvah*, the more complete the forgiveness.[3]

Resolve or Regret — Which Comes First?

3. If a person did an uncharacteristic wrong on a one-time basis he
   should first experience regret and then build up his inner defens-

---

1. *Rambam, Hilchos Teshuvah* 1:1.

2. Ibid. and 2:2,3; *Shaarei Teshuvah* 1:11.

3. *Shaarei Teshuvah* 1:9.

es to prevent a recurrence. However, if a person is easily ensnared in a certain wrongdoing on a regular basis, his first goal must be to rid himself of evil tendencies so that he will no longer repeat that wrong. Only after this has been accomplished should he contemplate and fully regret his past misdeed.[4]

> ❏ *A young man was aghast when some cholent fell on his new Shabbos suit. Overwhelmed with embarrassment, he ran to the sink and washed off the stain, thereby violating the Shabbos.*
> *He should first contemplate the awesome gravity of chillul Shabbos, until he fully regrets his action. Then he must resolve that under no circumstances will he ever violate the Shabbos again. He should take measures to ensure this, such as repeated review of the laws of Shabbos until they are fully mastered.*
> ❏ *Another young man regularly sleeps late on Shabbos, consistently missing the proper time for Krias Shema (reciting the Shema). His first move must be to change his habit, perhaps by asking a friend to "force" him to wake up on time. Only after he has broken the habit should he face his "regret" by contemplating the enormous loss of missing the time of Krias Shema even once.*

Interpersonal Wrongs

4. A person who has committed an interpersonal wrong (*bein adam l'chaveiro*) must meet a fourth condition crucial to the *teshuvah* process: he must ask the offended party for forgiveness.[5]

Neither Yom Kippur[6] nor death[7] can atone for interpersonal wrongs regarding which the offended party was not placated.

5. If the offended party refuses to grant forgiveness, the offender must repeat his plea at least three times. Each request must be stated in front of three people[8] and each reconciliation should be attempted in a different manner.[9] If the offended party still refuses, the offender is no longer required to persist, but should gather ten people and announce publicly that he has fulfilled the requirements for request-

---

4. Ibid 1:11.

5. *Yoma* 85b; *Rambam* ibid 2:8; *Orach Chaim* 606:1.

6. *Yoma* ibid.

7. See *Tefillah Zakah* in Yom Kippur *Machzor*.

8. Orach Chaim ibid.

9. Ibid. and *Mishnah Berurah* 606:3.

ing forgiveness. However, if the offended party is a rebbi who has taught him Torah, the requirement to ask forgiveness continues indefinitely until the offended party relents.[10]

6. When the offender sincerely asks for forgiveness, the offended person should grant it to him graciously.[11] It is forbidden to cruelly withhold forgiveness.[12]

If someone does not forgive others, he, too, will not be forgiven in Heaven for his iniquities.[13] It is part of the character of a Jew to forgive.[14]

However, if the offended party perceives that withholding forgiveness will benefit the offender, or if he is afraid that the forgiveness will cause damage to himself (i.e. despite the offender's current sincerity, he may repeat his actions at a future date), then he may refuse to forgive.[15] Even then, he should forgive him in his heart, since the offender is, at present, sincere in his request.

7. The *teshuvah* for an offense involving a loss of money must include full repayment when the offender is so obligated by *halachah*, unless the injured party waives the right to restitution.[16] If physical injury or mental anguish occurred along with the financial damage, then payment is not sufficient and the offender must also ask for forgiveness.[17]

> *One winter day, a boy threw a rock and broke the window of a classroom, leaving the students shivering in the cold. The principal told the boy that restitution would not be sufficient, and that he must ask the students' forgiveness for the discomfort he had caused them.*

8. A person who causes damage to many people and does not know to whom to make restitution, should engage in public works in the hope that the damaged parties will benefit as well. However, this does

---

10. *Orach Chaim* ibid. Note: As far as the asking of forgiveness is concerned, anyone who taught him Torah is considered his rebbi (*Mishnah Berurah* 606:7).

11. Ibid. *Rambam* says, "with a full heart and willing soul."

12. *Rambam, Hilchos Teshuvah* 2:10. Note: If the offended person refuses to forgive even after three times of requesting forgivesness (par. 5), then he is considered the sinner (*Rambam* ibid. 2:9).

13. *Rosh Hashanah* 17a, *Mishnah Berurah* 606:8. See *Shaar HaTziyun* 8, that for this reason a person should forgive even intentional wrongdoings. For then, in Heaven, they too will forgive him of his intentional sins.

14. *Yevamos* 79a.

15. *Orach Chaim* ibid. and *Mishnah Berurah* 606:10.

16. *Mishnah Berurah* 606:9.

17. *Rambam* ibid. 2:9.

not substitute for direct restitution; if he later finds an individual whom he has damaged he must make full restitution.[18]

> *Mr. B regularly cheated each customer in his store of a few pennies. After realizing the gravity of his sin, he gave each customer $20 in an attempt to cover the amount stolen. However, he was not satisfied, since he realized that he may have stolen more than $20 from some customers, or he may not have remembered every customer. Therefore, he undertook to help finance several public institutions in the city.*

9. If a person offended someone but does not know his current whereabouts, he should at least do what he can; i.e. resolve not to repeat the behavior, regret the past, confess his misdeed, and await the day when Hashem will help him to complete his *teshuvah*.[19]

When Forgiveness Is Achieved

10. Once the offended party forgives the wrong, he is forbidden to bear any further grudge over the incident.[20] At this point, the offender has fulfilled his obligation to placate the injured party.[21] However, if he realizes that the subject still harbors a lingering resentment, despite having extended his forgiveness, the offender should continue his attempts at conciliation until all traces of resentment are erased, even if it takes a number of years.[22]

> *David insulted Shlomo, who is very upset, and conveys his feelings to David. David, realizing the gravity of his behavior, asks Shlomo for forgiveness. If Shlomo agrees to forgive him, he is no longer permitted to harbor resentment toward David. If Shlomo has the self-awareness to realize that he will continue to harbor resentment, he*

---

18. *Bava Kamma* 94b; *Choshen Mishpat* 366:2.

19. The essence of *teshuvah* is to reconcile with Hashem. When a person wants to do *teshuvah* Hashem helps him. See *Chovos HaLevavos, Teshuvah*, Ch. 10. Thus, he should do whatever he can to express his desire for *teshuvah*, which is, in reality, the critical component of *teshuvah*. When the day comes that he will finally ask forgiveness of the injured party, he should then repeat the confession (*Shaarei Teshuvah* 4:18).

20. *Ohr Yisrael, Nesivos Ohr*, p. 58. Just as in monetary debts, where once the creditor forgives the debt he may no longer collect it, so it is with "debts" of wrongdoing; the act of forgiveness wipes away the "debt," and he no longer is permitted to bear a grudge.

21. Derived from above. Since the offended party can no longer harbor resentment, the offender has fulfilled his obligation.

22. Since, practically, there is still a lack of inner peace between the parties, the mitzvah of "pursue peace" still applies.

should say, "I can't forgive you yet because I still am very angry at you. Maybe we can try again in a few weeks." (Shlomo, on his own part, in order to fulfill the mitzvah not to bear grudges, must slowly work to overcome his resentment.) If Shlomo does forgive, but David sees that Shlomo still harbors resentment, David should continue his efforts until full reconciliation is achieved.

Forgiveness on Erev Yom Kippur

11. Prior to Yom Kippur, many people ask forgiveness of their friends and acquaintances for any interpersonal wrongs they may have committed in the course of the year. Routine forgiveness is usually granted. The fact that verbal forgiveness is legally valid, even if there is still lingering resentment, would seem to validate this custom. Therefore, even if a specific wrong was perpetrated, one is no longer required to ask forgiveness.

Anyone who forgives a friend on Erev Yom Kippur for "anything you did during the year" may no longer harbor resentment toward that person. Similarly, anyone who recites in *Tefillah Zakah*, "I hereby forgive all who wronged me," may no longer harbor resentment toward anyone.

This applies only to what society considers "normal" wrongs (e.g. a "slip of the tongue" or slightly degrading *lashon hara)*. However, if one person has caused serious damage to another, of which the subject is unaware when asked for general forgiveness (either he never knew, or he knew and forgot), then such a request is not sufficient and one must ask forgiveness specifically for the wrong perpetrated.[23]

> *If Reuven slandered Shimon, but Shimon was unaware that Reuven was the culprit, a general request for forgiveness is insufficient.*
>
> *Reuven had publicly insulted Shimon at the beginning of the winter. By the following Yom Kippur, Shimon had put aside the incident and is now on good terms with Reuven. Nevertheless, Reuven must specifically mention the incident and ask for forgiveness; a general request for forgiveness is insufficient.*

---

23. See *Bava Metzia* 66b, "Mistaken forgiveness is invalid." When people forgive in a standard way on Erev Yom Kippur they usually intend it for "standard" wrongs. However, an exceptional wrong that the offended party is unaware of is usually not included and the standard statement of *mechilah* (forgiveness) is mistaken and invalid regarding those wrongs, until they are specifically mentioned.

12. On Erev Yom Kippur it is proper for a person to forgive any wrongs done to him even if he was not asked.

> ... And I forgive anyone who wronged me ... and let no person be punished because of me (Tefillah Zakah).

If this form of forgiveness is not to the offender's benefit (e.g. he will interpret "foregiveness" as evidence that his offense was not serious, or worse, as permission to repeat the offense), one should at least make a concerted effort to be available to the offender so as to effect a reconciliation.

> There was once a butcher who slighted Rav. The gravity of the sin was multiplied by the fact that Rav was the greatest Torah sage of his time. On Erev Yom Kippur, when Rav saw that the butcher would not come to ask his forgiveness, Rav went to the butcher to give him the opportunity to do so.[24]

Teshuvah for Lashon Hara

13. Since *lashon hara* and *rechilus* are sins that affect other people, even Yom Kippur cannot atone for them unless the speaker appeases those he has harmed with his forbidden statements.[25] Even if the wronged parties are not aware of the incident, one is required to inform them in order to obtain their forgiveness.

Alternative to Asking Forgiveness

14. However, if the damage inflicted by one's *lashon hara*[26] can be repaired by persuading those who heard it not to believe the negative information imparted to them (or not to think less of the subject because of it), then one is not required to ask forgiveness.[27] Therefore, an individual who spoke *lashon hara* should go back to his listeners and attempt to repair the damage he has done. If successful, he is no longer required to ask forgiveness, since the damage caused by his *lashon hara* has been undone.

---

24. *Yoma* 87a.

25. *Chofetz Chaim, Hilchos Lashon Hara* 4:12.

26. Since in general the repentance for *lashon hara* and *rechilus* is the same, for the sake of simplicity we shall speak only of *lashon hara*, with the understanding that *rechilus* is also included unless there are aspects of repenting for *rechilus* which require special attention.

27. Ibid. *Be'er Mayim Chaim* 48.

One morning at Shacharis, Reb Yankel, a well-respected person in the community, publicly berated a certain beggar. David was quite upset and angrily repeated the story to his wife, Rachel, upon his return home. "Even though the beggar is a bit of a nuisance, how could a ben-Torah like Reb Yankel treat any human being that way?" he exclaimed. After a quick breakfast he left for work, and listening to a Torah tape in the car, he suddenly realized that the conversation with his wife was lashon hara. Furthermore, should she slip and tell her friends, he will then be unable to undo the damage. When he arrived at his office, he quickly called his wife:

David: Hello. I just got in to work.

Rachel: Is everything O.K.?

David: Well, remember the conversation we had this morning?

Rachel: About Reb Yankel?

David: Yes. Well, I realized it was lashon hara. So, first of all, please don't tell anyone about it.

Rachel: Of course.

David: (relieved) Now that it's just between us we have to think of a way to reinterpret the incident so that Reb Yankel will not be lowered in our esteem. I'll think about it today, and put myself in his position, and you should too. We'll talk about it tonight, O.K.?

Rachel: Fine.

15. Undoing the damage is preferable to appeasement for two reasons:

(a) It eliminates the damage caused by the *lashon hara* (a particularly serious concern in the case of *rechilus*, which often leads to public disputes and pointless hatred); and (b) it avoids the hurt and embarrassment likely to be felt by the subject when he hears what was said about him. However, in a case where it is not possible to do so, such as if the listeners cannot be persuaded to disbelieve what they were told earlier, or if they have since repeated the story to others, spreading the damage to the point where it can no longer be repaired, then the speaker is required to approach the subject and appease him despite the pain this will inflict. If, however, the revelation will result in great embarrassment to the subject, a rav should be consulted as to how to proceed.[28]

Mrs. P has two daughters: Leah, 16, and Rachel, 14. Leah and her friend Devorah have just returned from a Sunday afternoon outing.

Leah: Ima, I think Devorah and I had a conversation that wasn't right.

---

28. See *Orach Chaim* 606, *Mishnah Berurah* 606:3.

Mrs. P: Why, what did you talk about?

Leah: Well, we talked about Rachel. She really doesn't like Devorah, and I told her so.

Mrs. P: You did?! And how do you think Devorah is going to relate to Rachel now?

Leah: Well, she didn't like her before and this isn't going to help.

Mrs. P: Precisely ... So, isn't that rechilus? Didn't you learn about that in school last week?

Leah: You're right! What should I do now? I guess I'll have to ask Rachel for mechilah (forgiveness). That's not going to be easy.[29]

Mrs. P: Well, asking Rachel for mechilah would create a bit more harmony, but it would be even better to try to undo the damage. Why don't you call Devorah right now and try to help her figure out ways that she and Rachel can make peace. Tell her that it was a mistake to say that Rachel doesn't like her and that the whole situation really bothers you. Nobody likes discord and she will probably be very happy to cooperate. Try to figure out the root of the problem and maybe if everyone is open they can overcome their animosity.

Do Not Name the Listeners

16. In placating the subject of one's *lashon hara*, it is forbidden to name the people who listened to *lashon hara*, since the subject might resent them for failing to protest the insults on his behalf. This is *rechilus*, and is not permitted for the sake of obtaining someone's forgiveness. Thus, one must be extremely careful when asking forgiveness not to speak or even allude to *lashon hara* or *rechilus* about any other individual. Even if the subject threatens to withhold his forgiveness until the speaker reveals all the details of the incident, including the names of the listeners, it is forbidden to do so.[30]

> *Esther had failing grades in Bais Yaakov A, leading her parents to transfer her to Bais Yaakov B. No one in her new class was told the reason for her transfer so as to spare her embarrassment. However, Chaya, who lived in the same area, told a few classmates the truth.*

29. Note: She cannot ask for forgiveness by mentioning Devorah because that itself is *rechilus* (see par. 16).

30. It is axiomatic in Torah that it is prohibited to violate the Torah in order to achieve a certain goal, for the end does not justify the means. This is also not comparable to "beneficial *lashon hara*," where the statement itself produces benefit; here the statement produces animosity which the speaker is using as a means to achieve forgiveness.

When the teacher spoke to the class before Yom Kippur about the evils of lashon hara, Chaya decided to ask Esther for forgiveness.

Chaya: *Esther, how are you doing?*

Esther: *Fine, baruch Hashem, what's up?*

Chaya: *Well …Yom Kippur is approaching … and I have to ask your mechilah.*

Esther: *I don't understand. For what?*

Chaya: *Well … I told some girls in our class about what happened at the old Bais Yaakov.*

Esther: *Oh! How could you? I thought I was all settled here! And why didn't those girls tell you to be quiet … to give a new girl a chance … and maybe they told others the same lashon hara … Oy, I don't believe you did that to me.*

Chaya: *I'm so sorry … I feel even more miserable than you. Please forgive me.*

Esther: *I don't know … but it's before Yom Kippur … at least tell me which of those girls listened to lashon hara about me.*

Chaya: *You know I can't tell you … It would be rechilus. You are upset at them and could never feel the same about a girl who knows this about you, and might look down on you.*

Esther: *I can't forgive you unless you tell me which girls were there.*

Chaya: *I can't. It is assur (prohibited). Wait … I have an idea. I'll talk to the girls to try to undo the damage as much as possible. If you can be mochel all this, you stand a great chance this Yom Kippur because Hashem forgives those who forgive others.*

17. Even if the subject refuses to grant forgiveness because of the speaker's refusal to speak *rechilus*, the speaker is still required to persist in his efforts to placate the subject. If the subject is not placated, one should return at least three times, each time bringing three people with him.[31] With each attempt, he must be careful not to violate the laws of *lashon hara* or *rechilus*. If the subject still refuses to be placated after three attempts, one is not required to persist in his efforts.

When Asked Forgiveness

18. It is forbidden to callously withhold forgiveness, and when the subject feels that the speaker is asking sincerely he should for-

---

31. See par. 5.

give him immediately and graciously.[32] The subject should not ask for too many details about the incident — i.e. who was present, exactly what was said, etc. — since this puts pressure on the speaker to speak *lashon hara* and *rechilus* (or to lie). He thereby would transgress the prohibition against placing a stumbling block before a blind person.[33]

19. If the subject has a valid need to know the details, he is permitted to inquire. However, the speaker should not necessarily answer all his questions.

> *Reuven spoke about Shimon, a businessman, to Levi, his competitor, giving Levi an unfair advantage in the market. Shimon has a legitimate right to know exactly what was said about his affairs in order to devise strategies to minimize the damage, and is permitted to inquire about the pertinent details. However, Reuven should not answer without consulting a rav, because of the many halachic and practical considerations involved.[34]*

20. As explained, the subject is entitled to ask for information only if his practical interests are affected. Therefore, the proper way to respond when one is asked for forgiveness for unspecified *lashon hara* is to ask whether any practical consequences may have resulted that would require him to protect his interests. If the answer is in the negative, he should forgive his beseecher immediately for any affronts to his honor or similar slights, since it is the nature of the Jewish people to be kindly and forgiving.

If No Harm Was Done

21. The requirement to placate the subject of one's *lashon hara* applies only if it has caused him harm, e.g. a listener thinks less of the subject because of it, or, all the more so, if the subject's interests have been harmed. If, however, the listeners refused to believe the *lashon hara* in the first place, or gave the subject the benefit of the doubt, as the Torah requires, and did not draw any negative conclusions from the *lashon hara*, then the subject never suffered any damage at all. In

---

32. See par. 6.

33. See also Ch. 17 that this is certainly *avak lashon hara.*

34. Is the nature of what was revealed actually damaging or may it just prevent him from realizing extra profit? Will the competitor actually damage the subject? Will the words of the speaker now enable the subject to damage the competitor? Or perhaps the subject is trying to get information just to protect himself and will not damage the competitor at all?

such a case, the speaker is not required to ask the subject for forgiveness. Nonetheless, one is still required to do *teshuvah* by regretting the fact that he did wrong, confessing his sin to Hashem, and making a sincere commitment never to repeat such an action.[35]

> *Chani gave the principal negative information about Chaya. However, the principal, a wise person well versed in the Torah's outlook on life, discounted all the negativity in Chani's statement. Chani is not required to ask forgiveness; however, she must do her own private teshuvah.*

If There Is Still a Possibility of Harm

22. On occasion, one person has made statements about another and, although no harm has resulted yet, there is reason to fear that the subject will eventually suffer damage. For example, if the listeners do not consider the information to reflect badly on the subject, they will be likely to repeat it to others who will *then* think less of the subject themselves. The speaker should therefore immediately try to undo the damage and persuade the listeners not to repeat his words to others.[36] If he fails to do so, and the damage subsequently spreads, he will be obligated to ask the subject for forgiveness. Particular caution is required in the area of *rechilus* where damage is so much more inevitable, since *rechilus* by definition involves statements which are likely to cause conflict.[37]

> *Reuven has savings of $20,000 which he intends to use to support himself while he learns in kollel. In his circles, this is considered legitimate and even praiseworthy. Reuven's parents, however, would be aghast at this information, leading to a major crisis. If Shimon mentions this fact to Levi, Levi will see no problem in repeating it, for he views it as a legitimate form of behavior. However, Shimon should realize that his words may cause Reuven's parents to discover their son's intentions and lead to tension; therefore, he has spoken rechilus. He should immediately caution Levi from spreading it further, in order to avert a family crisis and not to violate the laws of rechilus. If Levi has already repeated the infor-*

---

35. *Chofetz Chaim, Hilchos Lashon Hara* 4:12.

36. Ibid. *Be'er Mayim Chaim* 41 (see discussion there if any legal obligation exists at this point to ask for forgiveness).

37. *Chofetz Chaim, Hilchos Rechilus* Ch. 4, *Be'er Mayim Chaim* 4.

mation, and Reuven's parents are informed, Shimon will have to ask Reuven for forgiveness.

Teshuvah for Believing *Lashon Hara*

23. A person who believed *lashon hara* does not have to placate the subject. Rather, he must undo the negative impression created in his heart and then do proper *teshuvah* (i.e. regretting the past, confessing to Hashem, and resolving not to repeat it).[38] If, however, he damaged the subject by spreading the news further or causing him any other form of hurt, then he must placate the subject.[39]

Teshuvah for a Life of Wrongdoing

24. Even if one has regularly offended people (through *lashon hara*, *rechilus*, verbal abuse, etc.) for many years and caused incalculable damage during that time, one should not despair, for nothing stands in the way of *teshuvah*.[40] No matter how low a person has stooped, Hashem is ready at all times to accept his *teshuvah*. Furthermore, Hashem desires and awaits his return.[41]

> *"And until the day a person dies You wait for him, if he will return to You, You will immediately accept him" (liturgy of Rosh Hashanah and Yom Kippur).*

> *"Let not a person who has done teshuvah imagine that he is far removed from the greatness of the righteous because of his sins and iniquities. It is not so; rather, he is beloved and desired before the Creator as if he had never sinned. Furthermore, his reward is great because he tasted sin and then left it, and overcame his evil inclination" (Rambam, Hilchos Teshuvah 7:4).*

> *How great is teshuvah. Yesterday (before he did teshuvah) he was distanced from Hashem ... if he cried out to Him he was not*

---

38. *Chofetz Chaim, Hilchos Lashon Hara* 6:12.

39. Ibid. See also *Nesiv Chaim* ad loc.

40. *Rambam, Hilchos Teshuvah* 3:14.

41. *Yechezkel* 18:23.

answered ... when he performed mitzvos they were taken away (i.e. they were unwanted) ... and today (after he has decided to return to Hashem) ... when he cries out he is answered immediately ... when he does mitzvos they are accepted with pleasure and joy...and furthermore, Hashem desires them (ibid. 7:7).

25. Although it may be impossible to recall the identity of all those who were harmed, one should at least make efforts to placate the ones whom one does remember having wronged. A person who wants to do *teshuvah* for years of wrongdoing should engage in four different activities:[42]

(a) He should rectify whatever he possibly can.

(b) He should take steps to distance himself as much as possible from repeating his old patterns of behavior. He should make efforts to avoid situations in which he will be tempted to repeat those wrongs, and should take active steps to ensure that his resolution to change his ways are carried out. For example, he should study *mussar* and the laws pertaining to the wrongs committed. If his personality led him to abuse others or speak *lashon hara,* he should examine the sources of the problem and get help to change his behavior patterns.

(c) Torah and acts of kindness are atonements for wrongdoing.[43] Thus, if a person wants to atone for previous behavior he should engage in Torah study and act with kindness to others.

(d) The righteous find favor doing precisely those activities with which they had previously sinned.[44] Thus, someone who wishes to atone for *lashon hara,* verbal abuse, cheating, etc. should try to teach and spread knowledge of these mitzvos and prohibitions and encourage others to observe them.

At the height of the ecstasy of rejoicing on Succos, those who repented said, "Fortunate are our older years that have atoned for our younger years."[45]

Most important is the need to firmly resolve that from now on these wrongs will not be repeated.

---

42. See *Shaarei Teshuvah,* the first *shaar* at length; cf. *Shemiras HaLashon* Part 2, Ch. 24.

43. *Shaarei Teshuvah* 4:11.

44. Ibid. 1:35, 50.

45. *Succah* 53a.

19

Guarding
One's Speech

1. A person is commanded to guard his speech, as the Psalmist says
   (*Tehillim* 34:12-14): *Come, my children, listen to me, I will teach you the
   fear of Hashem. Who is the person who desires life and loves days to see goodness? Guard your tongue from evil and your lips from speaking deceit. Turn
   away from evil and do good, seek peace and pursue it.* The Torah commands us to "choose life" (*Devarim* 30:19)[1] and this is, therefore, an
   obligatory mitzvah. Since a person's natural instincts will lead him to
   speak in a forbidden manner, this mitzvah compels us to create a
   "guard" around the spoken word through awareness of pitfalls and
   taking active measures to avoid them. Although each person is
   unique, requiring a unique strategy to accomplish this goal, certain
   basic principles do apply to everyone.[2]

2. The most crucial strategy for success in guarding one's speech is
   to understand and internalize a sense of its importance. From the

---

1. See *Shaarei Teshuvah* 3:17 that this is an obligatory mitzvah.

2. This chapter is based primarily on *Chovas HaShemirah* of the Chofetz Chaim. See also
   Halichos Olam, Ch. 23 fn. *alef*.

words of *Tehillim* quoted above, we derive that guarding one's speech is the first condition for achieving fear of Hashem and experiencing true meaning in life. Someone who makes a serious attempt to guard his speech will slowly come to an actual feeling of sanctity. He will also be repelled by all manner of forbidden speech, which will seem impure and repugnant. Therefore, when committing to guard one's speech, it is important to make a conscious effort to be sensitive to these awakening feelings of purity and sanctity.

> ***Father to family:*** *Let's make an experiment. For two hours we will avoid any forbidden speech: no lashon hara, no verbal abuse, etc. We will act in a kind and friendly manner and try to think only positive thoughts about each other, as the Torah prescribes. After the two-hour period we will each describe our feelings and impressions.*

3. A certain degree of failure is almost inevitable when a person begins to guard his speech. Furthermore, as he progresses and becomes more sensitive to his words, he will be even more aware of any lack of success in his efforts. These are positive signs of a greater level of sensitivity. A person should never be discouraged by failure; on the contrary, recognition of failure is in itself part of the mitzvah to guard one's speech. After repairing whatever damage was done (apologize, repent, etc.), he should continue and strengthen his "guard."

4. The following two mitzvos are particularly important, not only on their own, but also in helping us avoid forbidden speech and, in general, incorporating the Torah's ideals of interpersonal behavior into our lives. The first is the mitzvah of judging others favorably, as the Torah says (*Vayikra* 19:15), *With righteousness shall you judge your fellow.* Whenever we observe any failing in another Jew, we are required to look for ways to excuse him or at least to mitigate the severity of his fault or wrongdoing in our minds.[3]

5. The second of these is a negative commandment expressed by the prophet Zechariah: *You shall not think in your heart about the evil of your fellow* (*Zechariah* 8:17). Should unfavorable thoughts about another individual enter our minds, we should stop and remind ourselves that thinking badly of a fellow Jew is particularly hateful in Hashem's eyes, as expressed clearly at the end of the

---

3. See Ch. 2 for expanded discussion of this mitzvah.

verse: *for all these things I hate, says Hashem.* Instead, we are required to look for the good that exists in every Jew and to focus our thoughts on that goodness. As stated above by the prophet, the merit of this mitzvah — striving to overlook people's failings and only thinking well of others — has the power to bring the redemption closer. Realizing this, a person will surely prefer to choose this path than to allow himself to be in any way responsible for delaying the redemption. In addition, training ourselves to observe these two mitzvos makes it much easier to avoid the many forms of forbidden interpersonal behavior.

Common Forms of Forbidden Speech

6. Obviously, it is important to be able to recognize, and thus avoid, the various forms of forbidden speech. Following is a list of the ten most common categories, each with the chapter in which it has been explained.

(a) *Lashon Hara*: speaking evil of others — Chapter 5.
(b) *Rechilus*: causing animosity — Chapter 8.
(c) Falsehood — Chapter 10.
(d) Flattery: condoning a person's wrongdoings to him — Chapter 11.
(e) *Leitzanus*: mockery — Chapter 15.
(f) *Ona'as Devarim*: causing pain with words — Chapter 6.
(g) Causing embarrassment — Chapter 6.
(h) Arrogance — Chapter 16.
(i) *Machlokes*: feuding — Chapter 9.
(j) Anger — Chapter 16.

An easy way to remember these ten is LEAF (a person's conversation is compared to a leaf — see *Succah* 21b): **L** = *lashon hara, leitzanus;* **E** = embarrassment; **A** = animosity (*rechilus*), abuse, arrogance, anger; **F** = falsehood, flattery, feuding.

7. There are other forms of speech that, while less commonly found, are also forbidden. A person who knows that he is liable to falter in any of these areas should include them in his "guard." These categories are:

(a) Giving inappropriate advice, especially if the speaker's personal interest is served in some way. This is a particular problem facing *shadchanim,* brokers and salespeople.

(b) Coveting the property of another, i.e. trying to convince him to sell or give away his property against his wishes (see Chapters 30 and 37).

(c) Making false oaths.

(d) Cursing:*You shall not curse (even) a deaf person* (*Vayikra* 19:14).

(e) Committing to do a mitzvah and then not fulfilling the undertaking (see Chapter 55).

Building an Internal Guard

8. The most effective way to avoid the forbidden forms of speech is to fix a block of time each day, however short, to study and review the *halachos* and works of *mussar* relevant to guarding speech.

❏ Study the *halachos* for a few minutes before or after *davening* each day.

❏ Listen to pertinent tapes when in the car.

9. A person should make note of certain times when his guard is liable to slip, and devise measures to remind himself to beware.

❏ *A person who forgets himself at the shul's Kiddush on Shabbos may repeat to himself after davening, "Guard your tongue from evil and your lips from speaking deceit ..." (Psalms ibid.).*

❏ *If a person is susceptible when on vacation he should perhaps take along a book on the halachos of lashon hara and review it for a few minutes every day.*

If possible, one should designate regular times to "examine the ledger" and devise concrete resolutions for the future. Always make these resolutions small and attainable. It is not advisable to go too far, too fast.

10. It is also very helpful to firmly resolve to curb untoward curiosity about other people's lives.

A person should say to himself: Does anyone really know what's going on in my life? Who truly understands what is in the depths of my heart? How many people think they know my true motivations, but really know nothing? If people don't know what's going on in my life, how can I know what's really going on in theirs? Therefore, what is the point of curiosity, and seeking information, when I will never acquire the whole truth?

11. One should seek to associate with other people who are also careful with their speech. A group of like-minded individuals is a highly effective medium to provide encouragement for its members.

Applying the Guard

12. Even highly respected people may not always be careful in their speech. One should not allow their behavior to lead him astray. Nevertheless, while taking care not to learn from their example, one should still look for ways to judge such individuals favorably and assume that they do not realize the serious nature of the prohibitions involved.

13. A person should try to beware not to allow himself to become overly emotional when hearing of a situation not to his liking, since that would cause him to speak improperly. It is common to discover at a later day that he lacked a proper understanding of events in the first place and that his comments were unjustified.

> One of the great Torah Sages of recent times would walk out of the room when angered by a statement, until he felt able to respond calmly, and not from anger.

14. A person should train himself to accept life's events in good grace and to forgive others for any slights against him. This attitude is a sign of holiness, and the Sages have said that a person who forgives others will be forgiven by Hashem for his own actions. In addition, it is helpful in preventing anger and conflict.

15. It is also advisable to avoid undertaking any activity or filling a position that is likely to involve constant conflict (e.g. of leadership roles). It is almost impossible to avoid speaking and hearing forbidden speech in such situations. This is true even when dealing with the most humble and patient of individuals, and all the more so when ordinary people are involved.

> Mr. Black and Mr. Brown were both candidates for the position of chairman of the board of Mid-City Supermarket Chain Inc. Each rounded up their supporters for the final vote, which was very close. Mr. White suggested, "Let's have both of you serve as co-chairmen." Mr. Black refused, conjuring up images of constant feuding and lashon hara. "A joint position will not be good for the company, for me, or for Mr. Brown. No, it must be either him or me."

Limit Conversations With Certain People

16. One should be especially careful when conversing with people who are not careful in their speech or are otherwise weak in their observance of *halachah*, since they will often respond to comments about anyone, even their close friends, with *lashon hara*.[4]

17. One should not speak to a businessman about his competitors, nor to any craftsman or professional about his rivals, since it is to be presumed that they are antagonists. If circumstances require mention of a person's rival, he should take care to limit his words to no more than the minimum necessary.

In the Midst of a Danger Zone

18. If a person finds himself in a situation where *lashon hara* seems likely to ensue, he should do everything in his power to redirect the conversation to a safer topic. Even if he can avoid *lashon hara* only at the cost of great embarrassment, he should remember the words of the Sages that it is better to be thought of as a fool all one's life than to be wicked in Hashem's eyes for even one moment.

> *If a person were suddenly to learn that the food in his mouth was treife, he would unquestionably spit it out immediately, no matter how much embarrassment this would cause him.*
>
> *The Ramban writes that one hour in Gehinnom is worse than a lifetime of the suffering of Iyov.*

---

4. See *Shemiras HaLashon, Shaar HaTevunah*, Ch. 3.

⇉ Conflicting Values

Chapters 20-29

Helping Others vs. Helping Oneself

1. The Torah's commandment to help others, derived from the verses, *You shall love your fellow as yourself* (*Vayikra* 19:18) and *You shall go in His ways* (*Devarim* 26:9), can on occasion conflict with the mitzvah of taking care of and helping oneself. The Torah's guideline to resolve this conflict is *Let your brother live with you* (*Vayikra* 25:36), meaning that your life takes precedence over that of another.[1]

> *Two people were traveling in a desert. One of them had a jug of water containing only enough for one to survive. If they share the contents of the jug they will both die. Ben Peturah originally taught that they should share the water. Because each is prohibited from allowing the other to die, they must act to keep each other alive, regardless of the consequences. However, Rabbi Akiva taught, "Your brother shall live with you. Your life precedes your brother's." Therefore, the owner of the jug must drink the water and not share it.*

2. One's own interest takes precedence only if it is of the same relative importance as the proposed help to someone else. However,

---

1. *Ramban, Vayikra* 19:18; see *Nedarim* 80a.

one cannot refuse to help a person in need in order to accrue a greater profit or luxury for oneself.[2]

Mr. Diamond is a very wealthy person who has invested extensively in stocks and bonds. One morning he received a call from Mr. Green, the owner of a local store, stating that he desperately needed a three-month $20,000 loan to tide him over an especially difficult period. Mr. Diamond knows that Mr. Green's credit and word are impeccable, yet he is in a quandary because the loan would entail a $500 loss in revenue. Mr. Diamond knew that this was a question of halachah and consulted his rav, who determined that he must grant the loan. The rule that "your life and interests have precedence" does not apply because Mr. Green needs this loan to keep his business going. "For you," the rav explained, "the expected revenue is merely an additional profit and not crucial to your income."

Rabbi Abrams, the rabbi of a congregation in a small city, received a call that Reb Yankel, who was in a desperate financial situation, was arriving the next day to solicit funds for himself. Rabbi Abrams, who did not have a car available, approached Mr. Gold in shul that evening and asked him to pick Reb Yankel up from the airport. "But Rabbi," he answered, "I am supposed to go on vacation with my wife tomorrow morning." "Very well," answered the rabbi, "we will ask someone else. Enjoy your vacation." He spotted Mr. Silver and asked him to do the mitzvah. "But Rabbi," he, too, answered, "I am supposed to go on vacation with my wife tomorrow morning." "Nevertheless," answered the rabbi, "this is considered tzedakah, and you can postpone your vacation for a few hours or even a day in order to do the mitzvah. Please tell your wife you are following the Torah's teachings."

Chaim Abrams, the rabbi's son and a young Torah scholar in his own right, was puzzled by his father's behavior. Why did he give one answer to Mr. Gold and another to Mr. Silver? That evening at home he questioned his father, who answered, "The Golds have a large family and are under a lot of pressure. In their situation, a vacation is crucial for the family's well-being. Therefore, the rule of

2. *Nedarim* ibid. (*Tanna Kamma*); *Mitzvos HaLevavos* 2:8. See *Rambam, Mishnayos Bava Metzia* (Ch. 2, Mishnah 11); see also *Chasam Sofer, Yoreh Deah* 234.

"your life has precedence" applies here, and a vacation is, in a sense, considered tzedakah for them. The Silvers, on the other hand, do not have such pressures, and are only going to rest up. It won't matter if they lose one day of vacation. Therefore, the mitzvah of tzedakah to help this destitute person takes precedence.

3. This rule grants *permission* to put one's own interests first when another's interests are of the same relative importance. However, if a person decides to help someone at his own expense — even though one's own interests may be put first — this is indeed a fulfillment of the mitzvos of kindness.[3] Nevertheless, he *cannot* do so at someone else's expense or at risk to his own life or health.[4]

    In the previous example, it would be considered a mitzvah were the Golds to decide to delay their vacation to pick up Reb Yankel. However, if only one spouse is willing to do so while the other feels the need to go as planned, it is improper to convince the other spouse to forgo that need. Psychological pressure ("How can we not do such a mitzvah?") is not warranted. The implication is that our peace of mind, shalom bayis and providing a stable home for our children is not a mitzvah ... Only a "mitzvah" for others is important ... Sometimes, helping others makes one feel good whereas taking care of one's own self or family does not. On the other hand, this concept can be misused to avoid doing mitzvos. It is useful to ask oneself, "What does Hashem really want me to do?"

Uncertain vs. Certain Loss

4. If the relative importance to both parties is the same, yet one's own loss is uncertain whereas the other's loss is certain, one's own uncertain loss takes precedence over the other's certain loss.[5]

    Neighbor A: *May I borrow your car to go shopping?*
    Neighbor B: *My husband said he might come home in half an hour to go shopping with me. If he doesn't, you may have the car, but until I know, I can't lend it.*
    However, this should not be misused.

---

3. See *Bava Metzia* 33a (see also par. 5).

4. One cannot hurt someone in order to help someone else. See *Bava Kamma* 60b.

5. See *Choshen Mishpat* 426, *Pischei Teshuvah* 2; *Mitzvos HaLevavos* 2:6.

Neighbor A: May I borrow the car to go shopping?

Neighbor B: Well, maybe my husband will come home and need it. Maybe my child will be sick and need to go to a doctor, etc.

5. The Sages taught:[6] If a person is presented with a situation where he must choose between recovering his own loss and someone else's, one's own loss takes precedence, for the verse states, *There will not be a pauper within you* (*Devarim* 15:4). This can be interpreted as: "Make sure not to become impoverished," i.e. your loss takes precedence.

    Nevertheless, "Whoever is meticulous in this dictum will eventually come to it (poverty)." Rashi explains that even though the Torah does not compel a person to help another when he may lose out, he should nevertheless go beyond the letter of the law and not be overly meticulous in saying "mine is first" unless there is clearly a reason to predict loss. An overly meticulous person in this regard will remove from himself the yoke (obligation) of kindness and *tzedakah* and, in the end, will himself become dependent on others.

Avoiding Danger

6. It is permitted to place others' needs above one's own only when there is no danger to life. However, a person is not permitted to put himself into a dangerous situation in order to save someone else, even if that individual is in definite danger while the danger to oneself is uncertain.[7]

    > *If Reuven is drowning in the ocean, then Shimon, who is not a lifeguard, is not permitted to attempt to save him, since he cannot determine if he would thereby be putting himself in danger.*

7. However, with proper precautions, one may take measured risks in order to save someone who is in definite danger.[8]

    > ❑ *A lifeguard with proper equipment should attempt to save the life of a drowning swimmer, even if the water conditions are turbulent.*
    >
    > ❑ *After taking appropriate precautions, a doctor should treat a patient with a dangerous communicable disease.*

---

6. *Bava Metzia* 33a.

7. *Choshen Mishpat* 426, *Pischei Teshuvah* 2; *Mitzvos HaLevavos* 2:6.

8. Ibid.

8. A person is not permitted to risk his life for the sake of Torah and mitzvos.[9]

> *In the midst of battle, King David was unsure of a certain halachah. Three of his men went to ask the Torah scholars, but had to break through the enemy camp in order to reach them. It was considered inappropriate to put themselves in mortal danger, even for words of Torah. Therefore, King David refused to teach the halachah in their name, saying, "Thus we have learned from the beis din of Shmuel, 'Anyone who puts himself in mortal danger for words of Torah, we do not repeat those words of Torah in his name.' "[10]*

Therefore, for example, one is *not permitted* to speed excessively on a highway even for the sake of a mitzvah, such as learning on time or when traveling to a wedding.

Do Not Take Advantage

9. Although the precepts of kindness dictate that a person should sacrifice his own comfort or possessions for someone else's benefit, especially if that individual is in a position of greater need, it is nevertheless improper for the recipient to take undue advantage of the beneficence of others.[11]

> *If an elderly person or pregnant woman boards a crowded bus, it is incumbent on the able passengers to stand and offer their seats. However, if the person who has difficulty standing is aware that the bus is overcrowded, and that additional buses arrive regularly, he or she should not board the bus thinking that someone else will feel obligated to stand.*

---

9. Example is from *Bava Kamma* 61a. Note: During times of persecution when others try to force the Jewish people to abandon the Torah, the precedence of the laws of personal safety versus upkeep of Torah and sanctification of Hashem's Name is different.

10. Perhaps the reason is that the Torah is connected intimately with the "person." When a Torah scholar says over words of Torah, he and those words are bound forever; thus even after he passes away, when the words are repeated in his name his lips move in his grave. If someone endangers the "person" because of Torah, he minimizes the "person" aspect of the Torah-person relationship; thus the Torah is not repeated in his name.

11. See *Rambam, Hilchos Matnos Aniyim* 10:18.

21

Beneficial Lashon Hara

What Constitutes *Lashon Hara* — A Review

1. We have already explained that *lashon hara* is prohibited because it
   is "evil," meaning that it can cause people damage, embarrassment or disgrace. Even if it causes no such harm, *lashon hara* reflects the undesirable qualities of judging people unfavorably, accusing them wrongly, and gloating over their failings.[1] Furthermore, even casual *lashon hara* that emerges in the normal flow of a conversation with no harmful intent is prohibited.[2]

Lashon Hara for a Worthwhile Purpose

2. It is permitted to relate negative information for a worthwhile
   purpose, provided that all the conditions detailed in the following paragraphs are fulfilled. Such speech is not considered *lashon hara* because one's intention is good rather than evil.[3] Furthermore, there can sometimes be a mitzvah in relating such information.[4]

---

1. See Ch. 5 pars.1-3.

2. *Shaarei Teshuvah* 3:74.

3. *Chofetz Chaim, Hilchos Lashon Hara* 4:10-11, and *Kodesh Yisrael* 15:5-6.

4. *Chofetz Chaim* ibid.

One may relate negative information to prevent someone from getting involved in a detrimental situation, e.g. a harmful *shidduch*, partnership, job, friendship, etc.

However, even when speaking with a legitimate purpose, a person must be sure that his motivation is entirely positive as well. Any element of enjoyment in discussing other people's failings and misfortunes, or of personal dislike of the subject, is considered an evil motivation and these words are prohibited as *lashon hara*,[5] even if they may accomplish a worthwhile purpose.

> *The Young family has a long-standing grudge — justified, in their view — against Chaim Alter, a middle-aged divorced man. One day they heard that a shidduch was being proposed between Chaim Alter and Mrs. Rubin, a divorcee. Knowing Chaim Alter well, Mr. Young felt morally obligated to discuss Chaim's negative traits with Mrs. Rubin's brother, in order to prevent her from getting involved in a disastrous relationship. After a frank discussion, Mr. Young felt good about getting his true feelings about Chaim Alter "off his chest."*
>
> *Even if Mr. Young was correct in his assessment that the match was inappropriate, and should be stopped, his "enjoyment" of the conversation about Chaim Alter made him guilty of lashon hara. For the proper course of action, see paragraph 5.*

Conditions

3. Even if the speaker's intentions are entirely good, he must take care that the following three conditions are met.[6]

(a) Truth — Any statements he makes must be strictly true, and contain no element of exaggeration. Furthermore, if the subject is alleged to have violated the Torah, the speaker must be certain that his understanding of the relevant *halachos* is accurate and that he is applying them correctly to the case at hand. Often, the right or wrong status of an action depends on many intricate details, and an individual who makes a quick judgment based on superficial or secondhand knowledge of the facts is likely to err. Therefore, it is important both to investigate all the circumstances thoroughly and to consult with a qualified rav regarding any *halachic* considerations.

---

5. Ibid. 10:2, condition 5; see also par. 5 below.

6. Ibid. 10:2.

In Parshas Vayeishev Yosef misjudged his brothers' actions and con-cluded incorrectly that they were guilty of certain sins. He was guilty of lashon hara for relating this information to his father (Bereishis 37:2).

(b) Necessity — As a general rule, one may not relate negative information unnecessarily. Therefore, whenever possible, one should attempt to resolve a situation by speaking directly to the subject, thereby avoiding the need to relate unfavorable informa-tion. Where this is not possible, one may relate only that which is strictly necessary in order to accomplish the desired purpose. Even when it is legitimate to relate such information, it is forbidden to foster a more negative impression of the subject than required. Thus, one must carefully consider each point he intends to include to determine whether the desired outcome could be achieved without including that particular fact. If possible, it is preferable to construct the conversation in such a way that the relevant facts emerge on their own or through hints and allusions, provided, of course, that the listener will not misunderstand and make matters even worse.

(c) Avoid Excess Damage — One must also take care that what he says will not cause the subject any more harm or damage than the Torah allows under the circumstances. For example, if A tells B that C has stolen from B and B then maligns C in public, the result may very well be that C will no longer be able to show his face in the city or make a living there. Thus, even if A has told the truth and his intention was solely for a legitimate purpose (that C should repay B), his action still causes C far more damage than the Torah provides for this offense.[7] The Torah requires only that C repay what he stole, whereas public disgrace or loss of livelihood is certainly considered excess damage.

One evening in the dormitory of a Jerusalem seminary, Rivki noticed Chani enter Gitti's room, open her purse, and take out some cash. Rivki was knowledgeable in the laws of lashon hara and decided on a plan of action, rather than relating the incident to her friends.

(a) Ascertain the truth. Question: Did Gitti give Chani permis-sion to take the money? Or, perhaps, Gitti owed her the money and Chani decided to repay herself? Although this is not necessarily the

---

7. For assessment of the punishment of a thief see *Moed Katan* 17a, the story of Reish Lakish.

Torah way, it is not the same as theft. Rivki approached Gitti and discreetly ascertained that, from her point of view, this was not the case. Chani had apparently stolen the money.

(b) Approach the person directly. Rivki engaged Chani in conversation and gently led it to the evening's events. Chani denied the whole story.

(c) At this point, Rivki considered her options. Obviously, spreading the word among the student body would ruin Chani's future in terms of both jobs and shidduchim. This is a far greater damage than is called for by the Torah for this sin, and was ruled out.

Rivki pondered the following questions: What benefit is to be gained by repeating the story? To whom should she talk to gain these benefits? Is that person sufficiently discreet so that gaining these benefits will not cause damage to Chani?

Rivki decided that the two benefits were (a) helping Gitti recover her money, and (b) helping Chani to overcome her negative traits and to deal with her problems so that such behavior would not be repeated.

Rivki debated between confiding in the dorm mother and the principal, both fully capable of handling the situation. Although she considered the principal wiser, she trusted the discretion of the dorm mother more and chose to approach her first.

Rivki did not say, "I saw Chani steal," in case Gitti did owe her money or some other motivation existed. Rather, she chose to say only what she witnessed: "I saw Chani take money from Gitti's purse. Gitti knows nothing about it, and claims not to owe Chani anything. Chani denies the whole story. Please investigate this matter with discretion and handle the problem."

4. In a few special cases, leniencies are found regarding the application of some of the above three conditions.[8] However, *under no circumstances* can there be any compromise of the primary requirement on which this entire chapter is based, namely, that one's intention in speaking must be purely and entirely beneficial. Any speech based on evil motives such as dislike of a certain individual or the enjoyment derived from discussing another person's failings is *lashon hara.*

---

8. See par. 13 for leniency in the condition of truth. See Ch. 28 in regard to someone who is suspected of heresy or immorality.

The Dilemma of Helping Someone vs. Personal Dislike

5. If so, one may well ask what to do if he is required to speak out to prevent damage, and yet recognizes that he does in fact dislike the person about whom he must speak (or even that he enjoys spreading gossip). The best solution is to arrange for the matter to be resolved by another party who does not share his negative feelings. However, if this is not possible, silence is also wrong, because someone will be hurt by his inaction (e.g. by going through with a bad *shidduch* or partnership). In the face of such a dilemma, it is permissible to speak only if the following three conditions are met:

(a) He must firmly establish in his mind that the only justification for speaking negatively about others is when a clearly beneficial purpose will be accomplished. Thus, although he may have negative feelings, he *knows* on an intellectual level that the sole motivation for his speech is beneficial.

(b) He must take great care to relate only that negative information about the subject which is necessary to accomplish the desired purpose. (While this is true of all beneficial *lashon hara*, one must be doubly careful in this case because the emotions involved are a powerful driving force to relate more than necessary.)

(c) He must take care that his words be spoken *in a calm and detached manner that does not convey negative or emotional overtones*. Whenever possible, one should consult with a rav or other wise person who is capable of providing guidance.[9]

The Mitzvah to Help Others Improve Themselves

6. Any time one sees another Jew doing wrong or acting in an undesirable fashion, it is a mitzvah to attempt to show him how he has erred and to help him improve himself.[10] If a person has attempted unsuccessfully to correct someone in this fashion, or if he judges that his efforts will surely fail, then it is permitted (and indeed a mitzvah)

---

9. Once one concludes objectively (and sincerely, without self-deception) that his feelings are not affecting his decision, then the motivation of his speech is ruled to be beneficial and he is permitted to say what he has to, provided that he does not speak in a fashion where the unspoken message conveys his negative feelings. If time allows, someone in this situation is highly advised to study works of *mussar* on this topic (especially *Sefer Shemiras HaLashon* by the Chofetz Chaim). See *Kodesh Yisrael* 15:6,8.

10. See Ch. 3.

to discuss the matter with a discreet third party who is more likely to persuade the subject to correct his ways. Approaching the third party is acceptable because the intention behind their discussion is entirely beneficial.[11] Similarly, if one is unsure what steps can be taken to help someone improve himself, he may seek advice from a rav or any other wise and discreet person. If possible, he should safeguard the identities of the parties involved.

7. Even in these cases, however, one must take care to convey only the minimum required by the situation, as in paragraph 3(b) above.[12] It is also important to consider whether involving a third party might cause even more damage, e.g. if he reveals embarrassing information about the subject to others. Or, he may be liable to display anger to the subject, which is not only forbidden (as discussed in Chapter 3) but is also likely to do more harm than good. Thus, great care must be taken to turn only to a person of discretion who will approach the subject with sensitivity to his needs and nature. If such an individual cannot be found, no other one may be brought into the matter, even at the expense of leaving the situation unresolved.[13]

> Reuven, Shimon and Levi are all roommates and close friends in yeshivah. Yehudah, another friend, discovered that Reuven spends an hour of the afternoon seder reading books in his room. He asked the Rosh Yeshivah if he can approach Shimon and/or Levi to help convince Reuven to change his ways, as both are close friends who are the most likely to have a positive influence on him. The Rosh Yeshivah felt that Shimon is not sufficiently discreet and is liable to cause Reuven embarrassment by telling others, and that Levi is not very sensitive and may speak in a forceful, derogatory manner. Therefore, the Rosh Yeshivah decided that neither friend can be used and that another plan must be formulated.

8. Particular caution is required in the above case (a situation both easy and common to misjudge) in order to be certain that the action in question is indeed wrong or that the subject's behavior does actually need improvement.

---

11. See *Kodesh Yisrael* 9:2,4.

12. *Chofetz Chaim, Hilchos Lashon Hara* 10:2.

13. Since it is forbidden to cause someone embarrassment in the course of giving reproof (as discussed in Ch. 3), it is certainly also not permitted to cause any damage by discussing someone's affairs with an indiscreet third party for the purpose of giving reproof.

Perhaps Reuven has a difficult time focusing on his studies, yet he forces himself to concentrate through his inner drive to learn Torah. That one hour of reading in the afternoon may be the relaxation that enables him to learn the other nine hours of the study day.

If the subject in question is a Torah scholar one must take particular care to understand the true motives underlying his actions before concluding that he acted wrongly.[14]

9. Even if a person's knowledge of the problem in need of improvement is not direct, he is still allowed to relate what he has heard to a discreet third party who may be in a better position to influence the subject. The reason for this is that we are allowed (and even required) to react to *lashon hara* as if it contains some truth, *to the extent that it is necessary* to protect ourselves or others from harm, or to help people. However, he must make it clear that his knowledge of the matter is indirect, by saying, for example: "I have to tell you what I heard about this person. While we are not allowed to believe it, we are required to suspect that it might be true in order to do what we can to help him. Therefore, could you please investigate the matter and, if you feel it is appropriate, do what you can to persuade him of the need for improvement." In this case, a person must take great care not to appear to have concluded that the reports are definitely true.[15]

Father to principal: My son tells me that his friend, David, is associating with certain boys who are a very negative influence. Although we are not permitted to believe it, we are required to suspect that there may be some truth in the story and take the necessary precautions. For the sake of the students, please investigate.

Warning Others About People's Bad Traits

10. If one recognizes an undesirable quality in a certain individual, then it is a mitzvah to caution others, especially one's children and students, to avoid learning from that person's failings, and if necessary, to avoid contact with him entirely. This warning is not considered *lashon hara*, since the purpose is not to denigrate the subject but to protect others from acquiring his bad traits. However, it is

---

14. Ibid. 10:2, condition 2; *Be'er Mayim Chaim* 7.

15. Ibid. *Nesiv Chaim* 4, derived from *Rosh, Niddah* 9:5. See Ch. 13 for the *halachos* of believing *lashon hara*.

important to stress that it is permitted to relate such information only to protect them from undesirable traits and practices, and that they should not infer that *lashon hara* is allowed in other circumstances.[16]

Note: The educational wisdom of sounding these cautions is subject to many different factors, such as the problem at hand, the nature of the child/student etc. This *halachah* does not deal with *when* to make such a statement, but rather, *how* to make it when necessary. When appropriate, it is considered a mitzvah and not *lashon hara*.

> **Mother (to her son):** *I know that David doesn't listen to his parents and rebbi. This is not lashon hara because I am speaking to you for a good reason. He is not the right type of friend for you and can no longer come to the house. However, this does not mean that we can make fun of him and call him a "bad boy" or talk to the other boys about him. (See paragraph 12.)*

11. If one has not seen evidence of the undesirable quality himself but has only heard about it from others, then he is required to make it clear when speaking to people that his knowledge of the matter is indirect.

> *"I do not have direct knowledge of the matter but I heard that ..."*

Not to Cause the Subject Any Harm

12. It is essential to warn young people (and in many cases adults as well) that while they should avoid associating with the subject in order not to be influenced by his bad qualities, it remains strictly forbidden to cause him any harm or embarrassment, or to insult him either to his face or behind his back. If the speaker knows that his listeners are likely to ignore his warning not to embarrass the subject, then he should carefully weigh the benefits of speaking out versus the harm of the listeners reacting improperly.

> *A rabbi wishes to speak out against a certain group who act in a manner inconsistent with Torah values. He must carefully consider:*
> ❑ *What is the harm of failing to speak out (negative influences)?*
> ❑ *What dangers may ensue if he does speak out (lashon hara, rechilus, ona'as devarim, etc.)?*
> ❑ *Which is the greater potential danger?*

---

16. *Chofetz Chaim* ibid. 4:10.

❏ *Can he succeed in speaking out while avoiding both dangers?*
(Speak forcefully against the group, but simultaneously warn the
listeners against speaking lashon hara, creating machlokes, etc.)

13. If children or students have been warned against associating
with a particular individual, but they have not been deterred
from doing so, it is permitted to exaggerate the danger posed by the
subject, should this approach be judged more effective.[17] This strategy,
however, must be employed with wisdom and discretion.

> *My daughter is becoming friendly with a girl who is clearly a bad*
> *influence. If nothing else helps, I am permitted to exaggerate the nega-*
> *tive qualities of this friend so as to ensure that my daughter will no*
> *longer associate with her.*

If One Individual Is Thinking of
Forming an Association With Another

14. A person who is considering entering into an association (e.g. a
business partnership, employment, or *shidduch*) is permitted to
make inquiries about the proposed associate's character, circumstances, and other pertinent information. This is permissible in order
to make an informed decision, even though it might cause those being
asked to speak negatively about the subject. After all, a person is obligated to avoid situations that might lead to damage, disagreement,
disputes, or other forms of unpleasantness. Indeed, we are required to
do whatever possible to promote peace in the world and to forestall
disputes, as the Psalmist says, *Seek peace and pursue it* (*Tehillim* 34:15).

15. In making such inquiries, however, one is required to inform the
listener of his specific permitted purpose in asking. If he fails to
do so, the listener is likely to think that the questioner merely wishes
to hear *lashon hara*, and any negative information he relates will therefore be simply for the sake of disparaging people. The questioner is
then violating the commandment not to place a stumbling block
before a blind person by causing the listener to speak *lashon hara*.[18]
Many detailed considerations affect how the listener is to respond to
such inquiries, as we discuss at length in Chapters 25-28.

---

17. Ibid. *Be'er Mayim Chaim* 43.

18. *Chofetz Chaim* ibid. 4:11.

Mrs. Plonis (to husband): When you said that you were consider-
ing hiring Yankel, I decided to do my own investigation. I met his
sister yesterday at the store and spoke to her casually about him.
Well, I found out some really interesting information ...

Mrs. Plonis has violated the prohibition of placing a stumbling
block before the blind by inducing Yankel's sister to speak lashon
hara. The sister was unaware that the conversation may have been for
a beneficial purpose, and was therefore guilty of speaking lashon hara.
Mrs. Plonis' actions were prohibited even if the information could
only be extracted by means of such subterfuge.

Do Not Ask an Individual Who Dislikes the Subject

16. Even in cases where it is permitted to request information for a
     legitimate purpose, it is forbidden to question someone
believed to harbor dislike for the subject. This rule applies as well to
any member of the same profession or craft as the subject, as he is
presumed to have an instinctive feeling of envy or competitiveness
for others in the same field. Since it is human nature in such a case
to fabricate or exaggerate the facts to make the subject look even
worse, any information gained from such individuals is likely to be
distorted and unreliable.

> *David is investigating Chaim as a potential business partner. As*
> *Chaim's family owns one of the two butcher shops in town, David*
> *must not ask for information from the family that owns the com-*
> *peting store.*

17. One should not ask a person who dislikes the subject, even if
     one is certain that he will nevertheless not exaggerate at all. He
is still likely to derive enjoyment from relating unfavorable information about someone whom he dislikes or envies, thereby violating the
prohibition against *lashon hara* in any case. (In addition, the questioner violates the prohibition not to place a stumbling block before
a blind person.) Even if the speaker claims that his answer will be
unaffected by his dislike of the subject, he is not considered credible
in this matter.[19]

---

19. Ibid. in fn. However, if the person questioned is a person who greatly fears Heaven and
is meticulous about his speech, and there is no one else available to ask, the *halachah* may be
different. See *Halichos Olam* 5:13 and *Kodesh Yisrael* 15:6,8.

Warning a Gentile About Dishonest Jews

18. *Sefer Chassidim*[20] writes as follows:[21] "If a Jew and a gentile are together and the gentile says to the Jew, 'I plan to go to such-and-such a place where there are Jews and I am afraid that they might cheat me, so please tell me who is trustworthy and who is not,' the Jew should tell him, 'Do not have dealings with So-and-so.'" We can analyze the statement as follows: If the Jew claims ignorance and the gentile is cheated, the gentile will believe that Jews as a group are deceitful — a clear desecration of Hashem's Name. Furthermore, since it is forbidden for a Jew to cheat anyone, Jew or gentile, he will be preventing the dishonest Jews of that place from wrongdoing by warning this gentile. However, should the Jew tell the gentile not to get involved with specific individuals, the gentile will conclude that Jews are trustworthy, since this Jew gave him reliable information. Because the Jew's intention is to sanctify Hashem's Name, his statement is not considered *lashon hara*.

19. However, it is forbidden to speak if there is reason to suspect that the gentile will malign the Jew as dishonest and thereby cause him more damage than he deserves (by discouraging his customers and taking away his livelihood). This applies all the more if there is reason to suspect that the gentile will report the Jew to the authorities or cause him physical harm.[22] In any case, one must be certain that all the conditions described in paragraph 3 are fulfilled.

Stopping Ongoing Damage

20. If a person is being subjected to ongoing damage or distress, and knows that person A is responsible, and he believes that person B is capable of persuading A to cease his actions or to compensate him for his losses, he should not approach B without first confronting A directly.[23] Only if his attempts to resolve the problem directly with A prove unsuccessful, or if approaching A is unlikely to succeed, is he allowed to enlist B's help to intervene with A.

---

20. *Sefer Chassidim* by Rabbi Yehudah HaChassid, one of the *Baalei Tosafos*, is a classical work quoted often by the *Poskim*.

21. Paragraph 1086. See *Kodesh Yisrael* 15:7.

22. See *Chofetz Chaim, Hilchos Lashon Hara* 8:12.

23. Ibid. 8:10; *Be'er Mayim Chaim* 7.

21.   In this situation, however, the wronged party must be very care-
      ful to tell B only what is necessary to accomplish the permitted
purpose, for if his intention is also to vent his resentment or to take
revenge against A, then his words will be considered *lashon hara*. He
must also beware to speak only the truth and to say nothing which
could result in any harm to A. Thus, before involving B, he must be
certain of B's discretion and that he can be trusted not to spread
derogatory information about A.[24]

22.   Someone who is being subjected to ongoing damage and has
      heard rumors that A may be at fault may not believe the hearsay,
but is still allowed to suspect that it is true and take steps to verify the
information. If he cannot approach A directly, he may say to B, for
example, "I have heard that A is the cause of certain problems I am
experiencing; could you please investigate and, if it is true, use your
influence with A to persuade him to stop (or to compensate me for the
damage he has already caused)."[25]

Asking After Family and Friends in Other Cities

23.   If one has a child, close friend or relative in another city and
      wishes to keep abreast of his affairs out of genuine love and con-
cern for his well-being, then it is permitted to inquire of acquaintances
living in that city, as long as it is made clear that one's motives are
positive.[26] In such a case, the person being questioned is allowed to
answer truthfully, as long as his motives are beneficial as well. This
also applies to a teacher who maintains a close connection with former students and wishes to keep informed of their progress, especially if he can help them in any way to develop in a positive direction or
prevent them from straying.

   One of the sterling qualities of a righteous person is "to carry a
burden with one's friend." A righteous person is genuinely happy in
others' rejoicing, and sad with their pitfalls and misfortunes. When
such people hear negative news about another person they will not
think less of them, but will be saddened by their pitfalls.
Unfortunately, our hearts are not pure, and hearing about someone's

---

24. See *Rambam, Hilchos Dei'os* 6:8; *Halichos Olam,* Ch. 5 fn. *taf.*

25. *Chofetz Chaim, Hilchos Lashon Hara* 10:13; see also *Be'er Mayim Chaim* 34 which cites the
story of R' Gidel, *Kiddushin* 59a.

26. See *Zera Chaim* 4:11.

negative traits inadvertently involves some maligning of the person's character and therefore is *lashon hara*. Nevertheless, some relationships can come very close to the ideal. The Torah describes Yaakov's inner connection with his son Binyamin: *His soul is attached to his soul* (*Bereishis* 44:30). Similarly (*I Shmuel* 18:1), *The soul of Yonasan was bound with the soul of David, for he loved him as himself.* In such cases the source of questioning about the welfare of that close person is purely to "rejoice in his well-being and to be saddened by his pitfall or misfortune," with no trace of maligning character. A conversation in this spirit is not *lashon hara*.

24. However, this being a matter of personal discretion rather than a specific mitzvah, one must be absolutely certain that no harm will ensue from his questions.

> *Prohibited Situations:*
>
> ❏ *A mother inquires about a recently married daughter, and subsequently offers well-intentioned but less-than-helpful criticism of her behavior.*
>
> ❏ *A father who disapproves of his son's course in life asks about his affairs and draws additional fuel for his disfavor from the response.*
>
> *In these situations, any answer provided will be lashon hara. Therefore, before responding to such questions, one should ascertain the nature of the relationship between the involved parties, as well as the motives of the questioner.*[27]

25. It must be stressed that it is permitted to ask for or to give information only when the questioner is truly close to the subject and genuinely concerned for his well-being. If, however, he is merely curious and feigning genuine concern in order to glean information that he has no legitimate need to know, he is violating the prohibition not to place a stumbling block before a blind person. Any unfavorable information the speaker tells him is *lashon hara*.[28] Of situations such as this the Torah says, *You shall fear your G-d*, since only Hashem can know the sincerity of a person's intentions.

26. Particular care is required when asking a visitor from another city about mutual acquaintances (especially concerning their

---

27. Ibid.
28. Ibid.

spiritual affairs), because such conversations are liable to be full of *lashon hara* from beginning to end.[29]

> *"Shalom aleichem, old friend from my hometown ... How is Yankel? Does he learn at all? And Berel, does he come to shul? Is Mrs. Smith still angry at the whole world? Ah! And I bet Mrs. Ploni is still schmoozing about everybody."*

Asking a Rav

27. One is permitted to seek the counsel of a rav, or some other wise and discreet person, for guidance as to how to cope with a particular situation. Consulting a rav is not considered *lashon hara* as long as one is motivated solely by his own needs rather than the enjoyment of discussing other people's failings.[30] When asking the rav, one should omit any negative information that is clearly not pertinent. (If one is unsure if the information is pertinent he may mention it.)

Relieving One's Heart

28. A person who has suffered harm but has no recourse, and is forced to bear his distress with a heavy heart, is advised by the Sages[31] to relate his troubles to others. He is therefore permitted to discuss the situation with someone else, since his intention is to relieve the burden on his mind, even though he might speak *lashon hara*. However, the speaker is required to choose a listener well-versed in the *halachos* of *lashon hara* who will not judge anyone negatively on the basis of any unfavorable statements and will recognize that he is hearing a one-sided account. (See Chapter 13, "Accepting *Lashon Hara*," and Chapter 2, "Judging Others Favorably," for further discussion of these issues.) The speaker must also make certain that the listener will not repeat what he hears and that he understands that he is allowed to listen only for the sake of helping the speaker. If, however, one sees that the listener is not likely to observe these *halachos*, it is forbidden to speak to him.[32]

> *Mr. Solomon owns a grocery store in a neighborhood with many large families. The business does well but has a persistent cash flow*

---

29. *Chofetz Chaim, Hilchos Lashon Hara* 4:11, in note.

30. Heard from a *gadol hador.*

31. *Sanhedrin* 100b.

32. *Chofetz Chaim, Hilchos Lashon Hara* 10:14 fn.; see also *Halichos Olam*, Ch. 5 fn. *beis* (2).

problem because he has to extend credit and the customers are always late in paying their debts, forcing him to either delay payments to his suppliers or borrow money. He wished that he could talk about his problem, which weighed heavily on him, but felt that he would be speaking lashon hara by inadvertently maligning his customers. One day, Mr. Solomon met Reb David, who was very careful in the laws of lashon hara, and asked if he could speak to him about his problem. Reb David listened attentively and with a great deal of empathy, although he was unable to offer any practical advice on how to improve the situation. Mr. Solomon felt a lot better, but at the same time, Reb David did not conclude that the customers were bad people. He understood that they had difficulty managing their budgets and would all pay on time if they could.

Being Close to Someone Involved in a Conflict

29. It is an essential element of close relationships to share the difficulties of life. The closer the relationship, the greater the responsibility to share in the other person's trials and tribulations. The closest relationship is between a husband and wife, where the responsibility to share in each other's troubles is part of the essence of marriage. These are not merely norms of human behavior but are consecrated as Hashem's mitzvos: *You shall love your fellow as yourself,* and *You shall go in His ways.*

Just as Hashem is with a person in his troubles,[33] so must we be with a person in his troubles.

A Dilemma

30. This can cause a major dilemma regarding the laws of *lashon hara.*

If a man[34] is having trouble at work with his partner, boss or worker, who is making his life miserable, his wife should ask about his problems at the end of the day so that he can share them with her. On the other hand, this is an open invitation to speak *lashon hara,* a clear violation itself of *avak lashon hara* and of the Torah injunction not to place a stumbling block before the blind, because she is inducing him to speak *lashon hara.* So what should she do? How should the wife resolve this dilemma?

---

33. *Yeshayahu* 63:9, see also 66:13; *Tehillim* 91:15.

34. This is an example. It could be a woman having difficulties in her life, or two close friends, a parent and child, etc.

The Solution

31. There are two ways in which the man can legitimately pour out his troubles to his wife. One is if he is in need of advice. The second is if he needs to speak to someone in order to relieve his anxiety, as our Sages recommended, "Worry in the heart of a man, let him tell it to others." In both cases, the reason the man is speaking is for his own benefit, not to put down someone else.

Therefore, if a man comes home bitter and angry, his wife could initiate a conversation in the following way.[35]

> *"If you need to tell me about your troubles, I will be happy to listen to you. Remember, lashon hara for a beneficial purpose is permitted."*

By saying this she is encouraging him to talk in a permitted fashion and not inducing *lashon hara*. We can presume that he will listen to her and speak only for the stated purpose.[36] She, for her part, should mentally review the laws of accepting *lashon hara* and try to devise ways not to believe any negativity cast on the subject.

> ❏ *Perhaps he perceived that my husband did something wrong to him.*
> ❏ *Nebech, he probably wasn't brought up properly or was influenced to act in such a manner.*

In today's perverse society it is not difficult to find excuses for otherwise fine people who were influenced to act improperly.

However, she need not mention this positive thinking about the subject on her part if it is likely to make her husband even more angry.

This solution may be employed by anyone who wants to help a close friend in trouble. However, it is understood that if the motivation is to satisfy one's curiosity, and not out of a desire to help, it is absolutely considered *lashon hara*. Similarly, if this leniency is used as an excuse to publicize someone's evil character (e.g. I "needed" to tell Reuven, Shimon and Levi) it is absolute *lashon hara* as well. Only a person who is experiencing a serious problem with a certain individual, and genuinely needs to "talk it out" is permitted to do so for that express purpose. Of such instances the Torah states, *You shall fear your G-d*, for Hashem perceives a person's exact motivations, and will treat him accordingly.

---

35. Similarly, the man himself could say, "I need to talk about my problems."

36. See *Halichos Olam*, Ch. 20 fn. *zayin*.

32. Furthermore, this solution is valid only if the man has a basic fear of Heaven and is aware of the fundamental laws of *lashon hara*, because then we can presume that he will heed the words of his wife's preface and speak for the beneficial purpose stated. However, if someone habitually and willfully violates the laws of *lashon hara* (he doesn't "believe in it") we then presume that when he vents his fury his prime motivation is to put the other person down and degrade him in front of others. In such a case, it is forbidden for even a spouse or close relative to inquire about his troubles.

A Word of Advice

33. It is highly advisable for a couple (or other close friends or relatives) to prepare themselves in quiet times by studying these *halachos* so that they will be prepared to handle stressful situations in a permitted manner.

22

Defending Myself Against Accusations

1. If a person is asked in an accusing manner, "Who is responsible for this?" it is forbidden to reveal the identity of the perpetrator. Since the questioner views the act in a negative light, identifying the culprit violates the prohibition against *lashon hara*. Even if a person is falsely accused, he is still not permitted to reveal the identity of the true perpetrator, but is only permitted to say, "I did not do it." It makes no difference whether the questioner was personally harmed and wants to know who is responsible, or if he is merely curious; in all cases it is forbidden to reveal who committed the act.[1]

2. However, if the questioner has a legitimate need to know who was responsible for the act (e.g. in order to protect his interests in the future or to recover his damages), and if all the conditions of Chapter 21, paragraphs 3-6 are satisfied, then it is permitted to supply him

---

1. *Chofetz Chaim, Hilchos Lashon Hara* 10:17; *Hilchos Rechilus* 9:14. If A has no personal interest then the revelation of "Who did it" is *lashon hara*. If A has a personal interest, then the revelation will cause antagonism from A toward the perpetrator of the act and is considered to be *rechilus*.

with the information, even if he did not request it, and whether or not he suspects a specific person was involved.[2]

3. The result of saying "I did not do it" may be that the suspicion will now fall automatically on another individual. If the act was indeed improper and the accused justifiably wishes to clear his name, he is permitted to proclaim his innocence, even though this will inevitably shift the suspicion to someone else.

> *A rock came flying from the playground and smashed a window of the school building. The principal stormed out and found Reuven and Shimon in the area. He angrily confronted them, demanding to know who was responsible. Reuven is permitted to clear his name by saying, "I did not do it" (assuming it is true — see paragraph 7), but may not say, "Shimon did it."*

If the act was entirely proper, however, and the questioner is exaggerating its seriousness, then one should avoid saying, "I did not do it."[3]

> *Chani and Devorah rented an apartment. An elderly lady who lived downstairs was very sensitive to any noise. One evening at 10 p.m. Chani was talking on the telephone when the lady stormed upstairs and accusingly asked Devorah, "Were you talking?" In reality, no wrong was done, so she should not divert the lady's wrath from herself by saying, "I did not do it."*

A Group Decision

4. A person is allowed to deny his involvement in a matter only if he in fact played no role in it whatsoever. He is not permitted to do so, however, if he was part of a group that met to reach a consensus on an issue, even if he was vigorously opposed to the group's decision. Thus, a member of a *beis din* is not allowed to tell one of the litigants in a case that he personally supported his position but was overruled by his colleagues. The same principle applies to the governing committee of a synagogue, educational institution, business concern, or any other organization. Even if the accused wrongly suspects a person of "taking the other side," there-

2. *Chofetz Chaim, Hilchos Lashon Hara* 10:17.

3. *Be'er Mayim Chaim* 43.

by holding a grudge against him, he is forbidden to clear his name by saying, "I didn't do it."[4]

> *Mr. Gold, a top employee in the firm of Silver Brothers, received an end-of-the-year bonus much smaller than he thought he deserved. He cornered Mr. A. Silver to complain about this injustice and was told, "I agree that you deserved more, but I was overruled by my brothers." Mr. A has violated the prohibition of rechilus; as a member of a partnership, he must assume full shared responsibility for its decisions, and is not permitted to exonerate himself with Mr. Gold by blaming his brothers.*

5. The above-stated rule holds true only if the majority position is one sanctioned by the Torah. If, however, the action is forbidden under Torah law, then those in the minority are required to point out the error and do everything in their power to persuade the group to do what is right. If the majority refuses to be persuaded, the minority should not assume responsibility for an anti-Torah action.

> *An Israeli moshav decided to open its swimming pool on Shabbos. Mr. Green, a member of the governing council, publicly announced that he voted against the decision.*

Backing Out of an Agreement

6. A person who agreed to sell an item to A but then sold it to B before the transaction with A was completed may not reveal B's identity to A.[5]

> *Reuven has agreed to sell his car to Shimon, who requests three days to secure the required funds. Three days later Reuven tells Shimon, "I'm sorry, but I sold it to someone else." Shimon, very upset, demands to know who bought it, but Reuven is not permitted to reveal the name of the purchaser. It makes no difference whether Reuven sold the car to the other person intentionally or simply forgot about his commitment to Shimon. Since Shimon will bear a grudge against the purchaser in any event, his name cannot be revealed. Reuven should simply apologize and explain that he mistakenly sold it to someone else.*

---

4. *Chofetz Chaim, Hilchos Rechilus* 9:14.

5. Ibid. 9:15.

Accepting Blame — A Mark of Sterling Character

7. As discussed, there are situations where the Torah allows one to deny involvement in a particular act even though the suspicion will then be cast on another party. However, it is praiseworthy to refrain from doing so and to allow the blame to rest on oneself in order to spare the guilty party inevitable disgrace. Indeed, the Talmud relates several striking incidents in which some of the greatest Sages deliberately accepted blame in order to spare the guilty party from embarrassment.[6]

> *A woman appeared in the study hall of Rabbi Meir, turned to him and said, "One of the people here married me privately (and I therefore need a bill of divorce)." Rabbi Meir himself wrote her a divorce and every one of his students followed their teacher's example and wrote her a divorce as well, thus sparing the guilty person embarrassment (Sanhedrin 11a).*

8. See Chapter 29 for a discussion of a situation where a student in a classroom has done wrong and the teacher must determine who is responsible.

---

6. *Chofetz Chaim, Hilchos Lashon Hara* 10:17.

23

Relating the
Wrongdoing of Others

1. We have learned (Chapter 3) that when one sees another Jew
   doing wrong or conducting his life in an unfitting manner, it is a
mitzvah to attempt to correct him and to inform him that he is harming himself through his actions, as the Torah says, *You shall reprove
your fellow* (*Vayikra* 19:17).[1] Nevertheless, it is forbidden to relate
derogatory information about this person to others, even if one has
personally seen him do wrong, as this would constitute *lashon hara*.[2]

> **Reuven:** *Do you know what I saw Shimon do?*
> **Levi:** *Don't tell me ... speak to him.*

2. There are cases and aspects of wickedness which we may, and
   even at times should, publicize. In order to understand these
halachos, we will now discuss various levels of righteousness and
wickedness and the Torah way to react to them.

---

1. *Rambam, Hilchos Dei'os* 6:7.

2. *Chofetz Chaim, Hilchos Lashon Hara* 4:1.

Relating a Person's Past

3. It is a grave offense to malign a person who has mended his ways
    by saying that he behaved improperly in his early years. Similarly,
it is forbidden to describe someone's parents or ancestors as being disreputable, since he is thereby maligning their descendant, who has
not followed in their footsteps. Since this person has repented for his
misdeeds and/or does not imitate his parents' misdeeds, he is completely righteous in Hashem's eyes,[3] and no one has the right to disgrace him.[4]

> *The Sages have taught that even the totally righteous cannot stand
> in the place of those who have repented.*[5]

4. Therefore, those who in our times are called *baalei teshuvah*, hav-
    ing grown up in families distant from Torah and returned to the
ways of Torah on their own, deserve great respect. Unfortunately, as
some in our society fail to understand this, one should not divulge
information about the past of *baalei teshuvah*.[6] Similarly, converts are
held by our Sages in great esteem,[7] and their histories, too, should not
be divulged.

Beneficial Purpose

5. However, where a beneficial purpose exists, it can even be a mitz-
    vah to inform others of the past of such an individual.

> *If someone becomes friendly with a baal teshuvah and is ignorant of
> his background, he may unwittingly embarrass his friend or other-
> wise cause him discomfort. In such a case, it is a mitzvah to privately
> inform the person of his friend's background so that he can be sensi-
> tive to his situation and even give him any needed extra support and
> practical assistance.*[8]

---

3. *Rambam, Hilchos Teshuvah* 7:4.

4. *Chofetz Chaim* ibid.

5. *Berachos* 34b.

6. *Chofetz Chaim* ibid.; *Be'er Mayim Chaim* 1.

7. *Shaarei Teshuvah* 3:49 (see also *Rambam, Hilchos Dei'os* 6:4; *Reishis Chochmah, Shaarei Ahavah,* Ch.
1, where the love of a convert is incorporated in ten verses which speak of the love of Hashem).

8. See Ch. 21, "Beneficial *Lashon Hara*."

Say Nothing to a Rumormonger

6. It is best to remain silent if the person involved is known to enjoy
   talking about people and there is reason to suspect that he will
publicize any information he hears about his new friend. This consideration outweighs any beneficial purpose in speaking.[9] However, this
is an area in which it is difficult to formulate a general set of rules,
since many individual considerations exist in each case, with a great
deal depending on the public's attitude toward *baalei teshuvah* as well
as on the personalities and emotions of those involved. In cases of
doubt, the best recourse is to consult with a rav.

Without Beneficial Purpose

7. A cardinal rule in *lashon hara* is that it is forbidden to relate any
   information that would cause injury or embarrassment of any
kind were it to become generally known. Therefore, if the *baal teshuvah's* background is not known in his community it is forbidden to
reveal it, unless there is a specific beneficial purpose and the listener
is a person of discretion. If, however, (a) the information is generally
known except to a few scattered individuals, (b) the particular listener is a person of discretion who will not spread it further, and (c) the
listener appreciates that a *baal teshuvah* is worthy of esteem (so that
placing the information in his hands will not result in harm), then it is
permitted to relate the information to him, even without a specific
beneficial purpose.[10]

Respect for an Individual's Wishes

8. However, it is proper to remain silent if one knows that the person
   in question does not want information about his background to be
disseminated, since in general, a person's wishes are to be respected
unless a compelling reason exists to disregard them. Nonetheless, if
all the other conditions of paragraph 7 are met, it is not absolutely forbidden to speak.[11]

---

9. See Ch. 21 par. 3 (c).

10. Otherwise, it is forbidden even though the information is known; see *Rambam, Hilchos
Dei'os* 7:5; *Halichos Olam,* Ch. 11 fn. *zayin.*

11. See *Shevilei Chaim* 4:4; *Halichos Olam* ibid. fn. *ches.*

An Appearance of Impropriety — Can You Be Sure

9. If one sees a person speaking or behaving in a manner that seems wrong, he is required to interpret the situation favorably as long as it is possible to do so.

> *Mr. Gold is a member in good standing of the suburban Shomrei Shabbos shul. One Shabbos, someone spread the word that Mr. Gold was seen driving on Shabbos. The listeners are required to believe that even if true, he must have been driving to save someone's life.*

Does He Know It Is Wrong

10. An individual who is consistently seen transgressing a particular prohibition and whose behavior cannot be rectified through reproof (e.g. the subject will definitely not be swayed), still cannot be considered "wicked" until it can be ascertained that his actions are willful and not a result of ignorance. Unfortunately, not all mitzvos of the Torah are equally known for their severity when transgressed. Thus, while the prohibitions against eating *treife*, violating the Shabbos and immoral behavior are universally known among all mitzvah observers, others such as *lashon hara*, wasting time from Torah study and lack of adherence to some areas of *kashrus* are not as familiar. A certain type of ignorance causes many to consider these strictures applicable only to the very pious rather than incumbent on every Jew. If a person consistently violates one of the latter type of mitzvos, we must presume that he is not aware of the severity of his actions, and, in the area of interpersonal relationships, he is not considered "wicked."[12]

> *One day, Reuven visited the home of Mr. A, who was observant but unlearned, and noticed with distress that the non-Jewish help was cooking supper. (Food cooked completely by a non-Jew is forbidden; see Yoreh Deah 113.) He later met Shimon and related what he had seen. Shimon inquired if Mrs. A might have turned on the fire, making it permissible according to Ashkenazic custom, but Reuven claimed that this was not the case. "Well,"*

---

12. *Chofetz Chaim, Hilchos Lashon Hara* 4:3.

said Shimon, "it is not your job to tell me; that's lashon hara, a *worse offense. Mr. A surely does not know of this halachah, and he is not to be considered wicked, chas v'shalom. Since you witnessed this incident, why don't you figure out a way to explain the prohibition, perhaps by learning the relevant chapter in Yoreh Deah together with him!"*

If It Is Clear That Wrong Was Done

11. A Jew who is seen committing an act universally known to be prohibited (eating *treife*, adultery, etc.) and it is clear that his action was done deliberately, is not yet considered "wicked" if he is an average mitzvah-observing Jew, and it is forbidden to tell others about his actions as he might have already done *teshuvah*.[13] Since a measure of doubt exists, we are to assume that the person has done *teshuvah*, as is normally to be expected of a proper Jew.[14]

12. Nonetheless, a person who is pure of soul and therefore avoids contact with evil[15] is allowed to distance himself from the wrongdoer until it can be established with certainty that he has repented of his evil practice. Furthermore, someone who has seen this action is permitted to relate the incident to a sage[16] who is a "pure" person and is known to be discreet, *if* the witness knows that, in general, the sage trusts him implicitly. This person can then distance himself from the wrongdoer's company until he repents.[17]

> *Mr. Silver is one of the wealthiest and most prominent men in the Rebbe's shtiebel. One day, a beggar approached Mr. Silver demanding a large donation. Mr. Silver tried to talk to him but the beggar rudely persevered, whereupon Mr. Silver became infuriated, publicly slapped him on the face and threw him out the door. Chaim Gold, a cheder boy*

---

13. Since, after all, it is impossible to know if someone has done *teshuvah*, which is a matter hidden in a person's heart.

14. *Chofetz Chaim* ibid. 4:4.

15. This comes naturally to those who truly fear Hashem, as the Psalmist says, *O lovers of Hashem, hate evil!* (*Tehillim* 97:10); see Ch. 4 par. 8.

16. "Sage" here is an example of a wise and righteous person, but he/she does not have to be a scholar.

17. *Shaarei Teshuvah* 3:215; *Chofetz Chaim, Hilchos Lashon Hara* 4:4, *Be'er Mayim Chaim* 17; see *Kodesh Yisrael*, Ch. 9 at length; *Halichos Olam*, Ch. 11 fn. *lamed*.

who saw the whole incident, expressed his fury to his father. "How could Mr. Silver do that, especially to such a poor person! He violated the prohibitions against hitting a person and embarrassing someone publicly." Mr. Gold quietly explained to Chaim, "Mr. Silver is, in general, an upstanding Jew, and surely already regrets how he behaved in a fit of anger. Therefore, we have to treat him as we always have."

The following Shabbos, Mr. Gold insisted that Chaim go over to Mr. Silver and wish him "Good Shabbos" in a pleasant fashion. Chaim then ran over to watch the saintly Rebbe as all the people passed by to wish him a good Shabbos. When Mr. Silver approached, the Rebbe refused to give him his hand, instead closing his eyes, and quietly stating, "It is forbidden to gaze upon a wicked person."

Chaim, completely puzzled, ran to his father and related the Rebbe's actions. "And you told me to give him a pleasant 'good Shabbos'!" "Ah!" the wise father explained, "You were angry, and wanted to take revenge by treating him with disdain and avoiding him. It is prohibited to do so, since he probably regrets his action and has started to do teshuvah. The Rebbe, on the other hand, bears no personal anger toward him, but his pure soul is extremely sensitive to evil. Just wait ... by Yom Kippur the Rebbe will have influenced Mr. Silver to do teshuvah." As predicted, when Mr. Silver greeted the Rebbe on Yom Kippur, the Rebbe warmly took his hand and blessed him for a good year, knowing that he had done teshuvah.

When One May Tell a Third Party

13. If a person sees another Jew doing wrong, and judges that while the wrongdoer will not accept reproof from him, a family member or rav might be able to influence him, he may convey his knowledge to the third party in the hope of rectifying the situation. However, as discussed in Chapter 21 (paragraphs 6-9), this third party must be wise and discreet so that the matter will not come to be known publicly, causing the subject embarrassment. If he is not discreet, the matter should not be discussed with him.

14. This applies only in a situation where the subject is known to have periodically committed wrong acts but is not set in his evil ways. If, however, one judges that the wrongdoer is already set in his ways and is likely to continue them, then the *halachah* depends on the nature of the

wrong action observed. If it is one of the universally known transgressions (such as violating the Shabbos, eating *treife*, etc.; see paragraph 10), then one is permitted to relate the incident to a potentially positive influence even if the latter is not particularly discreet.[18] However, if the severity of the action involved is not widely understood but is mistakenly believed to be merely a stricture or commendably pious practice (such as laxity in Torah study, speaking *lashon hara*, *ona'as devarim*, etc.; see paragraph 10), then it should not be related to an individual liable to disseminate it, even if he may be able to influence the wrongdoer. Since the wrongdoer might not realize the extent of his transgression, the mere fact that he acted this way does not make him a wicked person, and there is no justification for causing him public disgrace.

15. There might be room for flexibility, even if the third party is generally not discreet, if one judges that when cautioned, he would speak only to the wrongdoer and not discuss the matter with anyone else.[19] In all such gray areas, however, one must seek the guidance of a competent *halachic* authority before taking any action.

> *Chaim and Yaakov were both fine students at the Eitz Chaim kollel. Yaakov left kollel to join a business firm, and soon rose to an executive position. Chaim noticed that Yaakov did not set aside time for Torah study. Mr. Smith, the highly successful president of the firm, learned Torah regularly and was greatly admired by Yaakov. Chaim judged that Mr. Smith was probably in a position to convince Yaakov to set aside time for meaningful Torah study. However, Mr. Smith was not known to be particularly discreet and Chaim feared that Yaakov's lack of learning would be publicized, embarrassing him and his family. Chaim consulted a prominent rav who knew Mr. Smith well. The rav judged that Mr. Smith would honor a request not to discuss the matter further, and told Chaim to go ahead and speak to him with that stipulation.*

If One Is a Witness

16. The Torah teaches (*Shemos* 23:1), *Do not extend your hand with the wicked to be a fraudulent witness.* As defined by Torah law (*D'Oraisa*), anyone who violates a prohibition associated with fraud, or who violates any Torah prohibition punishable by lashes is deemed

---

18. *Chofetz Chaim, Hilchos Lashon Hara* 4:6.
19. See *Kodesh Yisrael* 9:6; see also *Chofetz Chaim, Hilchos Rechilus* 9:12.

"wicked" and disqualified from being a witness.[20] Thus, if two qualified witnesses[21] see a person deliberately commit a transgression that disqualifies him from being a witness, they are required to testify about this before *beis din*. This applies if the wrongdoer's fitness to testify is of current practical relevance, e.g. he is to give testimony in a *beis din* or be an official witness to marriage or divorce proceedings or monetary transactions, or is himself acting as a *dayan* in a monetary case. However, if his suitability as a witness is not immediately relevant, then it is best that they not testify at once, as he might do *teshuvah* in the interim.[22]

> *Reuven, who was known as a generally pleasant person, often lost his temper at home, and, on occasion, would even strike his wife. He well knew that such physical violence is a Torah prohibition punishable by lashes that disqualifies a person from testifying in a court, yet in the heat of anger he would lose control. One day, he had a disagreement with his wife in the kitchen when his friends Shimon and Levi were in another room. Hearing the increasingly angry tone of the argument, they decided to walk into the kitchen, figuring that their presence would be a calming factor. Just as they entered the room, however, Reuven slapped his wife. Since Reuven was regularly employed by the local beis din as a witness, Shimon and Levi were obligated to go to the beis din and testify that he was disqualified from doing so. (Example continues in the next paragraph.)*

17. The above rule applies only to two qualified witnesses whose testimony is accepted in *beis din*. However, if the witnesses are unqualified (or if there is only one witness), they are forbidden to relate testimony to *beis din*; since it is unacceptable, it is considered *lashon hara* (and anyone who does relate such testimony is liable for corporal punishment).[23] Nevertheless, a person who has such information should privately inform anyone planning to use the wrongdoer as a witness, if he is confident that this individual will believe him and act accordingly, rather than reject the report out of hand.[24]

---

20. *Choshen Mishpat* 34:1.

21. The witnesses have to be adult males not related to each other nor to the defendant or the judge, and must not be in the category of the "wicked." See *Choshen Mishpat, Hilchos Eidus*.

22. *Chofetz Chaim, Hilchos Lashon Hara* 4:4, *Be'er Mayim Chaim* 16.

23. *Pesachim* 113b.

24. Cf. *Kiddushin* 66a; *Chofetz Chaim, Hilchos Lashon Hara* 4:4, fn.

If Shimon alone had seen the incident, he would be prohibited from testifying about it in beis din. Nevertheless, if he knew that Reuven was supposed to be a witness at a wedding that evening, it would be proper to advise the bridegroom to look for a replacement, unless he suspects that the bridegroom will reject his statement. (The bridegroom is entitled to do so; however, if the information is true, the wedding may be disqualified and he may not be considered married.) Moreover, even if there were no witnesses to his behavior, Reuven should disqualify himself from serving as a witness, if he himself recognizes that he has not properly repented.

A Person Who Rejects Even One Mitzvah

18. Everything we discussed so far applies to a Jew who is committed to observing all the mitzvos of the Torah, even if he slips and transgresses on occasion. However, there are individuals who refuse to accept one mitzvah or one *halachah*, and make statements such as, "I do not do this mitzvah," or "This *halachah* is not for me." Although he may observe all the other mitzvos of the Torah, he belongs in the category of *mumar l'davar echad* (rebel concerning one matter).[25] Such a person still has the full status of a Jew, since he believes in the Divine origin of all the mitzvos (including the one his desires have ensnared him into rejecting), but is classed not with righteous Jews but with the wicked. The rules of *lashon hara* are greatly altered with regard to wicked people, as explained below.[26]

Who Is Not Considered "Wicked"

19. Nevertheless, such a person is not classified as "wicked" in the area of practical *halachah* unless the mitzvah he rejects is well-known to all Torah-observant Jews. We can then be certain that he knows it is a commandment of Hashem and he knowingly and willfully rejects the authority of Heaven in this matter. If, however, the mitzvah involved is one of whose gravity not every Jew is aware (see paragraph 10), there is room to judge favorably and suspect that the

---

25. This is comparable to a servant who tells his master he will obey all the master's commands except one; even if he does everything else the master tells him to, he is still considered a rebel because he has rejected his master's authority over him (*Shaarei Teshuvah* 1:6).

26. *Chofetz Chaim* 4:7; see *Nesiv Chaim* 4:12; *Halichos Olam*, Ch. 11 fn. *kuf*.

individual in question believes it to be merely a stringency observed only by very pious people. The reason for this may be that he sees that others who are considered upstanding Jews also do not adhere to this mitzvah, even though it is, in reality, a very serious transgression. Therefore, even though he is rejecting the authority of Heaven regarding this one commandment, we still cannot classify him as a "wicked" person who may be disgraced in public.

> *Mrs. Ploni is a baalas lashon hara who constantly speaks about others in a negative light. Her friends have reminded her that lashon hara is a serious prohibition but she responds, "I do other mitzvos — this one isn't for me." The women asked a rav if she is to be considered "wicked," and if, as a "mumar l'davar echad" — she can be publicly embarrassed. The rav answered that if she is aware of the absolute prohibition against lashon hara, then she is indeed a mumar l'davar echad — but we don't know that. She may be thinking that many upstanding Jews speak lashon hara and the whole issue is an exaggeration. We must presume that she doesn't realize that lashon hara really is "treife" and we therefore cannot malign her in public. However, a habitual speaker of lashon hara, who knows that it is absolutely prohibited, is considered a mumar l'davar echad in Heaven, chas v'shalom.*
>
> *(Note: Even though the woman may not be publicly maligned, it is not permitted to have close associations with a baalas lashon hara. See example after paragraph 20.)*

Altering the Laws of *Lashon Hara* Regarding a "Wicked" Person

20. It is the nature of a human being to be highly influenced by his surroundings. Therefore, it is a mitzvah to create an atmosphere in the Jewish home and community that extols truth and abhors falsehood. When these values are absorbed into the essence of the society, the society achieves its purpose in creation. In an atmosphere where these ideals are revered, people are motivated to follow goodness and truth, and those who have acted in an evil way are motivated to change. In order to create and preserve such an atmosphere, any person who flagrantly abrogates a mitzvah of the Torah must be publicly disgraced, in which case the laws of *lashon hara* do not apply. Thus, the

prophets consistently denounced any deviation from the Torah, such as turning away from Hashem and injustice in society. Preserving an atmosphere that extols Torah values also contains a benefit for the sinner, for its existence creates a powerful motivation for him to change his ways and regain acceptance in society.[27]

> *Thus, maligning those who flagrantly violate the Torah serves as a tool to preserve Torah values and to motivate its violators to change their ways. These are powerful tools that can be put to good use but misused as well. In any unique situation that arises, a rav should always be consulted as to what is appropriate.*

Exposing a Person
Who Acts Like a *Tzaddik* in Public

21. The true wickedness of someone who acts righteously in public but is privately seen to reject even one mitzvah[28] should be publicized; we need not be concerned that we are speaking *lashon hara*. The Sages said that hypocrites, who cause a desecration of Hashem's Name, should be exposed so that people will not come to learn from them.[29]

The Need for Definite Knowledge

22. The above ruling applies only if there is definite knowledge of the subject's wickedness. It is forbidden, however, to spread unfavorable information acquired through hearsay, since it is forbidden to believe *lashon hara* heard from others. One must suspect that

---

27. *Chofetz Chaim, Hilchos Lashon Hara* ibid. Note: In our humble opinion, the seemingly insurmountable problems of crime and immorality in modern society are directly connected to the atmosphere created by the media. If there were a total ban on the reporting of crime and immorality, and all entertainment would shun these scourges, their levels would eventually drop drastically to the point of practical nonexistence. However, as a vacuum cannot exist, the newspapers and media would have to extol virtues and acts of kindness in their place, and thus create a positive atmosphere in society. Although this ideal is not within the reach of any one individual, the atmosphere in one's own home is an area over which a person has definite influence. Thus, we must heed the constant call of the Torah Sages to shun television, videos, and other such poisonous influences in our homes.

28. Note: There must be no doubt about his rejection of a mitzvah, for if there is any doubt, we must judge him favorably, as explained in Ch. 2.

29. *Chofetz Chaim, Hilchos Lashon Hara* ibid.

the negative reports are false or misleading and therefore one is forbidden to repeat them.

> The Rebbe, known as a saintly person, was seen ushering five men notorious for their criminal activities into his study. The next week they returned, and it soon became a weekly habit for these five men to meet with the Rebbe every Tuesday morning. Rumors swirled that the Rebbe was involved in crime, and was really just a hypocrite. When construction started on a new shul building, the rumors gained new impetus; the Rebbe was using "dirty" money for the project. One day the police came to speak to the Rebbe, and the rumors grew in strength; the Rebbe was being questioned about his criminal associations. People were sure that it was a mitzvah to discuss the matter in order to expose a hypocrite. The Rebbe remained silent and refused to answer when questioned about the weekly meetings, which only strengthened the rumors. Those "in the know" opined that the Rebbe was in financial trouble, causing him to stoop to such unsavory activities. And so it went until the newspapers carried the following headline: COURT SUSPENDS SENTENCE ON FIVE CRIMINALS BASED ON RABBI'S TESTIMONY OF THEIR REFORMED WAYS. Shortly afterwards, the new shul building was completed, and the Rebbe published a complete accounting of its funding. Not one penny came from these five men, but the saintly Rebbe welcomed five new congregants who had abandoned their lives of crime.
>
> Those "in the know" do not always know.
>
> "Everyone is saying ..." does not mean that they spoke the truth.
>
> Be extremely careful when "exposing the hypocrite" not to wrongly suspect the righteous in the process.

Required Conditions for Permitted *Lashon Hara*

23. In all cases where it is permitted, and even a mitzvah, to relate information about an individual's disgraceful behavior, the following conditions must be fulfilled. If any one of them is absent, the statement becomes pure *lashon hara* and is as strictly forbidden as any other *lashon hara* — *even though the subject is classified as "wicked."*[30]

(a) The sole intention must be to protect upstanding Jews from the influence of wicked people, or to motivate the wrongdoer to change

---

30. *Chofetz Chaim, Hilchos Lashon Hara* 4:4, *Be'er Mayim Chaim* 30, 32; see also *Kodesh Yisrael*, Ch. 14.

his evil ways through seeing the shame and dishonor to which wicked people are subject. It is forbidden to speak out of personal dislike, as the individual in question still retains the status of a Torah-observant Jew whom we are required to treat with respect and consideration except and to the extent that overriding circumstances require otherwise.

(b) It is also forbidden to relate this *lashon hara* in private, if the speaker publicly flatters the subject and attempts to win his favor. Thus, permitted *lashon hara* may be spoken only in the presence of three or more people. However, it is allowed to relate the *lashon hara* to individuals if there is reason to fear that the subject will seek revenge, or that a public quarrel will result.

(c) Even when *lashon hara* is permitted, it is forbidden to exaggerate the subject's wrongdoing, making it seem greater in any way.

(d) Likewise, when *lashon hara* is permitted, the speaker must be totally innocent of the fault he is criticizing in the subject. If he himself is occasionally guilty of the same fault, then he is forbidden from ascribing it to others. In such a case, he is considered to be simply gloating over the wrongdoer's faults, a form of *lashon hara*, rather than properly holding him up to disgrace.[31]

> *Mr. B, a respected person of means, was discovered to have secretly been a partner in a notorious gang of thieves.*
>
> *The rav of the city gathered a number of prominent people to an emergency meeting. He gave instructions that a special announcement in his name be made in every shul the following Shabbos denouncing Mr. B. However, the rav continued, the following crucial conditions must be met:*
>
> *(a) Anyone with a personal grudge against Mr. B is not permitted to make this announcement.*
>
> *(b) No one may discuss the matter privately with a friend before Shabbos.*
>
> *(c) This gang is involved in robbery, not murder. The announcement must be precise and not exaggerate the nature of the crime.*
>
> *(d) Finally, anyone with any irregularities in his own business is not permitted to make this announcement.*

---

31. *Shaarei Teshuvah* 3:219.

One Who Totally Rejects the Torah

24. The above restrictions apply only to an individual who basically acts as a proper Jew and whose failings are limited to one or several mitzvos. However, a Jew who totally rejects the Torah and behaves like a gentile, or even who practices the mitzvos but denies the Divinity of any part of the Torah, has the status of an *apikores*[32] and these restrictions therefore do not apply.

In Our Times

25. The situation today is radically different from any period in the past. Unfortunately, most Jews have grown up with little, if any, knowledge of the Torah and its commandments and no appreciation of the true meaning and spirit of Judaism. The status of a "wicked" person in terms of the laws of interpersonal relationships is practically non-existent, even among those raised in a genuinely Jewish environment. That status can be applied only after a person has been reproved and has rejected efforts to correct his faults. The ability to do so properly, gently and with sensitivity is rarely to be found in our time. Therefore, one should never gratuitously relate derogatory information about any Jew, except for the explicit purpose of creating a positive atmosphere by negating and disgracing negative influences (as explained in paragraph 20). Similarly, unless otherwise specified, one should be stringent regarding all the interpersonal mitzvos with all Jews, religious or secular.[33]

> *Sam was a member in good standing of his synagogue, until one day a rumor spread that he was engaging in prohibited behavior. Rabbi B was very disturbed and sent David, a devout Jew, to investigate the matter. A few days later David returned to the rabbi and reported that, to his chagrin, he believed that Sam had become a mumar l'davar echad, for when David asked about his behavior, Sam had become agitated and had answered, "Well, that mitzvah is not for me. I just don't believe in it!" The rabbi answered softly,*

---

32. A general term for someone who rejects the authority of Hashem and His Torah. Such a person, although born Jewish, is not privileged to be considered a fellow Jew regarding many laws of the Torah. *Chofetz Chaim, Hilchos Lashon Hara* 8:5.

33. See *Hagahos Maimoniyos, Hilchos Dei'os*, Ch. 6, *alef; Ahavas Chesed* (HaRav Y. Malin at the end of the *sefer*); *Chazon Ish, Yoreh Deah*, Ch. 2 (heard from a *gadol*); *Halichos Olam*, Ch. 11 fn. *nun.*

"My dear Reb David, according to you, he is a complete apikores, because saying, 'I don't believe in a mitzvah' is a denial of the Torah. But what does Sam know about emunah? He was raised in a non-Torah environment, and has no real understanding of 'fear of Hashem.' Has anyone ever explained to him that his whole being exists only to do the will of Hashem? No, he cannot be termed a rejecter of the Torah, having never really known it. We must help him learn that sin is defined as more than society's idea of poor behavior while ensuring that others don't copy his deviant ways."

The Approach to the Secular World

26. It is a mitzvah to create an atmosphere in the Jewish home and community that extols virtue, truth, and kindness. Therefore, crime, immorality, and, in general, any rejection of Hashem's Torah are negative values that must be eradicated. However, in so doing, one should focus only on the wrongdoer's *actions*, while treating the person himself as a *tinok she'nishbah* (a Jew captured by gentiles as an infant and raised under their influence) who does wrong only because of the influence of his surroundings. He should be treated with the fellowship that one extends to any Jew.[34] Similarly, it is incumbent upon a Jew to treat the people of all nations with dignity and kindness, while sharply rejecting their materialistic culture, as the verse says, *Its [the Torah's] ways are ways of pleasantness and all its pathways are peace* (*Proverbs* 3:17). Furthermore, the Psalmist says, *Hashem is good to all, and His compassion is on all His creations* (*Tehillim* 145:9).[35]

---

34. See *Rambam, Hilchos Mamrim* 3:3; *Kodesh Yisrael*, Chs. 14,20.

35. See *Rambam, Hilchos Melachim* 10:12; *Halichos Olam*, Ch. 26 fn. *kuf*, and Ch. 32 fn. *pei*.

24

Defending Justice

1. One of the pillars of the world is justice.[1] Hashem called Avraham "beloved" because he taught his descendants to perform deeds of righteousness and justice.[2] The prophet extols justice in a superlative way: *Champion the cause of the poor and impoverished ... for this is knowledge of Me, says Hashem* (Yirmiyahu 22:16). The performance of this mitzvah is not limited to a king, *beis din* or community; every individual must strive to right the wrongs of injustice and stand up for the truth. Indeed, it is an integral aspect of honoring Hashem.[3]

2. Therefore, if a person sees one person wrong another — by stealing, or causing damage, embarrassment, slander, cruelty, etc., and he knows that the offender has not rectified the damage (by returning the money, making restitution for the damage, or stopping the abusive behavior and apologizing) and thus the victim is still suffering — he should stand with the wronged party and not allow this injustice to continue.[4]

---

1. *Avos* 1:18
2. *Bereishis* 18:19.
3. *Shaarei Teshuvah* 4:5; see *Kodesh Yisrael*, Ch. 16.
4. *Shaarei Teshuvah* ibid. See also 3:221.

3. In such a situation, the preferred course of action is for the person who saw the wrong to privately approach the wrongdoer and attempt to convince him, in a gentle and friendly manner, that he has done wrong and needs to change his ways and make restitution for his actions.[5] If this approach is not effective, or if one judges that it is not likely to be so, the next recourse is to enlist the help of an individual better suited to approach the wrongdoer, as discussed in Chapter 21, paragraph 9.

4. Should these means prove unsuccessful, then it is permitted to publicize the wrongdoer's action in order to ensure justice. Consequently, the disrepute in which such individuals are held will be clear to all observers, who will then avoid similar behavior. It is also to be hoped that the culprit himself will be moved to repent and make restitution for his wrongs.[6]

> *Mr. and Mrs. A separated after years of an acrimonious marriage. Mr. A publicly announced that he would give his wife a get (Torah divorce), but postponed doing so in an effort to avenge himself by making her an agunah (a woman unable to remarry) or to at least extort a sizable sum of money in exchange for the get. When the rav got wind of Mr. A's true intentions, he immediately went to speak to him. He began by gently extolling the virtues of kindness and overcoming anger. When Mr. A refused to listen, the rav tried another tactic by vividly describing the tortures of Gehinnom awaiting a person who cruelly made a woman an agunah. When Mr. A remained adamant (I don't care if I suffer, as long as she feels the face of my anger!) the rav decided that it was necessary to publicize the matter. However, he refused to discuss it privately lest it be perceived that he had a personal vendetta against Mr. A (see paragraph 16). Before the Torah reading one Shabbos, he mounted the pulpit and addressed the large crowd, sharply condemning the specter of any man, and Mr. A specifically, inflicting an agunah status on a woman. Calling him "wicked" and "disgusting," he further stated that a community that tolerates such behavior has no right to identify itself with the children of Avraham Avinu, whose entire life was dedicated to kindness. He*

---

5. *Chofetz Chaim, Hilchos Lashon Hara, Ch. 10, Be'er Mayim Chaim 7.*

6. Ibid. 10:1. See *Kodesh Yisrael, Ch. 16.*

charged them with the need to expel this wickedness from their midst and constantly excoriate such behavior so that no one would dare even consider it. The rav ended with an emotional call to Mr. A, and the entire community, to return to the true Torah way and forever desist from behavior so uncharacteristic of the children of Avraham Avinu.

5. One must be certain before undertaking this course of action that doing so will not cause even greater problems. We will now discuss a number of essential considerations that must be taken into account in any such situation.

Pure Motives

6. The purpose of publicizing the wrong must be purely with the objective of righting it, rather than in order to derive enjoyment from disgracing the wrongdoer. One must also be certain that publicizing the incident will not simply cause or add fuel to public disputes. Therefore, it is not only futile to discuss it with people who do not disapprove of the wrong committed, but very likely to lead to greater controversy.[7]

> *In a meeting of the executive committee, Mr. Jones humiliated Mr. Smith by calling him an idiot. Mr. Robert, a member of the committee, privately tried to convince Mr. Jones to apologize. Mr. Jones refused, saying, "Considering what he did, he is an idiot!" Mr. Robert was furious, and decided not to let the matter rest. That Shabbos, after davening, he loudly declared, "I have an announcement." Surprised, everyone gathered to hear his words. "Mr. Jones," he began, "is a real rasha," and proceeded to detail all the insult and humiliation thrown at Mr. Smith. The reaction was mixed, with some people supporting Mr. Robert, and others minimizing the incident. "So he insulted him, big deal! These things happen all the time." And from others, "Wait till Jones hears this." Soon Jones did hear about it and a major feud erupted in town.*
>
> *Mr. Robert, although attempting to protect Mr. Smith and reform Mr. Jones, as well as prevent further shameful behavior, ended up causing discord and disharmony. He should have realized that his listeners did not feel as strongly as he about such behavior, and it*

---

7. *Chofetz Chaim* ibid. 10:4.

was useless to speak to them (and his words are therefore considered lashon hara).

7. Similarly, the incident should not be discussed with those likely to use it as fuel for intergroup rivalries (e.g. rival groups of Chassidim, Chassidim and *misnagdim*, or Ashkenazic and Sephardic groups).

> **Chaim:** *One of the ... ran away with a pile of other people's money.*
> **David:** *Well, what do you expect, all of the ... don't care about other people's money.*

In this scenario, one has not only thwarted the desired goal of bringing disrepute to wrongdoers, but has instead promoted dispute and senseless hatred among Jews.

Avoiding Hypocrisy

8. Anyone guilty of a certain offense is forbidden to speak out against it. He would only be proving himself a hypocrite who wishes not to rectify the behavior of wrongdoers, but merely to gloat over their failings.[8]

> *Rabbeinu Yonah (3:219) writes, "How can anyone not be ashamed to talk about someone else's vices when he is guilty of the same vice?"*

Necessary Conditions

9. Before one is allowed to speak, all the conditions discussed in Chapter 21, paragraphs 3-6 must be fulfilled. In the next few paragraphs, we will review these conditions and focus on certain particularly relevant aspects.

(a) One must be certain that the information being publicized is entirely accurate; therefore, the speaker must either have personally witnessed the incident, or else ascertain that it happened exactly as he was told.[9]

(b) The speaker must be certain that the Torah unequivocally forbids the action in question. This requires not only a thorough knowledge of all the relevant *halachic* issues, but often entails a clear analysis of the facts of the case as well as an understanding of the motives of the people involved. If a Torah scholar is involved, it is particu-

---

8. Ibid. 10:3.

9. See Chapter 13 as to when information heard can be believed and related.

larly important to reach a fundamental and comprehensive understanding of all the circumstances surrounding the incident before taking action.[10]

(c) Only that which is absolutely necessary to accomplish the desired purpose may be said and no more. Thus, if the same goal can be accomplished by omitting one or more aspects of the story, it is forbidden to publicize those points.[11]

(d) It is also forbidden to speak if publicizing the incident will cause the wrongdoer to suffer more severely than were he found guilty in a *beis din*. While having one's misdeeds publicized is generally a serious matter in itself, it is permitted in cases such as these because of the expected benefits to society at large and to the wronged party in particular. However, if the wrongdoer is likely to be disproportionately harmed for the gravity of his offense, then it is forbidden to say anything at all.[12]

> *Yanki, Yoni and Shimon were roommates in a yeshivah high school. In the privacy of their room, Yanki constantly hurled verbal abuse at his roommates, and would occasionally hurt them physically as well. Yoni and Shimon begged Yanki to stop but he refused to listen. They spoke to the Mashgiach and Rosh Yeshivah, who tried to intervene, but to no avail. The Rosh Yeshivah and Mashgiach met to review their options. They agreed that switching roommates would not help, as Yanki would only continue his abusive behavior with new victims. They then discussed publicizing the story, hoping that Yanki would be embarrassed and stop his behavior. It would also give the entire yeshivah a clear lesson on Torah values.*
>
> *They considered that (a) the information is clearly accurate; (b) Yanki's actions are absolutely forbidden by the Torah; and (c) Yanki has in no way made amends for his negative behavior.*
>
> *They then analyzed which aspects to publicize: the verbal abuse alone or the physical attacks as well? Furthermore, how will Yanki's future be affected? Will he ever be accepted in a yeshivah of higher learning or will this publicity close all doors to an otherwise bright, capable young man? Would Yanki agree to get help for his prob-*

---

10. Ibid. 10:2. A Torah scholar usually acts according to the Torah's guidelines; therefore, one should not decide that his actions were improper until a complete and thorough investigation is conducted on his actions and motivations.

11. Ibid.

12. Ibid. and *Nesiv Chaim* 8.

lems? Perhaps they should expel him from yeshivah without any public explanation. They ultimately decided to consult a wise Torah sage and follow his advice.

The End Does Not Always Justify the Means

10. Although it is a mitzvah to pursue justice by rescuing people from those who would harm them, one is not allowed to commit other transgressions in the process. For instance, it is forbidden to speak if the victim is unaware that he was wronged and would have remained ignorant were it not for the current publicity; in such a case, the revelation itself constitutes *rechilus*.[13]

> *Sam and David were the two main candidates for a lucrative job opening at the Jones Aviation Company. Sam, whose credentials were superior to David's, was more likely to get the position. However, David's brother Sol decided to ensure that the job go to his brother. He met with every member of the Jones Company board of directors and slandered Sam to the point that he would be considered a liability to the company. Indeed, at the next meeting, the job was given to David. Chaim knew the whole story, and asked a rav if he was permitted to publicize it. "Publicly embarrassing Sol for his lashon hara will bring people to appreciate the evil of such behavior," he stated. "Furthermore, Sol will be forced to apologize to Sam, and perhaps even help him find another job." "The only problem," answered the rav, "is that Sam has no knowledge of the incident. Publicizing it is a form of telling him, and would therefore be considered rechilus."*

However, it is sometimes necessary to inform a person that he is being wronged so that he can protect himself from future harm. Since the victim must be told, it is then also permitted to publicize the matter in order to accomplish the beneficial purposes described in paragraph 4.[14]

> *In the above example, if the board had not yet met, it may still be possible to undo the harm, and enable Sam to get the job. One could then go to speak to the members of the board describing the injustice of Sol's slander, even if Sam would then learn of the incident.*

---

13. It would seem that even if he did know about it but had not been so upset until it became a public issue, it would also be *rechilus*; see Ch. 8.

14. Ibid. 10:4; see also the fn. and *Be'er Mayim Chaim* 17,18.

11. It is irrelevant whether or not the victim has requested the information. When it is permitted to give him the information, it remains so even if he did not ask, and likewise, when forbidden, it is so even if he did ask.

12. It is forbidden to speak if there is any reason to fear that publicizing the matter will lead to the betrayal of the wrongdoer to secular authorities.[15]

> *If Sol (see example, paragraph 10) illegally bribed the members of the board, an action carrying a two-year jail sentence, then publicizing the incident would be prohibited as it would, in effect, send Sol to jail.*

The Wronged Party May Not Himself Speak

13. Although, as explained, it is permitted, and even a mitzvah, to publicize a wrong in order to promote truth and justice, *this mitzvah applies only to those who are not personally involved.* The injured party himself is forbidden to publicize the injustice, since he is judged to be seeking revenge rather than championing justice. He wishes to make his opponent look bad in people's eyes; indeed, the greater the wrongdoer's suffering, the happier he is. This also applies to the injured party's relatives and close friends, since they too feel the pain of his mistreatment and would enjoy disgracing the wrongdoer as well.[16]

> *Reb David, envious of Reb Noach's position, spread slanderous stories about him. Reb Noach feared for his reputation and begged Reb David to withdraw his statements. He also approached friends of Reb David to intercede, to no avail. He then asked a rav for permission to "reveal the truth" about Reb David. "Such behavior cannot be allowed to go unchallenged!" he thundered. The rav replied, "Although it is a proper action, you cannot undertake it. Instead, I will do it."*

14. If it is forbidden to speak of an actual injury one has suffered at another's hands, all the more so is it forbidden to relate the failure of others to do the favors required of Jews, such as lending money, giving *tzedakah*, or extending hospitality.[17]

---

15. Ibid. 10:4.

16. Ibid. 10:11.

17. Ibid. 10:12.

Unfortunately, it is very common for people to complain that the Jews in a certain city they have visited did not give them a proper reception ("They don't say 'shalom aleichem' there!" or "They were not very friendly," or "They were stingy in giving tzedakah," etc.) In doing so, not only do they fail to fulfill the mitzvah of giving others the benefit of the doubt, they actually speak lashon hara about an entire community, a far more serious offense than lashon hara about individuals.

Relatives Do Not Have Preference

15. The fact that the victim is a friend, relative, parent, rebbi, student or any other close associate of the witness to the wrong makes no difference as far as all the conditions and considerations described in this chapter (and elsewhere in this book) are concerned. Many people make the mistake of thinking that it is a mitzvah to publicize or avenge a wrong done to one of their relatives, when in fact it is usually a great transgression.[18]

❏ *"Everyone needs to know what they did to my father." (This is not a mitzvah, but rather involves a number of prohibitions.)*

❏ *"He spoke about me (my brother, friend); therefore I will speak about him." (This is a violation of the prohibitions against lashon hara, hatred and vengeance.)*

The Means of Defending Justice

16. When publicizing information about a wrong inflicted upon another, one must speak to an audience of at least three people. If he speaks privately to only one or two people, it could be suspected that the speaker is conducting his campaign in secret as a personal vendetta rather than for the purpose of establishing justice. It might also be suspected that the speaker is lying; were he telling the truth he would confront the wrongdoer directly. If that did not succeed he would at least spread the information in public rather than in secret, as is the way of liars.[19]

In the example cited in paragraph 4, the rav did not speak about Mr. A in private so that it should not seem as if he were conducting a personal vendetta.

---

18. Ibid. 10:4.
19. Ibid. 10:7.

17. If, however, the speaker has reason to fear the wrongdoer's wrath, then it is permitted to speak in private. Also, if the speaker has an outstanding reputation for integrity and is not afraid to speak the truth no matter who is present, then he is permitted to speak in private as no one would suspect him of lying or flattery.

In the above example, the rav could have even spoken privately if he commands so much respect from the entire community that no one would even entertain the thought that his words were not purely for the sake of Heaven.

Similarly, if the listeners are aware that the speaker has already confronted the wrongdoer directly without success, so that there is no reason to suspect any of the possibilities mentioned above, it is permitted to relate the information to only one person.[20]

After the speech, the rav may subsequently speak privately to individuals, for there is no more room for suspicion.

Forestalling the Damage Caused by *Lashon Hara*

18. Sometimes, a person sees someone spreading *lashon hara* about another individual, and judges that the speaker will probably continue doing so and that his *lashon hara* is likely to become generally accepted as true (since, unfortunately, we are all prone to believing *lashon hara*). Furthermore, it will be difficult to later correct that wrong impression, since people are inclined to believe the first account heard of an incident. In such a case, it is a mitzvah to approach all those who have not yet heard the *lashon hara* and to try to impress upon them the great wrong being done by the one who is spreading defamatory information about an individual with a presumption of innocence. When they eventually do hear the *lashon hara*, they will have been forewarned and will not believe it, and may even reprove the speaker regarding his behavior.

Mr. Green, who until now owned the sole kosher butcher shop in Midcity, became very worried when Mr. Brown opened a competing store. After some investigation, Mr. Green discovered that Mr. Brown had not always been religious. He spread the word around town, with the implication that the kashrus of such a person could

---

20. Ibid. 10:8,9.

not be trusted. Mr. Schwartz, who personally knew both Mr. Green and Mr. Brown, realized that Mr. Green was perpetrating a terrible injustice with his slander. He therefore called every single religious Jew in Midcity and explained that Mr. Green was spreading completely unjustified rumors about Mr. Brown, thereby completely neutralizing the effect of Mr. Green's slander.

19. The course of action described in paragraph 18 is allowed even if the subject of the *lashon hara* has no knowledge of what has been said against him, since it is to his benefit. Nonetheless, one must be certain before taking such action that all the conditions listed in paragraph 7 are met, as summarized below:

(a) One must have direct knowledge that the *lashon hara* was actually spoken, and is liable to be spread.

(b) One must know the *halachos* of *lashon hara* well enough to be certain that the statements in question definitely fall into the category of *lashon hara.*

(c) If the situation can be resolved by approaching the speaker of the *lashon hara* directly and attempting to persuade him of the wrong he is doing, then it is forbidden to say anything to others. (If, however, one sees that this will merely incite the speaker to speak worse *lashon hara* and to cause even greater conflicts, then it is better not to speak to him at all.)

(d) One must reveal only the minimum necessary to accomplish the desired purpose.

(e) One must be certain that speaking to others will not cause the speaker of the *lashon hara* greater harm than he would have had to suffer if he had been found guilty and punished by a *beis din.*

(f) Most importantly, one must take care that his motives in speaking to others are solely to accomplish the permitted purposes described in the previous paragraph and in the rest of this chapter, and not simply to derive pleasure either from spreading gossip or from any other personal interest.[21]

---

21. Ibid. 10:6.

25
Preventing Damage

1. If a person is about to engage in an endeavor that will surely prove to be disastrous, it is prohibited to stand by and take no action, as the Torah warns, *You shall not stand aside while your fellow's blood is being shed* (*Vayikra* 19:16).[1] We are not permitted to look away even if the endeavor will not be a disaster, but will involve some degree of loss, as the Torah says, *You shall not look away* (*Devarim* 22:3). Preventing damage to another person is an integral part of the mitzvah of returning lost objects. (See Chapter 37, paragraph 1.)[2]

2. Therefore, a person who sees someone about to associate with another (e.g. form a partnership, hire a worker, make a *shidduch*), and has knowledge that the subject is for some reason unsuitable for the proposed association, or that any harm will result from it, is obligated to inform the concerned parties in order to spare them the damage they would otherwise suffer.[3] This is not *lashon hara*, as explained in Chapter 21, since the motivation for the speech is not "evil" but rather a mitzvah.

1. *Choshen Mishpat* 426.

2. *Shaarei Teshuvah* 3:70; see also *Chofetz Chaim, Hilchos Rechilus* 9:1, *Be'er Mayim Chaim* 1; *Zera Chaim* ad loc.

3. *Chofetz Chaim* ibid.

3. Although it is a mitzvah to prevent an unsuitable association, someone who is not careful is liable to reveal information that is not necessary to accomplish the desired purpose. Relating any unnecessary negative information, however legitimate the purpose intended, is forbidden as *lashon hara* and *rechilus*. Therefore, we will now repeat points made in other contexts so that the reader will understand how to avoid *lashon hara* in the course of performing these mitzvos.

4. The overriding consideration is that one's intention in speaking must be solely to accomplish the beneficial purpose of helping people. It is forbidden to speak out of dislike of others. (See Chapter 21, paragraph 5 about what to do if one recognizes in himself a feeling of dislike for the subject in a situation where there is a legitimate purpose to be accomplished by speaking.)[4]

5. It is also critical to assess if relating the information in question will accomplish the desired purpose. If it does not, everything that was said will become unnecessary gossip retroactively.[5]

> **Mr. A:** *I don't think you should hire Yankel. He is …*
> **Mr. B:** *Thank you for the information.*
> *Two days later, Mr. B hires Yankel. Mr. A's words, as it turned out, were unnecessary character defamation.*

Even worse, the very fact that the words were spoken may have undesirable consequences.[6]

> **Chaim:** *Berel, don't marry Rochel. She is …*
> *A few days later Berel becomes engaged to Rochel. The following year, in the course of an argument, Berel exclaims, "Chaim was right when he said I shouldn't marry you!" (Berel has violated the prohibition of rechilus.)*
> *Chaim should have had more foresight in assessing whether Berel would listen to him before defaming Rochel.*

---

4. Ibid. 9:2 and *Be'er Mayim Chaim* 3.

5. Ibid. 9:2. Note: If the speaker made a reasonable judgment that the listener would heed his words, and then the listener did not, the speaker is not considered to be at fault, since he spoke with beneficial intentions. However, a person may unconsciously want to relate negative information to a party, and in his passion to do so misjudges the likelihood that the person will listen to him. This is retroactively considered to be *lashon hara*.

6. Ibid.

The Harm With the Benefits

6. On occasion, even though there is a beneficial purpose in speaking, a risk exists that in doing so, unfortunate consequences will result along with the benefits.

> **Chaim:** *Berel, don't marry Rochel. She is...*

> ❏ *Berel decides not to see Rochel any longer (the intended benefit). The next day, chatting with his friends at lunch, he tells them that he has decided not to continue seeing Rochel because Chaim says that she is ... It soon becomes public knowledge that Chaim has said that Rochel ...*

> ❏ *In another scenario, Rochel's father calls Berel and asks, "Why don't you want to see Rochel any longer?"*
> *"Well," Berel answers, "Chaim said that she is ..."*

In either case, it is easy to see that serious negative consequences may result.

7. Therefore, before speaking in such a situation one should caution the listener that he may not reveal the information to anyone else, even if asked directly. If one judges that this warning will be heeded, then it is permitted to relate the information. If this is not the case, it is forbidden to speak.[7] (Advice: Becoming the type of person who can be trusted to keep information to himself will help him to be told useful information, and vice versa.)

> **Mrs. G:** *Mrs. H, my Devorah needs a very bright young man. Is Yaakov A bright?*
> *Mrs. H knows that Yaakov is not very bright, but she does not trust Mrs. G not to relate this fact to the whole world, thus ruining Yaakov's reputation.*
> **Mrs. H:** *Well ... there are a lot of considerations in a shidduch, and I just don't see Yaakov as a match for your daughter.*
> **Mrs. G:** *But I do. I just want to know if he is bright.*
> **Mrs. H:** *(a) I have a principle when I don't envision a match: I do not discuss details because it could easily involve lashon hara. (b) I don't know. (c) (in desperation) Yes, he is bright, but I just don't see the match.*

---

7. Ibid. *Be'er Mayim Chaim* 5 and 9:12; see also *Halichos Olam*, Ch. 3.

Even though stating openly that Yaakov is not bright is the most likely way to stop the proposed shidduch, Mrs. H should not do so because of the risk of damage to Yaakov (see Chapter 28 for detailed laws regarding shidduchim).

Necessary Conditions

8.   If the following conditions are fulfilled, it is permitted to relate negative information in order to accomplish a worthwhile purpose.

   (a) The speaker must have definite knowledge that his information is accurate, and not knowledge based on mere hearsay or conjecture[8] (see paragraphs 9-18).

   (b) He may say only what is absolutely necessary to accomplish the desired purpose, and in particular must limit the negative impression created as much as possible. If matters can be arranged so that this purpose will be accomplished without saying anything, he is required to do so and is forbidden to relate the negative information.[9]

   In the above example, if Mrs. H believes that she can dissuade Mrs. G by saying that "it isn't a match" she will not relate that Yaakov is not bright even if Mrs. G can be trusted not to divulge this information to others.

   (c) One must be certain that the information he reveals will not cause the subject to suffer any greater harm or loss than is warranted by Torah law. For example, let us suppose that the association has already been finalized (e.g. the *shidduch* concluded, the partnership launched, or the prospective employee hired) and the question remains whether or not to relate the negative information in one's possession to the other party. Will the other party merely take steps to protect himself from harm or loss, or will he break a contract without further investigation on the basis of hearsay, a violation of the Torah law? In all such cases, a Torah authority must be consulted.[10]

   In a previous job as a financial executive, Mr. A committed certain errors that caused monetary losses to his firm. Now Mr. B has hired him in a similar capacity. If Mr. B is informed, he will believe the story, break the contract and fire Mr. A. It is unwarranted accord-

---

8. *Chofetz Chaim, Hilchos Rechilus* 9:2.

9. Ibid.

10. Ibid. 9:2,5.

ing to Torah law to break a contract on the basis of hearsay, and it is all the more unwarranted for Mr. B to ruin Mr. A's reputation or cause him other damage. Only if one is sure that Mr. B would consult a rav concerning his legal options, and avoid unnecessary damage, is it permitted to relate the information to him.

In a Case of Inconclusive Information

9. One who does not have direct personal knowledge of the unfavorable information but has only heard of it from others, is only permitted to suspect that the information might be true to the extent that it is necessary to protect himself or others from harm, but not to accept it as definite truth, as explained in Chapter 13.[11]

> *Levi is considering forming a partnership with Shimon. Reuven has heard that Shimon is dishonest, and should speak to Levi as follows: "I have heard that Shimon is dishonest. While it is forbidden to accept this as being definitely true, we are required to suspect that there might be some truth in it. Therefore, it would be wise not to enter into a partnership with him until the matter can be clarified."*

Considering the Risk of Ruining a Person's Livelihood or Reputation

10. Whenever one individual warns another about a third party (he is dishonest, lazy, not smart, etc.), he must consider the possibility that the third person could suffer greatly. The listener, upon hearing the warning, might pass it on to others so that they, too, should not engage that person in their affairs. Before long that person may acquire a reputation as an undesirable associate, and will find it impossible to make a living or find a *shidduch*. This situation is contrary to the Torah's injunction, *Let your brother live with you* (*Vayikra* 25:36), which commands us to help each other to sustain ourselves, and certainly does not allow us to undermine other people's means of livelihood, prospects of marriage, or advancement opportunities.

Conflicting Requirements

11. Thus, rather than be faced with a choice between these two seemingly conflicting requirements, one should strive to avoid the

---

11. Ibid. 9:2; *Be'er Mayim Chaim* 9.

dilemma. Statements can sometimes be worded in such a way as to prevent damage without destroying a person's reputation. However, there are times when there is no such option and the person must choose between saving one individual from a bad relationship or preserving another's reputation and dignity. In the following paragraphs we will discuss the situation in terms of business associations (partner, employee, etc.). The area of *shidduchim* is discussed in Chapter 28.

12. In these situations, we make a distinction between two cases: one in which the speaker knows with absolute certainty that the subject is dishonest and/or undesirable as an associate, and the other in which only hearsay or circumstantial evidence exists to that effect. In the second case, although we are forbidden to accept such evidence as absolute truth, we are nevertheless required to suspect that it may be true and to take steps to protect ourselves and others from harm or loss.

13. In the first case, where the subject is definitely known to be dishonest or undesirable for any other reason and is likely to cause damage to anyone who hires him, one is required to warn any potential employers or associates of the danger he poses.[12] Even if the result is that the subject cannot find employment and make a living, since he is, in fact, unsuitable in any such capacity, we cannot allow harm to come to others in order to preserve his reputation. Nonetheless, the Jews of the city have a responsibility to help him (as with any other person) find ways to support himself, in accordance with the mitzvah cited in paragraph 10.

14. It must be stressed that even though people in such a situation are allowed to protect themselves from loss by refraining from associating with or employing the subject, it is forbidden to cause him any other damage or loss. Even if someone is proven to be a thief, the Torah limits his punishment to returning what he stole, but does not permit causing him insult, anguish or embarrassment, and certainly does not allow others to persecute or harass him. (Rather, an obligation exists to make gentle and persuasive attempts to induce him to mend his ways, as discussed in Chapter 3.)

> *Mendy, who worked in a local store as a cashier, was caught pocketing some money and was immediately fired. Subsequently, whenever he applied for a job, his old employer, who knew Mendy well, felt*

---

12. This entire discussion is based on *Be'er Mayim Chaim* loc. cit.

obligated to inform the prospective employer of his history. He felt that, if tempted, Mendy would repeat his behavior. Thus, Mendy could not find employment, and furthermore, was ostracized to the point that he was no longer called up to the Torah. At a meeting of the shul's board of directors, the rav said, "Although it is proper that no one hire him because they do not want to suffer a loss, he is still to be treated like any other Jew who was caught committing a sin. He does not lose his status as a Jew, and he is to be called to the Torah as usual. No one is permitted to insult him or embarrass him in any way. Furthermore, it is our obligation to try to devise a way to help Mendy earn an honest living. Once he has a steady source of livelihood, we must then insist that he repay any stolen money."

Note: Sometimes, a community should ostracize an individual who has perpetrated an injustice in order to pressure him to rectify the wrongs he has inflicted on his victim. (See Chapter 24.) This, too, should be done *only* with the consent of a *beis din* or Torah sage. However, in this example, "Mendy" is no longer hurting anyone, and it is therefore wrong and prohibited to ostracize him.

15. In the second case explained in paragraph 12, however, there is no direct personal knowledge of the subject's dishonesty, only reports from others to that effect. On the one hand, if the reports were true, one would be required to warn potential employers or associates to be wary of the subject. However, if they are false, then anything one says to damage the reputation of this person is a gross injustice and *lashon hara*. Obviously, this situation presents a major dilemma.

Investigate

16. Therefore, if one hears such a report, the best recourse is to investigate the facts and attempt to either verify or disprove the negative information about the subject. If he is unable to do so by himself, he should enlist the help of other responsible people who in any case need to know the facts, for if the truth does not emerge, serious consequences could result.

17. If, however, the truth cannot be ascertained, one is left in a situation where taking action might cause an innocent person serious harm, while inaction could expose a number of people to potential losses. The Chofetz Chaim was unable to reach a resolution as to what

the *halachah* requires in such a situation. In a case like this we apply the principle that it is preferable to take no action. Nevertheless, one is strongly advised to consult a Torah sage in order to devise a strategy to minimize both the risk of harm to others and the possibility of injustice to the subject.[13]

> *Silver Electronics Inc. is planning to open a new outlet. One of the candidates for store manager is Jack, a charismatic young man. However, Mr. Gold, a friend of Mr. Silver, has heard that Jack is not very organized, and may exhibit a lack of efficiency that could cause losses to the company. Not knowing what to do, he consulted his rav, who told him to investigate further to verify the information. Jack may in fact be very organized and capable; perhaps the rumor was spread by an enemy. However, if after a few days the information cannot be verified, the rav advised him to return in order to determine a plan. Jack will surely not be hired before then, and in the meantime Mr. Gold should not say anything to Mr. Silver.*

Degrees of Potential Damage

18. The above discussion applies only to situations where the reports allege that the subject is liable to cause relatively mild forms of damage (e.g. that he is disorganized or careless with money). If, however, he is suspected of serious failings likely to have far-reaching repercussions (e.g. a candidate for a *shidduch* holds heretical views or comes from a disreputable background, a situation likely to cause a lifetime of damage, in addition to the effects on future generations), then it is even permitted to relate hearsay. However, in relating such information, one must make it clear that his knowledge of the matter is not definite. Therefore, even though we are required to suspect that the reports might be true, we cannot accept them as being conclusive.[14]

> *In the above example, if the rumor alleged that Jack had connections with drug dealers, Mr. Gold could immediately repeat it to Mr. Silver, stressing that he could not verify the information, but warning him to be careful.*

---

13. *Chofetz Chaim, Hilchos Rechilus* 9:2.

14. Ibid. and "Examples" 6; *Be'er Mayim Chaim* 9. For further discussion see *Halichos Olam,* Ch. 13 fn. *zayin.*

Poverty

19. Although it is permitted to relate information to prevent damage, poverty in and of itself is not a condition considered "damaging." Therefore, if one knows that a candidate for a partnership (or employment etc.) is poor, it is forbidden to relate anything that might damage his prospects, even if the prospective partner or employer is unaware of his financial status. In fact, taking such a person into a partnership and enabling him to improve his situation through his own efforts is one of the highest forms of *tzedakah* (see Chapter 50), from which the prospective partner will surely reap substantial blessings both in this world and in the next. Conversely, anything one does to interfere with such a great mitzvah is considered a grievous wrong.[15]

Direct Questioning

20. However, if, before any agreement has been concluded, one is asked directly by the prospective partner or employer about the person's financial condition, and the questioner makes it clear that he does not wish to associate with a poor person, the following considerations come into play: If one does not know with certainty that the subject is poor, it is forbidden to answer in a way that might harm his prospects. It is similarly forbidden to speak if one suspects that the matter might come to the subject's attention and result in conflicts. At the same time, since it is forbidden to lie in this situation,[16] the best course of action is to avoid answering at all.

21. If, however, one knows that the subject is indeed poor and is also sure that the questioner is discreet and no conflicts are likely to arise, it is permitted to reveal one's knowledge of the subject's financial condition. As stated, if there is any doubt about the subject's financial state, one should avoid giving a clear-cut response; i.e., "I do not know what to tell you because I am not familiar with his situation."[17]

Requests for Advice

22. However, if one is asked for *advice* concerning an association with the subject, then the answer must be based on how he him-

---

15. *Chofetz Chaim, Hilchos Rechilus* 9:2 and "Examples" in the fn. and in *Be'er Mayim Chaim* 2.

16. Misleading the questioner by giving him wrong information is a violation of the prohibition of "putting a stumbling block before the blind" (*Vayikra* 19:14).

17. *Chofetz Chaim* ibid., *Be'er Mayim Chaim* 1; see also *Shevilei Chaim* 27 and 28.

self would act in the questioner's situation. If one perceives that from a "practical" point of view, poverty would indeed be sufficiently detrimental in an association of this kind so that he himself would be deterred from contracting with the subject, then it is forbidden to advise another person to do so.

> *Mr. Simon is considering Mr. Gold as a partner in an investment firm. Chaim knows that since Mr. Gold has, of late, lost a great deal of money and is in dire straits, this could be just the opportunity to help him recover. However, the fact that Mr. Gold's assets are practically nil could be an important factor in impeding the growth of the proposed firm. Were Mr. Simon to merely mention to Chaim that he is considering a partnership with Mr. Gold, Chaim is forbidden to make any negative comments. If Chaim is asked for information on Mr. Gold's financial status, he should try to avoid the issue, but if Mr. Simon can be trusted to keep the information to himself, Chaim is permitted to reveal the truth. Should Mr. Simon ask for Chaim's advice as to whether he should take Mr. Gold as a partner, Chaim must reveal the fact that there is a negative aspect involved in the proposition.*

The Difference Between Offering Information and Giving Advice

23.   There is a fundamental difference between requesting information and asking for advice. The purpose of giving information is a desire to help, but one must be careful not to help one person at the expense of another. Thus, information that will cause damage to a poor person should not be offered (according to the guidelines set forth in paragraphs 20-21). This is merely considered withholding help, rather than inflicting harm. Moreover, it is not clear that the information itself is truly helpful, because an association with a poverty-stricken individual may bring great rewards.

However, if asked, and one offers less than the best advice, the Torah considers the adviser to have caused harm. This is prohibited, as the Torah says, *Before a blind person you shall not place a stumbling block* (*Vayikra* 19:14). Since we are admonished not to cause harm with poor advice, we must set aside all other considerations and contemplate the matter from a personal viewpoint. A person should say to himself, "If I would be in his position, and I had only my own interests in mind, how would I act?" Whatever the conclusion, that is the exact advice that one is *obligated* to give to another person. Any deviance, even arising from good motivations (e.g. to help a poor person), is considered harmful and violates the Torah's prohibition.[18]

24. The same applies also to issues related to *shidduchim*; when asked for advice one is required to weigh all the considerations involved exactly as if his own interests were at stake. Any advice that deviates from this formula because of a personal interest in the matter is a violation of the commandment not to place a stumbling block before a blind person. Sadly, it is common for people to allow personal interests to color the advice they dispense, without considering the Torah's requirements.

> *The following examples are common violations of the prohibition of placing a stumbling block before the blind (giving advice colored by personal interests):*
>
> ❏ ***Mr. Abrams:*** *What do you think of my hiring Reuven for the job?*
> ***Mr. Issacs*** *(who hopes that his son will get that job): Well, I can see a number of problems.*
>
> ❏ ***Mr. Jacobs:*** *Do you think that Shimon would be a good match for my daughter?*
> ***Mr. Levi*** *(who would like Shimon to meet his daughter): I honestly don't think it is such a good idea.*

Dealing With Threats

25. If one hears a person threatening to harm or insult another, or to cause him monetary or property loss, and there is reason to suspect that the speaker is likely to carry out his threat (since he has a previous record of committing similar acts), one is required to warn the intended victim to take steps to protect himself. However, before issuing such a warning, one must be certain that the necessary conditions are fulfilled (the intentions are beneficial — i.e. to promote peace, he states only what is true and necessary, and no excess damage will be caused).[19]

> *A speaker associated with the ABC association is scheduled to arrive in town for a lecture. The leaders of the anti-ABC movement*

18. *Chofetz Chaim* ibid. 9:3; see also *Nesivos Chaim* ad loc.
19. *Chofetz Chaim* ibid.

are planning a major demonstration during the speech, including heckling. Since they are well-known for such behavior, we can presume that this is not an empty threat. Therefore, we can inform the speaker in advance of their plans and advise him to perhaps reschedule his speech or change the location. (However, we need not mention the types of epithets and insults hurled by the anti-ABC movement, because we can accomplish the same goal without such negativity.)

26. If the speaker has not been known to act this way in the past, but one judges from his manner and the current circumstances that he seriously intends to carry out his threats this time, one is first required to speak to him in an attempt to dissuade him. If he accepts the admonition, then one should not speak to the intended victim. Since the speaker has no history of such behavior, it may be assumed that he was speaking out of anger; now that he has calmed down, he surely no longer intends any harm.

27. If, however, the speaker exhibits no sign of remorse, or if one judges from the outset that speaking to him will have no effect, then the intended victim should be warned to take steps to protect himself.[20]

28. Before taking action in such cases, however, the situation must be carefully assessed. A well-intentioned warning to either party can sometimes have the effect of further inflaming the conflict. The quarreling parties, rather than simply avoiding contact, will deliberately seek out additional and more destructive ways of inflicting harm on each other.[21] In such cases, one should obviously not approach either side. (If possible, one may cautiously enlist the help of a responsible neutral party to intervene and constructively resolve the conflict.)

In the above example, if we suspect that the ABC speaker will respond to the challenge by mustering a group of supporters to counter-demonstrate — a situation that could end in fighting — it is best not to get involved at all.

---

20. Ibid. in the note; also in *Be'er Mayim Chaim* 14.
21. Ibid. 9:4.

Misguided Behavior

29. Unfortunately, two types of misguided behavior are all too commonly found. On the one hand, some people who are asked for information about a particular person and assured that the request is being made *leto'eles* (for a beneficial purpose), immediately and without hesitation reveal everything they know about the subject. They do not consider what information is actually relevant to the matter at hand and what is not, which details are known to be definitely true and which are only hearsay, whether the questioner is discreet or likely to publicize the information, and if revealing this information is likely to cause the subject undeserved harm or loss.

"Oh, you need to know ... I'll tell you the whole story."

30. Other people are inclined to do just the opposite. Although they would readily reveal everything they know in response to a casual request for information (with no concern for all the prohibitions they are violating), the moment the questioner indicates that the matter concerns a *shidduch* or the like, they conceal their knowledge due to a misplaced desire to protect the subject from harm. In reality, however, denying the questioner information that he legitimately needs could be causing him unjustified damage.

Mrs. A: Why didn't you tell me this before they got married?
Mrs. B: Oh, I don't ever want to say anything to hurt a shidduch!

Rabbeinu Nissim mentioned this type of behavior in his *Vidui HaGadol* (Great Confession): "What You permit I have treated as forbidden, and what You forbid I have treated as permitted."

26

Shopping: Advice and Criticism

Direct Requests for Advice

1. A person is required to give the best possible advice if asked for his opinion regarding where to shop for a certain product. Even if the questioner is about to enter a particular store and asks if there is a better one for his needs, the person is required to offer his honest opinion (even though this will cause a loss of business to the first establishment). Advising the shopper against his best interests because of personal considerations (e.g. directing him to a store in which he or a relative has an interest) violates the commandment not to place a stumbling block before a blind person.[1]

2. The general rule is that when a person is asked for advice on any matter, he is required to give the best possible advice to the questioner, explaining exactly what he himself would do in a similar situation. Thus, just as one would be permitted to go to a less expensive store that he was reminded of as he was about to enter another, so too is it now permitted and *required* to advise the questioner in the same manner.

---

1. See Ch. 6 pars. 15-17.

Unsolicited Advice

3. If the same individual noticed an acquaintance entering a store that he knows to be generally more expensive than others, and his advice was not solicited, he should not say anything, since there is no reason to advance the customer's interests over those of the store owner. However, if the potential customer is a relative or very close friend (and the store owner is not), one should direct him to the cheaper store, since family members and intimate friends take precedence over others.[2] Similarly, a fellow Jew is considered a "relative" and takes precedence over a non-Jew.

> ❏ *Pizza shop A charges $2.00 a slice. Pizza shop B charges $1.75 for a slice of the same quality. If I am asked where to buy the cheapest pizza, I must direct the questioner to B (even if Mr. A is my close relative).*
>
> ❏ *If I see someone entering A I should not inform him that B is cheaper. (Why should I promote B's livelihood over A's?)*
>
> ❏ *If I see a relative or close friend about to enter A, I should inform him of the possibility of purchasing at B (unless A, too, is a close friend or relative, in which case they are considered equal and I should not get involved).*

4. In all of these cases, a person must be careful to say only, "Another store is cheaper," without implying that there is anything wrong with the first. Any suggestion that the store charges unreasonably high prices, or any other derogatory impression conveyed through tone or gestures, is considered *lashon hara*, since there is no legitimate purpose in casting such aspersions.[3]

> **Do not say:**
> *"This store is very expensive" or "That store is only for rich people."*
> *These nuances are all unnecessary.*
> **One can simply say:**
> *"You can get a better buy elsewhere."*

---

2. *Zera Chaim, Hilchos Rechilus* 9:10 (1-2), and *Kodesh Yisrael*, Ch. 17. Since the injunction *You shall love your fellow as yourself* applies equally to all fellow Jews, one should not interfere on behalf of one at the expense of another. However, if one is a relative (or very close friend — *Zera Chaim*), then the injunction *Do not look away from your flesh* (i.e. relative) (*Yeshayahu* 58:7) gives precedence to that relative.

3. *Chofetz Chaim, Hilchos Rechilus* 9:10.

5. It is strictly forbidden to publicize the fact that a particular establishment charges high prices, since doing so would discourage people from patronizing the store (see paragraph 16 for an exception to this rule). This kind of talk falls into the category of *lashon hara* since it causes damage to the store owner,[4] and also violates the words of the Torah, *Let your brother live with you* (*Vayikra* 25:36). This mitzvah commands us to help other Jews support themselves, and certainly does not allow us to harm their means of livelihood. It is, however, permitted to privately advise people to shop in less expensive stores under the conditions described above.

A Naive Customer and a Dishonest Storekeeper

6. If one knows that a potential customer of a certain store is naive in business matters and that the storekeeper is likely to trick him (e.g. by charging excessively high prices, offering inferior merchandise, or using inaccurate weights and measures), then one should try to dissuade that individual from shopping there. If at all possible, this should be done without actually revealing the storekeeper's dishonesty, since it is never permitted to relate *lashon hara*, even for a legitimate purpose, if another way exists to achieve the desired goal. This can be accomplished, for example, by telling him that another store is cheaper.

> *Reuven, who is not wise in the ways of the world, plans to buy a tape recorder. Mr. E, the generally honest owner of E Electronics, is likely to take advantage of Reuven and sell him an inferior product. Shimon, wishing to avoid speaking rechilus, suggests that Reuven patronize A Appliances, where this problem does not exist.*

7. If, however, one judges that there is no way to stop this shopper from buying in that particular store without mentioning the storekeeper's dishonest nature, then it is permitted to do so in order to protect the buyer's interests. Furthermore, one may warn him about the storekeeper's dishonesty even if they have already reached an agreement regarding a purchase.

> *If Reuven insists that he wishes to buy in E Electronics, Shimon may say, "I am afraid that he will cheat you."*

---

4. See *Rambam, Hilchos Dei'os* 7:5.

Even so, one must take care that all the relevant conditions are fulfilled (as summarized below in paragraph 15).[5]

8. Even if one is aware that the storekeeper's dishonesty will not cause the customer any monetary loss (e.g. the storekeeper will claim that a product is made by a certain well-known company, when it is actually another brand, although equal in value to the first), one is required to warn the customer because he will still be deceived.[6]

> *Shimon can say to Reuven, "He will cheat you," even if he will "merely" pass off a good quality brand X tape recorder as a top-name brand; he need not overcharge Reuven to be considered dishonest.*

If *Ona'ah* Is Involved

9. If the storekeeper's "custom" is to overcharge the customer, and one suspects that he plans to violate the prohibition against *ona'ah*,[7] then one is required to warn the customer. If the storekeeper usually overcharges by less than the amount considered *ona'ah*, nothing derogatory should be said. (If, however, there is a way to prevent the customer from buying in that store without revealing the storekeeper's deceptive intentions, one should do so.)[8]

> *If he suspects that the store will only overcharge slightly (e.g. $11.00 for a tape recorder worth $10.00), he can try to convince the customer to shop elsewhere, but cannot make any negative insinuations about the store owner ("He will overcharge you."). However, if he suspects that the overcharge will be more than a sixth (e.g. $12.00 for the tape recorder), he may even say, if necessary, "He could overcharge you."*

After a Sale Is Completed

10. The above applies only if the sale has not yet been finalized and one wishes to warn the customer in order to prevent *ona'ah*. Once the sale has been made, however, it is only permitted to speak if the subject will experience an actual positive benefit. The positive benefit can be either reversal of the transaction or prevention of future harm.

---

5. *Chofetz Chaim* ibid.

6. Ibid.

7. See Ch. 39 pars. 2-4 for a definition of what constitutes *ona'ah*.

8. *Chofetz Chaim* ibid. and *Be'er Mayim Chaim* 27.

Reversing a Transaction

11. If the motivation of the speaker is to help the purchaser reverse the transaction, three conditions must be met:

(a) He must be certain that the purchaser has a right to demand redress according to *halachah*.[9]

(b) He must judge that it is likely that this person will indeed do so. Many people do not take action in such a situation; they simply bear a grudge, or even worse, spread *lashon hara* about the storekeeper.

(c) He must judge that the purchaser will not overreact by, for example, seizing the storekeeper's property or arbitrarily refusing to pay money owed to him.[10]

Even though the purchaser has heard that he was wronged, he is not allowed to believe the information as being definitely true, but should verify it and then investigate the relevant *halachos* before taking any action.

> *If Reuven has already bought the tape recorder Shimon should say nothing if Reuven:*
>
> *(a) cannot return it according to halachah;*
>
> *(b) will not return it because that is not his nature; or*
>
> *(c) will take action against the store owner in a manner against halachah.*

Protecting From Future Harm

12. Even if the purchaser is unlikely to pursue his rights this time, if one judges that unless informed of the wrong suffered the purchaser is likely to return to the store and receive similar treatment, then it is permitted to warn him against such future loss. Similarly, even if it is doubtful that the purchaser will return to this particular store, but he is generally naive in these matters and likely to be exploited by others in the future, it is permitted to explain to him how he was deceived so that he will be better able to protect himself. However, if the purchaser cannot be relied upon to conduct himself according to *halachah* (e.g. he will withhold payment or seize property illegally — see previous paragraph), it is forbidden to say anything.[11]

---

9. See Chs. 39 (*Ona'as Mamon*) and 42 (Returning Merchandise) for detailed discussions of the *halachos* concerning reversal of a transaction.

10. *Chofetz Chaim* ibid. 9:11-13.

11. Ibid. *Be'er Mayim Chaim* 34 and *Shevilei Chaim* 25. See *Halichos Olam,* Ch. 15 fn. *tes.*

Continued from above example:

If Reuven already bought the item, but he is liable to be fooled again either by this store owner or others, Shimon should tell him the truth. This applies only if the reason he would not have told him otherwise were conditions (a) or (b) of paragraph 11. But if the reason was condition (c), he still may not tell him.

Praising an Already Completed Purchase

13. In paragraphs 10-17 we discussed the circumstances under which one should reveal to a purchaser that he was cheated. If those circumstances do not exist, however, it is a mitzvah to do just the opposite. He should speak positively about the purchase and point out its good features, even if this involves stretching the truth.[12]

> *The Sages taught:*[13] *How does one dance before the bride? (i.e. what does one say?). Beis Shammai say: The bride according to what she is (we mention her fine points but do not say an untruth). Beis Hillel say: The bride is pleasant and kind (we say so about every bride, even if it is an untruth). Beis Hillel proved the point as follows: If a person buys something in the market, we should praise it in his eyes, and not degrade it in his eyes.*

14. The following exchanges are examples of common behavior, and the correct ways to address these issues.[14]

> ### The incorrect way:
>
> **A:** *Look at my new suit.*
> **B:** *How much did you pay?*
> **A:** *X dollars.*
> **B:** *What! You were cheated!*
>
> *[B should have considered: (a) Perhaps the market price has recently changed. (b) Is there ona'ah? (c) Can A return the purchase? (d) Will he return the purchase? Is it worth his while to do so? (e) If he was indeed overcharged, and he can and will return the object, could the statement have been made without the negative put-down (ona'as devarim)?]*
> **B:** *(a) I'll tell you what to do: go and return it, and if he doesn't agree, force him to take it back!*

---

12. *Chofetz Chaim* ibid. 9:12.

13. *Kesubos* 17a.

14. Cf. *Chofetz Chaim* ibid. 9:13.

[Is he permitted to do so? Is B convincing A to do wrong and thereby violating the prohibition "Before a blind person you shall not place a stumbling block"?]

B: *(b) Did you pay for it yet? You wrote a check? Good. So if you can't return it, cancel the check.*

[If the sale is legally consummated and the buyer does not have the right to return the item, lack of payment constitutes theft.]

Later:

A: *I tried to return it, but the guy wouldn't take it back.*

B: *He is just a thief!*

[Who is the thief? Subsequent lashon hara and feuding can all be attributed to B's "wise" remarks.]

A far better way:

A: *Look at my new suit.*

B: *How much did you pay?*

A: *X dollars.*

B: *[Thinks: Sounds rather high ... but I don't know all the details yet.]*

B: *Looks like a very nice suit.*

[B finds out that A indeed overpaid but can legally return the suit according to the store's policy.]

B: *You know, A, that suit is really nice but I think you could have done better on the price. Why don't you return it and I'll take you to a store where it's less expensive.*

Conditions for Relating Derogatory Information

15. Relating derogatory information (e.g. to a customer regarding a storekeeper likely to defraud or overcharge, or to a customer who has already been tricked on a purchase) is permitted only if all the conditions and stipulations of the previous chapters are fulfilled. We will now summarize these conditions as they relate to the situations described in this chapter.[15]

(a) The motivation must be a genuine desire to help the customer rather than to vent one's dislike for any of the other parties involved. One must also be certain that speaking out will actually be to the customer's benefit.

(b) One must be certain that his facts are accurate and that the injustice actually occurred or is likely to occur based on known facts.

---

15. Ibid. 9:12.

(If knowledge of the incident is merely based on hearsay, see Chapter 25, paragraphs 9-17.)

(c) One must be certain that everything said is actually necessary to accomplish the intended purpose. If possible, one is required to resolve the matter by approaching the storekeeper in private and persuading him to act honorably as the Torah requires, and it is then forbidden to speak to the customer. If this is not feasible, one should attempt to bring about the desired result (i.e. preventing deception or recovering a loss) in some other fashion not involving negative speech at all, or at least by omitting some of the information he intended to convey.

(d) One must be certain that speaking out will not cause the guilty party to suffer a greater loss than the Torah allows under the circumstances. Thus, one must be certain that the customer will not take revenge on the storekeeper, or attempt to recover his loss in a way not sanctioned by the Torah. Furthermore, one cannot tell the customer anything if he is liable to spread *lashon hara* about the storekeeper. It is permitted to speak to him, however, if one judges that the customer will be discreet as cautioned, even though it is not his usual nature (as long as all the other conditions are fulfilled).

A Consistent Pattern of Dishonesty

16.   The third condition — that it is permitted to speak only if there is no other way to prevent the threatened harm — applies only to an isolated incident. If, however, one knows with certainty that a certain storekeeper regularly deceives his customers, then this fact should be publicized to protect the general public. Thus, it is permitted to warn a person seen entering that store about the storekeeper's dishonesty immediately, without seeking other strategies to protect the customer from harm. (This assumes that the other conditions are met: i.e. his intentions are to protect the public, he is sure of the facts, he does not add unnecessary details, and there will be no excessive damage — such as slander to the authorities.)[16]

---

16. Ibid. 9:10 in footnote.

27

Investigation of Shidduchim for the Involved Parties

The Proper Way to Make Inquiries

1. It is highly desirable for a person or family seeking a *shidduch* (marriage partner) to make inquiries about potential candidates to determine whether the two sides are well-suited; if conducted properly, such inquiries and the information they reveal are entirely legitimate and do not in any way fall into the category of *lashon hara*.

2. However, one is required to specify when making such an inquiry that it is for the purpose of a *shidduch*, so that both the questioner and the speaker will direct their focus properly. It is forbidden to solicit information as if one simply enjoys listening to derogatory information about people, since this approach would turn the speaker's response into *lashon hara*, as explained in Chapter 21, paragraph 15.[1] People tend to solicit information in a manner that causes *lashon hara* for two reasons: (a) They may wish to conceal the fact that they are interested in *shidduchim* or in pursuing this particular *shidduch*, or (b) they feel that they will not be given accurate information any other way. We will now discuss these two issues in detail.

---

1. *Chofetz Chaim, Hilchos Lashon Hara* 4:11.

Concealing Personal Interest in *Shidduchim*

3. If one wishes to conceal the fact that he is involved in *shidduchim*, he may simply state that he is asking for a beneficial purpose, without being specific as to its nature, or he may omit the fact that the inquiry is on his own behalf. This avoids the problem of *lashon hara* to some extent since he does actually have a legitimate need for the information. However, this approach can lead to various problems.

(a) The speaker might well relate information irrelevant to the purpose at hand, e.g. facts pertaining to job applications or business matters but with no relevance to *shidduchim*. Consequently, the speaker might easily disclose information that the questioner has no legitimate need to know and thereby transgress the prohibition against *lashon hara*.

(b) The questioner may state that he is asking for "the purpose of *shidduchim*" without specifying who the interested party is (thereby solving the previous problem). However, because the speaker is unaware of the individual's identity, he may give an inappropriate answer, since factors that render a candidate unsuitable for one person would not be considered drawbacks for another. Thus, in the end, the speaker may still reveal information that is not necessary for the decision at hand. However, this problem can be greatly limited by the speaker describing the candidate in general terms and outlining the qualities considered desirable in a partner. The speaker can also limit his answer to relevant details based on the information provided by the questioner.

4. The rule, therefore, is that as long as the questioner and speaker are conversing for a legitimate purpose it is not necessary to relate the exact nature of that purpose. However they must be aware of the problems of conveying unnecessary or inaccurate information. All such situations require discretion and good judgment.

Obtaining Accurate Information

5. Unfortunately, upon hearing that a *shidduch* is involved, many people do the exact opposite of what the *halachah* requires and deliberately distort the truth. Thus, someone who is really a weak and disinterested student is proclaimed a *"masmid"* (diligent student), or a selfish person is said to be a *"baal chesed"* (a person who engages in acts of kindness). Such misguided efforts to be helpful can cause serious and irreparable damage. They are also a violation of the commandment, *Before a blind person you shall not place a stum-*

bling block (*Vayikra* 19:14), which prohibits giving incorrect or unsuitable advice.

6. Although this sort of behavior makes it difficult for the serious-minded to form reliable judgments about candidates for *shidduchim*, it does not justify violating any of the Torah's prohibitions for the sake of obtaining accurate information. It remains forbidden to try to elicit the truth from a source by feigning disinterest and pretending to ask only because one enjoys hearing *lashon hara*.[2] Faced with this problem, the only course of action we can recommend is to seek out honest and truthful people who are willing to share accurate information with those who need it, or to find a knowledgeable friend who can be relied upon to tell the truth.

7. At such times, it is important to strengthen one's trust that Hashem will help those who want to obey His mitzvos and will protect them from any harmful consequences.[3] One can be certain that no harm will come from upholding the mitzvos of *lashon hara* and *rechilus*. Indeed, we are told that the reward for the fulfillment of these mitzvos is beyond the conception of even the highest angels. On the other hand, we usually see that no lasting good results from deliberate violations of His commandments.

❏ *Wrong:*

> *Oh, you learn in Midcity Yeshivah; do you know Yaakov A? What kind of fellow is he?*

❏ *Right:*

> *Oh, you learn in Midcity Yeshivah; do you know Yaakov A? I need to know what kind of fellow he is.*

❏ *Alternative:*

> *I need to know for a shidduch.*

❏ *Or:*

> *I need to know for a shidduch. The girl is looking for a boy who is* ... (see paragraphs 3-4).

---

2. Even though the listener's intent is legitimate, the speaker is unaware of that, and so, his intent is illegitimate and "evil," his words are *lashon hara* and the listener is guilty of causing this *lashon hara*. See *Chofetz Chaim, Hilchos Lashon Hara* ibid., *Mei Menuchos* 3; *Halichos Olam,* Ch. 17 fn. *gimmel.*

3. *Koheles* 8:5, *Those who guard a mitzvah will not know evil.* See *Bava Kamma* 50a (story of the daughter of "Nechunia the digger of wells").

The Permitted Length of an Inquiry

8. It is permitted to continue making inquiries as long as necessary to investigate a proposed *shidduch*. Even if one has already received many different reports about the candidate, further details may help clarify the overall picture.[4] However, once there seems to be a solid basis for making a decision, one should not persist in asking unnecessary questions.[5]

Accepting Negative Information

9. Even though it is permitted to *listen* to negative information about a candidate in order to then verify it, it is *forbidden to accept it* as definitely true and to think less of the candidate (or his family) on that basis. Since it is so easy and common to violate the prohibitions against accepting *lashon hara*, one is urged to take the following precautionary measures before making inquiries into a *shidduch*:

(a) Review the *halachos* concerning listening to and accepting *lashon hara* (see Chapters 13-14).

(b) Review the *halachos* concerning judging others favorably (see Chapter 2).

(c) Remind oneself before asking about a candidate not to accept any negativity that emerges (see Chapter 13, paragraphs 1-2) but only to suspect that the information might be true, and to take steps to verify it to the extent that it pertains to this particular *shidduch*. Should the information completely disqualify the candidate for the proposed *shidduch*, one should judge favorably and cease thinking about the individual in negative terms.

> *Rivki A fervently wishes to marry a serious ben Torah. Her parents made inquiries about Yanki B, who is reputed to be an accomplished scholar. After carefully sifting through all the information, Mr. A came to the conclusion that although Yanki has a brilliant mind, his diligence in learning and seriousness in life leave a lot to be desired. Mr. A discussed the information with Mrs. A and Rivki and decided that the shidduch was inappropriate. Mr. A then said, "Now we have to judge Yanki B favorably, as one never knows the whole story. In the context of his personal life challenges, learning Torah and upholding it may be*

---

4. *Mei Menuchos* 3, based on *Chofetz Chaim, Hilchos Rechilus* 5:3, *Be'er Mayim Chaim* 4.

5. Ibid.

very difficult. In Heaven, he may be considered a very righteous person for his struggle to lead a Torah life; since Jews are generally righteous, we must presume that this is the case. So, although he is not suitable for us, we cannot look down on him on the basis of our information."

Asking Others to Make Inquiries

10. If a third party is in a better position to obtain information than oneself, it is permitted to ask that person to act as a representative. If no such advantage exists, however, it is better to make the inquiries personally in order to limit the number of individuals who may potentially hear negative information. However, if the source is located in another city or is otherwise difficult to reach, one is not required to take the trouble involved, and may ask a trusted person in the area to inquire on one's behalf.[6]

Deception in *Shidduchim* Is Prohibited

11. Just as lying and deception are forbidden in all other kinds of transactions, so is it forbidden in *shidduchim* to deceive either party regarding any relevant facts or the financial commitments. This is included in the prohibitions against *geneivas da'as* (see Chapter 12) and *ona'ah* (see Chapters 6 and 39).[7]

Withholding Information

12. Although there are well-known incidents of *gedolei Yisrael* who have advised people to conceal various facts involving *shidduchim*, extreme caution is required in interpreting these stories and applying them to practical situations. Individuals who infer from such incidents excuses to withhold information as it suits them, may commit very serious transgressions of *ona'ah*, falsehood, deception and *geneivas da'as*.

13. Accordingly, we will discuss a few situations where it might be justified to conceal information about a candidate. It is important to emphasize, however, that what follows is *not intended as practical halachah, and that in all areas of doubt, the only safe course of action is to consult an authoritative rav, apprise him of all the particulars of the case, and follow his instructions exactly.* A Torah scholar who has spent his life plumb-

---

6. Ibid.

7. *Kehillos Yaakov, Yevamos* 38; *Mei Menuchos* 2.

ing the depths of Torah wisdom will often be able to propose a solution to a seemingly insurmountable problem in a way that does not involve transgressing any mitzvos, opening a path to a happy and fulfilling life.

14. For the purposes of *shidduchim*, people's shortcomings may be divided into two categories: (a) integral issues, i.e. those that will directly affect the life of the new couple and the family they hope to produce, such as personality problems, heretical views, physical or health issues (limited to the young couple), etc., and (2) tangential issues, i.e. those that will not affect the candidate's ability to raise a proper family, such as undesirable relatives in the family history. While defects of the latter kind might deter most people from concluding such a *shidduch*, they would not normally be sufficient to prevent the couple from leading a normal and rewarding life after marriage. Furthermore, once others see that the marriage is successful they will likely cease to be concerned with the matter. Although even the latter type of defect is difficult to conceal, a rav may find it appropriate in an extreme instance to permit withholding such information.[8] Even so, if one is asked a direct question about the candidate's situation, it is never permitted to tell a lie.[9]

Delaying Information

15. Sometimes a candidate for a *shidduch* possesses a minor problem that, if known at the outset, might deter people from even considering him, but which they would be willing to overlook once familiar with his strengths. In such a case, a Torah scholar may see fit to advise that individual to conceal the presence of the defect until the proceedings have reached the stage where the other party has gained an appreciation of the candidate's overall attractiveness and will not be deterred by this minor drawback.[10] However, the defect should be disclosed before the *shidduch* is concluded so that the other side will not later have reason to feel that they were deceived.

Financial Agreements

16. Once a *shidduch* is concluded, and an agreement reached on financial obligations, it is forbidden for either side to pressure the

---

8. *Yevamos* 45a. See *Kehillos Yaakov* ibid.; *Mei Menuchos* 2; *Halichos Olam*, Ch. 17 fn. *tes*.

9. Ibid.

10. Ibid.

other to give more than specified. This is included in the prohibition of *You shall not covet* (*Shemos* 20:14).[11]

> *Prior to the engagement, the parents of the bride agreed to buy the couple a three-room apartment in a less expensive area in Israel. Later, the groom's family sought to pressure them to upgrade to either four rooms, or to three rooms in a major urban area. If successful in their efforts, they have violated the tenth commandment, "You shall not covet."*

A Broken *Shidduch*

17. If a *shidduch* did not come to fruition (they did not get engaged, or the engagement was broken), each side must be very careful not to say *lashon hara* about the other.

> *"Why did they break up?"*
> **Do not respond:**
> *"Well, the other side ..."*
> **Instead:**
> *"They realized the 'chemistry' wasn't right."*
> **Or, simply:**
> *"It was just decided not to go through with it."*

However, if the questioner is asking for a beneficial purpose, it is permitted to reveal the truth, as explained in Chapters 21 and 25.

> *"My daughter is meeting that young man who broke up with your daughter. Why did they break up?"*
> *If appropriate, be truthful (bearing in mind to limit the negative details to what is necessary).*

Creating Harmony

18. Sometimes, even after a *shidduch* is concluded, doubts or resentments may linger with the families. Negative talk about the other side is both useless and *lashon hara* and is highly detrimental to the young couple. The mitzvah of all those involved is to bring harmony and joy into the life of the young couple. See Chapter 28, paragraph 36 for a discussion of proper conversations at weddings.

---

11. *Sefer Mitzvos HaKatzar* (Chofetz Chaim), Negative Commandment 40; for further discussion see Chs. 30 and 42.

Maintaining *Shalom Bayis*

19. The secret of maintaining a good marriage is to be constantly giv-
    ing, overlooking the other's faults and greatly appreciating his or
her positive aspects and kindness (see paragraphs 26-27). It is
inevitable that two people will have different styles and opinions. In
a good marriage, both partners are forthright, understand these differences, and negotiate them in a caring way to a peaceful mutually
acceptable solution. This is the definition of *shalom bayis* (peace in a
household),[12] and maintaining *shalom bayis* is one of the most important Torah obligations of a couple.

> *When our people were on a high moral and spiritual level, one of the
> "open miracles" was the mitzvah of the sotah waters. If a married
> woman secluded herself with another man, and it was not known if she
> had acted immorally, the husband would bring his wife to the Beis
> HaMikdash, and there she would drink the specially prepared sotah
> waters. If she had acted immorally, she would immediately fall sick and
> die; however, if she was innocent, she would be blessed with healthy
> children. Thus, the waters proved to the husband whether or not his
> wife was faithful, and if so, harmony was restored to the household.*
>
> *In the preparation of the sotah waters, Hashem's Name is erased
> into the water. This is to teach us how important shalom bayis is, for
> Hashem commanded His Name to be erased in order to create har-
> mony in a household.[13] Certainly, then, a human being can lower his
> own honor or ego in order to create harmony.*

20. Men and women naturally have different expectations in mar-
    riage. It is the obligation of each partner to fulfill the expectations
of the other.

> *The Rambam writes:[14]*
> *The Sages commanded that a man honor his wife more than him-
> self, and that he love her as himself. If he has financial resources he
> should generously spend on her according to his capability. He
> should not impose fear on her; rather, he should speak to her calmly
> and he should be neither sad (moody) nor wrathful.*

---

12. See *Alei Shur I*, pp. 257-258.

13. *Chullin* 141a.

14. *Rambam, Hilchos Ishus* 15:19-20.

They similarly commanded the woman that she should honor her husband exceedingly, that she should have awe of him, and that all her actions be according to his wishes. He should be in her eyes like a king, so that she should constantly strive to fulfill his desires and to distance that which is unpleasant to him. This is the way of the daughters and sons of Israel who are holy and pure in their marriage. In these ways their dwelling will be pleasant and praiseworthy.

Discussing Marital Conflict

21. If a conflict does arise between spouses, every effort should be made to resolve it. At such times, it is particularly important to be vigilantly on guard to observe all the *halachos* concerning forbidden forms of speech, including *lashon hara, ona'as devarim*, etc. Nothing should be discussed outside the home unless necessary, such as consulting with qualified sources of guidance (rabbanim, marriage counselors, etc.), or asking responsible outsiders to restore harmony. Even then, everything must be accomplished with utmost discretion and sensitivity. Speaking to a rav or marriage counselor is *not lashon hara*. Particular caution must be exercised not to involve any family members in the dispute (parents, siblings, etc.) since they are very likely to take sides and exacerbate the conflict, which is not only detrimental but is prohibited as *rechilus*.[15]

The Deterioration of a Marriage

22. If a marriage has, *chas v'shalom*, deteriorated to the point that divorce is a possibility or has already occurred (a time that acrimony and resentment usually take over), all the more caution is required to say no more than the minimum required in any discussion. The *yetzer hara* finds it very easy to persuade people who are steeped in anger and bitterness that it is permitted (and perhaps even necessary) to justify their own position by talking about the other side's failings and wrongdoings. Nevertheless, this is prohibited *lashon hara*, even if the story is publicly known.

Do Not Keep Troubles Bottled Up

23. People in such situations generally go through deep personal anguish, and the Torah does not expect them to keep their trou-

---

15. See Chs. 21 and 13 as to when and how such discussions should take place and how the outside parties are to relate to any information they hear.

bles bottled up inside. On the contrary, the Sages taught that a person with difficulties and worries should talk about them to others.[16] Furthermore, they taught that if a person is in trouble, he should publicize his situation so that others may pray for him.[17] However, none of these reasons justify speaking *lashon hara*.

Solution

24. The following are permissible times for discussing one's troubles.

> *(a) When seeking guidance for the purpose of sorting out problems and searching for solutions (see Chapter 21, paragraph 27).*
>
> *(b) When seeking to release tension by sharing feelings (see Chapter 21, paragraph 28). One must be careful that the listener is knowledgeable and careful in the laws of "believing lashon hara" (Chapter 13).*
>
> *(c) When trying to let someone know that he is in trouble. He can say, "I am having serious problems at home," or "I am getting divorced, and I'm in a lot of pain." The key is to concentrate on one's own problems, not on the other's failings and wrongdoings. This can (but need not) be coupled with requests for help ("pray for me," "I need a diversion," etc.).*

In difficult situations, in general, if one wishes to observe *halachah* (and enable his life to proceed happily and along Torah principles), the best course of action is to remain in constant contact with a rav and to seek his guidance on all matters, great and small, that arise.

Discussing Minor Conflicts

25. The above discussion relates *only* to serious marital problems.

However, minor conflicts in an otherwise stable marriage should not be discussed with anyone else at all, since even disclosing that a conflict has occurred is in itself *lashon hara* about the spouse. However, it is permitted to discuss even such small conflicts with an appropriate adviser if there is a beneficial purpose in doing so, as discussed in paragraph 21.

---

16. *Sanhedrin* 100b.

17. *Chullin* 78a.

Creating Harmony Through Appreciation

26. Every person has both strengths and weaknesses, and the key to
    a happy marriage is to look for and emphasize the other per-
son's strengths and at the same time overlook, or at least minimize,
their weaknesses. Successful marriages are built on the basis of rec-
ognizing and appreciating all the good that one receives from one's
spouse, and thinking of those things as favors done out of the goodness of his or her heart (rather than as rights that one *deserves*). If so,
each spouse must recognize an enormous debt to the other for all the
good received and to work constantly at giving as much as possible
in return. This mindset applies even to the normal services spouses
are required to provide for each other and their families (e.g. laundry
and cooking, earning an income, caring for and educating children,
etc.). Although "part of the job," these acts must be seen primarily as
favors and acts of kindness, thus placing a tremendous obligation on
each spouse.

> *The wife of the great sage Rabbi Chiya would deliberately try to irri-*
> *tate him. Nonetheless, if he found something that would please her,*
> *he would wrap it and bring it to her. Rav asked him, "But she irri-*
> *tates you!" He answered, "It is enough that they raise our children*
> *and protect us from sin."*[18] *Rabbi Chiya saw these as sufficient in*
> *themselves to earn a husband's appreciation.*

27. It would seem that such an attitude is also a fulfillment of the
    commandment to emulate Hashem's ways, Who also minimizes
people's failing and wrongdoings and always looks at the merits and
good deeds they have done in the past.

> *At a time when the Jewish people acted contrary to Hashem's will,*
> *He proclaimed through the prophet Yirmiyahu (2:1): I have remem-*
> *bered for you the kindness of your youth, the love of your bridal*
> *days, how you followed Me in the wilderness in an unsown land.*

---

18. *Yevamos* 63a.

28

Involvement in Shidduchim on Behalf of Others

1. The foundation of life is marriage. Our Sages taught that it is a mitzvah to make sure that marriage partners are a proper match so that they will have a home of harmony.[1]

They also advise us that finding a proper spouse can be exceedingly difficult,[2] and therefore, helping people find their match is a great mitzvah. On the other hand, the process is laden with potential pitfalls involving *lashon hara* and *rechilus*. A person should not say, "I do not want to get involved," in order to avoid *lashon hara*; instead, he should become well-acquainted with the relevant *halachos*, and then help people find a proper spouse.[3]

2. It is very difficult to state general rules to cover all situations regarding *shidduch* inquiries, since the proper course of action in each case will depend largely on the individuals suggested for the proposed *shidduch*, as well as on the inquirer and the person being

---

1. *Kiddushin* 41a.

2. *Sotah* 2a.

3. It is appropriate to pray to Hashem that one shouldn't fall into *lashon hara* pitfalls, and then trust in Him that He will help a person to fulfill His mitzvos properly.

asked. In this chapter we present overall principles and offer a general understanding of the basic *halachos*; however, it is essential to discuss all the particulars of a more complete case with a rav, and then to follow his instructions exactly.

Three Categories

3. Statements about *shidduchim* by non-involved parties fall into three categories:

(a) One of the parties (or their representative) has asked a third party for information about the proposed candidate:

❑ *What do you think of Yankel for Devorah?*
❑ *Does Yankel have a kind disposition?*

In this situation, advice is being sought, and one must respond with the best possible advice; otherwise it is a violation of the prohibition, *Before a blind person you shall not place a stumbling block* (*Vayikra* 19:14).[4] (However, there is a difference between requests for advice, "What do you think of A for B?" and requests for information, "Does he have a giving personality?" as will be explained later.)

(b) A third party has heard that a *shidduch* is being considered and volunteers negative information that he considers important for one of the parties to have:

> *"I heard that Yankel is being considered for Devorah. I'd better tell her family that ..."*

Since advice has not been asked, one should not speak unless there is a question of serious danger (e.g. probability of serious discord, abuse, divorce, etc.). If no serious danger is involved, and it is simply an opinion that "they could do better," then one should remain silent, because information that will help one party will harm the other. (An exception is discussed in paragraph 5.)[5]

(c) Outsiders discuss the *shidduch* purely for the sake of gossip, with no intention of helping those involved to make an informed decision.

> *"Did you hear that Yankel is almost engaged to Devorah? And he is ..."*

In this situation, any negative information disclosed is *lashon hara*.

---

4. *Mei Menuchos* 4, derived from *Toras Kohanim*; also *Chofetz Chaim, Hilchos Rechilus,* "Examples" 3.

5. *Mei Menuchos* 1 and 4.

When Advice Has Been Sought

4. If one has been asked his general opinion of a *shidduch* by one of the
    parties involved, he is required to give his best advice for that indi-
    vidual. Because the futures of two people are at stake, and they and / or
    their families have to decide whether they are right for each other, it is
    permitted to reveal any information, however detailed or sensitive,
    that is relevant to the question of their compatibility.[6] Later in this chapter
    we will discuss what is considered relevant and what is not.

Volunteering Information

5. If not asked, one should not speak to one of the parties unless it
    seems likely that the incompatibility is such that serious dam-
    age would result from the *shidduch* being concluded. Even though
    his perception is that one side "could have done better," and his
    intention is to "protect" one of the parties from harm, anything he
    says may well cause harm to the other side — and there is no rea-
    son to value the interests of one side over the other. If, however, one
    of the sides is a relative or very close friend (who has the same sta-
    tus as a relative for this purpose), then one is encouraged to relate
    information to them, and, in general, to help them find a suitable
    and appropriate *shidduch.*[7]

6. However, it is forbidden in all cases to remain silent if it seems
    likely that serious damage could result from a *shidduch.* He who
    does not speak out violates the commandment, *You shall not stand aside
    while your fellow's blood is being shed* (*Vayikra* 19:16), which obligates a
    person to act if he sees a Jew about to suffer damage. However, *if it is
    not clear that damage will result one should keep quiet;* often, a solid and
    respectable family is eventually established, even though the two
    sides appeared unsuitable at the outset.[8]

> *Ari, one of the best boys in his Midcity yeshivah, is very diligent
> in his Torah learning and has true yiras Shamayim (fear of
> Heaven). One day, his friend David heard that Ari is close to get-
> ting engaged to Leah A. David knew of Leah A through his sister
> and was aghast. He approached the Rosh Yeshivah and asked*

---

6. Ibid.

7. Ibid.; see also Ch. 26 for similar situations.

8. *Mei Menuchos* 1:2.

whether he should say anything to Ari. The Rosh Yeshiva asked, "Are you sure they are not compatible? Are you sure that she hasn't matured despite her behavior in her younger years? Perhaps today she really wants to marry a ben Torah. However, if you are sure that they are incompatible, and that Ari is blindly entering a situation laden with pitfalls, then, by all means, speak to him." (continued in paragraph 8)

Beneficial Advice

7. In relating negative information concerning a *shidduch* (whether one has been asked for information by one of the parties or volunteers it on his own initiative), one must make certain that all the conditions presented in Chapters 21 and 25 are satisfied. In the following paragraphs, these conditions are summarized, with a focus on how they apply to *shidduchim*. The foremost principle is that one is permitted to speak *only* if his intention is to sincerely help the parties involved find a suitable match. It is strictly forbidden to speak in order to vent dislike or envy toward any individual involved or to take any pleasure in discussing people's failings.[9]

> *Berel taunted Shmuel on a regular basis. Shmuel repeatedly begged him to stop, but to no avail. Shmuel thought to himself, "Berel will soon be looking for a shidduch. Then I'll be able to tell the truth about him — it will be for a beneficial purpose!" (Is Shmuel interested in saving someone from a bad situation or merely in avenging himself on Berel?)*

8. Similarly, one must assess that his information is actually needed for either party to make an informed decision. One should not provide the information, even if asked, if it will not make a difference to the *shidduch* (either because a decision has already been made or because the information will not carry that much weight).[10]

> *In paragraph 6, David must assess whether Ari is already committed to Leah in his heart, so that no matter what he says, Ari will go through with the engagement; if so, he should remain silent. Ari later meets David and says with a bright smile, "Guess what? I'm almost engaged to Leah A! So, what do you think?" If David real-*

---

9. *Chofetz Chaim, Hilchos Rechilus* 9:2.

10. See also Ch. 25 pars. 5-7.

izes that the question is rhetorical and Ari is not really interested in hearing negative information, he could pleasantly respond, "Nu ... when will there be a mazal tov?" (If he still worries for his friend, he should pour out his heart to Hashem — but not to his friend — that all should work out for the best.)

9. If one sees that the questioner is indiscreet and will publicize any information he is given, or will repeat it to the other side in the *shidduch* and provoke bad feelings, then one should not speak to that individual even if there is an otherwise valid reason to convey the information. (See Chapter 25, paragraphs 6-8 for further discussion of this matter.) Nevertheless, one should not allow a harmful *shidduch* to take place just because the candidate or one of his parents is lax with the laws of *shemiras halashon*. In such a case, another means should be devised to pass the necessary information on to a responsible family member or to otherwise achieve the desired effect without causing unjustified harm should the information reach the wrong ears.[11] (If unsure how to achieve this, one can consult a discreet person for ideas.)

> **Mr. A:** *I'm looking for a shidduch for my daughter. Does Berel B have middos tovos?*
>
> **Rosh Yeshivah thinks:** *(This is a difficult situation. Neither Mr. A nor his daughter are assertive people. Berel can be abrasive and could take advantage of an unassertive wife. But if I tell Mr. A that Berel does not have middos tovos he will spread the word in my name ... I have to figure out a way to prevent this shidduch without saying anything negative. However, he won't believe me if I just say that it's not a good shidduch. Both families are wealthy and are enticed by each other's wealth. I may have to cloud the matter as a delaying tactic.)*
>
> **Rosh Yeshivah:** *Uh ... Well, I think he is busy right now. I don't like to discuss my boys at all until we're dealing with something concrete. Let me speak to him and we'll talk another time.*
>
> *Later ...*
>
> **Rosh Yeshivah to Berel:** *Are you busy with a shidduch?*
> **Berel:** *No.*
> **Rosh Yeshivah:** *(I'd better think of a shidduch for him quickly so he can really be "busy.")*

---

11. See *Mei Menuchos* 4.

Rosh Yeshivah: O.K., I am bli neder going to keep my eyes open for you. By the way, someone may suggest Mr. A's daughter, but it isn't a good shidduch. I have a lot of experience and I can't explain it further. You are both fine individuals but are not a good match ... so please just politely decline.

Communication Awareness

10. A person who gives advice about *shidduchim* should be very sensitive to cultural nuances.[12]

    (a) In certain circles, no negative trait can ever be exposed in shidduch inquiries. If told that the prospective candidate is not of an angelic nature, the listener will immediately conclude that he is downright nasty. If it is discovered that the candidate once spoke with a therapist to resolve a temporary crisis, the listener will immediately presume that he is emotionally troubled. If the candidate does not have a strong constitution, the listener will wonder if he has a dreaded disease.

    (b) When asking, "Is he a masmid (diligent student)," what does the family want to hear? Do they want to hear that the candidate is entirely devoted to Torah and spends all of his free time in Torah study? Perhaps they want to hear that he learns during yeshivah hours and doesn't waste time. Or perhaps all they want to know is that he is an acceptable yeshivah student with a decent reputation.

    (c) When asking, "Is he/she a baal chesed (kindly person)," what does the family want to know? Are they searching for a person whose free time is spent visiting the sick and helping the impoverished? Perhaps they want an individual who has a giving personality. Or maybe they are simply looking for a pleasant person who gets along with people.

    Other common catchwords are:

    ❏ *"Baal middos tovos" (good personality traits — do they mean a person who is angelic, slow to anger, humble, modest, has a kindly disposition, or is just a decent person?)*

    ❏ *"Yirei Shamayim" (fears heaven — does it mean one who views himself standing before Hashem at all times and fears sin greatly, or simply a standard upright Jew who avoids the regular sins such as eating treife and violating Shabbos? Perhaps their definition falls somewhere between these two categories.)*

---

12. Ibid.

One way to partially avoid these problems is to be specific: He has this specific strong point in area A, in area B he is a little better than standard, area C is his weak point.

Necessary Conditions

11. In relating unfavorable information about a candidate for a *shidduch*, the following three conditions must be met:[13]

(a) Truth — one must be certain that everything he says is true.

(b) Necessity — one must be careful to say only what is strictly necessary to accomplish the desired purpose.

(c) No Risk of Harm — one must take care that what he says will not cause any unjustified damage.

In the following sections we will discuss each of these conditions as they apply to *shidduchim*.

Truth

12. In general, a person may say only that which he knows with certainty to be true. If unfavorable information about the candidate is known only through hearsay, the correct course of action depends on the nature of the information.

(a) If the information suggests that serious harm will result from the *shidduch* (e.g. that the candidate is of exceptionally bad character, holds heretical views, or flagrantly violates the Torah's standards of morality), then one should relate the information with the following qualification: "I have heard that this information is true, but I do not have direct personal knowledge of it. Therefore, while it is forbidden to accept it as absolutely true, you are required to suspect that it may be true." In such a case, one is required to warn the involved party in this way about the potential damage; failure to do so violates the commandment not to stand aside while someone's blood is being shed (*Vayikra* 19:16), which forbids us to remain inactive when seeing a Jew endangered.

(b) If the threatened harm is not very serious, one should first attempt to verify it personally; if he can do so, it is just like any other unfavorable information about which one has direct personal knowledge. If he cannot confirm it, however, then the *halachah* is subject to uncertainty, as discussed in Chapter 25, paragraphs 9-17. In such cases, it is best to excuse oneself from any involvement by saying that

---

13. See Chs. 21 and 25.

one does not know enough about the candidate to be informative. If the questioner persists and reminds the speaker that he has been closely associated with the subject, he should claim that even so, he does not have sufficient understanding of the subject's character to offer any meaningful insight. He should refer the questioner to others who know the subject better or are more insightful into human nature.

> *Rabbi G is a high school rebbi in the local yeshivah. His neighbors, the B family, are searching for a shidduch for their daughter.*
>
> **Mrs. B:** *Rabbi G, do you know if Yanki A (an older boy in the yeshivah) is a good shidduch for my daughter? Is he a masmid?*
>
> **Rabbi G thinks:** *(I've heard that he isn't a tremendous masmid, but I really don't know for sure.)*
>
> **Rabbi G:** *I don't know.*
>
> **Mrs. B:** *What do you mean you don't know! You are there every day — don't you know what's going on?*
>
> **Rabbi G:** *The laws of lashon hara dictate that a person should not speak unless he knows something with certainty. I do not know Yanki well enough; he may be among the top boys in the yeshivah, or he may not be. The person to ask is the Rosh Yeshivah, who knows all the boys well.*

13. If one knows that a candidate will cause grave harm, but one is also certain that the other side will not consider his defect to be so serious a drawback and will proceed with the *shidduch* anyway, then it might be justified to exaggerate the negative information in order to prevent the *shidduch* from taking place.[14] In practice, however, this must be done with wisdom and discretion, and if one has *any* doubts, he should consult a rav.

> *Ruth is a very impressionable young lady, who could easily marry either a fine, honest young man and have a fruitful life, or be caught up with a charismatic but irresponsible young man who could ruin her life. I've heard that she is seriously considering marrying Chaim, whom I know to be outwardly full of personality, but also highly untrustworthy. He is not likely to hold down a job and will probably get heavily involved in gambling, a pursuit that he has already dabbled in. His domineering personality will surely make Ruth's life miserable. If I tell Ruth the truth she will not believe me, so I am therefore permitted to exaggerate what I know of Chaim in order to spare her from a terrible mistake.*

---

14. *Chofetz Chaim, Hilchos Lashon Hara* 4, *Be'er Mayim Chaim* 43.

Necessity

14. An important rule in discussing *shidduchim* is to relate only what is absolutely necessary to accomplish the desired effect. This rule has four corollaries, as discussed below.

15. *One:* Only the information necessary to answer the question, and nothing more, should be supplied. Therefore, if asked a specific question, one should answer only that question and not volunteer other information (unless the defects are so great that one would be required to relate them even without being asked, as explained in paragraph 6). However, if asked a general question such as, "What is your opinion about the suitability of this person for a *shidduch*?" one is required to give a complete assessment of the candidate's suitability for the *shidduch* in question (as explained in paragraph 4).

> *Q.: Does Rachel have a fine character?*
> *(Do not answer: Yes, but she is not very bright.)*
> *A.: Yes.*
> *Q.: Is Chaim a ben Torah?*
> *(Do not answer: Yes, but his family is very poor.)*
> *A.: Yes.*
> *Q.: Is Chaim a ben Torah?*
> *A.: He learns very well but his character traits leave a lot to be desired.*
> *(If true, the answer is correct, since character is an integral part of a ben Torah.)*

16. *Two:* Beware not to relate misleading information. Before answering a question, one should attempt to determine the cultural meaning of the relevant term, and thereby understand exactly what information the questioner is seeking (see paragraph 10).

> *Q.: Is Sari a baalas chesed (kindly person)?*
> *(She wants to know if she will be a good wife, devoted to her husband and children. She is not interested in knowing if she helps people with their problems.)*
> *(Correct) A.: Yes, Sari is a baalas chesed.*
> *(Incorrect) A.: Sari is a good person and will be a very good wife and mother, but I can't really call her a baalas chesed.*[15]

---

15. See *Mei Menuchos* 4. This is incorrect even though it may be objectively true.

17. *Three:* The information is often totally irrelevant to the candidate's suitability as a spouse. For example, a girl's grades in school generally have no bearing on her abilities as a wife and mother.

> *Question to Teacher: I would like to know information about Debby for a shidduch.*
> *Teacher thinks: (Debby did under-average work, but she is a fine girl.)*
> *A.: Debby is a fine girl.*
> *Q.: How did she do in school?*
> *Teacher thinks: (This sounds irrelevant; I'll give a vague answer.)*
> *A.: Fine.*
> *Q.: I want to know specifically, was she in the top, middle or lower third of the class?*
> *A.: Why do you want to know? Is he a very brilliant boy who needs a brilliant wife?*
> *Q.: Yes.*
> *A.: Then she is not a match.*
>
> *Or:*
>
> *Q.: The boy, for some reason, insists on meeting only a girl who did very well in school.*
> *Teacher thinks: (This is a specific request, and I must answer straightforwardly.)*
> *A.: She is not a match.*

> *Question to Teacher: I would like to know information about Debby for a shidduch.*
> *Teacher: Well, her grades were very low (a highly inappropriate response).*

A former teacher's clearest recollections may be of an immature student completely incapable of paying attention in class. These unfavorable memories have no relevance at all to the girl's future as a wife and mother, and relating them can cause unjustified harm. However, a wise teacher may have noticed certain negative behavior trends that are highly relevant to the girl's future life.

> *Question to Teacher: I would like to know information about Debby for a shidduch.*

Teacher thinks: *(Debby never could sit still, she was always moving around or talking ... but she probably will make a wonderful wife and mother.)*

(Correct) A.: *I think she'll make a wonderful wife and mother.*

(Incorrect) A.: *Oh, I remember her in class, she was something else! ... but I'm sure she'll be fine in marriage. I think she'll make a wonderful wife and mother. (If it is irrelevant, don't mention it!)*

(Highly inappropriate) A.: *She never sat still in class. She was always moving around or talking.*

Question to Teacher: *I would like information about Chavi for a shidduch.*

Teacher thinks: *(Chavi was a very quiet girl in class ... but perhaps she just wasn't that interested in school. I don't really know how she was in general.)*

(Correct) A.: *In class she was a bit quiet, but I saw her only as a teacher. It may not mean very much, because people often act one way in the classroom and other ways in different situations. (Notice how the teacher conveyed a point that should perhaps be investigated — "she was a bit quiet" — but left open the possibility that this may not be negative or relevant.)*

(Incorrect) A.: *In class she was quiet, but I saw her only as a teacher. It may not mean much because she wasn't very interested in school work, so perhaps that's why she was quiet. (Notice how the correct answer limited the negativity to Chavi being a "bit" quiet and omitted a negative explanation for her behavior.)*

(Highly inappropriate) A.: *She is very quiet. (Unless she knows that she is quiet in all situations, she is implying a fact that may not be true.)*

18. Unfortunately, some people who hear that information is being requested "for a beneficial purpose" are quick to relate everything they know about the subject without stopping to think whether the information is relevant or not. As soon as the word *"shidduch"* is mentioned, they act as if none of the prohibitions against *lashon hara* apply, and take the opportunity to relate all the gossip they have ever heard about the subject. Conversely, when other people hear that a *shidduch* is involved, they fall silent and refuse to relate even legiti-

mately relevant information about a candidate. They may even go so far as to invent sterling qualities with only the most remote connection to the subject's true nature, claiming that they have no desire to damage a *shidduch*. Such behavior violates the prohibition against giving bad advice (*Before a blind person you shall not place a stumbling block* — *Vayikra* 19:14) and possibly also against failing to take action to prevent tragedies (*You shall not stand aside while your fellow's blood is being shed* — ibid. v. 16).[16]

19. *Four:* If one fact in particular will cause the inquiring party to lose interest in a *shidduch*, one should relate that fact and no more, even if certain additional information is relevant to the *shidduch* (since one should never relate derogatory information if there is another way to achieve the desired effect).

> **Q.:** *I am looking for a wealthy boy who knows how to learn.*
> **A.:** *He is not wealthy. (His learning skills have become irrelevant.)*

> **Q.:** *My daughter wants a husband who knows how to learn very well, but I cannot support someone in kollel. I want her to marry a professional. Is Chaim ever going to work? Is he a good learner? Is he a nice person?*
> **A.:** *Chaim plans to learn in kollel.*
> *Therefore, any further information is irrelevant.*

20. One should attempt not to relate minor negative information at the beginning of a *shidduch* because very often, after the candidates know each other, this minor point is easily overlooked.[17]

> **Parent to Rosh Yeshivah:** *I'm looking for a fine boy for my daughter. What do you think of Yankel?*
> **Rosh Yeshivah thinks:** *(Yankel is a really fine boy, and this could be a very good shidduch. He is missing one toe due to an accident. If I tell them now they may not agree to try, but once they know him they won't care.)*
> **Rosh Yeshivah:** *Yankel is a very fine boy. I'll recommend the shidduch to him.*

---

16. See ibid.
17. See *Kehillos Yaakov, Yevamos* 38.

21. Parents sometimes look for qualities in a *shidduch* that do not seem appropriate for their child. In some cases they do this to enhance their own social standing or for other extraneous reasons. However, they may genuinely hope to elevate their child through association with an individual of deeper spirituality. It is impossible to state fixed rules in these matters, and it is always desirable to consult with a qualified rav or other experienced person for guidance. In general, however, the welfare of the prospective partners themselves is of paramount importance.[18]

No Risk of Harm

22. In giving information about *shidduchim,* great care must be taken not to cause any unjustified damage. Before a *shidduch* is concluded, this can generally be accomplished by adhering to all the rules and principles presented above, i.e. by saying only what is both true and necessary to help the party or parties arrive at an informed decision, and also by ensuring that the questioner will not repeat any potentially damaging information except to those who legitimately need to know.[19]

23. However, once a *shidduch* has been concluded, any negative information heard by either side is likely to result in great damage. Such information can cause one of the sides to call the *shidduch* off entirely or, even if the marriage does take place, result in lingering resentment and estrangement and create strains on the marriage that can have a devastating effect on future generations, Heaven forbid. Thus, once a *shidduch* has been concluded, it is absolute *rechilus* (destructive talebearing, as explained in Chapter 8) to relate any negative information whatsoever to either party *even if one is asked directly.* To the contrary, after a *shidduch* has been concluded, it is a great mitzvah to praise the parties to each other so that they feel privileged to have completed a worthy *shidduch* leading to a bright future.[20]

> **Mrs. A:** *I get a mazal tov, my daughter is engaged to Chaim J.*
> **Mrs. B:** *Mazal tov, mazal tov, and he is such a good boy.*
> **Mrs. A:** *Yes, baruch Hashem, and you have probably known him for many years. So tell me, what was he like years ago?*

---

18. See *Mei Menuchos* 4.
19. See *Chofetz Chaim, Hilchos Rechilus* 9:11 and "Examples" 9.
20. *Kesubos* 17a.

Mrs. B thinks: (In elementary school he was wild, and not at all studious, until Rabbi G took him under his wing in high school and influenced him to change his ways ... but she doesn't need to know any of this ... especially since the shidduch is concluded.)
Mrs. B: Fine, fine, baruch Hashem you have such a wonderful boy for your daughter. May Hashem grant you to see much nachas.

24. However, if there is reason to believe that grave damage will result from the failings of one party of which the other is ignorant (such as heretical views, extreme personality problems, or flagrant immorality)[21] (see footnote), and on the basis of which that side would want to annul the *shidduch*, then it is a mitzvah to inform them; failure to do so is a violation of the injunction not to stand aside while someone's blood is being shed. In general, since an annulment of a *shidduch* is similar to the breaking of a contract, it should never be done without consulting a *halachic* authority for guidance as to whether and how to do so. Therefore, a general rule is that even such reports of potential grave damage should be related only if the injured party will subsequently consult a *halachic* authority as to how to proceed. In some situations, a person judges that the injured party will not consult a *halachic* authority, but rather, will take unilateral action. However, if he is silent, they may be in danger of needless suffering. In such cases, *one must consult a rav for guidance.*[22]

Financial Deceit

Introduction: Throughout the history of our people, the norm was for parents of the prospective partners to meet and discuss financial commitments to help the young couple. This was an integral part of the *shidduch*, with the *halachic* status of a legal agreement, and is still the custom today in many communities. In such cases, the *shidduch* has the added dimension of being a financial commitment.

---

21. If one has knowledge that a problem existed only in the past before the candidate matured, it is important to verify that it still exists, since young people often overcome many of their problems in the period before they reach marriageable age. This should be thoroughly investigated before one makes any statements.

22. If the candidate is even suspected of heretical views or flagrant immorality, the Chofetz Chaim permits revealing this even to someone who will unilaterally breach a contract (*Chofetz Chaim, Hilchos Rechilus* 9, "Examples" 11). See also *Nesiv Chaim, Hilchos Rechilus* 9:14 about someone who has a highly abusive personality. Nevertheless, usually the case at hand is not so clear-cut; therefore, the general rule should be not to proceed without the guidance of a rav.

25. If a person is aware that one side is acting deceitfully and does not plan to honor its financial commitments (see paragraph 27), then he is permitted to warn the other side even if the *shidduch* has been concluded, so that they can devise strategies to protect themselves from loss and receive everything to which they are entitled.[23] However, *one must be certain that they will not breach a contract (abrogate the shidduch) or in general, act in any way against the halachah.* People who are liable to act unilaterally without consulting a rav should *not be informed* of financial deceit perpetrated by the other side.

> *"If I tell them that the girl's father has no intention of giving the money that he promised, they are not going to ask a rav what to do, rather they will ..."*

26. If the *shidduch* has not yet been finalized, and one wishes to advise one side of suspected financial deceit on the part of the other side, one should do so only if he judges that his words will be used solely in a way sanctioned by *halachah*.

> ❑ *They will not go through with the shidduch.*
> ❑ *They decide to go through with it, but will proceed in a careful manner to avoid being deceived.*

However, he should say nothing if his words will be misused.

> ❑ *They will go through with the shidduch, and then engage in deceitful behavior in order to "outsmart" the other side.*
> ❑ *They will say, "He was right in what he said about you" (rechilus).*

27. It is forbidden to reveal information about one side's deceitful plans, either before or after the *shidduch* has been finalized, unless all three of the following conditions are fulfilled:

(a) One must be sure that the other side's plans are considered "deceitful" according to *halachah*. (When in doubt, consult a rav.)

(b) One must be completely certain that the party in question does not intend to meet its obligations. This can be done in any of three ways:

(i) Through definite knowledge that they are by nature dishonest and unreliable in such matters.

(ii) They have stated explicitly in one's hearing that they do not intend to fulfill their promises.

---

23. *Chofetz Chaim, Hilchos Rechilus* 9, "Examples" 8, 9.

(iii) Through personal knowledge that their financial situation is so desperate that they have no possibility of meeting their obligations. (However, the mere fact that they are poor is not in itself conclusive, since poor people are often more responsible about fulfilling their commitments than their wealthier fellows.)

(c) One should also consider whether the other side does not intend to perpetrate some deception of its own, since if both sides are acting dishonorably they cancel each other out and nothing should be said to either one.[24]

> *"I know that the girl's father will not keep his word and buy them an apartment, but I suspect that the boy's father does not intend to pay the money that he promised either. Therefore, I will say nothing."*

Knowledge of Health Problems

28. If one knows that one of the parties in a *shidduch* suffers from health problems of which the other side is unaware, it is permitted to reveal the information *before the shidduch is finalized*, provided that all the following conditions are fulfilled:

(a) One must be certain that the candidate actually suffers from a diagnosable illness, and not simply from a weak constitution or other general condition that is not overly significant.

(b) One may not exaggerate the seriousness of the condition.

(c) One must be certain that all the other necessary conditions for relating negative information for a beneficial purpose are met; in particular, one should consider carefully whether or not relating this particular information will accomplish the desired effect.[25]

> *Mr. A: If I tell the girl's side that he suffered from rheumatic fever, they will go through with the shidduch anyway, but at a future point, she may say during an argument, "Mr. A told me that you had rheumatic fever and you just hid this information from me."*

29. If one becomes aware that one side has withheld information about a health problem after the *shidduch* has been concluded, a qualified rav must be consulted to determine whether the Torah allows abrogating the *shidduch* on the basis of such a problem. If the

---

24. Ibid.

25. Ibid. "Examples" 6; *Be'er Mayim Chaim* 8.

shidduch may be annulled, it is permitted to tell the other side about the problem;[26] otherwise, it is forbidden.

The Candidate's Family

30. If one learns *after* a *shidduch* has been concluded that one of the sides withheld information about undesirable family members (e.g. that a close relative is known to have an "unsavory" reputation), *nothing should be said*. If the *shidduch* has not yet been concluded *and* the person who knows the negative information is a relative or close friend of the other side, and he believes that they would feel socially disgraced if they were to go through with the *shidduch*, then it would seem to be permitted to reveal this information to them in order to protect them from the hurt and disgrace involved.

31. If, however, it is not merely the family's social standing that is at stake but the actual compatibility of the couple (e.g. one partner would be unable to respect a spouse who comes from a non-observant family), then one is required to inform the other side rather than to allow a tragic error to occur.

It is important to stress that in all the situations described in this and the previous paragraph, no action should be taken without first consulting a qualified rav, since each case is different and requires special consideration.[27]

Qualities That Are Not Deficiencies

32. Certain qualities are commonly thought of as deficiencies in a candidate, but can actually be seen as strengths upon closer inspection. Thus, while one may think that he is required to tell a questioner that a candidate possesses these qualities, he may really be speaking *lashon hara*.

> *In some circles, a young man is considered naive and is even subjected to ridicule if he does not engage in the repartee common among his peers (often filled with lashon hara and leitzanus, and a source of great humiliation to its victims) or if he does not conform to the current fashions in dress. In fact, the Torah praises his behavior and condemns that of his detractors. Thus, it is lashon hara to relate that this candi-*

---

26. Ibid. "Examples" 10; *Be'er Mayim Chaim* 15.

27. See ibid.; *Be'er Mayim Chaim* 6 (referring to *Even HaEzer* 50:5 and *Beis Shmuel* 11); see *Halichos Olam,* Ch. 18 par. 28, fn. *dalet.*

date is held by his associates to be a fool and simpleton, and such talk often does great damage by making it difficult for him to find a shidduch. (Even if the person does find a shidduch, his new family may come to look down on him as a result of the bad name that has been circulated about him, and make his life unbearable.)

Before relating any unfavorable judgment about a candidate's character, it is important to think very carefully as to whether his qualities are truly undesirable from a Torah standpoint.[28]

However, if one side models such socially "undesirable" behavior and the other does not, they may be incompatible, and this should be pointed out without degrading any party.

Talking Without Purpose

33. Any time people discuss *shiduchim* and relate negative information about one of the parties without any purpose, solely for the sake of gratifying their curiosity about people or to gloat over their failings, they have violated the prohibitions against *lashon hara*.

> ❏ *"The shidduch is a miracle considering that she started out with such a reputation."*
> ❏ *"Who would have thought that such a fine girl would wind up with a boy like that!"*

In general, the Torah prohibits speaking in a negative way about any person unless there is a clearly worthwhile reason for doing so, such as helping the parents decide if a particular *shidduch* is suitable, or to help the sides adjust to each other. Each and every negative statement made in the course of a purposeless conversation constitutes *lashon hara*.

34. It must be stressed that just as it is forbidden to speak *lashon hara* about other Jews, it is no less forbidden to speak *lashon hara* about one's own children or students.[29]

> **Mrs. A:** *Mazel tov, my daughter is engaged. You don't know what this means to me. Nobody knows, but she used to …*
> **Teacher to friend:** *Mazel tov, Berel is engaged! I remember when he used to …*

---

28. *Chofetz Chaim, Hilchos Rechilus* 9, "Examples" 5.
29. *Chofetz Chaim, Hilchos Lashon Hara* 8:1.

Rejoice With Others

35. The Torah encourages us to rejoice when a *shidduch* is made, to overlook any shortcomings and focus instead on its positive aspects. Even if one thinks that harm might come from a particular *shidduch*, this does not justify spreading gossip in that regard. Rather, a rav should be consulted to determine whether and how the involved party should be informed. If he determines that they should be told, this is not blanket permission to inform others. If the rav decides that there is not sufficient reason to speak to the party, then one is required to keep his reservations to himself and should *daven* that no one suffers any harm through the *shidduch*.

> *Son: Did you hear, our neighbor Chaya is engaged to Yitzi … I know Yitzi, he's … How could they? I'm sure they don't know that he … wow, is this crazy news!*
>
> *Father: I see that you feel very emotional about this shidduch. Calm down, and ask yourself if there are any relevant halachos here.*
>
> *Son: Well, I guess there is a question of lashon hara, but I'm saying it "leto'eles" (for a beneficial purpose)!*
>
> *Father: And what is beneficial?*
>
> *Son: Well, if they knew what I know, maybe they would break up.*
>
> *Father: Are you allowed to say something that may break up this shidduch? After all, it's like breaking a contract. It could be that you are right, but you may also be wrong.*
>
> *Son: Well, I guess I have to ask the rav.*
>
> *Father: And even if he says that you should talk to them, you can talk only to the people involved, but not to anyone else.*
>
> *Son: And if he says I should be quiet?*
>
> *Father: Then you can't talk to anyone. But you can and should daven to Hashem … maybe He will help Yitzi straighten out and it will be a fine shidduch.*

36. It is especially important to note that at a wedding, it is not only forbidden but also contemptible behavior to speak or even hint at any failings on the part of either side. Sadly, it is not uncommon for people to make snickering remarks about the couple or their families.

> ❏ *"Her sister was a more attractive bride than she is."*
> ❏ *"So-and-so's gown was more tasteful than hers."*

❏ *"With a chasan like that, what do you expect?"*
❏ *"Well, that's the way these families are!"*

The Sages placed so much importance on promoting peace and harmony at a wedding that they required us to praise every bride, even if it is necessary to say a falsehood to do so. This is in order to make the new husband feel pleased with his bride and to encourage the families to be happy with each other. From this we can see the seriousness of the prohibition against the opposite behavior. Guests are not permitted to speak *lashon hara* even if no others are listening, and all the more so to say anything to a family member and arouse bad feelings between the sides. Thus, when arriving at a wedding, it is advisable to firmly resolve to speak only favorably about the couple and their families (unless one observes forbidden practices, in which case it is a mitzvah to prevent them, as discussed in Chapter 3). In this way, one can fulfill the important mitzvos of causing a bride and groom, and their families, to rejoice in one another, and of promoting peace and good feelings among people.[30]

---

30. Needless to say, one should exercise discretion and not offer excessive praise in a situation where it might provoke others to disparage them, as in Ch. 17, *"Avak Lashon Hara."*

29

Children in
Interpersonal Halachah

1. All the interpersonal mitzvos of the Torah apply equally to children and adults, and to the relationships between adults and children.[1] Just as it is forbidden to strike an adult or verbally abuse an adult so is it equally forbidden to do so to a child.

> *Mr. Silver slapped Chaim Gold. "He's just a child, and he deserved it," he rationalized. Mr. Silver has violated the Torah prohibition of striking a fellow Jew and is liable for the punishment of malkos (lashes), administered by beis din.[2]*

> *A group of teenagers played a prank on a child, leaving him confused and crying. Although they thought it was very funny and "just a*

---

1. It is axiomatic that "your fellow" includes all Jews — men and women, adults and children equally. See *Shulchan Aruch HaRav, Hilchos Talmud Torah* 1:13 that even a rebbi who wrongfully hits a child violates the Torah commandment not to strike another Jew and is liable for any damages.

2. Note: Punishment of "lashes" was applied in earlier times by the ordained *beis din* to anyone who, in front of witnesses, willfully performed an action that violated a negative commandment of the Torah. It indicates the severity of the prohibition.

joke," they have, in fact, violated the Torah prohibitions of abusing a fellow Jew (see Chapter 6) and "Do not to others what you would not want done to yourself" (see Chapter 1).

In addition, parents and teachers have special responsibilities to educate children.[3] Carrying them out can, on occasion, appear to be in conflict with the fulfillment of interpersonal mitzvos. In this chapter, an overview of relationships with children, we will discuss education in general, and training children in the area of interpersonal mitzvos in particular.

Educating Children

2. A parent is obligated to train his children to perform all the mitzvos in the Torah.[4] All interpersonal mitzvos (*bein adam l'chaveiro*) are included in this obligation.

> *Just as a parent must educate a child to daven, make berachos, "bentch" lulav on Succos and eat matzah on Pesach, so must he educate his child to love his fellow Jew, protect another person's property, judge others favorably, and, in general, to follow the ways of Hashem and be righteous in all of his dealings.*

A parent is obligated to raise his children to lead a life of Torah sanctity. This obligates him both to prevent a child from violating prohibitions and to train him to avoid them.[5]

> *Just as a parent must educate his child not to eat treife, and not to violate Shabbos and Yom Tov, so must he also educate him not to physically or verbally abuse others, not to speak lashon hara or engage in machlokes, not to damage the property of others and not to covet others' property, for all these are Torah prohibitions.*

3. The obligation of training children in the laws of interpersonal relationships is that much greater because, as adults, the relative ease or difficulty of the fulfillment of the laws depends a great deal on childhood training.[6]

---

3. See *Succah* 42a; *Shabbos* 121a; *Eruvin* 82a.

4. See *Orach Chaim* 343, *Mishnah Berurah* 343:3.

5. Ibid. See *Rambam, Hilchos Maachalos Asuros* 17:28.

6. *Chofetz Chaim, Hilchos Lashon Hara* 9:5 and fn.

A parent who trains his children to meticulously avoid evil in their speech will merit generations of righteousness and will merit "goodness" in this world and the next, as the Psalmist says (*Tehillim* 34:14): *Who is the person who desires life and loves days to see goodness? Guard your tongue from evil and your lips from speaking deceit.*[7]

The Parents' Example

4. It is a known fact that a child is much more apt to learn from a parent's action than from his words, as when a parent teaches one way but acts differently. If for no other reason, parents should train themselves to be meticulous in all the *halachos* of interpersonal relationships and in the wisdom of proper education.

5. A wise parent will seek to identify his own shortcomings and work to overcome them (by reading parenting books, learning communication skills, etc.). In our times, most people (even those raised in religious homes) have been brought up with varying degrees of exposure to non-Torah influences. Thus, attitudes and expressions that are anti-Torah insidiously enter our hearts and vocabulary; it requires a great deal of work and courage to slowly learn how to uproot them. However, we can do no less for ourselves and for our children.

> *A few minor examples:*
> ❏ *You are "bad" or "dumb."*
>   *(There are other ways to point out that a person made a mistake in his behavior or thought process without having to resort to ona'as devarim or lashon hara. Furthermore, statements such as these cause low self-esteem.)*
> ❏ *"If you don't listen, I'll beat you up."*
>   *(This is not the Torah way of addressing disciplinary problems. Furthermore, the parent is teaching the child a powerful lesson — when a person doesn't get his way, he resorts to abuse.)*
> ❏ *"That's stupid."*
>   *(The person feels "put down" and "low." The speaker has resorted to ona'as devarim and satisfied his lowly desire for "one-upmanship." This is a powerful example of the wrong way of relating to people's mistakes.)*

---

7. Ibid.

❏ *"We won! We're the greatest!"*

(Does it make a person "great" to be better than others in sports, studies, or any other competition? Greatness is achieved by true self-worth, not by victory over others. Furthermore, this is a direct violation of the prohibition to gain honor at the expense of others [see Chapter 16, paragraph 23]. A better alternative is: "We won! I'm so happy! It's a great feeling to win!" It is even more admirable in the presence of the losers to state only words that will not make them feel bad in any way, e.g. "It's not important who won, it was a fun game.")

❏ *"We are so proud that ..."*

(Many people are unaware that such a statement often may stem from a haughty sense of pride, an abomination in the eyes of Hashem. Pride indicates that a person's accomplishments are self-made and denies the Divine in human achievement. A parent who boasts, "We are so proud of our son's accomplishments in school," is teaching that a child's success is reason for the parent to feel haughty and superior. A far better alternative is: "We are so happy with his accomplishments." Thus, they are teaching that a person should be happy with his blessings, but not feel any superiority over others. An even better approach is: "We are thankful to Hashem that he was able to accomplish so much." Thus, the parent teaches a child how to view every success in life not with egoistic self-acclaim, but with humble recognition of Divine assistance, as the Torah says, "You shall remember Hashem for He has given you strength to succeed" [Devarim 8:18]. When a child displays good character traits, such as kindness or forgiveness, the parent should compliment him with words such as "great," "wonderful" or "well-done." There are times that saying to a child, "We are proud of you," can be an effective way of raising self-esteem. However, it is a phrase that should not be used indiscriminately.)

Note: Many such statements are learned from parents or teachers, who also have been influenced by the non-Torah values that have insidiously entered even the culture and language of Torah Jews. Also, since some of these statements are appropriate at times (see paragraph 19), people misinterpret the Torah to use them at inappropriate times; in fact, all they are then doing is following the norms of secular society. A person cannot excuse himself by saying, "Well, that's how others are." He must measure his words and example only by the yardstick of Hashem's Torah, and attempt, as much as possible, to uproot anti-Torah usage and lessons.

Educating Children to Avoid Speaking *Lashon Hara*

6. One of the most delicate issues in Torah education is how to teach children to avoid *lashon hara*. Although an adult who sees or hears negative behavior is not permitted to speak about it unless there is a specific beneficial purpose, a child cannot be limited in the same way. A child needs to relate his experiences to his parents or teachers, for they are his guide on how to relate to the world. Therefore, anything a child tells his parents or teachers, is, in a sense, for a beneficial purpose, and the parent or teacher does not have to stop him from speaking.[8] The parent may listen, but is not permitted to believe the *lashon hara*. Whenever possible, the parent should attempt to direct the child to view the incident from a more positive angle.

> **Child:** *Shimon fights all the time.*
> **Parent:** *That's sad. What do you think is bothering him that he feels a need to fight?*
> **Poor Parenting:** *He is a bad boy. (Focus on the action, not the person.)*
> **Poor Parenting:** *Shh … that's lashon hara.*

7. However, a parent must still teach a child the *halachos* of *lashon hara* and train him to avoid it. Therefore, if a parent feels that the time is appropriate to train the child in the *halachos* of *lashon hara*, he may refuse to listen in order to set an example and avoid hearing *lashon hara*.

> **Child:** *Shimon was fighting again today. All Levi did was touch his Gemara and he started.*
> **Parent (has already heard a few similar stories):** *We already talked about Shimon a few times. You can tell us what happens in yeshivah, but if we've already discussed it, then we're talking for no reason. That's lashon hara and I don't want to hear about it anymore. Of course, you should always come to us with any problem that affects you personally.*

---

8. See *Nesiv Chaim* and *Zera Chaim* on *Chofetz Chaim, Hilchos Lashon Hara* 9:5.

Note: There are no general rules, as each child and every situation is different. A parent must use his judgment, and, as with life in general, and educational issues in particular, pray for Divine assistance.

Sibling Squabbles

8. When siblings fight, one will usually go to the parent and proclaim how terrible the other is and what offense he committed. The *halachah* states that a person is not permitted to speak even beneficial *lashon hara* if there is some other way to resolve the issue. Whenever possible, one must first approach the wrongdoer to see if he will change his ways. Only after that has proven unsuccessful can one involve someone else — even if that "someone else" is a parent.[9]

> *In Parshas Vayeishev we learn that Yosef felt his older brothers were committing certain sins, so he told his father Yaakov about it with the beneficial intent of helping them mend their ways. However, since Yosef did not approach the brothers first, his words to Yaakov were deemed lashon hara.*

9. The *halachos* for children are not necessarily the same as for adults, as there is no clear barometer to measure when a parent's involvement is needed. Nevertheless, we can learn from the Torah some educational techniques that can be used to teach children how to properly fulfill the interpersonal mitzvos.

> **Yitzi:** *Yanki hit me and kicked me.*
> *(Mother — If I get involved, I'm teaching him that it's O.K. to "tattle." This not only encourages lashon hara, but teaches him not to be assertive. I want to teach him to speak up for himself and not need to speak lashon hara.)*
> **Mother:** *Go tell Yanki that you don't like to be hit.*
> **Yitzi:** *But he'll do it again.*
> **Mother:** *Go to him and tell him very clearly, without screaming: I DON'T LIKE TO BE HIT. If that doesn't help, come back to me. (At that point, she may have to get involved.)*

> **Leah:** *It's mine!*
> **Yitzi:** *No, it's mine. You grabbed it from me!*

---

9. *Chofetz Chaim, Hilchos Lashon Hara* 8:11 and *Nesivos Chaim* ad loc.

Leah: Ouch, he hit me.

Mother: (Taking the toy) I'm going to hold it for now. I want you both to go to the other room and figure out a way to make peace. Maybe Leah can have it first for 15 minutes and then Yitzi, or some other compromise. You are smart children and can figure out a way to make peace on your own. When I see you both smiling and agreeing on the compromise, I will be happy to give you the toy. (The mother has taught them that when a person has a disagreement, he must try to make peace with the antagonist rather than speak lashon hara and involve others in the fight.)

The same principles apply to teachers in a school setting. They, too, should try not to act immediately when fielding complaints (a possible violation of accepting *lashon hara*), but should teach the students how to make peace among themselves. Again, there are no general rules. In each case, a parent or teacher must use his or her judgment, and constantly pray for Divine assistance not to err.

Who Did It?

10. When some wrong or mischief occurs the natural reaction of a teacher or parent is to ask, "Who did it?" (The questioner does not expect the wrongdoer to come forward, but for others to reveal his identity.) The teacher may demand, "Whoever knows who did it should tell me now!" This is a call for *lashon hara*. The *halachos* as to how to respond to such a question vary, as discussed in Chapter 22. There are cases where a parent or teacher's main motive is curiosity or anger (i.e. who to punish), for the culprit's identity really doesn't make much difference. In such cases, asking "Who did it?" is a direct violation of the prohibition of *lashon hara*. However, there are times when the parent or teacher feels that the situation is educationally important, and as such, it is not considered *lashon hara* to elicit the necessary information. Nevertheless, Rav Moshe Feinstein wrote that it is wrong to do so because it causes the students to become lax in the laws of *lashon hara*.[10] Therefore, the teacher or parent should try acceptable methods of encouraging wrongdoers to volunteer the information, rather than demanding that some students reveal information about others.

---

10. *Igros Moshe, Yoreh Deah* II:103.

11. In an unusual situation, a teacher or parent may feel that the
    information is urgently needed, and the only way to elicit it is
by demanding that the students reveal their knowledge of the incident. In such extreme cases, the teacher or parent should first
briefly explain the difference between *lashon hara* and beneficial
speech, so that students should not feel that one can ever be lax in
the *halachos* of *lashon hara*.

When the teacher or parent hears the information, whether it was
elicited from a student or volunteered, the teacher or parent may
not believe it and act on it on that basis alone; rather, they must
attempt to verify it on their own. Acting solely on the basis of hearing certain information is a violation of the prohibition against
believing *lashon hara*.

12. A wise parent or teacher should recognize his serious responsi-
    bility to educate children to fulfill all the mitzvos of the Torah,
including those of an interpersonal nature. Thus, the teacher or parent will teach children the laws of interpersonal relationships at an
early age, and they will then be well aware of the differences between
prohibited and beneficial *lashon hara*.

> *After a grievous wrong was committed:*
> **Teacher:** *This is a very serious matter. Whoever knows who did it
> must tell me. It is not lashon hara — in fact, it is a classic case of
> beneficial lashon hara.*
>
> *(If the students have already studied the halachos of lashon hara
> and are well aware of their gravity, and have seen the teacher prac-
> tice them as well, then such incidents will not undermine their
> understanding of these halachos. On the contrary, the halachos
> become very much alive; they see that although lashon hara is usu-
> ally prohibited, it can also be a mitzvah.)*

Modeling Torah Behavior

13. A teacher must model Torah behavior. A teacher who acts in a
    way that is antithetical to the Torah, in effect, teaches his students
to take the Torah lightly.

> ❏ *If a teacher hurls a prohibited epithet ("stupid idiot") at a student
> (see paragraph 14), he teaches, in effect, that the Torah prohibi-
> tion against ona'as devarim is not to be taken seriously.*

❑ *If a teacher strikes a student (when prohibited — see paragraph 15), then he teaches, in effect, that the Torah prohibition against physical assault need not be taken seriously.*

❑ *If a teacher believes one child's word over another's (even when it is permitted to elicit information as in paragraph 11, or when a child volunteers the information) and acts on it without verification, the teacher is demonstrating that the prohibition against believing lashon hara is not to be taken seriously.*

❑ *If a teacher of Torah consistently favors one student in a class because of his natural brightness, he teaches, in effect, that Hashem values inborn genius over effort.*

An Introduction to Issues of Discipline

There are two common schools of thought in disciplining children. The "old" school believes in a firm, tough approach in response to wrongdoing, i.e. punishment and even hitting. The more "modern" school claims that these methods hurt children and destroy their self-esteem, and should be banned in order to create a more healthy, loving atmosphere for children. The old-schoolers retort that without appropriate punishment children have no limits and consequently do not develop into healthy adults, and point to the ills of modern society to illustrate the failure of the "modern" school. Furthermore, they quote *pesukim* in *Mishlei* and words of *Chazal* that encourage firm discipline and hitting to prove their contention that the newer approach is not in accord with Torah.

The truth is that neither school epitomizes the true Torah way. *Chazal* call a *cheder*, "*Beis Me'ahavai*" (*Makkos* 23b), a place that brings love between the Jewish people and their Father in Heaven, and love is only generated in an atmosphere of love. Furthermore, a child who is rebuked by an adult (parent or rebbi) whom he does not perceive as loving him will not absorb the intended lesson, and indeed, will regard the adult as being a *sonei ha'beriyos*, i.e. "he just doesn't understand people" (*Mishlei* 3:4, *Rashi*). Chastisement is in place only when the adult perceives a positive benefit for the child; otherwise, it is considered "killing" the child. (See *Mishlei* 19:18-19, explanation of the Vilna Gaon.)

Thus, the Torah teaches that a child needs limits and discipline. At times, punishment, and even hitting, is appropriate. However, only a rebbi or parent who truly loves the child and is acting with loving discipline for the child's benefit is permitted to carry out the punishment. Furthermore, it is not enough that the parent/rebbi loves the child; the child has to perceive and recognize that love, for then he will grow from the chastisement. Love is such a basic trait of the Torah personality that it is self-evident that it is necessary for a true Torah atmosphere. In a home or school based on such a true Torah atmosphere, then punishment — or even, for very serious infractions, hitting — is in place.

It should be noted that even in a loving atmosphere, many children may not thrive if they do not really fit into the class. There may be emotional or intellectual reasons why the child is experiencing trouble and either passively does not learn or actively disturbs. Such children's needs are usually not being fulfilled, and it is inappropriate to punish or hit them. In such cases, a different type of class setting is often appropriate.

In general, it is to be understood that any permission and encouragement of the Torah to discipline verbally or physically is entirely predicated on an atmosphere of love where the child feels the adult's love and recognizes that the parent or rebbi is acting for his benefit; the level of love determines the appropriate level of punishment. In the absence of the Torah ideal, physical punishment and/or verbal put-down are discouraged and may cause more harm than good.

Permission for Torah Teachers to Hurl Verbal Epithets

14. The Sages permitted, and moreover, *obligated* a rebbi to insult or embarrass a student who is not exerting sufficient effort in his studies or personality development, in order that he improve.[11] However, this is permitted only subject to certain conditions. If these conditions are not met, the rebbi violates the prohibitions against verbal abuse and embarrassing another person.[12]

(a) The rebbi must be sure that his student is not achieving his goal because of laziness. However, this approach is prohibited if the student did not understand the material because it wasn't explained properly, or because it is beyond this particular student's capabilities.

---

11. *Rambam, Hilchos Talmud Torah* 4:5.

12. See *Halichos Olam,* Ch. 26 fn. *ayin*(2), deriving these from *Rambam* ibid.

It is similarly prohibited if the student has difficulty concentrating (he has a headache or other problem that inhibits his concentration or he by nature has difficulty concentrating for long periods). Furthermore, if the rebbi is unsure whether the source of the problem is laziness or some extraneous reason, it is still prohibited. Only if the rebbi recognizes, to the best of his understanding, that the source of the problem is laziness, is he permitted and obligated to hurl insulting remarks.

(b) The specific issues involved must be important for the growth of the student. Thus a rebbi may employ these methods to push the child to learn Torah, or to exert himself to grow in the area of personality development and fear of Heaven. A teacher of girls may do so for personality development or to teach fear of Heaven, but not for Torah study. Similarly, these methods may not be used to push a student to exert himself in general studies (see footnote).[13]

(c) *Finally, and most importantly*, the rebbi must assess that the insulting remarks will have the desired effect; quite often, the remarks have the opposite effect of driving the student away from Torah.

Therefore, in modern times, it is highly inadvisable to use these methods, unless the students are mature enough to understand that the rebbi is acting for their benefit. Children, or even adults with low self-esteem, who hear "That was a stupid question!" translate this to "I am stupid and/or the Torah is not for me!" Thus, the rebbi is distancing them from Torah rather than bringing them closer.

> When the sage Levi asked his teacher, Rebbi (Rabbi Yehuda HaNasi), a certain question, Rebbi remarked, "It looks like there is no brain in his head."[14] Levi understood this to mean that Rebbi expected him to exert himself even further. Another time, when Rebbi said, "That's a question," Levi knew that he had exerted himself properly.[15] On yet

---

13. It is legitimate for a parent to strike a child in order to teach him a profession. If a child already has one profession it is legitimate to strike him in order that he learn a second profession (*Makkos* 8b). In modern times, when there are so many subjects that are studied, most of them irrelevant to the child's eventual source of income, we cannot presume that it is crucial for the child to know this material well, to the point of permitting what are otherwise Torah prohibitions of striking or verbally abusing a student. Furthermore, while a father has a mitzvah to teach his child Torah and a profession, and a rebbi has a mitzvah to teach Torah, a general studies teacher has no mitzvah to teach, and we find no precedent to permit such a teacher to strike or verbally abuse a student. However, if the student displays chutzpah or similar poor character traits, then it could very well be to the student's benefit to be "put in his place." One should ask a rav for guidance.

14. *Yevamos* 9a.

15. *Zevachim* 92b.

another occasion, Levi asked a certain question knowing that if his question was a point of debate, Rebbi would answer him in a calm manner, but if Rebbi did not consider it so, Rebbi would "act" angry and he would deduce from that another halachah.[16]

There was once a yeshivah high school student, who, although a good student, was consistently late, always with another excuse. One day, this student came late as usual, claiming that he overslept and missed his transportation. The rebbi, who was beloved and distinguished, was teaching Chumash and immediately commented from the parshah: "A'yeif min ha'aveiros" (Chazal comment that Esav was "tired" from his sins). [The rebbi knew his talmid and understood how he would take the remark.] The incident, which the student never forgot, made a strong impression on him and led him to realize that his excuses were not valid and that lateness would not be tolerated.

Permission to Strike a Child

15. The Sages permitted a parent or Torah teacher to strike a child[17] *when it is for the child's benefit and only when necessary.*[18] If no benefit exists, and it is done in order to gratify the parent or rebbi's anger, they violate the Torah prohibition of striking another Jew (which makes them liable for the punishment of *malkos* — lashes).[19]

16. The definition of "benefit" with regard to striking is the same as for verbal abuse: (a) The problem is some flaw in the child's behavior (e.g. laziness, chutzpah, failure to cooperate with parents). (b) The issue must be important for the child's development. (c) Most importantly, the parent or rebbi must calmly assess that striking will have the desired effect. If these conditions are not met, the parent or rebbi violates the Torah prohibition of striking another Jew.

In today's times striking usually has the opposite effect, and therefore, many educators believe that it should never be used.

---

16. Ibid. 30b.

17. *Bava Basra* 21a; *Makkos* 8b.

18. See *Halichos Olam*, Ch. 37 fn. *yud*, deriving this from *Makkos* ibid., and *Rambam, Hilchos Rotze'ach* 5:5.

19. See *Yoreh Deah* 245:10, *Pischei Teshuvah* 4; *Shulchan Aruch HaRav, Hilchos Talmud Torah* 1:13.

Before hitting a child, one should calm oneself internally and then explain to the child that sadly, because he ... (describe the behavior) he will now have to be hit. Usually, in such cases, a light spank is enough to have the desired effect. Besides being educationally sound, this type of spanking eliminates the possibility of violating the Torah prohibition of wrongfully striking a fellow Jew.[20]

17. A rebbi is only permitted to hit lightly.[21] Hitting in a cruel fashion, as an angry person beats an antagonist, is always prohibited and a rebbi who does so violates a Torah prohibition and is liable to *malkos* (lashes).[22]

When to Use Censure

18. Part of educating a child is to teach the severity of all evil such as immorality, injustice and cruelty. When referring to such evil phenomena or those who embody them, it is entirely proper to use very strong language in order to impress on the child/student the severity of the evil.[23]

- ❏ *"It is not right to embarrass someone." (Not very effective)*
- ❏ *"It is a terrible aveirah (sin) to embarrass someone." (The message has been conveyed that this is a very serious issue.)*

- ❏ *"He left his wife an agunah. That is not very fine. Keep away from him."*
- ❏ *"That wicked, cruel person left his wife an agunah. Keep far away from such scoundrels." (The listeners understand that such behavior should never even be contemplated.)*

If a parent/rebbi is careful not to misuse such language in any form of verbal abuse, the lesson will be that much more effective.

Mr. Gold was extremely careful in his speech, never speaking evil of others, nor using put-downs. Once, at the Shabbos table, the con-

---

20. The prohibition of striking a Jew is defined as doing so in an antagonistic way (*Rambam, Hilchos Chovel U'Mazik* 5:1). Someone who is inwardly calm and punishes by striking because of absolute necessity is safe from the possibility of violation of the prohibition (Rav Schwab explained how to hit a child).

21. *Bava Basra* 21a, *Rashi* s.v., *lo.*

22. See fn. 19.

23. See *Megillah* 25b.

versation centered on a contemporary issue of people who display cruelty toward others. Mr. Gold felt it an opportune time to teach his children the severity of such evil. He resorted to terms including "foul," "wicked" and "disgusting" when commenting on a relevant incident. His children, shocked at the severity of their father's language, had a lesson etched deep into their souls about the Torah outlook on such events.

Relating *Lashon Hara* About Children

19. Just as *lashon hara* about adults is forbidden, so is it forbidden about children, since they are also included in all of the Torah's commandments applying to "fellows." Therefore, it is forbidden to say anything that would harm a child's interests or cause him distress.

20. Relating normal childish behavior is not intrinsically *lashon hara*, because society considers such behavior normal and without negative implications.[24]

> ❏ *"Shimon will do anything to avoid doing his homework." (Normal children's behavior — the comment is not lashon hara.)*
> ❏ *"When Leah eats, her dress usually gets stained." (Normal behavior for a young child.)*

However, if a conversation will result in the child being embarrassed in front of teachers or by friends, it is forbidden.

> ❏ *If Shimon's neglect of homework would be reported to the teacher, he would be quite upset. (Therefore, it is lashon hara. A parent who conveys this information must assess that the listener will act with caution so that school personnel will not find out.)*
> ❏ *If Leah's eating behavior becomes known among her friends, she will be embarrassed. (Therefore, a parent should not mention it to someone if there is any possibility that it could be revealed to Leah's peers [e.g. a talkative mother whose daughter is in Leah's class].)*

Furthermore, one should not relate an excessive level of childish behavior that, if known, could stigmatize the child.

---

24. *Chofetz Chaim, Hilchos Lashon Hara* 8:3, and *Be'er Mayim Chaim* 5. See also *Shevilei Chaim* ad loc.; *Halichos Olam*, Ch. 19 fns. *dalet, hei.*

If Shimon yells and screams, and threatens his parents, they should not relate this behavior in normal conversation (unless they are talking for a beneficial purpose, e.g. to a child counselor, or to a close friend who will give them support or advice).

Even normal childish misbehavior should not be related by others, if one feels that the parents could be embarrassed by such reports.

If Leah's parents are extremely organized and meticulous, and will be embarrassed that their daughter does not know how to eat neatly, then her behavior should not be related to others.

Furthermore, when discussing children's typically childish actions in the course of everyday conversation, care must be taken that the adults who hear such reports will take them in the right spirit and that no harm will come to the child through them; if the child suffers in any way as a result of the conversation, it becomes *lashon hara.*

If I tell Mrs. A about Devorah, I know that she is insensitive enough to comment in ten years, "Devorah used to eat like a slob!" Therefore, I will not converse with Mrs. A about my children.

21. Normal conversations between friends about their children's doings are permitted, as long as there is no possibility of harm to the child. Generally, conversations about younger children do not cause them harm, and it is primarily in speaking about older children that more caution is required. In any case, parents should not hold such conversations in front of children, since the children might interpret these conversations as *lashon hara* and use them as an excuse to speak *lashon hara* themselves.

Although one may tell another adult that his 8-year-old rode his bike without his helmet, one should not say it to the 10-year-old brother, who will perceive that lashon hara about his younger brother is permitted.

Nonetheless, it is permitted to speak about very small children in the presence of older children, since they realize that such young children are not capable of behaving in a mature fashion.

One can relate to the children that the 3-year-old spilled water all over the floor. (One should be careful, though, not to embarrass him in front of others.)

22. Since even teenagers occasionally do not act in a mature fashion, it would seem that conversations about them in that regard do not fall into the category of *lashon hara*, as long as the listeners understand that such behavior can be expected[25] and will not think less of them when they reach adulthood or spread stories about their behavior.

> *She is just in a moody teenage state.*

In practice, however, it is best to refrain from such talk unless it is intended for the subject's benefit (e.g. to discuss educational strategies), since it could easily result in some form of harm or embarrassment to the subject, in which case it would be strictly forbidden.

Rechilus About Children

23. Just as *rechilus* about adults is forbidden, so is it forbidden to speak *rechilus* about a child.

> *If one sees two children fighting, one should carefully consider the situation before relating the incident to one of the parents. If one parent is the type who will take his child's side and hold a grudge against the other (and more so if he will abuse him verbally or physically) then it is prohibited to inform the parent of the incident — doing so violates the prohibition of rechilus.[26] However, it is permitted (and sometimes recommended) to tell this information to a parent who is the type whose goal is to promote peace and harmony and to educate their own and other children to better character traits.*

---

25. See *Halichos Olam*, Ch. 19 fn. *vav*.

26. *Chofetz Chaim, Hilchos Rechilus* 7:1

Financial Damages and Obligations

Chapters 30-37

30

Theft, Robbery and Coveting

1. The Torah prohibits stealing: *You shall not steal* (*Vayikra* 19:11); and robbery: *You shall not rob* (ibid. v. 13).[1] It is prohibited to steal no matter how small or insignificant the stolen object – even if it is worth less than a *perutah*.[2] However, one has to pay compensation only for an item worth a *perutah*.[3] The prohibition applies equally to the property of Jews and non-Jews.[4] Stealing from non-Jews is more serious than stealing from Jews because of the inherent desecration of Hashem's Name.[5]

2. It is forbidden to steal even if one's intention is only to play a joke on the victim or to annoy him. Even if one plans to return the object or to pay a fine of twice its value, it is still forbidden.[6]

---

1. "Stealing" is defined as taking something secretly to avoid detection (*geneivah*). Taking something openly without concern for who sees the theft is called "robbery" (*gezeilah*).

2. *Choshen Mishpat* 348:1. Note: A *perutah* is defined as the price of 1/40th of a gram of silver. It is usually worth approximately a penny.

3. Ibid. 348:2.

4. Ibid.

5. *Tosefta Bava Kamma* 10:7, quoted in *Beur HaGra* 348:1.

6. *Choshen Mishpat* 348:1.

3. The Torah considers stealing any amount from another person, even no more than a *perutah*'s worth, to be as if he were taking that person's life.[7]

4. The prohibition against theft does not apply to objects of no value that people would not mind being taken (e.g. a pebble, a thorn, or a leaf). However, if continuous removal of this object will result in damage, then it is praiseworthy not to take it at all.[8]

> *As Reuven was walking home with his father, he picked a leaf off a neighbor's tree. When his father glared at him in disapproval, Reuven defended himself by saying, "You know they don't care." "True," answered the father, "there is no prohibition because they don't mind and, in any case, one leaf has no value. But imagine if every passer-by took one leaf off that tree. Do you think they still wouldn't care? Therefore, we should refrain from picking off even one leaf as a pious stringency (middas chassidus). When it comes to 'theft' we should always be stringent!"*

Common Forms of Robbery

5. Although most people are not robbers in the classical sense, there are forms of robbery that some individuals do not consider to be theft. In the Torah's eyes robbery in any form is forbidden.

> ❏ *Using someone's property without permission.*
> ❏ *Eating food in a person's house or fruit from his garden without permission.*[9]
> ❏ *Picking flowers from property without being certain that there is no theft involved.*
> ❏ *A hired worker paid by the hour who wastes even a few minutes or uses the time for his own purposes.*[10]

6. It is forbidden to borrow someone's property without permission, even if one returns the object immediately after using it, and

---

7. Ibid. 359:3.

8. Ibid. 359:1.

9. Ibid. 359:7.

10. If a worker does or has done this, he/she should speak to the employer to straighten out the issue. Anything done with the employer's permission is, of course, permitted.

even if one knows that the owner will not need the object during the period of use.[11]

> **Father:** *David, whose bicycle are you riding?*
> **David:** *It's Avrom's bike. He's not home and anyway, he usually lets me ride it.*
> **Father:** *Return the bike immediately. Borrowing without permission is theft.*

7. It is forbidden to force someone to sell an object that he does not wish to part with, even if one is willing to pay the full price.[12]

> *If Reuven forces Shimon to give him his one of his possessions, he is guilty of robbery. If Reuven forces Shimon to exchange one of his possessions for money, he is guilty of a lesser form of robbery; even though Shimon has received the value of the object, he is no longer in possession of the object itself.*

Repaying Debts and Loans

8. A person who owes money (e.g. he borrowed money or owes wages, rent, etc.) or is holding someone else's property (he borrowed or rented property or an object) is required to follow the exact terms agreed upon. Thus, he must pay his debt or return the object at the time agreed upon.[13]

9. A person who refuses to pay a debt out of intransigence, not only violates the prohibition against robbery, but also the commandment, *You shall not cheat your fellow* (*Vayikra* 19:13). This commandment specifically covers cases of an individual who refuses to pay money or property, albeit that did not originally enter his possession through theft, but with the owner's consent, e.g. wages (he received the work from the laborer/artisan) or loans (he received the original funds from the lender).[14] A person who acts in such a fashion is called wicked, as the Psalmist writes (*Tehillim* 37:21), *The wicked one borrows but does not repay.* If he is a Torah scholar he commits the very grave offense of desecrating Hashem's Name as well, since such an individ-

---

11. Ibid. 359:5.

12. Ibid. 359:9.

13. See *Ahavas Chesed* Part 2, Ch. 24 for discussion of laws of repaying debts.

14. *Choshen Mishpat* 359:8.

ual is expected to be even more meticulous with the Torah's commandments than the average person.

Repaying Loans

10. Repaying a loan is a mitzvah that one is required to fulfill no less than any other obligatory mitzvah, such as *tefillin, shofar*, etc.[15]

11. This obligation is of paramount importance.

> *If a borrower fails to repay a loan on his own initiative and the lender must turn to beis din to recover his money, the beis din has the power to confiscate all the borrower's possessions (except his work tools), leaving him only enough funds to buy food for thirty days, clothing for twelve months, and rent for a specific period. In addition, the lender has the right to seize all other property belonging to the borrower, including his house, furniture and sefarim. The borrower may not even retain provisions for his wife and children, since everything he owns is considered collateral on his unpaid debt.[16]*

12. It is forbidden to squander borrowed money, leaving nothing for the lender to collect, even if the lender is very wealthy.[17] In general, it is advisable not to take a loan unless one has a compelling need for the money. The Sages cautioned us to treat other people's money as carefully as if it were our own.[18]

Danger to Life

13. In a situation where human life is at stake it is permitted to steal or damage another person's property, but one must then give compensation for any loss caused.[19]

> *Jack was threatened with his child's life unless he delivered $2,000 within the hour. Desperate, he broke into his neighbor's locked house and stole their money. Since he was saving a life, he was permitted to do so; nevertheless, he must subsequently pay back the money he stole as well as compensation for any damages caused.*

---

15. *Kesubos* 86a; see *Ahavas Chesed* ad loc.
16. *Choshen Mishpat* 97:23-29.
17. Ibid. 97:4, *Sma* 5; see also *Be'er Heiteiv* 2.
18. *Avos* 2:17.
19. *Choshen Mishpat* 359:4

The Prohibition to Covet

14. Two commandments in the Torah govern our attitude toward the property of others. One, *You shall not desire* (*Devarim* 5:18), forbids actively planning to possess another person's home, car, or any other possession. A person who thinks of ways to acquire the object in question and makes up his mind to carry out his plans violates this commandment, even if he takes no action to realize his objective.[20]

> ❏ *"I wish I had his ..." is not a violation of the prohibition.*
> ❏ *"This is how I plan to get his ..." is a violation of the prohibition.*

15. If one has not only made up his mind but actually carries through with an action to obtain another person's possession, even if he didn't steal it (i.e. he pressured the owner into selling or giving it to him, or used other people to exert such pressure), he violates an additional commandment, *You shall not covet* (*Shemos* 20:14).[21]

16. Thus, if a person made up his mind to obtain another person's possession he violates one prohibition. If he took action he violates two prohibitions, and if he actually stole he violates three prohibitions.[22]

17. It is forbidden to pressure the owner of an object to sell or give it away knowing that he would be ashamed to reject one's entreaties and would only relinquish it with reluctance. Such pressure is tantamount to coercion.[23]

> *Mr. Gold is good-hearted and has a soft side. However, there is a negative aspect to this character trait; he is easily persuaded to do things that he later regrets. One day, he put his second car up for sale with an asking price of $5,000, figuring that he would settle for $4,500. If an acquaintance knowingly takes advantage of Mr. Gold and "convinces" him by appealing to his soft nature (I can't afford more than $2,000, we really need the car, you're such a good person, etc.) he has violated the prohibition to covet. Although Mr. Gold does sell him the car, he really did not want to sell it for that price. (He may later admonish himself: "Why did I do it? If they*

---

20. Ibid. 359:10.

21. Ibid. See also *Sefer Mitzvos HaKatzar* by the Chofetz Chaim, Negative Commandment 40; *Halichos Olam*, Ch. 43 fn. *alef.*

22. *Choshen Mishpat* 359:12.

23. *Shaarei Teshuvah* 3:43.

needed a car they could have bought one for $2,000 or borrowed the money. I was just 'used' and I feel like a fool.") This type of psychological pressure is a form of coercion.

There are different situations in which people are especially apt to exert psychological pressure regarding financial arrangements.

When Yitzi and Rivki became engaged, each side pledged $15,000 toward the wedding and the expenses of starting the couple off. When it became apparent that additional money was needed, Yitzi's parents decided to pressure Rivki's parents to raise their commitment ("You know they need more, baruch Hashem you have enough, we made a mistake agreeing to this figure, etc."). They are permitted to ask, but not to pressure. If they do use pressure and succeed in procuring more funds, they have violated the tenth commandment, "You shall not covet."[24]

In the case of a person of respect or stature, however, merely asking someone to sell or give an object away is considered a form of pressure, since people are generally afraid or embarrassed to refuse such requests. Thus, such a person is allowed to make requests of this nature *only if he is certain* that the owner would not be embarrassed to refuse him. It is forbidden to even ask if there is any reason to think that the owner will accede begrudgingly.[25]

A police officer in Israel entered a silver store and spotted an item that he wished to purchase. He asked the price, which the store owner quoted in response. The officer offered a lower amount, and the store owner gave him the requested reduction. A prominent rav happened to be in the store and approached the officer. "Sir, excuse me, but you have violated 'You shall not covet.' You know that he is afraid to say no to you." The officer later returned to the store and paid the full price for the item. The rav later related the story as an example of "Yisrael kedoshim heim" (the Jewish people are a holy nation). [Story heard in Israel.]

Avak Gezel — Distancing From Robbery

18. A person may be offered a present, and knows that the giver cannot afford it, or does not really want to give it away, but is doing

---

24. *Sefer Mitzvos HaKatzar* ibid.

25. *Shaarei Teshuvah* ibid.

so out of embarrassment or some other external pressure. This is called *"avak gezel"* (literally: the "dust" of robbery). Although it is not considered legal robbery, there are some aspects of robbery involved and it is therefore forbidden.[26]

❏ *If a guest knows that a host does not have enough food to feed his own family, it is "avak gezel" to accept his hospitality.*

❏ *One should not accept an invitation if he senses that the host does not really want his company, even if the host extended the invitation on his own initiative and has enough food for his own needs.[27]*

❏ *A gabbai tzedakah (a collector of charity for the impoverished or for institutions) is forbidden to pressure or embarrass a person into giving more than he can afford. If he knows that a certain person characteristically does so and suffers as a result, it is forbidden to even ask him for charity. Those who violate this principle are considered "oppressors" of Jews and of them the verse is written (Yirmiyahu 30:20), "And I will punish all their oppressors."[28]*

Teshuvah for Theft — The Mitzvah of Returning Stolen Property

19. As long as a stolen object is still in its original form, a thief is obligated to return it to its owner rather than replace it or pay for it, as the Torah says (*Vayikra* 5:23): *He shall return the theft which he stole.* This applies even if the owner no longer expects to recover his loss. If, however, the stolen object has been transformed to the point that it cannot be restored to its original form (e.g. stolen flour was baked), or if the object has been used in construction and cannot be recovered without tearing down the building, then the thief may pay the owner the value of the object at the time of the theft.[29] If the owner lives in another locality, the thief is not required to send the money there but may instead inform the owner that the money is waiting for him.[30] If the owner is no longer alive, the thief is required to make restitution to his heirs.[31]

---

26. *Rambam, Hilchos Teshuvah* 4:4.

27. *Chullin* 7b.

28. *Bava Basra* 8b.

29. *Choshen Mishpat* 358:1, 360:1.

30. Ibid. 357:1.

31. Ibid. 357:4.

20. If a thief is ashamed to admit to his act, he may return the object to its place without informing the owner, as long as the owner is unaware of the loss. However, if the owner has already realized that he suffered a loss, then the thief must notify the owner of its return, even anonymously, in order to fulfill the mitzvah of returning the object.[32]

> *Reuven shoplifted from a store. If the owner is not aware that anything is missing, Reuven can simply replace the stolen goods in their place. However, if the owner is aware of what was taken, he must be informed of its return. If Reuven is embarrassed to admit that he took it, he may send an anonymous representative to say, "Someone took this and is now returning it."*

> *Shimon falsified a withdrawal from a bank account. If the owner of the account is unaware of the theft, Shimon can make amends by merely restoring the money. If, however, the owner is aware that something is awry, he must be made aware of the correction. However, he only needs to be informed that the account has been straightened out; no further details are necessary.*

> *Levi, working at the cash register, slipped some money into his pocket. As long as the owner has not yet checked the cash register Levi need only replace the stolen money. He can also replace the money even if the owner has already checked the register and is aware that it is missing, as long as the owner will realize that there is a surplus next time he checks, and that the amount missing has been replaced.*

21. It is particularly difficult to repent for theft from a large number of people, since it is usually impossible to locate and make restitution to each and every individual victim. For example:

❑ *A merchant who uses inaccurate weights and measures.*
❑ *A public official who abuses his position to favor his friends and relatives.*
❑ *A moneylender who charges interest.*

---

32. Ibid. 355:1.

If such a person wishes to repent for his actions, he is advised to fund public projects from which the entire community, including his victims, will benefit.[33] Nevertheless, if he can locate individuals from whom he has stolen, he is still required to make restitution and may not rely on public projects to fulfill his obligation to them.

Aiding and Abetting Thieves

22. It is forbidden to provide assistance to thieves.[34]

> ❏ *A locksmith is not allowed to duplicate a key if he has reason to suspect that it might be used to steal, or to store stolen property.*
> ❏ *It is forbidden to hold for safekeeping any object that appears to have been stolen.*

23. Similarly, it is prohibited to purchase stolen property since it rewards the thieves' wrongdoing and encourages them to continue. Concerning this matter, King Shlomo said (*Mishlei* 29:24), *He who shares with a thief is an enemy to his soul.*[35]

> *When it was discovered that Downtown Discount Dress Store Inc. acquired stock from a group of criminals who spirited merchandise out of factories, Mr. Silver forbade his family to shop there. "The Torah prohibits us from abetting sinners," he said. "The prohibition against stealing applies to Jew and non-Jew alike. Even if 'everyone' else buys there, we will not violate the Torah."*

However, it is permitted to buy a stolen object for the purpose of restoring it to its owner (since it is presumed that the owner would rather pay to recover his property than lose it entirely), provided that there is no other way to recover it.[36]

24. It is forbidden to make use of stolen property that remains in the thief's possession, even in a way that causes no harm to the property and to which the owner would not object.

> *It is forbidden to change stolen money, enter a stolen house for protection from the elements, or to cross a stolen lot to get from one place to another.*[37]

---

33. Ibid. 366:2.

34. *Choshen Mishpat* 356:1 in *Rema,* and *Sma* 3.

35. Ibid.

36. *Shulchan Aruch HaRav, Hilchos Geneivah* 9.

37. *Choshen Mishpat* 369:8.

25. It is forbidden to have any dealings with a well-known thief who has no visible source of legal income, and all of whose assets are presumed to be ill-gotten. One should not buy anything from him (as the object is likely to be stolen), sell anything to him, or even accept *tzedakah* from him (since all his money is suspect).[38]

26. It is forbidden to buy from a person who, although not known to be a "professional" thief, is suspected of having stolen merchandise.[39]

One may not buy from a watchman who furtively sells products from the warehouse that he is paid to guard.

In all such situations, any transaction is likely to be abetting a thief or his accomplices.

27. It is forbidden to buy anything or to accept a substantial gift from a married woman if there is reason to suspect that her husband is unaware of the transaction.[40] It is also forbidden to buy women's jewelry or clothing from a man if one suspects that he is selling his wife's articles without her consent.[41]

28. The Torah recognizes the authority of legal government action. Therefore, any money or property that the government has lawfully confiscated from anyone under its jurisdiction is not considered stolen, and one is allowed to derive benefit from it (even if the law itself is unfair or unjust).[42]

Reuven failed to promptly pay a small portion of his taxes and as a consequence, his property was confiscated. It was subsequently put on sale at an auction and Shimon bought it. Reuven took Shimon to the local beis din (rabbinical court) and demanded that he return his property. The court must determine if the law provides that property be confiscated as a consequence of not fully paying the tax. If the government officials were acting within the parameters of the law, even if the law is unjust and overly stringent, the property belongs to Shimon. If, however, the law does not provide for property seizure, but some other consequence such as monetary fines, then the gov-

---

38. Ibid. 369:4. See more details in *Choshen Mishpat* ibid. and *Shulchan Aruch HaRav* ibid. 12.

39. *Choshen Mishpat* 358:1-6.

40. Ibid. 358:5.

41. *Kitzur Shulchan Aruch* 182:11.

42. *Choshen Mishpat* 369:8.

ernment officials are in reality thieves. Shimon is considered to have bought property from a thief, and he has to return it to Reuven.

Inadvertently Exchanged Property

29. If one has left property (a coat, hat, umbrella, etc.) in a public place (e.g. a restaurant or shul) and returns to find that someone has mistakenly taken the item and left his own in its place, it is forbidden to use the other person's property. Instead, one must hold the item until its owner claims it and then return it to him. Similarly, if a dry cleaner gives someone another person's garment, it is forbidden to wear it even though one's own garment has been lost.[43]

Using the Property of Others

30. It is forbidden to use a person's property without his permission, even if the owner is a close friend and one is certain that he would not mind, and, even to the contrary, would be overjoyed that a friend is deriving enjoyment from his possessions.[44]

> *When visiting in a person's home, it is forbidden to take food from his pantry or produce from his garden without the owner's permission, even if he is a close friend who is only too happy to share his bounty with friends. Nevertheless, it is forbidden since the owner is presently unaware that his property is being taken.*

It is a mitzvah to make this *halachah* known to the public, since many people violate it out of ignorance.[45]

31. However, the transaction is permitted if it is common practice, because we presume that the owner consents to it.[46]

> ❏ *A small present or donation may be accepted from a married woman on the presumption that her husband is aware of and consents to her practice.*
> ❏ *Young members of a household can give a meal to their friends or let them make a local call, as is customary.*

---

43. Ibid. 136:2; see also *Halichos Olam*, Ch. 33 fn. *yud*(2).

44. *Kitzur Shulchan Aruch* 182:13 based on *Tosafos Bava Metzia* 22a, s.v. *Mar Zutra;* see *Choshen Mishpat* 358, *Shach* and *Kodesh Yisrael*, Ch. 28.

45. *Kitzur Shulchan Aruch* ibid.

46. Ibid. 182:14.

❑ *A regular guest who is accustomed to taking food with his host's knowledge is allowed to do so even if the host is not present and does not know what his guest is taking at that particular moment.*

Using the Money of Others

32. An individual who has been entrusted with money to make a purchase for another person is forbidden to use that money for his own purposes; if he "borrows" the money to buy the object for himself, the object belongs not to him but to the owner of the money, and his taking it is considered not a loan but a theft. If a person uses his own money to buy an object for himself that another person sent him to buy, his behavior is considered deceitful (since he agreed to buy it for the other person); nevertheless, the object still belongs to him.[47]

> *Mrs. A gave Mrs. B $100 and asked her to please go to the Midtown Dress Store and buy her two dresses from a sales rack of last year's stock marked down 75 percent. When Mrs. B arrived at the store, there were only two dresses left, and she decided to buy them for herself. If she "borrowed" Mrs. A's money to do so, she is considered a thief. If she used her own money, the dresses are hers, but she is considered to be deceitful.*

---

47. *Choshen Mishpat* 183:2-3.

31

Laws of Damages

1. Just as it is forbidden to steal from others, so is it also forbidden to damage their property.[1]

   Examples:
   ❏ *Breaking a window.*
   ❏ *Painting graffiti on a wall.*

   It is also forbidden to perform any action that, although not causing damage by itself, will eventually lead to damage.[2]

   Example:
   ❏ *Leaving another person's car door unlocked in an area where thieves are prevalent.*

   In the same way that causing damage through positive action is forbidden, so is causing damage through speech or writing.[3]

---

1. *Choshen Mishpat* 378.
2. *Bava Basra* 22b.
3. *Choshen Mishpat* 386:3, *Rema*.

Examples:

❑ *Giving poor advice that causes the person to lose money.*

❑ *Writing an incorrect sum on a deed.*

2. Damage can be caused not only through action but also through negligence, i.e. the failure to take a necessary action.

   A guest forgets to extinguish his candle before leaving the house and it is set afire as a result. The guest is liable for the damage caused.[4]

3. It is also forbidden to create a dangerous situation, such as digging a pit in a public thoroughfare or leaving broken glass in a place where it is likely to cause damage.[5]

   It is forbidden to pour liquid or leave fruit peelings on the ground in a public place where people are liable to slip and injure themselves.

4. The concept of "damage" includes any rendering of property distasteful to its owners.

   Littering paper wrappers and the like in a public or private place is forbidden.[6]

Removing Damage and Making Restitution

5. A person who creates a hazardous situation is required to remove the danger; as long as he fails to remove it, judgmental proceedings in a *beis din* should be taken against him to compel him to do so.[7]

6. Any individual who damages another person's property is required to make full restitution, unless the circumstances of the damage are completely out of his control.[8]

   ❑ *At a public fair where merchants laid out their wares for sale, Reuven inadvertently walked over some dishes and broke them. He is required to pay for them.*

   ❑ *Shimon was walking on the roof of his friend's cabin. He made a wrong move and slid to the ground, smashing a few outdoor vases. He is required to pay for them.*

---

4. *Pischei Teshuvah* 378:1 in the name of *Chavos Yair*.

5. *Bava Kamma* 2a, 28a, 50a.

6. *Rashi, Bava Kamma* 6a, s.v. *bimos hachama*.

7. *Choshen Mishpat* 386:3, *Rema*.

8. Ibid. 378:1-3.

> ❑ *Levi climbed up a ladder that had seemed quite sturdy when he checked it. However, he was not aware that one step had rotted due to infestation. When he reached that step, the wood cracked, and he fell and smashed the window. In this case, he does not have to pay for the broken window as the ladder was checked and presumed to be in good condition.*

However, if a person did not create damage directly, but rather caused damage indirectly, he is generally not liable for the resulting damage. Certain specific cases are exceptions, such as burning a document and thereby causing a person to lose the right to claim ownership of property or to collect a debt, etc.[9]

> *After Reuven opened Shimon's garage, a thief entered and stole his bicycle. Although Reuven's action is prohibited, he does not have to pay for the bicycle.*

7. The area of damage liability in *halachah* is very complicated, with many fine and intricate distinctions that are often difficult for the untrained observer to discern. It is therefore imperative that a person who finds himself in a situation where damages have occurred or might occur consult with a qualified *halachic* authority well-versed in these matters before taking any action.

> *It is a rare individual who is capable of viewing such matters with the detachment necessary to make rational decisions as to what the Torah requires, or even as to what is in his own best interest. Vital personal interests are often at stake, and the danger of acrimonious conflict lurks at every turn. Therefore, one should consult a rav and give him complete and accurate information to enable him to offer good advice and rule on the matter correctly.*

8. In our present exile, Jews throughout the world live under the domain of secular legal systems that, on occasion, may prevent a victim from claiming just restitution. Conversely, they often permit suing for restitution far beyond what the Divine Law considers just. Although these unjust laws are of human origin, still the *halachah* rules that "the law of the state is law."

However, this does *not* indicate complete abrogation of Torah law that is obligatory on every Jew. Therefore, in *all* cases of doubt, the only

---

9. Ibid. 386.

course of action for a person who wishes to live by the Torah is to consult a competent *halachic* authority and follow his exact instructions.

Hezek Re'iyah — Damage Through Sight

9. It is forbidden to observe another person's private space or activities, an activity from which two categories of damage arise. One is simply the natural discomfort a person feels at having his private activities observed by strangers. The second comes from the destructive forces (*ayin hara* — evil eye) unleashed by the envy that arises in people upon seeing the success of others. For this reason the Sages forbade standing in another person's field while its produce is in full growth, and we can apply the same principle to all other areas of activity.[10] Along these lines, whenever one person sees another engaged in his work, there is a praiseworthy custom that the observer give the worker, Jew or non-Jew, a blessing for success.[11] (This applies, of course, only if the work does not involve any violations of the Torah, such as dishonest practices, usury, desecration of Shabbos or *Shemittah*, etc.)

Mesirah — Informing

10. It is forbidden[12] to inform on any Jew to non-Jews or to Jews who do not conduct themselves in keeping with Torah law.[13] This is one of the most serious offenses in all of the Torah, and one who violates it forfeits his place in the World to Come[14] (unless he repents, as nothing stands in the way of sincere *teshuvah*). The offense includes not only physically delivering a Jew into the custody of non-Jews, but even merely making oral accusations or revealing information that would result in any harm to a Jew. Even if the Jew is wicked and a constant sinner, and even if he causes other Jews great difficulties, whether by word or deed, it is forbidden to hand over either his person or his money and property.[15]

11. However, if a Jew is threatening to inform on other Jews and the *only* way to protect them is to hand him over to the authorities,

---

10. Ibid. 378, *Sma* 4.

11. *Kitzur Shulchan Aruch* 183:6; see *Sheviis* 5:9; *Gittin* 62a.

12. *Choshen Mishpat* 388:9.

13. Ibid. 388:2, *Beur HaGra* 12.

14. Ibid. 388:9.

15. Ibid.

then it is permitted to do so. In addition, if an individual is causing harm to the community or is physically harming any individual Jew, then it is permitted to hand him over to the authorities in order to protect his victims.[16] It cannot be overemphasized, however, that in *all* cases a competent *halachic* authority must be consulted before any such action is taken — otherwise, one runs a great risk of transgressing this very serious offense of informing on other Jews without adequate justification.

12. An individual Jew who is engaging in illegal activities that could cause the entire Jewish community to suffer, must be warned to stop his activities. If he refuses to listen, then it is permitted to inform on him by stating that only this individual is involved.[17]

13. A person who provides information that leads to the confiscation of the money or property of another individual is liable to pay full damages for any loss he causes, even though he took no physical action but merely informed the authorities of its existence. Even if he was compelled to do so in order to protect his own money or property, this is not considered sufficient to relieve him of liability for loss caused to another Jew. However, he is exempt from damages if he was compelled through the use of force to disclose the information, provided that he only informed verbally. But if he personally delivered the money or property to the authorities he is liable for payment in all cases.

> *When the KGB threatened a community's leaders with torture, they caved in and informed on the whereabouts of a black-market store. Since they were so threatened, they are not liable for the financial loss incurred. However, had the KGB told them to "deliver the goods personally or else," they would have been liable for damages even though they acted to save lives.*

Even though danger to life permits a person to violate most prohibitions, including the prohibition against theft and damages, he must nevertheless subsequently pay for any damage that results.[18]

> *Joe was being pursued by muggers and ran into a liquor store, where he grabbed two bottles of whiskey and threw them at the muggers' heads. The shock and broken glass stopped them momen-*

---

16. Ibid. 388:10,12, *Sma* 30.
17. Ibid. 388:12, *Rema*.
18. Ibid. 388:2.

tarily, enabling Joe to get away. Even though his actions were entirely permissible because he was saving his life, he still must pay for the whiskey.

Protecting One's Property

14. If imminent danger is posed to a person's property, he is permitted to protect himself even if the steps taken will eventually cause damage to another individual. However, if one's property has already been damaged, one cannot recoup a loss at someone else's expense. Similarly, even if the damage has not yet occurred, one cannot directly damage the property of others in order to save his own.

15. Thus, it is permitted to make a barrier to protect one's property if floodwaters are approaching the vicinity, even though this action will inevitably divert the water to the property of others, as long as it is done before the flooding actually reaches one's own property. However, once the property becomes flooded and the damage has already been done, one may not drain out the water if it will eventually end up in someone else's property, since it is forbidden to help oneself by damaging another. Furthermore, even if the floodwaters have not yet reached one's property, he may not dig a canal to directly divert the water to some other property.[19]

> *If a fine or tax has been levied against two partners, it is absolutely forbidden for one partner or a representative acting on his behalf to divert it to the second partner. Since the penalty has already been finalized, the damage is done and one cannot recoup the loss at another's expense.[20]*

Watching Over Possessions

16. A person is required to watch over his possessions to make sure that they do not cause any damage. This applies to both animals and equipment, such as automobiles, machinery and tools.[21] One is also required to safeguard any fire (e.g. campfires, lit stoves) under his supervision to make sure that no damage is caused.[22] In the event that

---

19. Ibid. *Rema.* See also *Halichos Olam,* Ch. 33 fn. *ayin.*

20. *Choshen Mishpat* 163, *Shach* 18.

21. Ibid. 389.

22. Ibid. 155:1.

any of one's possessions does cause damage, he is required to consult a *halachic* authority to ascertain what compensation is required.

17. It is forbidden to incite a dog or other animal to attack a person; although the court would not require him to pay for damages, in Heaven he is considered liable.[23]

18. If one person stores his possessions on another person's property without permission from the owner, and the possessions suffer damage (e.g. the owner's animal ate the person's grains), the property owner is free of responsibility for all damages, since he had not granted his permission. Although the property owner is forbidden to damage the possessions deliberately,[24] he is allowed to remove them from his property.

> *Yanki left his bicycle in the Gold's driveway without permission. The next morning, when Mr. Gold pulled his car out, he accidentally destroyed the bicycle. Mr. Gold does not have to pay for the damage. However, it is forbidden for him to deliberately run over the bicycle, and if he does so, he must make restitution.*

Vicious Dogs

19. It is forbidden to keep a vicious dog,[25] even one that only frightens people with its bark but does not bite,[26] and even one that bites only when provoked,[27] unless it is kept on a metal chain in a fashion that makes it obvious that it is restrained.[28] If one must keep a watchdog to guard his property, he should keep it tied up during the day and allow it to run loose only at night when people are normally sleeping.[29] Anyone who keeps a dog where it is forbidden to do so prevents himself from performing acts of kindness (since poor people will be afraid to approach his house) and is the subject of a curse.[30]

---

23. Ibid. 395:1.

24. Ibid. 378:6, 393:1.

25. Ibid. 409:3.

26. Lest a pregnant woman miscarry because of fear (*Rashi, Bava Kamma* 79b, s.v., *es hakelev*).

27. *Pischei Choshen, Nezikin* 6:43 (96) derived from *Choshen Mishpat* 395:1.

28. *Pischei Choshen* ibid. (97) derived from *Choshen Mishpat* 409, *Sma* 5.

29. *Choshen Mishpat* 409:3.

30. *Bava Kamma* 83a; *Shabbos* 63a.

Dangerous Obstacles on Public Thoroughfares

20. It is forbidden to leave a dangerous obstacle, such as stumbling blocks or glass objects that are likely to break, in a public thoroughfare or even on one's own grounds. A person who left in such an area broken glass that was later kicked by passersby or animals to a place where it is likely to cause harm, is liable for any damage it causes. The person who kicked the glass is liable only for damages caused directly by his kick.[31] If a passerby picks it up and then deliberately leaves it either in the same spot or elsewhere, this second person is liable for any damage it causes.

> *Reuven left a glass bottle on the street. Shimon, while running across the street, inadvertently sent the bottle flying, cracking a car window. Later, a child tripped and fell on the broken glass. Shimon is liable for the broken car window (since the damage occurred directly from his kick) while Reuven is liable for the child's injuries.*[32]

Public Property

21. Just as it is forbidden to damage property belonging to an individual, so is it forbidden to damage property belonging to the public. Thus, actions such as writing graffiti and leaving refuse or litter in public areas are all forbidden. Refuse and litter must be disposed of in designated places in accordance with local custom.[33]

22. In localities where the custom is to bring out refuse for sanitation pickup shortly before the collection time, one is required to abide by these and similar rules. In modern times, since sewage systems exist in all areas, it is forbidden to dispose of waste water in a public area. However, if local practice so tolerates, it is permitted to pour clean water in a spot where it will drain off quickly. It is similarly permitted in rainy weather, when it will not be noticed.[34]

---

31. *Choshen Mishpat* 411.

32. However, it could very well be that if Shimon were driving a car and hit the bottle, causing it to fly off and break something, Reuven is responsible for all damages. Since it would have been dangerous for a driver to swerve on the road to avoid it, Shimon could be completely exonerated from liability.

33. *Choshen Mishpat* 414:1, 2; see also fn. 6 above.

34. *Choshen Mishpat* ibid.; see *Aruch HaShulchan* ad loc. and *Pischei Choshen* 8:38.

People of Authority

23. People in positions of authority should be particularly careful not to cause damage to others. An official charged with the responsibility of fixing fines and punishments must take great care that all his actions be for the general welfare and not for personal reasons. Such individuals must also be especially careful not to take respect for others lightly.[35]

Damage With Words

24. One should always be careful with one's words, and in particular, not to speak of negative events befalling another person, because words can have a spiritual impact.[36]

> *For example, refrain from stating:*
> ❏ *"I wish he were dead."*
> ❏ *"I hope he goes broke."*

---

35. Cf. *Rambam, Hilchos Sanhedrin* 24:9.
36. *Kitzur Shulchan Aruch* 33:14.

32

Assault

Categories of Damage

1. The Torah specifies five categories of compensation for bodily damage: (a) *nezek* (damage), any permanent loss of functioning, such as the loss of a limb or an injury that renders it permanently unusable; (b) *sheves* (idleness), loss of work time; (c) *ripui* (healing), medical and related expenses resulting from an injury; (d) *tzaar* (distress), the pain and discomfort caused by an injury; and (e) *boshes* (embarrassment), the social embarrassment resulting from an injury.[1] The Torah forbids causing any of these categories of injuries and damages.[2]

2. Besides the prohibition against injuries, the Torah also forbids striking any Jew in a hostile manner. One who transgresses this

---

1. *Bava Kamma* 83b.

2. See *Tur Choshen Mishpat* 378 with regard to damages; see also *Rashi, Gittin* 21b, s.v. *lo.*

commandment is liable to punishment by *malkos* (lashes)[3] and is disqualified from giving testimony in *beis din*.[4]

> *Although Reuven wanted to honor his good friend Shimon to be a witness at his wedding, the rav disqualified him; since Shimon was known to slap people on occasion, he was disqualified from being a witness.*

3. Even raising a hand to strike a Jew without actually delivering a blow is enough to brand someone as wicked and to disqualify him from giving testimony in *beis din*.[5]

4. So serious is this offense that the Sages said that slapping a Jew on the face is tantamount to doing so *kivyachol* to the Divine Presence.[6]

> *The Talmud relates the story of a man who was summoned to beis din for constantly hitting people, for which the beis din ordered that his hand be amputated. This punishment was derived from the verse, "A haughty arm shall be broken" (Iyov 38:15).*[7]

5. The five categories of damages listed in paragraph 1 are independent of each other, and it is possible for one injury to involve any combination of them. For example, if one person strikes another, although *nezek* and *sheves* may not be applicable (if there is no loss of functioning or work time), the assailant can still be required to compensate his victim for *ripui*, *tzaar* and *boshes*.[8] Alternatively, if one person gives another a poison which causes skin discoloration, he would be liable only for *ripui* (and possibly also *boshes*, depending on the nature of the discoloration).[9] If someone shaves off all of another person's hair, he is liable only for *boshes*.[10] Each case is judged individually, based on the specific facts and circumstances.

---

3. *Choshen Mishpat* 420:1. If he caused injury to the extent that he is liable for financial restitution, he pays but does not receive lashes.

4. Ibid. 34:2.

5. Ibid. 34:4 in *Rema*.

6. *Sanhedrin* 58b.

7. Ibid.

8. *Choshen Mishpat* 420:3.

9. Ibid. 420:10.

10. Ibid. 420:12.

6. It is forbidden to startle someone by jumping at him suddenly in the dark, shouting in his ear, etc. Similarly, it is forbidden to spit at a person, call him wicked, or use other objectionable names.[11]

Hitting a Child or Student

7. A father is permitted to strike his sons and a teacher his students, if he judges it necessary for their benefit (i.e. to correct bad habits).[12] If, objectively, it is not for their benefit, or will not be effective, hitting a child is a Torah prohibition.[13]

8. A teacher is permitted to strike a student only lightly in a way that will not injure him, and even that is allowed only if he judges that it will genuinely be of benefit to the child. Great caution is required to be sure that physical punishment does not have a negative effect, which is unfortunately very common. In any case, it is forbidden for a teacher to strike a student viciously or to deliver any form of harsh blows. Striking a student unnecessarily is prohibited no less than striking any other Jew, and the teacher is liable for punishment of *malkos* or can be required to pay damages, as discussed above.[14] (See also Chapter 29.)

Physical Force in Self-Defense and Preventing Wrongdoing

9. A person who is being hit by another individual has the right to strike back in order to protect himself, but he must take care to apply no more force than necessary. Someone who strikes another person in self-defense when he could have saved himself in some other fashion, is liable.[15]

10. If one sees one Jew striking another, and he judges that the *only way* to stop the attacker is to strike him, one is permitted to do so in order to prevent the attacker from sinning further.[16]

---

11. Ibid. 420:32, 38.

12. *Bava Basra* 21a.

13. Cf. *Makkos* 8b.

14. *Bava Basra* 21a, *Yoreh Deah* 245:10 and *Pischei Teshuvah* 4; *Shulchan Aruch HaRav, Hilchos Talmud Torah* 1:13.

15. *Choshen Mishpat* 421:13.

16. Ibid.; see *Kodesh Yisrael*, Ch. 15.

11. Similarly, if one sees an individual for whom he bears responsibility (e.g. his own child or *talmid*) in the process of doing wrong
and there is *no other way* to prevent the subject from continuing, he is
allowed to strike him and/or punish him in order to stop him from
his wrongdoing, provided that this will be effective.[17]

12. However, if the subject is not his responsibility (e.g. not from his
family), usage of force to prevent wrongdoing is prohibited, as a
person cannot arbitrarily set himself up to become a magistrate to
enforce Torah and justice. Nevertheless, if a person is physically
assaulting another individual, then anyone may strike the assailant in
order to prevent further damage, as discussed in paragraph 10.[18]

Asking Forgiveness

13. Even if a person pays full compensation for injuries he has
inflicted, he must still ask his victim for forgiveness. If the person asks to be forgiven one or two times and shows that he regrets
his action and does not intend to repeat it, then the injured party
should be gracious in granting him pardon. Granting forgiveness is
highly praiseworthy,[19] while withholding one's pardon is considered an act of cruelty unworthy of a member of the holy nation.[20]

---

17. *Choshen Mishpat* 421:13 in *Rema*. See *Halichos Olam*, Ch. 37 fn. *nun* for reference to *Terumas HaDeshen*.

18. *Yam Shel Shlomo, Bava Kamma* 3:9. Note: A *beis din* may use force to prevent wrongdoing. Similarly, a person who is highly regarded as a great sage, may, if he finds it necessary, use force (ibid.). See also *Kodesh Yisrael*, Ch. 15.

19. *Mishnah, Bava Kamma* 92a; *Rambam, Hilchos Choveil* 5: 9-10.

20. *Rambam* ibid.

33

Preventing Danger and Harm

1. Any person who sees another Jew in trouble is required to help him
by any means at his disposal. If this requires exerting himself physically he is required to do so, and if it involves hiring others to participate in the effort he is required to do this too. One who fails to help
another Jew in need violates the commandment, *You shall not stand aside
while your fellow's blood is being shed* (*Vayikra* 19:16), which prohibits
standing by idly and not rescuing a fellow Jew who is in danger.[1] This
mitzvah applies not just to mortal danger but to any situation in which
a Jew is threatened with any significant misfortune.[2]

> *Joe S, an Orthodox Jew, was hired by a brokerage firm. He had bril-
> liant business acumen and rose rapidly through the ranks. The old-
> timers in the company watched the rising fortunes of this young reli-
> gious person with envy and plotted to discredit him and force him
> out. The firm's accountant, also a religious person, got wind of the
> plot after noticing some obvious discrepancies in the books. He
> turned to his rav for advice, and was told that he was required to do*

---

1. *Sanhedrin* 73a, *Choshen Mishpat* 426.

2. See *Zera Chaim, Hilchos Rechilus* 9:1, and *Halichos Olam*, Ch. 36 fn. *alef*.

everything in his power to thwart their plans, including trying to persuade them to retract, bribing them, revealing their plans to others and convincing others to help, etc.

Moishi was not well-liked in his seventh-grade class. One day, a group of boys plotted to really "get" him by coming early to school the next day with sticks, forming a line and giving him the "treatment" as he walked in.

Although Yanki, another boy in the class, was also not very fond of Moishi, he still felt that he was obligated to warn him of the trap in order to avoid violating the prohibition of "You shall not stand aside while your fellow's blood is being shed."

2. Anyone who rescues even one Jew from harm is considered to have preserved an entire world.[3]

3. If delivering another Jew from harm requires spending money to hire others, one is entitled to recover his expenses from the person he has saved, if the latter has the money to pay him.[4]

Helping Other Travelers on the Roads

4. The Torah commands us, *If you see the donkey of someone you hate crouching under its burden, would you refrain from helping him? You shall help him repeatedly* (*Shemos* 23:5). From this we learn that we are not allowed to leave even a hated individual (and all the more so a person for whom we have no particular enmity) helpless in the middle of the road, but are commanded to relieve his distress and restore him to a normal functional state. If one fails to do so and leaves such a person floundering, he transgresses this mitzvah and also violates the commandment, *You shall not see the donkey of your brother or his ox falling on the road and hide yourself from them; you shall surely stand them up, with him* (*Devarim* 22:4).[5]

5. Since animals are no longer in general use today, we shall focus our discussion of the practical applications of this mitzvah on those *halachos* that are relevant to more common situations.

---

3. *Sanhedrin* 37a.

4. *Choshen Mishpat* 426, *Sma* 1.

5. Cf. *Rambam, Hilchos Rotze'ach* 13:1-2.

6. If one sees a person carrying a load so heavy that it falls, it is for-
    bidden to ignore him and one is required to lend assistance.[6]
Similarly, if one sees a vehicle from which cargo or other possessions
are falling and whose owner is at a loss as to how to secure them, one
is required to stop and help.[7]

7. If a group is traveling together in different cars and one car breaks
    down and needs repairs, the others are not allowed to leave that
individual alone and continue on without him. However, if this will
cause serious delays, they may proceed.[8]

Driving Carefully and With Courtesy

8. One is required to obey traffic laws, because, besides the obliga-
    tion to observe local law, danger to life is involved. A person who
does not drive carefully is, in effect, being reckless with the prohibition against murder. Furthermore, a Jew must always act with courtesy when driving in order to sanctify the Name of Hashem.

Ma'akeh — A Guardrail on a Roof

9. It is a mitzvah to erect a guardrail on one's roof, as the Torah says
    (*Devarim* 22:8), *You shall make a fence for your roof and you shall not
place blood in your house* (i.e. without a fence, a person could fall off the
roof). This railing must be at least ten *tefachim* high (approximately 40
inches) and sturdy enough to support an adult leaning on it.[9]

Other Kinds of Danger

10. This mitzvah applies not only to a roof, but to any other place
    such danger exists. Anyone who fails to provide proper protec-
tion violates the negative commandment, *You shall not place blood in
your house* (ibid.).

---

6. If one has to help an animal that is overloaded, certainly one has to help a person who
is overloaded.

7. Helping to reload an animal is for the benefit of the owner; therefore it makes no difference whether the carrier is an animal or motor vehicle. Note: Whatever one does to help
alleviate physical overload of a person or animal must be done free of charge. However,
when one helps reload an animal or vehicle, one may charge the owner for the work at the
rate that a worker would receive.

8. *Choshen Mispat* 272, *Sma* 20.

9. *Choshen Mishpat* 427:1,5.

❏ *An individual who has a pit in his property is required either to erect a ten-tefachim railing around it or to cover it in such a way that people will not be able to fall into it.*[10]

❏ *Possession of an unstable ladder, a vicious dog, or anything else which creates a danger to himself or others is a transgression of the commandment, You shall not place blood in your house.*[11]

Protecting One's Self

11. We are commanded, *Beware and guard yourself carefully* (*Devarim* 4:9). This mitzvah enjoins a person to watch his health and general well-being and forbids putting oneself into any dangerous situation or harming oneself in any way.[12] Some people feel that they can be reckless and act in a dangerous way if they are putting only themselves at risk. Besides being a violation of this mitzvah, such behavior is a contradiction of one of the essential principles of the Torah. The Torah does not consider a person to be a proprietor over himself in the way that he owns money or property. Rather, the self of a person belongs to Hashem, and the person is encharged with its safety and upkeep. Any dangerous tampering with his self will have to be reckoned with before his Owner.[13]

Preserving Property

12. Even though a person owns his property, he is still forbidden to destroy it senselessly. Thus, any individual who breaks a dish, tears a garment, renders food inedible, throws money away, or otherwise destroys any object that could be of use to people, violates a negative commandment, *Do not destroy its trees* (*Devarim* 20:19).[14]

13. Even if a person has no use for an object, he should not throw it away if it could be of use to others.[15]

---

10. Ibid. 427:7.

11. *Bava Kamma* 15b.

12. *Choshen Mishpat* 427:8,9.

13. *Radbaz* on *Rambam, Hilchos Sanhedrin* 18:6; cf. *Bava Kamma* 92a.

14. *Rambam, Hilchos Melachim* 6:10.

15. *Yevamos* 44a: "One should not spill out water from his well when others need it."

Living Creatures

14. The Torah forbids hurting any living creature, and on the contrary, requires us to alleviate their pain. However, a person is not required to spend money on animals, and he does not have to feed hungry stray animals. Nevertheless, it is proper to throw a small amount of food toward a hungry stray dog, thereby emulating the Creator Who has mercy on dogs (see footnote) but may then hit it with a stick so that the dog should not continue to come.[16] If an animal is causing a human any kind of anguish, or if the animal is needed for medical or research purposes, it is even permitted to kill it without concern for its distress or suffering, just as the Torah allows the slaughtering of animals for human consumption.[17]

---

16. *Shulchan Aruch HaRav, Hilchos Tzaar Baalei Chaim* 3,4. The dog has difficulty finding its food so Hashem created this animal in such a way so that it takes 72 hours to digest its food.

17. Ibid. Note: The human being is the purpose of Creation, and all other creatures are created for him. Hashem gave the human being mastery over the earth and its creatures (*Bereishis* 1:28). However, acting with cruelty to animals violates the sense of compassion that is within the soul, and the Torah forbids it.

34

Relationships With Neighbors

1. Conflicts of interest between neighbors provide one of the most fertile grounds for unpleasantness among people. These conflicts usually occur when people care only about their rights, but not their obligations. The Torah gives us guidelines and specifies our obligations towards others; any violation of these is a form of "damage" to a neighbor and is tantamount to stealing. Neighbors who follow the ways of the Torah will avoid the conflicts that lead to pointless hatred.

2. The Torah forbids any act that results in damage to a neighbor, even if it takes place entirely on one's own property. For example, one may not position a drain spout so that it spills water onto one's neighbor's property without his permission. However, if the drain spout was in place at the time one first occupied the property, one may leave it there since the neighbor is presumed to have already given his consent.[1] The rules concerning preexisting conditions are many and detailed, and a qualified rav should be consulted in any case of doubt or disagreement.

---

1. *Choshen Mishpat* 153.

Invasion of Privacy

3. It is forbidden to "stare" into a neighbor's house or yard, since any intrusion into a person's privacy is considered a form of damage. Therefore, it is forbidden to build a new window overlooking a neighbor's property where one did not exist before, unless that section of his property is already exposed to public view.[2] (In all questionable cases a rav should be consulted.)

4. Although one has every right to stand in a public thoroughfare adjacent to a private property, it is forbidden to intentionally position oneself to observe the "goings-on" in people's homes or even in their yards.[3] Even if the intention when standing in that position is not to observe the neighbor's activities but only for one's own unrelated purposes, it is still forbidden to act in any way that gives the appearance of a thief "checking out" a property.[4]

Preventing Damage

5. Homeowners have the right to prevent a neighbor from doing any dangerous activity on his property (e.g. start a fire) if such actions place their property in danger as well.[5]

6. If water from an apartment runs into the apartment on the floor beneath and causes damage, the neighbor on the upper floor is required to stop causing damage, e.g. by repairing a leak. However, if rainwater runs from an upper apartment to a lower one, the lower neighbor is responsible for protecting himself from any damge.[6]

7. Any activity, even one occurring entirely on one's own property, that causes dust, dirt, smoke, fumes or any other noxious or harmful emission to blow onto a neighbor's property is forbidden without the neighbor's explicit permission. Therefore, one must take care not to start bonfires, trash fires, etc., in a place where the smoke is likely to cause inconvenience or distress to the neighbors.[7]

---

2. Ibid. 154:3.

3. Ibid. 154:7 in *Rema*.

4. Ibid. 154:4 *Rema* and *Sma* 14.

5. Ibid. 155:1.

6. Ibid. 155:4.

7. Ibid. 155:34, 36.

Keeping a Building Quiet

8. If one resident in a shared courtyard (or in an apartment building with a common entrance) wishes to open a store, medical clinic, or any other center of activity that will attract large numbers of visitors, the other residents have the right to prevent him from doing so on the grounds that the increased volume of traffic in the common areas will disturb them. Even if only one individual objects while all the others have given their consent, that resident has the right to block the enterprise.[8]

9. The above rule does not apply to mitzvah-related activities, such as institutions of Torah learning or synagogues, and therefore, neighbors do not have the right to interfere.[9]

10. This rule applies only to damage caused by increased traffic volume in the common areas. Within the confines of a private home, however, it is permitted to perform loud activities (such as hammering) and the neighbors have no right to object.[10]

11. However, if the neighbor is elderly, unwell, or otherwise particularly sensitive to disturbances, he has the right to object to any loud activity that causes him pain or distress because of his low level of tolerance.[11] Even if the unwell person originally consented to the disturbing activity and only later realized that he could not tolerate it, he still has the right to insist that it stop.[12]

> If Reuven wants to work at home with a loud machine that causes headaches to his neighbor Shimon, Shimon has the right to prevent Reuven from doing this work when he (Shimon) is at home.

12. If an individual regularly works with noisy machines in his home, and subsequently a neighbor becomes unwell and sensitive to the noise, there is a disagreement among the *halachic* authorities as to who is required to accommodate whom, and a rav should be consulted.[13] However, if a healthy person moves into a dwelling located next to a

---

8. Ibid. 156:1, 2.

9. Ibid. 156:3.

10. Ibid. 156:2 in *Rema*.

11. Ibid. and 155:15 *Rema*.

12. *Bava Basra* 23a, *Choshen Mishpat* 155:41.

13. See *Nesivos Chidushim* 156:7 and *Beurim* 155:13; *Chazon Ish, Bava Basra* 13:11.

workshop and later develops a condition that does not allow him to tolerate disturbances, he cannot protest since he took occupancy with the knowledge that such activities would occur there.[14]

13. All the rights and prohibitions discussed in this chapter apply only to unusual activity not common among the majority of people. However, no one has the right to protest disturbances caused by the ordinary activities of neighbors.[15]

❏ *An infirm person cannot object when his neighbor's children cry at night, since this is part of the normal course of living.*

❏ *A noise-sensitive person cannot object to the sound of his neighbor's air-conditioning system. However, he can object to loud music.*

Competition

14. When a person wishes to open a business in the vicinity of an already existing one of the same nature, the current proprietor has the right to object in certain circumstances on the grounds that the newcomer will interfere with his business and undercut his source of income (see *Choshen Mishpat* 156). Therefore, one should ask a rav before taking any step that might affect another person's livelihood.

---

14. *Pischei Choshen, Nezikin* 13, fn. 24.

15. *Chazon Ish* ibid.

35

Employer-Employee Relationships

Reaching a Clear Agreement

1. Before hiring any worker, including one hired to perform a certain task in one's home or business, it is highly advisable to reach a clear and unambiguous agreement with him as to exactly what work he will be expected to perform and how much pay he is to receive. If no clear agreement exists, the prevailing pay rate for such work in the region is applied, and should the employer pay anything less, he is guilty of theft and cheating. The prevailing rate for any given type of work can be difficult to determine; therefore, if no agreement was reached at the outset, the only way for the employer to avoid the possibility of wrongdoing is to pay the worker whatever compensation he demands.[1]

   Note: All rules in this chapter apply to any kind of worker, even an individual hired to do minor household work and the like, and even if only a miniscule amount of payment is involved.

2. In the absence of a clear agreement, conflict is liable to result, causing bad feelings and leaving each side with the belief that it

---

1. *Ahavas Chesed* 10:14 in the comment at the end of the chapter.

has been wronged by the other. Even if the parties decide to compromise their position in order to avoid further unpleasantness, one side or the other would be transgressing the prohibitions against stealing and cheating if they did not actually forgo their claims. Therefore, the best course of action is to fix a pay rate and state clearly what work is expected at the beginning of the employment. A Torah scholar has to be especially careful in these matters, since a situation of a worker with any grounds to think that a Torah scholar has cheated him out of what is rightfully his, can result in a desecration of the Name of Hashem.[2]

> **Housewife:** *How much will this job cost?*
> **Worker:** *Don't worry, it won't be expensive … we won't end up going to a rav!*
> *This is highly inadvisable.*

Conditions of Employment

3. When an employer hires a worker, the employment is subject to the standard conditions of employment prevalent in that area, unless otherwise specified. For example, if the custom is for workers to be provided with meals, the employer is required to do so. Similarly, working hours must follow the local custom, and even if the employer is willing to pay overtime rates, he cannot force the worker to work longer or different hours than is considered normal in that area. In short, any deviation from the prevailing practice must be stated clearly at the time that the worker is hired.[3]

> *Mr. A is expanding his house. The first day of work the foreman approaches Mr. A and states, "My workers expect coffee and cake at 10 o'clock." Mr. A declares, "I never heard of such a thing!"*
> *The halachah is that one must investigate local practice. If it is clearly on the side of the workers, Mr. A must provide coffee and cake. If not, Mr. A does not have to provide the refreshments.*

> *Mr. B hired a new secretary for his office. She expects a one-hour lunch break every day, but he wants to allow her only a few minutes*

2. Ibid.

3. *Choshen Mishpat* 331:1-2.

348 / JOURNEY TO VIRTUE

to eat a sandwich. The halachah is that local custom prevails, and anyone who wants to veer from the custom should state so clearly at the time of the hiring.

Mrs. C is making a simchah, and announces to her househeld help: Since the wedding is this week, I need you to stay two extra hours on Friday. I know that it is difficult for you, so I'm willing to pay double for those two hours — but you must stay.

Household help: Thanks for the offer, but I really don't want to stay those extra hours on Friday.

Unless local custom is clearly on Mrs. C's side, the household help is within her rights and cannot be coerced to work extra hours.

Working Diligently

4. Just as it is prohibited for an employer to cheat his workers, so are workers required to do their work as diligently as they are able, as did Yaakov, who served his father-in-law Lavan with all his might in spite of the poor treatment he received.[4] Furthermore, they are prohibited from wasting time on the job[5] which is a form of stealing.[6]

> *When the Sages greeted Abba Chilkiyah he did not even return their greeting because he was in the middle of a workday and did not want to waste even a moment from his employment.[7]*

A worker is not allowed to deprive himself of food or sleep (e.g. by taking on an additional job at night or fasting) if this will impair his work efficiency during the day.[8] This applies to all employees, but in particular to teachers of Torah, who must consider themselves employed by the Master of the Universe.[9]

---

4. Cf. *Bereishis* 31:6-7: *With all my might I served your father, yet your father mocked me and changed my wage a hundred times.*

5. *Choshen Mishpat* 337:20.

6. *Mesillas Yesharim*, Ch. 11.

7. *Taanis* 23b.

8. *Choshen Mishpat* 337:19.

9. *Yoreh Deah* 245:17, *Rema* and *Beur HaGra* 30.

Withdrawing From an Agreement

5. If an employer or a worker withdraws from an agreement before the work has commenced, neither one can claim compensatory damages from the other if no monetary loss was suffered by either side.[10] However, each side may have a legitimate complaint that they now have to exert time and effort to find a new employer/employee.[11] If one side does stand to suffer a monetary loss from the cancellation of the agreement, or if work has already begun, that side can make a claim for damages. A rav should be consulted to determine the *halachah* for assessing these damages.[12]

> *If a person orders a taxi, and then cancels it, the driver is entitled to some compensation if the cab has already left the station to pick up the passenger.*

The Mitzvah to Pay an Employee

6. Once a worker has completed his work the employer is required to pay him. If the employer fails to pay the worker, he violates the commandment, *You shall not cheat your fellow* (*Vayikra* 19:13).[13] (A person who fails to repay a loan on demand also violates this commandment in addition to the prohibition against stealing.[14]) Withholding payment owed to a worker is considered tantamount to having taken his life and is a transgression of five separate commandments.[15]

---

10. See *Choshen Mishpat* 333:1, *Sma* 1 that someone who withdraws from his word is considered "lacking in faith"; see Ch. 41.

11. Ibid. This is from the *Mishnah Bava Metzia* 6:1, "They only have on them complaints." Rav Yisrael Salanter explained: A person is not permitted to have complaints and to be upset at someone for no reason. However, if one person wronged another and did not yet beg for forgiveness, the wronged party is permitted to feel upset and angry at him. Thus, the Torah legislates when one person is permitted to have a complaint against another, and when this is not permitted (*Ohr Yisrael, Nesivos Ohr*, p. 115).

12. *Choshen Mishpat* ibid.

13. *Ahavas Chesed* 10:14. The *halachos* pertaining to paying a worker on time are located in *Bava Metzia* 111, 112 and *Choshen Mishpat* 339. Since the Chofetz Chaim condensed these sources and elaborated on them in *Ahavas Chesed*, Chs. 9-10, similar to the *Mishnah Berurah*, we will quote the source in *Ahavas Chesed* for the remainder of the chapter.

14. *Choshen Mishpat* 359:9.

15. (a) *You shall not cheat your fellow* (*Vayikra* 19:13); (b) *You shall not rob* (ibid.); (c) *A worker's wage shall not remain with you overnight until morning* (ibid.); (d) *You shall not oppress an impoverished worker* (*Devarim* 24:14); (e) *The sun shall not set upon him* (without his wages) (ibid. v. 15); and a positive commandment, *On that day you shall pay his wage* (ibid.).

Paying the Same Day

7. It is a mitzvah to give a hired worker his pay on time, and an employee who delays payment violates the commandment, *On that day shall you pay his wage; the sun shall not set upon him* (*Devarim* 24:15).[16] Similarly, it is a mitzvah to pay the rental fee for an implement, work animal, house or field on time, and someone who fails to do so violates the relevant commandments.[17] For these purposes, if the work or rental is completed during the day, one is required to pay before sunset, and if it is completed at night, one is required to pay before the following daybreak. A person who fails to pay on time for work completed at night transgresses the commandment, *A worker's wage shall not remain with you overnight until morning* (*Vayikra* 19:13).[18]

> *Mr. Schwartz catered a winter weekend convention. He hired David as supervisor of all the waiters and instructed him to remain at the hotel until it was entirely clean. As it turned out, David stayed until 7 p.m. (after nightfall). Since Mr. Schwartz was no longer on the premises, David went home. If Mr. Schwartz remembers at any time of the night that he has not yet paid David, even if it is the middle of the night and he is already in bed, he must get up and go pay David in order to avoid transgressing a prohibition of the Torah. Another alternative is to call David and ask him to waive his right to be paid immediately (mechilah) so that he can wait to pay him the next day.*[19]

These time restrictions apply to workers hired for longer periods as well (e.g. on a weekly, monthly, or even yearly basis). Once the work period ends, one has only until the end of that day or night to pay for the work.[20]

---

16. *Ahavas Chesed* 9:1. See also *Zohar HaKadosh* quoted by the Chofetz Chaim in the introduction of the chapter, which says that for the violation of this prohibition of paying on time a person's "sun could set" before his time, *chas v'shalom*. In contrast, someone who pays his poor worker, and in general helps the poor fellow, will be granted extra years.

17. *Ahavas Chesed* 9:5; see also *Nesiv HaChesed* 14,15.

18. *Ahavas Chesed* 9:1,2.

19. See *Nesiv HaChesed* 29. A person who wishes to go beyond the letter of the law (*lifnim me'shuras hadin*) will pay that day even if the worker is willing to wait, as Rav Hamnuna did; see *Zohar HaKadosh* quoted by the Chofetz Chaim in the introduction to Ch. 9 of *Ahavas Chesed*.

20. *Ahavas Chesed* 9:4.

8. This commandment to pay the worker on time applies only if the worker has already asked for his pay (see paragraph 9)[21] and if the employer has the funds with which to pay him.[22] If, however, the worker has not yet requested his fee, or if the employer does not have cash available, the employer does not violate the prohibitions mentioned above if he does not pay that day. If the employer does not have cash, but has objects that can be converted to cash, he is obligated to sell them in order to raise the necessary funds to pay his workers on time. Similarly, if the owed wage is a small amount and the employer has only a large bill, he must change the bill to pay his worker on time. Furthermore, if he can borrow money he should do so in order to pay his workers.[23]

❏ *Mr. Black was short on the cash needed to pay his factory workers on Friday. Even though a large check was due to arrive the following Tuesday, he did not wait; instead, he sold some stocks to raise cash and pay his workers.*

❏ *Mrs. White's household help was leaving in two hours, and was to be paid $20. Since Mrs. White only had a $100 bill, she went to the bank to get change.*

❏ *Mr. Green asked Shimon the handyman to fix the sink. Having no cash available, he borrowed $50 from a neighbor to pay Shimon.*

According to some opinions, if the worker has not requested his pay, one still fulfills a positive commandment by paying him on time.[24]

When the Worker Is Considered Not to Have Asked for His Pay

9. When a worker does not ask for pay, the prohibitions are lifted *only if it is clear that the worker does not necessarily care whether he is paid immediately*. However, if the omission of demand for pay by the worker does not imply that the worker does not care about being paid immediately, the commandments remain in place.[25] If a worker is unable to claim his pay for any reason, the employer is required to pay him as soon as the work is finished even if no claim is made.

---

21. Ibid. 9:11.

22. Ibid. 9:7.

23. Ibid. See *Nesiv HaChesed* 21.

24. *Ahavas Chesed* 9:11.

25. *Nesiv HaChesed* 29, 32.

If a worker had to rush to a doctor or similar appointment immediately after he finished his job, the employer must pay him or at least make the money available to him[26] on that day, whether or not the worker had asked to be paid. However, if the worker specifically said that he does not mind being paid later, it is permitted to delay payment.

Similarly, once one finishes using a rented tool or machine, he is required to pay the rental fee on time; the owner cannot claim payment immediately upon completion of the work since he does not know exactly when the work was finished.[27]

Shimon rented some construction equipment from Reuven for a few days. When he is finished using it, he must pay Reuven on that day and not delay, unless Reuven specifically says that he does not mind a delay in payment.

A worker who comes to the employer's door, but does not say anything, is considered to have asked for payment. Since it is possible that he was simply embarrassed to ask, the omission does not imply a willingness to defer payment, and the commandments remain in effect.[28]

Daughter: Mommy, the babysitter is at the door, ready to leave.
Mother (to herself): I'm busy with the laundry. She didn't ask to be paid now, so I can wait until next time.
Mother: Tell her to have a good Shabbos and I'll pay her next time.
The mother's reasoning is incorrect. "Standing at the door" is the equivalent of asking to be paid, and the worker must be paid that day.

When the Commandments Do Not Apply

10. If an employer specifically states when hiring workers that he will pay them only when he has money available, he is permitted to do so.[29] If he customarily pays through an agent (e.g. a bank) then the commandments do not apply.[30] (However, see paragraph 16 for relevant Rabbinic injunction.)

---

26. An employer does not have to go to the employee to pay him. It is sufficient to inform him that the money is available. *Ahavas Chesed* 9:11, *Nesiv HaChesed* 31.

27. *Ahavas Chesed* 9:1.

28. *Nesiv HaChesed* 29.

29. Ibid. 13.

30. *Ahavas Chesed* 10:5. See ibid. Ch. 10 for other variable cases, e.g. if an agent hires on behalf of an employer.

Item for Repair

11. If one gives a garment, vessel or implement to a worker for repair
     and the worker returns it during the day, the owner is required to
pay for the work that same day; if it is returned at night he must pay
the same night. However, as long as the item remains in the repairman's possession, the customer is not required to pay, even if the work
has already been completed for several days. Even if the repairman
notifies the owner to come and claim his item and pay his debt, the
owner is not considered to be in violation of the commandments listed
above while the item is in the repairman's possession.[31]

Defining the Period of Payment

12. Even if a worker does not finish his work until the very end of the
     day, the employer is still required to pay him before sunset in
order to fulfill the mitzvah of paying a worker on the same day, and
also to avoid violating a negative commandment of the Torah.

> *In our times, when people usually do not work until sunset (in the
> summer), one must be careful to pay before sunset.*

If this occurs late Friday afternoon, the worker must still be paid
before sunset,[32] even if one has to forgo Shabbos preparations in order
to do so.[33] If a worker finishes his work after sunset but before nightfall, the employer is advised to pay him immediately. If he did not pay
before nightfall, he should at least pay him that night.[34]

Paying and Rewarding Children

13. All of the above rules apply no less to children. Failing to give a
     child any promised reward (be it money, food or a trinket) for
doing a service, even for a minor errand such as delivering a small
item, is a violation of the commandments mentioned above, including
those against theft and the requirement to pay a worker on time.
Many people transgress in these matters out of ignorance.[35]

---

31. Ibid. 10:1, *Nesiv HaChesed* 2.

32. *Ahavas Chesed* 9:2.

33. Shabbos preparations are a mitzvah derived from the Prophets while paying a worker
avoids prohibitions of the Torah and is a commandment of the Torah. Therefore, the Torah
law takes precedence.

34. Ibid. See *Nesiv HaChesed* 7,8.

35. *Ahavas Chesed* 9:5. See *Nesiv HaChesed* 16.

Mother to children: Whoever cleans the backyard will get ice cream.

If the children complete the job, the mother must give them the ice cream that day. If there is no ice cream in the house she must go buy it (unless it is Shabbos). If she does not give them the ice cream that day she violates the relevant commandments. If she does not give them an ice cream altogether she violates the five prohibitions and positive commandment mentioned in footnote 15 (You shall not rob, You shall not cheat your fellow, etc.).

The mother may say at the outset: "Whoever cleans the backyard will get an ice cream but not necessarily today." Although she must eventually give them the ice cream, she is not bound by time constraints.

Have the Money Ready

14. If an employer knows that he will not have the money to meet his payroll, he may not hire workers unless he informs them explicitly at the outset that he is unable to pay them on time.[36] If the employer will not be present to pay his workers when they finish their work, he should make sure that the money will be available for them.[37] In any case, it is always advisable to have money on hand well in advance of the time he will need it.[38] If an employer is overdue in paying his workers, he is not allowed to spend money on other expenditures unless he also has enough for the payroll.[39]

Although Mr. Dale, owner of Dry Goods Inc., was offered an excellent deal on merchandise for cash, he refused to make the purchase because he would then not be able to pay his workers on time.

Paying the Entire Sum

15. Even if the employer has paid his workers nearly the full amount he owed them, as long as any amount remains outstanding he is still considered to be in violation of the mitzvah not to delay payment, not to rob, etc.[40]

---

36. *Ahavas Chesed* 10:12.

37. Ibid.

38. Ibid. 9:9.

39. Ibid.

40. Ibid. 9:10, 10:14.

Although the babysitter was owed $11.50, Mrs. A did not have any small change and only gave her a $10 bill. If the babysitter is not "mochel" the delay, Mrs. A must find the change that day/night.

An employer who has some money on hand but not enough to cover all of his debts to his employees is required to give them what he has; if he does not do so, he violates the commandment of delaying payment.[41]

After the Due Time

16. The mitzvah not to delay paying workers does not extend beyond the end of the first night (or day) in which the payment is overdue. Nevertheless, the employer is still required to pay his workers as soon as possible. Until he does pay them, he transgresses a Rabbinic injunction, as derived from the verse, *Do not say to your fellow, "Go and come back, and tomorrow I shall give," if you have it with you (Mishlei 3:28).*[42] Similarly, if the commandments are not applicable (see paragraph 10), the employer still transgresses this injunction for any delay in payment.[43]

A person who owes money, and possesses the money to pay, is not permitted to say, "Leave now and come back tomorrow."

Precedence in the Absence of Sufficient Funds

17. If an employer does not have money to pay all his workers the total amount they are owed, workers who are poor have precedence over their better-off co-workers, even if the better-off ones have asked to be paid and the others have not yet asked for payment.[44] If none of the workers are poor then the employer should pay each one an equal proportion of what is owed to them. Even if some workers have not yet claimed their pay, it is presumed that they will eventually do so. However, if the employer knows that certain workers consented to forgo immediate payment he is allowed to pass them over in favor of the others.[45] A relative of the employer has no precedence over any other employee, even if both are poor.[46]

---

41. Ibid. 9:10.

42. Ibid. 9:12.

43. Ibid. 9:13.

44. Ibid. 10:8,10. We presume that the poor workers will also ask to be paid shortly.

45. Ibid. 9:8.

46. Ibid. 10:9.

The principal called a teachers' meeting and announced that, unfortunately, the school would not be able to pay full salaries for the next month. He hoped that within two months the situation would straighten out, but for the upcoming month everyone would get only 60 percent of their salary. The principal's daughter, a teacher in the school, would be treated no different than anyone else (for that is the halachah).

18. If an employer is in arrears to two employees, one who worked that day and one who worked on an earlier date, and he has only enough money to pay one of them, that day's worker takes precedence. The Chofetz Chaim leans towards the opinion that this is true even if the worker from before is poor and the worker from that day is well-off.[47]

Loss Caused by a Worker

19. It is praiseworthy for an employer to forgive his workers for any loss they cause him, even if their actions were negligent and they can legally be made to pay for damages. It is a mitzvah for the employer to waive his rights, as derived from the verse, *So that you may walk in the ways of good people (Mishlei 2:20).* It is a special mitzvah to go even further and give the worker his wages even if the action resulted in the job not being completed at all, especially when he lives in poverty, as this verse concludes, *and the ways of the righteous you shall guard.* This is the way of righteous people who follow Hashem's ways by going beyond what is required of them in matters of *tzedakah* and justice.[48]

Rabbah bar bar Chana hired porters to carry a casket of wine, which, through negligent handling, was broken. He thereupon seized their cloaks as reparations. They came to Rav who ordered Rabbah bar bar Chana to return their cloaks. When he asked, "Is this the din?" Rav answered, "Yes, because it says 'So that you may walk in the ways of good people.' " The workers then said to Rav, "We are poor, we worked all day, and we are hungry with nothing to eat." Rav ordered Rabbah bar bar Chana to pay their wages. When Rabbah asked, "Is this the din?" Rav answered, "Yes, because it says, 'and the ways of the righteous you shall guard.' "[49]

---

47. Ibid. 10:11.

48. *Bava Metzia* 83a; *Kitzur Shulchan Aruch* 185:5.

49. *Bava Metzia* ibid.

36

Safeguarding Money and Objects

1. When a person accepts an object for safekeeping, he is required to guard it conscientiously from loss, theft, or mishap, from the time he accepts responsibility for it. If he is negligent in protecting it, he is required to pay for any damage that ensues.[1] However, he is only required to guard it if he has taken responsibility.

> **Reuven:** *Can you please watch my bike?*
> **Shimon:** *Yes.*
> *Shimon has taken responsibility for the bike and must lock it up and guard it from mishap.*

How Does One Accept Responsibility?

2. Even if one does not accept responsibility explicitly but says, "Leave it with me," or any similar statement implying that he intends to watch the object, this also constitutes an acceptance of responsibility.[2] A statement such as, "You can put it down," or "Here's

---

1. *Choshen Mishpat* 291:1.

2. Ibid. 291:2.

my house," does not imply that he accepts responsibility, and he has no obligation to watch it nor is he liable for any loss.[3]

> **Mrs. A:** *I would like to leave my jewelry in your house.*
> **Mrs. B:** *You can put it wherever you want.*
> **Or:** *My house is open to you. You can do whatever you like.*
>   *Mrs. B has not taken responsibility.*

However, even if he has not accepted responsibility, the mitzvah of returning a lost object to its owner requires him to protect the object if it is in danger of being damaged, and the same applies to any property belonging to a Jew wherever one happens to see it.[4]

> *In the above example, if there are thieves in the vicinity, Mrs. B must lock the door and take other precautions to prevent loss, as every person is required to do to protect someone else's property.*

3. If, however, the owner of the object asks someone to take it with him to another place, then even an expression such as "Put it down," or "Here's my car," is considered an acceptance of responsibility. Since the owner obviously does not intend to accompany the second person, if he does not safeguard the object, it will surely be lost.[5]

> **Reuven:** *You're driving to Chicago? Could I send this package along with you?*
> **Shimon:** *You can put it in the car.*
>   *Shimon has accepted responsibility.*

> *At the airport:*
> **Reuven:** *I have to go someplace for a few minutes. Could you please watch my baggage when you sit down?*
> **Shimon:** *Put it down.*
>   *Shimon has accepted responsibility.*

4. A guardian also includes a person who rents or borrows an object; he, too, is required to guard the object itself from all damage while he has use of it.

---

3. Ibid. Note: In such a situation the right course of action is to prevent misunderstanding by advising the owner that one does not accept responsibility.

4. See Ch. 37 par. 1.

5. *Choshen Mishpat* 291:2, see *Sma* 5. See also *Halichos Olam*, Ch. 47 fn. *gimmel.*

The Required Level of Care

5. When a person accepts responsibility for watching an object, he is required to treat it with the same care that people normally take with their own possessions, i.e. keeping it in a safe place and protecting it from theft and mishap.[6] Even if one treats his own possessions carelessly and does not watch them properly, he is still required to treat objects that have been entrusted to him with due care.[7]

> *Mr. Brown lived in a tropical climate, where it was considered proper care for a car to be covered during the midday hours so as not to expose it to the hot sun. Mr. Brown often neglected to protect his own car in this manner. However, when Mr. Silver went on vacation and asked Mr. Brown to take care of his car for the duration of the trip, Mr. Brown dutifully covered Mr. Silver's car every single day in order to protect it.*

When an Object May Be Entrusted to Other People

6. When one has been entrusted with an object for safekeeping, he is not allowed to turn it over to a second person for watching without permission, unless it is known that the owner himself is accustomed to leaving the object in that person's care, or if the transfer of care is done in the owner's presence and he does not object.

> **Reuven:** *I'm going away with my parents for a vacation. Could you please watch my bike?*
> **Shimon:** *Sure, I'll lock it up in our garage.*
>   *A week later.*
> **Shimon's parents:** *Shimon, we are going on a two-day trip.*
> **Shimon:** *Oh! I want to come along. I'm watching Reuven's bike, but I'm sure Levi will watch it for me.*
> **Parents:** *But the halachah is that you are not permitted to leave it with Levi without permission from Reuven.*
> **Shimon:** *I guess I'll have to work hard to locate Reuven by telephone and get his permission.*
>   *Or:*

---

6. *Choshen Mishpat* 291:2.

7. Ibid. 291:14. Note: Although all guardians are expected to watch the objects properly, a paid guardian is expected to be even more diligent; see *Bava Metzia* 93b and *Poskim* for a few detailed differences between paid and unpaid guardians.

Shimon: But in this case I don't have to. Reuven always leaves his bike with Levi, but since Levi wasn't around, he left it with me. So we have proof that Reuven would be happy to leave it with Levi.

However, it is assumed that when a person entrusts his possessions to someone else for safekeeping, he gives tacit consent to have them left in the care of the guardian's wife and older children, but not under the guardianship of children who have not yet reached the age of bar/bas mitzvah.[8]

Mr. Gold left valuables with Mr. Silver. While Mr. Silver was away, thieves broke into the home and stole the valuables.

Mr. Gold: *The very fact that you were away indicates negligence. I left valuables with you, not your wife and children.*

Mr. Silver: *The halachah is that as long as you do not specify otherwise, leaving an object with a person gives tacit consent to leaving it with his family, provided that the guardian is a legal adult (i.e. bar/bas mitzvah).*

Subletting

7. Someone who rents or borrows an object has no right to rent or lend it to others without the permission of the owner. There is no distinction in this regard between fixed property (houses, land, etc.) and movable property. This rule applies even to a *Sefer Torah* or another mitzvah object; although one might presume that the owner would allow his property to be used for a mitzvah, it is still forbidden without his permission.[9]

The Golds lived in a rented house. They were planning to go away for the summer and were hoping to either sublet the house or swap houses with a resident of a resort area. Both are forbidden without the owner's permission.

A new shtiebel opened in town. The gabbai of the shtiebel asked the president of the Midtown Synagogue if they could borrow a Sefer

---

8. *Choshen Mishpat* 291:21,26.

9. Ibid. 342:1, see 316:1; *Rambam, Hilchos Sechirus* 5:5; *Raavad* and *Maggid Mishneh*. See *Halichos Olam*, Ch. 48 fn. *zayin*, explaining that it seems that in modern times the *Rambam* would agree with *Raavad*.

Torah for Simchas Torah. The president answered that since the Sifrei Torah were privately owned and on loan to the synagogue, they could not be lent out without permission of the owners.

Personal Use of an Entrusted Object

8. It is forbidden to make personal use of an object one is holding for safekeeping, even if it does not in any way affect the object's value or future usability. If the guardian uses the object without permission, his action is considered to be theft. It is all the more so forbidden to keep the object for oneself, which is considered outright theft.[10]

Money Entrusted for Safekeeping

9. It is forbidden to make use of money entrusted to one for safekeeping in an enclosed manner (e.g. a sealed envelope or a tightly bound bundle) since this indicates that the owner wishes his money to remain intact. Use of this money is forbidden just like any other object entrusted for safekeeping. If, however, there is no such indication, the guardian is allowed to use the money; if he does so, it has the status of a loan that he is required to repay even if it is lost or damaged through circumstances beyond his control. If he does not make use of the money, he still has the status of a paid guardian (*shomer sachar*, as explained in paragraph 11), since, in any case, he benefits from having the right to use it.[11]

> *If one person gives another cash to "please hold for me," and the cash is in a closed envelope, one may not borrow it. If the cash was merely handed over, one may borrow it and replace the bills when the owner returns.*

Liability for Loss or Damage

10. In the next paragraph, we state a number of general rules as to when someone holding an object for safekeeping is required to pay for loss or damage to the object. In practice, however, there are usually many detailed and intricate considerations that must be taken into account before making a final determination of liability;

---

10. *Choshen Mishpat* 292:1.

11. Ibid. 292:7, *Sma* 18, *Shach* 12.

it is therefore always advisable to consult with a *halachic* authority in any given situation.

11. If an object being held for safekeeping is stolen, lost, or otherwise destroyed and the guardian had been negligent in his duty to guard the object, he is required to pay compensation for the loss.[12]

> ❏ *If a bike was stolen, was it properly locked?*
> ❏ *If valuables were lost, were they properly stowed away?*
> ❏ *If a house was broken into, was a door or window left open?*

If there was no negligence, however, liability depends on the terms under which he accepted responsibility for the object.

(a) If he is watching the object as a favor without pay (*shomer chinam*), he is free from any liability (see footnote).[13]

(b) If he is being paid to watch the object (*shomer sachar*) or is renting it, he is normally required to pay in cases of loss or theft. However, if the loss was caused by unavoidable circumstances, he is free of liability.[14]

> ❏ *If thieves broke into the house he is liable.*
> ❏ *If he was mugged on the street he is not liable.*

(c) If he borrowed the object, he is required to pay for all categories of loss or damage.[15]

> *He is required to pay the owner of the object even if he was mugged.*

In all of these cases, if the object's owner was working for the guardian at the time the object was entrusted for safekeeping, the guardian (i.e. the employer) is not required to pay.[16] Furthermore, if the object was rented or borrowed, and it broke during normal usage, the renter or borrower is free from liability.[17]

---

12. Ibid. 291:1.

13. Ibid. Note: The owner has the right to demand that the guardian take an oath to prove the veracity of his claim that he was not negligent and that the object was lost or stolen without fault. Failure to take the oath causes the guardian to be liable to pay for the object. In the text, however, the discussion focuses only on liability where the circumstances are known but not where the facts themselves are a matter of dispute between the parties.

14. Ibid. 303:2-3.

15. Ibid. 340:1.

16. Ibid. 346:1.

17. Ibid. 340:1.

Mrs. A: I'm making a simchah. Could you please help me in the kitchen?

Mrs. B: Sure, I'll come right away.

Mrs. A: By the way, could I borrow your necklace to wear during the simchah?

Mrs. B: Sure.

If the necklace gets lost or is stolen, Mrs. A is not liable since Mrs. B was "working" for her at the time she borrowed it.

If a borrowed bike or car breaks down during usage, the borrower is not liable if there is no negligence involved.

Craftsmen Who Receive Objects for Repairs

12. An individual who takes in objects for repairs or cleaning has the status of a hired watchman as long as he is working on the items. After his work is completed, he retains the status of a hired watchman if he insists on receiving payment before relinquishing the objects. If, however, he indicates that he does not require immediate payment (e.g. by stating, "You'll take it and pay me when you want to"), then until the owner picks up his object the workman is considered to be keeping it as a favor to the owner (and is not liable for loss or theft unless he was negligent, as in paragraph 11). If he has told the owner to take his object and disclaims any further responsibility for it, he bears no liability for it whatsoever.[18]

Returning an Entrusted Object

13. When one returns an object that he has been holding for safekeeping, he must take care that the object actually enters the owner's control, or that of his wife who manages the household. If one returns the object to other members of the household, the *Poskim* differ as to whether the guardian's liability has thereby been terminated.[19]

Borrowed Objects

14. Because a borrower bears greater responsibility than other kinds of guardians, his liability does not terminate unless he returns the

---

18. Ibid. 306:1.

19. See *Choshen Mishpat* 72:31, *Shach* 136; 291:21 *Rema*; 120:7 *Beur HaGra*; 340 *Nesivos* 13.

borrowed object directly to its owner and not to the owner's wife or children, unless the owner's wife manages his fiscal affairs, or if the owner gives him specific permission to do so or to send the object back with some other person.[20]

Period of Borrowing

15. If an object is lent for a specific time period, the lender cannot insist on its return once the borrower takes the object into his possession (by picking it up, driving the car, etc.) until the specified time. If no time period was specified, the lender has the right to demand that the object be returned to him whenever he wishes.[21]

16. If an object was lent for a specific time period, the borrower may no longer use the object after that period is over.[22] However, he must still guard the object and his status changes to that of a paid guardian (as in paragraph 11). Therefore, the rules of returning the object are the same as those of a guardian (paragraph 13).[23]

Deviating From Owner's Instructions

17. It is forbidden to deviate in any way from the owner's instructions concerning a borrowed object or to make any use of it except as the owner allows; anyone who does so is considered a thief. It is also forbidden to keep an object any longer than was originally agreed upon, unless the owner gives his express permission.[24]

---

20. Ibid. 340:8, *Rema*; *Nesivos* 13.

21. Ibid. 341:1.

22. Ibid.; see *Nesivos* 1.

23. Ibid. 340:8.

24. *Ahavas Chesed* Part 2, Ch. 22.

37

Returning Lost Objects

Lost Objects

1. The Torah states, *You shall not see the ox of your brother or his sheep stray, and hide yourself from them. Rather you must return them to your brother (Devarim* 22:1). We are therefore required to make an effort and extend ourselves to save another person's property from loss. Thus, a person who sees a lost object is required to return it to its owner.[1] In other situations as well, we are obligated to rescue the endangered money or property of other people (e.g. a field about to be flooded).[2]

> *The eighth-grade boys were playing ball in the school playground when one boy noticed that a friend's bike was parked unlocked outside the schoolyard. He went and told the rebbi, who, within seconds, was outside bringing the bike to safety. When the student asked the rebbi why he didn't just tell one of the boys to bring in the bike, he answered, "Rescuing endangered property is not just a 'good deed' — it is an obligatory mitzvah. We are commanded to exert ourselves to make sure that other peoples' property should not be endangered. Any procrastination would have meant further endangering the bike and that would have been a violation of this mitzvah. That is why I ran out so quickly."*

1. *Rambam, Hilchos Aveidah* 11:1.
2. *Bava Metzia* 31a.

Similarly, one is required to help a lost person find the way to his destination.[3]

> On his way to school, Chaim met an elderly Jew who told him that he came from another city, was supposed to go to Mr. A's house, and was hopelessly lost. Chaim tried to explain the directions, but when he saw that the man was confused, he walked him all the way to Mr. A's house. He then rushed to school, but still arrived late. When questioned, Chaim told his rebbi the story. The rebbi praised him for doing this mitzvah and excused his lateness.

All the more so are we required to expend efforts to save another person and to help him in times of trouble. All these mitzvos are included in the commandment to return a lost object and the accompanying prohibition that forbids looking away.[4]

Jews and Non-Jews

2. The mitzvah of returning lost objects and extending oneself to save another person's property is related to the mitzvah of *You shall love your fellow (Vayikra 19:18)*. Even though that commandment applies only to fellows Jews who have entered a covenant to follow the ways of Hashem, the traits developed thereby are nevertheless extended universally to include all mankind. Similarly, the mitzvah of returning lost objects is stated only with regard to your "brother" in the Torah. However, the traits are, at times, extended universally.

> ❏ *The Sages taught: If one sees objects belonging to a non-Jew on the street, one should bring them to safety because the ways of the Torah are ways of peace.*[5]
> ❏ *A lost object of a non-Jew should be returned in order to sanctify the Name of Hashem.*[6]

The Obligation to Return the Object

3. From the verse quoted in paragraph 1 we derive three mitzvos that apply to an individual who sees a lost object.[7]

---

3. *Bava Kamma* 81b.

4. *Shaarei Teshuvah* 3:70.

5. *Choshen Mishpat* 266:1.

6. Ibid.

7. Note: An object has to be worth a *perutah* (see Ch. 30 fn. 2) to be included in the mitzvah of returning lost objects.

(a) He may not take it for himself (included in the prohibition not to steal).

(b) He is obligated to make efforts to return the object to its owner.

(c) If he ignores the object, he transgresses the commandment, *"You shall not look away"* (*Devarim* 22:3).[8]

4. An item has the status of a lost object that must be returned only as long as its owner still hopes to recover it. However, once he abandons hope of ever seeing it again (by commenting, "It's too bad that I've lost it," "Forget it," or similar statements), then the object is subsequently considered ownerless and anyone who finds it is allowed to keep it. However, if at the moment the finder picked it up the owner had not yet given up on it, then the obligation on the finder to return the object remains in force even after the owner does give up.[9]

> *As the seventh-grade boys were cycling down Main Street, one of them suddenly braked, calling to the others, "Look over there!" Quickly, they all parked their bikes and gathered around the find, a color Game Boy. "We could have a great time with that," said one boy, "but we have to check it for any simanim (identity marks)." They carefully looked and sure enough found a piece of tape with the letters C.G. on it. "I bet you that's Chaim Gold," said one boy. "He lives a few houses down from me and owns one of these." The boys raced over to Chaim Gold's house, rang the bell, and presented him with his game when he opened the door. "Thank you, thank you so much," he said. "You did a real mitzvah." Suddenly, he stopped to think, and then continued, "I really appreciate the effort you made. But, the truth is, I must confess that when I didn't find it this morning I gave up on it. I figured it was lost and no one would return it, so the game really belongs to you." "What time was that?" asked the boys. "Hmm, about 10 o'clock," he answered. "Did you, by any chance, pick it up before 10 o'clock? Then it is still mine." "Well," they answered, "we picked it up about a half hour ago, around 12 o'clock." The boys were not sure what to do, and decided to ask a rav. (Continued in paragraph 8.)*

When a Lost Object May Be Kept

5. It can be assumed that the owner has given up hope of finding a lost object, if *all* the following conditions are met: It must have no

---

8. Ibid. 259:1.

9. Ibid. 262:3.

identifying marks or features (see Chart A); it must be apparent that it was not left in that place intentionally but rather was dropped or left there unintentionally (see Chart B); the object must be one whose absence the owner is likely to have noticed, either because of its weight and bulk or because it has significant value (since it is presumed that a person checks his pockets frequently to be sure his valuables are intact) (see Chart C). If any one of these conditions are missing one may not keep the object.[10]

CHART A

IDENTITY MARK	NO IDENTIFYING MARK
❑ Wallet with name ❑ Briefcase with indelible ink mark ❑ Sweater placed in a specific place (the location becomes the identity mark), e.g. the edge of the fence on the right side	❑ Unmarked standard bill ❑ Unmarked common piece of clothing ❑ Store-bought food

(In all cases of uncertainty a rav should be consulted.)

CHART B

PLACED INTENTIONALLY	LEFT UNINTENTIONALLY
❑ Coat left in a room	❑ Coat found on the street

CHART C

PRESUMED OWNER NOTICED LOSS	PRESUMED LOSS NOT NOTICED
❑ Wallet ❑ Case of fruit	❑ One fruit fell out of a shopping bag

6. If an object has an identifying mark, then it is forbidden to keep it for oneself, even though it is obvious that it fell from the owner's possession accidentally. The owner will undoubtedly hope that it will be found by an upright Jew who will fulfill the mitzvah of returning

---

10. Ibid.

it, since he will be able to positively identify it. If the finder is not expert in the *halachos* of lost objects, he must consult a rav as to what constitutes positive identification.

7. However, if the place where the object was lost is frequented predominantly by people who do not keep mitzvos (non-Jews or Jews who do not keep mitzvos), it may be presumed that the owner has given up hope of recovering it (since he will assume that it was found and kept by a non-observer). Therefore, a Jew who finds the object is allowed to keep it. In practical terms, in an area that does not have a majority of religious Jews, one is obligated to return objects lost only in a synagogue, *mikveh*, school or any similar place frequented mainly by religious Jews.[11]

8. Even though there is no obligation to return the object in areas frequented by non-Jews or irreligious Jews, it is praiseworthy for the finder to waive his rights and to return it to the owner if a Jew comes forth to claim it with positive identification.This is included in the general mitzvah that a person do more than the strict requirements of the law.[12] Furthermore, according to some opinions, a finder may even be compelled to return the object to its owner (in order to fulfill this mitzvah). However, if the finder is poor and the owner wealthy, then it is not necessary to go beyond the requirements of the law.[13]

> *(Continued from paragraph 4.)*
>
> The boys approached the rav, told him the story, and asked him what to do. The rav listened intently to their story, thought for a minute, and then answered, "I must compliment you on your alacrity at performing mitzvos and your desire to follow the din. The halachah is that the game is yours. However, since you know who the owner is, it is a mitzvah to go beyond the strict requirements of the law and return it to him. I highly recommend that you do so."

9. If an object was lost under circumstances that would have rendered it valueless in any case (e.g. if it was about to be washed away in a flood), the finder has the right to keep it even if it has distinguishing features. Even in this situation, however, it is praisewor-

---

11. Ibid. 259:3.

12. *And you shall teach them … the deeds that they should do* (*Shemos* 18:20) [they should extend themselves to do more than absolutely required], *Bava Metzia* 30b; cf. Ch. 2 pars. 21-22.

13. *Choshen Mishpat* 259:5. See also *Beur HaGra* 15, *Kitzur Shulchan Aruch* 187:2.

thy for the finder to waive his rights and to restore it to the owner if his identity is known. Furthermore, if the local *beis din* orders that it be returned, one is required to do so. Also, if local law requires its return, then since the Torah commands us to follow the laws of the local governing authority, we must do so.[14]

An Object Left Intentionally

10. If there is reason to suspect that the object was left in its place intentionally (and all the more so if there is conclusive evidence that this is the case), then a number of specific considerations apply, as described in the following paragraphs:

11. If the object was found in a safe place where people are accustomed to leaving their belongings (e.g. a coatroom or tool shed), then whether the object has identifying marks or not, one should simply leave it in its place and not touch it. The general rule is that whenever there is a possibility that the owner purposely left it there, and intends to recover it, one should not pick it up. This prohibition applies whether the owner is Jewish or non-Jewish.[15]

12. If one has already picked the object up, but has not yet brought it home, he should return the object to its place. If he has already brought it home (i.e. he has left the premises long enough that the owner could have come searching for it and not found it) then he should not return it to its place but should do as follows: (a) for an object with identifying features, he should follow the procedures described in paragraph 18 for advertising that he has found it; (b) an object that does not have identifying features must be kept it in his possession until the prophet Eliyahu comes to tell him what to do with it.[16]

Note: The prophet (*Malachi* 3:23) teaches us that Eliyahu will come before Mashiach. It is our tradition that difficult questions in Torah will be posed to him. The *halachah* is that a person who is in possession of a lost object and has no way of identifying the owner, should keep it until Eliyahu comes and instructs him about what to

---

14. *Choshen Mishpat* 259:7.

15. Ibid. 260:9; see *Nesivos* 4, *Sma* 266:4, *Shach* 260:5. See also *Halichos Olam*, Ch. 46 fn. *lamed*.

16. *Choshen Mishpat* 260:10. See also *Rema* and *Shach* 31, 32. Note: The *halachah* quoted in the text in pars. 12-14 is according to the *Rema*. The *Rambam* and *Mechaber* have a different view. A Sephardic Jew who customarily follows the *Mechaber* should consult a rav for guidance.

do. If the object will spoil (e.g. food), see paragraph 21. For other difficulties with storage, consult a rav.

13. If the object was found in a place where people are less likely to leave their belongings but might still do so (e.g. on a path, in a field, in a school hallway), and it has identifying features, one should take it and advertise it, as explained below. If it does not have identifying features, however, he should leave it in its place. If he has already picked it up and brought it home, he must keep it until Eliyahu comes. However, if he is still at the site, then according to some opinions he should put it back where he found it while others say that he must take it home and keep it until the arrival of Eliyahu. A person who follows either opinion has support for his position.[17]

14. If the object was found in a place where no one would deliberately leave such an item (e.g. a public thoroughfare), one should take it and treat it as if it had accidentally fallen from its owner's possession, as described in paragraphs 3-7. Thus, if it has identifying features one should advertise that it has been found, while if it does not have identifying features and there is reason to presume that the owner has abandoned hope of recovering it, the finder may keep it for himself. If there is no reason to make such a presumption, however, it should be kept until the arrival of Eliyahu.[18]

Beneath the Dignity of the Finder

15. If it would be beneath the finder's dignity to pick up the lost item (e.g. because he is a Torah scholar or some other highly distinguished person), he is exempt from the mitzvah of making an effort to return it to its owner. The determining criterion is whether the finder's sense of dignity would inhibit him from saving such an item from loss if it were his own property; if so, he is excused from picking it up in order to return it to another owner as well. However, if his status would not prevent him from taking action to protect a similar item of his own, then he is expected to do the same for others.[19]

16. Some opinions permit a Torah scholar to be stringent with himself and return an object even though it is below his dignity.

17. *Choshen Mishpat* 260:10.
18. Ibid.
19. Ibid. 263:1.

WHAT SHOULD ONE DO?

LOCATION OF OBJECT FOUND	IF THE OBJECT HAS IDENTIFYING FEATURES	IF OBJECT HAS NO IDENTIFYING FEATURES
Common place to leave belongings (e.g. coatroom, tool shed).	1. Do not take. 2. If picked up but one is still on premises, put it back where it was. 3. If taken home, advertise the lost object.	1. Do not take. 2. If picked up but one is still on premises, put it back where it was. 3. If taken home, keep until Eliyahu comes.
A place less likely but still possible to leave belongings (e.g. on a side path, in a school hallway).	Pick it up and advertise.	1. Do not pick up. 2. If picked up but still on premises: Some opinions — put back where it was. Others say — take it home and do as in 3. 3. If taken home, keep until Eliyahu comes.
An area where it was definitely not left but fell or was forgotten (e.g. a public thoroughfare).	Pick it up and advertise.	Can pick up. If we can presume the owner already gave up on his object, it belongs to the finder (see paragraph 4). If not, keep until Eliyahu comes.

Others prohibit a Torah scholar from acting below his dignity; if he wishes to be stringent, he may pay for the object from his own funds.[20]

Payment Should Not Be Accepted

17. One who finds a lost object is required to return it to its owner without taking payment. If this would cause him to suffer any kind of loss, a rav should be consulted.[21]

---

20. Ibid. 263:3.

21. Ibid. 265.

Advertising a Find

18. One who finds a lost object with distinguishing marks or features is required to make an announcement in synagogues and *batei midrashim* that he has found it.[22]

> *Customarily, signs are posted in these places as well as other public areas where they will be widely read.*

19. If one has advertised the found object and the owner does not come forward, one must keep the object in his possession until the arrival of Eliyahu.[23]

20. A finder who is holding onto an item awaiting an owner is considered a legal guardian of the object and is responsible for its care and upkeep until it is returned to the owner.[24]

21. If a found object is likely to depreciate in value (e.g. through food spoilage), he should sell it and keep the proceeds until the owner comes to claim it.[25] If keeping the object and caring for it costs the finder money, many considerations come into play and a rav should be consulted.[26]

---

22. Ibid. 267:3.
23. Ibid. 267:15.
24. Ibid. 267:1,16,17.
25. Ibid. *Sma* 30 and *Shach* 16.
26. *Choshen Mishpat* 267:21-22.

✳ Honest Commerce

Chapters 38-43

38

General Rules of Business Practice

1. It is forbidden to defraud or deceive people in business transactions. Thus, a seller is required to inform prospective purchasers of any defect in his merchandise even if the defect would not affect the price in any way. It is also forbidden to claim that merchandise is of a particular well-known brand name when it is actually of another brand, even if the second one is of equal quality. Even if the seller is asking a reasonable price for the merchandise in question, it is still forbidden to make false claims or to deceive the buyer in any way. In all these matters, it makes no difference whether the buyer is a Jew or a non-Jew.[1]

> *Gold's Menswear normally sells Italian designer suits for $600 and Brand-X suits for $300. Being short on cash, Mr. Gold announces a big end-of-year sale, with the designer suits to be sold for $150. On the day of the sale, he mixes some Brand-X suits in with the Italian ones, rationalizing that $150 is a very good price even for the Brand-X suits. Although it is indeed an excellent price, it is still forbidden to deceive customers in this way.*

---

1. *Choshen Mishpat* 228:6.

2. The use of false weights or measures, whether in transactions with a Jew or a non-Jew, is a violation of the commandment *do not commit a perversion in ... measures of length, weight or volume* (*Vayikra* 19:35).[2] This is a particularly severe offense, since in order to repent properly one has to make restitution to everyone cheated, and it is generally impossible to locate each individual in order to do so. In such cases, one is advised to fund public projects (so that the victims may benefit from them) but this does not have the full effect of proper restitution.[3] It is prohibited to even own a perverted measure (e.g. broken commercial scale); one must either fix it or dispose of it.[4]

> *The Sages taught[5] that someone who keeps unfair weights or measures in his possession will lack sufficient means to provide for his needs, while one who holds to strict and exacting standards of honesty will be supplied with all his needs in full measure. Elsewhere they stated[6] that a person who wishes to become wealthy should conduct his business dealings faithfully and ask for mercy from the One Who controls all wealth, as the prophet says, "Mine is the silver and Mine is the gold," says the God of Hosts (Chaggai 2:8).*

3. The Torah requires us to give a small amount more than strictly required when weighing or measuring merchandise for sale.[7]

> *When a certain ben Torah in Eretz Yisrael opened a retail food store, he sought the advice of a great scholar as to how to conduct the business in the optimal Torah fashion. The gadol advised him to give away ten grams of merchandise for every kilo sold (i.e. 1 percent) in order to be sure to avoid inadvertent theft.*

4. A merchant is required to measure his commodities in accordance with the local custom, without any deviation.[8]

---

2. Ibid. 231:1.

3. Ibid. 231:19.

4. Ibid. 231:3.

5. *Bava Basra* 89a.

6. *Niddah* 70b.

7. *Choshen Mishpat* 231:14.

8. Ibid. 231:8.

In ancient times commodities were measured by the size of the container; some contained a "lug," a "kav," etc. The buyer would bring the appropriate container to the seller, who would fill it up. In some places the custom was to fill a container until it was overflowing, while in other places the custom was to level it off at the top. When dealing in commodities such as flour the difference was appreciable. The Sages ruled that it was required to fill a container to overflowing where the custom was to do so, even if the buyer agreed to accept a smaller quantity at a lower price. Conversely, where the custom was to level off the commodity one was not allowed to fill the container to overflowing, even if the buyer agreed to pay a higher price. The Sages were concerned that a visitor to the city might notice the transaction and mistakenly think this to be the local custom, and thus inadvertently come to cheat or be cheated in his own local transactions.

5. The leaders of a community are responsible for appointing officials to inspect businesses and examine their measures and scales, with the power to fine or punish violators at their discretion.[9]

6. It is forbidden to adorn and embellish merchandise in order to deceive customers into thinking it is more valuable than it actually is.[10]

   Examples:
   ❏ *Polishing old dishes to make them appear new.*
   ❏ *Mixing a few spoiled fruits in with good ones in order to sell them for the regular price.*

7. A business may use "gimmicks" to attract customers provided there is no deception, since the competitors may be doing so as well.

   A storekeeper may give out nuts and candies to children in order to accustom them to buy from him.[11]

8. Advertisements should portray the true value of the item and not be misleading. Similarly, when a salesman is trying to convince an individual to buy a product he should portray the true value of the item without any deception.

---

9. Ibid. 231:2.

10. Ibid. 228:9.

11. Ibid. 228:18.

9. One may charge less than the going price for an item in order to attract customers, and his competitors have no right to attempt to prevent him from doing so.[12]

10. Any form of market manipulation that causes the price of essential commodities to rise excessively is forbidden. He who does so is branded as wicked,[13] and the leaders of the community have the authority to appoint officials to punish such individuals at their discretion,[14] as with those described in paragraph 5 who use deceptive weights and measures. They are considered as reprehensible as those who lend money at interest, and they transgress the commandment to *Let your brother live with you* (*Vayikra* 25:36).[15]

11. In general, it is especially important in business matters to consult with a rav when any shadow of a doubt exists since people whose personal interests are involved are highly prone to mislead themselves.

---

12. Ibid.

13. *Yoma* 83a.

14. *Bava Basra* 89a; *Choshen Mishpat* 231:21.

15. *Choshen Mishpat* 231:21. The commandment to "Let your brother live with you" gives each Jew a responsibility to help other Jews thrive financially. A person who manipulates the market, thereby causing prices of essentials to rise, undermines the financial stability of his brothers.

39

Ona'as Mamon

General Rules of *Ona'ah*

1. The term *ona'as mamon* refers to the sale of an item for an unreasonably high price or its purchase for an unreasonably low price relative to the market value,[1] when the other party involved in the transaction is unaware of the discrepancy.

> *On their way to a family picnic, the Greens stopped at the neighborhood grocery store and bought a six-pack of soda at 45¢ a can. Later, at a highway rest area, they found the same soda available at $1 a can. When young Chaim exclaimed, "That's highway robbery!" Mr. Green patiently explained that this was a reasonable price for the soda; if they had charged $2, that would have been excessive.*

The laws of *ona'ah* apply equally whether one actively deceives the other party as to the item's true worth, merely takes advantage of the other party's ignorance, or even does so innocently without realizing that the price is unreasonable. A purchase or a sale at an unfair price violates the negative commandment *You shall not cheat your fellow* (*Vayikra* 19:13). Even if the seller himself was tricked into paying an

---

1. Thus, a refreshment stand in a park would reasonably charge more for a can of soda than a large supermarket would.

unfair price for the item in question, this does not give him the right to take advantage of others. Furthermore, because this is a form of theft, one is required to refund any unfair gain realized in a transaction, whether or not any deliberate deception was involved.[2] In the remainder of this chapter we will discuss in detail specific applications of these rules.

What Constitutes *Ona'ah*

2. If the discrepancy between the market value of an item and the amount paid is exactly one-sixth of the total[3] (according to *either* of the two computation methods described in the footnote), the law of *ona'ah* applies — the transaction stands, but the aggrieved party is entitled to a refund of the discrepancy between the amount paid and the market price.[4]

> Yitz the Butcher received an order for meat from some newly observant Jews in a nearby town. Realizing that these customers were not familiar with the price of kosher meat, Yitz upped his usual price of $5 a pound to 6. This is clear ona'as mamon and the buyers are entitled to a refund.

Mekach Ta'us — Erroneous Sale

3. If, however, the discrepancy is not exactly equal to one-sixth according to either of the computation methods described in footnote 3, then we always compute the discrepancy relative to the market value of the item (*method one* in footnote). If the discrepancy computed in this fashion is more than one-sixth, the transaction is considered a *mekach ta'us* (an "erroneous sale") and the aggrieved party has the right to insist that the transaction be annulled and the money and merchandise be returned to their original owners. (According to some opinions, either party has the right to insist on nullifying the sale.)[5]

---

2. *Rambam, Hilchos Mechirah* 12:1; *Tur* and *Shulchan Aruch Choshen Mishpat* 227:1; *Kitzur Shulchan Aruch* 28:3.

3. In method one, the proportion is computed relative to the value of the item; thus, *ona'ah* occurs if an item worth $60 is sold for exactly one-sixth ($10) either more or less than its value, i.e. either $50 or $70. Under method two, the proportion is computed relative to the amount paid; thus, if $60 is paid for an item worth exactly one-sixth ($10) either more or less than the amount paid ($50 or $70), we say that *ona'ah* occurs.

4. *Choshen Mishpat* 227:2.

5. Ibid. 227:4.

Yankel inherited a very old sefer from his grandfather. One day he showed it to his friend Berel, who offered him $100 for it on the spot. Yankel immediately accepted the cash and closed the deal. Ten minutes later, however, he told David, a Judaica expert, about the sale and David said that the sefer was worth at least $150. This is a case of mekach ta'us, and Yankel has the right to reverse the sale.

Mechilah — Forgiveness

4. If the discrepancy is less than one-sixth, the Sages determined that in business transactions it is difficult to establish the market price to any great degree of accuracy and people therefore have to be willing to accept such discrepancies.[6] Once the Sages determined this to be the common practice, they did not allow exceptions to the rule and did not grant anyone the right to claim redress for a discrepancy of less than one-sixth.[7]

The Best Way to Act

5. The above-stated rule regarding discrepancies of less than one-sixth applies only when a transaction has already been concluded in genuine ignorance of the market value of the item. If, however, one of the parties was aware of the market value and deliberately adjusted the price slightly to realize an unfair profit, the *halachah* is unresolved as to whether or not this falls into the prohibited category of *ona'ah*. Therefore, a person should be stringent upon himself in both directions. On the one hand, one should be careful never to deviate from the fair value of the goods in which he deals, since doing so may violate a Torah commandment; and if he has already inadvertently done so, he should be strict with himself to return the unfairly received excess to the other party. At the same time, if unfair advantage was taken of him, he should accept his loss and not take any steps to recover money on which he possibly has no claim.[8]

---

6. Ibid. 227:3, *Sma* 2.

7. *Sma* 14.

8. *Choshen Mishpat* 227:6, *Sma* 14. See *Even HaAzel, Hilchos Geneivah* 7:12 who brings Rambam's opinion that he definitely violates the prohibition of *ona'ah*. However, see *Halichos Olam*, Ch. 40 fn. *hei*, that, according to the Rambam, the violation of the prohibition does not necessarily entail an obligation to reimburse.

Reuven sells electronic products. Shimon, who is unfamiliar with the field, came into the store one day to buy a portable CD player. Reuven, telling himself that Shimon will not know the difference, charged him $38 for a $35 item. Shimon later found out that he had been cheated. Since the ona'ah was less than one-sixth, Shimon refrained from demanding that Reuven return the difference. On the other hand, Reuven may have violated a Torah law through his behavior and ought to return the extra money.

Until When a Claim May Be Made

6. The seller's obligation to refund an excess payment (in the case of *ona'ah*) or to reverse the transaction (in the case of *mekach ta'us*) does not extend indefinitely. It applies only for the period of time reasonably required for the buyer to show his purchase to an expert for an appraisal or to seek the advice of his relatives or other trusted advisers. If he waits longer than this time, however, he loses his rights to claim restitution, unless he can demonstrate that he was prevented from seeking the necessary information by extenuating circumstances.[9] (See also paragraph 11.)

Mrs. A bought a dress from Debby's Dress Store. Two weeks later, when Mrs. B was visiting, Mrs. A showed it to her. Mrs. B immediately commented that the dress was overpriced. Since Mrs. A should have asked for advice earlier, she lost her rights to restitution; it is forbidden for her to pressure Debby into taking back the dress or refunding the money. (See Chapter 42 — Returning Merchandise.)

7. However, the seller's right to claim restitution from the buyer generally extends indefinitely, since the item is no longer in his possession and he has no way of verifying the fairness of the price he received for it. If, however, the price of the item in question is known in the marketplace and he did not make any effort to inquire, his right to claim restitution expires after a reasonable time. Similarly, if at some point the error was brought to his attention and he failed to take action, his right to claim restitution expires.[10]

Mr. Diamond sold a diamond ring to a friend for his son's kallah for $5,000. Two months later, at sheva berachos, the chasan thanked Mr.

---

9. *Choshen Mishpat* 227:7.

10. Ibid. 227:8.

Diamond for the beautiful ring. Mr. Diamond smiled and, turning to the kallah, asked to see it again. When she displayed it he became quite agitated; he had inadvertently sold a $10,000 ring for $5,000. If this is true, then even though two months have passed, Mr. Diamond is entitled to claim "mekach ta'us" and they must either return the ring, pay its full price, or accept a less expensive ring.

8. If the seller quotes a price that is obviously far below market value, so that it is apparent that he wants to sell the item at any price he can get, he cannot later claim that this was a *mekach ta'us* and demand that the transaction be reversed.[11]

Debby's Dress Store advertised a $50 sale on selected dresses. Debby put all the originally $100 dresses on one sales rack for $50. The $200 suits were not on sale, but she inadvertently put two suits on the sales rack. She later began to regret the whole sale.

She cannot claim mekach ta'us for the $100 dresses that were on sale.

She can claim mekach ta'us for the two $200 suits that were mistakenly put on the wrong rack.

A Change in Market Price

9. In all cases, when one party of a transaction is required to pay money or to reverse the transaction, we look only at the price that prevailed at the time of the transaction. Even if there is a change in the market price so that based on the new price a different ruling would apply, we enforce the appropriate ruling based on the original circumstances.[12]

If an item worth $4 dollars was sold for 5 (so that normally the transaction would be reversed) and afterwards the market value rose to 7, the buyer still has the right to annul the transaction. However, the overcharging seller is not allowed to exploit the situation to his advantage by claiming that since he overcharged, the sale is annulled and he can now charge $7.

If an item worth $5 was bought for 4 and the prevailing price then dropped to $3, only the aggrieved seller has the right to reverse the transaction. However, the buyer cannot cancel the sale on the basis

---

11. Ibid. 227:9.
12. Ibid. 227:10-11.

that "mekach ta'us" existed so that he will now be able to purchase the item for $3.

This applies also in cases of actual *ona'ah,* i.e. the discrepancy is exactly one-sixth. The transaction stands but the aggrieving party is required to refund the excess money.[13]

If a $5 item was sold for 6, the seller has to return the dollar even though the price subsequently rose to 7. He cannot say that since the item is now worth $7 "you should be happy that you bought it for 6." Rather, since an item was worth $5 at the moment of sale and was sold for 6, $1 still must be returned.

10. The laws of *ona'ah* are independent of whether either or both of the parties have any expertise in appraising the worth of the merchandise involved.[14]

The Types of Merchandise Covered

11. The laws of *ona'ah* apply to all forms of movable property, including books, gems and precious stones, electronic equipment, automobiles, etc. Thus, one is well advised to seek out a knowledgeable appraiser as soon as possible after a purchase, since one's right to make a claim of *ona'ah* lapses after a reasonable time has passed, as explained in paragraph 6. However, if the buyer made reasonable efforts and could not locate an expert at the time of the transaction, and only contacted one long afterwards, at which time he was told that the price was unfair, his right to reverse the transaction remains in effect since he was heretofore unable to clarify the facts.[15]

Mr. Gold visited an old scribe who showed him a 150-year-old Megillah. When Mr. Gold expressed interest in purchasing it, the scribe, who did not know much about the value of antiques, sold it to him for $2,000.

Four months later, Mr. Gold located an acquaintance who collected Judaica and brought him the Megillah for his opinion. The collector said that the Megillah was worth a maximum of $1,000, and Mr. Gold had overpaid. Even though months have passed since the

13. Ibid. 227:12-13.

14. Ibid. 227:14.

15. Ibid. 227:15.

purchase, Mr. Gold may claim mekach ta'us and demand his money back since he could not locate an expert in this field earlier.

Stipulating Exceptions to *Ona'ah*

12. If either party makes a general statement at the time of the sale that the rules of *ona'ah* do not apply to this transaction, the words have no effect and the rules of *ona'ah* remain in effect.[16]

> *A storekeeper decides to hang a sign stating, "All sales in this store are made with the understanding that the laws of ona'ah do not apply." The sign is ineffective and the laws of ona'ah still stand.*

If, however, the seller states explicitly that he is overcharging, i.e., "I realize that this item for which I am charging $200 is actually worth only 100, and it is sold with the understanding that the laws of *ona'ah* will not apply to this transaction," then the laws of *ona'ah* do not apply, since the buyer knowingly consents to pay an unfair price.[17]

A Good-Faith Sale Is Protected

13. If a seller conducts his transactions in good faith, by stating for example, "I paid X dollars for this item and am making a profit of Y by selling it to you at this price," then the buyer cannot later claim that he paid an unfair price.[18]

Real Estate

14. In transactions involving real property, slaves (in times past), and notes of indebtedness, the laws of *ona'ah* do not apply, although it is still forbidden to sell such properties at an unfair price. Some authorities rule that the transaction can be reversed if the discrepancy is at least half the value of the property involved.[19]

Sale Through an Agent

15. Additional considerations apply to transactions conducted through agents; a rav should be consulted in cases of uncertainty.[20]

---

16. Ibid. 227:21.
17. Ibid.
18. Ibid. 227:27.
19. Ibid. 227:29, *Sma* 51.
20. *Choshen Mishpat* 227:30.

Rentals

16. The rules for purchases apply to rentals as well; therefore, the laws of *ona'ah* do not apply to the rental of housing or land. Similarly, hired workers are also not subject to the laws of *ona'ah*, since it is analogous to previous practices of purchasing servants for a specific period of time.[21]

> *If a question of ona'ah arises regarding a worker hired along with his equipment, such as a car with a driver, an assessment should be made as to how much of the total price applies just to the car, and restitution should be made for that part of the amount overcharged.*[22]

Work Done Under Contract

17. Work done under contract is subject to the laws of *ona'ah*. Thus, when one pays a tailor for a custom-made suit, the tailor's status is that of a contractor rather than of a hired worker, since he is being paid for his output however long time it may take him. Therefore, the laws of *ona'ah* do apply to the transaction.[23]

---

21. Ibid. 227:32, 33, 35.

22. Ibid. 227:33, *Rema*.

23. *Choshen Mishpat* 227:36.

40

Keeping One's Word

The Requirement to Keep One's Word

1. The Sages established the rule that even though one has paid money to purchase an object, the object is not considered "acquired" until he lifts it up or performs some other legal act of acquisition. Thus, even after money changes hands in a transaction, until an act of acquisition takes place the actual ownership of the object does not change and either side may cancel the sale. To do so, however, is to dishonor one's word and is considered behavior unbecoming an upright Jew,[1] as the prophet says, *The remnant of Israel will not perform iniquity, will not speak falsehood, and words of trickery will not be part of their speech (Tzefaniah 3:13).*

> *Mr. Jacob agreed to buy Mr. Shapiro's car, and gave a down payment with the intention of picking up the vehicle the next day. That night, Mrs. Jacob convinced her husband to back out. If he listens to her, he has dishonored his word, and is subject to the curse of the beis din (see paragraph 2).*

---

1. *Choshen Mishpat* 204:1,4.

The Curse of *Beis Din*

2. Our Sages commanded the *beis din* to pronounce the following curse on a person who dishonors his word:

> *"The One Who punished the generation of the Flood, and the generation of the Dispersal, and the people of Sodom and Gomorrah, and the Egyptians, who drowned in the sea — may He punish those who do not stand by their word."*[2]

Other Forms of Acquisition

3. Similarly, even if no money changes hands but the buyer marks the merchandise to indicate his purchase, or shakes hands with the seller to affirm his intention to complete the sale, then either of the parties who backs out is subject to the curse of *beis din* as described in paragraph 2. If the custom in that locality is that such acts constitute finalization of a sale, then the sale is considered final.[3]

> *In some businesses, a handshake is considered a finalization of a sale.*

The Object Is Lost or Damaged

4. If the object is lost or damaged after payment is made (even if the seller is not at fault), the buyer can annul the sale without being subject to the curse of *beis din*, since the seller is no longer in a position to deliver the object.

> *Avi went with his father to Mr. Abrams' bicycle store. They chose a bike, paid for it at the counter and waited for the worker to carry it to the car. As he approached the parking lot, the worker was accosted by a thug who grabbed the bike, jumped into a van, and sped off. After they recovered from the incident, Avi and his father returned to the store to pick up another bike. The store owner said that he was very sorry, but since they had already paid, it was their bike that was stolen.*
>
> *However, according to halachah no act of acquisition was made. Therefore, even though the item had already been paid for, Avi is permitted to cancel the acquisition and Mr. Abrams must make full restitution.*

---

2. Ibid. 204:4.

3. Ibid. 204:6.

If the object sold still exists but there is a risk that it will be lost or suffer major damage, the sale should be annulled only by mutual consent. However, one side that unilaterally cancels the agreement is not subject to the curse of the *beis din* since there are *halachic* authorities to support that position.[4]

> *Kibbutz Ploni decided to go into the dairy business. When they found out that Moshe's cow farm was experiencing a cash flow problem, Kibbutz Ploni offered to buy 100 cows for cash at a 30 percent discount. Moshe took the cash and promised to deliver the cows within five days. Two days later the news was full of reports that a deadly cow virus had hit Israel and no one knew how many cows would be infected. The Kibbutz members met and decided that the time wasn't right to go into the dairy business and they should cancel the deal. There is a disagreement among the halachic authorities if it is permissible for them to unilaterally do so, and therefore, they should try to work it out with mutual consent. If Moshe refuses to cancel the deal, they should trust in Hashem that He will guard those who keep his commandments, take the risk, and not cancel. However, if they do unilaterally cancel, the beis din would not pronounce a curse on them, since some authorities hold that it is permissible.*

No Money Was Exchanged

5. When two parties have verbally agreed to conclude a sale at a given price without any exchange of money or formal act of acquisition, if one party later decides to annul the sale, the curse of *beis din* is not applied. Nevertheless, it is still improper to dishonor one's word, and this is considered a lack of faith.[5] Here, too, the verse, *The remnant of Israel ...* is applicable.[6] If the market price has changed, the authorities disagree as to whether backing out of the deal is considered lacking in faith. Therefore, it is best to stand by one's word, since this accords with most opinions.[7]

> *David agreed to buy Ari's computer. If he later hears of a sale where a comparable computer is being sold at a cheaper price, according to*

---

4. Ibid. 204:2; see *Bach* and *Shach* 3.

5. *Choshen Mishpat* 204:7.

6. *Rashi, Bava Metzia* 49a, s.v. *mishum; Shaarei Teshuvah* 3:183.

7. *Choshen Mishpat* 204:11, *Rema;* see *Shach* 8; see also *Halichos Olam,* Ch. 41 fn. *yud alef.*

most authorities he should still keep his word to Ari. If he does not do so, he is considered "lacking in faith."

Offering to Give a Gift

6. If one person offers to give another a gift, and the recipient is expecting him to give it, then if the donor changes his mind and does not do so, he is considered lacking in faith. This applies only to small gifts; however, if the gift involved is a substantial one, it is assumed that the recipient did not fully expect to receive it and therefore the donor is not considered lacking in faith.[8]

> *At the annual bazaar Rachel wanted to buy a watch that cost $10. When she checked her pocketbook she found that she had only $9. Leah reassured her, "Don't worry. I'll give you the dollar." Leah must keep her word.*

Nevertheless, one should never offer any gift, even a substantial one, unless he genuinely intends to fulfill his word, since the Torah forbids insincere speech.[9]

7. The above rule applies only if the statement was made to an individual who is financially secure, but if it was made to a poor person, then the gift is considered *tzedakah*, the offer has a status similar to that of a vow and it is absolutely forbidden to retract it.[10] Even if one merely decides in his mind to give a gift to a poor person, the Torah requires him to carry out his decision.[11]

8. Similarly, if one phrased his offer as a "promise," then even if the favor or gift is very large he is still required to fulfill his word since the recipient expects him to do so. If he fails to fulfill his word, he is considered lacking in faith. In addition, if a group of people told one person they would give him a gift, they are required to fulfill their offer and are considered lacking in faith if they fail to do so.[12]

---

8. *Choshen Mishpat* 204:8; see *Bava Metzia* 49a. See also Ch. 10 par. 11 for further discussion.

9. *Bava Metzia* ibid.

10. See Ch. 55.

11. Ibid. See *Yoreh Deah* 258:11, *Rema.*

12. *Choshen Mishpat* 204:11.

One must keep one's word if the following statements were made:

❏ *I promise ...*

❏ *At our meeting we decided to give you ...*

The Ways of the Pious

9. It is considered *middas chassidus* (an act of piety) to make good on everything one says even in situations where it is not considered "lacking in faith" to back down on one's word.[13]

> *Rav stated, "Whenever I instruct someone in my household to give a present, I do not retract my word."[14]*

However, if circumstances later change to such an extent that one would not originally have made the offer had the new conditions prevailed at the time, then there is no reason to fulfill one's offer even as an act of piety (*middas chassidus*).[15]

> *Rav Kahana was involved in a sale, which Rav held was halachically permissible to annul, but the pious would still refrain from doing so. However, when the market price changed significantly, Rav advised Rav Kahana to annul the sale.*

Fearing Heaven

10. An individual who fears Heaven is careful to carry out even those acts he decides in his mind to do for the benefit of others, even if he has not revealed his intention to anyone else. Therefore, when a person who fears Heaven decides to sell an object at a particular price, he should not take more than he had decided to accept for it, even if the buyer offers him more. In doing so he earns the praise of the Psalmist: *He speaks the truth in his heart* (*Tehillim* 15:2). Similarly, if a buyer who fears Heaven decides to pay a certain amount for an object, he should not change his mind even if the seller is willing to accept a lesser amount.[16]

---

13. *Rambam, Hilchos Dei'os* 5:13. See *Yerushalmi Sheviis* 10:4, *Rash* ibid. It would seem that this is included in the mitzvah of following in the path of Hashem (*Devarim* 28:9). See *Rambam* ibid. and 1:5-6.

14. *Yerushalmi Sheviis* ibid.

15. Derived from the story of Rav and Rav Kahana, *Bava Metzia* 49a.

16. *Kitzur Shulchan Aruch* 62:17. See also *Makkos* 24a and *Bava Basra* 88a.

Rav Safra had an object to sell. One day while he was reciting Krias Shema, someone came to buy it and offered him a particular price. Since Rav Safra was in the middle of saying Shema, he did not respond. The man, thinking Rav Safra was holding out for a higher price, raised his offer. When Rav Safra finished saying Shema he sold the object for the original price, since at the time the man made the first offer Rav Safra had made up his mind to accept it.[17]

---

17. *Rashi* on *Makkos* 24a.

41

Preempting Others

When One Purchaser Attempts to Preempt Another

1. If one person has put effort into securing the purchase or rental of an object (be it movable property or real estate, and whether the seller is a Jew or non-Jew) and has agreed on a price with the seller, then a second person who comes and buys or rents it before the first person concludes the transaction is considered "wicked" for appropriating that which another has taken the trouble to attempt to acquire. This intruder should have instead put his resources into endeavors that do not interfere with other people's efforts. An announcement should be made in the synagogues that he has perpetrated a wicked act.[1]

> *Reuven saw an attractive house on sale for a very reasonable price and moved quickly to close the deal. The next day he met with the seller and they reached a verbal agreement on price and terms, and set a time to meet again the following day to sign a formal agreement. Shimon heard about Reuven's plans and just a few hours before Reuven's second meeting with the seller, contacted the agent and bought the house on the spot. For this Shimon is considered a "rasha"(wicked person).*

1. *Choshen Mishpat* 237:1 and *Sma* 1.

2. However, if the first buyer and the seller have not yet agreed on a price (e.g. if the seller is still asking for more than the buyer is willing to pay), it is permitted at this stage for another person to purchase the object.[2]

Obtaining a Gift or Ownerless Object

3. If one person is attempting to acquire an object that has no owner, or to obtain a gift from someone, and another person intrudes to divert the object or the gift to himself, some are of the opinion that the second person is not considered wicked. The object is not being offered for purchase but falls into the category of a windfall gain, a gain that cannot be acquired elsewhere, and everyone therefore has a right to try to be the first to obtain it. According to other opinions, however, the second person is still considered wicked for depriving the first person of something he put effort into obtaining and that could have added to his income.[3]

> Mrs. Gold redecorated her house and was giving away her old table. Mrs. Silver called and told Mrs. Gold that she was interested and would come with a van to pick it up at 4 p.m. At 3 p.m. Mrs. Diamond visited Mrs. Gold, noticed the table, and asked to take it. When Mrs. Gold did not object she took it on the spot.
>
> If Mrs. Gold had stated or implied to Mrs. Silver, "I will give it to you," then she must keep her word; since the table was being given away in any case, the offer to give it to Mrs. Silver is considered a "small gift" and she must therefore keep her word. If Mrs. Diamond persuades Mrs. Gold to give it to her, she violates the prohibition of "Before a blind person you shall not place a stumbling block" by convincing her to do wrong.
>
> However, if Mrs. Gold did not imply that she would reserve the table for Mrs. Silver, then the question of whether Mrs. Diamond was permitted to acquire the table for herself depends on the two opinions mentioned above. Mrs. Diamond, therefore, is not wrong for acquiring the table for herself, but she would be praiseworthy, hearing the circumstances, if she would refrain from doing so.

---

2. *Rema* ibid.

3. *Rema* ibid. See also *Bach*. Although the authorities lean toward the first opinion, it is preferable wherever possible to be stringent as in the second opinion. See *Halichos Olam*, Ch. 42 fn. *gimmel*.

4. In the above case, if the object is commonly available and easily affordable, so that the first person who saw it could easily obtain it elsewhere, then anyone has the right to take it, even according to the second opinion.[4]

> *One day at lunch in the camp dining hall, Reuven notices an extra roll on the table. Even though he saw it first, Shimon is allowed to take it.*

5. According to some opinions, the lenient opinion is relevant even to purchases, if they are sold for an unusually low price.[5]

> *According to this opinion, if one person is about to buy the last item at a 50 percent-off sale, another shopper may attempt to acquire it for himself.*

Preempting Employees

6. A person is forbidden to try to persuade an employer to hire him for a particular position if the result is that the present employee will lose his job (one who does so is called wicked) unless the employer has let it be known on his own initiative that he does not wish to retain the present employee.[6]

7. It is forbidden to hire an employee away from his present employer unless one believes that no equally capable workers are available and unless the employee is not bound by contract to his present job. Even this is permitted only according to the lenient opinions mentioned in paragraph 3.[7]

> *Mrs. Gold is an exceptionally qualified math teacher who has taught at Bais Yaakov of Newville for many years. The English principal of Bais Yaakov of Midcity, hearing that Mrs. Gold's contract is up for renewal, asks the school's rav if they are allowed to make her a more attractive offer in order to get her to come work for them. Since she is considered to be outstanding in her field, the rav decides that the lenient opinion applies to this case and therefore he cannot tell them not to do it.*

---

4. *Rema, Choshen Mishpat* 237:1.

5. *Rema* (but *Shach* disagrees).

6. *Choshen Mishpat* 237:2; see also *Nesivos HaMishpat, Chiddushim* 5.

7. *Choshen Mishpat* ibid.

8. The administration of a particular yeshivah may hire a rebbi away from another school or locality if they consider him to be uniquely qualified, unless he is bound by contract to his present position.[8]

Renewing a Rental Contract

9. If a Jew who has been renting a dwelling from a non-Jew wishes to renew his contract at the end of the rental period, a *cherem* of Rabbeinu Gershom Meor HaGolah[9] forbids all other Jews from offering the non-Jewish landlord more money for the dwelling in order to secure it. All similar infringements on the positions of others are also forbidden.[10]

---

8. The *Nesivos* states that this is permitted only according to the lenient opinion. See *Halichos Olam*, Ch. 42 fn. *tes*.

9. Rabbeinu Gershon Meor HaGolah (literally: the light of the exile) was the great luminary of European Jewry in the 10th century C.E. He enacted various laws that he enforced with a *cherem* (excommunication). These laws have generally been universally accepted, at least by European Jewry. See *Choshen Mishpat* 237:1, *Rema*.

10. Ibid. *See* also *Pischei Teshuvah* and *Nesivos* ad loc.

42

Returning Merchandise

General Principles

1. Once a sale has been finalized, the item belongs to the purchaser
   and the money to the seller. To "reverse" a transaction is, in reality, to perform an entirely new transaction, in which the item is actually sold back to the original seller. This new sale is like any other
transaction; both parties must agree to the transaction, and each one
is forbidden to pressure the other to conclude a sale against his will.[1]
Applying pressure to conclude a sale is a violation of the tenth commandment (*Shemos* 20:14), *You shall not covet* (see Chapter 30, paragraphs 14-17). Therefore, once one has purchased an object, it is forbidden to pressure the seller to accept it in return.[2] Furthermore, a distinguished person is forbidden under any circumstances to even ask

---

1. *Choshen Mishpat* 359:10-12.

2. Pressuring someone to make a sale or purchase, is, in effect, coveting his possessions or his
money and is a violation of the tenth commandment, *You shall not covet* (*Shemos* 20:14; see Ch.
30). In this instance, the purchaser who returns the item covets the money of the seller in
exchange for the item, and thus, violates the prohibition. Furthermore, by pressuring the salesman to accept a return that he is not legally bound to do, the purchaser causes the salesman
anguish and violates the prohibition of causing anguish (*Vayikra* 25:17, see Ch. 6) and the mitzvah of loving your fellow as yourself. For further discussion see *Halichos Olam*, Ch. 43 fn. *alef*.

to return merchandise since the seller is likely to be embarrassed to refuse him, and this, too, constitutes a form of pressure.[3]

2. However, if the prevailing practice in the locality is to accept returns, then it is allowed, as long as one is certain that this is indeed the custom. In addition, if the parties make an explicit agreement at the time of the sale to allow returns (usually within a specified time period), then it is permitted to return the item. Agreed upon conditions take precedence over local custom. Therefore, if a store posts a "No Returns" sign, it is prohibited to pressure the storekeeper to accept a return, no matter the local custom. It is always wise to clarify the store's return policy at the time of a sale.[4]

> *Mrs. Schwartz has bought herself a dress for her daughter's wedding. The store policy is to allow returns only within ten days of purchase. After days of agonizing, she finally decides on the eleventh day to return the dress. She approaches Mr. Lifshitz, the store's owner, and beseeches him time after time, "I just can't wear this to my daughter's wedding." After a few rounds of this bombardment, Mr. Lifshitz caves in and agrees to take it back. Mrs. Schwartz has violated the tenth commandment, "You shall not covet." She should have made her decision before the ten-day limit expired; once it has already passed, she should try to sell the dress herself or find some other means of resolving her problem without violating the Torah's commandments.*

Returning Defective Merchandise

3. Regarding merchandise that turns out to be defective, the buyer has to ascertain what the *halachah* allows him, as discussed in the remainder of this chapter. If the sale may be annulled, he is permitted to return the merchandise and claim a refund. If, however, the sale is ruled to be valid, the buyer is not allowed to pressure the seller to accept the item for return.

Mistaken Amounts

4. If one purchases a commodity by weight, measure or count, and later discovers that he has received the wrong amount, then although the quantity has to be adjusted, the sale remains in effect. For example, if a person pays for 100 apples and upon counting them

---

3. *Shaarei Teshuvah* 3:43.

4. Cf. *Ahavas Chesed* Part 1, 10:14 fn.

finds that there are actually 101, he must either return the extra apple or pay for it, but he does not have the right to nullify the sale because of the error. Similarly, one who is supposed to pay a certain sum and later discovers that he has inadvertently paid either more or less, is required to pay for any deficiency and is permitted to claim a refund for any excess he has paid, but the sale itself stands.[5]

> *The Schwartz family ordered ten pounds of shemurah matzah from Bakery X at $15 a pound. Three days before Pesach, Bakery Y, realizing that they had an excess of matzos, announced a sale of matzah at $10 a pound. Meanwhile, it was discovered that Bakery X had mistakenly sent eleven pounds of matzos to Mr. Schwartz, who thought that he had a pretext to cancel the entire purchase. However, his rav told him that this was a mistake; although he must return the extra pound of matzah, the sale stands. (Example continues in paragraph 5.)*

5. If, however, a box labeled as containing 100 apples turns out to contain only 99, some opinions say that since the buyer never obtained possession of the specified order, he has the right to return his merchandise and to demand a refund of the entire sum.[6]

> *If Bakery X had delivered ten boxes of matzos, each supposed to contain one pound, and upon inspection it was discovered that they each weighed only 14 ounces, then, according to some opinions, Mr. Schwartz may cancel the entire sale (see note). On the other hand, if each weighed 18 ounces or only nine boxes of matzos weighing one pound each were delivered, then although the relevant adjustments must be made (either to return, deliver, or adjust the price), the sale stands.*

Note: Since this is not the unanimous view of the authorities, a buyer who finds himself in such a situation should, preferably, not force the seller to reverse the sale.[7]

Defective Merchandise

6. If an item is sold that later turns out to have a defect of which the buyer was unaware at the time of the sale, the buyer always has the right to demand that the sale be annulled and his money returned

---

5. *Choshen Mishpat* 232:1.

6. *Sma* ibid. 4.

7. See *Maggid Mishneh, Hilchos Mechirah* 15:1.

to him. However, once he learns of the defect he must stop using the item immediately. If he continues to use it after realizing that it is defective, he is presumed to waive his right to a refund unless he informs the seller of the defect and the seller gives him permission to continue to use it temporarily, in which case the buyer's right to a refund remains in force.[8]

> As soon as Chaim arrived home with his newly purchased bicycle, he noticed that the frame was slightly bent. If he wishes to return the bicycle, he must stop riding it immediately; should he continue to use it, he forfeits his right to return it unless he has received specific permission from the seller.

7. If the item sold is of a kind which commonly contains a certain defect that does not interfere with its normal use, and the buyer could easily have discovered the defect at the time of sale but failed to inspect the item, then even though the seller did not inform him of the defect, we presume that the buyer was willing to accept the existence of such a defect. He therefore does not have the right to return the item.[9]

> David purchased a new sefer without inspecting it carefully, and later realized that the cover was bent and discolored due to direct exposure to sunlight. He is not allowed to return the sefer since he should have paid attention and noticed this defect at the time of purchase.

What Is Considered a Defect

8. The definition of a defect is determined by the prevailing local practice. If a particular defect is considered serious enough in that locality to warrant returning the merchandise, then the buyer always has the right to return the flawed item,[10] even if it is very costly and the defect lowers its value by only a slight amount.[11]

9. A buyer who discovers a defect in his purchase but is willing to keep it as is, cannot force the seller to reduce the price. The most required of the seller is to accept the item for a return and refund the purchase price.[12]

8. Ibid. 15:3; see *Glosses of R' Akiva Eiger,* also *Pischei Teshuvah* 1.

9. *Sma* ibid. 10; see also *Pischei Teshuvah* ibid.

10. *Choshen Mishpat* 232:6.

11. Ibid. 232:4.

12. Ibid.

Leah noticed a slight rip in the inner binding of her new school note-book. She is permitted to ask for a reduction in price, but if the sell-er refuses, her only options are to pay the full price or to return the notebook for a refund. It is prohibited to pressure the seller to give her a reduction.

10. In the case of a defect caused by external factors that can be removed, completely restoring the item to its original condition, the seller has the right to pay any repair or cleaning costs and insist that the sale remain in effect.[13]

On a visit to Eretz Yisrael Yankel saw a beautiful apartment for sale. After returning to New York, he decided to buy it and contacted a lawyer in Eretz Yisrael, who concluded the deal. He was unaware that the night before the papers were signed, there was a fire outside the building in the course of which several windows were shattered and the façade blackened. When Yankel heard about this, he lost all interest in living there. However, if the seller is willing to pay all the expenses of restoring the apartment to its original condition, the sale stands and Yankel cannot withdraw from the deal.

Damaged Food Products

11. Food that is discovered immediately after purchase to be spoiled or infested with insects and the like may be returned for a refund. In a case where the problem is only noticed later, an expert should be asked if it is possible to determine in whose possession the spoilage occurred. If the expert is confident that the damage occurred before the sale, then the buyer has a right to return the mer-chandise for a refund. The sale stands, however, if there is any pos-sibility that the problem began only after the merchandise came into the buyer's possession. If the buyer has not yet paid for the mer-chandise, a number of considerations come into play and a *halachic* authority should be consulted.[14]

Chaya bought a fresh loaf of bread on Monday, charging it to her account at the bakery. On Tuesday she noticed that the bread had started to turn moldy, but the bakery refused to take it back and demanded payment. Since it is uncertain as to whose possession the

---

13. Ibid. 232:5.

14. Ibid. 232:11 and 16; see also *Sma* ibid. 35.

bread was in when the damage occurred, the bakery owner should consult a rav.

Non-Kosher Food

12. If the purchased food turns out to be forbidden to eat, the seller is required to accept its return and refund the purchase price. If the problem is discovered only after the food has been eaten, the seller is required to refund the purchase price if a Torah prohibition is involved, even though the food is no longer in existence. However, if the prohibition is Rabbinic, the seller does not have to refund the value of any food already eaten. If it was forbidden not only to eat, but to have any benefit from the food in question, the merchandise never had any monetary value whatsoever, and the seller is required to refund the full price.[15]

> *A week after Pesach, Mrs. Cohen bought a package of macaroni from her local store and served it to her family. The next day, she discovered that the store had mistakenly obtained the macaroni from a non-religious Jewish distributor, in whose possession it had been over Pesach. Mrs. Cohen was very upset and demanded a refund from the store. Although the product had already been consumed and eating chametz that was in a Jew's possession over Pesach is only a Rabbinic prohibition, she is still entitled to a full refund, since any form of benefit from the chametz is prohibited and the macaroni is considered to be totally valueless.*

If the Seller Was Cheated

13. A person who unknowingly sells defective merchandise that he has just bought from a supplier, is nonetheless responsible for the quality of what he has sold. The seller is required to accept it in return from the buyer and refund his money, regardless of whether or not he is ever able to obtain a refund from the supplier who sold him the defective merchandise in the first place.[16]

> *Reuven, a used car dealer, purchased a vehicle from Shimon, who said it was two years old and had only 40,000 miles. Reuven, in turn, sold the car to Levi, who then showed it to a mechanic. Levi*

---

15. *Choshen Mishpat* 234.

16. Ibid. 232:18, *Rema*.

was told that it was really eight years old and had more likely been driven 140,000 *miles. Levi took the car back to Reuven and demanded a refund. Upon investigation, Reuven discovers that Shimon, the original seller, is nowhere to be found. Reuven must accept the car back and return the full purchase price to Levi.*

How to Refund

14. If a seller is required to give a refund for defective merchandise, he must give it in the form of money rather than as merchandise or other property, unless he does not have the money.[17]

> *Rivki buys a dress from Mrs. Black's clothing store and then notices that it has a serious defect. When she returns it, Mrs. Black must give her a cash refund and cannot insist on giving her a credit towards another purchase unless Rivki agrees. Only if Mrs. Black has no cash on hand and no money in her bank account is she allowed to insist that Rivki accept other merchandise instead of cash.*

Merchandise of the Wrong Quality

15. In the case of merchandise sold as being of one type that later turns out to be of another, the seller is required to accept it for refund. If merchandise represented as good quality turns out to be inferior, the buyer has the right to reverse the sale, but not the seller. Conversely, if merchandise sold as being of an inferior kind turns out to be a better type, the seller has the right to reverse the transaction but not the buyer.[18]

16. If merchandise is sold as being of good quality and actually is of good quality, the buyer cannot claim that he wanted only the very *best* quality and demand a refund. Similarly, if the seller makes it clear that the merchandise is of poor quality and it turns out to be of the worst quality, the buyer cannot demand that the sale be reversed.[19]

> *Reuven asked for a top-quality CD player at the electronics store. When he showed his purchase to his friend, the friend told him that although the quality was very good, it was not the best. Reuven cannot return the CD player and demand a refund. However, if Reuven*

---

17. Ibid. 232:23, *Rema.*

18. *Choshen Mishpat* 233.

19. Ibid.

had paid the price for the top-of-the-line model, he has been over-charged and the rules of "ona'as mamon" apply (see Chapter 39).

Shimon asked for a "standard" inexpensive tape recorder, and the store owner brought out the lowest grade item, made completely of cheap plastic. Within days the tape recorder started to fall apart – quite normal for that quality machine. Shimon cannot claim that although he did ask for a cheap tape recorder, he did not mean the very lowest grade. However, if Shimon paid the price for a better than rockbottom quality item, the rules of "ona'as mamon" apply.

In both cases, if Reuven or Shimon had specified: "I want the very best CD player," or "I want an inexpensive tape recorder, but not the lowest grade; I want it to last for a while," then they each have the right to demand a refund for the delivery of wrong merchandise. However, even with such specification, there are cases in which the seller does not have to take back the merchandise, and a rav should be consulted.

In these two cases, if there is a difference in price between the expected quality and the quality actually received, the buyer is entitled to an adjustment for the difference. If the difference is more than one-sixth, however, the transaction can be reversed as a *mekach ta'us*, as described in Chapter 39 paragraph 3.[20]

Prohibition to Deceive

17. In all of the above cases in which the Torah allows a transaction to be reversed, this is intended only as a way of resolving a situation that should have been avoided in the first place. It is strictly forbidden, however, for a seller to deceive a buyer into thinking that he is receiving one type of merchandise when it is actually another, even if the second kind is not inferior to the first, and even if after the sale has been concluded, the Torah allows it to remain in force.[21]

---

20. Ibid., *Sma* 3.
21. *Choshen Mishpat* 228:6.

43

The Torah Court

Promoting Compromise

1. Whenever disputes arise, the Torah strongly encourages the parties to make concessions among themselves in order to reach a compromise.[1]

2. If the parties in a dispute are unable to resolve their differences on their own, they may decide that each side will select an independent party to represent their respective interests, and these chosen parties will then meet and attempt to work out a compromise. (This may be done within the framework of a *beis din*, although it is not required.) The "judges" must attempt to produce a fair compromise, since it is just as forbidden to impose an unfair compromise as it is to make an unfair ruling.[2]

> *"Judges" who are chosen to work out a compromise (and certainly to hand down a ruling) and are partial, or use anti-Torah methods of favors, bribery, extortion or any other form of unfairness, are in gross violation of a number of Torah prohibitions.*[3] *Even if*

---

1. *Choshen Mishpat* 12:2.

2. Ibid.

3. There are people who mistakenly believe that if each side picks one of the judges, that judge may act as an attorney and use various tricks in an attempt to win the case for his "client." However, *Tur Choshen Mishpat* 13 in name of the *Rosh* sharply refutes such behavior,

"scholarly in Torah," they are not considered "Torah scholars" and one should not rise for them or honor them in any way, since their actions are a gross violation of the Torah[4] (see paragraphs 11 and 14).

Secular Courts

3. If the parties cannot work out a compromise, and feel compelled to turn to a court, the Torah requires them to go to a *beis din* composed of qualified Torah scholars and *forbids* going to a non-Jewish court, even if they know that the non-Jewish law will produce the same result as Torah law in their particular case. This is forbidden even if both parties had previously agreed (either verbally or in writing) to judge any disputes that arose in a non-Jewish court. A Jew who brings a case with another Jew before a non-Jewish court is thereby rejecting the authority of the Torah, (except as provided for in paragraph 4).[5] Similarly, it is forbidden to go to a court whose judges are Jewish but who apply secular non-Torah laws; for this, too, is a rejection of the Torah. (In fact, it is an even greater rejection of Torah when perpetrated by Jews.) Even if a majority of the Jews in a community choose to be governed by an alien legal system, their preference has no weight as far as the Torah is concerned and any action taken by the legal institutions they establish is considered to be theft and oppression, as well as insurrection against the Torah and the One Who gave it.[6]

It is equally forbidden to go to a secular court in Israel and in the Diaspora.

4. If one needs to take legal action against a Jew who refuses to submit to the Torah's jurisdiction, one should first summon him to a *beis din*. If he refuses to appear, one can then request the *beis din's* permission to institute proceedings in a secular court.[7]

5. A Jew who possesses information relevant to proceedings in a secular court and knows that his testimony would result in a Jew

---

calling such people *"chasrei da'as"* (lacking in basic understanding of Torah) and considering them in violation of not showing favoritism in justice (*Devarim* 1:17). All the *Poskim* accept the ruling of the *Rosh* as quite obvious and self-evident.

4. See *Yoreh Deah* 243:3.

5. *Choshen Mishpat* 26:1.

6. *Chazon Ish, Choshen Mishpat, Sanhedrin* 15:4.

7. *Choshen Mishpat* 26:2.

being made to pay more than required by Torah law in such a situation, is forbidden to testify. He should testify, however, if refusal to do so will result in a desecration of Hashem's Name.[8]

Proceedings of a *Beis Din*

6. It is forbidden for one of the parties to discuss the case with any of the judges unless the other party in the dispute is present as well. A judge who hears one side of a case without the other being present violates the prohibition, *You shall not accept false words* (*Shemos* 22:1).[9] (This is the same prohibition that prohibits accepting *lashon hara*; in both situations, the words may be true, but the method of conveying information is that of slick falsehood.)

7. The judges must treat the parties equally.[10]

    ❏ *It is forbidden for the judge to talk to one side harshly and to the other softly, or to let one party speak at length and instruct the other to "keep it short."*

    ❏ *If one party is dressed in elegant attire and the other in rags, the judge must tell the finely clothed person to either dress the other party as himself or to dress like the other party.*

    ❏ *They must also be equally standing or sitting.*

8. Bribery is forbidden in any form, even to encourage a judge to render a fair decision. A judge who accepts a bribe violates an explicit commandment, as the Torah says, *You shall not accept a bribe* (*Devarim* 16:19), while a person who gives a bribe violates the commandment not to place a stumbling block before a blind person.[11]

9. The Sages were extremely meticulous not to judge any individual who did them even a slight favor.[12]

    Mar Ukva was once presiding over a case in the courtroom, and there was some distasteful matter on the dirt floor. A man came over and covered it (so that Mar Ukva should not have to see it). When Mar Ukva asked him what brought him to the court he replied that

---

8. Ibid. 28:3.
9. Ibid. 17:5.
10. Ibid. 17:1.
11. Ibid.
12. *Kesubos* 105b.

he had a case pending. Mar Ukva immediately disqualified himself from the case.

⊰⊱

Rabbi Yishmael, the son of Rabbi Yose, had a sharecropper who brought him a basket of fruit from his (Rabbi Yishmael's) field every Friday. One week, he came on Thursday; when Rabbi Yishmael questioned the early delivery, he answered that he had a case pending before him and thought, as he was coming to Rabbi Yishmael anyway, he would do him the favor of bringing his fruit a bit earlier. Rabbi Yishmael not only refused to accept the fruit, but disqualified himself from the case, appointing other Sages to handle it. As he paced nearby and overheard the proceedings, he realized that his thought patterns were, "If the sharecropper would claim such and such, he could win the case." Catching himself, he exclaimed, "Let the bribe-takers' souls leave them! Here I didn't take anything, and even if I would have, it would have only been what is rightfully mine. Even so, since it was done in the manner of a small favor, I found myself desiring that the sharecropper win his case; surely those who actually take bribes, how much more so are they biased!"

10. There is a rule in Torah law that the burden of proof in a dispute falls on the party who wishes to take money or property that is in another person's possession.[13] This rule can, on occasion, have the effect of giving the upper hand to an individual who has wrongly taken another person's money, since the plaintiff may have difficulty finding evidence to support his claim, however true it may be. Even if one knows that the only way of recouping money rightfully his is by lying, or that if he speaks the truth he will be unjustly forced to pay money, it is still forbidden to make any false claims or statements. If the judges feel that there is falsity in the claims, and following legal protocol will not lead to a truthful verdict, they should withdraw from the case.[14] A person must integrate into his soul the knowledge that even if a human *beis din* cannot enforce a fair solution in such cases, Hashem knows what is right and will see to it that Divine Justice will ultimately prevail.

---

13. *Bava Kamma* 46a.
14. *Shevuos* 31a.

Qualities of a Judge

11. In appointing a *beis din*, the members of a community must be certain that each of the judges possesses *all* of the following qualities: Torah wisdom, humility, fear of Heaven, disdain for money, love of truth, the respect and esteem of others, and a reputation for uprightness in all his actions.[15] Appointing a judge who is not qualified violates the commandment, *Do not show favoritism in judgment* (*Devarim* 1:17), which forbids appointing a person as a judge because he is wealthy, a friend or a relative. It is forbidden to rise in the presence of an unqualified judge who has received his appointment through bribery or nepotism, or to show him any other form of respect; on the contrary, one should treat him with disrespect. Concerning such a judge the Sages said, *Do not make for yourselves idols of silver or of gold* (*Shemos* 20:20).[16]

> *When a judge appointed by the powerful house of the Nasi was found to be unlearned, Yehudah bar Nachmani exclaimed, "Woe to those who say to wood, 'Arise,' and to a silent stone, 'Wake up.' Will he teach? He is bound by gold and silver, there is no spirit within him!" (Chabakkuk 2:19).[17]*

12. In a community where no suitable judges exist, the best and the wisest of the available candidates should be appointed to form a *beis din* to judge disputes that arise to the best of their ability. Although a tribunal of this sort lacks scholarly qualifications, it is better to bring disputes to such a *beis din* that attempts to adjudicate compromise and Torah law according to their best ability, than to a secular court, which is absolutely prohibited, as discussed in paragraph 3. Once a community has empowered a *beis din* composed of its most suitable members, no one may dispute its authority.[18]

13. The community is obligated to honor and revere the members of a *beis din*, and the members, in turn, are not permitted to act frivolously in public. A person who has been appointed to a position of leadership may no longer perform work publicly, participate in parties, or imbibe alcohol in public to a point approaching drunkenness.[19]

---

15. *Choshen Mishpat* 7:11.

16. Ibid. 8:1.

17. *Sanhedrin* 7b.

18. *Choshen Mishpat* 8:1, *Rema*.

19. Ibid. 8:3.

To Champion Justice

14. The institutions of justice are basic to Torah Judaism. The righteous are extolled for being vigorous in championing the rights of the poor and underprivileged and ensuring that justice is carried out.[20] The prophets consistently denounced the people for any minor flaws in justice.

> *Rabbi Yose ben Elisha said, "If you see a generation with many tragedies, go and check the judges of Israel, for every punishment that occurs in the world comes because of the judges of Israel."*[21]
>
> Note: *This statement apparently includes both individual judges who act inconsistently with Torah standards and the state of justice institutions in general, for when people do not seek to carry out Torah justice, true justice will suffer.*

One of the saddest features of many contemporary Torah communities is the lack of public acceptance of the authoritative jurisdiction of righteous judges. The Jewish people pray constantly for the return of justice as in days of old[22] and that merit will be an intrinsic part of the ultimate redemption.[23]

---

20. Avraham (*Bereishis* 18:19), Moshe (*Shemos* 2:12,13,17), Iyov (*Iyov* 29:12,14,17), David (*II Shmuel* 8:15), Shlomo (*I Melachim* 3:9,28), Yehoshofat (*II Divrei HaYamim* 19:5-11), Yoshiahu (*Yirmiyahu* 22:15,16), Mashiach (*Yeshayahu* 11:4).

21. *Shabbos* 139a.

22. *Shemoneh Esrei*, 11th *berachah*.

23. *Yeshayahu* 1:27.

❯ Respect and Honor

Chapters 44-47

44

Honoring and Revering Parents

1. The Torah commands a person to (a) revere his parents and (b) honor his parents. Great care is required to do so properly, since the Torah compares the honor and reverence of parents to that of Hashem. The Torah writes, *Honor your father and your mother* (*Shemos* 20:12), and also *Honor Hashem* (*Mishlei* 3:9). Elsewhere it says, *A man shall fear his mother and his father* (*Vayikra* 19:3), and also *You shall fear Hashem, your G-d* (*Devarim* 6:13). Just as the Torah commands us to honor and fear Hashem, so too, does the Torah command us to honor and fear our parents.[1]

> *Three partners participate in creating a person: Hashem, the father and the mother. When a person honors his parents, Hashem considers it as if He Himself were dwelling among them and they were honoring Him.*[2]

The Mitzvah of Reverence

2. It is forbidden to stand or sit in the father's regular place in shul, among his friends or in the home. It is forbidden to disagree with a

---

1. *Kiddushin* 30b.
2. Ibid.

parent in his presence. One may not even agree with a parent because that implies that the child may question the parent's opinion or action.[3]

> *Mrs. Schwartz was discussing a certain matter with Mrs. Gold. Her daughter Miriam, after respectfully asking if she could speak, mentioned a point supporting her mother's viewpoint but did not say "my mother is right because ..."*

According to some opinions, one should not openly disagree with a parent even when the parent is not present.[4] However, when the parent is not present one may respectfully state the truth as he sees it, even if it contradicts the parent's position.[5]

> ❏ *Do not say: My father is wrong.*
> ❏ *Rather: I believe that ...*

A son may learn Gemara with his father even though this usually involves debates and contradictions.[6] Nevertheless, the son should conduct these debates with respect.

3. One may not refer to a parent by name, even after the parent is no longer alive, but rather call him *Avi Mori* (my father, my teacher) or a similar respectful formula.[7] However, if asked by someone who does not know his parent's name, he is permitted to state in a respectful manner, "I am the child of So and so."[8]

> *When the gabbai in shul asks a person for his name, he may answer Ploni ben Reb Ploni.*

4. One should not call others who have the same name as a parent by name in the parent's presence; if the parent's name is uncommon, one should not call others by it even if the parent is not present.[9] According to other opinions, however, one may call others by a shared common name even in the parent's presence, and it is only forbidden to call others by the parent's name when the name is uncom-

---

3. *Yoreh Deah* 240:2.

4. Ibid., *Shach* 2; note, however, that *Taz* 3 and the *Gra* 3 disagree.

5. See *Halichos Olam*, Ch. 50 fn. *hei.*

6. *Pischei Teshuvah* 1 to *Yoreh Deah* 240.

7. *Yoreh Deah* 240:2.

8. *Pischei Teshuvah* 2 to *Yoreh Deah* 240.

9. Ibid., according to the opinion of the *Shulchan Aruch* and the *Rema.*

mon and the parent is present.[10] Since revering parents is a *mitzvah D'Oraisa* (a commandment of Biblical origin) one ought to follow the stringent opinion.

> *David was going to his friend, Chaim, for Shabbos. Since Chaim's father's name was David, they made up a code name for Chaim to call David at the Shabbos table.*

> *Yaakov's father's name was Abaye, and he had a friend named Abaye as well. Even in school, Yaakov called his friend "Aby" in order to avoid the possibility of violating the mitzvah of revering one's father.*

The Mitzvah of Honor

5. One shows his parents honor by serving them food and drink, dressing them, and in general performing all the services a personal servant performs for his master.[11]

> *Rabbi Tarfon's mother went for a walk in her courtyard on Shabbos. Her shoe broke and could not be fixed on Shabbos. Rabbi Tarfon placed his hands on the ground for his mother to step on, and thus he continued until his mother reached her bed.*
>
> *One day Rabbi Tarfon took ill. His mother asked the Sages to pray for him, mentioning this story to show the extraordinary extent to which he honored his mother. The Sages replied that even if he would have multiplied that honor a thousandfold, he would not have reached half the extent of honor that the Torah expects a child to give a parent.[12]*

One must take care to do all this in an agreeable and respectful manner, for if any resentment is displayed about serving the parent, then even if one serves only the choicest foods, he will be called to account and be punished for it.[13]

> *There are children who feed a parent delicacies and inherit Gehinnom and others who tie them to a mill to work and inherit Gan Eden:*

---

10. *Shach* 3 to *Yoreh Deah* 240.

11. *Yoreh Deah* 240:4, *Rema*.

12. *Yerushalmi Pe'ah* 1:1.

13. *Yoreh Deah* ibid.

One man fed his father delicacies of fowl every day. When his father asked, "From where do you have all this?" the son replied, "Old father, eat and be quiet, like dogs eat and are quiet."

Another man was working at his mill and soldiers came to draft people to work for the king. The man said, "Father, you work the mill and I will go instead of you to work for the king."[14]

6. When referring to a parent, one should speak as if one is in awe of the parent and anxious to show him proper honor.[15] If one needs a service or favor, and knows that those involved will do it to honor his father, then even if he knows that they would do it to honor him as well, he should request it in his father's name rather than his own in order to show honor to his father.[16]

❏ *Were I to say, "Please do this for my sake," they will be honoring me.*

❏ *However, if I say, "Please do this for my father's sake," they will be honoring my father.*

7. One is required to rise as soon as one hears one's parent's voice and becomes aware that he or she is present, even if the parent is not yet in sight.[17]

Rav Yosef stood up when he heard his mother's footsteps and said, "I will stand for the Divine Presence." (Honoring a parent is equivalent to honoring Hashem.)[18]

Honor at Whose Expense

8. Although a child is required to serve his parents food and drink, he is not required to offer these items at his own expense, but at theirs. If the parents are indigent, however, the child is required to support them as part of his *tzedakah* responsibility. However, one should use one's own funds if possible, rather than *tzedakah;* the Sages even placed a curse on anyone who can afford to support his parents as a personal expense and uses *tzedakah* funds for that purpose.[19] If both parents and child are indigent, then according to some opinions,

---

14. *Yerushalmi Pe'ah* ibid.

15. *Rambam, Hilchos Mamrim* 6:4.

16. *Yoreh Deah* 240:6.

17. Ibid. 240:7; see *Gilyon Maharsha.*

18. *Kiddushin* 31b.

19. *Yoreh Deah* 240:5; see also *Kodesh Yisrael,* Ch. 31.

the child is obligated to collect charity or to hire himself out as a work-er in order to support his parents.[20]

9. Even though a child is not required to care for his parents at his own expense, he is obligated to take time from his work to serve their needs. Unless this will cause him to become impoverished, he is obligated to do so even though it will cause financial loss.[21] According to some opinions, even if it will cause him to become impoverished, he is still required to take time from his work to serve his parents.[22]

> *Father: Yankie, could you please drive me to the airport?*
>
> *Although Yankie will lose a day's work, he must serve his father. However, according to the first opinion, if Yankie would thereby be in danger of losing his job, which could impoverish him, then he is permitted to refuse.*

Extent of Reverence and Honor

10. The Sages gave us examples of the extent to which we are required to demonstrate reverence for parents, and from this example we can extrapolate other lessons.

> *A man dressed in very distinguished clothing was sitting at the head of a prestigious gathering when suddenly his parent came up to him and tore at his clothes, slapped him on the head, and spat in his face. The son may not act angry or cause the parent any pain or embar-rassment, but must sit quietly, in fear of the King of all kings Who so commanded him.[23]*
>
> *Note: The Sages do not say that the son should not feel anger; it is quite natural for the child to be angry at a parent. A person who bears angry feelings toward a parent should try to alleviate them in*

---

20. Tosafos, Kiddushin 31a from the *Talmud Yerushalmi,* also *Smag* and *Smak; Chazon Ish, Yoreh Deah* 149; see also *Kodesh Yisrael* ibid.

21. *Yoreh Deah* 240:5, *Beur HaGra* 14 in name of *Ramah.*

22. *Yoreh Deah* ibid. permits it only if he doesn't have food for that day. The *Bach* prohibits even this for this is the opinion of many *Rishonim.* But see *Kodesh Yisrael* ibid. that there are other *Rishonim* who hold like the first opinion. Note: With regard to other mitzvos (e.g. vis-iting the sick, comforting mourners, bringing a bride to the *chuppah* etc.) the *Poskim* unani-mously agree with the first opinion. Therefore, if someone knows of a sick person or mourn-er who needs visitors and there is no one else to do it, one should take off from work to do the mitzvah but one does not have to endanger his job (*Beis Yosef, Yoreh Deah* 240; *Taz* 7).

23. Ibid. 240:3. See *Kiddushin* 31a.

other ways, but is forbidden to carry out acts — stemming from the anger — that cause pain to the parent.

11. A parent who is asleep with the key to the child's store under his pillow, may not be awakened by the child, even though he stands to forfeit a large profit. However, if the parent will himself suffer a loss or be unhappy over this, then it is a mitzvah to disturb the parent's sleep in order to make him happy. It is also a mitzvah to awaken one's father to go to shul to *daven*, or for other mitzvah-related activities, since both parent and child are required to give honor to Hashem.[24]

Parents Contradicting Each Other

12. If both parents ask a child to give them a glass of water, the father takes precedence, since both the mother and the child are required to honor the father. If the parents are divorced, however, then they have equal precedence; according to some opinions, the child may show preference to whomever he wishes, while others say that he should not prefer either one but should leave the water in front of them and let them serve themselves.[25]

13. A child who does something at his mother's request and is then asked by his father who told him to do it, should not answer if he senses that the father will be upset with the mother, even if this will cause his father to be upset with him.[26] Apart from the lack of respect to the mother, a prohibition against *rechilus* is also involved. He should therefore not listen to his father, since one is not allowed to obey a parent if it will result in a transgression.

Married Women

14. Although both men and women are obligated in the mitzvah of honoring parents, a married woman is exempt from honoring her parents since she is under her husband's domain. Nevertheless, if her husband so permits, she is required to honor her parents to the extent that she is able.[27] The husband has his own mitzvah to honor his parents-in-law (see paragraph 33).

---

24. *Kitzur Shulchan Aruch* 143:4; see the story of Dama ben Nesina, *Kiddushin* 31a.

25. *Yoreh Deah* 240:14; see *Pischei Teshuvah* 12 in the name of the *Maharshal*.

26. *Kitzur Shulchan Aruch* 143:6.

27. *Yoreh Deah* 240:17, *Shach* 19.

15. On occasion, a parent may ask a son or daughter who also has children for a favor, and listening to the parent will interfere with his or her own parenting responsibilities. Since feeding and providing for one's children is a mitzvah,[28] it would seem that this takes precedence, because the obligation to honor a parent does not supersede a mitzvah. Nevertheless, a person should attempt to do both to whatever extent possible.

Note: It is highly educational for a child to see parents go out of their way to honor their own parents.

Honoring Parents After They Have Passed On

16. The mitzvah of honoring parents extends after their death. When mentioning a parent during the first twelve months after departure, one should add the phrase, *"Hareini kaparas mishkavo/ah* — May I be an atonement for his/her repose" (i.e. for any sins committed during his/her lifetime for which atonement is now required). After twelve months, when the parent has already received any needed atonement (since even the wicked are not sentenced to more than twelve months in Gehinnom), one should add the phrase (both in speech and in writing), *"Zichrono/ah livrachah lechayei haOlam Haba* — May his/her memory be a blessing for the life of the World to Come."[29] According to some opinions, it is permitted to use this second formula even during the first twelve months, but the first formula ("May I be an atonement" etc.) certainly may not be used after this period has ended.[30]

17. In a situation where one's father had ordered him to perform a certain task after his death and the widow (his mother) objects, there are differences of opinion in the *Poskim* and a rav should be consulted.[31]

Mitzvos Supersede Honor of Parents

18. If a parent tells a child to violate the Torah, whether a positive or negative commandment or even a Rabbinic one, the child may not listen. This is derived from the verse, *A man shall fear his*

---

28. *Kesubos* 49b, 50a.

29. Some use the acronym *zatzal* which stands for *zecher tzaddik livrachah*, "the memory of a righteous person is a blessing."

30. *Yoreh Deah* 240:9 and *Shach* 9.

31. Ibid. *Pischei Teshuvah* 11; see also *Kodesh Yisrael*, Ch. 32.

mother and his father, and you shall keep My Sabbaths, I am Hashem, your G-d (Vayikra 19:3). Even though Hashem commanded us to fear our parents, we are not to obey a parent who tells us to violate the Sabbath. Concerning all other mitzvos as well, this verse tells us, *I am Hashem, your G-d;* both you and your father are required to honor Hashem, so do not listen to your father if he tells you to violate any of the commandments. The Rabbinic commandments also have the force of Hashem's words, as the Torah says, *You shall act according to the Torah they shall teach you and the judgment they shall say to you; do not deviate from the word they shall tell you to the right or the left (Devarim 17:11).*[32]

> *A person whose father orders him not to speak to a particular person or not to forgive someone for a certain action, whereas the son is willing to be reconciled, is not permitted to obey his father in this matter, since it is forbidden to hate another person (see Chapter 4), nor bear any grudge (see Chapter 7). Thus, the father is ordering him to disobey the Torah, and he may not listen to him.*[33]

19. If a father tells a son to serve him and the son is presented with another mitzvah that must be done immediately, the child should serve his father if he can arrange for others to do the second mitzvah. If there is no one else to do the other mitzvah, then the son should. However, if the son has already started to do the other mitzvah, he is in any case exempt from the mitzvah of honoring his father until he finishes, since a person who is involved in one mitzvah is exempt from performing others.[34]

> *When Berel took sick, his close friends Yitzi and Yanki undertook to bring him food and medicine, visit him and attend to his general needs. On a day that Yitzi was planning to care for Berel, his father called saying that he needed him at the office. If Yitzi can get Yanki or someone else to take care of Berel he should go to his father's office, but if there is no one else to do so, he should attend to Berel. If he already has started his mitzvah of caring for Berel, then he need not look for someone to replace him, because a person involved in one mitzvah is exempt from other mitzvos.*

---

32. *Yoreh Deah* 240:15.

33. Ibid. 240:16.

34. Ibid. 240:12.

Torah Study, *Davening*, and Marriage Supersede Honoring Parents

20. If a father objects to his son's plan to go to a different location for the sake of success in his Torah studies (even if the father is worried that the other city is dangerous), the son is not required to listen, since Torah study takes precedence over the mitzvah of honoring parents.[35] Even if he is unsure if his learning will improve, he does not have to listen to the father.[36] Similarly, if he wants to *daven* in a certain shul where he feels that he will concentrate better, and the parent objects, the child does not have to listen to the parent.[37] In addition, if a child wishes to marry a certain individual, and the parent objects, the child is not required to listen to the parent.[38]

Rebuking a Parent

21. If one sees his father violating the Torah in some form, the son should not tell his father of his wrongdoing outright but should say, "Father, does the Torah tell us such and such?" as if he were simply asking a question. This avoids the embarrassment of a father being chastised by his son.[39]

> If the father is about to speak lashon hara, the son could say, "Daddy, according to the halachah is this considered lashon hara?"

22. Even if one's parent does not uphold the Torah at all, one should still honor and revere him.[40]

> Rachel, wife of Yaakov, did not merit to raise her youngest son Binyamin because she upset her father Lavan (even though her intentions were purely to prevent him from idol worship).[41]

---

35. Ibid. 240:25. We see this in the case of Yaakov, who spent fourteen years after he left his father studying Torah in the yeshivah of Ever and then went to work for his uncle Lavan in order to build a family. Later, he was punished for the additional twenty-two years he spent away from his father with twenty-two years of grief for his missing son Yosef, but was not punished for the fourteen years he spent studying Torah.

36. *Pischei Teshuvah* 22.

37. Ibid.

38. *Yoreh Deah* 240:25, *Rema*.

39. Ibid. 240:11.

40. Ibid. 240:18. Although some hold that there is no obligation of honor as long as one does not actively upset them (see *Rema* and *Shach* 20), it would nevertheless seem that since today most non-observant Jews do not have the status of "wicked" (see Ch. 1 par. 5), there would be unanimous agreement that there is an active obligation of honor and reverence.

41. *Yoreh Deah* 241:4; *Shiurei Berachah* in name of *Zohar*.

Striking or Cursing a Parent

23. A person who strikes and wounds a parent or who curses a parent using one of Hashem's Names, even after the parent's death, is liable to the death penalty. One who strikes without wounding or curses without using one of Hashem's Names, while not liable for the death penalty, is nonetheless violating a negative commandment of the Torah, a serious matter in itself.[42]

24. Someone who mocks or makes light of a parent, even through a hint, is subject to the Torah's curse, *Accursed is one who degrades his father or his mother* (*Devarim* 27:16). *Beis din* has the authority to punish such a person with beating or any other punishment it deems appropriate.[43]

> *(With inappropriate nuances): "That's the way my mother is ... what can you do ..."*

25. A child should not remove a thorn stuck in his parent's skin if someone else is available, since this might cause a wound. If the son is a doctor, he should not operate on a parent if there is another doctor equally capable of performing the surgery. However, if no other equally qualified doctor is available, he may do whatever is necessary to heal the parent.[44]

If a Parent Is Mentally Unstable

26. One should care for a parent who becomes mentally unstable until normalcy is restored. If the parent's state is beyond one's ability to deal with, one should arrange for others to provide the appropriate care.[45]

Parents' Relationship With Children

27. A parent is not allowed to impose excessive burdens on his children or to be exacting in his demands for honor, for these things eventually will cause the children to violate their obligations of honor and reverence. A parent should instead forgive slights and ignore

---

42. Ibid. 241:1.
43. Ibid. 241:6.
44. Ibid. 241:3.
45. Ibid. 240:10.

infractions, since a parent is allowed to yield his honor.[46] On the other hand, parents are obligated to train children to honor them, just as they are obligated to train children to perform all the other mitzvos.

28. Although a parent's waiver of his right to honored treatment exempts the child from punishment, the son still has a mitzvah of honoring his parents.[47] If, however, a parent *orders* a child to act in a way not in keeping with the parent's honor, the child is required to obey.[48]

> ❏ **Father to son:** *When I enter the room you do not have to stop what you are doing and stand up for me.*
> *The son does not have to stop his activity and rise; however, if he does so, he merits a mitzvah.*

> ❏ **Father to son:** *When I enter the room, I do not want you to stop your activity and stand up for me.*
> *The son may not stop his activity and stand, for that would be disobeying his father's request.*

29. A son is permitted to accept services from a father who wishes to perform them for his son, unless the father is a *ben Torah*.[49]

30. It is forbidden for a parent to strike a child who is mature enough to consider himself an adult and will resent the blows (either in words or in actions). Instead, the parent should offer constructive criticism in a way that will effectively bring the child to change his ways. A parent who strikes a mature child is subject to *nidui* (ostracism), since he violates the commandment against placing a stumbling block before a blind person, i.e. he incites the child to strike back, verbally or physically, which is prohibited. (See footnote.)[50]

Other Adults Included in the Mitzvah

31. A person is required to honor his father's wife, even if she is not his mother, as long as his father is alive, and similarly to honor

---

46. Ibid. 240:19.

47. Ibid. *Pischei Teshuvah* 16 in the name of the *Radbaz*.

48. *Kiddushin* 31b, *Tosafos*, s.v. *R' Tarfon*; story of *R' Yishmael*.

49. *Yoreh Deah* 240:25.

50. Ibid. 240:20; see also *Kitzur Shulchan Aruch* ibid. 18 (*Birchei Yosef* in name of *Ritva*). See *My Child, My Disciple* by Rabbi Noach Orlowek, who cites Rabbi Shlomo Wolbe that nowadays even a three-year-old is liable to hit back and is therefore considered to be as an "older child." See also Ch. 29 for a discussion of this issue.

his mother's husband as long as his mother is alive. It is fitting to continue to honor step-parents even after the parent passes away.[51]

32. A person is required to honor his older brother (whether through his father or his mother), even if he himself is more learned.[52] The term "older brother" as used here refers to the oldest male in the family who can assume the father's role as head of the family.[53] There are those who hold that there is no requirement to honor an older sister, apart from the general rules of proper behavior to respect anyone older than oneself (see footnote).[54] According to some opinions, one is required to honor an uncle, whether on his father's side or his mother's.[55]

33. A person is required to honor his parents-in-law, as they are considered like parents.[56]

> King David addressed King Shaul as "Father" since he was his father-in-law.

34. A person is required to honor his grandparents, although the obligation to honor parents is greater.[57]

35. A non-Jew is not obligated by this mitzvah. Nevertheless, even a non-Jew is expected to honor his parents and not treat them with any disregard.[58]

> Cham was punished for not showing respect to his father Noach.

Thus, a non-Jew who converts to Judaism, although not obligated by the Torah commandment to honor his parents,[59] should nevertheless continue to do so as before.[60]

---

51. *Yoreh Deah* 240:21.

52. Ibid. 240:22.

53. Ibid. *Beis Lechem Yehudah* in the name of *Kavanas HaArizal*; see also *Kodesh Yisrael*, Ch. 34.

54. *Yoreh Deah* 240:22, *Pischei Teshuvah* 19. However, if an older sister takes an active part in caring for a younger child, there is a general obligation of appreciation toward an individual who made an effort to care for and raise someone else — see *Sotah* 49a; *Halichos Olam*, Ch. 50 fn. *reish* (2).

55. *Birchei Yosef* in the name of *Rabbeinu Yonah*, *Sefer HaYirah*, and *Sefer Chareidim*.

56. *Yoreh Deah* 240:24, *Taz* 19.

57. Ibid. *Rema*; see also *Kodesh Yisrael*, Ch. 33.

58. *Yad Avraham* on *Yoreh Deah* 241:9.

59. A person who converts is legally considered like a newborn child without connection to previous relatives.

60. *Yoreh Deah* 241:9.

True Mutual Respect

36. A person who truly wishes to honor his parents should devote himself to Torah and good deeds; this is the greatest honor one can accord them since it brings them praise for raising such a child. A child who does not go in the proper path, however, is a disgrace to his parents and causes them great degradation.[61]

37. Similarly, a parent who truly wishes to help his children should devote himself to Torah and good deeds and act in a way that casts honor upon his family, while a person who does not follow in the path of uprightness causes his children to suffer disgrace. There is no greater way to help one's children in life than to mold oneself into a *tzaddik*, for the merit of a *tzaddik* endures for a thousand generations.[62]

---

61. *Kitzur Shulchan Aruch* 143:21.
62. Ibid.

45

Honor and Reverence of Torah Scholars

Honoring Hashem — The Purpose of Creation

1. The sole purpose for which we are created is to honor Hashem and to sanctify His Name, as the prophet says, *All that is called by My Name, indeed, it is for My glory that I have created it, formed it and made it* (*Yeshayahu* 43:7). It stands to reason, then, that any individual who desecrates Hashem's Name and spurns His Word negates the very reason for his existence.[1]

2. Sanctifying Hashem's Name means that our every action and speech convey the conviction that serving and fearing Hashem and upholding His Torah is the basis of everything that is good and dear and worthy, as King Solomon wrote, *For this is all of the man* (*Koheles* 12:13). In order to perpetuate the service of Hashem, there must be those individuals who devote themselves to studying His Torah day and night, for they preserve it for the Jewish people in every generation. We are therefore obligated to honor our Torah scholars, for by doing so we are honoring Hashem and affirming our belief that serving Him is the basis and sole purpose of our existence.[2]

---

1. *Shaarei Teshuvah* 3:143.

2. Ibid. 3:148.

Note: A scholar of Torah who does not fear Heaven or belittles the Torah or its mitzvos is not considered a "Torah scholar" and one should not honor him.[3]

3. A person is required to honor all Torah scholars, even those who are not one's teachers. He is also required to honor his Torah teachers even if they are not great Torah scholars. Through honoring them all we show honor to the Torah.[4]

Reverence for Torah Scholars

4. The verse *You shall fear Hashem, your G-d* (*Devarim* 6:13) contains the superfluous word *"es."* This teaches us that we are required to fear not only Hashem but Torah scholars as well, both one's teachers and all other Torah scholars. The Sages taught, *The fear of your rebbi should be like the fear of Heaven* (*Avos* 4:12).[5]

5. It is a serious transgression to hold Torah scholars in contempt, to slight their honor or to hate them. Jerusalem was not destroyed until its Sages were scorned. He who slights a Torah scholar loses his portion in the World to Come, is called an *apikores* and is included among those whom the Torah describes with the phrase, *He has scorned the word of Hashem* (*Bamidbar* 15:31).[6]

6. A person who speaks *lashon hara* about a Torah scholar violates not only the prohibition against *lashon hara* but also the serious injunction to fear Hashem, as discussed in paragraph four.[7] This mitzvah prohibits slighting even Torah scholars of lesser stature than oneself; although one is not actively required to show fear of those lesser than himself, it is nevertheless forbidden to slight them in any way. We see this from the rule that a Torah scholar is allowed to sit while testifying before a court (whereas all other witnesses are required to stand) even if he is of lesser stature than the members of the court, since it would be a slight to the honor of the Torah knowledge he possesses to require him to stand.[8]

---

3. *Yoreh Deah* 243:3.

4. *Rambam, Hilchos Talmud Torah* 5:1 and 6:1.

5. *Tosafos, Bava Kamma* 41a, s.v. *es.*

6. *Rambam, Hilchos Talmud Torah* 6:11; *Sanhedrin* 98b.

7. *Sefer Chofetz Chaim,* Positive Commandment 8 and *Be'er Mayim Chaim* 10.

8. *Shevuos* 30b; *Choshen Mishpat* 28:5; see *Kodesh Yisrael,* Ch. 35 and *Shevilei Chaim* 7.

7. From the mitzvah of *You shall fear Hashem, your G-d*, a person should learn to hold Torah scholars in awe and be fearful lest he mistakenly slight one of them. Sadly, many unthinking people are unaware of this prohibition and are quick to speak disparagingly of the leaders of groups other than their own, such as Chassidic Rebbes, Roshei Yeshivah, or other Rabbanim. Anyone who fears Hashem must take great care not to learn from these individuals, since the Torah not only prohibits speaking disrespectfully about Torah scholars but even merely listening to such statements; when we hear people speak in this fashion we are required to protest immediately.[9]

> *Rabbi Elazar, the son of Rabbi Shimon bar Yochai, was not buried after he passed away. For years his body lay in the attic of his house and remained completely fresh, to the point that one could pull out a hair and the body would bleed. Two people in litigation would stand in front of the house; each would state his position and a voice would come from the attic pronouncing the decision. One day, Rabbi Elazar's wife saw a worm in his ear. He appeared to her in a dream and told her that this was not the beginning of his body's decomposition, but happened because he once heard a Torah scholar slighted and did not protest as much as he should have.*

8. The Torah relates (*Bamidbar* 12) that Miriam spoke to her brother Aharon, criticizing the fact that Moshe separated from his wife Tzipporah. Miriam was unaware that Moshe's level of prophecy required him to separate from his wife. Although she spoke with good intent, she was nevertheless punished with *tzaraas* (a Divine retribution resembling leprosy that caused her impurity, forcing her to temporarily leave the Israelite camp). The essence of her sin lay precisely in taking lightly the awe that she and Aharon were expected to have for their brother Moshe, as Hashem chastised them, *Why did you not fear to speak against My servant Moshe?* (ibid. v. 8). As *Rashi* explains, it would have been wrong to speak against Moshe even had he not excelled in being Hashem's servant, since he was a Torah scholar. It would also have been wrong to speak against any of Hashem's servants, even if they were not leaders of Moshe's caliber.

---

9. *Bava Metzia* 84b.

46

Honoring One's Rebbi

Categories of Rebbis

1. There are four categories of rebbis (teachers of Torah), each of which requires a different degree of honor: (a) a *rebbi muvhak* (principal rebbi); (b) a *rebbi she'eino muvhak* (rebbi who is not one's principal rebbi); (c) Torah scholars of roughly equal stature who learn from each other; and (d) a rebbi who is not a Torah scholar, from whom one learned as a child.

Rebbi Muvhak

2. Greater honor and fear is required for a *rebbi muvhak* than for any of the other categories. A *rebbi muvhak* is defined as the rebbi from whom one acquired most of one's wisdom in Torah.[1] When a person is privileged to become a Torah scholar, his *rebbi muvhak* is considered

---

1. *Yoreh Deah* 242:30. If someone's learning is limited to *Chumash*, then his *Chumash* rebbi is his *rebbi muvhak*; if he has achieved Mishnah, then his Mishnah *rebbi* is his *rebbi muvhak* etc. In today's times, when students advance through yeshivah changing rebbis each year, it is quite possible for an adult not to have a *rebbi muvhak*. However, it is wise to educate children to act toward the rebbi of their grade as to a *rebbi muvhak*. An adult who studies Torah under a rebbi should give him extra deference as well.

to be the teacher from whom he learned how to analyze the Torah to the depth required to extract correct *halachah*.[2]

3. One is expected to have greater honor and fear for his rebbi than for his father, since a father gives him life only in this world, while the rebbi from whom he acquired Torah gives him life in the World to Come.[3] Therefore, all the forms of honor and fear required for a parent (not calling him by his name, standing in his presence, etc., as discussed in Chapter 44) are also required for a rebbi.[4]

4. One is required to act toward his rebbi with awe, and should therefore not speak to the rebbi as he does to other people. In greeting a rebbi one should bend over slightly and say with reverence, "*Shalom alecha, rebbi u'mori*" ("Greetings, my rebbi and my master").[5]

5. One should not remove his *tefillin* in the presence of his rebbi. He should not recline in his presence but should sit up straight as in the presence of a king.

> *Although there is an obligation to recline at the Seder, a student who is in the presence of his rebbi may not do so without permission from the rebbi.*

One should not sit down until his rebbi tells him to, and if he is sitting he should not stand up to leave without first receiving his rebbi's permission. When one leaves his rebbi's presence, rather than turn around and walk away as usual, he should back away from the rebbi while still facing him.[6]

> *When Rava left the presence of his rebbi, Rav Yosef, he backed away so far that his toes were stubbed and the threshold of Rav Yosef's door was red with his blood. When Rav Yosef (who was blind) was informed of this, he said, "May it be the will of Hashem that he will be head of the entire yeshivah of the city." (Rava gave extraordinary honor to the Torah, therefore he will rise to the heights of Torah) (Yoma 53a).*

---

2. Ibid. *Rema*. It would seem that in today's times scholars privileged to study under a Torah sage who taught them the profundities of Torah analysis in wide areas of Torah are to consider him a *rebbi muvhak*. See *Kodesh Yisrael*, Ch. 35.

3. *Rambam, Hilchos Talmud Torah* 5:1.

4. *Yoreh Deah* 242:15.

5. Ibid. 242:16; see also *Rema, Beur HaGra, Birchei Yosef* and *Pischei Teshuvah* 11.

6. *Yoreh Deah* ibid.

6. One is required to rise to his full height as soon as his rebbi is seen approaching, even from a distance, and to remain standing when he leaves as long as the rebbi's figure can be seen in the distance. If the rebbi is riding it is considered as if he is walking by and one is required to stand.[7] However, if one's rebbi is called to the Torah reading, one is not required to remain standing the whole time the rebbi is standing.[8]

7. If two people are walking with their rebbi or any great Torah scholar, the rebbi should be in the middle, with the greater person on his right and the lesser on his left.[9] Both should be slightly behind him.[10]

8. A *talmid* (student) is required to perform for his rebbi all the services a personal attendant usually performs for his master. A rebbi who does not permit his *talmid* to serve him is considered as if he prevented his student from doing kindness and causes him to take lightly his obligation to fear Hashem. A *talmid* who takes his rebbi's honor lightly causes the Divine Presence to withdraw from the Jewish people.[11]

9. One should not give honor to a *talmid* in the presence of his rebbi unless the rebbi honors him as well, or unless it is clear that the rebbi will be honored by the honor his *talmid* receives.[12]

10. A rebbi does not have to stand in the presence of a *talmid*, even if the *talmid* himself is a Torah scholar. Nevertheless, we find that Rabbeinu Meir of Rottenberg used to show even his lesser students some measure of honor,[13] in keeping with the Mishnah's teaching, *Let your student's honor be as precious to you as your own* (*Avos* 4:12).

Rebbi She'eino Muvhak

11. The above-stated rules pertain only to a *rebbi muvhak*; however, it is sufficient to give a *rebbi she'eino muvhak* the honor one gives for other Torah sages, such as standing when he comes within four *amos*

---

7. Ibid.

8. Ibid. 242:18.

9. Ibid. 242:17.

10. *Shach* 38.

11. *Yoreh Deah* 242:19, 20.

12. Ibid. 242:21 and *Shach* 39.

13. *Yoreh Deah* ibid., and *Rema* 244:8.

etc. For these purposes, a *rebbi she'eino muvhak* is considered anyone from whom one has learned any amount of Torah. Even if the "rebbi" is of lesser stature than the *"talmid,"* one is required to accord him a certain amount of honor, such as standing in his presence, since one has learned at least one fact of Torah from him. Furthermore, when two Torah scholars learn together and each has learned at least one thing from the other, they are required to stand in each other's presence.[14] The Sages taught, *Anyone who learns from his colleague (even just one thing) is required to treat him with honor (Avos* 6:3).

> *Rabbi Akiva had 24,000 students who all died between Pesach and Shavuos because they did not give each other sufficient honor.[15] (That is why this period is considered a period of mourning.)*

12. Although one is required to give *honor* even to a *rebbi sh'eino muvhak* of lesser stature, the requirement to display *awe* for a rebbi does not apply unless the rebbi is of significantly greater stature than oneself. Moreover, there is a general obligation of awe for any great Torah Sage, even if a person has never learned anything directly from this sage (see Chapter 45, paragraph 3).[16]

13. From all that has been discussed about the honor and fear required for one's rebbi, we can see what a very serious offense it is to treat a rebbi with any degree of disrespect. Such behavior is considered tantamount to *apikorsus*[17] (see Chapter 45, paragraph 5).

14. Even when a rebbi waives his right to honor, it is still a mitzvah for the student to give the rebbi honor, and it is certainly forbidden to act disrespectfully toward him. Although a Torah scholar may waive his right to honor, he may not allow others to insult him.[18]

Teachers of One's Youth

15. Someone who studied under a teacher of Torah as a child, and grew up to become a Torah scholar, is required to honor the rebbi of his youth only if the latter is also a Torah scholar, in which case he

---

14. *Yoreh Deah* ibid. 242:30; see also *Beur HaGra* and *Mishnayos Bava Metzia* 2:11 with *Rambam's* commentary.

15. Cf. *Yevamos* 62b.

16. *Rosh, Perek Arvei Pesachim* 20; *Orach Chaim* 472:5. See also *Kodesh Yisrael* loc. cit.

17. See *Eruvin* 62b, *Rashi,* s.v. *nahi* and 63a, *Rashi,* s.v. *amar.*

18. *Yoreh Deah* 242:32 and *Gilyon Maharsha.*

has the status of a *rebbi she'eino muvhak*. If the teacher is not a Torah scholar, however, one is not required to stand in his presence but is expected to treat him with some degree of deference.[19]

Teachers of Trades and Other Areas of Knowledge

16. These rules apply only to teachers of Torah, and are based on honor for the Torah and for those who uphold it. However, the various forms of respect and awe discussed are not relevant to teachers of a trade or profession, or to any secular branch of knowledge. To the contrary, it degrades the Torah's honor to revere teachers of other fields in the same way that we honor those of Torah. Nevertheless, the Sages implied[20] that apprentices and the like are required to honor their masters and teachers, though only out of *derech eretz* (proper behavior).[21] Sadly, many young people act disrespectfully towards teachers of secular studies, and this is wrong, as the Sages said, *Do not be scornful of any person* (*Avos* 4:3). Children must be taught that such behavior is a mark of the wicked, as King Shlomo wrote, *When the wicked man comes, insult comes* (*Mishlei* 18:3). Respectful treatment, on the other hand, is a mark of the righteous.[22]

---

19. *Birchei Yosef* on 242:30.

20. *Pesachim* 108a.

21. Someone without *derech eretz* is called a *"boor"*; cf. *Avos* 2:6; *derech eretz* is very basic to being part of a normal Torah society; cf. *Kiddushin* 40b.

22. *Mesillas Yesharim*, Ch. 22.

47

Honoring Sages, Elders, Kohanim and Peers

1. The Torah writes: *In the presence of an old person you shall rise and you shall honor the presence of a sage and you shall revere your G-d, I am Hashem* (*Vayikra* 19:32). This teaches us two distinct *halachos*: to honor every Torah scholar (since the word *seivah*, old person, as used in the Torah, has the meaning of those wise in Torah), and also to honor every elderly person, meaning anyone who is 70 and older.[1]

2. The term "honor" as used here includes speaking with deference, extending a hand of support to an elderly person, and standing up from the time the person comes within four *amos* until he goes by.[2]

3. The requirement to stand up for a sage or an elderly person applies only in a place where respect is appropriate, but not in a public comfort facility, bathhouse, etc.[3]

4. A worker is not required to interrupt his work to stand up for an honored person; if he is working in someone's employ he is not allowed to do so.[4]

---

1. *Kiddushin* 33a; *Yoreh Deah* 244:1; *Avos* 5:25.
2. See *Rambam, Hilchos Talmud Torah* 5:9; *Chofetz Chaim*, Introduction to Positive Mitzvos 8; *Halichos Olam*, Ch. 53 fn. *beis*.
3. *Yoreh Deah* 242:4.
4. Ibid. 242:5.

5. It is forbidden for one to act as if he does not see a person whom he is required to honor. (This is why the above-cited verse concludes *and you shall revere your G-d*, to teach us that Hashem judges us according to our thoughts.) It is not fitting for a Torah scholar to make people rise for him, and, if possible, he is advised to choose a path that minimizes people's inconvenience.[5]

6. A person who is engaged in Torah study is required to stand up out of respect for a Torah scholar.[6]

7. Two Torah scholars or two elderly people are not required to rise for each other, although it is a mitzvah for them to give each other some degree of honor (e.g. to act as someone about to stand). Similarly, a young Torah scholar is not required to stand for an elder who is not a Torah scholar, although he should accord him some degree of honor.[7]

Respect for an Elder Who Is Not Learned in Torah

8. The Torah's command to show respect for an elder and to stand up for him applies even to an elder who is not learned in Torah. However, one should not stand up for an elderly person who does not keep the mitzvos of the Torah.[8]

Respect for Elderly Gentiles

9. It is proper to show some amount of respect to an elderly gentile as well and to extend to him a supporting hand[9] in consideration of his age and experience in life, because he has presumably seen many of Hashem's wonders in the course of his years.[10]

Preferring a Torah Scholar's Merchandise

10. When a Torah scholar has merchandise to sell, no other merchant should be allowed to sell his wares until the Torah scholar has finished selling his own. However, if there are other merchants pre-

---

5. Ibid. 242:3, 6.

6. Ibid. 242:11.

7. Ibid. 242:7, 8.

8. Ibid. 242:1.

9. Ibid. 242:7.

10. *Kiddushin* 33a, and *Rashi*, s.v. *herpatki*.

sent who will not respect this *halachah* (e.g. gentiles or non-observant Jews), then it is permitted for a Torah-observant Jew to sell his merchandise. In such a case, since the other Jew's refraining from sales will not cause any advantage to the Torah scholar, the other Jew need not sustain needless losses.[11]

A Torah Scholar Is Exempt From Taxes

11. An outstanding Torah scholar (relative to his time, as defined in the next paragraph) is exempt from all forms of communal taxes, even if he is wealthy.[12]

> *Until modern times, governments would tax the community as a whole; Torah scholars were exempt, and the rest of the community was required to pay the tax for them.*

12. For these purposes, a person is considered a Torah scholar if he knows how to analyze Torah issues rigorously and is familiar with most of the major issues in Talmud and *halachah*. Furthermore, Torah study must be his main vocation; while he may engage in some trade or business, he must devote as much time as possible to Torah study, limiting his business activities to the minimum required to support his family without seeking to amass wealth.[13]

13. A person who does not take his performance of mitzvos seriously, however much Torah knowledge he may possess, does not have the status of a Torah scholar and is no better than the least weighty member of the community.[14]

Respect for Kohanim

14. The Torah writes concerning Kohanim, *You shall sanctify him* (*Vayikra* 21:8), from which we learn that we are to show respect to Kohanim because of their special sanctity. Thus, we are to honor them by giving them the first *aliyah* at the Torah reading; by allowing them to speak first at public gatherings, lead *Bircas HaMazon*, be served the first portion at meals; and by according them all similar honors.[15]

---

11. *Yoreh Deah* 243:4.

12. Ibid 243:2.

13. Ibid.; see also *Pischei Teshuvah* 3.

14. *Yoreh Deah* 243:3.

15. *Gittin* 59b; *Orach Chaim* 201:2.

Use for Personal Service

15. One may not use a Torah scholar for personal service, even one who only reviews *halachos* constantly,[16] and also not a Kohen,[17] unless they waive their right to honor. In any case, however, they should not be allowed to engage in undignified activities.[18]

Preference of Torah Scholar Over Kohen

16. Someone worthy of honor for his Torah knowledge takes precedence over a Kohen. An ignorant Kohen is not to be given preferential treatment over a Torah scholar as a regular practice, but this may be done on occasion with the permission of the Torah scholar.[19]

Honor to All People

17. The way of Torah is to honor every person, as the Rambam writes, "One should never let people's honor be a light matter in his eyes."[20] The Sages also told us not to be scornful of any person,[21] and, further emphasizing the matter, warned us to make the honor of our peers as important to us as our own.[22] In general, insulting people is a trait associated with the wicked, as King Shlomo writes, *When the wicked man comes, insult comes* (*Mishlei* 18:3). In contrast, the righteous give honor to every individual.[23]

---

16. *Yoreh Deah* 243:6, *Rema*.

17. *Orach Chaim* 128:45, *Rema*.

18. *Mishnah Berurah* ibid. 175.

19. *Orach Chaim* 201:2.

20. *Hilchos Sanhedrin* 24:10, taken from *Berachos* 19b.

21. *Avos* 4:3.

22. Ibid. 2:10. See commentary of *Rabbeinu Yonah;* see also *Avos* 4:12, *Let the honor of your friend be as fear of your rebbi.*

23. *Mesillas Yesharim*, Ch. 22.

⇒ Financial Kindness

Chapters 48-55

48

Lending Money

The Obligation to Lend Money

1. The Torah teaches, *If there shall be in your midst a destitute person …
you shall not harden your heart or close your hand from your destitute
brother. Rather you shall open your hands to him* (to give him outright,
and if that is not possible or called for[1]) *or you shall lend him his requirement, whatever he is missing* (*Devarim* 15:7,8). Furthermore, the Torah
says, *If you shall lend money to My people, to the impoverished who (dwell)
with you* (*Shemos* 22:24). The Sages understood through the oral tradition that the word "if" in this verse actually denotes an obligation.[2]

> *One morning after shul, Mr. Cohen, a salaried employee, approached
> Mr. Weiss, a wealthy businessman, for a $3,000 six-month loan. If
> Mr. Weiss has the money available, he must lend it, since he knows
> that Mr. Cohen is trustworthy and will return the money (see para-
> graph 10). It is forbidden for Mr. Weiss to refuse.*

The mitzvah of extending loans is greater than the mitzvah of *tzedakah*
(charity) because the recipient of a loan will not feel embarrassed.[3]

---

1. See *Rashi* ad loc.
2. See *Rashi* ad loc.; *Choshen Mishpat* 97:1; *Ahavas Chesed* 1:1.
3. *Choshen Mishpat* ibid. See *Rashi, Shabbos* 63a, s.v. *gadol.*

"Someone who lends is greater than someone who gives tzedakah, and someone who invests (so that the recipient will be able to build his own business) is greater than both of them."[4]

2. This mitzvah includes lending money to wealthy people who are in need of cash. The above-cited verse mentions lending to the poor only to indicate that poor borrowers take precedence over wealthy ones.[5] Even poor people, if they happen to have money on hand, are obligated to lend it to others who are in need.[6]

> *Reb Yidel, a poor person, went collecting for funds to marry off his daughter. When he returned home a month before the wedding, he was able to lend the money to another person who needed it for three weeks.*

3. A person who has the cash available, but does not lend it to a poor person, not only transgresses the positive commandment mentioned above, but also violates the negative commandment (*Devarim* 15:9), *Beware lest there be a lawless thought in your heart, behold the Shemittah year is approaching* (which cancels debts[7]) *and your eye will see with disfavor your poor brethren* (who request a loan).[8] One violates this commandment if his reason for withholding the loan is based on fear of loss from the *Shemittah* year; it is certainly prohibited to withhold a loan if no such fear exists. Such thoughts are called lawless (*bli-yaal*).[9]

4. The obligation to lend money to others is even greater if the borrower is faced with any danger because of his lack of money. In such a situation the negative commandment, *You shall not stand aside while your fellow's blood is being shed* (*Vayikra* 19:16) also applies.[10]

---

4. *Shabbos* 63a.

5. *Ahavas Chesed* 1:1; see also *Kodesh Yisrael*, Ch. 38 for a discussion as to whether lending money to wealthy people is included in the mitzvah of *If you shall lend money* or is simply included among the acts of kindness we are required to do for all Jews. Note: The laws of precedence in loans, *tzedakah* and kindness in general are stated in Ch. 54.

6. *Ahavas Chesed* 2:1.

7. When Hillel saw that people violated this prohibition, he enacted *prozbul*, which enables people to collect those debts on which the *prozbul* was arranged. See *Sheviis* Ch. 10.

8. *Ahavas Chesed* Introduction, Negative Commandment 1. The Sages taught that the words *hi'shameir* and *pen* both indicate negative commandments; thus, someone who closes his heart and does not lend money to those in need actually violates two negative commandments.

9. *Shaarei Teshuvah* 3:67.

10. *Ahavas Chesed* 2:3.

Examples:

❏ *A person who needs to be ransomed.*

❏ *A sick individual in need of medical treatment that he cannot receive due to lack of finances.*

❏ *A person who owes money and the creditors make his and his family's life miserable.*

5. The mitzvah of *Let your brother live with you* (*Vayikra* 25:36) obligates us to help ensure that every fellow Jew has a means of sustenance. Thus, if someone asks for a loan so that he can build a business from which he can sustain himself, the obligation to help him is much greater. Similarly, if one sees a fellow Jew on the verge of financial collapse, one is obligated to rescue him through loans, outright gifts, or any other means.[11]

> *The prophet says of someone who lends to a poor person in need, "Then you shall call and Hashem will answer" (Yeshayahu 58:9).*[12]

How Much to Apportion for Loans

6. Although the Sages prohibited us from lavishing more than a fifth of our income on *tzedakah*, this restriction applies specifically to gifts but not to loans.[13] On the contrary, it is a mitzvah to devote as much of our resources as we can afford to them, although one is not required to overextend himself and lend more than he can afford, since one's own needs take precedence over those of others.

7. Similarly, if one can afford to do so, it is a mitzvah to give the borrower as much money as he needs and for as long a time as he needs it. Nevertheless, if one cannot afford more, any amount one lends is still a mitzvah, even if only for a few hours should doing so help the borrower.[14]

> *"Can you lend me $20 until tonight?"*

How to Lend

8. Doing kindness for others is one of the mitzvos that has no upper limit,[15] and even if one has given handouts to a hundred paupers

---

11. Ibid. Positive Commandment 3.

12. *Yevamos* 63a.

13. *Ahavas Chesed* 1:4.

14. Ibid. 1:5-6.

15. *Pe'ah* 1:1.

in one day, one should not feel resentment when the hundred and first person knocks on his door to ask for a loan or a gift. To the contrary, one should feel happy, since the Torah promises that for each needy individual a person helps he will receive a direct blessing from Hashem. One should therefore rejoice over every pauper who comes to his door just as one would rejoice over an opportunity for a business deal from which he earns an enormous profit.[16]

> *Mr. Gold runs the town's free-loan society. There are constant knocks on the door every evening and Mr. Gold treats each request with respect. When his children complained about the constant disturbances, Mr. Gold answered, "Imagine each person who knocked on the door as bringing us $100. You would, of course, welcome each knock. In reality, each one brings a blessing from Hashem. How happy we should be with each knock."*

9. Just as with *tzedakah*, loans should be extended graciously and without any bad feelings.

> *A person should always strive to treat his unfortunate fellows in the exact same way he would want to be treated if he were forced to be dependent on others for the same favor.[17]*

Unsafe Credit

10. If the lender does not trust the borrower, he should not grant a loan unless he will receive adequate collateral. The mitzvah to lend money includes a loan where one takes collateral.[18]

11. Even if one considers the borrower completely trustworthy and does not insist on collateral, the loan must still be made in the presence of a witness or a note of indebtedness given (handwritten is adequate), in order to avoid a possibility that the borrower will forget his debt.[19] However, if the parties stipulated that should the loan be forgotten, the obligation of repayment will be canceled, then witnesses are unnecessary.

> *The Sages taught: "Whoever lends money without witnesses violates the commandment not to put a stumbling block before the*

---

16. *Ahavas Chesed* 1:7.

17. Ibid. Part 2, Ch. 23.

18. Ibid. 1:8; see also the end of *Nesiv HaChesed* 13.

19. Ibid.

blind (by inducing a dishonest person to borrow and then to deny that he borrowed) and causes curses to himself." (When someone claims that he is owed money but has no proof, people do not believe him, and they curse him for trying to collect money that is not his.)

Rav Ashi was told that Ravina was extremely meticulous in fulfilling every dictum of the Sages. One Friday afternoon Rav Ashi sent Ravina a messenger requesting to borrow 10 zuz to buy a small piece of land that had just become available. Ravina replied, "Please send me either witnesses or a note of indebtedness." Rav Ashi answered, "You ask this even of me?!" Ravina responded, "Surely you, who are so busy with Torah study, could forget, and I will cause curses to myself."[20]

Collection

12. Once the stipulated period is over, the lender may demand to be repaid. Even if he is unsure if the borrower has the funds to repay him he may demand payment. However, if he learns that the borrower does not have funds at present, he is prohibited from demanding payment because that is a form of harassment, and is a violation of the negative commandment, *Do not act toward him as a creditor* (*Shemos* 22:24). Furthermore, he is not allowed to even pass in front of the borrower, since merely being reminded of a debt one cannot repay is enough to embarrass a person.[21]

Responsibility of the Borrower

13. Just as a lender is forbidden to harass a borrower, a borrower who has money is also forbidden to delay paying his debts, as King Shlomo wrote, *Do not say to your fellow,"Go and come back, and tomorrow I shall give," if you have it with you* (*Mishlei* 3:28).[22]

Note: If the borrower has no funds, the creditor takes (with the permission of *beis din*) objects or real property in lieu of payment. This applies even if the creditor is very wealthy and the borrower is impoverished.[23]

---

20. *Bava Metzia* 75b.

21. *Rambam, Hilchos Milveh* 1:2-3; *Choshen Mishpat* 97:3.

22. *Rambam* ibid.; *Choshen Mishpat* ibid.

23. *Choshen Mishpat* 97:5,23.

14. It is forbidden to spend borrowed money on non-essentials, for the money may be lost and the lender will be unable to collect. It makes no difference if the lender is very wealthy; a person who does this thing is called wicked, as the Psalmist writes (*Tehillim* 37:21), *The wicked one borrows but does not repay.* In general, one should not take a loan unless he has a great need for the money. If there is no great need, and he is borrowing for some luxury or risky enterprise, he must inform the lender of the purpose of the loan. The Sages cautioned us to treat other people's money as carefully as if it were our own (*Avos* 2:17). If one knows that the individual seeking a loan is not responsible concerning money *it is better not to lend to him at all* than to do so and then have to pursue him to collect it, since one is then likely to violate the commandment not to act as a creditor (as discussed in paragraph 12).[24]

Commitment to Lend

15. A person who says that he will lend a sum of money to a poor person or to anyone who is presently short on cash must keep his word, since any statement of intent to do a mitzvah is equivalent to a vow.[25] However, if one offers a loan to a wealthy person for a long period (e.g. for investment purposes), there is no obligatory mitzvah involved and one may renege on it, unless an actual promise was made or the recipient is relying on him.[26] Similarly, if one states his intention to set aside a particular sum for the benefit of others (and even more so if one actually sets the money aside), it is forbidden to go back on the commitment.[27]

Cash Available

16. The obligation to lend out money applies whenever one has extra cash on hand. However, one is not required to borrow in order to lend to someone else, although if he does so, he has fulfilled a mitzvah.[28]

> *Rabbi Green has lent Mr. Smith a considerable sum of money out of his monthly paycheck.*

---

24. *Rambam* ibid.; *Choshen Mishpat* 97:4, *Sma* 5, *Taz* ibid.

25. See Ch. 55.

26. See Ch. 10.

27. *Ahavas Chesed* 1:11.

28. Ibid. 1:12.

> **Mrs. Green:** *Are we really obligated to lend money that we need for our living expenses?*
> **Rabbi Green:** *No. However, we don't need half the money until the second half of the month. This money is just "cash on hand" and if someone trustworthy needs to borrow it for two weeks, we are obligated to lend it to him.*

17. A person who has deposited funds (e.g. cash in a safe deposit box or funds in his own bank account) is considered to have cash on hand, and if someone requests a loan he is required to collect the funds and lend them. If, for some reason, he does not wish to do so, he is required to borrow money elsewhere in order to lend this petitioner. (Since he has cash he is obligated to lend it and must somehow procure the funds.) Similarly, if one has cash on hand but does not wish to use it (e.g. to avoid family conflicts), he is required to borrow elsewhere to lend his petitioner. According to some opinions, a person who is himself owed money and the time of repayment has come, is considered to have money on hand.[29]

18. If the petitioner of the loan needs the money urgently to avoid financial collapse or any similar emergency, then even if there is no cash available one is required to borrow money if necessary in order to fulfill the mitzvah of *Let your brother live with you* and *You shall not stand aside while your fellow's blood is being shed* (see paragraphs 4-5).[30]

Note: If there is reason to suspect that the money will not be returned, then one should consider the money as *tzedakah*; he should borrow and/or give according to the pertinent parameters of *tzedakah*, as explained in Chapter 51.

> *A variety of mishaps put the B family of Midcity in major financial distress. The bank was threatening to foreclose on their home and other creditors were regularly harassing the family to pay their debts. Mr. B's regular paycheck couldn't begin to cover their debts, let alone put bread on the table.*
>
> *The rabbi called an emergency meeting with some prominent members of the shul. After assessing the B family's financial situation, they concluded that a $250,000 interest-free loan was needed to cover their debts, which they should be able to repay over twenty years. Five people promised to immediately donate*

---

29. Ibid.; *Nesiv HaChesed* 21.
30. See *Nesiv HaChesed* 20.

$10,000, and if the Rabbi could procure loans for the rest they would guarantee repayment.

The Rabbi immediately organized a committee to procure a $1,000 loan from each of the 200 members of the shul. The Rabbi said that even someone who at present has no cash available is obligated to borrow in order to lend the money so as not to stand aside while their "fellow's blood is being shed."

19. Someone who is holding other people's money in trust may not lend it out to others even if he has permission to use the money, unless he is willing to commit himself to return the entrusted money upon demand (whether or not he is able to call in the loan). However, he is not required to make such a commitment in order to fulfill the mitzvah of lending out money. However, if he is in possession of borrowed funds for which he has no immediate personal need, and someone comes to request a loan from him, he is required to lend him this money, provided that doing so will not in any way endanger his ability to repay his own debt on time.[31]

No Obligation to Give Credit

20. Credit from a store or business is not considered a loan, and a storekeeper therefore has no obligation to give credit for his merchandise. If, however, a poor person approaches him and asks for goods on credit so that the loan is a fulfillment of the mitzvah of *Let your brother live with you*, then the storekeeper is required to do so.[32]

In the Silver warehouse:
David Silver: Father, why did you give Mr. A credit? You always say that you don't like selling on credit.
Father: Because I had to.
David: But credit is not a loan, so there is no obligation.
Father: Yes, but Mr. A's business is not very strong. He doesn't have cash available, and if I don't give him goods on credit then he will have to borrow from the bank with interest; his profit margin is too small to do that. Therefore, the mitzvah of "Let your brother live" obligates me to help him as much as I can, which in this case means selling him the goods on credit.

---

31. *Ahavas Chesed* 1:13; *Nesiv HaChesed* 24.

32. *Ahavas Chesed* 2:5.

Lending by a Spouse

21. A married woman is not permitted to lend money without her husband's permission, unless she knows that his nature is not to object to loans, or unless the loan is so small that people would generally not mind. Spouses should encourage each other to do mitzvos, and a woman who advises and encourages her husband to fulfill the mitzvos of kindness in financial matters shares in his eternal reward. In contrast, she will be called to judgment for discouraging her husband from lending money when it is appropriate.[33]

Earning Livelihood With Loans on Interest

22. Even an individual who makes his living by lending money at interest, e.g. to gentiles or to Jews by means of a *heter iska* (where the funds are not considered a loan but an investment with the possibility of profit or loss), is included in the obligation to give poor people interest-free loans to the extent that his resources allow.[34]

When Engaged in Torah Study

23. If an individual engaged in Torah study is approached by people wanting to borrow money, and there is no one else to lend it to them, then he has to interrupt his studies in order to do this mitzvah. In defining "no one else" it makes no difference whether others do not have money to lend, or merely do not wish to lend to this person.[35]

---

33. Ibid. 2:2.

34. Ibid. 2:3; see also Ch. 54 for further discussion.

35. *Ahavas Chesed* 2:4.

Lending Objects

1. The mitzvah of kindness covers all kinds of favors and acts of
   kindness one can do for others, including lending out one's tools,
   utensils, dishes, car and all other types of objects to those who need
   them.[1] One fulfills this mitzvah even when lending out minor objects
   such as small kitchen utensils, pencils, screwdrivers, etc.[2]

   > *They will not ask in Heaven why a person did not lend a large sum
   > of money if he could not afford it, but they will ask why he did not
   > lend out a tool to a neighbor.*[3]

2. One who does not lend an object because of laziness violates the
   mitzvah of kindness; one who does not lend an object because
   of dislike violates the prohibition against hatred as well. If one does
   not lend his possession because that person once did not lend to
   him or do him some favor, he has also violated the prohibition
   against revenge.[4]

---

1. *Ahavas Chesed* Part 1, 1:2.
2. Ibid. Part 2, Ch. 23.
3. Ibid.
4. Ibid.

❏ *"I just don't like him; I'm not going to lend this to him."*

❏ *"After what he did to me, I'm supposed to lend him my car?"*

3. If one is concerned that the borrower will not care for or use the object properly, he is not required to lend it to him.[5] Similarly, if one expects to need the object himself, he may refuse to lend it out or to insist that it be returned by a specified time.[6]

4. One who is asked to lend out an object of any kind should not react with reluctance, but should rejoice and thank Hashem for giving him an opportunity to extend kindness to others.[7] Hashem desires kindness, as the prophet said, *For He desires kindness (Michah 7:18).*

This applies in particular if the borrower is poor, since the lender is also fulfilling the mitzvah of *tzedakah* (see paragraph 8), for which he is assured of a blessing directly from Hashem, as the Torah says, *For because of this thing He will bless you (Devarim 15:10).*[8]

5. The rewards for kindness are measured according to the time and effort invested.[9]

> *Examples:*
>
> ❏ *Bringing the item to the borrower, if necessary.*
>
> ❏ *Paying attention to the true needs of the other person.*[10]

6. A woman is not required to obtain her husband's permission to lend kitchen utensils and other objects that are commonly lent and borrowed among neighbors.[11]

7. When the Jewish people merited the apparent Divine Providence of "a touch of leprosy,"[12] those who avoided lending objects to neighbors were exposed.

---

5. This *halachah* is derived from the analogous one in *Ahavas Chesed* 1:9 concerning lending money.

6. See *Bava Metzia* 62a, "Your life precedes your brother's life." See Ch. 20, "Helping Others Versus Helping Oneself."

7. *Ahavas Chesed* Part 2, Ch. 22.

8. Ibid. Part 1, 1:7.

9. *Succah* 49b.

10. *Rashi* ad loc., s.v. *ella.*

11. *Ahavas Chesed* Part 1, 2:2.

12. "A touch of leprosy" is a Divine disease that is not at all connected to the physical illness of leprosy; it is rather Divine retribution and a lesson for those afflicted with spiritual maladies

Reuven: Do you have any extra big pots? We are gathering in my home for a simchah.

Shimon: Sorry, I do not even have enough for myself.

A short time later "a touch of leprosy" appeared on the walls of Shimon's house. A Kohen was summoned and ordered everything cleared out of the house before he arrived. All the neighbors pitched in to help. Shimon's face turned beet red as Reuven watched them remove ten huge pots.

The Chofetz Chaim concludes that although in our times we do not merit the "touch of leprosy," Hashem has other ways of exposing such people.[13]

Other Mitzvos Involved in Lending Objects

8. If the borrower is poor and lacks the means to obtain the object in any other way, one is obligated to lend it to him under the mitzvah of *tzedakah*. Even though the lender will receive the object in return, he is still credited with the mitzvah of *tzedakah* since the poor person needs it now. Indeed, because this mitzvah costs the lender less than other forms of *tzedakah*, the obligation is greater than it would be if the giver were never to receive the item back. Similarly, if the use of the object will help the borrower earn his livelihood, the lender is also fulfilling the mitzvah of *Let your brother live with you (Vayikra 25:36).*[14]

> *Reuven barely manages to support his family as a salesman. One day his car breaks down, requiring extensive repairs that he can hardly afford. He certainly cannot afford to rent a car for the week his car will be in the garage, but if he does not continue working he will lose a week's income and possibly even his job. Shimon usually drives to work, but for that week, decides to commute to his office and lend his car to Reuven.*
>
> *Shimon's wife: But how will you get to work?*
>
> *Shimon: Public transportation and cabs.*
>
> *Shimon's wife: Are you really obligated to do that?*

---

such as *lashon hara*; see *Tazria-Metzora*. (I heard from HaRav S. Schwab the translation and explanation of *"nega tzaraas"* as *"a touch of leprosy,"* meaning that although there is outward similarity, the two are not at all related.)

13. *Ahavas Chesed* 1:2.

14. Ibid. 1:3, *Nesiv HaChesed* 7; also Part 2, Ch. 22.

Shimon: *The mitzvos of tzedakah, and "let your brother live with you," are an absolute obligation to whoever can afford them. Reuven earns about $1,000 a week with the use of his car. I am not obligated to give him $1,000 because I can't afford it. However, the $50-60 that it will cost me to go to work without a car I, baruch Hashem, can afford. Therefore, I am obligated to give him "whatever he is missing" (Devarim 15:8).*

Shimon's wife: *Do the expenses count as tzedakah money?*

Shimon: *It usually costs me about $20 a week for gas. If it will cost me $50 this week, then $30 will be tzedakah money. The extra trouble of buses and cabs … that is for my eternal reward.*

9. Someone who lends out Torah-related books for others to study fulfills not only the mitzvah of doing kindness, but also the mitzvah of encouraging and supporting Torah study, and is assured of a *berachah* from Hashem for supporting Torah.[15]

---

15. *Ahavas Chesed* Part 2, Ch. 22; see *Kesubos* 50a.

50

Categories of Tzedakah

1. _Tzedakah_ (literally: righteousness[1]) is defined as giving a needy person what he needs, as the Torah says, _You shall open your hand to him [and give him] whatever he is missing (Devarim 15:8)._[2] Thus, one should notice the needs of the total person and help him accordingly. The Sages taught that whoever gives money to a poor person receives six blessings, but whoever gives him pleasant words as well receives eleven blessings.[3]

> _A destitute person approached Mr. Gold after davening and asked him for some money for breakfast. Mr. Gold, who was talking to his neighbor, quickly put his hand in his pocket and gave the poor person $5._

---

1. The word _tzedakah_ is related to _tzedek_, which means righteousness; the person who is righteous is called a _tzaddik_. To help someone is not a merciful act of grace, but is within the parameters of right vs. wrong. This is one of the most fundamental teachings of the Torah — that a person is created to do right and to avoid wrong. Therefore, helping someone is intrinsic to a person's _raison d'être_. Viewing "charity" as a merciful act of grace on the part of the wealthy who give at their whim is antithetical to all of the Torah. Rather, _tzedakah_ is an "obligation" fundamental to a person's existence. Wealth is given to a person for the purpose of _tzedakah_ (see _Eruvin_ 86a).

2. See Ch. 51 for detailed _halachos_ of "fulfilling his need."

3. _Bava Basra_ 9b. Someone who needs to ask for a handout feels diminished; by adding pleasant words one can give him the self-regard to make him feel "whole."

> *Mr. Gold has given him the money he needs for breakfast. However, he has not offered the emotional support implicit in that request, and his mitzvah of tzedakah is incomplete. If he would have momentarily given his complete attention and said, with a smile, "Enjoy it," or "Have a good day," he would have shown the destitute person that he has worth, and fulfilled "all his needs."*

⁇

> *Mr. Silver was in debt and his income barely covered his expenses. With his son's bar mitzvah, he decided to make a very small Kiddush; even that would cost him $500, which he didn't have. Not wanting to go further into debt, he privately approached Mr. Smith to ask if he could help him. Mr. Smith warmly wished him mazal tov, blessed him that he should see nachas from his son and gave him $100. Since Mr. Smith could easily have afforded the entire $500, his mitzvah, too, is incomplete. He should have realized that Mr. Silver was really asking for the whole amount and given it to him. He would have then fulfilled "all his needs."*

2. The righteousness of *tzedakah* is an outgrowth of the basic Divine-like emotion of compassion implanted in the human being. Thus, the Torah warns, *You shall not harden your heart or close your hand toward your destitute brother (Devarim 15:7).*

3. Although in a specific sense, *tzedakah* refers to financial help combined with moral support, in a wider sense, any help rendered to a person in need is considered righteous *tzedakah*.[4]

> *When the Babylonian general Nevuzaradan freed the prophet Yirmiyahu from jail, this too was considered tzedakah.*[5]

4. The twin characteristics of righteous giving (*tzedakah*) and truthful justice (*mishpat*) are the legacy of Avraham Avinu,[6] the foundation of the Torah, and an emulation of Hashem's Providence.[7] The

---

4. See *Tosafos Bava Basra* 10b, s.v. *vayavei* and *Maharsha* ad loc., s.v. *lefi*. (Note: According to the first opinion in *Tosafos* any "help" rendered to the cause of Hashem's truth is also included in righteous *tzedakah*.)

5. *Tosafos* ibid.

6. *Bereishis* 18:19.

7. *Tehillim* 33:5, from whence is derived the eleventh *berachah* of *Shemonah Esrei*. See also *Succah* 49b.

specific mitzvah of *tzedakah* is intrinsically related to righteous *tzedakah* in the wider sense (see paragraph 3) which is one of the foundations of Hashem's Providence. Thus, the Sages used superlatives when describing the mitzvah of *tzedakah* (especially in its highest forms; see paragraph 11).

❏ *Tzedakah is greater than all the offerings, as King Shlomo said, "Doing tzedakah and justice is more dear to Hashem than sacrifice" (Mishlei 21:3).*[8]

❏ *Israel's redemption will come through tzedakah, as the prophet says, "Tziyon will be redeemed with justice, and its returnees with tzedakah" (Yeshayahu 1:27).*[9]

❏ *Tzedakah can save a person from death and abrogate evil decrees.*[10]

❏ *Whoever continuously gives tzedakah will merit sons who possess wisdom, wealth, and understanding of Aggadah (so that they will be able to influence people).*[11]

❏ *Someone who avoids giving tzedakah is compared to an idol worshiper and is called "wicked" and a "sinner."*[12]

❏ *A door that doesn't open to the poor will open to a doctor.*[13]

❏ *The mitzvah of tzedakah requires more heedfulness than does any other positive commandment, since this mitzvah is the sign of a righteous descendant of Abraham, as the Torah says, "For I know him that he will command his children ... to guard justice and tzedakah" (Bereishis 18:19).*[14]

5. No one need ever worry that giving *tzedakah* will impoverish him or cause him any other harm, as the prophet says, *The act of tzedakah is peace (Yeshayahu* 32:17). Anyone who has compassion on others is assured that Hashem will have compassion on him, as the Torah says, *He will give you compassion and have compassion on you and cause you to multiply (Devarim* 13:18). The very fact that a person is hardhearted is in itself grounds to suspect that he is not Jewish. All Jews, whether born Jewish

---

8. *Succah* ibid.

9. *Shabbos* 139a.

10. Ibid. 156b. *Bava Basra* 9b, 10a.

11. *Bava Basra* 10a.

12. Ibid.; *Rambam, Hilchos Matnos Aniyim* 10:3.

13. *Kitzur Shulchan Aruch* 32:1 quoting *Yerushalmi.*

14. *Ramban* ibid. 10:1.

or those who have joined the Jewish people, are considered brothers, as the Torah says, *You are sons to Hashem, your G-d (Devarim* 14:1), and if one brother does not have compassion on another, who will?[15]

6. Hashem is close to the cries of the poor, as we read, *You hear the cry of the poor (Iyov* 34:28). We have to be particularly careful when poor people cry out to Hashem since they have a special covenant with Him, as the Torah says, *It shall be when he cries to Me I will hear, for I am compassionate (Shemos* 22:24). Just as we wish for Hashem to hear our cries, so should we also hear the cries of the poor.[16]

7. One should not think that giving *tzedakah* will deplete his funds, since in any case one's money does not belong to him but is only given in trust from Hashem to use in accordance with His wishes. Furthermore, the world is a continual cycle where nothing is permanent, and even if one now enjoys comfortable circumstances, it is very likely that in the course of time either he or his descendants will be forced to accept *tzedakah*.[17]

> *Rabbi Chiya told his wife, "When a poor person comes, be sure to be ready with bread so that when your children go knocking on doors, they will also find that favorable reception of the bread ready for them." She asked him, "Are you cursing them?" (that they will be poor). "No," he answered, "but the Torah says, 'For this thing (tzedakah) you shall be blessed'; the word 'biglal' is similar to 'galgal' (cycle) which means that Hashem runs the world in a cyclic way — that the rich become poor and vice versa."[18]*

8. The Sages have said that one must keep giving *tzedakah* as many times as he is asked since the Torah says, *For because of this thing, Hashem, your G-d, will bless you in all your deeds and in your every undertaking (Devarim* 15:10). Thus, one should never be upset if the same pauper returns to him time after time; indeed, one should feel as much joy each time as if an important customer were coming to buy more and more goods, since the pauper brings a blessing from Hashem with his every approach (see footnote).[19]

---

15. Ibid 10:2.

16. *Tur Yoreh Deah* 147 (from various sources).

17. Ibid.

18. *Shabbos* 151b.

19. *Ahavas Chesed* 1:7. Note: This *halachah* should not be misconstrued to allow a collector of *tzedakah* to pressure a person to give more than he can afford, for the Sages taught (*Bava Basra* 8b)

9. If a poor person asks for *tzedakah* and one has nothing to give, one should use an apologetic tone and attempt to conciliate him. It is forbidden to speak harshly to a poor person or to raise one's voice toward him, since he is depressed and broken-hearted over his situation, and the Psalmist has said (*Tehillim* 51:19), *A broken and humbled heart, O G-d, You will not despise.* Woe unto anyone who causes a poor person shame or disgrace, as we read, *I am a Father to the anguished (Iyov* 29:16).[20]

Exhorting Others to Contribute

10. A person who exhorts others to give *tzedakah* has a greater reward than the giver himself. Of those who collect and distribute *tzedakah* the prophet says, *Those who bring righteousness to the public will shine (in the future) like the stars (Daniel* 12:3).[21]

The Eight Levels of *Tzedakah*

11. The following are the eight levels of *tzedakah*,[22] starting with the highest:

(a) The highest level is helping a person to support himself so that he does not have to be dependent on the gifts of others. This is derived from the verse, *You shall strengthen him … so that he can live with you (Vayikra* 25:35), meaning that we are to strengthen someone's position so that he can provide for his own needs and not be forced to ask for handouts.

> *This can be achieved by:*
> ❏ *Giving or lending the capital needed to establish a steady income.*
> ❏ *Taking him into a partnership.*
> ❏ *Hiring him.*

There are times when one cannot do this personally but knows of someone else who can. He must do his utmost to help secure the position with that other individual.

---

that collectors of *tzedakah* who torment the givers of *tzedakah* will be punished. Rather, it is to teach us the proper approach to *tzedakah* — who is the real "receiver." If a person considers himself fortunate to merit to give *tzedakah* he will never tire of the beggars who come daily to shul and the collectors who come monthly to the door; he will instead thank them for giving him another opportunity to fulfill the mitzvah, and for bringing him blessings.

20. *Rambam* ibid. 10:2.

21. *Bava Basra* 8b.

22. The eight categories are listed in *Rambam, Hilchos Matnos Aniyim* 10:7-14 and in *Yoreh Deah* 249:6-13.

The Sages taught, "Let the poor be your household help."

One should not go to employment agencies for household help if any of his brethren, young or old, could do the same job and needs the income.

(b) The next form of *tzedakah* is giving to a poor person when neither the giver nor the recipient knows who the other one is; this is considered a "pure mitzvah."

There was a special chamber in the Beis HaMikdash devoted to this kind of tzedakah; the righteous would anonymously place money or utensils there, and poor people of respected families would take without anyone realizing their identity.

There is a similar practice in our times of giving to established *tzedakah* funds, but one should be careful to give only to those organizations whose administrators are known to possess Torah wisdom (so as to properly distribute the funds), and are completely trustworthy like Rabbi Chananya ben Tradyon.

Rabbi Chananya ben Tradyon was a famed gabbai tzedakah (administrator of tzedakah funds). He had two purses in his pockets, one for tzedakah and one for his own funds. One time he confused these purses, and then gave both of them to tzedakah.[23]

(c) The next form of *tzedakah* occurs when the giver knows who the recipient is, but the recipient does not know the identity of his benefactor.

These were Sages who had the practice of secretly leaving money under poor people's doors so that no one would know who had given it.[24]

This method is especially appropriate if one does not know if the administration of the established *tzedakah* funds is reliable.

(d) The next form occurs when the recipient knows the identity of his benefactor; the giver, however, does not know who receives his gift.

Some of the Sages used to wrap money into bundles and drop them as they were walking so that poor people could come and take them without feeling embarrassed.[25]

---

23. *Avodah Zarah* 17b.

24. *Kesubos* 67b, story of Mar Ukva.

25. Ibid. 67b.

(e) The next form is to give *tzedakah* to a poor person before he asks for it.

(f) The next form is to give *tzedakah* to a poor person after he asks for it.

(g) The next form is to give less *tzedakah* than appropriate, but with a pleasant manner.

(h) The lowest form of *tzedakah* is to give begrudgingly, in a resentful manner, since this transgresses the commandment, *You shall surely give him, and let your heart not feel bad when you give him (Devarim 15:10).* Furthermore, one should never boast about the *tzedakah* one gives.[26]

12. Included in the mitzvah *of tzedakah* is providing for the needs of one's older children, whom one is no longer required to support, in order to enable them to learn Torah.[27] Supporting one's parents is also considered *tzedakah;* the closer one is to the recipient the greater is the obligation to give him *tzedakah.*[28]

13. One should give *tzedakah* before each prayer.[29]

---

26. *Yoreh Deah* 249:13, *Rema;* see also *Halichos Olam,* Ch. 57 fn. *tes.*

27. *Rambam* ibid. 10:16.

28. Ibid.

29. *Bava Basra* 10a; *Orach Chaim* 92:10.

51

Procedures for Giving Tzedakah

1. The Torah writes, *If there shall be in your midst a destitute person, any of your brethren in any of your cities, in the Land that Hashem your G-d gives you, you shall not harden your heart or close your hand from your destitute brother. Rather, you shall open your hand to him (to give him) or you shall lend him (if he is embarrassed to accept a gift, give it as a loan; Rashi), his requirement, whatever he is missing (Devarim 15:7,8).* Thus, we are commanded to open our hands and to give him whatever he is missing. On the same theme, the Psalmist writes, *All eyes look to You, and You give them their food in its proper time (Tehillim 145:16).* Just as Hashem provides each creature in the world with whatever he lacks, so are we commanded to provide each person with what he lacks.[1]

2. "Whatever he is missing" is defined according to the particular needs of the individual. If he lacks food, one is required to feed him; if he lacks clothing one is required to clothe him; if he lacks household utensils one is required to buy them for him; if he lacks a

---

1. See *Kesubos* 67b; *Teshuvos Rashba* III:380, cited in *Beis Yosef* at the end of *Yoreh Deah* 250.

spouse one is required to search for one and provide him (or her) with marriage expenses.[2]

3. Although we are obligated to make up that which a needy person lacks, we are not obligated to make him wealthy[3] (i.e. to give him more than what he lacks). Nevertheless, each person has his own unique needs and we are required to understand the depths of those needs in order to alleviate his feelings of being "diminished" by the necessity to accept handouts.

> *There was once an honored gentleman who regularly made his way around town on his horse with a servant crier running before him to announce his presence. One day, he lost his fortune, was forced to sell both his horse and servant, and became dependent on handouts for his basic necessities. The sage Hillel made sure that tzedakah funds be appropriated not only for his basic necessities, but even to rent a horse and a servant crier to run before him. On a day that no servant was available to be rented for the poor gentleman, Hillel himself ran before him announcing his presence.[4]*

The benefactor should not say that an impoverished person living on public funds ought to lower his standard of living in order not to be a burden on the public.

> *An impoverished man once came to Rava asking for food. When Rava asked what his usual standard meal was, the man replied, "A fat chicken and old wine." Rava asked, "Is it right to burden the public funds?" The man answered, "Do they feed me? Hashem feeds me as the verse says, 'All eyes look to You, and You give them their food in its proper time.' The fact that the giving of food is singular (its time) and not plural (their time) shows that Hashem gives each individual sustenance to meet his exact needs." Just then Rava's sister, whom he hadn't seen for thirteen years, arrived with a gift of fat chicken and old wine. Rava, recognizing the Divine Providence, apologized and said, "Come, eat."[5]*

Nevertheless, a person living on public funds should, on his own, try to limit his expenses as much as possible.

---

2. *Rambam, Hilchos Matnos Aniyim* 7:3.

3. Ibid.

4. *Kesubos* ibid.

5. Ibid.

HaGaon HaRav Yerucham Gorelick and another Torah scholar were sent to South America during World War II to raise funds for the Vaad Hatzalah (the aid organization for refugees). They were scheduled to return to the United States on a flight that left once a week. There were two alternative ways to get to the airport: to take a cab (which would cost money), or to have someone drive them (however, the driver could not promise to get them to the airport on time for the flight). Reb Yerucham insisted on accepting the ride even with the risk that they miss the flight, reasoning that unless absolutely necessary, public funds should not be spent. Sure enough, as their car approached the airport, the plane was taking off. His friend was very upset; his reaction changed dramatically, however, when the plane crashed.[6]

Note: People who need to learn how to stabilize their budget and cut expenses should consult a rav; this is *not* the job of the benefactor. Some people need a certain standard to keep up their spirits, while others really need help in managing their fiscal affairs – the rav will decide if and how to proceed.

Providing the Needs of the Poor — the Responsibility of the Individual or the Community?

4. A wealthy person is not required to provide all the needs of the poor people who collect door to door[7] because they can rely on the community as a whole to provide that which they are lacking. However, the public may not make up the needs of a particular individual, either because they are very great (e.g. he failed to raise enough funds for his yeshivah, has large medical expenses, or incurred large debts from the marriages of a few children) or because he is unable to reach a sufficient number of people. If one has sufficient means to provide for all this person's needs, then one is required to do so.[8] Furthermore, when a collector is going from door to door, although the individual benefactor is not required to provide for all his needs, it is still forbidden to turn him away empty-handed.[9]

---

6. Heard from a *talmid*.

7. *Yoreh Deah* 250:3, *Shach* 4.

8. This is evident from *Shach* ibid. 1.

9. See par. 7.

Coercing a Poor Person to Turn to the Public

5. An individual with means who is approached privately by a needy person who has not gone around collecting is required, according to some opinions, to give him what he lacking; it is forbidden to force him to collect and allow his misfortune to become known to the public.[10] According to other opinions, if the populace will provide for the person's needs, the wealthy individual is not required to do so, and the needy person can thus be compelled to let his misfortune be known to the public.[11] However, if one knows that the community will not provide for his needs, either because of a lack of numbers or of sufficient means, then the responsibility falls upon the individual. Similarly, if the needy person approaches the administrator of a charity fund or the community as a group, they are required as a "community" to provide him with his needs.[12]

An Individual Who Cannot Provide "All His Needs"

6. If an individual is approached by a poor person who needs more than he can give, he should still give as much as he can. The amount depends on the donor's situation. While the ideal is to give a fifth (of one's income) to *tzedakah*, the standard is to give one-tenth; a person who gives less is considered stingy.[13] Even within the parameters of a fifth and a tenth there may be others who take precedence for his *tzedakah* funds, as explained in Chapter 54. Even limited by these parameters, however, a person should give as much as he can. This applies only to those who can afford it; a person who is himself needy is exempt from giving large amounts. Nevertheless, even a pauper subsisting on gifts is required to give some *tzedakah* to other needy people.[14] One who can give only a small amount should still do so, for that small amount is as great a mitzvah as a much larger sum given by a wealthy person.[15] However, an individual who totally lacks what

---

10. Cf. *Rashi, Bava Basra* 9a, s.v. *ain nizkakin*; see also *Tur* and *Beis Yosef* loc. cit. with *Shach* and *Beur HaGra* who rebuts the *Shach*.

11. *Beis Yosef* and *Rema* 250:1, supported by *Shach* 1.

12. Ibid.

13. *Rambam* ibid. 7:5; *Yoreh Deah* 249:1.

14. Ibid.

15. *Kitzur Shulchan Aruch* 34:2; see *Menachos* 110a.

he needs for himself and his family is not required to give, since maintaining a basic livelihood for oneself always takes precedence over providing for others.

> *A person's personal obligations take precedence over tzedakah. There are individuals who ask for reductions in yeshivah tuition and contribute large amounts to tzedakah; they should rather pay full tuition and give less to tzedakah.*

7. Even if one is not required to give more than a small amount (e.g. if he is himself poor or if the needy person is collecting door to door, as described in paragraph 4), he is still required to give something. It is forbidden to turn a pauper away empty-handed, as the Psalmist says, *Let not the oppressed turn back in shame* (Tehillim 74:21).[16]

> *It is highly praiseworthy to make sure to keep some money in one's pocket for the poor people who come to his shul, office, etc.*

8. A person who offers the needy person a small amount commensurate with the *halachah* and with his means, only to have it thrown back at him in an effort to procure a larger sum, need not submit to these tactics. The donor may simply state that he can offer only that amount and will take it back if it is insufficient. In general, one must give *tzedakah* according to Torah guidelines and not fall prey to the emotional tactics or advertising ploys of individuals or institutions.

> *A wise person who has tzedakah funds to distribute will be in contact with a rav to advise him how to distribute them according to the Torah.*

9. The Torah does not view *tzedakah* as "spent" or "wasted" money. It is, rather, "invested," bringing eternal merit to those who give it justly and wisely.[17] Just as an investment banker will not invest large sums until he researches a company and is sure of its stability and profit-making ability, so too must a *tzedakah* distributor be aware of *halachic* priorities and not allocate a large sum until he is sure of the money's exact destination. Therefore, it is appropriate to inquire about a *tzedakah* solicitor and ask for references.

---

16. *Rambam* ibid. 7:7; *Yoreh Deah* 249:4 in *Rema*. It is interesting to note that this verse is actually phrased as a request that Hashem not turn us, His oppressed people, away empty-handed, and the Rambam infers from this that we, too, are not allowed to turn someone away empty-handed. Otherwise, how can we ask Hashem not to turn us away empty-handed?

17. *Bava Basra* 9b.

The prophet Yirmiyahu, when cursing the wicked men of Anasos, said, "When they give tzedakah it should be given to unworthy people," thus minimizing their merit.[18]

When told that their money was not given to a worthwhile cause, some people will shrug their shoulders and say, "Well, it's their problem if they fooled me." In reality, it is the donor's problem, for he has squandered tzedakah money and lost potential merit. The same people would react differently when investigating stocks and bonds; if they make a poor investment they feel it as their loss.

10. A person who has absolutely nothing to give is still obligated to empathize with the needy person and to offer solace over his misfortunes. It is absolutely forbidden to scold a needy person.[19] Even if the recipient becomes upset over a small donation, the donor is still required to placate him and to explain patiently and pleasantly that he cannot give more, or that he is giving what is appropriate for his means.

11. It is a mitzvah to set money aside for *tzedakah* purposes, i.e. a fifth or tenth of one's income even if there are no people in need of immediate help.[20] This mitzvah is discussed further in Chapter 52.

Needs of the Poor

12. During the week, a needy person away from home should be given two meals a day and a place to sleep if he so requires, and on Shabbos, he should be given three meals (and a place to sleep). This is the minimum required for a needy stranger, but if one knows him personally as a person of distinction, he should be given as much as is appropriate to his status.[21]

13. Anyone who asks for food should be fed immediately with no attempt to verify that he has a genuine need. However, if a person

---

18. Ibid.

19. *Yoreh Deah* 249:3, *Rambam* ibid. 10:5.

20. *Yoreh Deah* 249:1; see also *Bartenura* on *Pe'ah* 1:1.

21. *Yoreh Deah* 249:9, derived from a Mishnah in the last chapter of *Pe'ah.* In the olden days, people were accustomed to eating two meals per day. One could ponder if the *halachah* in today's times is different, since most people are accustomed to eating breakfast, lunch and supper.

asks for clothing one should first verify his needy status. If one already knows him to be needy, he should be given clothing immediately.[22]

How to Support the Needy of a City

14. In a city with a large needy population the wealthy members of the community may seek to compel them to go around collecting while the middle-class residents propose supporting the poor with a progressive tax to be paid by each person in proportion to his resources. The latter view should prevail, since the Torah requires every Jew to give *tzedakah* according to his financial ability.[23] This tax is compulsory; each person can be forced to give an amount appropriate to his situation. Thus, even an immensely wealthy person who contributes large sums, but not as much as he should, can be punished for his failure to give, while someone who gives in accordance with Hashem's blessing makes himself worthy of further blessings.[24]

15. The best way to give *tzedakah* is through an anonymous fund, where the donor and recipient are unaware of each other's identities, provided that the administrator of the fund is known to be wise in Torah law and scrupulously honest. It is forbidden to contribute to a fund that is not administered by someone with these qualities.[25]

Needy Relatives

16. Each person has an obligation to support his needy relatives.[26]

Therefore, communal *tzedakah* funds are not required to support those needy people who have wealthy relatives. This applies even if the wealthy relative contributes to the fund; since he has a responsibility to provide for his needy relatives, public funds are exempt from supporting them.[27] However, this does not apply if the wealthy relative is unable to support his poor relations for any reason, or if he is unwilling to recognize his Torah obligation to do so.

---

22. *Yoreh Deah* 251:10.

23. Ibid. 250:8 and in *Rema*; see also *Teshuvos Rashba* 3:380.

24. *Rashba* ibid.; see also *Kesubos* 49b and 66b; *Rema* ibid.

25. *Yoreh Deah* 256:1 in *Rema*, based on *Bava Basra* 10b.

26. See Ch. 54 for discussion of precedence among relatives.

27. *Yoreh Deah* 257:8.

In these cases, the obligation reverts to the communal *tzedakah* funds, and the needy person in question has the same status as all other needy people in the city.

17. All of a person's *tzedakah* donations should not be directed to just one relative or one needy person at the expense of all others.[28] If a person of limited means has a relative whom it is his Torah obligation to support (e.g. a member of a *kollel* or a poor family), he should direct the bulk of his funds to the impoverished relative but should still apportion a small amount of money for distribution to *tzedakah*.

18. The rule that relatives take precedence applies only when the donor is giving from his own funds, but a person who distributes money entrusted to him by others must be stringent not to show any favoritism to his relatives or friends.[29] If one knows that the administrator of a *tzedakah* fund gives preferential treatment to his friends and relatives, this might be sufficient grounds not to contribute to that fund, as discussed in paragraph 15; a rav should be consulted.

> *Reb Yankel distributes the communal tzedakah funds and allocates $300 to every solicitor for a poor bride. One day his brother, who barely made ends meet, asked him for a donation to help marry off his daughter. Reb Yankel is not permitted to give more than the usual $300 from community funds. However, from his own tzedakah funds he is encouraged to give what he can. Furthermore, he can solicit extra donations from people for his brother.*

The Work Hazards of a *Tzedakah* Administrator

19. A *tzedakah*-fund administrator need not be concerned if he is subjected to insults in the course of his work (either from the needy who complain of unjust treatment or from the wealthy who feel they are being taxed unfairly); to the contrary, as long as he is careful in applying the Torah's guidelines, the merit of his activities increases many times from any unpleasantness he suffers.[30] However, he must be careful not to solicit *tzedakah* from a person who cannot afford to give but out of embarrassment will do so when asked.

---

28. Ibid 257:9, and *Shach* 19.

29. *Yoreh Deah* 257:10.

30. Ibid 257:7.

Giving *Tzedakah* — An Awesome Responsibility

20. The Sages related the following stories:

> *Rabban Yochanan ben Zakkai was leaving Jerusalem (after the Destruction) accompanied by his students, when they saw a young lady searching for barley kernels among the dung of animals belonging to Arabs (to avoid starvation). When she noticed them she ran over and pleaded, "Rabbi, support me."*
>
> *Rabban Yochanan asked, "Who are you?"*
>
> *She said, "I am the daughter of Nakdimon ben Gurion." (He was an immensely wealthy, extremely righteous person.[31])*
>
> *Rabban Yochanan asked, "What happened to the wealth of your father?"*
>
> *She answered, "Rebbi, don't they say in Jerusalem the parable 'Salt your money by giving it away'?" (I.e. If you want your wealth to last, give it to tzedakah, so that there will be blessing in the wealth.)*
>
> *Rabban Yochanan asked: "And what happened to your father-in-law's wealth?"*
>
> *She answered: "The loss of one caused the loss of the other." (The partnership of the two was doomed because of the lack of tzedakah of one of them.)*
>
> *She said: "Rebbi, do you remember when you signed my kesubah (marriage contract)?"*
>
> *Rabban Yochanan turned to his students, saying, "I remember when I signed her kesubah and I read 'one million golden dinars brought into the marriage from her father's house aside from what her father-in-law gave to the couple.'"*
>
> *Rabban Yochanan cried out, "Fortunate are you Yisrael – when you fulfill the will of Hashem, no nation can have any power over you, and when you don't fulfill the will of Hashem, He hands you over to a lowly nation, and not even the people but the animals of that nation." (She was searching for food morsels among the dung of the Arabs' animals.)*
>
> *The Gemara asks: Did Nakdimon ben Gurion not give tzedakah? We learned that when he went from his house to the house of study, his servants would put silk under him, and as he passed, the poor would pick up the cloth (so that they not be embarrassed by the lavish gifts).*

---

31. Cf. *Taanis* 20a about his extreme righteousness, and *Gittin* 56a about his immense wealth.

The Gemara offer two answers: (1) He did it for his own honor (his motivations weren't pure, but were tainted by self-aggrandizement); (2) although he gave lavish gifts, it was not sufficient; based on his wealth, he could have given more.[32]

... And Its Grand Rewards

There was a righteous man named Binyamin who administered the local tzedakah fund. Once, during a time of famine, a woman approached him for support, and he answered, "There is nothing in the fund." She said, "Rebbi, if you do not support me, a woman and her seven children will die from starvation." So he undertook to support her from his own funds.

One day, Binyamin was struck by disease and lay dying. The Celestial Angels said to Hashem, "You said that whoever saves one life from Israel, it is as if he saved an entire world. And the righteous Binyamin who supported a woman and her seven children should die with shortened years?" Immediately, the evil decree was torn up and twenty-two years were added to his life.[33]

In times of famine, King Munbaz (a righteous convert) opened the treasuries and distributed his royal fortunes to the poor. His family complained, "Your forefathers constantly accumulated and added to the royal treasures and you 'waste' them!"

He replied, "My forefathers accumulated treasures in this lowly world and I have accumulated treasures in the upper world.

"My forefathers accumulated wealth in a place where others could take them but I have accumulated wealth in a place where no stranger can take them.

"My forefathers accumulated wealth that produced no fruit, but I have accumulated wealth that produced fruit.

"My forefathers accumulated treasures of money and I have accumulated treasures of lives.

"My forefathers accumulated for others (they eventually died, and left the wealth for others) while I have accumulated for myself.

---

32. *Kesubos* 66b.

33. *Bava Basra* 11a.

"My forefathers accumulated wealth in this world and I have accumulated wealth in the World to Come."[34]

21. The Sages said[35] that one should keep giving even if the same needy person comes back a hundred times. The Chofetz Chaim added that one should rejoice every time one gives as if it were an opportunity to earn a great fortune, since each time earns him Hashem's blessing for himself and his household, a value far beyond our ability to imagine.[36]

The Very Best for the Mitzvah

22. A general rule regarding mitzvos is that one should apportion the very best. This is derived from the verse, *all the "chalev" (the best parts of the animal) to Hashem (Vayikra* 3:16), and is true not only of sacrifices but of all mitzvos. Thus, if an individual or a group builds a synagogue or a *beis midrash,* they should take care to make it as pleasing and attractive as possible. Similarly, one should serve a poor or hungry person the best and tastiest food, give him the finest clothing, and make available premium lodging. The same principle applies to all mitzvos: whatever its form, it should be done with the best materials and in the finest possible fashion.[37]

---

34. Ibid.

35. *Bava Metzia* 31.

36. *Ahavas Chesed* Part 1, 1:7 (see *Ahavas Chesed* Part 2 for the immense rewards of *tzedakah* and kindness).

37. *Rambam, Hilchos Isurei Mizbe'ach* 7:11.

52

Laws of Ma'aser

1. As we have explained,[1] one should ideally give every poor person
    who approaches him enough money to provide for all his needs.
    However, since that is not usually possible, one must put aside some
    money for *tzedakah*. The Torah encourages a person to donate a fifth
    of his income to *tzedakah*, although a tenth (*ma'aser*) is considered an
    acceptable standard for average people.[2]

    > *A young man starting out in business went to the Steipler Gaon to*
    > *discuss the proper amount of tzedakah to give. When the young man*
    > *mentioned "chomesh" (a fifth) the aged sage lifted his saintly eyes*
    > *and exclaimed "A fifth? Not everyone merits this!" ("Chomesh! Lo*
    > *kol echad zocheh lazeh.")*

2. With so many needy individuals and causes, the mitzvah to regu-
    larly set aside a fifth or a tenth of one's income for distribution to
    tzedakah is highly recommended. This mitzvah is called *ma'aser kesafim*
    (tithing one's money).

    The Sages taught that the merit of giving *ma'aser* enriches a person.[3]

---

1. Ch. 51.

2. *Yoreh Deah* 248:1.

3. *Taanis* 9a. See also *Tosafos* there about the neglect of this mitzvah.

According to some opinions, it is permitted to "test" Hashem regarding this mitzvah, while others forbid this practice.[4] The Chofetz Chaim concluded that a person may test Hashem in this (provided that it is performed properly).

> *The advantage of regularly apportioning a tenth or fifth of one's income rather than simply giving tzedakah, is that by doing so one sanctifies his business enterprise by making Hashem a partner; 10 or 20 percent is thus the Partner's share. It is worthwhile to explicitly have this point in mind at the time one accepts upon himself the mitzvah of giving ma'aser — that one wishes to enter into a partnership with Hashem so that a share for Hashem is in all his work. Fortunate are those who do so.*[5]

Calculating Ma'aser

3. When a person first resolves to undertake this mitzvah, he is advised to stipulate that he is doing so *"bli neder"*[6] in the event that he is unable to carry it out for some reason at any point. This will also help in case he earns income whose exact amount is difficult to calculate. If he knows that such income is likely, he should stipulate that he does not intend to keep an exact accounting of his earnings and *ma'aser* obligations so that he will be allowed to approximate his *ma'aser* donations.[7]

4. If a person who starts a business is given a certain amount of capital, or if someone receives an inheritance, that money should be tithed, and any subsequent new income should be tithed as well.[8]

5. In determining *ma'aser* obligations, a person should deduct from his profit any losses suffered in his business operations, and figure the *ma'aser* only from the net income.[9]

6. All donations to the poor may be counted as *ma'aser*, even small amounts given to beggars who come to the door.[10] On the other

---

4. *Yoreh Deah* 247:4 in *Rema*; see also *Pischei Teshuvah* 2.

5. *Ahavas Chesed* Part 2, 20:6.

6. The words *bli neder* mean that he does not wish this commitment to have the status of a vow; see Ch. 55.

7. *Ahavas Chesed* Part 2, 18:2,3.

8. Ibid. 10:1.

9. Ibid. 18:2.

10. Ibid.

hand, the expenses of educating one's children may not be taken from *ma'aser* funds, since these are obligations and *ma'aser* money may not be used to pay debts.[11] (However, if one lacks money for both, the mitzvah of fulfilling one's obligations takes precedence over the mitzvah of giving *tzedakah*, and even more so over the mitzvah of taking *ma'aser*.)

7. If one calculates that *ma'aser* was not yet taken on all income received to date, he should do so immediately and give it to the needy as soon as possible.[12] If no needy causes are known, or if one originally stipulated that he will distribute *ma'aser* money when he sees fit,[13] he may keep the *ma'aser* money in his possession until distribution. While holding this money, one is allowed to borrow it to use for his own needs. (It is advisable to keep accurate records of all money owed to *ma'aser*.) Once approached by a poor person, however, he is required to give him any borrowed *ma'aser* money; if he does not have cash on hand, he is required to borrow money from others to pay off this debt.[14]

8. The *halachah* is unclear as to whether a person who did not so specify is allowed to apply *tzedakah* given in excess of a tenth (or fifth) of his income toward future *ma'aser* obligations. Therefore, it is best to stipulate when beginning the mitzvah that any *tzedakah* given in excess of his *ma'aser* may be counted against any future *ma'aser* obligations.[15]

To Whom Should *Ma'aser* Be Distributed

9. *Ma'aser* is *tzedakah* and should be directed only to purposes that are considered true *tzedakah*[16] (i.e. the needy and Torah support). It should not be used for other mitzvos (e.g. buying a *lulav*, purchasing *sefarim*, writing a *Sefer Torah*, or financing the shul's electric bill). The order of preference with regard to *tzedakah*, as presented in Chapter 54, applies equally to *ma'aser*.

> *One can pay for the performance of mitzvos, such as buying aliyos, with ma'aser money provided the funds are allocated to tzedakah (e.g. distribution to the poor or supporting Torah study).*

11. Ibid. 19:2.
12. Ibid. 18:2.
13. See Ch. 55 par. 16.
14. *Ahavas Chesed* ibid.
15. Ibid.
16. *Yoreh Deah* 249:1, *Rema, Pischei Teshuvah* 2 in name of *Chasam Sofer; Yoreh Deah* 231, 232.

However, a person may stipulate at the start of the mitzvah of *ma'aser* that it can also be used for non-*tzedakah* mitzvos which he could not otherwise afford (e.g. helping pay the expenses of a shul, establishing a Torah lending library), and it is then permitted.[17] A person who wishes to establish a free loan fund with *ma'aser* money but did not stipulate so should consult a rav.[18]

10. A person who does not have a poor relative or other pressing cause should preferably use his *ma'aser* to promote Torah study by supporting dedicated students of Torah, just as the original *terumos* and *ma'aseros* were given to Kohanim and Leviim, the mainstays of Torah at the time.[19]

> The Chofetz Chaim wrote[20] that one can test Hashem with both *ma'aser* from produce and *ma'aser* from personal income because the *ma'aser* is used to support those who study Torah, thus enabling them to study with greater diligence. As the prophet Malachi said, "Bring the *ma'aser* to the storage and there will be food in My house (the houses where Torah is studied) and please test Me, if I won't open for you the windows of Heaven and I will pour on you blessings until you will say 'enough' " (Malachi 3:10). (The Sages add, "You will tire from saying, 'Enough! Enough!' ")
>
> In particular, those who apportion a fifth of their income toward *ma'aser* should divide that fifth into two tenths and reserve the first for Torah, leaving the remainder for other mitzvos.[21]

The Upper Ceiling of *Tzedakah*

11. The Sages taught that a person who wishes to "squander" his money on *tzedakah* should not give away more than a fifth.[22] An individual who squanders his income and possessions is liable to become needy himself, and a person is enjoined to protect himself so that he should not become a burden on others. However, there are a number of exceptions to the rule of the "fifth," and such indi-

---

17. See *Chasam Sofer* ibid. Note: Although such a stipulation permits the money to be used for any mitzvah, the more appropriate mitzvah is to give the *ma'aser* for *tzedakah* (ibid.).

18. See *Ahavas Chesed* Part 2, 18:1.

19. Ibid. 19:1.

20. Ibid. 18:1 (fn.).

21. Ibid. 19:3.

22. *Kesubos* 50a.

viduals are permitted and sometimes even required to go above that upper ceiling.

They are:

(a) Those who are "very wealthy"; i.e. if they give more they will still not be in danger of becoming needy.[23]

(b) Those who waste money on unnecessary luxuries. The Sages said not to "squander" more than one-fifth of one's money on mitzvos, but if a person is squandering money in general, the rule is not applicable to him.[24]

(c) Those contributing to any cause that involves danger to life. Although one's life comes before someone else's, and similarly, one's needs come first as well, one's finances do not come before the lives of others.[25] However, no one person has to assume full responsibility for what is a communal responsibility, unless the community does not fulfill that obligation. In all such cases, one should consult a rav.

> A person who falls into one of these categories and has already donated a fifth of his income, is still obligated when approached by a needy individual to fill "all his needs" to the extent that he is able. Similarly, someone who normally gives a tenth (ma'aser) and is approached by a needy person is still required to "fill his needs" to the extent that he is easily able to. The Torah obligation of "filling the needs of your impoverished" is not abrogated by giving a tenth of one's income in regard to those who can easily afford more – until one reaches the point of a fifth. After that point is reached, he should not give more unless he falls into one of the above-mentioned categories.[26]

(d) Furthermore, the ceiling of a fifth relates only to tzedakah for the needy, but does not apply to Torah support.[27]

> Rabbi Meir earned three selas a week; two were used for the support of his family and the third to support Torah scholars. When asked why he did not save any money as an inheritance for his children, he answered, "If they will be righteous they will be like David said

---

23. *Ahavas Chesed* ibid. 20:1.

24. Ibid. 20:5 fn.

25. Ibid. 20:2.

26. See ibid. 19:4 and fn. at length. See *Rambam, Hilchos Matnos Aniyim* 7:5.

27. *Ahavas Chesed* 20:4.

(Tehillim 37:25), 'I have not seen a righteous person left alone and his children begging for bread' (i.e. Hashem will provide their sustenance). And if they won't be righteous, why should I leave my possessions for those who are the enemies of Hashem?"[28]

The relationship between Yissachar and Zevulun[29] (the patrons of Torah and those who dedicate themselves to Torah study) is that of partners: One is entitled to invest as much as he desires into a partnership and to reap a commensurate reward.[30]

The Chofetz Chaim writes: "From this we can see how a person should conduct himself in such a partnership: When a representative of Torah approaches someone, he should be treated with respect as if he were a partner in a business deal from whom one has realized an enormous profit. If one gives the scholar a cheerful reception, he will ultimately merit to rejoice in the World to Come in the scholar's portion in Torah, unlike those short-sighted people who give their support to Torah begrudgingly and with a sour countenance. As a person treats others, so will he himself ultimately be treated in the next world. The wise person will take heed."[31]

---

28. Ibid. from *Midrash Koheles*.

29. The members of the tribe of Yissachar were known for being immersed in Torah study. Thus, the giants of Torah study emerged from this tribe (see *I Divrei HaYamim* 12:32). The members of the tribe of Zevulun were seafaring businessmen (who also engaged in Torah study, see *Shoftim* 5:14). Zevulun and Yissachar created a partnership; Zevulun would share all earnings with Yissachar, and in return, the eternal earnings of Yissachar's Torah study would be shared by Zevulun. Yissachar and Zevulun have thus always been considered classic examples of Torah scholars and patrons of Torah.

30. *Ahavas Chesed* ibid.

31. Ibid.

53

Accepting Tzedakah

Standards of Eligibility in Earlier Times

1. Based on the standards of their time, the Sages set forth the following guidelines as to who was entitled to receive *tzedakah*: anyone who had 200 *zuz* on hand, or 50 *zuz* working capital, was considered to have enough to support himself for a year and was not entitled to receive *tzedakah*. A person with less than that amount was considered poor and was allowed to accept *tzedakah*. A poor person is not required to sell his utensils and clothing (even if they are valuable) and live off the proceeds in order to be eligible to receive *tzedakah*. However, this rule applies only to those who receive *tzedakah* from private sources; those who wish to benefit from public *tzedakah* funds are required to sell any valuables, including gold and silver eating utensils, and are then eligible for *tzedakah* only if they remain under the poverty level (i.e. in earlier times, having less than 200 *zuz*).[1]

Under Present Conditions

2. Under the changed conditions that prevail today, there is no fixed threshold corresponding to the 200-*zuz* figure set by the Sages,

---

1. *Yoreh Deah* 253:1.

and a poor person is allowed to continue collecting until he has sufficient funds to provide for his family's needs from the profits.[2]

Becoming Ineligible

3. An individual who is classified as "poor" (i.e. in the Sages' time owning less than 200 *zuz*) is entitled to accept any sum, even 1,000 *zuz*, if it was given at one time. However, if he had 199 *zuz*, and was given one *zuz*, and then 999 *zuz*, he is not permitted to accept the latter, since at that moment he is no longer classified as "poor." Nevertheless, a person who embarked on a trip to solicit funds is not required to return home after raising 200 *zuz*, spend some of the funds and then re-embark on his trip in order to continue collecting. Rather, he is permitted to visit all the places as originally planned and is not required to stop collecting after accumulating 200 *zuz*.[3]

4. One should not give *tzedakah* to a wealthy person who refuses to spend money on his own needs and deprives himself of necessities.[4] However, the *tzedakah* administrators should ensure that his innocent family members do not suffer.[5]

Use of Excess Funds Collected

5. If a collection undertaken to pay off the debts of a particular needy person (or to ransom a captive) receives more than the amount required, the recipient is entitled to keep the excess. However, when a collection is undertaken for the benefit of poor people or captives in general, then any excess must be set aside for other such individuals. The administrators of the fund can sometimes be granted flexibility in changing this general rule; a rav should be consulted.[6]

Those Unwilling to Accept *Tzedakah*

6. It is permitted to "deceive" a genuinely needy person who does not wish to accept *tzedakah* by extending him a loan and then not insisting on repayment if he does not have enough money.[7]

---

2. Ibid.
3. Ibid. 253:2.
4. Ibid. 253:10.
5. See *Rashi, Kesubos* 67a, s.v. *yeish lo.*
6. *Yoreh Deah* 253:4.
7. Ibid. 253:5.

The Sages taught us to be sensitive to a person's feelings. If possible, a poor person should be asked for security on a loan. When he responds that he has nothing to offer, the administrators should "agree" to the loan without security. The very fact that security was requested will give him the feeling that he received a bona fide loan and not tzedakah.[8]

7. A Torah scholar should be supported in accordance with the honor of his status. If he is unwilling to accept *tzedakah*, he should be given a share in a business enterprise which will provide for his needs (e.g. by acquiring low-priced merchandise on his behalf and selling it at a profit so that he will be able to live off the proceeds). If he is adept at business himself, he should be helped to operate a business in a way that will not seriously compromise his Torah learning.[9]

Tzedakah From Non-Jews

8. Accepting charity openly from non-Jews constitutes a desecration of Hashem's Name, and it is forbidden, but if done discreetly it is permitted. However, if one has a severe need, and there is not enough available from either Jewish sources or discreet non-Jewish sources, then it is permitted to accept charity even openly from non-Jewish sources.[10]

9. The administrator of a *tzedakah* fund is required to return a donation from a non-Jew. If this cannot be done without arousing the donor's enmity, the donation should be discreetly distributed to needy non-Jews; this is not considered deception since providing for non-Jews is within the scope of the Jewish concept of *tzedakah*. If the donor specifies that his donation may only be given to Jews, however, then his wishes must be fulfilled, since it is forbidden to deceive him.[11]

10. This rule applies specifically to *tzedakah*. However, a donation to a synagogue may be accepted from a non-Jew, just as offerings were accepted from non-Jews in the time of the *Beis HaMikdash*.[12]

---

8. *Kesubos* 67b.

9. *Yoreh Deah* 253:10.

10. Ibid. 254:1.

11. Ibid. 254:2 in *Rema* and *Shach*.

12. Ibid. in *Rema*.

11. According to some opinions, it is forbidden to accept *tzedakah* from a *mumar l'hachis* (a person who willfully transgresses the Torah).[13]

Do Not Become Dependent on *Tzedakah*

12. A person should always strive to avoid taking *tzedakah* and should endure difficulties in order not to be dependent on others for support. The Sages taught us that it is better to make Shabbos like a weekday (i.e. to forego any special purchases for Shabbos) than to accept *tzedakah*. Even a distinguished person who becomes impoverished should avoid being dependent on others by going to work (at a degrading occupation, if necessary).[14]

Attitudes Toward Receiving *Tzedakah*

13. Anyone who is not truly in need and engages in deception in order to receive *tzedakah* is assured that at some point during his lifetime he will be genuinely forced to accept *tzedakah*. On the other hand, an individual with a legitimate need for *tzedakah* (e.g. the elderly, disabled, unemployed or one who requires supplementary income to make ends meet or to finance his children's weddings) who refuses to accept help out of pride, is compared to a murderer. Any difficulties he imposes on himself and his family are counted as sins and transgressions. However, a person on the "borderline" of poverty who technically needs *tzedakah*, but pushes himself so as not to be a public burden, is assured that he will ultimately support others during his lifetime. Of such a person the prophet said, *Blessed is the man who trusts in Hashem (Yirmiyahu 17:7).*[15]

14. In our time, it is generally not possible for Torah scholars to develop their full potential if they divert time from Torah in order to make a living. It is therefore better to accept support from others than to take time away from Torah. Even a scholar with minimal resources that barely suffice to support a meager lifestyle, but will not allow proper dedication to his studies, should accept outside support and study Hashem's Torah with an easy mind. Any hardships such a person brings upon himself in order to be financially independent are simply for the sake of satisfying his own

---

13. Ibid. in *Rema*, though *Shach* 5 disagrees.
14. Ibid. 255:1.
15. Ibid. 255:2, and *Shach*.

pride and stubbornness.[16] (However, even though hardships should be avoided, excess spending of public funds is improper — see Chapter 51, paragraph 3.)

Throughout the ages, and especially today, the survival of the Jewish people as a nation has depended on the existence of yeshivos and those who study in them. It follows that supporting yeshivos is tantamount to supporting and preserving the Torah and through it the nation itself, and is therefore the greatest mitzvah there is.[17] Clearly, a Torah student should not leave yeshivah in order to be independent of the tzedakah funds specifically established to support those who toil in Torah.[18]

The very great mitzvah to support those who toil in Torah to the extent of one's ability, includes not only financial aid, but also lending encouragement and appreciation to their vital national service. Not only should one speak to the Torah heroes themselves with encouraging words, but in conversations with friends and associates as well. By doing so, one earns enormous merit in Heaven, for one of the most important purposes of man's creation is to proclaim, through words and actions, that serving Hashem is the foundation of our existence.[19] We must recognize that Torah scholars constitute the foundation upon which the Torah rests and are the source of survival of the Jewish people, whose raison d'être is living a life of Torah. There are those who view fundraising on behalf of Torah scholars as "just another way to earn a living" — one that does not necessarily command respect. Moreover, in their eyes, a Torah scholar is engaged in Torah study merely to "earn a living." Clearly, however, many more lucrative pursuits are open to them, so their devotion to Torah is unquestionably due to a commitment to preserve Torah in the world, which is really nothing less than preserving the world itself. Furthermore, honoring Torah scholars is tantamount to honoring Hashem Himself.[20]

---

16. *Karyana D'Iggarta* (*Selected Letters of HaRav Yaakov Yisrael Kanievsky, The Steipler*), no. 52.

17. See *Shaarei Teshuvah* 3:148.

18. See *Kesef Mishneh* on *Hilchos Talmud Torah* 3:10.

19. *Shaarei Teshuvah* ibid.

20. Ibid. See also *Nefesh HaChaim* Part 4 at length.

54

The Rules of Precedence for Acts of Kindness and Tzedakah

1. The Torah teaches (*Shemos* 22:24): *If you shall lend money to My people to the impoverished who (dwell) with you.* We derive from this that there are rules of precedence when a person performs an act of kindness (e.g. lending money or giving *tzedakah* to the poor, and in one's business dealings such as choosing where to buy or sell a product).[1]

2. The following rules of precedence are derived from the words of the *pasuk: My people* — a Jew over a non-Jew; *the impoverished* — over the non-impoverished; *with you* — those who are close to you over those further from you. The latter has two connotations: A relative who is close to you takes precedence over a non-relative (and a closer relative over a more distant one, e.g. a child or parent before a sibling) and those who dwell in your city take precedence over those living in distant areas. There is also the additional factor of honoring the Torah, which gives preference to Torah scholars over others.[2] This chapter details the laws of preference, their conflicts and resolutions.

---

1. *Bava Metzia* 71a.
2. *Yoreh Deah* 251:9.

"My People" — Jews and Non-Jews

3. Just as we are required to help needy Jews, it is also a mitzvah to help needy non-Jews, for the Torah teaches us to emulate Hashem Who is good to all, and to live a life of peaceful relationships.[3]

4. Nevertheless, if both a Jew and a non-Jew need *tzedakah* and one cannot adequately assist both, one is required to give to the Jew first. Similarly, if both a Jew and a non-Jew ask for a loan, with each offering acceptable security (collateral, guarantors, etc.), the Jew must be given precedence, even if interest will only be paid by the non-Jew, and even if the Jew is not poor and simply needs a loan.[4] However, according to some opinions, if one stands to realize a large profit from the non-Jew's interest and the Jew is not poor, one is not required to give preference to the Jew.[5]

5. A person whose income (full or partial) is based on investment returns (e.g. through loans to non-Jews at interest or investment bonds in a non-Jewish corporation) is not required to lend his capital to Jewish borrowers, since his own livelihood takes precedence over other people's. Nonetheless, if a poor Jew requests a loan and one can afford to deduct that potential interest from his income, he is required to give the Jew precedence as an act of *tzedakah*. One is especially required to do so if the Jew needs the loan for his basic livelihood, based on the mitzvah of *Let your brother live with you* (*Vayikra* 25:36). If one is able to do so but does not, he also transgresses the negative commandment, *Beware, lest there be a lawless thought in your heart* (*Devarim* 16:9).[6]

> *Rabbi Gold, a rebbi in the Midcity Elementary School, approached Mr. Schwartz, a wealthy man who was president of an investment agency, for a $20,000 loan so that his wife could start a small business. Mr. Schwartz had no extra cash; however, his business did have investment money. Since the expected revenue from $20,000 is about $1,500, which he could easily afford for the sake of a mitzvah, he is obligated to lend these business funds so as to enable Rabbi Gold to enhance his family's ability to earn a living.*

---

3. Ibid. 251:1; see also *Shach* 2.

4. *Ahavas Chesed* 5:1, 2, 5.

5. Ibid. in the name of *Shaar HaMishpat*; see also *Kodesh Yisrael*, Ch. 38 for a lengthy discussion of this issue.

6. *Ahavas Chesed* 5:3.

When the Non-Jew Asks First

6. The rule that in a case of limited funding a Jew is preferred over a
    non-Jew applies only if both requested a loan at the same time. If
the non-Jew asks first, one is permitted to give him the loan at interest, unless one definitely knows that a Jew will soon approach him, in
which case, one should not give the loan to the non-Jew.[7] This applies
only to loans, but in the area of *tzedakah* a Jew takes precedence over
a non-Jew, even if the Jew does not approach him at all. The reason for
this is that we have an obligation to support all Jews in need, whether
or not they approach us personally. As there are unfortunately many
needy Jews, every Jew is considered to have a constant responsibility
for them even if they do not come forward.[8]

7. Although it is our responsibility to help the numerous needy
    Jews, we should also give a small amount to a non-Jew who
approaches us for a handout. Such a contribution is not likely to
affect us very much and by doing so we are fulfilling the Sages' dictum to support needy non-Jews.[9] However, a situation where a non-
Jew requests more than a small amount should be handled with discretion and if possible, a rav should be consulted. Giving a substantial gift to a non-Jew can at times result in a sanctification of
Hashem's Name, and it may even be possible to forestall a dangerous situation by doing so.[10]

Preference in Buying and Selling

8. In all other matters too, Jews are to be given precedence over non-
    Jews. Thus, when buying, selling or renting property in which
both a Jew and non-Jew are interested and offering similar terms (or
even if the non-Jew is offering slightly better terms), it is a mitzvah to
close a deal with the Jew. However, if a non-Jew offers the going price
for an object and a Jew offers less, there is no mitzvah to prefer the
Jew, who is underpricing, over the non-Jew (this applies to sales, purchases, rentals, and other kinds of transactions).[11]

---

7. Ibid. 5:4.

8. See ibid. *Nesiv HaChesed* 8.

9. Otherwise it would be almost impossible to fulfill the Sages' instruction to support needy
non-Jews. See also *Bava Basra* 8a, story of Rabbi Nassan bar Amram.

10. See *Yoreh Deah* 251:14.

11. *Ahavas Chesed* 5:6-7, *Nesiv HaChesed* 12.

If a house is for sale and a Jew offers $200,000, while a non-Jew offers $201,000, there is a mitzvah to sell it to the Jew. However, if the non-Jew offers $220,000, there is no mitzvah to sell it to the Jew.

The "going price" for a certain computer is $500. A non-Jew is offering $500 while a Jew is willing to pay only $480. The owner does not have to sell to the Jew since he is underpricing.

An item sold in a supermarket for considerably less than in a small Jewish store may be purchased at the cheaper price. However, if the difference is only slight, it is a mitzvah to patronize the Jewish store.

Two stores, one owned by Jews and one not, are selling the same object. If the non-Jew is offering a slight discount or sale, one still has a mitzvah to buy it at the Jewish-owned store. However, if the savings involved are considerable, it is permitted to buy it from the non-Jewish store. If there is a set "going price" for the item (i.e. all stores generally charge the same), and the Jew overcharges even slightly, there is no mitzvah to buy from him.

Lending vs. Renting

9. If a Jew wishes to borrow an object while a non-Jew is willing to
     pay the owner a rental fee, it is permitted to rent it to the non-Jew
even if it is only for a small amount.[12] However, a poor Jew who wishes to borrow the object takes precedence, as the additional mitzvos of *tzedakah* and helping a fellow Jew earn a living are involved.[13]

If a non-Jew is willing to pay $50 for the use of Reuven's car for a week, and a Jew asks to borrow the car gratis, Reuven may give it to

---

12. This situation is not to be compared with the choice between lending money to a non-Jew at interest or to a Jew without interest, as discussed in par. 2. When one lends money, the amount received in return is exactly equal in value to what was lent out, while in lending objects, the object's value is diminished through wear and tear. See *Ahavas Chesed* 5:8, *Nesiv HaChesed* 13 for another difference between lending money and objects.

13. *Ahavas Chesed* ibid.

the non-Jew. However, a Jew who needs the car for the sake of his income (e.g. he cannot work without a car and his is being repaired) takes precedence.

"The Impoverished" — Needy and Less Needy

10. If two Jews request *tzedakah* or a loan, or if one can do business with two people, one very poor and the other not as needy,[14] the poor person takes precedence. This is true even if he is from a different city and is not related, while the other individual is from one's own city and is a relative. The same rule applies to someone who does not presently qualify as poor (see Chapter 53, paragraphs 1-2), but is in financial danger of losing his income; one is required to help him first as well.[15]

Food vs. Clothing

11. If approached by two poor people, one asking for food and the other for clothing, preference should be given to the one in need of food.[16] The Chasam Sofer writes that a person lacking food is categorized as poor compared to one who has food, and therefore has first priority even if he is from another city and is not a relative.[17]

With You — Relatives and Those in Geographical Proximity

12. A relative takes precedence over a neighbor, and a neighbor over others.

> *A person with a relative (son, brother, etc.) who wants to devote all his time to learning Torah cannot force this relative to desist from these plans, and is obligated to prefer him over all other tzedakah causes. However, one is not obligated to help him beyond the parameters of tzedakah, nor is one obligated to try to earn more money to support him.*

The poor of one's own city take precedence over the poor of other areas. Someone is considered a resident of one's city if he has either

---

14. Ibid. 6:13.

15. Ibid. 6:1.

16. *Yoreh Deah* 251:7.

17. *Teshuvos Chasam Sofer, Yoreh Deah* 234. See also *Halichos Olam*, Ch. 63 fn. *dalet*.

spent twelve months there, purchased a dwelling, or come with the intention of living there permanently.[18]

> *Local tzedakah causes come before those from out of town, unless funds are needed for cases of extreme poverty that do not exist locally (as described in paragraph 11).*

13. If a needy relative is able to acquire the necessary assistance from others without difficulty while a non-relative has no one else to turn to, the non-relative takes precedence.[19]

> *Rabbi Gold is supported by his brothers, who feel privileged that their sibling devotes all his time to Torah. Since he is well supported, Rabbi Gold consistently refuses financial aid from his own congregants, who are willing and able to support him. However, if the Gold brothers are approached by another Torah scholar for support, they cannot decline with the excuse that their brother needs them, since he is able to procure other means of support.*

14. The rules of precedence among relatives are: parents over children, children over siblings, and siblings through one's father over siblings through one's mother. All of these take precedence over other relatives.[20]

Honoring Sanctity

15. We are obligated to honor Hashem in all our endeavors; doing so reinforces one's inner Awe of the Majesty of Hashem and demonstrates a person's greatest value.[21] Therefore, in the area of preference regarding *tzedakah* and kindness, those whom we honor because of their special sanctity take first precedence.[22]

16. The obligation of honoring the Torah and its scholars is especially important, since the existence of the Torah, the Jewish people and the world is dependent on them. The flourishing of Torah is synonymous with the flourishing of its scholars; by according Torah scholars honor, others will aspire to join their ranks and Torah will

---

18. *Yoreh Deah* 251:3; *Ahavas Chesed* 6:2.

19. *Ahavas Chesed* 6:3.

20. Ibid. 6:4, from *Yoreh Deah* ibid.

21. *Mesillas Yesharim*, Ch. 19; *Shaarei Teshuvah* 3:147-148,156.

22. *Horayos* 13a; *Yoreh Deah* 251:9.

flourish. Furthermore, the Torah Sages are the natural leaders of the Jewish people and therefore should be accorded proper honor. Honoring our Sages is equivalent to honoring Hashem.[23]

17. A Torah scholar in need of aid takes precedence over other impoverished cases, even though the others may be in greater need. Thus, a Torah scholar who needs clothing precedes someone else who needs food (provided the latter has some basic provisions and his life is not in danger). The wife of a Torah scholar is equivalent to him and also takes precedence.[24]

18. A parent takes precedence over a Torah scholar.[25] Some *Poskim* hold that a relative or the local poor take precedence over a non-related or geographically-removed Torah scholar. However, the final *halachah* is unclear and a rav should be consulted.[26]

19. It would seem that the disagreement cited in the previous paragraph is relevant only when the issue is precedence for a Torah scholar over other needy individuals because of his honored status. If, however, one's motivation in wishing to support a Torah scholar is to acquire a share in his Torah study (a person who does not properly fulfill his obligation to study Torah should support others who do and is considered as if he himself had studied, *Yoreh Deah* 246:1), he is, in reality, supporting himself, and one's own life takes precedence over the life of another.[27]

---

23. See *Shaarei Teshuvah* ibid.

24. *Yoreh Deah* ibid.; *Ahavas Chesed* 6:6.

25. *Yoreh Deah* 251:9, *Shach* 17; *Ahavas Chesed* 6:7.

26. See *Ahavas Chesed* ibid., *Nesiv HaChesed* 14. See *Halichos Olam*, Ch. 63 fn. *yud*.

27. Those who think that learning Torah is a voluntary mitzvah are mistaken, for in reality, learning Torah is an all-inclusive obligation greater than all other mitzvos combined (*Yerushalmi Pe'ah* 1:1). Every man is obligated to spend every free moment studying Torah (see *Yoreh Deah* 246:1, *Beur HaGra* 1). However, we are also obligated to live Torah lives, which is the sum total of all our life affairs. Furthermore, most people, by nature, need some periods of relaxation; see *Mesillas Yesharim*, Ch. 1 (in reference to "wordly pleasures"), *Shaarei Teshuvah* 2:9 (even an extremely elderly person who no longer has the faculties to enjoy worldly pleasures should enjoy the sun, for *kotzer nefesh* [frustration] prevents a person from fulfilling his spiritual tasks). Nevertheless, every person is obligated to devote a part of every day and every night to Torah study (*Yoreh Deah* ibid.). The obligation is all-encompassing; a person must study the entire Written and Oral Torah and spend his life delving into its depths according to his ability (ibid. 246:4). The Torah itself is so vast and diverse that every Jew can find his niche of Torah study. Unfortunately, modern lifestyles leave very little time for Torah study (the *Rambam* suggests spending three hours a day learning *Tanach*, three hours learning Mishnah, three hours learning Gemara, and three hours a day pursuing a

A person who does not properly fulfill his obligation to learn Torah, either because he does not know how, or because his affairs are overly time-consuming, should, to the best of his ability, support a needy Torah scholar and afford him the opportunity to learn without financial pressure. This type of tzedakah precedes all others, even that of the local poor or relatives.

20. Other factors being equal, a Kohen takes precedence over a Levi, a Levi over a Yisrael, and a Yisrael over a *mamzer*.[28] This applies, however, only if the two are equal in Torah wisdom; a *mamzer* who is a Torah scholar takes precedence even over an unlearned Kohen Gadol.[29]

The Needy of Eretz Yisrael

21. The needy of one's own city take precedence over the needy of other cities, even the residents of Eretz Yisrael (Land of Israel — see footnote).[30] Nevertheless, if one does contribute to the needy of other cities, the needy of Eretz Yisrael take precedence over the needy of other countries,[31] and the needy of the old city of Jerusalem (which has special sanctity) come before the needy of other cities of Eretz Yisrael.[32]

---

livelihood). Nevertheless, the obligation to set aside time every day and every night remains in force, as does the obligation to at least attempt to study the entire Torah. A person whose affairs leave him no time for serious study, or one who was never privileged to learn how to study, can fulfill his obligation by enabling someone else to learn. He thus receives a share of the other person's Torah (ibid. 248:1) but he is not absolved from his own obligation to study whatever or whenever possible. This support is not merely *tzedakah*; its purpose is to fulfill one's own obligations. Since it is not *tzedakah* there is no limit of a fifth of one's income (*Ahavas Chesed* Part 2, 20:4 in the name of *Shitah Mekubetzes, Kesubos* 50a); just as a person spends for all his needs (food, clothing, housing, etc.) so must he spend on his own Torah study obligations. Therefore, this is obligatory, even if spending this money precludes one from giving substantially to *tzedakah*, for one's own needs precede *tzedakah*.

28. A *mamzer* is someone born of an illicit relationship where both parents are Jews but *halachic* legal marriage between them is impossible (e.g. adultery with a married woman or incest with a close relative mentioned in *Vayikra* Ch. 18).

29. *Ahavas Chesed* 6:6 from *Yoreh Deah* ibid.

30. *Yoreh Deah* 251, *Shach* 6 in the name of *Bach*. Note: "The Land of Israel" is legally defined as any land sanctified by Joshua and the people of Israel after the Exodus from Egypt. Some land subsequently conquered by King David is also considered Eretz Yisrael, but only *mi'd'Rabbanan* (from Rabbinical origin — the "Rabbis" are King David and his *beis din*). See also next fn.

31. *Yoreh Deah* 251:3, in the name of *Sifri*. Note: Not all of modern day Israel is included in Eretz Yisrael. See *Poskim* for the *halachic* boundaries.

32. *Teshuvos Chasam Sofer, Yoreh Deah* 234; see *Halichos Olam*, Ch. 63 fn. *tzadi*.

Torah and Eretz Yisrael

22. However, any Torah institution or Torah scholar, even one out-side of Eretz Yisrael, takes precedence over residents of Eretz Yisrael, and even over residents of Jerusalem who are not Torah scholars.[33] Furthermore, residence in Eretz Yisrael and Jerusalem lends precedence only because of the special sanctity inherent in those places and the mitzvos which can be fulfilled by those dwelling there. It is therefore relevant only to those who embody that sanctity by being particularly careful in their observance of Torah and mitzvos.[34] However, those residents who abuse that sanc-tity by flouting Torah and mitzvos only exacerbate their transgres-sions and would be better off living outside Eretz Yisrael;[35] they cer-tainly are not entitled to any precedence regarding *tzedakah* and other forms of assistance.

An Individual Who Cannot Afford *Tzedakah*

23. When a conflict arises between one's own life and those of oth-ers, the rule is that one's own life takes precedence; someone whose resources are inadequate for his own needs is exempt from the requirement to help others.[36] This is only true regarding needs of an equivalent nature. Thus, tuition for one's own children comes before subsidizing tuition for others. Providing a healthy physical, emotional, and spiritual environment for one's own children also comes first. However, luxuries do not precede *tzedakah* — quite the opposite. The Chofetz Chaim writes[37] that anyone who spends money on luxuries probably cannot exempt himself with giving only a fifth of his income to *tzedakah*, since he is already spending money unnecessarily.

24. Therefore, someone with inadequate resources who is approached for a loan by two people, one a needy person who will pay no interest and the other wealthy and offering interest (either

---

33. *Chasam Sofer* ibid.

34. Ibid.

35. *Teshuvos Maharam MiRottenberg* (Berlin ed.) 9, 14. "Those who go there (Land of Israel) to live with frivolity I say about them, 'You have come and defiled my land,' but to those who go for the sake of Heaven and live there with sanctity and purity there is no limit to their reward."

36. *Yoreh Deah* 251:3.

37. *Ahavas Chesed* Part 2, 20:5 in fn.

a non-Jew or a Jew by means of a *heter iska*[38]), does not have to give the needy person precedence. However, great care is required to be certain that the lender is genuinely unable to afford the free loan, since a person can easily convince himself that he is incapable of an action that he really can accomplish, and he who consistently avoids helping others for fear of being impoverished when there is really no such danger, increases his risk of actually falling into poverty.[39]

A Relative Plans to Ask for a Loan

25. Let us say that a person is approached by a needy non-relative for a loan and knows with certainty that a needy relative will soon approach him as well. Assuming that he cannot help both, he is permitted to refuse the non-relative so that he will be able to lend the money to his relative (even though he has not yet asked explicitly). However, if it is not certain that the relative will approach him, there is no excuse to deny his petitioner. If neither the relative nor the non-relative are needy, and they both need loans, the *halachah* is inconclusive as to whether one has a right to refuse the non-relative before he has heard explicitly that the relative plans to request a loan.[40] These rules apply only to loans, whereas regarding *tzedakah*, a relative always comes first.[41]

> *Mr. Silver, who just won the lottery, has been approached by many tzedakah funds for sizable contributions. He has turned them all down because he has two brothers who are in desperate need of funds, and although they haven't yet asked him, they take precedence. (The brothers are not necessarily preferred over funds that support Torah — see paragraphs 18 and 19. However, if the brothers themselves are full-time Torah scholars, they do take precedence.)*

26. If approached by two people, one of whom has relatives who are in a position to help him, one should give precedence to the other. However, if the first person claims that his relatives are unwilling to help, then the two are to be treated equally.[42]

---

38. A *halachic* redefinition of a loan in terms of an investment whereby the "lender" is really investing money with a risk of profit or loss. Thus, the "interest" is not defined as interest on a loan, but rather, as profit on a successful investment.

39. *Ahavas Chesed* 6:9.

40. Ibid. 6:11, *Nesiv HaChesed* 18.

41. See par. 6.

42. *Ahavas Chesed* 6:12.

Mrs. A to Husband: Why did you give tzedakah to Chaim Black? You know he has wealthy parents.

Mr A: True, but since they don't help him he is the same as anyone else.

Not His Own Money

27. If one person gives money to another to be distributed in the form of *tzedakah* or loans, then the relatives of neither individual take any precedence in terms of receiving help.[43]

> *Mr. Gold just received a sizable amount of money from Mr. Silver to establish a general free-loan fund. Although both Mr. Gold and Mr. Silver have brothers who are in need of loans, these brothers do not take precedence over any other person.*

---

43. Ibid. 6:13.

55

Vows Concerning Tzedakah and Mitzvos

(Note: The term "vow" as used in this chapter is to be understood to include all commitments having the force of a vow, whether or not the word "vow" is specified in making them, as discussed in paragraph 2.)

The Torah's Commandment

1. The Torah states, *When you make a vow to Hashem, your G-d, you shall not be late in paying it* (*Devarim* 23:22), and also, *You shall observe and carry out what emerges from your lips, just as you vowed a voluntary gift to Hashem, your G-d, whatever you spoke with your mouth* (ibid. verse 24). From these verses we learn that anyone who makes a vow either to bring an offering or to donate an item of value for sacred use, or to give *tzedakah*, is obligated to fulfill his commitment. An additional negative commandment, *If a man takes a vow to Hashem … he shall not desecrate his word* (*Bamidbar* 30:3), also warns us not to desecrate commitments made for sacred purposes, including *tzedakah*.[1]

---

1. *Rosh Hashanah* 6a; *Yoreh Deah* 257:3. Note: There are two types of *nedarim* (vows); see *Ramban* on *Bamidbar* 30:3, and *Rambam* at the beginning of *Hilchos Nedarim*. Vows of *tzedakah* are similar to those of sacrifices and funds for the *Beis HaMikdash*.

What Constitutes a Vow

2. Any time a person commits himself to give to *tzedakah*, whether or not the word "vow" itself is spoken, the commitment is considered to be an actual vow that he is required to fulfill.[2]

> *Examples of statements having the force of a vow:*
> **To solicitor:** *I will give you* $100.
> **At synagogue appeal or parlor meeting:** *I will donate* $1,000.
> **To oneself:** *I'm going to contribute* $500 *to that cause.*

3. Even if one merely made up his mind to give *tzedakah*, he is required to do so as if he actually spoke aloud.[3] However, as long as one has not reached a mental decision, thoughts have no legal validity.

4. There are two types of commitments to *tzedakah*. In the first, a person commits *himself* to give *tzedakah*.

> ❏ *I will donate* $18 *to tzedakah.*
> ❏ *We will give a car to a poor person.*

In the second, a person commits the *money* or *object* to *tzedakah*.

> ❏ *This* $18 *will go to tzedakah.*
> ❏ *I will donate this sefer to the school.*
> ❏ *We will give this car to a poor person.*

Both types are equally considered a vow. However, should the money or object be lost, there is a difference between the two types of commitments.

In the former case, where one commits *himself* to give, he is required to fulfill his commitment under any circumstances; if money is set aside and lost before it can be given to *tzedakah*, he is required to replace it. In the latter case, however, if money or an object designated for *tzedakah* later gets lost he is not required to replace it, since his commitment covered only that specific cash or item.[4]

> *Mr. Gold left* $1,000 *cash in an envelope for the representative of a yeshivah, and instructed his son to give it to the man when he came*

---

2. *Yoreh Deah* ibid.

3. Ibid. 258:13, *Rema;* see also *Choshen Mishpat* 212:8 and *Beur HaGra.*

4. *Kinim* 1:1; *Megillah* 8a.

to the door. The son, however, misplaced the envelope. Mr. Gold asked the rav if he must replace it, and was told, "If you said (or mentally decided) that you would give $1,000 to the yeshivah you must replace the money. However, if you said (or mentally decided) that you would give this $1,000 to the yeshivah, then you do not have to replace the money."

Note: Nonetheless, if he borrowed dedicated tzedakah money for his personal use (as discussed in paragraph 18) and subsequently lost it, then even if the commitment was limited to "this money," he is still required to "pay back" his loan and replace the money to tzedakah.

Avoid Making Vows

5. The wisest policy is never to make vows of any kind so as not to risk violating a serious transgression by failing to fulfill them. Therefore, if possible, one should not commit oneself to give; one should simply give.[5] However, in a public gathering where each person is asked to pledge a certain amount, one should join in the public mitzvah. Nevertheless, he should still be careful to avoid vows by stating explicitly that his pledge is *bli neder* (i.e. does not have the force of a vow). In such a situation, even though he does not actually verbalize a commitment, he still receives a reward for the statement since he joined the public mitzvah and encouraged others to pledge as well.[6]

> The Sages taught: If a person says he will give, and then he gives, he gets reward for the words and reward for the deed. If he didn't say he will give, but he tells others to give, he will be rewarded for those words. Even if he doesn't tell others to give, but he mollifies the impoverished with words he will be rewarded, because the verse says (Devarim 10:15), "For because of this davar (literally 'thing,' but also explained to mean dibbur — words), Hashem will bless you."
>
> (We learn that Hashem rewards words of tzedakah or any mitzvah, and it is therefore proper to say "I will do a mitzvah." However, in order to avoid a vow one should say he will do it "bli neder" (without any force of a vow).

---

5. *Yoreh Deah* ibid.

6. *Sefer Derech Emunah, Hilchos Matnos Aniyim* 8:1 in the name of *Ahavas Chesed* Part 2, Ch. 16, in fn.

Vowing in Times of Distress

6. It is permitted to make vows in times of distress or danger.[7]

> *When fleeing his brother Esav, Yaakov said, "If Hashem will be with me, and watch me on my journey, give me bread to eat and clothing to wear ... And all that You give me I will tithe to You"* (*Bereishis* 28:20-22).

Commitments to Do Mitzvos

7. Any statement of intention to learn Torah or perform a mitzvah has a force similar to a vow and one is required to fulfill what he has stated,[8] unless he specifies that his commitment is *bli neder*.

> ❏ *I will learn this chapter of Mishnah.*
> ❏ *I will get up to daven in the first minyan.*
> ❏ *I will host these guests for Shabbos.*
> ❏ *I will attend your wedding.*

However, any statement that is not a mitzvah does not have to be fulfilled. There are people who mistakenly say *bli neder* indiscriminately.

> ❏ *I will go shopping.*
> ❏ *I will go on vacation.*
> ❏ *I will cook this.*

However, the following statements do have to be fulfilled:

> ❏ *I will go shopping for you (a person who needs the help).*
> ❏ *I will make you a meal (the recipient is a guest or is ill, or is in need of help).*

If the mitzvah was intended to help someone, and that individual waives the favor, one need not take any further action.[9]

> **Mrs. A to Mrs. B (who is ill):** *I'm sending you a meal.*
> **Mrs. B:** *Thanks.*

---

7. *Yoreh Deah* 203:5.

8. *Nedarim* 8a; *Yoreh Deah* 213:2. Note: If one cannot fulfill his word to learn Torah or do the mitzvah, he may sometimes make a *hataras nedarim*. See also *Yoreh Deah* 211:2 for the effectiveness of *Kol Nidrei* on Yom Kippur and statements of Erev Rosh Hashanah. Thus, in all such cases a rav should be consulted.

9. See *Yoreh Deah* 232:20.

Later, Mrs. B calls: My mother came and cooked supper, so I don't need your help today. Thanks for the offer!
Mrs. A has no further obligation.

Tzedakah on Condition

8. If one states his intention to give *tzedakah* if he performs a specified action (or fails to perform it), then if he fulfills the condition he is required to give the *tzedakah*, whether or not the action in question involved a mitzvah. This applies to any other statement of intention to do a mitzvah as well.[10]

> ❏ *If you let me take the car, I will learn afterwards for two hours.*
> ❏ *If I don't take you shopping, I will give $10 to tzedakah.*
> ❏ *If I miss Krias Shema even once, I will daven with the first minyan for a month.*

Whose Vows Are Legally Valid

9. Any person who has reached the age of mitzvos (13 for boys and 12 for girls), who makes a statement that constitutes a "vow" is halachically required to fulfill it. Furthermore, any statement constituting a vow made a year before the bar or bas mitzvah (boys — 12 years old; girls — 11 years old), is also considered a *halachic* vow, provided the child understands the meaning of a vow. Any statement made before that period has no *halachic* validity; nevertheless, it is educationally wise to obligate the child to keep his word in order to teach the serious nature of vows and oaths.[11]

10. The Torah teaches that a man may abrogate his wife's vows on the day that he hears of them. However, this applies only to vows that are related to her person or their relationship.

> ❏ *A vow pertaining to her well-being:*
> *I will fast every Monday and Thursday for a month.*
> ❏ *A vow pertaining to their relationship:*
> *I will not wear any of the nice dresses that my mother gave me —*
> *I'm giving them to tzedakah.*

---

10. Ibid. 258:10, and *Mishnah Berurah* 562:51,53,54, both cited in *Derech Emunah, Hilchos Matnos Aniyim* 8:2.

11. *Yoreh Deah* 203:5.

However, vows that do not pertain to either of these categories are valid even if the husband would want to abrogate them.[12] However, a woman usually cannot pledge money without her husband's permission.[13] In some cases, a woman can make a pledge that she will not be obligated to fulfill unless she becomes single (i.e. widowed or divorced).

> *Mrs. A pledged $1,000 to tzedakah. When her husband heard, he was categorically opposed and abrogated the vow. On the one hand, the abrogation is invalid. On the other hand, Mrs. A has no independent access to funds and cannot fulfill her vow. However, if she ever becomes single she would be obligated to donate that $1,000 to tzedakah.*

In all such cases, a rav should be consulted.

11. The Torah teaches that a father may abrogate the vows of his daughter from the age of 12 to 12 ½. Some *Poskim* say that this applies only to some types of vows and others say that it applies to all vows.[14] In all cases, a rav should be consulted.

When Is a Vow Fulfilled

12. If one makes a vow to contribute an unspecified sum to *tzedakah*, he fulfills his vow with any amount greater than a *perutah*. However, if he specified an amount, he must give that amount. If he does not remember exactly how much he vowed to contribute, he is required to give the maximum amount that he could have pledged.[15]

> **Mr. A:** *I agreed to contribute when they were soliciting for a poor bride yesterday. I don't remember if I said $18, $36, or $50. What should I do?*
> **Rav:** *Could you have said $75?*
> **Mr. A:** *No, I definitely would not have said more than $50.*
> **Rav:** *In that case, give $50.*

How Soon *Tzedakah* Must Be Given

13. From the verse mentioned in paragraph 1 ... *you shall not be late in paying it*, we derive that it is forbidden to delay fulfilling a

---

12. Ibid. 234:55.
13. Ibid. 248:4, 5.
14. Ibid. 234:58.
15. Ibid. 258:3.

vow. Therefore, one who makes a vow to give *tzedakah* without specifying a recipient is required to distribute it immediately if needy people or worthy Torah institutions exist in his city (or give it to funds established to channel *tzedakah* to the needy of other cities). If he does not do so, he is in constant violation of the commandment not to delay fulfilling vows. However, one who vowed to give *tzedakah* to a particular needy person or institution is not in violation of the commandment until the recipient is available to collect the funds.[16]

14. If a person stated his intention to give *tzedakah,* and there are no needy people in his vicinity, he is required to put the money aside and keep it until a proper recipient becomes available.[17]

> *A person who lives in an area where there are no needy people should send the money immediately to a tzedakah fund in another locale.*

15. A person who makes a pledge in shul where the payments are customarily made to the shul's officers, is not required to pay until they request payment. Once it is requested, however, it must be given immediately; he remains in violation of the prohibition of delaying payment until he does so. If the officers are not aware of one's vow, he is required to tell them so they will know to request payment.[18]

16. It is permitted to set aside money for a *tzedakah* fund with the intention of distributing it as one sees fit to the various needy people who may present themselves over time. In such cases, even though one is not supporting the local needy, it is not a violation of the prohibition to delay *tzedakah* since the funds were originally designated on the condition that they be distributed according to the decision of the fund administrator (in this case, the person himself).[19]

17. One can avoid any possibility of violating the prohibitions of desecrating a vow or delaying its fulfillment by specifying that all commitments are made *bli neder* and that any money set aside does not become *tzedakah* until it actually reaches the hands of the recipient. This was the advice of the *Chazon Ish.*[20]

---

16. Ibid. 257:3.

17. Ibid.

18. Ibid., *Shach* 7.

19. *Yoreh Deah* ibid.

20. See *Derech Emunah, Tziyun Halachah* (8:72) who writes that such was the advice of the *Chazon Ish* in order to avoid any doubt of transgressing the mitzvah.

Borrowing *Tzedakah* Money

18. The contemporary custom permits borrowing money set aside as *tzedakah* for personal use (even by one merely administering the fund), as long as he is sure that there will be absolutely no delay in distributing it to any needy person who presents himself.[21]

Note: It is a wise practice to keep a written record of money borrowed from *tzedakah* funds.

---

21. *Yoreh Deah* 259, *Pischei Teshuvah* 4; see also *Derech Emunah, Hilchos Matnos Aniyim, Tziyun Halachah* (8:123) who writes that the *Chazon Ish* permitted this.

Personal Kindness

Chapters 56-59

56

The Mitzvah of Extending Hospitality

1. The verse (*Vayikra* 19:18), *You shall love your fellow,* obligates a person to perform acts of kindness.[1] Furthermore, the Sages explained that in the verse, *And you shall teach them the path they should tread (Shemos* 18:20), "the path" refers to acts of kindness.[2]

    Acts of kindness are greater than *tzedakah* in three ways: *tzedakah* involves only money while kindness involves both money and physical effort; *tzedakah* helps only the poor while kindness can benefit the wealthy as well as the poor; and last, *tzedakah* helps only the living while acts of kindness can benefit the departed as well as the living.[3]

2. Although acts of kindness include all the various ways people can help one another, the Sages enumerated a number of kindnesses as specific mitzvos:
    (a) hospitality to guests and escorting them upon their departure;
    (b) visiting and tending to the needs of the sick;
    (c) attending to the needs of the dead, including assisting in the funeral, burial and eulogies; and

---

1. *Rambam, Hilchos Aveil* 14:1.

2. *Bava Metzia* 30b.

3. *Succah* 49a.

(d) helping a bride and groom celebrate their marriage, sharing in their rejoicing and helping them establish a life together.

The Mitzvah of Hospitality

3. The Sages extolled the mitzvah of hospitality.

> *Extending hospitality to wayfarers is greater even than receiving the Divine Presence, as we see from Avraham who interrupted his conversation with Hashem and ran after three passersby, begging them to accept his hospitality (Bereishis 18:3).[4]*

> *Sarah (see Bereishis 18:1-14) and the Shunamis (see II Kings 4:8-17), both childless, were rewarded with children because of this mitzvah.[5]*

4. A community can compel its members to participate in the mitzvos of hospitality to wayfarers and *tzedakah* to the impoverished.[6]

5. Even though there is a mitzvah to extend hospitality to both the rich and the poor, receiving poor guests is more important since it includes the mitzvah of *tzedakah* as well.[7]

> *When one feeds a poor person, he is considered as having brought an offering on the Altar. If his guest is a poor Torah scholar, he is considered as having brought the daily Tamid offering.[8]*

6. Sadly, we often encounter the exact opposite of the Torah ideal, and wealthy visitors are greeted warmly and showered with honor and attention, while the poor, especially the downtrodden and dispirited, are received far less graciously.[9]

> *Torah scholars are sometimes forced to travel to distant places to solicit funds. Some represent Torah institutions, while others must raise funds for wedding expenses and other mitzvos. The reward of those who receive them and accord them honorable treatment is very great.*

---

4. *Shabbos* 127a; see also *Ahavas Chesed* Part 3, Ch. 1, for discussion of the importance of this mitzvah and sources. This chapter is mostly from *Ahavas Chesed*, Chs. 1 and 2.

5. *Tanchuma, Parshas Ki Seitzei.*

6. *Yoreh Deah* 256, *Shach* 1.

7. *Ahavas Chesed* Ch. 1, in the name of *Yesh Nochalim* and *Maharil.*

8. Ibid., from *Chagigah* 27a and *Berachos* 10b.

9. *Ahavas Chesed* ibid.

7. The mitzvah of extending hospitality to guests applies even when the host is ill. He should still expend as much effort as he can to see to his guests' needs, just as Avraham exerted himself on behalf of his guests even though he was ill, recovering from circumcision at an advanced age. Similarly, one should educate his children to distinguish themselves in this mitzvah, as Avraham did with Yishmael.[10]

How to Emulate the Hospitality of Avraham and Sarah

8. One should seek out guests and treat them with great warmth, as if each one were a wealthy person from whom one stands to realize a great profit.[11]

> Avraham ran after wayfarers to invite them in.

9. When guests arrive, one should immediately allow them to wash if they need to.[12]

> Avraham said, "Take water and wash your feet."

For this reason one should make sure that his facilities are kept clean and attractive for their use.

10. When guests arrive, one should offer them an opportunity to rest from the exertions of their journey.[13]

> Avraham said, "And they should rest under the tree."

However, if they do not need to rest, they should be served a meal immediately, in case they are hungry and too embarrassed to ask to eat.[14]

11. If one sees that his guests wish to remain only a short while and then continue on their way, he should suggest that they eat only a small amount rather than delay them with a full meal.

> Avraham said, "I will fetch just a loaf of bread ... and shortly after you will be on your way."

---

10. Ibid. Ch. 2; see *Bereishis* Ch. 18 (and *Rashi* to v. 7).
11. Ibid.
12. Ibid.
13. Ibid.
14. Ibid.

At the same time, guests often decline offers of food out of politeness or embarrassment, but when a meal is placed in front of them they are actually quite happy to eat.

> *Avraham, in fact, served an entire meal with delicacies. (Righteous people say little and perform a great deal.)*

Nonetheless, if the guests genuinely do not want to eat, they should certainly not be pressed to do so; the only considerations should be fulfilling the guests' needs and wishes.[15]

12. Guests should be offered one's best foods and should be served as expeditiously as possible. Once part of the meal is ready it should be served immediately rather than withheld until other dishes are available, just as Avraham did.[16] A host should not consider it beneath his dignity to personally serve his guests.[17]

> *Avraham, who had been coronated Prince of G-d by all the nations, did not consider it beneath his dignity to serve his guests even though he believed them to be low and uncouth idol worshipers. He, in turn, learned from Hashem Who provides for every creature.[18] How much more so should ordinary hosts treat ordinary guests with honor and deference.*

13. Guests should receive cheerful treatment and not be burdened with any of the host's worries or concerns.

> *Mr. Schwartz, while serving his guests a lavish meal, related how his business was failing and he would have to declare bankruptcy. The guests did not feel very comfortable.*

Even if the host is not a wealthy person, he should act as if he were and not make his guests feel as if they are an imposition, or lower their spirits in any other way. On the contrary, a host should always attempt to boost his guests' spirits and try to convey an impression of regret that he cannot provide for them more lavishly, in order to give them a sense of importance.[19]

---

15. Ibid.
16. Ibid.; see *Rashi* to v. 8.
17. Ibid.
18. See *Kiddushim* 32b.
19. *Ahavas Chesed* ibid.

14. The host should serve his guests generous portions and not watch them closely or in any way make them self-conscious about how much they are eating. For the same reason, he should slice the bread and serve the other foods himself, since if they had to help themselves they might feel too embarrassed to take as much as they really want and thus go hungry.[20]

15. Guests should be given the best beds available, since the more comfortable one's bed, the better one rests.

> In general, the host should always keep in mind how he would want to be treated in his guests' position and extend food, drink, lodgings, and honor to them in the same way he himself would want to be received.[21]

16. If one knows that another homeowner in the city can offer a visitor better accommodations or food, (or if the guest will derive some other advantage from staying elsewhere), the guest should be encouraged to lodge with the other host since this is to his benefit. If, however, no one more capable exists or if one knows that the other hosts in the city will not receive this particular visitor, then one should invite the guest and treat him as well as possible. The fact that a person is not capable of giving a guest the treatment of which he is worthy does not excuse him from the mitzvah, and he should do as much as he is capable of doing.[22]

Propriety

17. The mitzvah of hospitality does not override the Torah's strictures concerning propriety. Thus, a male host may receive other males as guests and a female hostess other females, and hosts of either gender may receive couples as guests; likewise, a married couple may receive guests of either gender or other couples. However, a single female hostess should not receive male guests, nor should a single male host receive female guests.[23] Similarly, when a poor man comes to the door, the woman of the house is not permitted to let him enter,

---

20. Ibid.

21. Ibid.

22. Ibid.

23. We find that the women of Moav were not blamed for not being hospitable to the women of Israel, since that would have entailed going into the desert, which was considered inappropriate (*Yevamos* 79a).

violating the laws of *yichud*. She should instead refer him to a man to feed him or otherwise provide his needs in a manner appropriate to Torah propriety. It goes without saying that if the man is unknown to her she should not let him in.

Escorting Guests

18. Once a guest has eaten and drunk and is ready to leave, the host is obligated to escort him on his way.[24]

> *The reward for escort is greater than all (other mitzvos of kindness). Avraham instituted the mitzvah of escort, for after his guests ate and drank he escorted them on their way. The mitzvah of hospitality is greater than receiving the Divine Presence, and escort is greater than hospitality.*[25]

19. When a host escorts his guest he: (a) shows the guest's importance to him; and (b) shows him the way. Even if the guest knows the way, the host is still obligated to escort his guest for the first reason. Although escort is defined minimally as four *amos* (approximately eight feet) and even that amount of escort brings great reward, the Sages nevertheless required that guests be escorted specific distances, depending on the relationship between the host and the guest: A rebbi is required to escort his students to the edge of the city; an ordinary person is required to escort his equal until the *techum Shabbos* (approximately 0.7 mile from the last dwelling in the city); a student is required to escort a rebbi one *parsah* (approximately 2.8 miles) and his *rebbi muvhak* (primary teacher) three *parsa'os* (approximately 8.4 miles). In practice, however, the custom is for the guest to excuse his host from escorting him these distances and to accept an escort of only four *amos*. The guest should not excuse the host from this minimal distance, since this mitzvah protects the guest from all kinds of harm on his journey.[26]

> *Rav Yehudah said in the name of Rav: Whoever accompanies his friend four amos in the city saves him from harm. Ravina accompanied Rava bar Yitzchak in the city; thereafter, Rava was about to be harmed, but was saved as a result of Ravina's escort.*[27]

---

24. *Rambam, Hilchos Aveil* 14:2.

25. Ibid.

26. *Sotah* 46b. *Rambam* ibid. 14:3. *Choshen Mishpat* 427, *Sma* 11. *Ahavas Chesed*, Ch. 2.

27. *Sotah* ibid.

It would seem that these four *amos* start only after one emerges into the public thoroughfare, but does not include the distance covered within one's own property, courtyard, apartment building, etc.[28]

20. We see that the basic mitzvah of providing an escort involves walking minimally four *amos* with a guest and, if needed, giving him directions to his destination. If one honors the guest by escorting him further, that is an additional mitzvah. Conversely, if one is unable to provide an escort, but does give directions, that too is a mitzvah. When one finally parts from a guest, one should part with words of Torah.[29]

21. Each of the four activities involved in receiving guests — providing food, drink, lodging, and escort — is an independent mitzvah. If the host can do nothing else (e.g. the guest stays only a few minutes and is not hungry), he should still accompany the guest on his departure.[30] However, a guest who needs food and lodging must be provided with all his needs.

> *A person who was known to be very hospitable to guests was struck by tragedy when a fire burned down his house. People wondered why the merit of the mitzvah had not saved him. When the question was posed to a Torah Sage he answered, "'Eshel' is the acronym describing Avraham's hospitality: alef, shin and lamed, stand for achilah (food), she'siyah (drink), and linah leviyah (lodging and escort). This man, while being very hospitable, neglected to escort his guests, and his mitzvah, specifically the 'lamed' aspect, was therefore incomplete. Thus, only the alef and shin remained, spelling aish (fire)."*[31]

22. The mitzvah of escorting applies not only to guests, but to anyone else as well. This mitzvah can be fulfilled simply by giving a stranger directions, and all the more so by walking with him the

---

28. The *Sma* ibid. writes that the custom is to escort to the "gate" or at least four *amos*. It seems that the "gate" refers to the gate of the Jewish street in the ghetto, and that is why he concludes "or at least four *amos*" [which is merely within the city (*Sotah* 46b), but does not reach the "gate"]. However, as long as the guest is within the host's property he has not left at all, and accompaniment is not "escort."

29. *Berachos* 31a (the *Gemara* says "*dvar halachah*" but the subsequent story indicates that the intention is any words of Torah).

30. Derived from par. 22.

31. *Ahavas Chesed* ibid. in fn.

distance of four *amos*. In all these cases, the reward for the mitzvah is limitless.[32]

> When the men of the tribe of Yosef wanted to capture a city they could not find its entrance, whereupon they spotted someone and asked him. Because he showed them the entrance with his finger they saved him; he thereupon left and built the city of Luz which lasted for centuries. World conquerors did not destroy it and even the Angel of Death was not permitted to enter the city. Instead, when old people in Luz had no more desire to live, they left the city and then died. All this was a reward for the escort lifting a finger; how much more for the mitzvah of escort by foot and troubling oneself to show a person the way.[33]

Rooms for Guests

23. Any person who is able to do so should set aside a room in his home for guests, to be available at least for them to sleep, even if it is used for other purposes during the day. Although individuals may not have the resources to build special facilities for travelers, the community as a whole has an obligation to provide accommodations and food for them. It is a time-honored and worthy tradition in Israel to maintain societies to attend to the needs of travelers; fortunate are those who have a share in this mitzvah.[34]

---

32. *Sotah* 46b. The story in the example quoted from *Sotah* indicates that one does not have to be a "host" to perform the mitzvah of "escort"; rather, any person who needs escort or directions is considered as a "guest" to the one who possesses that knowledge and shows him the way.

33. Ibid.

34. *Ahavas Chesed* ibid. It would seem that the existence of commercial hotels does not relieve a community of this obligation, since many travelers do not have the means to stay in hotels. Therefore, each community should be sure to provide facilities worthy of the children of royalty, since all Jews are the King's children.

57

Tending to the Needs
of the Sick

The Mitzvah of Visiting the Sick

1. It is a mitzvah to visit someone who is ill, just as Hashem visited
   Avraham when he was recovering from his circumcision. There
   are no social distinctions, and even great and esteemed individuals
   are obligated to visit sick people of lower standing.[1]

2. The primary objective of this mitzvah is to help the patient with all
   his needs.[2] For example:

   ❏ *Calling a doctor.*
   ❏ *Obtaining medicine.*
   ❏ *Keeping him company.*
   ❏ *Buoying his spirits.*
   ❏ *Shopping or cleaning his house if needed.*
   ❏ *Praying for his recovery and well-being.*

---

1. *Yoreh Deah* 335:1,2; *Ahavas Chesed* Part 3, Ch. 3.

2. See *Ahavas Chesed* ibid. (Note: The practical details of *Bikur Cholim* are many and varied.
See "The Healing Visit" by Shafros and Zuchner for excellent insights and practical applications of this mitzvah.)

3. Someone who visits a sick person and does not pray for him has not fulfilled the mitzvah properly.[3] The Sages taught that one should not pay a visit during the early part of the day (when illnesses are generally at their mildest and the visitor will not be stirred to pray earnestly), nor in the last part of the day (as the patient is often at his worst then, and one might despair of his recovery and not pray for him properly).[4]

> *Although one can and should pray for a sick person even from a distance, the Sages insisted that prayers be said in the presence of the patient. The heart is moved more by what one sees than what one hears, and the more heartfelt the prayer, the more effective it is. Furthermore, since the Divine Presence rests on an ill person, prayers offered at his bedside are more likely to be accepted.[5]*

Visit for the Patient's Benefit

4. A person should visit only if doing so will be to the patient's benefit.[6]

> *One should not visit a patient with intestinal disorders or other conditions that cause him embarrassment.[7]*

Even if a visit will not be to the patient's benefit, one should still observe as much of the mitzvah as possible by stopping by the home or hospital and asking after his well-being, inquiring whether anything is needed and by rendering any possible assistance. He should listen to the accounts of the patient's troubles and pray for his recovery and well-being. Although this can largely be accomplished with a telephone call, and that, too, is considered a mitzvah, the kindness and effort of a personal visit is far greater and more effective. However, a person who for some reason is unable to visit should, at a minimum, call.[8]

---

3. *Yoreh Deah* 335:4.

4. Ibid. Note: If one is only able to visit at these times because of other commitments, it is better to go then than not to go at all (*Ahavas Chesed* ibid.).

5. See *Igros Moshe, Yoreh Deah* 223.

6. See fn. 7. See *Rambam, Hilchos Aveil* 14:5, who writes that the reason for not visiting a sick person during the early part of the day is that in the morning his needs are being attended to (as is the practice of modern hospitals, where doctors make their rounds and supervise patient treatment in the mornings). Accordingly, visits should be planned in accordance with the patient's actual schedule.

7. *Yoreh Deah* 335:8.

8. Ibid. *Ahavas Chesed* Part 3, Ch. 3; *Igros Moshe* ibid. 223.

It is often a lift to the patient (and/or his family) just to know that someone cares enough to come by, even if the patient was not in a condition for visitors.

Failure to Visit

5. The Sages taught that failure to visit a sick person is likened to murder.[9]

> *A student of Rabbi Akiva once became ill, and, for some reason, the Sages did not visit him. When Rabbi Akiva discovered this situation, he personally went to visit. Seeing that the patient was lying in the midst of dirt, Rabbi Akiva arranged for the premises to be cleaned. The student said, "Rabbi, you have given me life." Thereupon, Rabbi Akiva went to the beis midrash and taught that failure to visit the sick is tantamount to murder.[10]*

Even with doctors and nurses caring for patients in hospitals, there are still many needs that a visitor can attend to, and even more so if the patient is home (e.g. to provide company, prepare food for the patient or family, shop, pay bills, help care for children, etc.). Furthermore, a visitor may have knowledge of a particular doctor or treatment that could be helpful to the patient. This applies particularly if the sick person is poor or otherwise disadvantaged and one is able to arrange better care or more effective forms of treatment (in such a case, the mitzvah of *tzedakah* is involved as well). Ill people are also more likely to need help in maintaining the daily functioning of their families — there may even be no food in the house. Someone in a position to help who ignores a needy sick person violates the commandment, *You shall not stand aside while your fellow's blood is being shed (Vayikra 19:16).*[11]

6. Many communities have a society for tending to the needs of the ill (*Bikur Cholim*). Since it is not possible for each individual to see to these needs, the society shoulders the communal responsibility of tending to all who require its services. This function is highly commended; fortunate are those who have a share in the mitzvah.[12]

---

9. *Nedarim* 40a.

10. Ibid.

11. *Ahavas Chesed* Part 3, Ch. 3.

12. See ibid.

The Sages taught that those who visit the sick are saved from the judgment of Gehinnom, merit special Divine Providence to be saved from the Evil Inclination, are guided through life's troubles, are honored by all, and are helped to acquire good friends who will stand at their sides.[13]

Visiting the Sick

7. Upon being informed that a person is ill, relatives and close friends who are frequently in his home should visit immediately. Those less close to him should wait three days to avoid affecting his *mazal* by drawing attention to his illness. A person may sometimes be saved immediately if there is no public focus on his illness.[14] If, however, circumstances indicate differently (e.g. the patient wants visitors, has no close family or friends or they will not visit, or the illness struck suddenly and may be overwhelming him), then even less close associates should visit him immediately.[15]

8. A sick person may be visited even a number of times on the same day, for the more a person performs this mitzvah the more praiseworthy he is,[16] as long as the visits are not an imposition on the patient.

9. If for some reason the patient is lying on the floor, the visitor should not sit on a chair that is higher than him since the Divine Presence resides above the patient's head, as the Psalmist said, *Hashem will sustain him on the bed of his misery (Tehillim* 41:4). If the patient is lying on a bed, however, it is permitted to sit on a chair or bench.[17]

Spiritual Help and Prayer

10. Everything that happens to a person is Divinely ordained; there are no "coincidences." Illness is an indication of danger for the person who is sick, with the danger varying according to the gravity of the illness. Therefore, a person who is sick needs a greater measure of good deeds and prayer.[18]

---

13. *Nedarim* 40a.

14. *Rashi* ibid., s.v. *delo.*

15. *Yoreh Deah* 335:1. See "The Healing Visit" p. 37, quoting HaRav Chaim P. Sheinberg, and HaRav Elyashiv.

16. *Yoreh Deah* 335:2.

17. Ibid. 335:3.

18. *Shabbos* 32a.

Rav Yehudah said in the name of Rav: A person should always ask for mercy that he not take ill, for once he takes ill they (in the Heavenly tribunal) say, "Let him bring merits to be acquitted."[19]

11. Others, too, are enjoined to pray for their friend and contribute spiritually to his welfare with additional *tzedakah*, Torah and mitzvos.[20]

12. Anyone who has the ability to ask for mercy for an individual in need and does not do so is called a sinner. If the person in need is a Torah scholar one must beg for Hashem's mercy to the point where, figuratively, "one makes oneself sick."[21] Therefore, one should make a habit in the daily *tefillah* of heartfelt prayer for the sick in the *berachah Refa'einu*.

David said of his associates who turned against him: "And when they were sick, I donned sackcloth, I afflicted my soul with fasting" (Tehillim 35:13).

Praying While Visiting the Sick

13. It is incumbent upon a visitor to utter a prayer for the patient's recovery.[22]

The Sages taught: "Whoever visits a sick person causes him to live (because he prays for him)."[23]

14. When praying for mercy in the patient's presence, one may pray in any language (however, if not in his presence, the prayer should preferably be in Hebrew).[24] He should pray that the patient be granted a recovery among all other sick Jews so that the combined merit will help his prayers find acceptance.[25] Therefore, one says to the patient: *"May the A-mighty have compassion on you among all sick Jews."*

On Shabbos and Yom Tov (when prayers do not include personal requests because of the peaceful sanctity of the day), it is proper to

---

19. Ibid.
20. See *Nedarim* 40a.
21. *Berachos* 12b.
22. *Yoreh Deah* 335:4.
23. *Nedarim* 40a.
24. *Yoreh Deah* 335:5, see *Taz* 4.
25. Ibid. 335:6.

say: "*Shabbos (Yom Tov) prevents us from crying out, but the healing is soon to come, His compassion is great and rest in peace.*"[26]

15. Someone who has a sick person in his house should go to the sage of the city (e.g. the Rosh Yeshivah or the senior rav) to ask him to pray for mercy for the patient. The custom is to make the blessing *Mi she'beirach* in shul on behalf of a sick person.[27] (The congregation should make a point of answering "Amen" with the intention of affirming the prayer for the patient's recovery.)

16. There is a custom to give a gravely ill person an additional name, so that a decree issued against the patient under his old name will not have force on the person bearing the new name.[28] (This should be done with the advice of a rav.)

Healing — The Obligation and Its Parameters

17. A doctor is obligated to heal the sick to the best of his abilities.[29]

> One may ask, "Since healing is in the hands of Hashem, why does the doctor have an obligation to heal?"
>
> Hashem created a world of "cause and effect" directed by Him alone.[30] This reality gives a human being the most basic aspect of his humanity: free will. Because a person eats, he feels satiated; therefore, he can choose to do the mitzvah of feeding the hungry. Because he has money he can buy food and clothing; therefore, he can choose to give tzedakah to the poor and alleviate their plight. A disease is cured by a certain medication; therefore, a doctor can prescribe it and perform the mitzvah of healing the sick. This is the purpose of creation: to choose that which is right and to avoid wrong.[31] Thus, the world of "cause and effect" is the framework within which a person can operate his "free will."
>
> If a person wrongly exercises free will by recklessly exposing himself to disease or danger, he violates the basic injunction to guard his life and health which were Divinely bestowed to accomplish his life's

---

26. Ibid.

27. Ibid. 335:10, *Rema*.

28. Ibid.

29. *Yoreh Deah* 336:1.

30. See *Bereishis* 2:4, *Rashi*, s.v. *Hashem*; *Orach Chaim* 5.

31. *Devarim* 30:15.

tasks. He then deserves the effect of illness or accident that he chose to bring upon himself.[32] However, Hashem may decide to bring illness even on a person who acted very responsibly, and directs the cause and effect toward that end.

If Hashem wants a person to be fed, He will cause him to meet his kindly benefactor. Similarly, if Hashem wants an ill person to recover, He will cause him to meet the doctor who will heal him. However, if Hashem does not wish the person to be healed, He will direct "cause and effect" that way.

Thus, Hashem alone directs "cause and effect." Our task in life is to exercise free will. A doctor can choose to treat a patient, exercising his free will for "right"; he has chosen to fulfill Hashem's mitzvah of returning a person to life and health.[33] If he chooses "wrong," and does not treat the patient, his negligence is considered tantamount to murder.[34]

18. Even if a sick person already has one doctor treating him, other doctors should take an interest in his case, if possible; one can never know in whose hands Heaven will place the merit of curing this particular patient (see footnote).[35]

19. A person should not practice medicine unless fully qualified to do so. (Every doctor therefore has a *halachic* responsibility to maintain his medical knowledge at a high level.) If one doctor knows that a more expert doctor is available to treat a particular patient, he should consult with him or defer to his more qualified colleague.[36]

---

32. See *Kesubos* 30a.

33. *Yoreh Deah* ibid.

34. *Nedarim* 40a.

35. *Yoreh Deah* 336:1. Note: The wording of *Shulchan Aruch* indicates that even if a person is being treated by a doctor, another physician cannot refuse to treat him, as one cannot know who will have the merit of curing this individual. Thus, a person who has a regular doctor, and chooses to turn to someone else for a certain illness, should not be refused treatment because he ought to see his own doctor. However, if a person is already being treated, he obviously cannot be treated by two doctors simultaneously. Nevertheless, the concept of each doctor's responsibility to do his utmost for any patient — as one never knows whom Heaven will merit to bring about a cure — indicates that he should not avoid taking an interest in a given case; perhaps his approach will work for a particular patient. This is the reasoning for the text.

36. Ibid. Note: The wording of *Shulchan Aruch* is that only an expert is permitted to engage in healing; there should be no one greater in his field. The implication is that only the best doctor in town should engage in healing (just as only the greatest scholars in the area should rule on Torah questions). In the context of modern medicine, a doctor has a minimal obligation to consult with someone more expert than himself on any medical question that is not clear cut.

20. A doctor who inadvertently causes damage to a patient is required to compensate him.[37] A doctor who inadvertently kills a patient is considered an inadvertent murderer (see *Bamidbar* Chapter 35).[38] Nevertheless, a doctor should not refrain from treating patients out of a fear of making mistakes, nor should he worry that he may have made a mistake, since he is performing a mitzvah.[39] However, if he knows that he has harmed someone,[40] he should consult a rav for advice.

21. The Torah does not allow a doctor to charge for treating fellow Jews since one is not permitted to charge money for the performance of a mitzvah.[41] Today, however, when doctors practice full time and rely on their medical income to continue their work, they are permitted to accept payment for their services.[42]

22. Similarly, it is forbidden to charge an unreasonable price for medications that are needed by a sick Jew.[43]

> A Torah Jew should be aware that the Torah does not permit profiteering on medications.[44]

Conflicting Schedules

23. A person who is studying Torah is obligated to visit the sick only if the mitzvah cannot be accomplished through others.[45] (This and the following *halachos* apply to all the mitzvos of kindness: comforting mourners, rejoicing at a wedding, etc.) Part of the mitzvah of visiting the sick is to utter a prayer at their bedside. Since there is no limit to prayer, nor can one person's prayer be replaced by another's,

---

37. The patient may not have a clear right to collect damages in *beis din*; in Heaven, however, the doctor is held liable. (See *Yoreh Deah* ibid.)

38. Ibid.

39. *Ramban, Toras HaAdam; Shach* 1,3.

40. See *Yoreh Deah* ibid.

41. Ibid. 336:2, see also *Shach* 4.

42. This is comparable to the practice of Rabbanim and teachers who receive pay even though, strictly speaking, accepting money to teach Torah is not permitted. Since they teach full time and cannot do other work, they can continue teaching only if an income is provided.

43. Ibid. 336:3.

44. See also the end of Ch. 39.

45. *Yoreh Deah* 246:18.

the prayer aspect of visiting the sick is considered a mitzvah that cannot be carried out by others.[46]

24. Involvement in one mitzvah exempts a person from getting involved in another.[47]

> Since it is a mitzvah for a mother to care for her small children,[48] she is exempt from the mitzvos of kindness if doing so will interfere with her children's care.[49]

25. If an individual cannot visit a sick person unless he takes off from work (e.g. visiting hours are only during his working hours) he is still obligated to do the mitzvah unless there is a danger of losing his job and being thrown into poverty.[50]

26. When faced with a choice between the mitzvos of visiting the sick and comforting mourners, one should first visit the sick in order to pray for Hashem's mercy for the patient, provided that he will later be able to comfort the mourners as well. If, however, there is time for only one of the mitzvos, then comforting the mourners takes priority, since it is a kindness to both the living and the dead.[51]

Visiting Others

27. One should also visit non-Jews who are ill, since the kindly character traits that the Torah develops in a person extend to all human beings.[52]

28. One should not visit a sick enemy, nor pay a condolence call on an enemy in mourning so as not to seem to be gloating over his misfortune, although each case depends on the individuals involved and the nature of their relationship. However, it is not considered gloating to attend an enemy's funeral, since this is the end that awaits every human being.[53]

---

46. *Igros Moshe, Yoreh Deah* 223.

47. *Orach Chaim* 38:8, *Rema.*

48. *Kesubos* 49a, 50a.

49. At a certain moment a mother may not be involved with her children; however, she needs this time to rest up or prepare for them, and she is considered "involved in her mitzvah" and exempt from other mitzvos. See *Orach Chaim* 38, *Beur Halachah,* s.v. *im tzarich.*

50. *Yoreh Deah* 240, *Taz* 7.

51. *Yoreh Deah* 335:10, *Rema, Shach* 11.

52. Ibid. 335:9.

53. Ibid. 335:2, *Rema, Shach* 2.

Patients With Serious Illnesses

29. A person afflicted with a serious illness should pay extra attention not to leave the world with unfinished affairs. *There is no reason to fear* that attending to these affairs will "cause" one to die.[54] To the contrary, adding mitzvos to one's treasury of mitzvos is a merit for life.

> ❏ *Perhaps this person lent money or items to others or borrowed money or items and subsequently forgot about them.*[55]
> ❏ *He should also ask forgiveness from anyone he has offended.*[56]

There are many *halachos* relevant to a dangerously ill person; the family should be in constant contact with a rav for guidance regarding specific situations.

30. A patient nearing death should be told to confess his sins; one should tell him that many have confessed and did not die, and many have not confessed and died. Confessing one's sins is itself a merit to live, and he who confesses has a place in the World to Come. If he cannot confess verbally he should confess in his heart, and if he does not know how to confess he should state, "Let my death be an atonement for all my sins." These statements should not be made in front of ignoramuses, nor women or children, lest they break down crying and the patient's spirit, too, will be broken.[57]

> *The following is the confession of a person nearing death:*
> *"I admit before You, Hashem, my G-d and the G-d of my fathers, that my healing and death are in Your Hands. May it be Your will that I should be healed completely, and, if I will die, may my death be an atonement for all my sins, iniquities and rebelliousness that I have sinned and rebelled before You. Give me a portion in Gan Eden, and give me merit for the World to Come which is hidden for the righteous." (If he so desires, he can continue with the entire confession of Yom Kippur.)*[58]

31. A person who ministers to a patient's spiritual needs by urging him to repent while there is still time can have the immeasurable

---

54. Ibid. 335:7.

55. Ibid.

56. *Ahavas Chesed* Part 3, Ch. 3.

57. *Yoreh Deah* 338:1.

58. Ibid. 338:2.

merit of saving him from harsh judgments and the fires of Gehinnom and winning for him eternal life. Of such an individual the Psalmist says, *Fortunate is the one who contemplates the needy* (*Tehillim* 41:2). Both courage and sensitivity are required to find the most effective approach to stir the patient to confess his sins and ask Hashem for mercy without causing him undue distress. A patient with resources should be reminded to give generous *tzedakah,* as King Shlomo wrote, *Tzedakah saves from death* (*Mishlei* 10:2).[59]

---

59. *Ahavas Chesed* ibid. Note: A person who can use his resources for eternity by arranging in his lifetime to use them for the mitzvos of upholding Torah and *tzedakah* after his death, thus constantly gains merit. A person should not wait for illness, but should arrange this when he is still healthy. He should not rely on his children, who may think that since their father has passed on, he no longer has any use for his resources. See *Ahavas Chesed* Part 3, Ch. 4 for further elaboration.

58

Comforting Mourners

The Importance of Mourning

1. The death of a Jew is comparable to the burning of a *Sefer Torah*, as there is no Jew who does not possess some measure of Torah and mitzvos.[1]

2. A person who fails to mourn as the Sages commanded, and acts as if nothing of great significance occurred, is considered cruel. A mourner should instead realize that Hashem's trait of justice has struck very close to him, with the purpose of moving him to examine his deeds and repent.[2]

> *And know and understand that afflictions from Hashem are for a person's benefit; for if a person sinned and did what Hashem considers evil, the afflictions from Hashem have a dual purpose. The first is to atone for his sins and remove them … and the second is to remind a person to retract from evil paths. But if he doesn't accept these afflictions and accept the Heavenly rebuke, woe to him, woe to his soul, for he has suffered afflictions but his sins have not been for-*

---

1. *Shabbos* 105b, Rashi, s.v. *she'nisraf.*

2. *Rambam, Hilchos Aveil* 13:12.

given, but rather his punishment has been doubled (because of the sin of not repenting) (Shaarei Teshuvah 2:3).

3. The Sages taught: "When one member of a group dies, the entire group has to worry."[3]

    Although there is no obligation to mourn a friend or associate, one must engage in introspection.

Eulogizing the Departed

4. It is a great mitzvah to deliver a fitting eulogy for the departed,[4] for this brings him honor.[5] The Sages said that anyone who is lax in eulogizing a Torah scholar deserves to be buried alive, and will not live a long life. On the other hand, when one cries over any upright Jew, Hashem counts his tears and preserves them in His storehouse.[6]

Who Should Attend the Funeral

5. If there are not enough men to attend to the burial of a Jew (i.e. to prepare the body for burial and form a *minyan* for *Kaddish*), even if he did not study Torah at all it is permitted to interrupt Torah studies for both the funeral and burial. For a person who did learn regularly (even if he studied only Scriptures or Mishnah), his honor demands the presence of up to 600,000 people;[7] thus, that many individuals may interrupt their Torah studies to do him this honor. If the departed had the merit of teaching Torah to others, his honor is unlimited, and there is therefore no limit on the number of people who may interrupt their studies to accord him this honor.[8]

    Note: In any situation where it is permitted to interrupt Torah study for the sake of a funeral, one should do so.

6. The previous paragraph focuses only on interrupting Torah studies to attend a funeral. However, anyone who works is required to leave his job in order to participate in this mitzvah for any Jew.[9]

---

3. Ibid.

4. *Yoreh Deah* 344:1.

5. *Rambam* ibid. 12:1.

6. *Shabbos* 105b; see also *Rambam* ibid. 12:2, who modifies the Gemara slightly.

7. Since the Torah was given in the presence of 600,000 men, it is fitting that the same number be present when someone who possessed Torah is escorted from the world.

8. *Yoreh Deah* 361:1-2.

9. Ibid.

Note: It would seem from the *halachah* that all the inhabitants of a city are obligated to attend every funeral. However, in large cities, not even great Torah scholars go to each one. As the deeds of our Sages demonstrate Torah teachings, one cannot obligate a person who lives in a large city to attend every funeral. Nevertheless, a person should do so within his own community circles. Furthermore, if one sees a passing funeral one must join for at least four *amos*, as discussed in paragraph 7. One is not required to travel to another city to attend a funeral.

7. Anyone who sees a funeral in progress and does not join the procession for at least four *amos* is considered to be mocking the departed.[10]

> *"One who makes fun of a poor person insults his (the poor man's) Maker" (Mishlei 17:5). A departed person is considered poor, and anyone who escorts him is honoring Hashem.*[11]

A person who is unable to join the escort for some reason is still required to stand when the procession passes by, just as one is always required to stand in the presence of those involved in performing a mitzvah.[12]

8. Children are never to be interrupted from their Torah studies for this or any other mitzvah, up to and including the building of the *Beis HaMikdash* (since the world continues to exist only in the merit of the Torah that emerges from their mouths which are as yet unsullied by sin).[13]

Comforting Mourners

9. It is a mitzvah to comfort mourners. This is considered a kindness to the living as well as the dead.

> *Hashem himself comforted Yitzchak after Avraham's death.*

Those coming to comfort are not allowed to speak until the mourner speaks, as we find that Iyov's friends did not speak[14] until he spoke to them. As soon as the comforters see that the mourner no longer wishes their presence, they are not allowed to remain.[15]

---

10. Ibid 361:3.

11. *Berachos* 18a.

12. *Yoreh Deah* 361:4 and *Taz* 2; see also *Pischei Teshuvah* 3 and *Chiddushei R' Akiva Eiger.*

13. *Yoreh Deah* 361:1, see also *Shach* 6 and *Beur HaGra* 3.

14. See *Iyov* 2:13, 3:1 and 4:1.

15. *Yoreh Deah* 376:1.

10. When not actually comforting the mourners, one should not speak at all.

> *When Aharon's two sons were killed, the Torah says, "Aharon was silent." (Silence indicates the humility of a mortal in the face of a Divine decree.)*

It is not even proper to speak Torah in a house of mourning, except as it relates to the issues of mourning; it is certainly wrong to engage in idle talk and banter.[16] People should speak about the departed's good qualities, the meaning of life or other appropriate topics. (Those who learn from and appreciate the finer qualities of the departed as an inspiration for their own life certainly bring great merit to the departed. See paragraph 15.)

11. Mourners and sick people are not required to stand up as a mark of honor for any visitors, even for those whom one normally honors by rising.[17]

12. When one person wishes to stand as a gesture of respect for another, it is considered common courtesy for the second person to tell the first to sit. However, one does not say this to a mourner or a sick person, since the implication is that he sit and remain in his current position of mourning or illness.[18]

13. A mourner should not say, "I am so bad. I deserve more tragedy. I haven't yet been punished for all my wrongdoings."[19]

14. One should not say, "What can you do — we can't change what Hashem does," since this implies that it would be desirable to change Hashem's actions if we could. Rather, we have to accept Hashem's decrees with love.[20]

> *This can be illustrated with the following parable:*
> *Two paupers, Reuven and Shimon, having no proper housing, were forced to sleep on a park bench and begged for a few dollars to buy some food. Mr. Gold, a wealthy person, noticed these two paupers one day and decided to help them — each in a different way. He*

---

16. Ibid. 378:7.
17. Ibid. 376:1, *Rema*.
18. *Yoreh Deah* 376:2.
19. Ibid., *Rema*.
20. Ibid.

presented Reuven with a sizable check and promised a similar check each month. Reuven was thrilled with the possibility of a normal life and couldn't thank Mr. Gold enough for his kindness. He could now rent an apartment, buy decent food and clothing, and stop begging. Every single month Mr. Gold's check arrived in the mail, and Reuven thanked him profusely each time.

For Shimon, however, Mr. Gold decided to arrange a system of support whereby he would receive an anonymous bank check each month. Shimon, too, was thrilled with his new life, but had no idea of his benefactor's identity.

This continued month after month, year after year, until the day, ten years later, when the checks stopped. Both Reuven and Shimon heard that Mr. Gold was involved in the cessation of their checks; their reactions, however, were very different. Reuven knew that Mr. Gold, his great benefactor, was a very kindly person and must have a very good reason for stopping the checks. He certainly wasn't angry with Mr. Gold, whose actions were always done out of kindness. Shimon, however, did not know the name of his benefactor; he only knew that Mr. Gold had stopped his checks. He was very angry, exclaiming, "That rasha (wicked person) caused me to lose my source of livelihood."

Many people are like Shimon and do not know their Benefactor. The fact that a person is alive, healthy, and has food to eat is taken for granted. However, as soon as something bad happens, they relate it to Hashem and are very angry at Him. How then can they accept His Decree with love?

However, if, like Reuven, a person realizes the truth, and all through the years sees his health, livelihood, and life itself as manifold kindnesses of the Great Benefactor Who loves His creatures, he can begin to understand that this Benefactor performs only kindnesses. What we see as bad and evil are really kindnesses too, even when we cannot fathom how and are feeling sadness and pain. Even in times of trouble, such a person will continue to love his Loving Benefactor Whose every action is one of kindness; His Kindness is Truth, and His Truth is Kindness. He will thus be able to accept the Divine Decree with love.

Kindness to the Departed

15. There are a number of things we can do to give pleasure to the soul of the departed and to help it in the next world. While some apply only to the departed's children, there are many that can

be undertaken by any friend or relative. In the remainder of this chapter, we will summarize six categories of activities, in ascending order of importance, as presented in *Succas Shalom* by HaGaon R' Eliyahu Gutmacher.[21]

(a) When a son says *Kaddish*, receives the honor of *Maftir* on Shabbos, or leads the services on *Motza'ei Shabbos*, he redeems his parent from Gehinnom by sanctifying Hashem's Name in public. Also, answering *Amen, Yehei Shemei Rabba* with proper concentration helps ameliorate judgments decreed against parents for not answering properly.[22]

(b) As a general rule, leading the services is even more helpful to the departed's soul, but only if one knows how to do so properly and does not garble the words or speak too softly for the congregation to follow. Otherwise, it is better to refrain from leading the services.

(c) Active performance of mitzvos (giving *tzedakah*, lending money or objects, helping a person in need, hospitality, etc.) helps *even more*. (Whenever possible, people should make a point during their lifetime of directing their children to devote themselves to one particular mitzvah.) Some people erroneously think that saying *Kaddish* and leading the services are the only means of giving the departed pleasure, and as a result engage in disputes in shul over the right to do so. Such individuals should be informed that by excelling in mitzvos, especially those of benefit to the public, during the mourning period or on a *yahrzeit*, they can do far more to help the departed's soul than through *Kaddish* and *tefillah*. Such mitzvos can also be performed by anyone to help the soul of any departed person.

> *A person who lost a close relative or friend could think of a mitzvah that needs to be done (such as establishing a free-loan society, or aiding distressed people, new mothers, or children with learning problems) and try to do it as a merit for that person. (Since the departure of that person and the desire to do him a kindness is what spurred the person to the mitzvah, the departed shares in its merit.)*

---

21. A giant 19th-century Torah scholar in both the revealed and hidden aspects of Torah.

22. Translator's note: See *Mateh Efraim, Hilchos Kaddish Yasom* 4:8, who writes that even though a woman cannot say *Kaddish* for a parent, by listening carefully and answering *Amen, Yehei Shemei Rabba* with full force (i.e. concentration and the intention to affirm what is being said) she can achieve the same effect as if she had said the *Kaddish* herself.

(d) Still more beneficial to the soul of the departed is Torah study, at least of *Mishnayos* and preferably of Gemara and *halachah,* since the study of applied *halachah* has enormous power to elevate the soul of the departed.[23] In any case, it is helpful to study *Mishnayos* with a commentary that mentions the *halachos* which emerge from the *Mishnayos.* Before starting to study one should say, "For the elevation of the soul of So-and-so the son/daughter of So-and-so."

A person who cannot learn can pay someone else to learn for his relative or friend.

(e) It is even more helpful to the departed to engage in this learning with a *minyan.*

(f) It is desirable to combine Torah and *tefillah,* e.g by studying before or after *Shacharis* or between *Minchah* and *Maariv.* After finishing learning, someone should say the Mishnah (*Makkos* 3:16), "Rabbi Chananya ben Akashya says ..." followed by *Kaddish d'Rabbanan.*

16. The *Zohar* (cited by *Kitzur Shulchan Aruch* 26:22) states: "*The mitzvah of honoring parents can be fulfilled by serving them food and drink, but these apply only during the parents' lifetimes, and then a child is obligated to do so. However, if you would think that children are exempt from this mitzvah when the parents have departed, this is not so, for even though they are dead, the child has an even greater obligation to honor them. If the child goes in a corrupt path, it is certainly a discredit to the parents and he certainly dishonors them. But if the child goes in the path of righteousness and acts honorably, it is certainly an honor to his parents, both in this world as regards other people and in the next world before Hashem, and Hashem will have mercy on them and give them an honored place.*"

---

23. There is a widespread custom to study *Mishnayos* in particular since the word Mishnah contains the same letters as the word *neshamah,* soul.

59

Rejoicing at Weddings

1. It is a mitzvah to bring joy to a *chasan* (groom) and *kallah* (bride) at their wedding.[1]

> *When Hashem created Adam and Chavah in the Garden of Eden, He brought Chavah to Adam with joy, so that they should rejoice with each other.*[2]

This is an obligatory mitzvah of kindness. One may interrupt one's Torah study in order to bring rejoicing to a couple.[3]

> *When a wedding procession passed, Rabbi Yehudah would interrupt his Torah studies and go with his students to dance for the bride*[4] *and bring the couple joy.*

---

1. *Berachos* 6b; *Kesubos* 17a.

2. *Bereishis* 2:22; *Berachos* 61a.

3. *Kesubos* 17a.

4. In ancient times, the *kallah* would be betrothed for a period before the actual "wedding," which was a procession from the home of the girl to her new husband's home accompanied by her family and friends. This entourage constituted the "wedding procession," and anyone whom they passed was obligated to join them for a short period. These "guests" sang and "danced in front of the bride," i.e. in front of the procession, to join in their

2. The essence of this rejoicing is described by the prophet Yirmiyahu:

> It was months before the final destruction; the Ten Tribes were long gone. The Babylonian soldiers had already captured the countryside and were laying siege to Jerusalem. The weary Judean soldiers were fighting both famine and the Babylonians — and the atmosphere was very gloomy. In a walled area near the Beis HaMikdash, the great prophet Yirmiyahu was incarcerated for prophetically advising the people to surrender and save their lives. From this jail, he sadly watched his own prophecy come true.
>
> Suddenly, there was a visitation from Hashem. "Call to Me, and I will answer you, and I will show you great and mighty things which you do not know ... So says Hashem, the G-d of Israel, about the houses of this city which are destroyed because of the hordes (of soldiers) and the sword ... I will bring them healing ... So says Hashem ... It will again be heard in this place, which you say is desolate from man and beast, in the cities of Judah and the streets of Jerusalem ... a voice of joy and a voice of happiness, a voice of chasan and a voice of kallah, a voice saying 'Thank Hashem for He is good, for His kindness is eternal,' bringing a thanksgiving offering to the House of Hashem ... " (Yirmiyahu 33:3-13).

When Hashem wanted to describe the opposite of death and desolation, He described a life of joy, happiness, *chasan* and *kallah*, thanking Hashem for His Eternal kindness and goodness — this is the

---

rejoicing. Their participation created an atmosphere of a major event occurring, giving a feeling of importance to the future wife and mother in Israel. Thus, the Sages decreed that it is obligatory to interrupt even one's Torah studies for the bridal procession. When the *kallah* and her entourage reached her new husband's home they would feast there for a week in order to provide an atmosphere of joy as they began to establish their new home. At the feast the essence of the mitzvah was to provide words of happiness and encouragement (see paragraph 4).

For the past many hundreds of years the custom has been to betroth and marry simultaneously in a specific place under a canopy (e.g. the courtyard of the shul). Thus, the *chuppah* (marriage canopy) has taken the place of the entourage (see *Even HaEzer* 65, *Beis Shmuel* 3), and one is obligated to attend in order to bestow importance on this major event and to join in the happiness of the wedding. However, it would seem that the main obligation to attend a wedding is either when there are not enough guests to convey a feeling of importance and happiness (see paragraph 7), or if one is a close friend whose presence is of importance to the *chasan* or *kallah* and will bring them happiness. The presence of a certain person may only be of great importance to a parent or grandparent; this is included in the mitzvah of kindness to a "fellow" Jew (see Ch. 1). Although attending any wedding is a mitzvah, it would seem that interrupting Torah study in order to attend a wedding is an obligation only in the two specific cases described above. One is not technically obligated to travel to a wedding in another city; however, it is often a great mitzvah to do so depending on the circumstances.

essence of pure life. All sorrow and destruction are the result of man's folly, his lack of appreciation and misuse of his life. However, "life" in its essence is constant joy and happiness with the Source of life, and constant appreciation of His kindness and goodness. This, too, is the essence of groom and bride, on whose harmonious union dwells the Divine Presence, and from whom springs new life. Their rejoicing is the rejoicing of the essence of life with the Source of life, appreciating His goodness and kindness and reflecting and emulating these traits, bringing harmony and serenity to their own lives. This is the rejoicing which the Holy Nation brings to each of its sons and daughters as they embark on establishing a new home.

3. The primary purpose in attending a wedding is not to have a good time or to enjoy the meal and refreshments, but rather to bring the joy of Torah life to the young couple.[5]

> *The Sages said that anyone who enjoys a wedding feast and does not help the couple rejoice thwarts the five "voices" evoked by the prophet: a voice of joy, a voice of happiness, a voice of chasan, a voice of kallah, a voice that says, "Thank Hashem for He is good" (Yirmiyahu 33:11). A person who does bring the couple joy will merit Torah and it is considered as if he had brought a thanksgiving offering and as if he had rebuilt one of the ruins of the desolate Jerusalem.*

4. Although one sings and dances at a wedding, the main reward of bringing joy to the couple is with words.[6] Words of happiness and encouragement give them high spirits; it is especially important to endear the couple and the two families to each other.

> *When one dances before the kallah, what does one say? The kallah is na'ah and chasudah (indicating that she radiates attractiveness and kindliness). This is said for every kallah even if she does not stand out in these qualities.[7]*

Conceivably, the *kallah* could be made attractive in the *chasan's* eyes when men gaze at her, creating the impression that society considers his wife highly attractive; this is absolutely forbidden.[8]

---

5. *Berachos* 6b.

6. Ibid. See *Rashi*, s.v. *mili.*

7. *Kesubos* 17a.

8. Ibid. It is a Torah prohibition for a man to gaze at a woman because of her attractiveness. The Gemara discusses whether this is permitted for the ulterior motive of endearing the *kallah* to her husband, and the decision was handed down that it is forbidden, and thus a Torah prohibition.

5. In particular, one should take care not to defeat the whole essence of the mitzvah by belittling the couple or their families or through any other form of *lashon hara*. On the contrary, one should do everything in his power to endear all the parties to each other and encourage them to cooperate in every possible way in establishing the new family.[9]

6. The Sages went to extreme lengths at weddings in singing praises to Hashem and creating a joyful atmosphere.[10] Although the Sages have forbidden song and music in memory of the destruction of the *Beis HaMikdash*, the universal practice is to accompany weddings with joyful songs of praise to Hashem for all His kindnesses.[11] Nevertheless, the Sages warned not to overdo the levity so that people should not forget the fear of Heaven.

> At the wedding of the son of Mar, the son of Ravina, he saw the Sages going too far. He shattered an expensive white glass cup as a reminder to the people not to forget themselves.[12]

Disadvantaged Couples

7. The importance of the mitzvah is multiplied many times when there are special circumstances or the couple is in some way disadvantaged, e.g. if the parties are orphans, impoverished, or have parents who rather than helping their children, leave them to fend for themselves. In such cases, there is a very great mitzvah to help the

---

9. See Ch. 28 par. 36.

10. *Berachos* 30b-31a.

11. *Rif* ad loc. There are opinions that music is generally forbidden, while others hold that it is forbidden only at a party or similar circumstances. However, singing songs of praise to Hashem at weddings is universally accepted (*Orach Chaim* 560:3).

12. *Berachos* ibid. *Rashi* indicates that the over-rejoicing made it "appear" that they were forgetting the yoke of Heaven, and smashing the glass served as a reminder. On our level, it would be an accomplishment not to completely forget the yoke of Heaven.

Note: In reality, the ultimates of rejoicing and fearing Hashem are not at all contradictory. Quite the opposite, they are highly complementary, and one leads to the other; thus, there should be no concern that "over-rejoicing" will lead to levity. However, this is true only of a pure soul, within which fear and love of Hashem and Torah and the joy of life all merge into one. The Sages teach us that such absolute purity will not exist in this world until the future redemption; therefore, every person, even sublime souls such as the Talmudic Sages, must guard that the joy of mitzvah not spill over into joy of *aveirah*. How much more so in our lowly generation; while we must search for joy in our life through Hashem, His Torah and mitzvos, and our souls need that joy for their very sustenance (which even on our level is coupled and complemented by fear of Heaven), at the same time we must guard that it not spill over into the sort of false transient rejoicing that leads to *aveirah*.

couple rejoice,[13] as well as to provide the needy families with financial and other material assistance to make weddings for their children and establish them in homes of their own.[14] There is no limit to the reward of providing assistance so that people can marry.[15]

> *It is only permitted to sell a Sefer Torah for two reasons: to provide funds for Torah study or to help a needy person get married.*[16]

Mitzvah With *Aveirah*

8. Doing a mitzvah does not permit one to commit transgressions.

> *A person should not attend a wedding[17] if he knows that improper activities will take place there and he is likely to transgress the commandment of the Torah, "Do not follow your eyes …" (Bamidbar 15:39) that prohibits a man from "gazing" at a woman. (See footnote.)*[18]

9. On some occasions, a person's presence may be sorely needed, yet the Torah does not permit the violation of any transgressions.

> *There are couples who need great encouragement, but they or their families may be unaware of the Torah way of separating men and women. In such cases, a rav should be consulted; perhaps there is some way to attend while simultaneously avoiding transgressions.*[19]

---

13. *Ahavas Chesed* Part 3, Ch. 6.

14. Ibid.

15. *Pe'ah* 1:1.

16. *Even HaEzer* 1:2; see *Beis Shmuel* 2.

17. *Ahavas Chesed* ibid.

18. *Even HaEzer* 21:1. According to Western culture's view of morality, only actual physical acts are considered immoral while merely "looking" is deemed innocent. The Divine Torah, however, views the human being as an elevated G-d-like being whose every faculty is sacred. His sensual feelings are sacred as well, to be used for his spouse alone as expressions of deep love. When misused, they become expressions of animalistic feelings, stripping the woman of her status as a person and classifying her as a mere object for his whim. By dressing in provocative style, she too, in essence, denies her own humanity and proclaims herself an animal object. Denying one's own elevated G-d-like humanity is called *ra* (evil) and is anathema to Hashem. (Note: Notice the common denominator between this *ra* and *lashon hara* (evil gossip). The subject, as a person, is irrelevant in both; one person says or does as he feels while the other's feelings and humanity become completely irrelevant.) We are commanded to sanctify ourselves to the greatest possible extent. Therefore, going to a place where one will be exposed to women who dress or act immodestly is forbidden. See also fn. 19.

19. See *Bava Basra* 57b that passing near a river where women launder clothing (and thereby may be improperly exposed) is prohibited, even if he turns the other way, since he could have chosen a different route. It is permitted, however, if there was no other route, provided

Funeral or Wedding

10. When faced with a choice between attending a funeral or a wedding one should give precedence to the funeral,[20] although some are of the opinion that participating in the *chuppah* takes precedence.[21] However, if given a choice between comforting mourners sitting *shivah* and going to a *sheva berachos* (and it is not possible to do both), one should comfort the mourners, as King Shlomo writes, *The heart of the wise is in the house of a mourner and the heart of the fool is in the house of feasting* (*Koheles* 7:4).[22]

---

that he does not "gaze" improperly. Although all weddings where immodesty takes place should be shunned, the mitzvah of attendance is so great in some cases that, in effect, there is "no other route." Thus, if there is any way to avoid transgressions he should attend. Obviously, this depends on the strength of character of the individual as well as the extent of immodesty at the wedding. A rav should be consulted for advice in all such situations.

20. *Rambam, Hilchos Aveil* 14:8.

21. *Ramban* quoted in *Kesef Mishneh* ad loc.

22. *Kesef Mishneh* ibid.

❧ Emulating Hashem's Ways

Chapter 60

60

Emulating
the Ways of Hashem

1. The Torah commands us to follow Hashem's ways, i.e. to attempt to emulate His qualities to the best of our ability. We learn this mitzvah from the verse, *You shall go in His ways* (*Devarim* 28:9). The Sages offer us guidance as to how to observe it: "Just as Hashem is compassionate, you should also be compassionate. Just as He does acts of kindness for people such as comforting mourners, visiting the sick, and rejoicing with a bride and groom, so too should you do these things." While the Sages chose these activities as examples, there is really no limit to the ways in which Hashem's attributes find expression, and no limit to the ways in which we can emulate them if we only make the effort to look.[1]

> *A great Torah scholar once visited Rav Yisrael Salanter. After spending some time together, the visiting rav arose to take his leave. Rav Yisrael prepared to leave as well, holding a packet of money. Curious, the visitor inquired as to Rav Yisrael's destination. Rav Yisrael replied that the money belonged to Rav Ploni and he was taking it to him. The rav asked, "Why travel all that way when you could send it with someone else?" Rav Yisrael answered, "In my*

---

1. *Rambam, Hilchos Dei'os* 1:6.

opinion, I am obligated to take it myself." The visiting scholar, who was quite close to Rav Yisrael, commented, half in jest, "If this were a Gemara I would also know it." Rav Yisrael countered accordingly, "Perhaps it isn't in your Gemara, but it is in mine!" Highly curious, the rav begged Rav Yisrael to explain the riddle.

His answer was as follows: The Gemara states[2] that toward the end of King David's life there was a three-year famine. David beseeched Heaven to reveal the cause of the famine and he was then given two reasons: first, that the people did not eulogize King Shaul properly, and second, that when King Shaul killed the Kohanim of Nov, no amends were made for the great suffering of their servants, the Givonim. The Gemara comments that the two reasons seem contradictory; the first teaches the righteousness of King Shaul as he was not properly eulogized, while the second mentions his sin of killing the Kohanim of Nov and all the subsequent suffering. The Gemara's answer is that this is an attribute of Hashem; when He mentions a person's sins He simultaneously mentions his greatness.

"I, too," said Rav Yisrael, "must criticize Rav Ploni for behavior that, in my opinion, was amiss. As I am obligated to emulate the ways of Hashem, I have to honor the target of my criticism for the greatness that he does have. By troubling myself to travel to this rav and return the money to him personally, I am honoring his Torah learning and good deeds at the same time that I criticize him."

Rav Yitzchak Blazer (one of Rav Yisrael's great students) commented: The "ways of the world" are the opposite: when making a positive comment about an individual, people are "careful" to limit the praise by mentioning a negative trait as well. Rav Yisrael, on the other hand, learned this Gemara and applied it to his own life to emulate Hashem and do the opposite![3]

2. In the last three verses *of Sefer Michah* the prophet alludes to thirteen principal traits of Hashem's goodness and mercy: *O God, Who is like You, Who bears iniquity and passes over transgression for the remnant of His heritage? He does not retain His wrath eternally for He desires kindness. He will again be merciful to us; He will suppress our iniquities and cast into the depths of the sea all their sins. Grant truth to Jacob, kindness to Abraham, as You swore to our forefathers from ancient times (7:18-20). The*

2. *Yevamos* 78a.

3. *Ohr Yisrael, Nesivos Ohr* pp. 116-117.

giant Sage and Kabbalist, Rabbi Moshe Cordevero, elaborates in his *Tomer Devorah* on these thirteen traits of Hashem and explains how they can be emulated by every person in practical daily life.

3. The *first* attribute is derived from the phrase *0 God, Who is like You.*

Hashem has infinite patience and tolerates those who insult Him, as seen from the fact that He maintains the existence of the entirety of Creation at all times, so that even at the very moment that a person sins, Hashem continues to give life and health not only to the sinner, but to the very limb or organ committing the sin.

> *The following story illustrates what "should happen" when a person uses a limb to rebel against Hashem.*[4]
>
> *King Yerovam ben Nevat, who led the Ten Tribes astray, was standing at his altar serving idolatry, and Hashem sent a prophet to rebuke him. When Yerovam heard the words of the prophet he stretched out his arm and ordered, "Grab him!" Immediately, Yerovam's arm became paralyzed, until he meekly begged the prophet to pray to Hashem that his arm return to its former vigor. (Although Hashem did not paralyze the arm for serving idolatry, it was paralyzed in order to honor the righteous.)*

Hashem could well say that someone who wishes to sin against Him should utilize his "own" resources rather than Hashem's, and thus deprive at least the offending limb of its life force. Yet He does not do so; even as the sin is being committed, He continues to bestow His goodness and sustenance on the sinner, and on the offending limb itself.

We should learn from this to tolerate people who offend and annoy us, and to keep doing kindness for them even as they continue to upset us.

4. The *second* attribute is associated with the description *Who bears iniquity.* The Sages taught[5] that each time a person sins, he acquires (i.e. creates) an accusing angel which goes before Hashem and says, "So-and-so created me." Since no being can continue to exist without Hashem's consent, it would seem only reasonable for Hashem to be unwilling to sustain destructive forces in the world and so send the angel back to the sinner who created it to live from his resources. The accuser, returning to the sinner, would then either take his life, or

---

4. *I Melachim* 13:4-6.

5. *Avos* 4:13.

exact some other form of punishment until its destructive energy was expended. Yet Hashem does not do so but continues to sustain this destructive angel, just as He sustains the entire world, until the sinner repents of the sin that brought the accuser into being — thereby destroying it — or until it is eventually destroyed by the sinner's suffering in this world or the next.

> *This quality of Hashem's teaches us to be patient even as the evil perpetrated by a person continues to exist, until the one who caused it rectifies the evil, or until it ceases on its own.*

5. The *third* attribute is suggested by the phrase *and passes over (cleanses) transgression.* Hashem Himself cleanses the stains that a transgression leaves on the sinner, as the prophet says, *When Hashem will wash off the dirt of the daughters of Tziyon, and the guilt-blood of Yerushalayim He will cleanse from its midst* (Yeshayahu 4:4).

> *People may ask, "Why should I rectify the damage caused by another's wrongdoing?" However, Hashem Himself cleanses the stain created by people's sins. (Furthermore, the knowledge that the King Himself will come to cleanse us should make us ashamed to commit any further wrong.)*

6. The *fourth* quality is described as being *for the remnant of His heritage.* This tells us that Hashem considers Israel to be His own children and says, "What can I do to them; they are My children after all, and if any harm befalls them, I will also suffer!"

> *We, too, should act as if all Jews were close relatives, wishing them only good and the same degree of honor and respect that we would like for ourselves. After all, we are all parts of one collective soul originating from the same source in Heaven. This is the basis of the mitzvah of ahavas Yisrael, which requires us to love our fellow Jews in just the same way as ourselves. Thus, we should desire the well-being of others and want everyone to think well of them; certainly, we ourselves should never speak ill of others. We should react to anything that happens to them, good or bad, exactly as if it were happening to us, just as Hashem "feels" our well-being or distress as His own.*

7. The *fifth* quality is seen in the statement, *He does not retain His wrath eternally.* From this we learn that when a person persists in sinning, Hashem does not remain angry with him, as the verse states,

He will not feud forever, nor will He bear grudge eternally (Tehillim **103**:9). Hashem tempers His anger and waits for the sinner to repent, **some**times treating him gently and other times harshly, but always **moti**vated by love for His people Israel.

> *We should also react in this manner — even in situations where we are allowed to show anger. For example, when a reprimand is called for, we should restrain ourselves and not remain angry any longer than necessary. In this vein we can understand the following mitzvah: If you see the donkey of someone you hate crouching under its burden, would you refrain from helping him? You shall help him repeatedly (Shemos 23:5). The Sages taught[6] that this mitzvah applies even if the animal's owner is known to be wicked and even if one has personally seen him commit one of the sins for which we are allowed to hate him. Nevertheless, one is commanded to overcome one's negative feelings and help him; perhaps what he needs is warmth and kindness. All this is included in the quality of "He does not retain His wrath eternally."*

8. The *sixth* attribute is stated as *for He desires kindness.* Even if there is an evil decree on the Jewish people, the merit of the kindness that people bestow on each other can save them, or at least partially abate the decree. Hashem, seeing this kindness, will have compassion on His people, because *He desires kindness.* Thus, at the time of the destruction of the *Beis HaMikdash,* when there was a decree of total destruction, Hashem had compassion on the Jewish people because of the kindnesses that people did for each other and preserved a remnant to start anew.[7]

> *We, too, should treat people in the same fashion: Even if someone treats us badly or upsets us, we should still try to focus on his positive qualities or on the good deeds he has done for us or others, and, overcoming our negative feelings, treat him with kindness. If, for example, a man's wife does something upsetting to him, he should say, as the Sage R' Chiya did,[8] "It is enough (for a husband) that a wife raises his children and saves him from sin." Similar statements can be made in any other situation: "That favor he once did for me (or for someone else) or his one good quality is enough on its own to*

---

6. *Pesachim* 113b.

7. *Vayikra Rabbah,* Ch. 26.

8. *Yevamos* 63a.

make him worthy of favorable treatment." This is what is meant by "desiring kindness."

Note: People who reject Torah, even partially, are sometimes granted very fine personal qualities so as to enable them to ensnare people in their evil ways.[9] One must be very careful not to use this trait of "He desires kindness" to mask the words and actions of those people who are anti-Torah. If confused or unsure as to how to relate to a particular person, one should consult the righteous who spend their time in Torah and mitzvos, and who have the clarity of vision necessary to offer guidance as to whom one should avoid in mind and deed.[10]

9. The *seventh* attribute is *He will again be merciful to us.* It is human nature that someone who sustains an injury and later forgives his assailant still nurses residual resentment over the hurt suffered; the forgiveness is never complete. Hashem, however, is different: when He sees that a sinner genuinely wants to repent and to forswear his sin, He draws the penitent even closer than before, as the Sages taught,[11] "In the place where penitents stand, not even the completely righteous can stand."

> *We should try to emulate this behavior as well; if a person who has upset us genuinely wants to make amends, we should not bear a grudge or harbor any remnant of our previous anger. If someone truly wants to be restored to our good graces, we should treat him with even more kindness than we did prior to the upset. We, too, can say, "In the place where penitents stand not even the completely righteous can stand," and treat people who want to rectify the wrongs they have perpetrated as though they were completely righteous and never did anything to upset us.*

10. The *eighth* attribute is described by the phrase, *He will suppress our iniquities.* This alludes to the fact that the mitzvos a person does are allowed to enter into Hashem's inner quarters where He, *kaviochol,* can take pleasure in them, while sins are not granted entrance but are instead "suppressed." The mitzvos that have entered are built into a great structure of reward, while sins become part of the abhorrent Gehinnom. Therefore, Hashem does not allow Himself to be "bribed"

---

9. *Even Sheleimah* 4:11,13 (in name of Vilna Gaon).

10. See Commentary of Vilna Gaon on *Mishlei* 11:9.

11. *Berachos* 34b.

with mitzvos into forgiving sins. For example, if a person has forty mitzvos to his credit and ten sins on his account (and did not repent for them during his lifetime when he had the opportunity), Hashem does not take ten of the mitzvos to cancel out the ten sins, leaving him credit for only thirty mitzvos. Instead, the person is made to suffer for all his sins so that he can receive full reward for each and every mitzvah.

The rationale for this is that the sins are of no eternal significance, as we see that Hashem suppresses them and does not let them enter His quarters. If so, how can a mitzvah, whose place is in the purely spiritual realms, be canceled out by a base and ignoble sin? Although Hashem pays exacting attention to a person's each and every action, whether good or bad, He still does not suppress the good but rather elevates it to the higher worlds to be transformed into a worthy structure. Sins, on the other hand, do not receive such treatment but instead are suppressed and denied the benefits of entrance into the inner quarters.

> We, too, should follow Hashem's example in our interactions with others and not ignore people's good qualities while emphasizing their bad ones. On the contrary, we should "suppress" people's bad qualities and exclude them totally from our thoughts, while keeping their good qualities at the forefront of our minds. We should not use the rationalization, "So what if he's done some good? He's also done a lot of bad!" as an excuse to forget someone's good qualities. Rather, we should seize upon any grounds to excuse and overlook a person's bad side, and at the same time not allow ourselves to forget any of the good in him. This is the way of Hashem, Who suppresses our iniquities.

11. The *ninth* attribute, expressed as *and cast into the depths of the sea all their sins,* can be explained as follows: When Israel sins, Hashem sends the nations of the world to punish them so that they will repent. The nations, however, don't act with the intention of being agents of Hashem; they simply pour their wrath and venom onto Israel. Therefore, after the nations have performed this function, Hashem punishes them for their sins. The nation of Israel, on the other hand, characteristically returns to Hashem through their suffering. When this happens, Hashem does not merely forgive them, but casts all their sins onto their enemies, just as the sins of the people were placed onto the goat "for Azazel" on Yom Kippur in the time of the *Beis HaMikdash.*[12] Thus, after Israel is judged and punished,

---

12. See *Vayikra* 16:21,22.

Hashem regrets, so to speak, their punishment, and avenges the suffering of His beloved people. The prophet Yeshayahu compares the wicked to the sea (cf. 57:2: *The wicked are driven like the sea*). Thus, casting Israel's sins onto the wicked can be described figuratively as *casting their sins into the depths of the sea*.

> We should also behave this way toward others. If we witness the suffering of people who perpetrated evil, we should withdraw our negative feelings toward them and treat them as brothers. Once they have undergone punishment or disgrace we should draw them close, have compassion on them, and rescue them from their enemies. In emulating this quality, one should desist from condescending statements such as, "They deserve all their difficulties because of their wrongdoing," and, like Hashem, be kind and compassionate.

12. The *tenth* attribute is called *Grant truth to Jacob.* "Jacob" refers to the masses of Torah-true Jews who are faithful to Torah and live a life of truth. The "truth" of Torah is a life of justice, fairness, and compassion, and thus, Hashem, too, acts toward them with these qualities of Torah truth.

> We, too, should treat people with Torah truth, fairly and compassionately, and never deviate from just behavior toward others.

13. The *eleventh* attribute is [He gives] *kindness to Abraham.* "Abraham" refers to those remarkable people who express their extraordinary love for Hashem by acting far beyond what is required of them. Hashem, too, treats them with extraordinary kindness beyond the norms of justice and compassion. In other words, Hashem *gives kindness to* [those who are like] *Abraham.*

> Similarly, although we must be fair, just and compassionate to all, we should go above and beyond the normal requirements when dealing with people who are exceptionally good and generous like Abraham. We should treat them with greater kindness and patience, extend extra friendship and respect toward them, and make a consistent effort to associate with them.

14. The *twelfth* attribute is derived from the phrase, *as You swore to our forefathers.* There are so many unworthy people, and yet, Hashem still has compassion on them. The Sages taught[13] that the

---

13. *Berachos* 7a.

verse, *And I shall grant "chein"*[14] *to those that I shall grant it, and have compassion on those that I shall have compassion* (*Shemos* 33:19), teaches us that Hashem has a "treasure" of compassion which He grants freely to those who are undeserving. The rationale is: "They still have the merit of their forefathers, to whom I swore;[15] therefore, even if the children are unworthy, I will still guide them with compassion until they eventually reach their lofty destiny."

> *We, too, should not insult a wicked person, nor react with cruelty, since he, after all, is also descended from Avraham, Yitzchak, and Yaakov. Although such individuals may themselves be unworthy, their ancestors were highly worthy; an affront to the descendants is an affront to the ancestors as well.*
>
> *Note: One should not overlook the evil of the wicked; see Chapters 4 and 23. However, one who is not actually engaged in "distancing from evil" should constantly remind himself that even the wicked are children of Avraham, Yitzchak and Yaakov and treat them accordingly with respect and compassion, thus emulating this attribute of Hashem.*

15. The *thirteenth* attribute, expressed in the words *from ancient times*, applies in circumstances where the merit of our forefathers has been depleted and is insufficient to bring compassion on the Jewish people. It was of such a situation that the prophet wrote, *I have remembered for you the kindness of your youth, the love of your bridal days* (*Yirmiyahu* 2:1). Because of this quality, Hashem remembers our love for Him in ancient times and the many mitzvos we have done since we came into existence, and together with all the other attributes of compassion with which He conducts the world, He fashions one great treasury of compassion. Thus, this final attribute encompasses all the others.

> *Even if we cannot manage to employ any of the arguments suggested in the preceding sections, we can still be guided by this principle,*

---

14. *Chein* seems to denote special affinity and love for a person just because "he is who he is." When Noach found *chein* in the eyes of Hashem (*Bereishis* 6:8), it does not mean that he was absolutely perfect and worthy of being saved, but rather that his personality was one that Hashem "liked" — i.e. he had an inner desire to do the will of His Creator. When Shechem asked to find *chein* in the eyes of Dinah's brothers (*Bereishis* 34:11), he was asking them to "like" him and follow his wishes even though he was not deserving of their friendship.

15. See *Bereishis* 22:16-18.

and say, "At some point in this person's life he was an upright person who had not yet done wrong, even if it was only as a newborn infant." This alone should provide adequate reason to be kind to him, pray for his well-being, and do him favors.

When a person emulates these "thirteen attributes" of Hashem, he will merit that these attributes of compassion will be opened toward him in particular, and to the world in general.

In times of crisis, individual or national, a person's greatest possible contribution is to invoke Divine compassion through prayer, tzedakah and deeds. By emulating Hashem's attributes of compassion, he will be "opening the gates" for Divine compassion on His beloved people.

Thus, a person should constantly remind himself of these verses in *Michah* containing the "Thirteen Attributes" and apply them to his owh life when appropriate, thereby bringing Divine compassion to the world.

This volume is part of
THE ARTSCROLL SERIES®
an ongoing project of
translations, commentaries and expositions
on Scripture, Mishnah, Talmud, Halachah,
liturgy, history, the classic Rabbinic writings,
biographies and thought.

For a brochure of current publications
visit your local Hebrew bookseller
or contact the publisher:

Mesorah Publications, ltd

4401 Second Avenue
Brooklyn, New York 11232
(718) 921-9000
www.artscroll.com